SAP® ERP Financials User's Guide

 PRESS

SAP PRESS is a joint initiative of SAP and Galileo Press. The know-how offered by SAP specialists combined with the expertise of the Galileo Press publishing house offers the reader expert books in the field. SAP PRESS features first-hand information and expert advice, and provides useful skills for professional decision-making.

SAP PRESS offers a variety of books on technical and business related topics for the SAP user. For further information, please visit our website: *www.sap-press.com*.

Subbu Ramakrishnan
Manufacturing Finance with SAP ERP Financials
2009, 584 pp.
978-1-59229-238-7

Naeem Arif, Sheikh Tauseef Muhammad
SAP ERP Financials: Configuration and Design
2008, 467 pp.
978-1-59229-136-6

Mitresh Kundalia
Segment Reporting with Document Splitting in the SAP General Ledger
2009, 131 pp.
978-1-59229-265-3

Paul Theobald
Migrate Successfully to the SAP General Ledger
2009, 218 pp.
978-1-59229-296-7

Heinz Forsthuber, Jörg Siebert

SAP® ERP Financials User's Guide

Galileo Press

Bonn • Boston

Galileo Press is named after the Italian physicist, mathematician and philosopher Galileo Galilei (1564–1642). He is known as one of the founders of modern science and an advocate of our contemporary, heliocentric worldview. His words *Eppur si muove* (And yet it moves) have become legendary. The Galileo Press logo depicts Jupiter orbited by the four Galilean moons, which were discovered by Galileo in 1610.

Editor Eva Tripp
English Edition Editor Stephen Solomon
Translation Lemoine International, Inc., Salt Lake City, UT
Copyeditor Ruth Saavedra
Cover Design Jill Winitzer
Photo Credit Masterfile/RF
Layout Design Vera Brauner
Production Editor Kelly O'Callaghan
Typesetting Publishers' Design and Production Services, Inc.
Printed and bound in Canada

ISBN 978-1-59229-190-8

© 2010 by Galileo Press Inc., Boston (MA)
1st Edition 2010

1st German edition published 2009 by Galileo Press, Bonn, Germany

Contents at a Glance

Contents

4   Accounts Receivable Accounting 163

6   Bank Accounting 323

7   Closing Operations 383

Introduction

SAP ERP Financials User's Guide is devoted to a detailed discussion of the application components used for Financial Accounting (FI) in SAP ERP Financials. This book seeks to provide support for everyday use of FI and to give you useful tips based on practical experience.

The first edition of this book was published in 2002. This book is based on the current release of SAP, SAP ERP 6.0 (formerly SAP ERP 2005), and is aimed at both beginners and experienced SAP users. Many SAP customers are in the process of upgrading to the new release, and SAP ERP 6.0 is poised to replace R/3 Release 4.6C as the most widely used SAP release.

Target Audience

This book is geared towards readers with a basic knowledge of accounting. For experienced SAP users, it also provides an introduction to the new features of SAP ERP 6.0. Both sets of readers will benefit from the many practical tips and examples included.

Structure of This Book

This book comprises seven main chapters, which are outlined below:

Chapter 1 provides an overview of the new features in the latest release of SAP ERP Financials.

Chapter 2 is devoted to general ledger accounting (SAP General Ledger). General ledger accounting is always at the heart of any accounting system. This chapter familiarizes you with the basics, including concepts such as client, chart of accounts, company code, business area and profit center. It also provides guidelines for making optimal use of the master data and transaction data in the SAP system. Finally, it explains the significance of the SAP General Ledger, and closes with a customer report by Accenture.

Vendor payables are managed in accounts payable accounting, that is, in SAP FI-AP component. We discuss this topic in detail in **Chapter 3**, which includes an in-depth discussion of four alternative options for entering A/P invoices. This chapter also explains how automatic payment transactions are organized by means of detailed descriptions of the SAP payment program. The chapter ends with a discussion of reports that allow you to monitor critical changes to master records and an analysis that allows you to keep track of due dates for payables.

Chapter 4 is concerned with the subject of accounts receivable accounting (SAP FI-AR component). Efficient systems for managing receivables are always in demand, in particular in economically challenging times. In addition to FI-AR, Release 6.0 provides three new receivables management features in the area of Financial Supply Chain Management (FSCM). Risks are evaluated using credit limits with SAP Credit Management. Dunning by telephone is becoming an established dunning procedure, alongside dunning by written correspondence. SAP Collections Management provides an ideal solution for this purpose. If invoices are not paid in full, SAP Dispute Management allows you to create an electronic dispute case file to clarify the issues involved.

Asset accounting constitutes the subject of **Chapter 5**. The SAP Asset Accounting (FI-AA) subledger accounting module is used for managing complex fixed assets both physically and by value. This chapter provides detailed explanations of the SAP concepts of chart of appreciation, depreciation area and depreciation term. An example is provided to illustrate how several master records can be created simultaneously in a single work step and how the acquisitions postings for these assets may appear. Intercompany transfer, depreciation and asset retirement posting then bring the asset lifecycle to a close.

Chapter 6, Bank Accounting, begins by taking a closer look at master data. Bank accounting (FI-BL) is certainly not a new topic. A function has been added in the new release to simplify the exchange of data media and account statements with the individual house banks. Our discussion of bank accounting also includes check deposits, bill of exchange management and, finally, the main liquidity forecasting reports.

Chapter 7, Closing Operations, which runs to almost 200 pages, explains how closings can be completed as quickly as possible ("fast close"). The software provides support for recurring periodic activities, such as foreign currency valuation, the reclassification of receivables and payables or interest calculation. An Accrual Engine is also available as of SAP Release 4.7, while a tool for intercompany reconciliation is provided as of SAP ERP.

Practical documentation is provided in the **Appendices** to supplement the main chapters in this book. Here you will find a summary of all menu paths used in the book. In addition, an example of a structured closing procedure document is provided to accompany Chapter 7, "Closing Operations." Finally, the Appendices also include a glossary and a beginner's guide to using the SAP system.

How to Use This Book

Each of the chapters in this book is a self-contained unit that can be read in isolation. This leaves you free to skip individual chapters and to focus on the topics that are of most interest to you personally.

The following special icons are used in this book to help you find your way around:

- ▶ This icon warns you of a possible problem. Take particular care when tackling this task or using the function in question. **[!]**

- ▶ This icon indicates an example. We use examples frequently throughout the book to illustrate the topics and functions under discussion. **[Ex]**

- ▶ This icon indicates a tip. We use this icon to draw your particular attention to important information that can facilitate your work. **[+]**

Acknowledgements

Writing a book is never a simple task, and writing a technical book about complex application software like FI requires a great deal of commitment, not only from the authors. Many friends and colleagues supported us throughout this project by providing advice, information, and corrections. We would like to take this opportunity to thank them all sincerely.

The support of our families in particular proved invaluable. The revision of this book in the current edition could never have been completed without a large measure of patience. Special thanks are therefore due to Eva Siebert, Adriana and Hans Tacheci, to whom this book is dedicated.

Jörg Siebert and **Heinz Forsthuber**

"You have to know the past to understand the present." With this guiding principle in mind, we provide an overview in this chapter of how the SAP ERP Financials solution has developed over time. A summary of the new features in the latest release of SAP ERP Financials is also included here.

1   Overview

In 1972, five former employees of IBM—Claus Wellenreuther, Hans-Werner Hector, Klaus Tschira, Dietmar Hopp, and Hasso Plattner—founded a small enterprise called SAP in the town of Weinheim in Baden-Württemberg in Germany. In 1977, SAP moved to the nearby town of Walldorf. From the outset, accounting software was one of SAP's core solutions. The design of SAP Financial Accounting was influenced to the greatest degree by Claus Wellenreuther.

SAP's first software packages, R/1 and R/2, contained a component called RF. This acronym stood for Real-Time Financial Accounting. This version offered general ledger accounting with subledgers for vendors, customers and assets. Back in the days of R/2, the graphical user interface was largely shaped by the mainframe computer and its character orientation.

The RF component

An early transaction for master data entry is shown in Figure 1.1.

Some of the concepts developed in these early days have been preserved in the current SAP release.

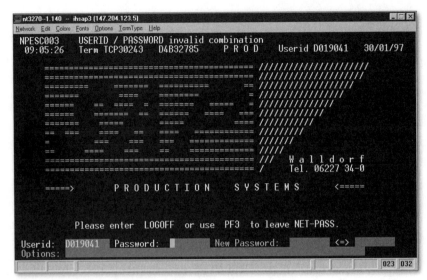

Figure 1.1 R/2 User Interface

1.1 Reports and Transaction Codes

RFBILA00/
RAGITT00

Any current reports that start with the letters "RF" have their origins in the old RF component. For example, the current SAP release still includes a balance-sheet report called RFBILA00. Reports starting with the letters "RA" originate in the same period, with RA standing for the Asset Accounting application. An example of one of these reports is the asset sheet history RAGITT00. If you are searching for reports in SAP ERP Financials in general or in the Asset Accounting subcomponent in particular, it is therefore useful to start your search with RF* or RA*.

The transaction
code principle

In the earliest days of SAP, you could only operate the software using report names and transaction codes. There were no printed folders outlining all functions and their corresponding transaction codes to help SAP users find their way around the system. Another aspect of the earliest solution that has survived alongside report names is the use of transaction codes. The following list provides examples of the transaction codes you will find in the current release:

▶ FB01 – Financial Accounting, Post Document

▶ FB02 – Financial Accounting, Change Document

- ► FB03 – Financial Accounting, Display Document
- ► FD01 – Financial Accounting, Create Customer
- ► FD02 – Financial Accounting, Change Customer
- ► FD03 – Financial Accounting, Display Customer
- ► FK01 – Financial Accounting, Create Vendor
- ► FK02 – Financial Accounting, Change Vendor
- ► FK03 – Financial Accounting, Display Vendor
- ► KS01 – Cost Accounting, Create Cost Center
- ► KS02 – Cost Accounting, Change Cost Center
- ► KS03 – Cost Accounting, Display Cost Center

Today, these codes still enable fast access to several SAP functions. However, the significance of transactions has declined owing to the manageability of menu paths and their associated navigational structures. This book will therefore focus more on menu paths than on individual transaction codes. An index of menu paths used in this book is provided in the appendix, as is an index of all transaction codes mentioned (keyword: "Transaction"). In addition to these functional throwbacks to earlier times, several other basic design principles have survived to the present day. These include real-time processing and the document principle.

1.2 Real-Time Processing and the Document Principle

Even in the earliest SAP releases, the real-time processing of information ensured simultaneous processing of information in the general ledger and subledgers in Accounting. According to the real-time principle, all connected modules are checked for error-free processing before a posting transaction. This applies to purchasing, sales and distribution, travel expenses, cost accounting, and many other areas.

In SAP's infancy, end-of-day processing was the norm in most enterprises. However, with end-of-day processing, posting checks took place at a late stage after data entry, and error sessions were created for correc-

End-of-day processing and error sessions

tions. As a result, the filed physical documents had to be gone through a second time, which necessitated an additional manual processing step. A document principle could only be usefully applied once real-time processing was in place. According to the document principle, any posting document only ever needs to be viewed once. If all of the information it contains is correct at this time, the document can be posted electronically and the physical document can be filed away.

Even today, some software solutions on the market have not fully mastered the concept of real-time processing and the document principle. In these solutions, a periodic job retrieves the posting documents every five to ten minutes for checking and processing.

If the current SAP system informs you directly that an error has occurred in the additional account assignment cost center when you are entering an accounts payable (A/P) invoice, this is always thanks to the principle of real-time processing, which is still in place today.

1.3   SAP R/3 Replaces SAP R/2

Client/server software

The R/2 generation of software was designed for use on mainframes, and it reached the end of its lifecycle in the mid 1990s when personal computers with the client-server model began to supersede the mainframe. Taking the RF component as its starting point, SAP developed the components FI (Financial Accounting) and CO (Controlling) in addition to a new technical (client-server) infrastructure in its subsequent release, R/3. The features of real-time processing, the document principle, and transaction codes were preserved in the new release, which also included several improvements.

Graphical user interface

One noteworthy improvement was a new graphical user interface (GUI), which served, above all, to make it easier for all new SAP users to use the business applications. Thanks to this new GUI, users could navigate their way around the system with a logically structured application menu, which represented a welcome alternative to the transaction codes that had previously been the only navigational option available. The menu structure in FI is shown in Figure 1.2.

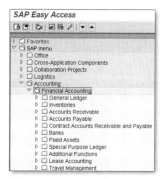

Figure 1.2 SAP Application Menu in Financial Accounting

In addition to the enhanced graphical user interface, the introduction of Microsoft Office integration represented another step forward in R/3. This meant that you could, for example, open data in Microsoft Excel® from the SAP system directly, while still maintaining the reference to the underlying database. The range of applications for the Excel Inplace function was rooted largely in reporting (see Figure 1.3).

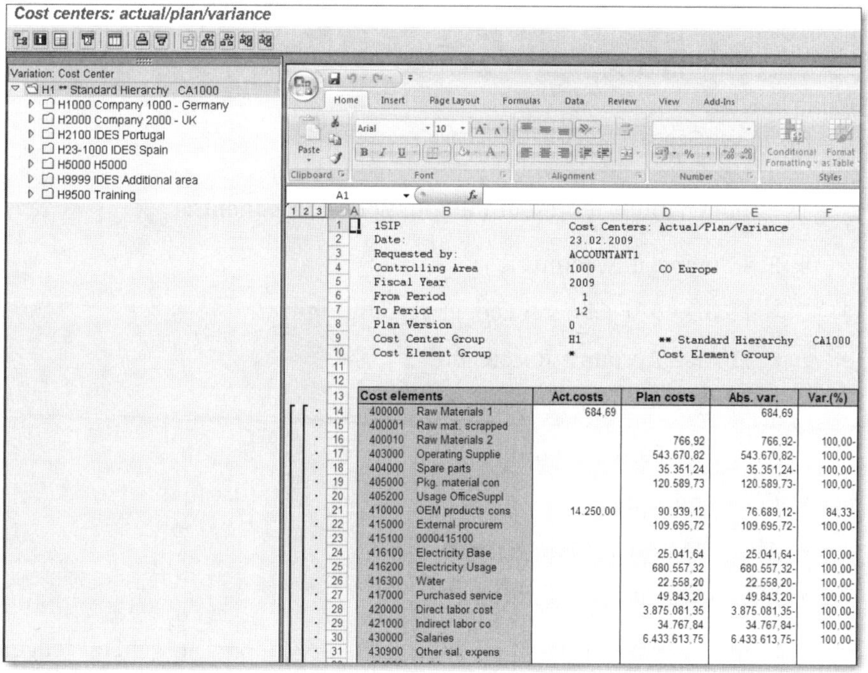

Figure 1.3 Microsoft Excel in the SAP System

Additional improvements were included in a later R/3 release. For example, applications containing a range of information were rendered more manageable with the introduction of tab pages (see Figure 1.4).

Figure 1.4 Tab Pages

A cross-section of the Financial Accounting area

Figure 1.5 shows some of the components contained in R/3 with a focus on Financial Accounting.

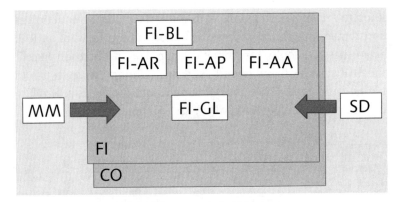

Figure 1.5 Representation of Components in SAP

The abbreviations represent the following components:

- FI – Financial Accounting
  - FI-GL – SAP General Ledger accounting
  - FI-AR – Accounts Receivable
  - FI-AP – Accounts Payable
  - FI-BL – Bank Accounting
- CO – Controlling
- MM – Materials Management
- SD – Sales and Distribution

A look at the various components

The figures gathered from all subledgers are merged in general ledger accounting (FI-GL), and financial statements are created on this basis.

Accounts Receivable (FI-AR) has a real-time connection to the general ledger and enables receivables management at the level of customer and line items. New transactions are transferred from the Sales and Distribution module (SD) in the form of invoices. FI-AP, Accounts Payable, manages an enterprise's vendors and payables. If the MM component (purchasing) is also used, new A/P invoices can be checked against purchase orders and good receipts directly. Bank Accounting is based on a "virtual subledger." Bank accounts are mapped using the general ledger, with only the cash journal having the character of a small subledger. The CO component (Controlling) is much more complex than can be described here. A further distinction is made between Cost Element Accounting, Cost Center Accounting and Cost Object Accounting in this area. The major components of CO are listed below:

▶ CO-OM – Overhead Cost Management

▶ CO-PC – Product Costing

▶ CO-PA – Profitability Analysis

These topics are not discussed further in this book. For more information, we recommend *Product Cost Controlling in SAP ERP* by John Jordan (SAP PRESS).

All of these components are based on a shared database. The main benefit of this design is that master data, for example, customer master data for the FI and SD components, only needs to be stored once. The same applies to the purchasing process and vendor data for the FI and MM components. This shared architecture is of particular advantage to process steps that straddle different departments in an enterprise, such as a credit limit check or a check for A/P invoices. The document principle ensures that the information from all relevant modules is checked in real time and then made available as required. As a result, Controlling has immediate access to information about revenue and expense items. The same holds true for Bank Accounting, where future cash outflows can be determined in real time from data relating to purchase requisitions, purchase orders, and vendors, and future cash inflows can be determined in real time from orders and invoices. This aspect of integration is described in detail in this book in the chapters devoted to Accounts Receivable, Accounts Payable and Bank Accounting.

Shared master data

1.4   Integration

Standard user
interface

All SAP users can access functions in Financial Accounting, Materials Management, Sales and Distribution, or Controlling from a standard user interface, provided that they have the user authorizations required to do so. This represents one of the key benefits of an integrated system. In specific use cases, this helps track the document flow. You can, for example, jump from the due date analysis in Accounts Receivable to the Sales and Distribution component. A similar drilldown is conceivable in reporting, for example, from the liquidity overview in Accounts Payable to Materials Management. These two examples demonstrate the benefits in terms of integration offered by a standard user interface used in conjunction with the internal document flow. These possibilities would be barely conceivable in other software solutions based on "information silos" and interfaces.

1.5   SAP ERP Replaces SAP R/3

Despite the success of the R/3 client-server solution introduced the early 1990s, it gave way to its successor in 2003. This was mySAP ERP. Since then, the prefix "my," which emphasized the software's adaptability and thus also its possibilities in terms of personalization, has been dropped. These days, we refer simply to SAP ERP (note that this merely represents a name change and not a new release).

Technical basis:
SAP NetWeaver

This new generation of software was distinguished by its new technical infrastructure, SAP NetWeaver. SAP NetWeaver is the new SAP Basis, which represents the technical platform for the software and places SAP ERP on a broader footing. It also enables new functions in the various areas of application software. SAP NetWeaver essentially supports integration at the following four levels:

▸ **Integration of persons**
Browser-based interfaces became more widely used as part of the general development of the Internet. This type of interface is also used in SAP NetWeaver Portal, which unites SAP and non-SAP applications in a single user interface and makes these accessible to the user in a single logon procedure. Some of these portal roles are

described in addition to the R/3 options in Chapter 4, Accounts Receivable.

▶ **Integration of information**

SAP reporting in R/3 was efficient and versatile. However, it was not suitable for data that originated outside of the SAP system. Furthermore, an analytical examination of characteristics or dimensions of your choice was not possible. SAP Business Information Warehouse (BW), which was later renamed SAP NetWeaver® Business Warehouse, was designed to meet this information requirement. This book deals mainly with conventional R/3 reports. However, a selection of BW reports is discussed to give you some idea of the capabilities of this tool.

▶ **Integration of processes**

Today, in light of the current possibilities of data communication, it is almost impossible to imagine that all business processes were once covered by a single software solution. A business software solution usually interacts with other IT systems to create process efficiency. Taking bank communication as an example, this book explains in detail how payment media and account statements are exchanged directly between the SAP ERP system and the connected house bank system.

▶ **Runtime environment**

In addition to the SAP-specific programming language ABAP, the new runtime environment also incorporates Java, the programming language commonly used in Internet applications. A Java application is illustrated in Chapter 4, Accounts Receivable, using an example based on SAP Biller Direct.

Based on this integration, the new SAP Basis also ushered in a technical shift from client-server software to service-oriented software. The mono lithic R/3 application was split apart, giving rise to a range of versatile components. Open standards present opportunities for implementing end-to-end processes across enterprise and software boundaries.

SAP's accounting product is now known as SAP ERP Financials. In addition to applications for Financial Accounting and Controlling, this

SAP ERP Financials

umbrella term also includes many additional functional areas, which are listed below:

- **Financial Accounting**
  The FI component allows you to manage and represent all financial accounting data, record business transactions in accordance with the document principle, use an integrated data flow, make financial accounting data available in real time, and effect automatic postings to the general ledger. All of these topics are discussed in this book.

- **Controlling**
  CO offers functions for coordinating, monitoring, and optimizing business activities. CO is closely integrated with both FI and the Logistics modules. As a result, all data that is relevant for cost accounting is automatically incorporated into those areas also.

- **SAP Financial Supply Chain Management**
  SAP FSCM consists of functions for receivables management, credit management, and electronic invoice processing. FSCM seeks to optimize working capital by monitoring and enhancing the cash flows from purchase order to payment and, in the opposite direction, from order receipt to cash receipt. Some of the relevant products (SAP Dispute Management, SAP Collections Management, and SAP Credit Management, and SAP Biller Direct) are also discussed in this book.

- **Treasury**
  SAP Treasury and Risk Management optimizes transactions on capital markets and internal and external payment transactions. Securities, cash transactions, foreign exchange transactions, and derivative transactions are covered by the corresponding subledger. This book covers one small aspect of these payment transactions by examining the topical subject of SEPA and the SAP Bank Communication Management solution.

A solution for Enterprise Performance Management is also provided. It offers functions for strategy management, consolidation and enterprise planning. The palette of solutions is completed by a solution for Governance, Risk and Compliance (GRC). The SAP BusinessObjects GRC solutions offer functions for access controls, process controls, risk management, international trade (SAP BusinessObjects Global Trade Services) and a component for compliance with environmental regulations and employee protection law (SAP Environment, Health, and Safety [EHS] Management).

R/3 customers planning a release upgrade are not obliged to install and activate all of these components at once. On the contrary, they can specifically select the components they require for processing their business transactions. As an initial step, many enterprises implement a technical transition first without immediately activating the new functional features.

1.6 New Features in SAP ERP Financials (Release 6.0)

SAP Release ERP 6.0 is the source release for new SAP customers and the platform for a target release for existing customers. This, the new edition of *SAP Financials Handbook*, is based on the latest release and aims both to impart a basic knowledge of SAP ERP Financials and to highlight the new features of ERP 6.0 compared with 4.6C. The main new functional features are listed below:

- **SAP General Ledger**
  The most noteworthy new feature in the latest ERP release is certainly the revamping of the core component of SAP ERP Financials. Chapter 2, General Ledger Accounting, examines the essential role played by FI-GL and places this new feature in context.

- **Accrual Engine**
  Accrual and deferral postings are discussed in more detail in Chapter 7, Closing Operations. Previously, these could only be posted with recurring entries. A new alternative is now offered by the Accrual Engine.

- **Intercompany reconciliation**
  Business relationships within a corporate group generate intercompany posting documents. These then need to be reconciled as part of closing operations. New features in this area are discussed in Chapter 7, Closing Operations.

▶ **Electronic tax return for tax on sales and purchases**
A small change is presented by the electronic tax return for tax on sales/purchases. Previously, the only option was to submit hard-copy documents to the authorities. Chapter 7, Closing Operations, describes the steps involved in this integrated electronic process.

▶ **Receivables management**
Receivables management, which is often referred to by the acronym FSCM (Financial Supply Chain Management), has been significantly updated in the new SAP ERP release. With new applications for credit, collections, and dispute management, as well as SAP Biller Direct, the new release is better equipped to support business processes. The potential offered in this area is demonstrated in Chapter 4, Accounts Receivable.

▶ **Bank communication**
The SAP Bank Communication Management (BCM) solution is indicative of the fact that the enhancement packages contain more than mere functional enhancements of existing programs. This completely new solution is delivered with Enhancement Package 2 and enables a direct exchange of payment media files and account statements between house banks. Functional enhancements of the solution are delivered with Enhancement Package 4. The details are provided in Chapter 6, Bank Accounting.

▶ **Self-service option for asset inventory**
This scenario was developed for SAP Germany and serves as an example of what can be achieved using the new underlying infrastructure of SAP NetWeaver. An insight into this option is provided in Chapter 7, Closing Operations.

▶ **Improvements in the depreciation posting run and in the periodic posting run for APC values**
This new feature is not immediately obvious to users because the runtime of the programs has been optimized with a new architecture. The depreciation run process step is described in Chapter 7, Closing Operations.

▶ **Worklist for exchange rate maintenance**
An option of working via worklists was developed to facilitate the maintenance of exchange rates. This option is demonstrated using an

example of foreign currency valuation in Chapter 7, Closing Operations.

The new features briefly sketched above are described in detail in the individual chapters in this handbook. Note, however, that each of these is representative of what has changed in SAP ERP Financials as a whole. A detailed overview of these changes is provided by the SAP ERP Solution Browser. This technical tool is available free of charge on the Internet at *http://solutionbrowser.erp.sap.fmpmedia.com/* and is not limited to the SAP ERP Financials application area. Figure 1.6 illustrates the options provided by this tool. On the left of the screen, you enter the source and target releases. You then limit your selection to a specific application, and the corresponding delta functions are listed.

Solution Browser

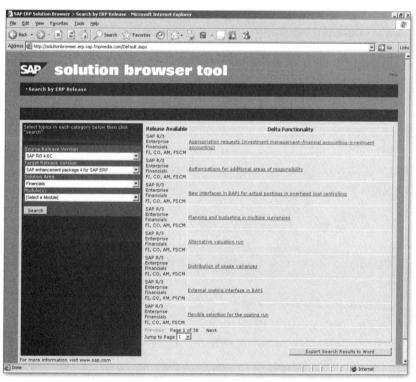

Figure 1.6 SAP ERP Solution Browser

A further level of detail is provided by a description of the functional enhancements, together with a list of business benefits (see Figure 1.7).

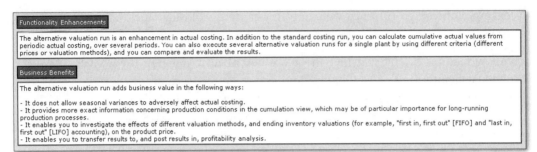

Figure 1.7 The Solution in Detail

Additional information is provided in the Release Notes, which run to several hundred pages. The next section provides a brief description of points to note when upgrading to the new release.

1.6.1 Release Upgrade

No problems with versioning

Thanks to the architecture of the SAP solution, no versioning problems arise between the various modules within a release, such as SD, MM, FI, and CO, because all are delivered in the same version. In the past, a release upgrade always constituted a major project for customers and always involved a significant investment of time and money. Customer-specific programming and updates were particularly time-consuming. In many cases, extensive testing, modifications, and user training were required.

[+]   **SAP Releases**

The sequence of new SAP releases over recent years is outlined below:

- R/3 4.0
- R/3 4.5
- R/3 4.6
- R/3 4.7 (also known as R/3 Enterprise)
- ERP 5.0 (formerly known as mySAP ERP 2004 and ECC 5.0 (Enterprise Core Component))
- ERP 6.0 (formerly known as mySAP ERP 2005 and ECC 6.0)

It was often the case that a release upgrade was put on the back burner owing to the investment required, even if some of the new functions would have improved processes. From the perspective of overall cost, it was much more cost effective to skip one or more releases. One CIO perfectly summed up a prevalent customer attitude as follows: "You [SAP] can touch my ERP core system once every five years—and make that a Saturday please." On the flip side, many heads of enterprise want to see their processes improved on a frequent basis (once every quarter)—which gives rise to a classic conflict between stability on the one hand and dynamic changes and improvements on the other.

Enhancements based on a stable core

Another concern that was consistently voiced by SAP customers in the past relates to functional changes within an ERP system. For example, a customer may have needed to use a new function in the SAP ERP Financials area without having the slightest interest in the new functional features in Payroll, Materials Management, or Sales. It was previously the case that, after a release upgrade, the new functions in all areas were visible and, in some cases, immediately active. SAP customers wanted to avoid this "big bang" approach. Their preference was for small projects, where it was easy to compare the project costs and benefits.

The concept of enhancement packages was developed in response to these two challenges. With this concept, the system core remains stable and process improvements can be made without a release upgrade. This means that small functional improvements are possible within one area without a big bang.

1.6.2   Enhancement Package

The idea of a stable core and functional enhancements in the form of small packages is not new to SAP. Back in Release 4.7, extension sets offered a similar option. However, the extension set approach was unsuccessful, partly because the various SAP industry solutions (numbering approximately 27) necessitated changes to the ERP core. Furthermore, the new SAP Basis component, SAP NetWeaver, simultaneously gave rise to a new infrastructure that also had to be taken into account. The experience demonstrated that it is no easy task to maintain a stable core while developing new functions. Nevertheless, conditions are now favorable

Take two

for the enhancement package concept. Since 2005, this approach has offered the possibility of making functional enhancements to the SAP ERP 6.0 core. Enhancement Packages 1 to 3 are now in general release, and Enhancement Package 4 is to be delivered to the first customers in the middle of 2009. A schedule is already in place for 2010 and 2011 with the release of Enhancement Packages 5 and 6.

System status You can check which release and enhancement package you are using by selecting System Status in the menu bar. A small window then opens, in which the release number is indicated as shown in Figure 1.8. In our example, the release is SAP ERP 6.0 with Enhancement Package 4.

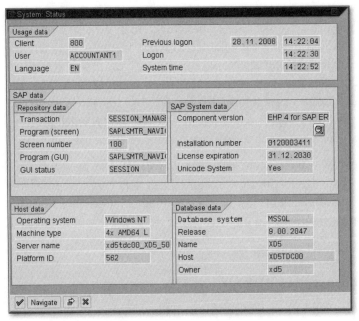

Figure 1.8 Release Overview

Because the new functions are encapsulated by topic and are initially inactive, they must be activated by each customer in Customizing. The menu path TOOLS • CUSTOMIZING • IMG • EXECUTE PROJECT • F5 • SAP CUSTOMIZING IMPLEMENTATION GUIDE • ACTIVATE BUSINESS FUNCTIONS brings you to the business function sets that represent the functional enhancements of the enhancement packages that are technically implemented in the SAP system. Activating individual business functions generates new Customizing menu paths in the SAP system and makes the new functions visible in the applications.

Figure 1.9 also shows the interdependencies that exist between new functions. For example, Enhancement Packages 2 and 4 both contain enhancements of the general ledger. However, Package 4 builds on Package 2, so it only makes sense to activate both packages together. This approach means that SAP customers can implement functional enhancements as part of small, manageable projects. As a result, the alternative big bang approach is now a thing of the past.

Interdependencies

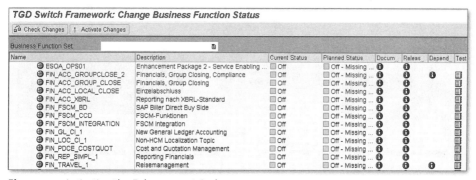

Figure 1.9 Activating the Enhancement Packages

However, these projects must still consist of the necessary steps of design, configuration, testing, and "go live," regardless of this technical innovation.

Enhancement packages provide a cornerstone for a sustainable generation of software. In the next section, we will briefly touch on SAP's maintenance strategies.

1.6.3 Maintenance Strategy

To ensure planning security for customers for the SAP ERP release, SAP informs customers well in advance about the duration for which it will guarantee maintenance of the solution. This notice is important, in particular when it comes to changes made to the software to meet legal requirements. The current situation is shown in Figure 1.10.

As you can see, standard maintenance is guaranteed until 2015. For an additional charge of 2% of the maintenance fee, standard maintenance of SAP ERP 6.0 can be extended until 2017.

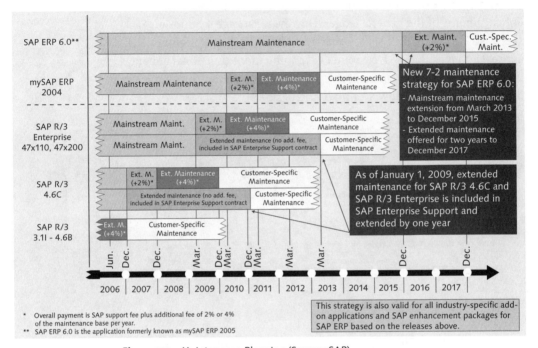

Figure 1.10 Maintenance Planning (Source: SAP)

1.7   Conclusion

It is useful to take a brief look back at past developments to determine where we stand at present. The maxim "You have to know the past to understand the present" certainly holds true for many aspects of life. In the context of SAP ERP and the SAP ERP Financials solutions, knowledge of the past helps us understand and, more importantly, assess the current situation. Software is a long-term investment, so it is hardly surprising that some older functions like report names and transaction codes have survived to the present day. When SAP R/2 was replaced by SAP R/3, many key principles such as integration and real-time processing were preserved and simply placed on a new footing, namely, client-server architecture. In addition to the technical infrastructure, new, user-friendly graphical navigation options, MS Office integration, and tab pages helped increase productivity for SAP users. A similar leap forward led to the replacement of SAP R/3 with SAP ERP. In this case, the new SAP Basis, SAP NetWeaver, provided an even broader platform for the gradual integration of persons, information, and processes based on a service-oriented architecture. SAP ERP 6.0 is the recommended target release and provides a starting point for implementing functional packages of enhancements—the Enhancement Packages.

The following chapters focus on the functions in General Ledger accounting, Accounts Payable accounting, Accounts Receivable accounting, Asset Accounting, and periodic closing operations.

General Ledger accounting forms the core of finance and account-
ing. This fact remains unchanged in Release SAP ERP 6.0. There
is now also an additional option that can be used to define this
central element—the SAP General Ledger.

2   General Ledger Accounting

This chapter deals with the basic business principles of general ledger
accounting and describes the FI-GL (SAP General Ledger) component.
We explain many organizational terms generally, such as client, company
code and controlling area, business area, and chart of accounts, and place
them in the overall context. Because the structure of efficient accounting depends greatly on the characteristic values of master and document
data, we also dedicate some sections to these topics.

The main new feature in SAP ERP 6.0 is the SAP General Ledger. In a separate section we will examine the exact meaning of the group of topics in
more detail and which companies might find them worthwhile to use.

2.1   Basic Principles

In the main area of accounting in SAP the accounting-relevant data of
a company is entered, controlled, shared, and documented. Within
accounting, a distinction is made between an external accounting area
(FI component) and an internal accounting area (CO component). The
external accounting area includes general ledger and administrative
accounting with statutory subledgers, and the internal accounting area
covers cost and activity accounting. The two areas of financial accounting
(accounting) and cost and activity accounting are often enhanced by the
statistics and planning areas.

External/internal
accounting

2.1.1 Cost and Activity Accounting

Accounting provides the cost and activity accounting with the relevant expense and revenue postings. Cost and activity accounting adds costing-based valuation approaches and clearings, which are also to be posted on the G/L account of a shared chart of accounts, to this data material. This enables Controlling to be coordinated with all individual transactions and general ledger accounting in the SAP system. Statistics provide operational evaluations using comparison calculations contrasted with earlier periods or companies from the same industry. The statistics are used as the source for planning the activities of a company to obtain a basis for future decision-making.

The following tools ensure integration between accounting and cost accounting:

▶ Common chart of accounts

▶ Consistent document principles with single document posting based on the real-time principle

▶ Parallel account assignment features for general and subledgers and cost and activity accounting

▶ Reconciliations regarding periodic and transaction-related documents and totals

▶ Mutual clearing flow from general ledger accounting and subledger accounting into the systems for cost and activity accounting

Particularly close relationships exist here between:

▶ General ledger accounting (G/L accounting, expenses) and overhead cost management

▶ Asset accounting and project controlling (investment management)

▶ Inventory accounting and product cost by order or period

▶ Profitability analysis with all accounting systems

This book focuses on Financial Accounting (external accounting), the tasks and development of which we explain in the next section.

2.1.2 Objectives of General Ledger Accounting

The main task of general ledger accounting is to provide an overall view of external accounting and, as a result, of accounts. Recording all business transactions (primary postings and settlements from internal accounting) in a software system that is integrated with the business areas of a company ensures that the accounting data is always complete and accurate. The important factor is that the general ledger is regarded as complete verification of all business transactions. It represents the main current element of financial reporting. You can access individual transactions at any time in real time using documents, line items, and transaction figures at various levels, such as:

Transactions in real time

▶ Accounting data

▶ Journalizing

▶ Totals and transaction figures

▶ Balance sheet and profit and loss statements (P&L)

The balance sheet is a key element of accounting and gives a brief summary of the assets and liabilities of a company. It provides information about the size, type, and composition of the assets of a company measured in money at a specific time and establishes how much borrowed capital and company capital has been used to finance the assets. The balance sheet is broken down into individual balance sheet accounts at the beginning of a fiscal year. These are used to settle each balance sheet item separately in a clear and consecutive way.

2.1.3 Configuring the System

Within the framework of the system configuration (Customizing) in the implementation phase, the delivered standard SAP system must first be adapted to meet the specific requirements of the customer. The internal organization of the SAP customer and the predefined structures in the SAP system must be covered in this process. This applies to the static structure of the company and to the particular functions of the SAP system that you can use to automate existing business processes in the company. Customizing an SAP system primarily involves setting the contents of specific tables that have control functions in the SAP system.

System configuration or Customizing

SAP evaluation groups The main evaluation groups of an SAP system from the perspective of Financial Accounting are the client, generally the corporate level, the chart of accounts, and the company code, normally the level of the individual company. When you use the CO component (Controlling) it also contains the controlling area organizational unit where the cost and activity accounting requirements and consequently all internal business transactions are mapped.

2.1.4 Client

The client is the highest hierarchy level in the SAP system. Each client is a self-contained unit with separate master records and a complete set of tables. All entries are saved separately according to client to ensure that processing rules are consistently observed. A client is therefore a designated unit of system use of the standard SAP software. You can only process and evaluate data within one client. You therefore cannot evaluate customers of different clients in a dunning run. Specifications that you make at the client level apply to all organizational structures of this client (company codes, business areas, and so on). Access authorization is assigned separately per client. To enable a user to work in a client, you must create a user master record within the client.

2.1.5 Chart of Accounts

Account number and name The chart of accounts is a systematically structured directory of all G/L account master records required in one or more company codes. The chart of accounts contains the account number, account name, and control information for each G/L account master record. You can use any number of charts of accounts within a client. You may need to do this if company codes belong to different industries or nationalities. The charts of accounts used within a client form the chart of accounts list.

2.1.6 Company Code

Level of consolidated financial statement A company code is the smallest organizational unit for which a complete self-contained set of accounts can be drawn up. This includes recording all relevant transactions and generating all supporting documents required for a statutory consolidated financial statement (balance sheet and P&L statement) and reporting. A company code is therefore an independent accounting unit. You can set up almost any number of company codes for a client. You must assign each company code exactly one operating chart of accounts that can be used by several company codes.

2.1.7 Business Area

A business area is an organizational unit within a client that is not subject to any legal requirements. It describes a separate area of operation or responsibility in the company. Business areas are only suitable for internal purposes, in particular for evaluating and analyzing internal data. As a level of financial accounting, the business area primarily forms a dependent organizational unit within a client. Thus, you can save, manage, and evaluate all transaction figures and results (balance sheet and P&L statement) for each business area. Owing to internal clearings, business areas can represent any result levels (divisions, plants, sales organizations, and so on) in a structured way according to business-relevant contents.

Area of operation or responsibility

2.1.8 Profit Center

Profit centers are management-oriented divisions of the company and therefore are used for the internal control of sales and acquisition of activities from other departments. Another important task of profit center accounting is to determine specific key figures (return on investment, cashflow, working capital). Results that are determined according to the cost-of-sales or period accounting approach are shown on profit centers. Cost and revenue-bearing objects in the system (internal order, sales order, profitability segment, asset, cost center) are assigned to exactly one profit center each. When entering documents, you can use additional account assignments to map each result-relevant business transaction to the related profit center. If an account assignment object is not assigned, the corresponding costs and revenues within profit center accounting are posted to the dummy profit center that must be available as a master record like every real profit center in the SAP system.

Company within the company

2.1.9 Controlling Area

A controlling area is the organizational unit within a company for which complete, self-contained cost accounting can be performed. The controlling area structures a company from the perspective of controlling. Controlling is viewed as a managerial function with the task of supplying information to the decision-makers in the company. The focus here is mainly on the economic situation of the company, usually structured according to the following areas of responsibility:

▶ Planning and control of costs

▶ Planning and control of equity holdings adjustments

▶ Determining costing

Unlike Financial Accounting, which is subject to restrictive legal guidelines, internal accounting does not have any external regulations. Because you can structure cost accounting based on the ideas of management, you can make allowances for special scenarios and requirements of a company. To ensure that data is transferred in real time from Financial Accounting, each controlling area must be assigned to at least one company code. The following applies in this case:

▶ Company codes and the controlling area use the same operating chart of accounts.

▶ If company codes work with different currencies, the company code objects use the company code currency as the object currency.

The company is divided into individual areas of responsibility within the controlling area. Within SAP, these are:

▶ Cost center

▶ Adhering to a cost budget (cost controlling)

▶ Profit center

▶ Business success

▶ Investment center

▶ Investment framework (profit center with assets)

These general accounting structures and tasks must be represented in the context of the FI-GL component.

2.2 FI-GL Component

The component for general ledger accounting, SAP General Ledger, is rarely viewed in isolation. Value flows involved in general ledger accounting begin in other SAP ERP components such as MM (Materials Management), SD (Sales and Distribution), and PP (Production Planning). In addition, the general ledger supplies values to Controlling. An example of some of the subject matter is outlined briefly below:

Value flows in the SAP system

Goods Receipt/Invoice Receipt (MM)

In the purchasing process you normally receive the requested goods first, and this leads to an increase in material stock. An automatic entry to a reconciliation account is executed accordingly on the material stock account in the general ledger (account determination in material master). The entry is offset on the goods receipt/invoice receipt account (GR/IR) that is cleared again by posting the liability on the vendor account when the invoice is received.

Purchasing process

Goods Issue/Outgoing Invoices (SD)

The goods issue and outgoing invoices sales process runs in a similar way in Accounts Receivable. Here too, SAP General Ledger only receives values from connected components.

Sales process

Asset Acquisition from Asset Accounting (FI-AA)

When a vendor acquires an asset, the SAP system creates a posting with some automatically derived posting items. The balance sheet account (class 0) determined using the account determination key in the master record of the asset increases its value by the amount invoiced by the vendor. The entry is offset on the vendor account and in parallel on the reconciliation account (liabilities) stored in the vendor master record.

Asset accounting

Settling a Production Order from Production Planning (PP)

Production planning

As is the case with all order types, a production order settlement is structured according to a certain logic in the SAP system. The costs accumulated on the production order are grouped according to a stored system and settled using a defined rule. The production order is credited using the primary "Plant activity" cost element, and the settlement correspondingly increases the "finished products" stock.

Value Flows in Controlling (CO)

The Material Withdrawal Through Cost Center and Depreciations from Asset Accounting examples below explain in more detail the value flows that flow from general ledger accounting into other components.

Material Withdrawal Through Cost Center

Additional account assignment

When you enter a material withdrawal, the SAP system clears amounts and values between different objects. A price that is used to evaluate a goods movement (normally the standard price) is stored in the material master record. You must specify the material number and withdrawn quantity when you enter a material withdrawal. The value of the goods movement is calculated as a product from the quantity with the stored price of the material. The value of the material stock is now reduced accordingly in the SAP system, and an automatic entry to a reconciliation account is executed on the material stock account. The entry is offset on a primary cost element (G/L account in FI) that requires a mandatory additional account assignment on a CO object.

Depreciations from Asset Accounting

Accumulated depreciation account for decreases in value

When you post depreciations within Asset Accounting, values are also transferred from Financial Accounting to Controlling. We look at two depreciation areas in this example: the commercial valuation approach and the costing-based valuation approach. The indirect method involves posting the commercial depreciation on the accumulated depreciation account (balance sheet account), not on the balance sheet account, and thereby reducing the value of the asset. The entry is offset on a neutral expense account (P&L account). This ensures that the asset balance sheet value is reduced and the corresponding amount is included in the P&L statement. You post the costing-based depreciation on a primary cost element. This leads to the relevant amount being transferred to cost accounting by an additional account assignment (CO object). The entry is offset on an accumulated depreciations P&L account. Because the two accounts in question are profit and loss accounts the costing-based depreciation remains cost-neutral.

Regardless of how the values end up in the general ledger, the SAP General Ledger component forms the core of accounting at the level of individual financial statements. The SAP General Ledger in SAP ERP gives you a second option to organize general ledger accounting. For more detailed information, refer to Section 2.6, SAP General Ledger in SAP ERP Financials. Irrespective of whether you use the classic or new general ledger in the SAP system, the definition of master data or performance of manual postings looks 99% identical.

SAP General Ledger

2.3   Master Data

Financial Accounting uses G/L accounts as the basis for creating the balance sheet and P&L statement. A distinction is made here between balance sheet accounts and P&L accounts. You manage receipts and issues for a stock on balance sheet accounts, and you close them at the end of the fiscal year using the financial statement. The balance on a balance sheet account is carried forward to the new fiscal year. In contrast, you enter expenses and revenue for a company on P&L accounts. You close them using the P&L statement, and they have a zero balance at the start of each fiscal year. The collection of all G/L accounts used by a company is called a general ledger, and the account number in this case is a search criterion. Postings are sorted in chronological sequence within the account. You create the balance sheet and the P&L statement from the general ledger. Subledgers describe a general ledger account (known as the reconciliation account). When you create a new account, you must first specify an account group, which is why you also need at least one account group. Accounts that require the same master record fields and number range are created with the same account group. An account

Balance sheet accounts and P&L accounts

group is a group of properties that controls the management of master records. The account group controls the screen layout when you enter master data, and it defines the number ranges for the account name (internal or external assignment, numeric or alphanumeric, and which account interval).

2.3.1 Setting Up G/L Account Master Data

Two parts   G/L account master data consists of two parts, one specifically for charts of accounts and another specifically for company codes. The definitions in the chart of accounts area relate to cross-company code functions. All company codes to which this chart of accounts is assigned use this information. For example, the account number is assigned once at the level of the chart of accounts. Among other things, the information in the chart of accounts controls how master records are created in company codes. This is why you always enter the chart of accounts area first when you create a G/L account. The area specifically for company codes contains company-specific characteristics. You use these definitions to control how you enter accounting documents (field status group) and manage accounting data (manage open items, display line items) or control the currency you can use to post the account (account currency).

You can therefore enter data gradually in two steps. In the following example (Figure 2.1), the data in the chart of accounts is maintained first and is subsequently followed by the data in the company code.

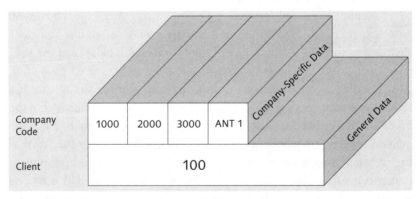

Figure 2.1 Structure of the G/L Account Master Data

Organization of Account Maintenance   **[+]**

Companies that are centrally organized define their chart of accounts data centrally. Employees of individual companies subsequently maintain the area of the relevant company code. The chart of accounts area in this case is not maintained by company code employees. In companies that are organized locally, both areas are normally created and maintained by employees in the individual company codes. The organizational structure required in each case for maintaining accounts is controlled by authorization management.

The entire master record for a G/L account is often defined centrally.

2.3.2 Maintaining G/L Accounts of Chart of Accounts Segment

The chart of accounts segment defines the account system and only exists once within a client. You select the menu path ACCOUNTING • FINANCIAL ACCOUNTING • GENERAL LEDGER • INDIVIDUAL PROCESSING OF MASTER DATA • IN CHART OF ACCOUNTS (Transaction FSP0) to maintain data.

Numbers for G/L accounts are assigned with classes 0 to 9 by the chart of accounts. The account number assignment in this area is therefore controlled externally.

Structure of Assigning Numbers   **[+]**

You can also have alphanumeric numbering, although this is less common because having nonalphanumeric numbering means you can enter data for posting transactions much more quickly using the numeric keypad on the keyboard.

The example in Figure 2.2 shows the chart of accounts segment of G/L account 113100 (Deutsche Bank domestic).

Click on the DISPLAY button to display an already existing G/L account master record. The CHANGE button correspondingly enables you to change a master record, and the CREATE and CREATE WITH TEMPLATE buttons enable you to enter a new master record. We explain the most important master record fields in the following list:

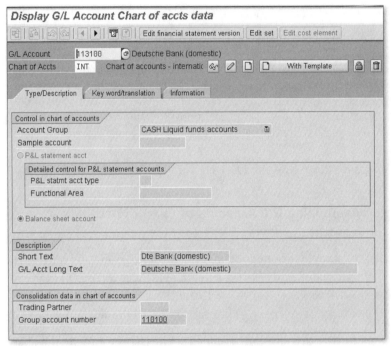

Figure 2.2 Chart of Accounts Segment—Type/Description

▸ **Account Group**

This field controls the screen layout of the area specifically for company codes when you create or change the master record and the assignment of account numbers. You use account groups to determine the status of master record fields centrally. You can hide fields here or define them as required entry or optional fields. An account group applies in all company codes that use this chart of accounts. The G/L account in the example belongs to the CASH account group (liquid funds accounts). This has implications for subsequently entering master data into company code segments.

▸ **Sample account**

If you want to create the account using a sample account, you enter the corresponding account number here.

▶ **Balance sheet account/P&L statement acct**
  Here you specify whether the G/L account is a balance sheet account or a P&L statement account. The balance on a balance sheet account is carried forward to the new fiscal year. With P&L statement accounts, you must specify the account to which the balance is carried forward for the new fiscal year.

▶ **Group account number**
  You can link up to three charts of accounts with each other in the SAP system. In this example, rather than transferring the individual bank or cash accounts for a subsequent consolidation of individual financial statements, the liquid funds are consolidated in consolidation item (group account) 110100.

Additional master record fields are located on the other tabs. Figure 2.3 displays the KEY WORD/TRANSLATION tab.

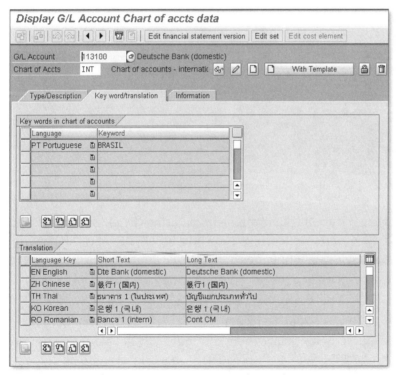

Figure 2.3 Chart of Accounts Segment—Key Words/Translation

Maintenance
language for
account names

In practice a stored principle maintenance language is not sufficient for the different account names. A translation is particularly necessary when an operating chart of accounts is to be used in several countries. Depending on the logon language, you can search for translated account names directly. You can also use key words to store key terms of an international account assignment manual for search queries.

The next tab, Information, mainly provides information about the master record history. The example in Figure 2.4 shows that the G/L account was created in 1992 by user SAP in the INT operating chart of accounts.

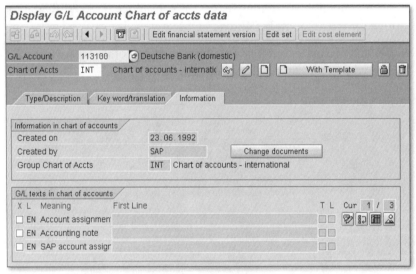

Figure 2.4 Chart of Accounts Segment—Information

Changes can be
traced

All changes since this time can be traced using change documents. You go to the overview of changes shown in Figure 2.5 by clicking on the Change documents button. You can see that four fields were changed there in the past.

Detailed logging

You can double-click to trace the field changes of the account group. As proof of the results you can use the overview in Figure 2.6 to see that there were two changes in the meantime. By double-clicking on the entry from 1996 you can display details about the user profile.

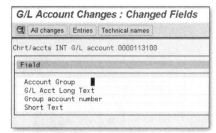

Figure 2.5 Change Document—Overview

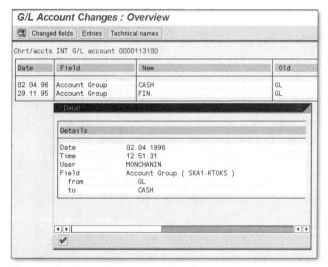

Figure 2.6 Change Document—Detail

This type of logging occurs for all changes to master and transaction data. You can therefore clearly trace who did something and when in the SAP system. In addition to the chart of accounts segment you can store information in the G/L account master record at the company code level.

2.3.3 Maintaining G/L Accounts of Company Code Segment

A chart of accounts and company code segment must exist to enable an account to be posted. You select the menu path ACCOUNTING • FINANCIAL ACCOUNTING • GENERAL LEDGER • MASTER DATA • INDIVIDUAL PROCESSING • IN COMPANY CODE (Transaction FSS0) to maintain data.

The Control Data tab in Figure 2.7 displays important information that is required for a local specification at the company code level.

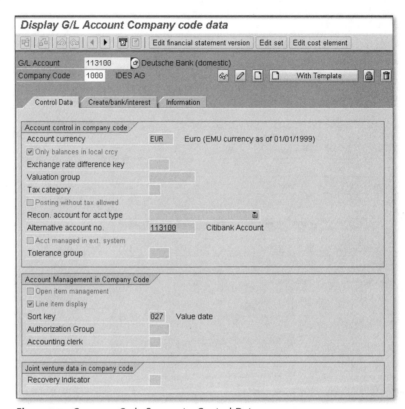

Figure 2.7   Company Code Segment—Control Data

▶ **Account currency**

If the currency key is the same as the local currency (company code currency) for a balance sheet account, a posting can be made into any currency at the document level. Transaction figures in this case are managed in the local currency. If you choose another currency key for a balance sheet account, transaction figures are managed in the local currency and the foreign currency. However, you cannot post into another currency. You can nevertheless make a posting into any foreign currency for P&L statement accounts, balance sheet accounts with open item management, or reconciliation accounts. Transaction figures in this case are managed in the local currency and in each posted foreign currency for information purposes.

▶ **Recon. account for acct type**
At least one reconciliation account must exist in the G/L accounts area for each subledger accounting (customers, vendors, and assets). An account type entry in this field identifies the G/L account as a reconciliation account. The assignment of an account to subledger accounting is defined in the corresponding master record. You cannot post reconciliation accounts manually.

▶ **Open item management**
You can clear open items for an account if you can assign an identical offsetting amount to the account. To do this you must first select this field in the master record. You are also required to display the line items. This is only useful if the account has debit and credit items that are to be assigned to each other (for example, clearing accounts). There is a guarantee for accounts with open item management that the documents can only be archived when all document items have been cleared. If open item management is defined retrospectively, this entry will only apply for documents posted after this change. However, the corresponding account must have a zero balance at the time of the change.

▶ **Line item display**
The line item display is the display of the document items for the account. You must select the corresponding G/L accounts for which you want to display line items. In this case you can use an index to connect the account with the related line items in the document file. In the dialog you can then access the item volume of the account where you can display specific fields using selection conditions. You can use the line item display to go to individual document items.

Displaying Line Items   [+]

Displaying line items for reconciliation accounts does not generally make sense. All details are contained in the subledger accounting and do not have to be recovered again in general ledger accounting. Alternative settings cost unnecessary memory.

▸ **Sort key**
You use a sort key to display line items. By default the SAP system sorts line items based on the content of the Assignment field in the document. When a document is entered, the key entered here controls which document field is copied into the Assignment item field if this is not filled manually or automatically.

[+] **Using an Alternative Account Number**

You can use this additional account number for different statistical purposes, for example, if you have created a new chart of accounts; the previous G/L account number is nevertheless useful for search queries or evaluations. Alternatively, this account number fulfills legal requirements from countries such as France or Spain where the state specifies a chart of accounts for which a financial statement is to be drawn up.

To enter more data for the company code segment you switch to the next tab, which you can also call using the [F8] function key.

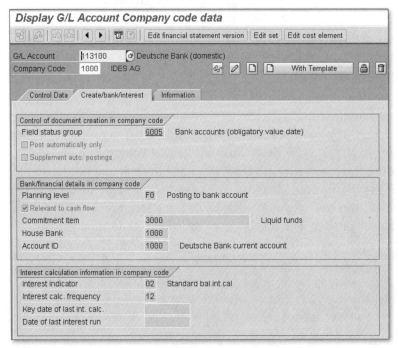

Figure 2.8 Company Code Segment—Create/Bank/Interest

Figure 2.8 shows the corresponding screen with the Create/bank/interest tab that contains additional master record fields:

▶ **Field status group**
Along with the field status group stored in the relevant posting key, the field status group entered here jointly controls the screen layout and therefore optional and required entry fields when you enter documents.

▶ **Interest indicator**
If you want the interest on a G/L account to be calculated automatically, you must enter the interest calculation indicator here.

▶ **Interest calc. frequency**
This entry determines the intervals (in months) in which balance interest (automatic process) will be calculated on the account.

▶ **Key date of last int. calc./Date of last interest run**
If balance interest is calculated automatically on the account, the SAP system stores the corresponding date here after each interest calculation run.

The next tab contains summarized information about the company code segment of the G/L account. The example in Figure 2.9 shows the user profile and creation date of the master record. Account 113100 is a component of the INT operating chart of accounts. The GKR local country chart of accounts against which the alternative account number is checked is assigned to company code 1000.

You use the | Edit financial statement version | button to define where you want the G/L account to be shown in a financial statement. You can store an account in one or more versions. G/L account 113100 (Deutsche Bank) with a debit balance appears on the assets side of the financial statement, as displayed in Figure 2.10.

Identifying the account in the financial statement version

57

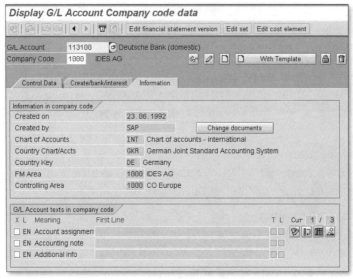

Figure 2.9 Company Code Segment—Information

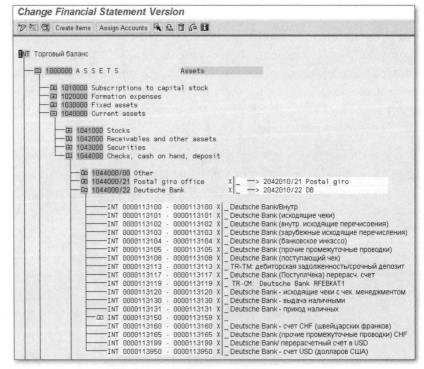

Figure 2.10 Assets Side of Financial Statement Version

If there is a liability rather than a receivable from the bank, the bank account must be shown on the liabilities side for a credit balance. Figure 2.11 illustrates this situation.

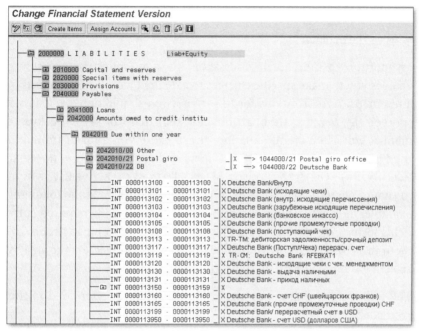

Figure 2.11 Liabilities Side of Financial Statement Version

You do not need any manual transfer postings here for the period end. The SAP system recognizes the total balance of the account and, owing to the maintained financial statement version, can automatically decide which item is to be shown.

No manual transfer postings

2.3.4 Changing G/L Account Master Data

With the exception of the Account number field, you can change all fields of the G/L account master record. However, you must take certain prerequisites into account for the following fields:

▶ You can only change the Currency key and Tax category for accounts that were not yet posted.

▸ You can only define an account as a Reconciliation account if it has a zero balance. You can only undo this definition retrospectively if the account has not yet been posted.

▸ You can only set or undo the Open item management indicator if the account has a zero balance.

▸ Mass data changes

In addition to individual processing, the new collective processing enables you to make specific changes to a defined worklist of accounts in a few steps. Authorizations for this transaction should only be assigned sporadically because although this is a tool that can save you lots of manual work in a credit situation, it can cause you a lot of trouble if used incorrectly. You can select the menu path ACCOUNTING • FINANCIAL ACCOUNTING • GENERAL LEDGER • MASTER DATA • COLLECTIVE PROCESSING to change chart of accounts data or company code data. In the following example, the field status group responsible for specifying required entry fields for posting documents is to be changed in the company code segment in a collective process for all bank accounts. You access the area by selecting the menu path or Transaction OB_GLACC12.

Warning message

The following warning once again illustrates the care required in this context:

Note that you can change many objects simultaneously in mass maintenance. The system performs a consistency check when you save your changes. The changes then take immediate effect on all selected objects. Therefore proceed carefully.

When you confirm the warning message, the selection screen shown in Figure 2.12 appears.

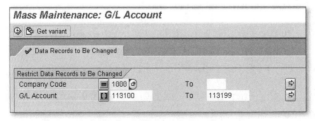

Figure 2.12 Selection for Collective Processing

In the example, the bank accounts for company code 1000 are to be selected as a worklist in the area from 113100 to 113199. The current contents of the company code segments for these accounts are displayed when you execute the selection using the ⌨F8 key (see Figure 2.13).

You can see that there are differences in the Field status group column. To store a uniform G001 specification for all selected accounts, select the column and enter this new value in the upper area of the screen. The data is transferred when you select the ⊞ icon, and the mass data is changed when you select Save.

Implementing field changes

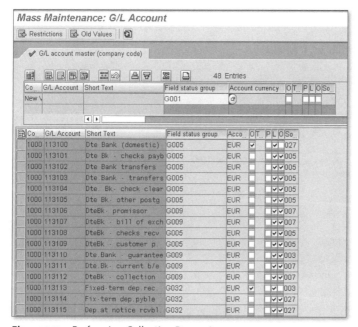

Figure 2.13 Performing Collective Processing

A new warning message indicates the effects of this step:

> *You want to save changes. Changes will immediately affect all selected objects. You cannot undo this step.*

Most master record changes are implemented manually and individually. Although technically possible, blocks are not generally assigned for G/L accounts with collective processing.

2.3.5 Blocking G/L Accounts

If you no longer want to use G/L accounts or if they were created by mistake, you can use the options illustrated in Figure 2.14. You can essentially block G/L accounts at two levels:

▶ **At chart of accounts level**
In the chart of accounts you block a master record for creation in the company code and an account for posting and planning.

▶ **At company code level**
In the company code you can only block an account for posting. You can set and undo the blocking indicator at any time.

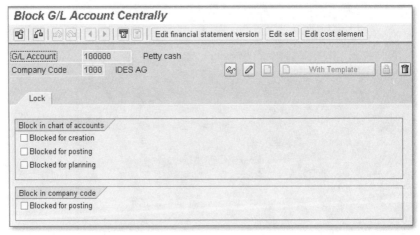

Figure 2.14 Blocking a G/L Account

Archiving master data
You can archive master records that you no longer require. When you archive master records, the data is extracted from the database, deleted, and put in a special file. However, you cannot physically delete master records immediately. To do this you first need to block this account for posting. You must then select the master record for deletion. Before the master record is deleted the system checks that it has no saved transaction figures and that the account was not posted in a past period and current period. After having focused on G/L account master data in the previous sections, we want to concentrate on transaction data on the following pages.

2.4   Documents in the SAP System

Documents exist at the center of the SAP system as the basis for process-   Related unit
ing and as documentation of individual business transactions. Each business transaction is stored in the system as a transaction-related posting
document. The document forms a self-contained and related unit (sym-
bolized by a unique document number). A consistent document structure, unique posting rules, and strictly formal and content-based checks
ensure that each posting document only enters the SAP system correctly
and completely for saving and further processing. This guarantees that all
account stocks and summary data of the FI component of the SAP system
result from single documents that are continuously posted correctly.

In this section we will first look at the layout of a typical SAP accounting
document. We will then explain the controlling factors of a document
(document type or posting key). We will discuss posting transactions in
other sections in this chapter.

2.4.1   Document Layout

The SAP system is consistently based on the document principle. This
has the following significance in the entire system:

▶ Each business transaction is entered and documented in a single posting document.

▶ Posting is only possible for zero balances (with the exception of statistical documents such as down payment requests).

▶ Each document contains a document number unique to the relevant
company code.

▶ Document numbers can be assigned internally (by the system) or
externally (entered by the user) depending on the business transaction.

The consistent document principle ensures that all integrated systems   Consistent
with their posting-relevant transactions or line items are linked to one   document principle
another at the transaction level and in an audit-proof way for every
business transaction entered in the SAP system. You can also offset all
summary data based on this principle and the analysis of this summary

data up to the single document. As the data basis for all individual transactions and summary updates, this complete document logic fulfills the crucial requirement for the German Generally Accepted Principles of Computer-Assisted Accounting Systems (GAPCAS) as part of the German Generally Accepted Principles of Data Processing (in Accounting) (GAPDP).

The FI component provides all the options of document management. You can display, change, cancel, and archive the posted documents directly using report analyses.

Structure of document header and item

Each document has a document header and 2 to a maximum of 999 document items or posting items. The document header contains information for the whole document such as document date and number. It also contains control parameters such as the document type. Document items only contain data for which the validity area is limited to the relevant document itself, for example, the posting key, account number, and amount. The other type of data that appears in the document items depends on the transaction in question and the account used. For example, a G/L account line will require data different from a customer or vendor line.

2.4.2 Document Header

Figure 2.15 shows the document header for an accounting document. The information contained in the document header is relevant for the whole document and cannot be limited to specific document items. Some values in the document header even have a direct effect on individual document items. This includes the Document Type, Currency, and exchange rate, which affects all document item amounts. There is also a record of the SAP user (Entered by field) who entered the document and the date (Entry Date field) and time (Time of Entry field) it was entered.

Below is a description of some of the fields in a document header:

▶ **Document Type**
The document type classifies the business transaction.

▶ **Doc. Header Text**
Text field for information valid for the whole document.

▶ **Document Date**
In the SAP system this is the creation date or date of the relevant business transaction (for example, the invoice date).

▶ **Posting Date**
The posting date in the SAP system is the date when the document is assigned to accounting or updated on the accounts. The date must be in an allowed posting period. When you enter a document, the current date is specified as the posting date. We discuss period control in more detail in Chapter 7, Closing Operations.

▶ **Posting Period**
This describes the period when accounts are updated (the current month is specified). The posting period is automatically derived from the posting date.

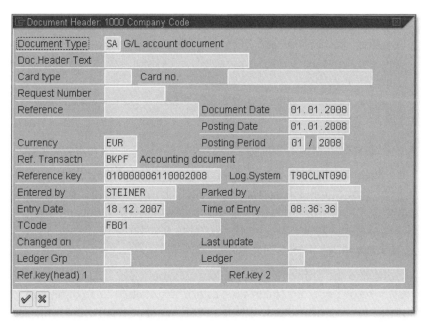

Figure 2.15 Document Header

▶ **Reference**

The reference is a reference number that is valid for all posting items and is transferred to the Assignment field when you store the 009 key (external document number) as a sorting criterion in the master record of the customer/vendor.

▶ **Currency**

The currency that the document is posted in is specified here (also transaction currency).

2.4.3 Document Type

Classifying the subject matter

Each document header contains a document type, which classifies accounting documents. The document type has the following functions:

▶ Differentiates business transactions.

▶ Provides information about the type of posted business transaction and is therefore simultaneously used for documentation purposes (storage criterion).

▶ Specifies the accounts to which you can post a document (checks the account types used for the posting, for example, the C account type for customers).

▶ Restricts the posting keys that you can use (controlling factor for document items).

▶ Assigns document numbers and controls document storage.

Each document type is assigned a document number range from which a document number is allocated for the relevant document when you enter it. The document type also controls whether the document number is assigned internally (by the system) or externally (by the user or feeder system).

Checking against allowed account types

To illustrate the properties of a document type, Figure 2.16 displays the master record of a document type as it is maintained in a configuration context in the SAP system. When a DR document type is used, the settings in Figure 2.16 assign a document a document number from the 18 number range, the interval limits of which are defined at a different level. If no selections are made in the Account types allowed area, account

66

types are deliberately excluded from document entry. All account types are allowed in this example. The standard SAP system includes the document types listed in Table 2.1.

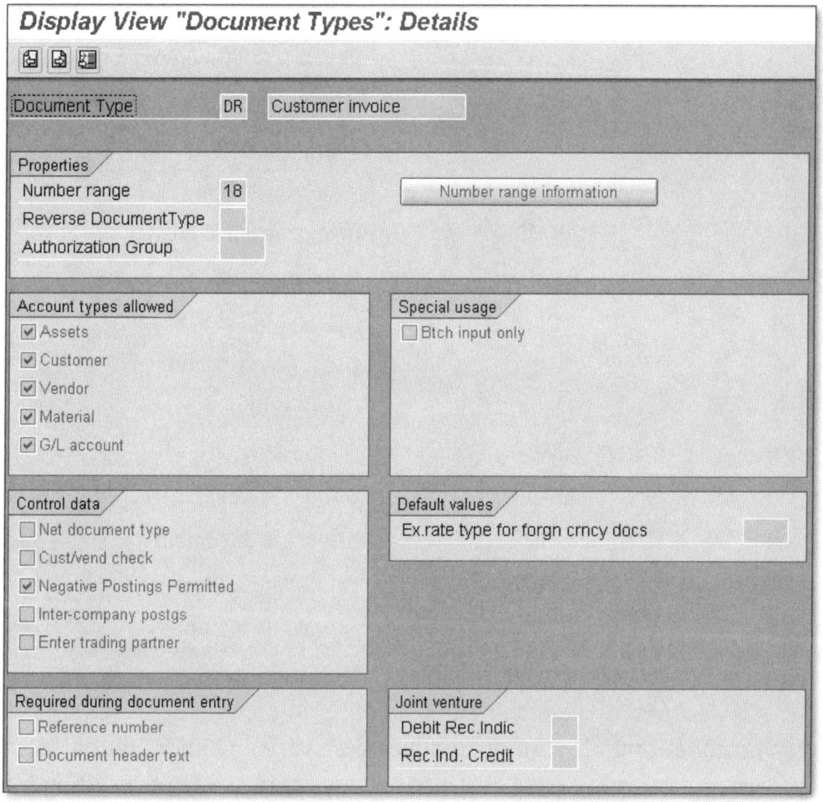

Figure 2.16 Settings for the DR (Customer Invoice) Document Type

Document type	Account type	Description
AA	ADKMS	Asset posting
AF	AS	Depreciation posting
DA	DS	Customer document
DB	ADS	Customer recurring entry
DG	DS	Customer credit memo

Table 2.1 Document Types

Document type	Account type	Description
DR	ADKMS	Customer invoice
DZ	DS	Customer payment
KA	AKMS	Vendor invoice
KG	AKMS	Vendor credit memo
KN	AKS	Vendor net
KR	AKMS	Vendor invoice (gross)
KZ	AKMS	Vendor payment
RE	AKMS	Invoice receipt (gross)
RN	AKMS	Invoice receipt (net)
SA	ADKMS	G/L account document
SB	DS	G/L account posting
SK	S	Cash document
WA	AMS	Goods issue
WE	AMS	Goods receipt
WI	AMS	Inventory document
X1	ADKMS	Permanent document
X2	ADKMS	Sample document

Table 2.1 Document Types (Cont.)

The document number uniquely identifies every document within a fiscal year and company code. Because documents may be in the system for a long time, sufficiently large document number intervals are required. The system ensures this with the following options:

▶ Number ranges are defined per company code, which means each company code can use the same number ranges.

▶ Document numbers can be up to 10 characters long.

▶ Number ranges are defined on a fiscal basis, so the same numbers can be assigned consistently every year.

Maintain Number Range Intervals

🔲 Interval 🔲

NR Object   Accounting document

Intervals

No	Year	From number	To number	Current number	Ext
01	1992	0100000000	0199999999	0	☐
01	1993	0100000000	0199999999	0	☐
01	1999	0100000000	0199999999	100013204	☐
01	2000	0100000000	0199999999	100001663	☐
01	2004	0100000000	0199999999	100013927	☐
01	2005	0100000000	0199999999	100003782	☐
01	2006	0100000000	0199999999	100003364	☐
01	2007	0100000000	0199999999	100010061	☐
01	2008	0100000000	0199999999	100001638	☐

Figure 2.17 Number Ranges in Company Code 1000

2.4.4 Document Items

A document item only contains information about the relevant posting item. This always includes the posting key, amount, and account number. Depending on the posting transaction, additional information such as the payment term or an additional account assignment such as a cost center is added.

Significance of posting key

Display Document: Data Entry View

🔲 🔲 🔲 🔲 ℹ️ Taxes 🔲 Display Currency 🔲 General Ledger View

Data Entry View

Document Number	1900000000	Company Code	1000	Fiscal Year	2009
Document Date	19.01.2009	Posting Date	19.01.2009	Period	1
Reference		Cross-CC no.			
Currency	EUR	Texts exist	☐	Ledger Group	

Co...	Item	PK	S	Pers.No.	Account	Description	Amount	Currency	Assignment	Tx	Cost Center
1000	1	31			1000	XYZ Ltd	25.000,00-	EUR	19000000002009	V0	
	2	40			417000	Purchased services	5.000,00	EUR	0000001000	V0	1000
	3	40			417000	Purchased services	5.000,00	EUR	0000002100	V0	2100
	4	40			417000	Purchased services	5.000,00	EUR	0000004120	V0	4120
	5	40			417000	Purchased services	10.000,00	EUR	0000004279	V0	4279

Figure 2.18 Document Items

In the individual document items you can double-click to go to a line of the displayed document (see Figure 2.18). The following fields are displayed here:

▶ **Posting key (PK)**
This key determines which data can be entered (for example, customers, G/L accounts), how the posted data is processed further, and how the entered data is updated (debit or credit).

▶ **Account number (Account)**
This account is updated based on the posting key (for 40 or 50 the G/L account with the entered number, for 01 the customer account with the corresponding number).

▶ **Amount**
The document item amount is specified here depending on the display variant in the document currency (transaction currency) or local currency.

▶ **Additional account assignments**
You can enter the relevant CO account assignment objects here (order, cost center, and so on).

▶ **Assignment**
This is the first criterion for sorting individual items within the display of account items. In this case a sort key is stored in G/L account 417000, and it copies the number of the cost center (1000 in this example) into the Assignment field.

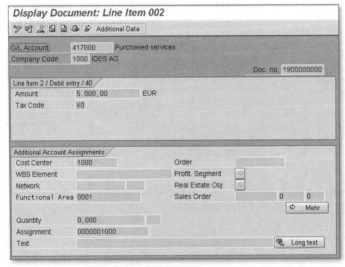

Figure 2.19 Details of a Document Item

2.4.5 Posting Key

Figure 2.20 summarizes the properties of a posting key. In the following subsections we describe some of the posting keys (PSTKY), which are provided in the standard system, separately according to component and area of application.

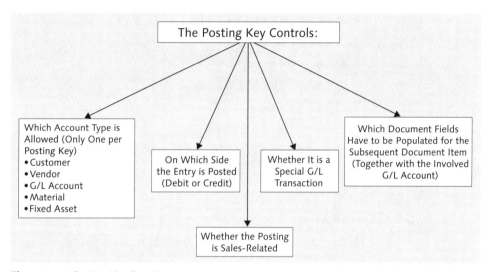

Figure 2.20 Posting Key Functions

Accounts Receivable Accounting

The posting keys displayed in Table 2.2 are available with the specified properties in accounts receivable accounting in the standard SAP system.

PSTKY	D/C	Description
01	Debit	Invoice
09	Debit	Special general ledger
11	Credit	Credit memo
15	Credit	Incoming payment
16	Credit	Payment difference
18	Credit	Payment clearing
19	Credit	Special general ledger

Table 2.2 Posting Keys (Customers)

Accounts Payable Accounting

Table 2.3 shows the posting keys provided in the standard SAP system for the accounts payable accounting component.

PSTKY	D/C	Description
21	Debit	Credit memo
25	Debit	Outgoing payment
26	Debit	Payment difference
27	Debit	Clearing
29	Debit	Special general ledger
31	Credit	Invoice
36	Credit	Payment difference
39	Credit	Special general ledger

Table 2.3 Posting Keys (Vendors)

G/L Account Postings

You can use the following posting keys for G/L account postings:

PSTKY	D/C	Description
40	Debit	G/L account posting
50	Credit	G/L account posting
81	Debit	Costs
85	Debit	Inventory changes
86	Debit	GR/IR debit
91	Credit	Costs
96	Credit	GR/IR credit

Table 2.4 Posting Keys (General Ledger)

Subledgers for Asset Accounting and Materials Management

Asset accounting and materials management subledgers are delivered in the standard SAP system with the posting keys shown in Table 2.5.

PSTKY	D/C	Description (Account Type)
70	Debit	Debit assets (A)
75	Credit	Credit assets (A)
89	Debit	Stock receipts (M)
99	Credit	Stock issues (M)

Table 2.5 Posting Keys (Assets and Materials)

2.4.6 Special G/L Indicator

The special G/L indicator informs the system that a certain special G/L transaction is to be posted. Figure 2.21 shows the special G/L transactions that are delivered preconfigured in the standard SAP system. The important special G/L transaction for bill of exchange management is described in detail in Chapter 6, Bank Accounting.

Definition of special G/L transactions

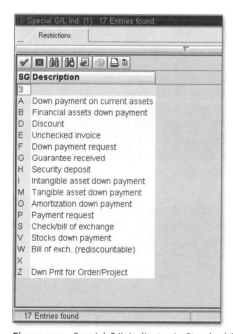

Figure 2.21 Special G/L Indicator in Standard SAP System

2.5   Document Entry

Posting key and
field status group

The document type defines the document number (number range) and influences the posting key and allowed accounts through the account types. The posting key entered defines the appearance of the next screen in conjunction with the field status group. You enter additional data on this screen, for example, the amount, an additional account assignment, or a payment term. You then enter posting keys and account numbers for the next document item, which in turn defines the layout of the next screen.

2.5.1   Entering G/L Account Postings

In Release 4.6 of the SAP system there are basically two transactions available for entering a G/L account document: one in the form already known from earlier releases and the other in the single-screen transaction (SAP Enjoy transaction) available since Release 4.6. In the following sections we explain these two versions using an example that we first want to introduce briefly here.

[Ex]

Cash Document for Purchasing Office Material

An employee purchases books that he or she needs to carry out his or her duties. The expense amounting to €100 is reimbursed in cash from the central cash office when the corresponding document is presented. When the accounting document is created, the cost center of the employee is also to be debited simultaneously.

The posting occurs in the general ledger on the Central cash office G/L account and on a corresponding expense account. The Cost center CO object in this case is debited with the amount from the expense account posting.

Traditional Procedure

First, we will describe the traditional form of entering documents in the SAP system. You can access this area by selecting the menu path ACCOUNTING • FINANCIAL ACCOUNTING • GENERAL LEDGER • POSTING • GENERAL POSTING (Transaction F-02) (Figure 2.22).

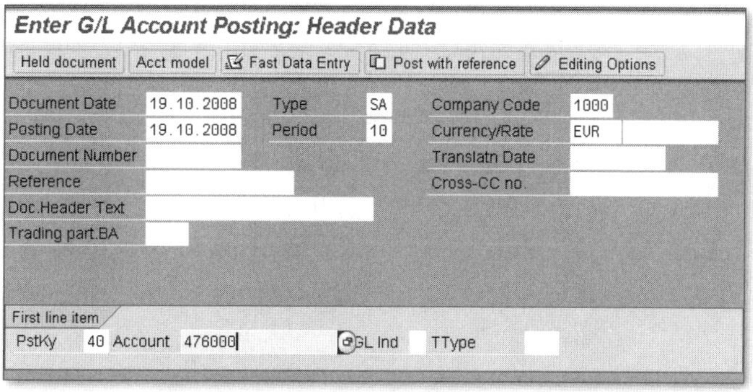

Figure 2.22 Entering G/L Account Postings—Initial Screen

The first two entries for a document item define the relevant account and posting side (debit or credit). In this example these are posting key 40 (debit G/L account) and the account number of the G/L account in question. When you press the ⌷Enter⌷ key, the screen shown in Figure 2.23 appears.

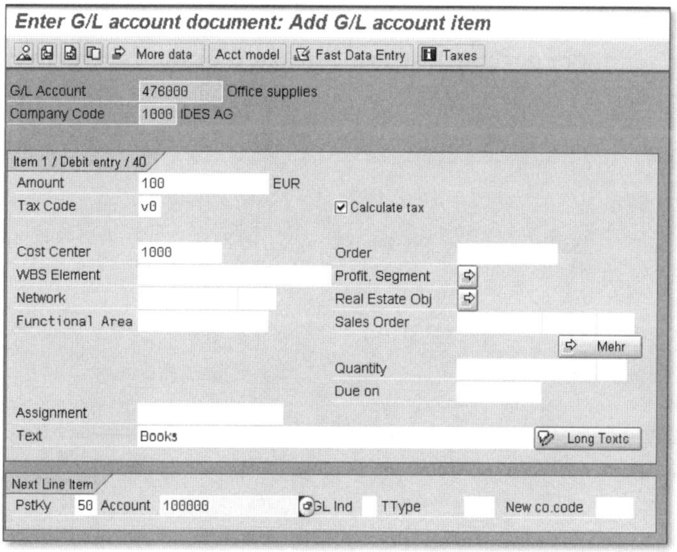

Figure 2.23 Entering G/L Account Postings—First Item

After you enter the first item of the G/L account posting, you must then enter the posting key and account number of the next document item before you press the ⌷Enter⌷ key. The screen shown in Figure 2.24 is then displayed.

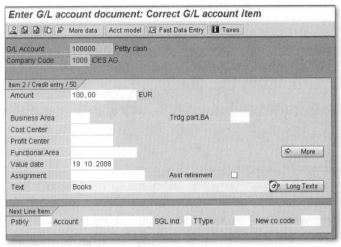

Figure 2.24 Entering G/L Account Postings—Second Item

You can display the document before it is posted in the system by selecting the menu path DOCUMENT • SIMULATE.

From this display area, you can still change all of the data for an entered document or add more document items. You can post the document if there is a zero balance.

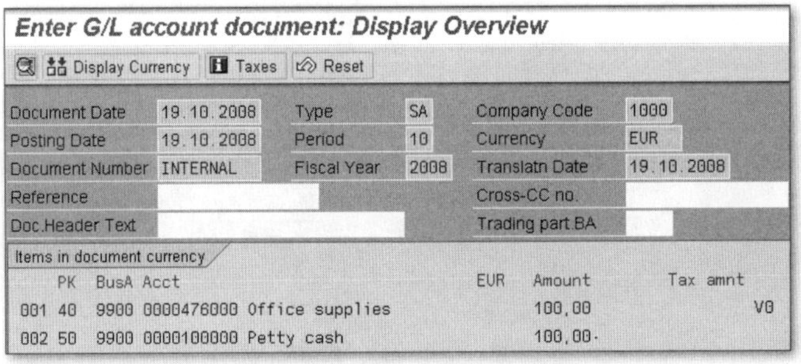

Figure 2.25 G/L Account Posting – Document Display

New Single-Screen Transaction (SAP Enjoy Transaction)

A new transaction for entering G/L account documents has been available since SAP Release 4.6. This single-screen transaction enables you to enter and post all data for a business transaction (header and item data), which used to be displayed on several pages, completely on one screen. You access the new transaction within general ledger accounting by selecting the menu path ACCOUNTING • FINANCIAL ACCOUNTING • GENERAL LEDGER • POSTING • G/L ACCOUNT POSTING (Transaction FB50).

In principle, this new SAP transaction is nothing other than a slightly visually refined fast data entry that was also available in earlier releases. The screen for entering postings consists of four areas in this case:

Fast data entry in a posting screen

▶ Data for the document header

▶ Data for individual document items

▶ Procedural documentation to help make it easier to enter documents

The structure for entering documents using the new transaction is displayed in Figure 2.26. Like the previous fast data entry version, you can only enter G/L account items in the data of individual document items.

The traffic light display indicates the balance in the document currency:

▶ **Red**
The balance does not equal zero.

▶ **Yellow**
The balance has not been checked (initial status).

▶ **Green**
The balance equals zero.

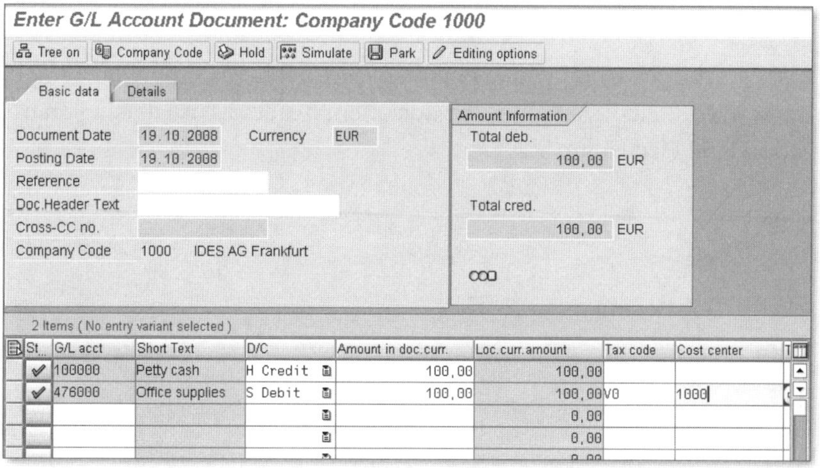

Figure 2.26 G/L Account Posting in Enjoy Transaction

Document items are entered in the table. You have different editing options here:

- You can derive the debit/credit indicator using the plus and minus signs of the amount (setting in the editing options).
- You can individually configure the entry table using the table settings (corresponding button beside the table).
- You can use other options from the function key menu under the entry area.

In the Tree on area you can select entry variants, account assignment templates, or held documents. You can do this in a number of ways:

- By double-clicking
- By using the context menu (right mouse key)
- By using the menu bar

2.5.2   Entry Tools

Simplifying the manual assignment of accounts

The SAP system has a number of entry tools to support you when you manually enter documents. In this section we describe the two most important entry tools, fast data entry and the account assignment model.

Fast Data Entry

Fast data entry enables you to enter G/L account items simply on a single input screen. First, you enter the document header as usual using Transaction F-02 (see Figure 2.27).

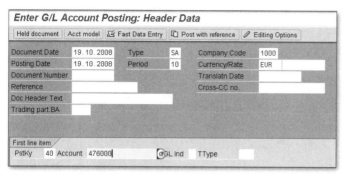

Figure 2.27 Fast Data Entry—Header Data

When you click on the Fast Data Entry button, the SAP system goes to a simplified display for entering documents.

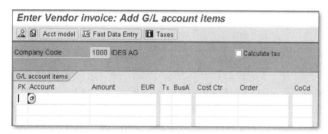

Figure 2.28 Fast Data Entry—Item Data

You can then enter G/L account items quickly and simply.

Copy and Paste   **[+]**

The example in the fast data entry works without default values, which you can nevertheless copy into the lines simply by copying and pasting. If you use one column in a spreadsheet for the posting key and one for accound numbers, you can copy these contents using the `Ctrl` + `C` key combination and paste them directly into the fast data entry in the SAP system using `Ctrl` + `V`.

Account Assignment Model

An *account assignment model* is a template for entering documents. It can contain any number of G/L account items that may be incomplete, and you can therefore enhance, delete, and change them when you enter a document. You can call any number of account assignment models. You can also switch here between entering document items in the normal way and entering them using account assignment models. You can add equivalence numbers to account assignment models. When you use an account assignment model, in this case only a total amount is specified, which is always distributed proportionally on the items of the account assignment model. You create an account assignment model by selecting the menu path ACCOUNTING • FINANCIAL ACCOUNTING • GENERAL LEDGER • POSTING • REFERENCE DOCUMENT • ACCOUNT ASSIGNMENT MODEL menu path (Transaction FKMT).

In the initial screen shown in Figure 2.29 you must enter a key containing up to 10 characters. The account assignment model is stored under this key. If you want to display or change an existing model, you can use the input help key to get an overview of existing models.

Distributing amounts
To define the account assignment model with equivalence numbers, you select the field of the same name. You must specify a currency key if amounts are to be defined in the model. You can subsequently only use the model for postings in the specified currency. If you do not want to define any amounts, you leave the Currency field shown in Figure 2.29 blank, which means you will be able to use the model for any currencies.

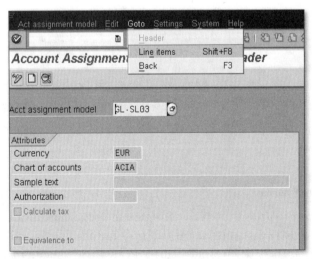

Figure 2.29 Creating an Account Assignment Model—Initial Screen

Account assignment models are not linked to a company code. They can contain document items for different company codes. You can also specify external company codes (which are managed in other systems) or omit the company code. In the latter case, the company code is set dynamically when you use the account assignment model.

You specify a chart of accounts if no company codes are to be defined in the items of the model but the system is to check that the specified accounts exist. You only use sample text of an account assignment model for documenting the relevant account assignment model. No data is obtained for the document from this text; in particular, it is not transferred into the document header or document item text. You select the menu path GOTO • ITEMS to go to an entry screen for the items of the account assignment model (see Figure 2.30).

Provided you have not yet entered an item, you can modify the entry screen. You can change the entry screen by selecting the menu path SETTINGS • ENTRY SCREEN. Once you have defined the entry screen, you can enter the individual contents of the account assignment model.

Preparing provision postings

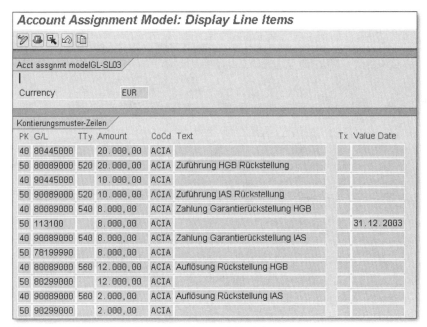

Figure 2.30 Items of the Account Assignment Model

The example relates to preparing provision postings. Accounts for additions, transfer postings, and reversals are stored in the account assignment model. Only the posting amount varies, and you cannot store it.

When you use an account assignment model, an entry is supported in list form. Like the fast data entry of G/L account items, you can structure the entry screens individually. A scroll function is also supported in these screens. You can overwrite all data in the entry screen when you use an account assignment model. You can also add more items without needing to change to normal entry mode. The account assignment model we just discussed in the example was selected using Transaction F-02. Figure 2.31 illustrates this process.

When you confirm a selection by pressing the ⌷Enter⌷ key, values for the account assignment model are transferred to the G/L account items (see Figure 2.32).

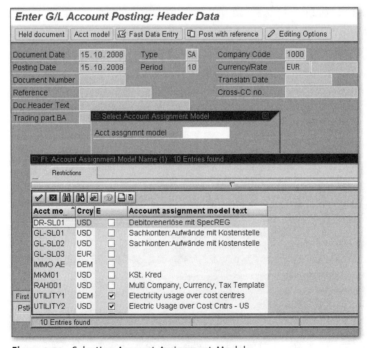

Figure 2.31 Selecting Account Assignment Models

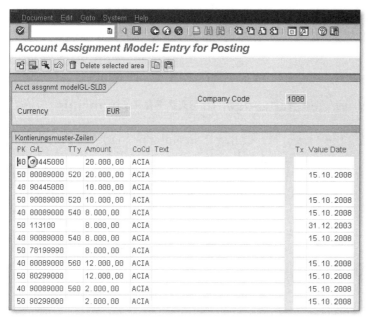

Figure 2.32 Transferring Contents

When you use an account assignment model with equivalence numbers, you cannot enter any amounts into the items. Two input fields appear in the header section of the screen for this purpose, where you enter the debit or credit amount to be distributed (see Figure 2.33). The system distributes the amounts to the items. You can subsequently post the document by clicking on the SAVE button.

Figure 2.33 Account Assignment Models with Equivalence Numbers

The same entry tools are available and master data is maintained in the same way regardless of whether you use classic or new general ledger accounting.

2.6   New General Ledger in SAP ERP Financials

Remodeling the core of accounting is an ambitious task. All other components such as subledgers, valuation programs, and in particular, integration with other components like SD (sales & distribution) or MM (materials management) must be tailored to this new center of accounting. Business processes including the preparation of financial statements would not run seamlessly in the company without this harmonious interaction. The existing general ledger in SAP R/3 has proven its worth over the years and will remain in SAP ERP.

2.6.1   Overview

Flexible solution   The new general ledger is optional and connects the solutions distributed across several applications in SAP R/3. SAP customers would have to implement several components to fulfill international and/or industry-specific standards. To avoid this, a new flexible solution was created for the general ledger in SAP ERP. This solution combines the general ledger, including the cost of sales ledger, profit center accounting, special ledger, and consolidation preparation ledger. The new general ledger is based on a broader standardized data basis. For example, a G/L account, functional area, and profit center are included in one data record. This enhances the quality of data, reconciliation measures become unnecessary, and period-end closing can be performed more quickly. Above all, the new general ledger creates transparency and increases the quality of data.

Parallel Financial Reporting

Accounting standards such as International Financial Reporting Standards (IFRS) have been mandatory since 2005 for consolidated financial statements of companies listed on the stock exchange, but regulations also still apply at the level of individual financial statements. Parallel financial reporting has increased in importance in this context. But where and how do you efficiently record and save the valuations of the different accounting standards and make them available for reporting? To date, SAP R/3 offered three options:

- ▸ Accounts
- ▸ Special ledgers
- ▸ Company codes

The account solution is the mapping option used by the majority of customers and the one recommended up to now by SAP. For customers with a very large number of accounts with valuation differences, maintaining a parallel ledger to the general ledger in the special ledger application was one alternative to the account solution. We advise against using the company code solution, because this is only supported by asset accounting and is not being further developed by SAP. A fourth option is available with the new general ledger as of SAP ERP. You can use it to map several ledgers, provide them with contents using a standardized posting transaction (for example, Transaction FB50,) or evaluate them for the balance sheet and P&L statement (Report RFBILA10) using standardized reporting. The new Ledger Group field in the document header determines which ledger is filled when you post manually.

In the SAP menu you can use Transaction FB50L or select the menu path Accounting • Financial Accounting • General Ledger • Posting • Enter G/L Account Document for Ledger Group to enter posting documents for individual accounting standards. The manual business transaction for a provision posting is used for the example in Figure 2.34. A provision posting is entered exclusively for Ledger Group L5, which represents the IAS valuation approach. The selection in the new

Transaction for ledger groups

Ledger Group field is used for this purpose. The displayed ⌷F4⌷ input help shows other alternatives that would also be possible. For more information about how provision postings are dealt with in the closing process, see Chapter 7, Closing Operations.

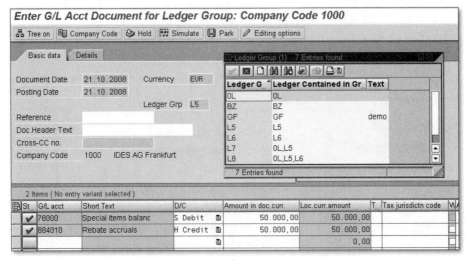

Figure 2.34 Provision Posting per Ledger Group

New evaluations   The new general ledger also includes a number of new evaluations that specifically enable you to display individual ledger contents in a financial statement. The menu path ACCOUNTING • FINANCIAL ACCOUNTING • GENERAL LEDGER • INFO SYSTEM • GENERAL LEDGER (NEW) provides a balance sheet report that displays the information shown in Figure 2.35. You can see that the IAS valuation approach for the L5 ledger was again selected exclusively there. The account just posted for provisions appears in the liabilities section of the balance sheet, which is structured in accordance with commercial law.

Individual segment balance sheets are also supported for every profit center, business area, or segment.

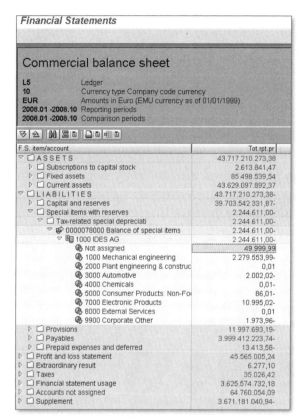

Figure 2.35 Report RFBILA10 for a Ledger Group

Document Splitting

In addition to the legal company code characteristic, other aspects for mapping financial statements are possible, for example, in the area of energy supply, where legislation, in addition to legal business units, insists on segment balance sheets to monitor previous energy monopolies. When you update the new general ledger, you can also activate a document split (online split). Unlike a financial statement adjustment for which complex totals postings are performed retrospectively, document splitting enhances the original document with the segment information in real time. The objective of this enhancement is to project account assignment objects into document rows where they were not originally assigned, for example, the profit center from the revenue lines into the

Enhancing with segment information

receivables line. This option increases the transparency of the postings and enables you to create additional internal financial statements. Collective posting for the financial statement adjustment is therefore no longer necessary because all information is already available at the document level.

Example In the following example we explain the principle of splitting documents in more detail. A receivable over €1,100 including a EUR 100 tax portion is split between the two profit centers, JB1 with €400 and JB2 with €600, in the revenue items. In practice, these could be two different activities for the customer that are represented internally across profit centers (in other words, company within the company). Irrespective of whether this transaction is integrated through the SD component or entered manually in the FI component, the new general ledger with an active document split can generate the document displayed in Figure 2.36.

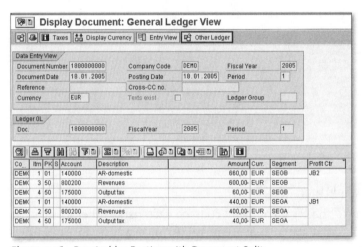

Figure 2.36 Receivables Posting with Document Split

In the new general ledger the information for the revenue lines is projected and split into the receivables and tax lines. This information can be inherited for an incoming payment posting (this is described in more detail in Chapter 6, Bank Accounting) (see Figure 2.37).

Complete financial statement for segments in real time The customer pays with a 3% cash discount and reduces not only the receivables amount, but also the tax amount. This adjustment posting can also relate to the original invoice information at a ratio of 4 to 6.

Complete financial statements for segments are possible in real time with a new active general ledger and a document split. Figure 2.38 shows a financial statement for profit center JB1, and Figure 2.39 shows one for profit center JB2.

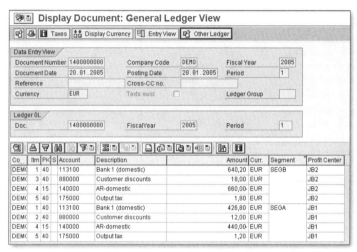

Figure 2.37 Incoming Payment with Document Split

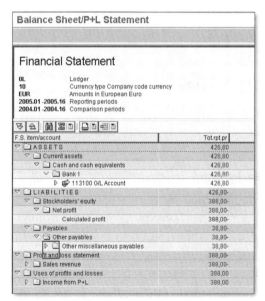

Figure 2.38 Financial Statement for Profit Center JB1

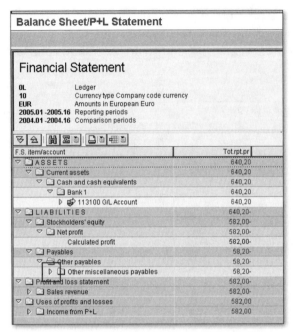

Figure 2.39 Financial Statement for Profit Center JB2

There are other factors in favor of the new general ledger besides parallel financial reporting and document splitting. We discuss these in more detail in the next section using a customer example.

2.6.2 Evaluation Report for Accenture GmbH

The basis for implementing the new general ledger successfully involves selecting and allocating the use of the new functions correctly.

Customer Description and Background

The project we conducted was initiated by the corporate accounting department of a world-leading retail and services group (with approximately 11.5 billion turnover and about 53,000 employees in the 2007/2008 fiscal year). As part of harmonizing the corporate chart of accounts worldwide, a decision was made to replace the traditional third-party software with SAP ERP Central Component (ECC) 6.0 for the German/Dutch accounting system group (approximately 550 future SAP users). The scope of the project involved 84 legal entities in 13 locations mainly in Germany, with their main field of business in the area of multichannel retail (catalog, Internet, stationary retail).

Challenges for the Project

One of the complex challenges for the project involved harmonizing the accounting carried out at 13 locations to facilitate implementing the information from corporate accounting uniformly across the locations. The new harmonized corporate chart of accounts had to be detailed further to map a global, operationally usable chart of accounts in SAP ECC 6.0. The new processes should also increase efficiency potential considerably, because the decision to implement an SAP system was based on a preinvestment analysis. The new global requirements also included mapping parallel financial reporting in accordance with local accounting standards (for example, German, UK, and U.S. GAAP) and IFRS, which meant reimplementing the P&L statement based on cost-of-sales accounting. The implementation of transferring both accounting standards to the SAP EC-CS corporate reporting system every month and the need to take into account other already emerging international system rollouts completed the requirements.

Harmonization in Accounting

Constitutional Project Decisions

From the perspective of Accenture, the introduction of the new general ledger with its new functions meets the needs of the market, which, owing to heightened requirements in financial reporting, requires more flexibility when accounting is being mapped using standard software. Examples of heightened requirements include managing different parallel financial reporting standards owing to a globalization of systems and the creation of complete financial statements at the segment level. The introduction of the new general ledger on the market by SAP essentially does not change the need to identify constitutional questions early in the design phase, develop possible solutions for them, and ultimately choose an alternative option.

Heightened requirements

Many of these decisions occur in the same way for all customers but may have completely different results depending on the customer's situation and the required debit situation. The new general ledger adds additional alternatives, each with their own advantages and disadvantages, to the toolbox of the project team specifically for these constitutional decisions. We therefore recommend that you carefully weigh up traditional solution alternatives again and assess them on the basis of the new general ledger. Especially for customers who migrate from systems other than SAP, the choice to move to a new function of the new general ledger may only be the second-best alternative from a procedural point of view. The implementation project described here was formed by the following constitutional decisions relating to the new general ledger.

Parallel Financial Reporting

Obviously, the primary requirement from the very beginning of the project was to be able to map two parallel valuations simultaneously. Depending on the subsidiary company, this was the relevant country-specific financial reporting (for example, in accordance with German GAAP, UK GAAP, Dutch closing statement), and financial reporting in accordance with IFRS for group reporting. Secondary objectives were to minimize operational expenses in accounting for entering accounting material and creating closing statements, comply with generally accepted accounting principles, maximize the transparency of implemented solutions, and maximize functions in all financial reporting (ledgers).

Several alternatives The following activities were analyzed and evaluated with a view to their practical feasibility:

▸ Mapping using account logic

▸ Mapping using account delta logic

▸ Mapping using the new functions of parallel ledgers

When you map using account logic, there is a single general ledger, in other words, a single data store where you post the information of local financial reporting (for the sake of simplicity, abbreviated to GAAP from here on) and information in accordance with IFRS. The customer also mapped this variant in the original accounting system with what is known in the project as the "Mickey Mouse" solution. Most information is posted in accordance with IFRS and GAAP. This information is posted on the G/L accounts that are only allowed for common information (Mickey Mouse's head).

The left ear is reserved for HGB information only (for example, tax-based adjustments), and the right ear is reserved for IFRS information only (for example, the activation of software created in-house). Therefore, postings only have to be entered twice for information that must be updated differently between the two accounting standards. Owing to the main disadvantages of this solution already being used by customers (namely, adding duplicate accounts to the chart of accounts, presenting the same contents in the different ears, and the possibility of creating value shifts owing to inadvertent postings between the accounting standards), the analysis of the mapping using parallel ledgers was carried out with great interest.

"Mickey Mouse" solution

Obvious benefits include the clear separation of financial reporting into two different data stores and the prevention of duplicate accounts if the same information is to be posted in a different amount. The information can therefore no longer be mixed up. We can compare the operational posting expenditure with that of the "Mickey Mouse" account solution, because it enables the new general ledger to update the same information simultaneously in both ledgers. In an ECC 6.0 Release without Enhancement Package 3 (EhP3 was still in the ramp-up phase), however, the restrictions that open items could only be managed in the leading ledger (for example, clearing provision accounts), and the Controlling ledger (for example, for cost-of-sales accounting) could only be compared in the leading ledger proved to be disadvantageous. Because of these disadvantages (which SAP nevertheless partially removed in Enhancement Package 3) and the convenience of not having to change the posting logic during the implementation, after intensive consideration the tried-and-tested account solution was eventually chosen.

Restrictions in Enhancement Package 3

Introducing the P&L Statement According to Cost-of-Sales Accounting with Real-Time Integration of CO with FI

When a P&L statement is introduced in accordance with cost-of-sales accounting, this immediately raises the question in retail as to which reporting dimensions, such as customer group, article, material group, distribution channel or branches, are to be used for reporting. Customer

Different reporting dimensions

analysis showed that a solution developed in-house already existed for the detailed contribution margin accounting and profitability analysis, and this is why the requested reporting dimensions were limited to the company code. All other dimensions of the customer-specific profitability analysis were filled from other operational systems. First, the alternative for mapping using the profitability analysis (CO-PA) that was suitable for the customer-specific multidimensionality of the reporting dimensions was therefore discarded because of the considerable implementation effort required and the process changes needed when entering posting data.

In addition to the number of reporting dimensions, the requirement to manage a subfunctional area had to be met. This meant that the type of costs incurred had to be taken into account under the actual functional area, for example, sales and administration costs. This requirement could be mapped using a multiplication of the relevant income statement accounts with the functions and through the classic variant using the functional areas object.

Mapping option using accounts The variant to multiply out accounts would inevitably have led to the chart of accounts being extended. Therefore, this variant was rejected next because the necessary extension of the chart of accounts clashed with the objective of the project to reduce the number of accounts. Furthermore, the previously exclusive benefit of this variant in particular no longer exists owing to the new CO-FI real-time integration of the new general ledger. The benefit in question was that, by posting to accounts that had been multiplied out, the P&L statement in accordance with cost-of-sales accounting was also in real time when the classic general ledger was used (and there was no waiting for the postings from the reconciliation ledger). In the end, the choice was made in favor of mapping using functional areas and using the new CO-FI real-time integration, for which the functional areas are stored in the material costs master or cost center master and all relevant information for cost-of-sales accounting can therefore be derived automatically in the background without additional operational effort when accounting documents are entered. The information for the subfunctional area mentioned above is contained in the FI G/L account or CO cost element to ensure that the combination of G/L account and cost element and functional area meets the content-related requirements of cost-of-sales accounting.

Customer-Specific Fields of the New General Ledger

When customer-specific fields are used, the requirement to obtain all financial evaluations from one data source, in accordance with the "one truth" basic principle, competes with the objective to minimize the complexity of the accounting system and thereby ensure that it operates efficiently. Every additional reporting dimension also has to be entered, which adds an extra level to the summary record tables. Consequently, these two objectives must again be weighed against each other for every customer during the design phase. The requirement that emerged in our case was that Financial Accounting had to enter data relating to article numbers and the material group and forward it to a downstream profitability analysis.

Additional reporting dimension

However, a transfer of master data for articles and material group into Financial Accounting and a consequent synchronization between these two systems was ruled out because of the complexity of the master data. Nevertheless, the existence of suitable master data stored in the SAP system is a useful prerequisite for customer-specific fields. In this situation, therefore, the best alternative remaining for the customer was to use a free text field (in this case, "assignment") where the article number or material group can be entered. This approach is in no way a solution to be recommended for the vast majority of SAP customers but is intended to show that an unconventional solution can be productive.

Profit Center Accounting, Segment Reporting, and Online Document Split

The integrated profit center accounting in the new general ledger offered the greatest benefit for our customer. It fulfills a wide range of requirements, and the customer was able to use it to map the defined branch and shop network, to make its own P&L statement, and the most important balance sheet items such as material stock, available for each location. Profit center accounting was also used as the basis for segment reporting, in particular for companies that hold shares in different segments. Furthermore, foreign commission companies were mapped through profit centers.

With future requirements in mind, the online document split was activated when the system was configured, and the "Zero Balance for Profit Center" setting was selected when the document splitting characteristics were set. These technical functions, which run in the background, already completed an important preparatory step for future requirements such as activity reporting, because the SAP system can now map complete financial statements at the profit center level. As a result, new business models can be mapped separately and reported without creating a separate legal entity and therefore without creating a new company code based on profit centers. This enables the customer to "control" new activities based on the same profitability key figures even before divestment, and therefore reduces investment costs when developing new business areas.

Empirical data from this and other projects conducted by Accenture and information from SAP show that the online document split initially requires a high level of configuration effort during the project phase, which must be considered when planning the project within the framework of creating the business case and planning resources. Mechanisms must also be implemented for the subsequent operation that will prevent problems from occurring if, for example, there is a lack of profit center information that would necessitate carrying out postprocessing when updating documents, which would involve significantly higher operating costs.

Special Ledger and SAP CO-OM as Enhancement to the SAP General Ledger

Similarities to special ledger

In principle, the structure of the SAP General Ledger is similar to that of a special ledger. There are two cases that deviate from the basic principle of mapping only one truth if possible and consequently mapping all accounting-relevant information in the general ledger. First, the cost center and internal order accounting was mapped in SAP CO-OM in the classic way owing to allocations across company codes, the use of established CO standard reporting, and planning functions. Second, a special ledger that represents the data basis for the EC-CS interface was also introduced despite the new general ledger. There were two main reasons for this decision:

▸ As required by corporate accounting, the (sub)functional area was able to be implemented into a "real" G/L account posting on the group account using special ledger derivation rules.

▸ This enabled us to achieve greater flexibility when mapping the segment assignment of profit centers, which we would no longer be able to change in the SAP General Ledger in the profit center master record in the standard SAP system as soon as postings took place.

Project experience shows that the new general ledger integrates superbly with traditional techniques such as a special ledger or overhead cost controlling, which represents unprecedented flexibility in the development of the accounting solution.

Conclusion

The functions of the new general ledger considerably extend the wide range of tools provided by the SAP system and offer the project team greater flexibility when mapping customer requirements. From the perspective of Accenture, with the introduction of the SAP General Ledger, the focus is still on the processes and on determining the most important future reporting requirements. System functions, regardless of whether you select the new or classic version, must support this in the best possible way. From our point of view, it is therefore extremely important in the design phase to carefully consider the customer requirements and how the new functions can be used effectively.

Extending existing functions

In particular, enhanced options (such as customer-specific fields and the online document split) to add additional account assignment information to the posting data creates a need for greater discipline when entering posting data. All feeder systems and users must be able to access the additional information to enable them to specify it for the relevant posting. It is essential that these requirements are taken into account when interfaces, processes, and training are being designed.

Overall, it is also worthwhile to introduce the new general ledger from another perspective. There is still a lot of activity in the development of the new general ledger by SAP, which means you will be able to benefit from future improvements and enhancements to functions without any great effort. This will facilitate the SAP strategy to provide new functions in enhancement packages at short intervals that can be gradually implemented with little effort.

2.7 Evaluations in General Ledger Accounting

Reporting here depends greatly on whether you use the classic or SAP General Ledger. In the SAP ERP information system there is a separate folder in each case containing reports that are used either for the classic or SAP General Ledger. Formatted reporting based on SAP NetWeaver BW also extracts its data from one of these storage locations. We use an example of a journal and a balance sheet report on the following pages to illustrate evaluations in general ledger accounting.

2.7.1 Journal

Chronological sequence of business transactions

All business transactions are posted (books of original entry) chronologically in the journal (daybook, compact journal). The posting data entered chronologically in the journal is transferred from the accounts of the general ledger (balance sheet accounts and P&L accounts). The single-column journal is the original form of journal and includes all transactions in one column (separated according to debit and credit). Let's take a look at an example (see also Figure 2.40 to Figure 2.43).

[Ex] **Example of a Retail Company**

A retail company buys goods worth €1,000 on credit from a supplier (non-cash). This company then sells retail goods worth €500 to a customer for €1,200.

Date	Posting Explanation	G/L Accounts	
		Debit	Credit
08/12/00	Goods Purchased on Credit	1,000.00	1,000.00
08/14/00	Goods Picked for Sale	500.00	500.00
08/16/00	Goods Sold on Credit	1,200.00	1,200.00

Figure 2.40 Single-Column Journal

Summarizing receivables and liabilities in a single column makes it difficult to get an overview of the credit transactions. To remove this flaw the books of original entry were first separated into postings on subledger accounts and other G/L account postings. This resulted in the two-column journal: one column for subledger accounts and a second column for other G/L account postings. The appearance of our example therefore changed, as shown in Figure 2.41.

Date	Posting Explanation	Subledger Accounts		G/L Accounts	
		Debit	Credit	Debit	Credit
08/12/00	Goods Purchased on Credit		1,000.00	1,000.00	
08/14/00	Goods Picked for Sale			500.00	500.00
08/16/00	Goods Sold on Credit	200.00			1,200.00

Figure 2.41 Two-Column Journal

During development one specific column each for customer posting and vendor posting was added beside the G/L accounts, which resulted in a three-column journal. This was used in the majority of copying procedures (automatic entry to reconciliation account). Figure 2.42 illustrates the change.

Journals with three and four columns

Date	Posting Explanation	Customer		Vendor		G/L Accounts	
		Debit	Credit	Debit	Credit	Debit	Credit
08/12/00	Goods Purchased on Credit				1,000.00	1,000.00	
08/14/00	Goods Picked for Sale					500.00	500.00
08/16/00	Goods Sold on Credit	1,200.00					1,200.00

Figure 2.42 Three-Column Journal

In the four-column journal the G/L Accounts column was split into one for balance sheet accounts and one for P&L accounts. This meant that the profit or loss made up to a certain period could be determined to some degree of accuracy (without limiting nonoperating and other unrelated influences). This is illustrated in Figure 2.43.

Date	Posting Explanation	Customer		Vendor		G/L Accounts		P&L Accounts	
		Debit	Credit	Debit	Credit	Debit	Credit	Debit	Credit
08/12/00	Goods Purchased on Credit				1,000.00	1,000.00			
08/14/00	Goods Picked for Sale						500.00	500.00	
08/16/00	Goods Sold on Credit	1,200.00							1,200.00

Figure 2.43   Four-Column Journal

The multiple-column journal ultimately had 6 to 12 columns that were used as group columns. Because the ledger sheets could be moved using a relevant function and lines and columns in the spreadsheet could be adjusted to the journal sheet, the postings could be grouped in the journal according to certain factors (chart of accounts).

Let's look at the example of the business process that was presented in different forms of the journal in this section. A company buys retail goods on credit for its retail warehouse, a portion of which are then withdrawn from the warehouse and sold to a customer on credit.

First, we receive retail goods from our vendor (sender), which we deposit in our retail warehouse (recipient). We then withdraw the ordered goods from the retail warehouse (sender) and deliver them to our customer (recipient of goods). Finally, we invoice our customer (recipient of invoice) for the delivered goods. In this case the sender is the sales order created in the SD component. It now shows that the stock of retail goods has increased by €500. It also shows that the profit was made through the sale of the retail goods.

In addition to the display in the journal form, accounting-related evaluation options enable you to get an overview of the financial, assets, and profit situation of a company.

2.7.2 Balance Sheet

The balance sheet compares and contrasts assets and capital (liabilities). Liabilities provide information about the origin of funds, and assets inform us about the utilization of funds. The balance sheet only contains information about values, not quantities. Assets consist of fixed assets and current assets (stocks, receivables, means of payment), capital from capital and reserves, and outside capital (bonds, liabilities, provisions). In addition to assets on the left and liabilities on the right, the balance sheet usually also contains accruals and deferrals. They are used to distinguish profit or loss from one period from that of the next period. For example, these are contributions paid in advance (prepaid expenses) or rents received in advance (deferred expenses). In both cases, the payment relates to a transaction that will only have an effect in the next period. At the beginning of a fiscal year, there is an opening balance sheet that contains assets and liabilities for the balance sheet key date. The balance sheet items are transferred to individual balance sheet accounts. Business transactions are posted on the balance sheet and P&L accounts throughout the year.

Origin of funds and funds utilization

There are different evaluation programs in the SAP system that you can use to create a balance sheet. We describe two options in detail in the following example. You can select the menu path ACCOUNTING • FINANCIAL ACCOUNTING • GENERAL LEDGER • INFO SYSTEM • GENERAL LEDGER REPORTS • BALANCE SHEET/PROFIT AND LOSS STATEMENT/CASH FLOW • GENERAL • ACTUAL/ACTUAL COMPARISONS in SAP ERP for the classic general ledger.

After you select the company code and balance sheet and P&L structure used, the sample report shown in Figure 2.44 is displayed.

The values of the individual accounts are displayed in account items in a similar tree structure to assets and liabilities. Amounts for the current fiscal year 2008 are compared with the previous year, and the difference is shown in the Variance line in absolute values. If you have to investigate an account item amount, the 🔲 icon enables you to drill down to the line items of G/L accounts. In the example, this is the case for the total value of the Commerzbank Frankfurt item (see Figure 2.45).

Comparison for year

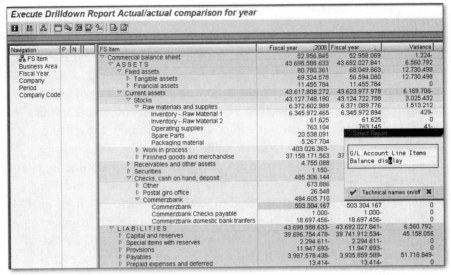

Figure 2.44 Display as Balance Sheet Drill-Down Report

G/L Account Line Item Display

G/L Account 113300 Commerzbank
Company Code 1000

St	Assignment	DocumentNo	BusA	Type	Doc. Date	PK	Amount in local cur.	LCurr	Tx	Clrng doc.
✓	19941212	1400000037		DZ	12.12.1994	40	13.293,59	EUR		
✓	19941220	2000000193		ZP	20.12.1994	40	844.642,53	EUR		
✓	19941231	100007419		SA	31.12.1994	50	66.528,95-	EUR		
✓	19950102	100004095		SA	02.01.1995	50	11.411,09-	EUR		
✓	19950102	100004096		SA	02.01.1995	50	52.090,36-	EUR		
✓	19991231	100012301		SA	31.12.1999	50	484.642,76-	EUR		
✓	20001231	100001342		SA	31.12.2000	40	0,01	EUR		
✓	20071211	1400000222	1000	DZ	11.12.2007	40	5.807.184,49	EUR		
✓	20071211	1400000223		DZ	11.12.2007	40	497.253.719,31	EUR		
* ✓							503.304.166,77	EUR		
** Account 113300							503.304.166,77	EUR		

Figure 2.45 Drill Down to G/L Account Line Items

The total value displayed beforehand is reflected here in the line items.

Formatted reporting in SAP NetWeaver BW If you require less detailed information, SAP NetWeaver BW is also particularly suitable for accounting-related evaluations. You can create management reports very simply using the formatted reporting available there. This is illustrated clearly in the example in Figure 2.46.

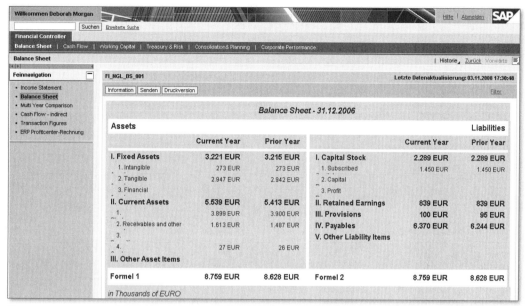

Figure 2.46 Formatted Reporting

Irrespective of whether you use reporting in SAP ERP or SAP NetWeaver BW, sufficient standard reports are provided to ensure that the information requirements of every target group can be met.

2.8 Conclusion

General ledger accounting creates the basis for a functioning SAP Financial Accounting system. The basic question as to whether you want to use the classic or SAP General Ledger sets the course very early on in this context. Evaluations in SAP ERP and SAP NetWeaver BW make the sets of figures clear and transparent. With SAP NetWeaver BW you can make the reports available in a corresponding format for management.

Accounts Payable manages payables. This chapter describes the points of contact between SAP ERP Financials and the purchasing department. It also details how to perform efficient postings. Information on standard evaluations and the automatic payment run rounds off the chapter.

3 Accounts Payable Accounting

This chapter explains the basic business principles of accounts payable accounting, describes the SAP subledger, FI-AP (Accounts Payable), and then details various posting procedures, such as the various options for entering incoming invoices. It introduces four alternative transactions for entering documents, namely, general posting, fast data entry, single-screen transaction, and integrated invoice verification. If the incoming invoices are available in the SAP system, the program provides different options for the payment run for paying vendor invoices in an optimal manner. The main new feature in Release ERP 6.0 is accounts payable accounting in the context of payment transactions and bank communication. For more details, refer to Chapter 6, Bank Accounting. Reporting ensures transparency for the presentation of the essential information in sample reports for critical master data changes, open items, due date analyses, and in the accounts payable information system.

3.1 Business Principles

For subledger accounts you differentiate between vendor accounts or vendors and customer accounts or customers. In contrast to general ledger accounting, in which you only manage the total of payables for the financial statement, you use Accounts Payable Accounting to manage all details regarding business transactions, such as invoices, credit memos, and outgoing payments. The interaction between the purchasing department and accounts payable accounting assumes a significant role here. At

Accounts payable management as a continuous business process a very early stage, purchase requisitions or purchase orders lay the foundation for successful invoice verifications. You also have to ensure a correct documentation of the goods receipt, because it is used as the basis for releases for payments of invoices. The FI-AP component keeps and manages account-based data of all vendors. Furthermore, it is an integral part of the purchasing system. Purchase orders, deliveries, and invoices are managed based on vendors and update vendor evaluations.

3.2   FI-AP Software Component

Features   FI-AP (accounts payable accounting) ensures that legal obligations to keep records are fulfilled for reliable accounting but also serves as the information source for an optimal purchasing policy and supports the enterprise's liquidity planning owing to the direct integration with cash management and forecasting. Account analyses, due date forecasts, and further standard reports are available for the open item management. You can customize the correspondence according to the individual requirements of your enterprise. The payment program automatically pays due payables and closes the corresponding items. To document the processes in accounts payable, you can use account balances, journals, balance audit trails, and numerous standard reports. For key date valuations you revaluate foreign currency items, determine vendors on the debit side, and scan the balances established this way for remaining terms.

3.3   Master Data

This section focuses on the vendor master record. The data contained therein is required for handling business transactions in the accounting area and in the purchasing area.

3.3.1   Structure of the Vendor Master Data

Division of the master record into three parts   The master data of vendors is made up of three parts. The general data is maintained at the *client level*. This data is available for all company codes. At this level, you specify the name of the subledger account in subledger accounting, the tax number, and the bank details. Data that is important for individual company codes is specified in the *company code area*. This includes the account number of the reconciliation account in the general ledger, the terms of payment, and the settings for the dunning procedure. Figure 3.1 shows the basic structure of a vendor account.

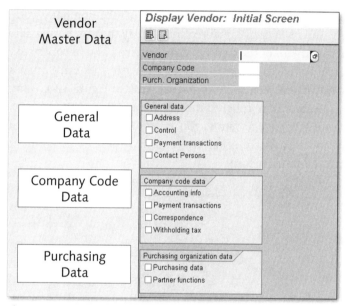

Figure 3.1 Structure of the Vendor Account

For the integrated use with the MM module (materials management), you are provided with additional fields for the vendor master record. These fields contain information that you require to handle business transactions in the purchasing component. In this area, you enter data on requests, on purchase orders, and for invoice verifications. This data can vary in each defined purchasing area and is only used by applications of the MM module. This data includes conditions (for example, purchase order currency, terms of payment, or minimum purchase order value), sales data (sales person including telephone number), and control parameters.

3.3.2 Creating a Vendor Account

You create vendor master records by selecting the menu path ACCOUNT-
ING • FINANCIAL ACCOUNTING • ACCOUNTS PAYABLE • CREATE MASTER DATA
(Transaction FK01).

Central/
decentralized
maintenance of the
master record
Alternatively, you can enter the general data and the company code
data separately. However, you can enter and display the purchasing data
within the vendor menu in the Central Maintenance only. In contrast to
the maintenance of the customer accounts, the system doesn't open a
dialog box but navigates you to an initial screen (see Figure 3.2). Here,
you can enter the account number of the vendor and the company code.
When you create a vendor account, you must also specify an account
group, which controls the internal and external number assignment
when creating the master record.

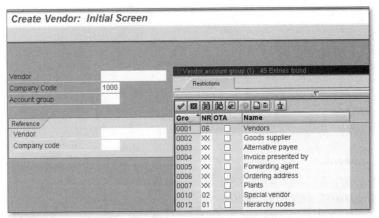

Figure 3.2 Maintaining a Vendor Account—Initial Screen

When you press the [Enter] key, the SAP system displays the screen
shown in Figure 3.3.

▸ **Name and Street Address**
  The reports and correspondence in the SAP system access this address
  data. Depending on the report, it then appears in the address and
  salutation of correspondence or in the report lists.

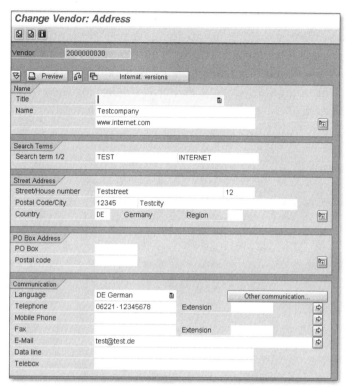

Figure 3.3 Maintaining a Vendor Account—Address Data

- ▶ **Search Terms**

  In this field, you can enter a freely selectable term that is used for the search for master records with the matchcode. To ensure that the field is filled uniformly, it is recommended that you specify rules. For the standard matchcode, this is the primary key with which you can search for master records most rapidly.

- ▶ **Language (Communication)**

  Here, you define the language in which the correspondence is written.

- ▶ **Account control (Customer)**

If a business partner is both a vendor and a customer, you're provided with the option to have the system clear receivables and payables automatically (automatic payment program or dunning). In this case, you must enter the account number of the customer in the vendor master

Clearing processes with vendors that are also customers

record and vice versa (see Figure 3.4). If these fields are filled, the system displays the Clearing field in the account management for the data of the company code. Clearing is not possible until this field is activated. In the example, the vendor is also a customer. Here, a link to customer account 1000 including subsequent clearing was selected. The effects of this become particularly obvious in Section 3.7, Automated Payment Transactions.

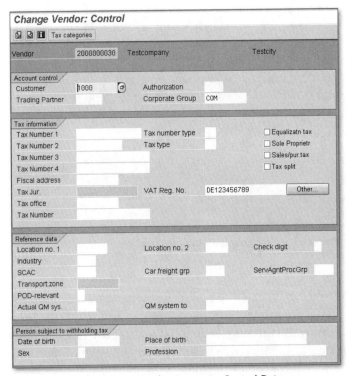

Figure 3.4 Maintaining a Vendor Account—Control Data

Payment transaction settings If you press Enter, the system takes you to next entry screen (see Figure 3.5):

▸ **Bank Details**
If the automatic payment program is supposed to consider a vendor, you need to enter the bank details. For automatic debits, the corresponding field must also be selected.

▶ **Alternative payee**

If you enter the account number of the vendor here, all payments are made using the bank details of this business partner (bank transfers, automatic debit, credit memos). This field exists in the general part, in the company code area, and at the document level. The specification that is more detailed applies (from the general area to document level).

▶ **Bank type**

If you define multiple bank details in a vendor master record, you can differentiate them by means of any four-digit abbreviation (partner bank type). If you want to pay an open item using specific bank details of the vendor, you must define the corresponding abbreviation in the line item. The payment program of the SAP system then controls the specified bank details of the vendor.

▶ **IBAN**

In many cases, you can determine the IBAN from the bank key and account number. Because this procedure is not necessarily unique, you should always verify it. Chapter 6, Bank Accounting, provides more information on the IBAN and SEPA.

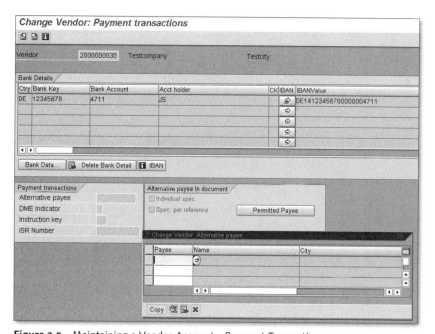

Figure 3.5 Maintaining a Vendor Account—Payment Transactions

When you press ⌈Enter⌋, the system navigates you to the maintenance of the company code area of the vendor account—to the account management data first (see Figure 3.6):

▶ **Reconciliation account**
Each posting to an account of subledger accounting automatically creates an entry to the general ledger. This integration is ensured through the reconciliation account. The field status group in the master record of the reconciliation account specifies the screen layout for document entry. The items of the vendor's account are managed in the currency of the reconciliation account.

▶ **Sort key**
You use sort keys to display line items. Usually, the SAP system sorts the documents in the line item display based on the content of the Assignment field in the document. This sort key controls how the Assignment field is automatically filled during document entry if it is not populated with a value from another source.

▶ **Authorization**
In this field, you can specify who receives change or read authorization for this account.

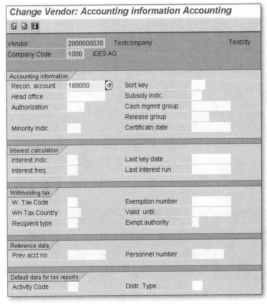

Figure 3.6 Maintaining a Vendor Account—Account Management (Accounting)

When you press ⌈Enter⌋, the system takes you to the settings for the payment transactions in financial accounting. The system now displays the screen shown in Figure 3.7.

▶ **Payment terms**

This key is used for orders, purchase orders, and invoices and provides information about dunning and payment transactions. The value entered here is used as a default value for the document entry.

▶ **Tolerance group**

To map different rights for the processing of business transactions, you can assign accounting clerks to so-called tolerance groups. You make specifications for the granting of cash discounts and for the handling of payment differences for each tolerance group. This entry affects dunning and the entry of payment transactions. For manual closing, the payment differences are accepted by the system up to the defined tolerance, and the items are closed.

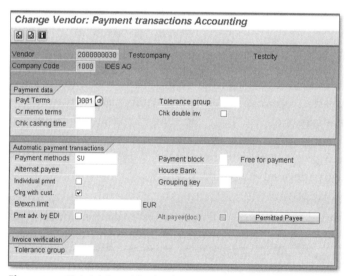

Figure 3.7 Maintaining a Vendor Account—Payment Transactions (Accounting)

▶ **Checking double invoices**

If you select this field, the system checks, when a document is entered for this vendor account, whether the invoice or credit memo has already been entered. This check is supposed to prevent users entering invoices or credit memos twice by mistake. Depending on the content of the Reference document header field, the system checks whether there is a document in the SAP system that corresponds to the following content:

▶ If the Reference field in the document header is empty, there has to be a document in the SAP system that contains the same values in the Company Code, Vendor, Currency, Document Date, and Amount in Document Currency document fields.

▶ Otherwise, the company code, vendor, currency, document date, and reference number have to be identical.

▶ **Payment methods**
Here, you can find the payment methods that are allowed for this vendor if the automatic payment program is used. If a payment method for the incoming payment is entered here, for instance, B (bank direct debit) or A (automatic debit), this business partner is not considered in dunning.

▶ **Payment block**
An entry in this field causes a block of the account for payment transactions. In the automatic payment program, the block is effective if it is set either in the master record or in the document. If the block is set in the master record, all open items of this customer are transferred to the exception list. The * blocking key (asterisk) causes the system to ignore all open items of the account; the + key (plus) causes the system to ignore all open items for which no payment method has been explicitly specified in the document.

▶ **Individual payment**
This checkbox determines that all open items of this vendor are paid or collected separately. This prevents multiple open items clearing jointly with one payment medium.

Dunning vendors When you press ⌈Enter⌋, the system takes you to next entry screen (see Figure 3.8). You can also dun vendors. This is particularly useful if the payables are less than the receivables.

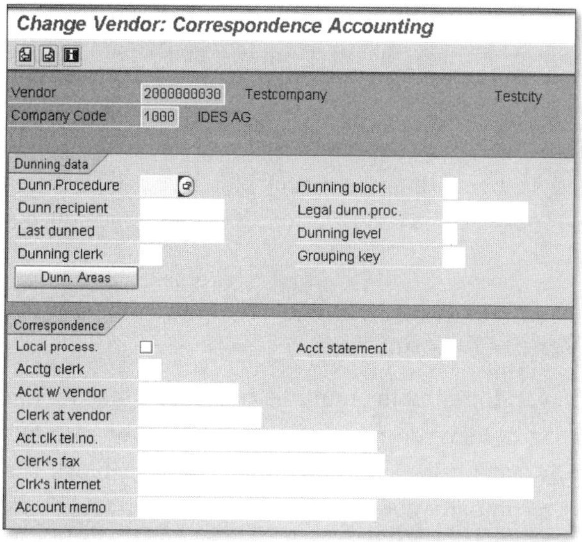

Figure 3.8 Maintaining a Vendor Account—Correspondence (Accounting)

▶ **Dunning Procedure**
If this business partner is supposed to be considered in the automatic dunning procedure, you must define a dunning procedure here. The entry is used as a default value for the document entry.

▶ **Dunning block**
If you select this field, this business partner is not included in the dunning proposal of the automatic dunning program.

▶ **Dunning level**
This field is usually set by the dunning program. In exceptional cases, you can change the dunning level manually. The dunning level influences the next dunning run. If the dunning level is 0, the system uses the specified minimum number of days to calculate the days in arrears; for all other dunning levels, the system uses the grace days. The days in arrears define the date for the next dunning run of this account.

▶ **Dunning clerk**
The specified name is printed on the dunning notices. The dunning clerk does not have to be identical to the accounting clerk.

▶ **Accounting clerk**
The name that corresponds to the defined ID appears on all corre-

spondence documents sent to the business partner. Additionally, it is printed on the dunning notices, if the Dunning clerk field is not filled.

With these specifications, two of three possible parts of the vendor master data are maintained at the *client* and *company code* level. If a vendor account is no longer supposed to be used, various blocking mechanisms are available.

3.3.3   Blocking a Vendor Account

Central block   The master record of a vendor contains multiple fields for blocking the account. This makes it possible to centrally block an account for accounting and purchasing. For accounting, you have the option to block the account in one or more company codes. A dunning or payment block can be set at the company code level. You can set and undo the blocking indicator in the subledger at any time. Figure 3.9 illustrates a central block, which is available under the menu path ACCOUNTING • FINANCIAL ACCOUNTING • ACCOUNTS PAYABLE • CENTRAL MAINTENANCE • MASTER DATA • BLOCK/UNBLOCK menu path (Transaction XK05).

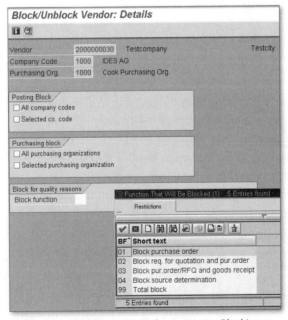

Figure 3.9   Maintaining a Vendor Account—Blocking

For vendors, you can set posting blocks and purchasing blocks. The block for quality reasons differentiates again between blocks for purchase orders; for requests and purchase orders; for purchase orders, requests, and goods receipt; and for source determinations and total blocks.

In addition to the options for defining master data for accounts payable and blocking it at any time, an option for one-time vendors is also available.

3.4   One-Time Vendor

The SAP system provides a special master record type for one-time or sporadic vendors. In contrast to the "regular" master records (customers and vendors), this master record does not contain specific data of the business partner, such as the address and bank details. This information is entered separately during document entry. When posting to a one-time account, the system automatically navigates to a master data screen where you can enter the specific data of the business partner (see Figure 3.10). Master records for one-time accounts are stored separately in a specific account group. The system hides the specific fields of the business partner when the master data is entered (see Figure 3.11).

One-time vendor

If you decide to use one-time accounts, you should create multiple one-time accounts, because the large volume of postings to a one-time account can easily lead to confusion. In this case, you should group the business partners according to defined criteria (first letter, area, industry). These criteria assume a particular role, because it is critical for postings or clearings to quickly find the appropriate account of the business partner and the corresponding item.

You maintain one-time accounts the same way you maintain customer or vendor accounts. The open items can be dunned using the dunning program and processed using the payment program. The functionality of these special accounts is only limited in some aspects. For example, clearing is not possible for a customer that is also a vendor. Once you've defined the basis with the master data and clarified the use of one-time vendors, it is time to have a look at an integrated business transaction in accounts payable accounting.

Limited functionality

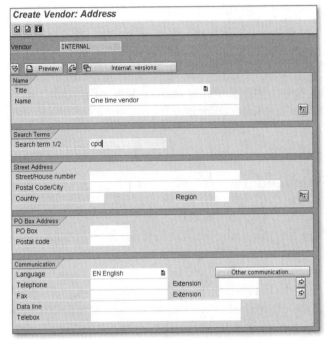

Figure 3.10 Personal Data in a One-Time Document

Figure 3.11 Master Record of a One-Time Account

3.5   Overview of the Integrated Business Transaction

Accounts payable in the context of integrated business transactions usually concerns the individual steps from purchase orders to outgoing payments (purchase to pay). Integration also means that the information flow involves different departments. This example includes the departments of purchasing, accounts payable accounting, controlling, and treasury. Figure 3.12 illustrates the various departments at four levels.

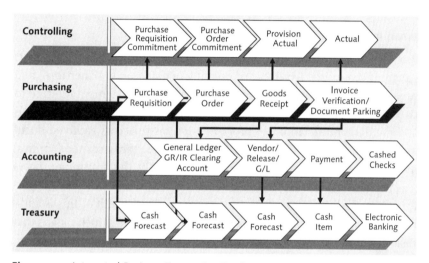

Figure 3.12   Integrated Business Transaction Purchase to Pay

Ordering Process

The ordering process in this example starts with a purchase requisition. Before you can generate a purchase order for the vendor, this internal approval process ensures clarity and transparency. The purchase requisition defines exactly at which price goods or services may be ordered, and an approval of the purchase requisition requires a dual-control or three-control principle. This early implementation facilitates later invoice verifications. Additionally, the purchase requisition enables the involved departments, controlling and treasury, to obtain an overview of the expected expenses or cash outflows.

Purchase requisition

Goods Receipt

GR/IR account   If goods have been received for this purchase order, the goods receipt is not only based on quantities but also documents the exact value of the goods for the purchase order. If no vendor invoice that corresponds to the goods receipt is available at the end of the month, this value serves as the basis for accrual and deferral postings. You can find a detailed description in Chapter 7, Section 7.3, Automatic Maintenance of the GR/IR Account.

Incoming Invoice

Processing of incoming invoices is one of the traditional areas in accounts payable accounting. Services are usually documented in paper form and sent by post: "No posting without document." This statement referred to paper documents in the past. Longer legally stipulated retention periods and the demand for more comfortable options to access archived documents ruled out microfilming. Today, enterprises store a scanned, optical image of the original document. Up until recently, this scanning process was performed quite late in the process, but now a lot of enterprises perform it at the beginning of the process chain. The benefit of this is additional transparency and an acceleration in processing, which means that cash discounts are no longer lost thanks to timely processing and payment. However, the implementation of this requires a central inbox for incoming invoices. Once the invoices have been scanned, they find their way through the enterprise as optical documents via the workflow.

OCR   In addition to the implementation of a central inbox and an early scanning process, the optical recognition and interpretation of paper invoices is the next step on your way to an optimized process. Owing to the performance of today's computers, OCR (optical character recognition) allows for default account assignment of the accounting document. Provided that the system finds the corresponding purchase order for the invoice and provided that there are no price differences or quantity variances, the system can automatically post the document in the background.

EDI   If a large invoice volume is involved, the transfer of invoice data via EDI (electronic data interchange) including a subsequent printout of the collective invoice has become established as a process. These are one-to-one connections between customers and vendors. In some industries, for example, in the automotive industry, this procedure is already widely used. Summarized, you can distinguish between the following types of processing incoming invoices:

- Manual processing with late scanning
- Manual processing with early scanning, so that an optical image is provided for the workflow in the enterprise
- Automatic processing and early scanning via OCR, which also creates default account assignments in addition to the optical image
- Automatic processing where large invoice volumes are transferred via EDI

Payment

If goods and invoices have been received and the invoice verification has a positive result, the automatic payment program is responsible for making the payments at the optimal time. The payment run includes the planned liquid funds (see Chapter 6, Section 6.5, Payment Transactions and Bank Communication) and cash discounts and due dates for net payments of invoices. Because the accounts payable accountant is involved in this process, the following sections discuss the manual and automatic payment transactions.

Cashed Checks

Cashed checks enable specific evaluations. You can evaluate when and whether vendors cashed the received checks and even indicate this as an average value in the master record.

In integrated SAP ERP systems, it is always advantageous to consider the entire business process. The task area of an accounts payable accountant has critical connections to other departments in your enterprise.

3.6   Entering Incoming Invoices

You can use several transactions to post incoming invoices in the SAP system. For example, you can enter an incoming invoice in the SAP system either in the logistics area in the MM module or within the accounting area in the FI-AP component.

3.6.1   General Posting

The general FI-AP posting transaction has basically been provided since the days of the R/2 system (formerly Transaction TB01). The menu path in SAP ERP is ACCOUNTING • FINANCIAL ACCOUNTING • ACCOUNTS PAYABLE • OTHER POSTINGS • GENERAL INVOICE (Transaction FB01).

The most important fields for entering a document header are the following:

▸ **Document Type and Currency/Rate**
Depending on the business transaction

▸ **Company Code**
Of the respective enterprise

▸ **Document Date**
Relevant date of the process

▸ **Posting Date**
Date for updating the accounts

▸ **Reference according to external specification**
Usually invoice number of the vendor

The first two entries for a document item (posting key and account number) define the relevant account and posting side (debit or credit). In Figure 3.13, these are posting key 31 (credit posting to a vendor account) and the corresponding account number of the vendor in the SAP system.

Required entry fields

Pressing ⌷Enter⌷ takes you to the next screen (see Figure 3.14). The vendor's payables account controls the selection of the fields for the entry screen and their ready-for-input status. For entering a vendor item you require other fields than for entering a G/L account item. In this example, the Business Area field has the Mandatory Entry field status.

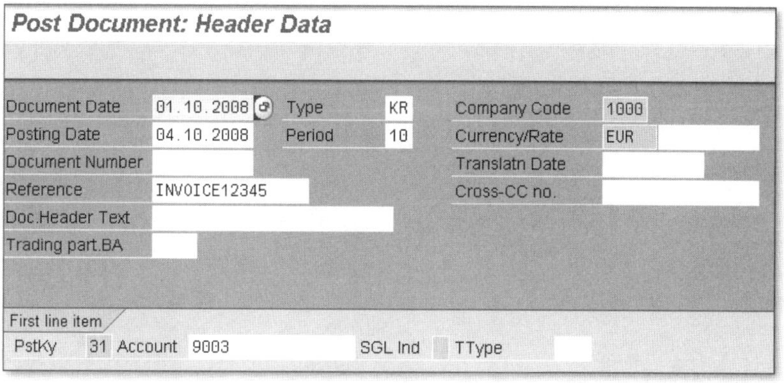

Post Document: Header Data

Document Date	01.10.2008	Type	KR	Company Code	1000
Posting Date	04.10.2008	Period	10	Currency/Rate	EUR
Document Number				Translatn Date	
Reference	INVOICE12345			Cross-CC no.	
Doc.Header Text					
Trading part.BA					

First line item

PstKy 31 Account 9003 SGL Ind TType

Figure 3.13 Incoming Invoice—Initial Screen

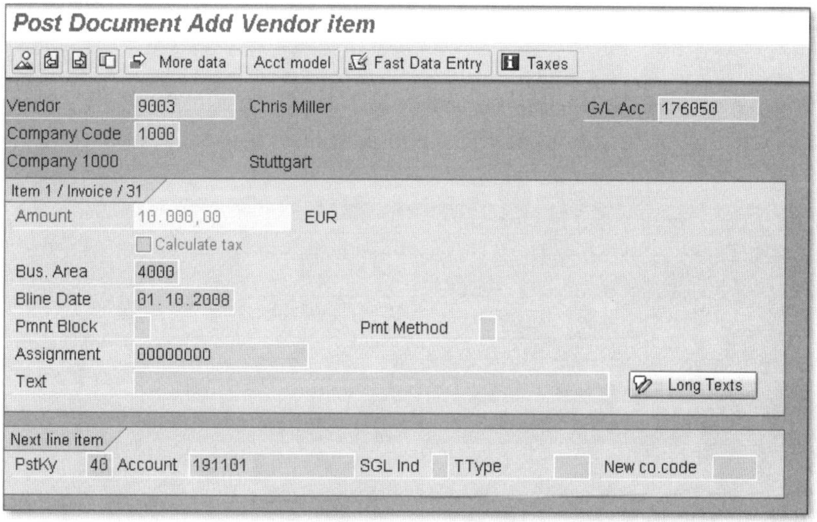

Post Document Add Vendor item

More data | Acct model | Fast Data Entry | Taxes

Vendor	9003	Chris Miller	G/L Acc	176050
Company Code	1000			
Company 1000		Stuttgart		

Item 1 / Invoice / 31

Amount	10.000,00	EUR
	☐ Calculate tax	
Bus. Area	4000	
Bline Date	01.10.2008	
Pmnt Block		Pmt Method
Assignment	00000000	
Text		Long Texts

Next line item

PstKy 40 Account 191101 SGL Ind TType New co.code

Figure 3.14 Incoming Invoice—Vendor Item

After you have entered the vendor item, first enter the posting key of the document item, which is 40 in this example (debit posting to a G/L account), and the corresponding account. When you press `Enter`, the system takes you to next screen (see Figure 3.15).

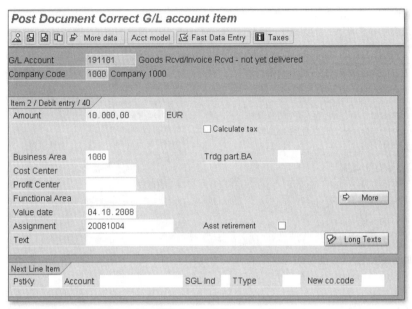

Figure 3.15 Incoming Invoice—G/L Account Item

You can display the document item, which has been automatically generated by the SAP system, via the menu path DOCUMENT • SIMULATE.

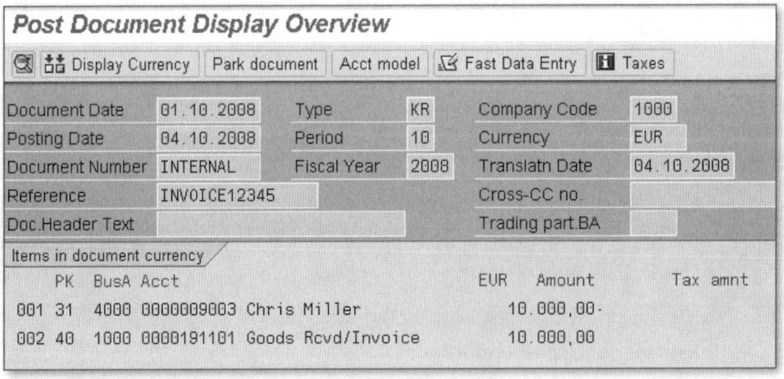

Post Document Display Overview

Document Date	01.10.2008	Type	KR	Company Code	1000	
Posting Date	04.10.2008	Period	10	Currency	EUR	
Document Number	INTERNAL	Fiscal Year	2008	Translatn Date	04.10.2008	
Reference	INVOICE12345			Cross-CC no.		
Doc.Header Text				Trading part.BA		

Items in document currency

PK	BusA	Acct		EUR Amount	Tax amnt
001 31	4000	0000009003	Chris Miller	10.000,00-	
002 40	1000	0000191101	Goods Rcvd/Invoice	10.000,00	

Figure 3.16 Incoming Invoice—Document Display

Figure 3.16 shows the posting from the example, which the system generates after you click on the SAVE button. The G/L accounts involved are a material stock account for goods receipt, the "payables" account for invoice receipt, and the typical interim account, "GR/IR clearing account," which is usually directly cleared when the invoice receipt is entered. In addition to Transaction FB01, the SAP system provides you with further options.

3.6.2 Single-Screen Transaction in FI

Since Release 4.6, accounts payable accounting has provided a new entry option. In contrast to the general posting, this concept is supposed to simplify the entry process by displaying all information in one screen. Furthermore, information, such as posting key, document type, selection of the tax key, and so on, is predefined and hidden. You can find the new "single-screen transaction" via the menu path ACCOUNTING • FINANCIAL ACCOUNTING • ACCOUNTS PAYABLE • POSTING • INVOICE (Transaction FB60).

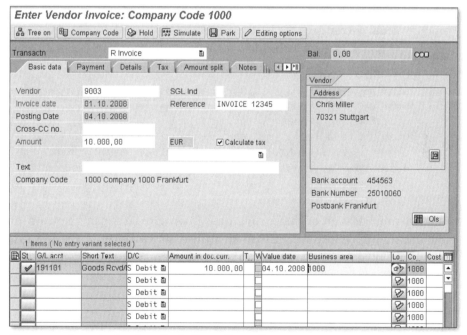

Figure 3.17 Incoming Invoice—Single-Screen Transaction

The tabs contain the following functions:

▶ **Basic data**
This refers to general document data.

▶ **Payment**
Here, you specify data for the payment transactions.

▶ **Tax**
If the invoice contains multiple tax codes and the tax amounts are supposed to be copied from the invoice, you can enter them here.

▶ **Details**
Here, you specify additional fields for the business partner line, such as assignment number and business area.

▶ **Notes**
You can define additional notes for the open item. The system assigns the text to the receivable or payable and not to the complete document.

▶ **Local currency**
This tabs appears if postings are made in a foreign currency or if parallel currencies exist in the company code.

[+]

Changing the Transactions

If an accounting document is supposed to include multiple vendor items, you must change to the traditional entry process using the menu path ENVIRONMENT • COMPLEX POSTING. Now you can enter additional vendor items in the footer. However, you cannot return to the single-screen transaction from this "complex posting."

A simplification of the posting transaction provides many benefits for users who sometimes have to enter incoming invoices in the SAP system. When speed is relevant, the fast data entry provides considerable advantages.

3.6.3 Fast Data Entry

You can find this transaction in the menu path ACCOUNTING • FINANCIAL ACCOUNTING • ACCOUNTS PAYABLE • POSTING • IR/GU FAST ENTRY • INVOICE

(Transaction FB10). This entry option is solely designed to enable a fast data entry via the keyboard. The system hides information or input fields that are not absolutely necessary. The predefined settings shown in Figure 3.18 are configured by the accounts payable accountant at the beginning of a work day and thus don't have to be made again.

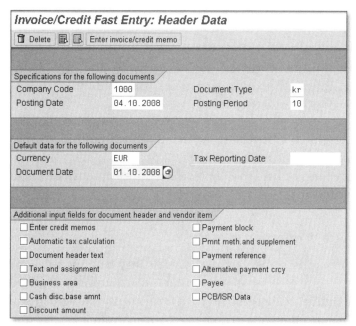

Figure 3.18 Fast Data Entry—Predefined Settings

Pressing ⌈Enter⌋ takes you to next screen, the actual fast entry screen. Figure 3.19 shows a screen that is populated with a minimum of information. You can easily access all field information using the Tab key. The system displays the vendor item first and then offsetting items including additional account assignments.

Number of Offsetting Items   **[+]**

The number of offsetting items is not limited to six lines. If they are filled with values, you can use the Page Down key for scrolling. In total, 999 line items are available.

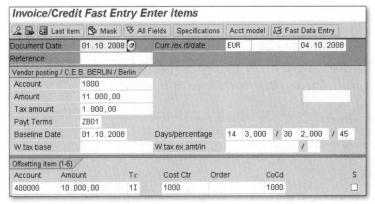

Figure 3.19 Fast Data Entry—Entering Items

The entry transactions described so far, that is, general posting (Transaction FB01), single-screen transaction (FB60), or fast data entry (Transaction FB10), can only be used to a limited extent; the entry transaction in the MM logistics module may close this gap.

3.6.4 Invoice Verification in MM

In different enterprises, different departments may be responsible for the logistical invoice verification. This business function can be provided either in the purchasing department or in accounts payable accounting. In SAP ERP, the required transaction and the menu path are defined in the MM module: LOGISTICS • MATERIALS MANAGEMENT • INVOICE VERIFICATION • DOCUMENT ENTRY • ADD INCOMING INVOICE (Transaction MIRO).

Particularly if an invoice refers to a previously created purchase order (with purchase order reference), you can quickly decide on posting and subsequent payment. Transaction MIRO supports you in identifying price differences and quantity variances between the purchase order and the invoice. Furthermore, the system sets payment blocks automatically in defined cases. This can make sense in the following cases, for example:

▶ No goods receipt is available for the invoice receipt.

▶ An invoice amount, for example, that is larger than $10,000, has to be checked by two persons.

▶ Spot checks are carried out, for example, for each tenth invoice.

The example in Figure 3.20 shows an invoice receipt with purchase order reference. When you enter purchase order number 4500018601, you need to enter additional information on the amount and quantity.

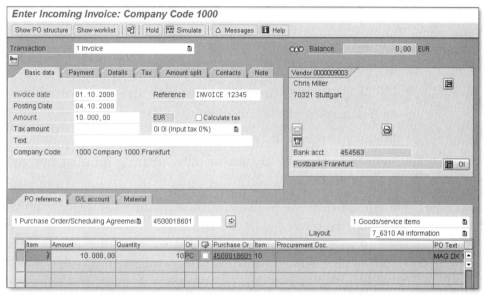

Figure 3.20   MM—Adding an Incoming Invoice

The Simulate button enables a simulation of the future posting procedure, which is illustrated in Figure 3.21. G/L account 191100 (GR/IR clearing, external procurement) is posted on the debit side, and the payables of the vendor account are posted on the credit side.

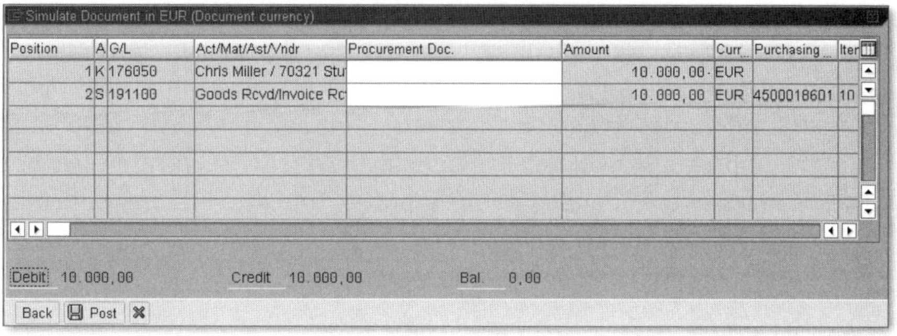

Figure 3.21   MM—Simulating a Document

Once incoming invoices have been entered in the SAP system, you can start the payment process for paying the vendor.

3.7 Automated Payment Transactions

The *payment transaction* concept refers to the processing of the incoming and outgoing payments of an enterprise. This specifically includes:

- Incoming payments via debit memos
- Outgoing payments via bank transfers or checks
- Incoming checks with manual check preposting
- Incoming payments via bank transfers, returned debit memos, and returned checks

Accounting and process view
You can structure the payment transactions in an enterprise according to various aspects and issues and separate the individual processes. You distinguish between the accounting view and the process view. The accounting view—as usual—differentiates between incoming payments and outgoing payments. The process view, in contrast, differentiates between incoming and outgoing payment processes. The outgoing process is usually triggered via a payment run by your company, and the corresponding information (bank, account, amount, and so on) is defined by the SAP system and passed on to third parties. This includes bank transfers and outgoing checks to third parties (outgoing payments) but also debit memos that are collected by third parties (incoming payments). The incoming process instead is triggered by third parties, and the corresponding information is provided from the outside (banks, vendors, customers). This includes bank transfers and incoming checks by third parties (incoming payments) but also debit memos that you collect from third parties (outgoing payments). Consequently, SAP's automatic payment program manages the outgoing payments of an enterprise but also processes the outgoing payment process and thus includes both outgoing payments and incoming payments (debit memos). In this context, the payment program has the following functions:

- Selection of the due and open items
- Posting of payment documents (accounting documents)

▸ Generation of payment lists and logs

▸ Generation of payment media (check forms, payment advice notes)

Before you can execute Transaction F110 for the payment program, you need to implement some basic settings.

3.7.1 Payment Methods in SAP Systems

A payment method in the SAP system defines which procedure (check, bank transfer, bill of exchange, and so on) is used for payment. The specifications for a payment method are made during the system configuration at two levels. There are basic settings that depend on the country; that is, settings for "US" (United States) apply to all company codes with headquarters in the United States. In addition, there are checks that you can define individually for each company code and enterprise.

Maintaining the Payment Methods in the Master Record and/or in an Open Item	[+]
You can define payment methods in the master record of a business partner and in individual items. If you have specified a payment method in the open item, it overwrites the specification in the master record. A payment method that is entered in the open item doesn't have to be included in the master record. However, the payment method of a payment run must always be defined either in the master record or in the open item to have the system include the item in this payment run.	

Which specifications from the master record of the business partner are inevitably required is defined for each country. If *one* of the necessary specifications is not provided in the master record, you cannot use this payment method. For the C payment method (Check), a complete address must be maintained in the master record. Otherwise, the C payment method is not valid for this business partner. Furthermore, under which conditions this payment method can be used is defined in the individual company codes for each payment method. The following also applies here: If *one* required condition is not met, you cannot use this payment for the respective open item. These defined checks affect the following specifications:

Payment method: Check (C)

▶ Minimum and maximum amounts

▶ Allowed business partners abroad (country code in the master record)

▶ Allowed bank details abroad (country code in the bank master record)

▶ Allowed foreign currency

The payment program only selects the payment method for which you specify a minimum or maximum amount if the payment amount doesn't fall below the minimum amount and doesn't exceed the maximum amount.

[+]

> **Exception to the Rule**
>
> Minimum and maximum amounts don't apply if the payment method is explicitly indicated in the open item. In this case, the defined payment method is also used even if the payment amount falls below the minimum amount or exceeds the maximum amount.

A brief look at the exception list is sufficient to determine whether a condition that was met was the cause for not including an item in the proposal list. The following section now discusses the payment block reasons.

3.7.2 Payment Block Reasons

A payment block is an indicator that you can use to block accounts or individual items for payment. The system indicates the payment block in the master record of the business partner or in the document item. The standard SAP system provides numerous block reasons, which map why no payment is supposed to be made in this specific case.

A due open item may be included in the exception list for several reasons. A brief look at the exception list is sufficient to determine why an item is not included in the proposal list.

[+]

Note in the Log of the Proposal List
If a payment block is set, the system displays the error message "Account blocked for payment" or "Item blocked for payment" in the exception list for the corresponding open item.

You can remove or set payment blocks during the processing of the payment proposal. However, you cannot remove and set all payment blocks in a proposal. The restrictions for the respective block reason are defined in Customizing. For the example in Figure 3.22, it is specified that the V payment block cannot be removed during the processing of the payment proposal. If the block reason " " (Free for payment) is not selected, the account cannot be manually blocked in the payment run.

Display View "Payment Block Reasons": Overview

Block ind.	Description	Change in pmnt prop.	Manual payments block	Not changeable
	Free for payment	☑	☐	☐
*	Skip account	☐	☐	☐
A	Blocked for payment	☑	☑	☐
B	Blocked for payment	☑	☐	☐
N	IP postprocessing	☐	☐	☐
P	Payment request	☐	☑	☑
R	Invoice verification	☑	☐	☐
V	Payment clearing	☐	☑	☐

Figure 3.22 Using the Payment Block Reasons

If you have implemented the basic settings for the payment methods and payment block reasons, you can access the payment program.

3.7.3 Accessing the Payment Program

You access the initial screen of the payment program via the menu path ACCOUNTING • FINANCIAL ACCOUNTING • ACCOUNTS PAYABLE • PERIODIC PROCESSING • PAY (Transaction F110).

First, enter the date of the payment run and an identification feature. You can add a sequential number to the identification feature to distinguish between different runs on the same date.

ID and bank
communication

The example illustrated in Figure 3.23 displays 01/12/2008 as the day of the execution and the ID of the person responsible, that is, JS2. The Identification field is provided with a new function and meaning in the context of bank communication. For detailed information, refer to Chapter 6, Bank Accounting.

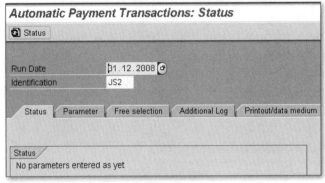

Figure 3.23 Initial Screen of the Payment Program

To enter the parameters and navigate to the respective tab. You have to specify the complete company codes (four digits) and separate them by a comma. In addition to single values, you can enter intervals. No blanks are allowed between the defined company codes or intervals. The required payment methods must be indicated without any separators. The posting date of the next payment must run to check the due date of the payables. If an item is due on the date of the next payment run, it will be paid in this payment run. Receivables (debit memos) can generally not be paid before the baseline date for payment. They are paid once the due date is reached or expired, independent of when the next payment run is supposed to be executed. You additionally have to enter the vendors or customers that the SAP system is supposed to include in this payment run. This can be done in single values or intervals. The parameters illustrated in Figure 3.24 consider all posting documents until 01/12/2008 in company code 1000. The payment run is supposed to clear the payables using a payment document with 01/12/2008 as the posting date. All due payables of a vendor are supposed to be paid via check or bank transfer. 10/12/2008 is defined as the date for the next payment run; that is, the system selects all items with a due date for net payment before this date.

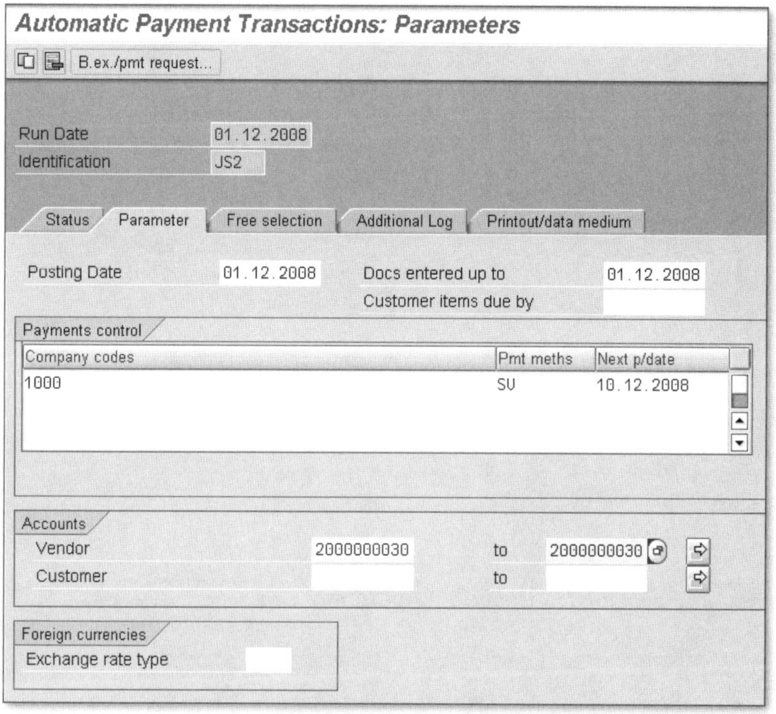

Figure 3.24 Parameters of a Payment Run

The Free selection tab navigates you to the entry of further selection criteria. Here, you can define fields at the document level or from the master records of the business partners as additional selection criteria. You enter the name of the database field in the Field Name field. The system supports the search process for the corresponding field name with the F4 search help. If you select the Exclude values field, this payment run doesn't include the documents with the corresponding criterion. The setting in Figure 3.25 doesn't define any restrictions.

In the payment run, you can define restrictions for the additional log. The log displays the processing logic of the payment program with the corresponding level of detail (see Figure 3.26).

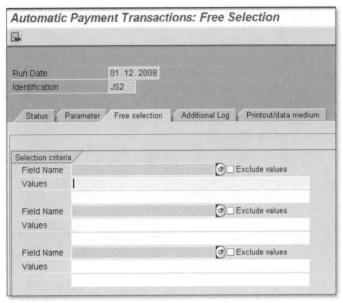

Figure 3.25 Free Selection

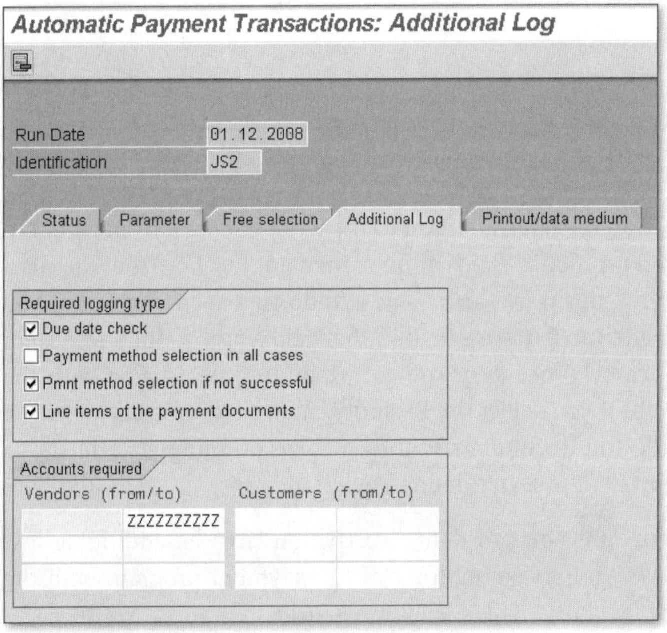

Figure 3.26 Additional Log

Additional logs should only be used in exceptional cases. The corresponding tab displays the details of the additional log. The system only creates an additional log for the payment run if at least one of the following checkboxes is selected:

▶ **Due date check**
Defines that the due date check is logged for open items.

▶ **Payment method selection in all cases**
Ensures that the selection of all payment methods and all banks is documented in the log. You can then use the log to trace the procedure for the payment method selection.

▶ **Payment method selection if not successful**
Defines that the attempted selection of the payment method and banks is only documented in the log if no allowed payment method or bank has been found. The log enables you to identify whether corrections have to be implemented in the master record of the business partner or in the configuration of the payment program.

▶ **Line items of the payment documents**
Ensures that the log outputs all posted documents including the corresponding items. In the case of payment proposals, the document items that the system would generate for the following payment are output.

The PRINTOUT/DATA MEDIUM TAB navigates you to the configuration of the print output of proposal lists, release lists, and checks. For each payment method, there is a payment medium program that enables you to print payment forms (see Figure 3.27).

These settings must be saved with the SAVE button. Then, navigate to the STATUS tab. It displays the status message "Parameters have been entered" (see Figure 3.28).

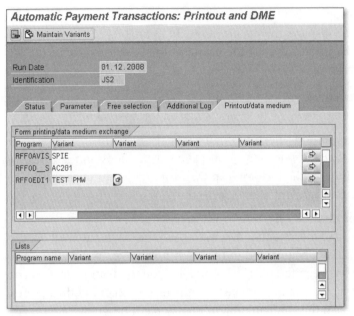

Figure 3.27 Output and Data Media Tab

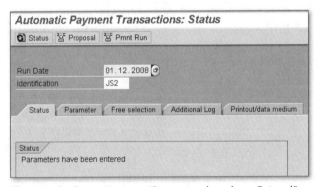

Figure 3.28 Status Message "Parameters have been Entered"

Once all parameters have been entered, you can schedule the payment proposal.

3.7.4 Payment Proposal

Based on the defined parameters, the SAP system determines the outstanding payments for the vendor or customer. Here, the generated payment proposal is the first step. For this purpose, click on the 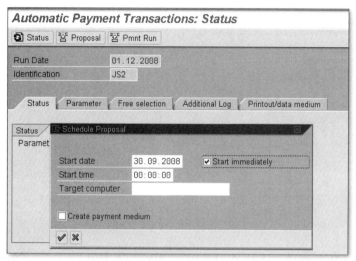 Proposal button. The Schedule Proposal dialog box opens (see Figure 3.29).

Figure 3.29 Schedule Proposal Dialog Box

When you select the Start immediately option and press Enter, the processing is performed in the foreground. You can retrieve data of this payment run using the proposal list, which stores a wealth of information, for example, an overview of all payments and line items.

At the end of this list, you can find a list of the payment amounts, sorted by the following criteria:

▶ Business areas

▶ Countries

▶ Currencies

▶ Payment methods

▶ Banks

The two-level procedure with a proposal list to be processed and a subsequent generation of the data medium can also be shortened, if required. Then, the system generates the payment medium directly without using a proposal list. The following example illustrates the two-level procedure. Here, the proposal list is processed first, and then the payment medium is generated. The status message in Figure 3.30 indicates that the proposal run created a payment proposal.

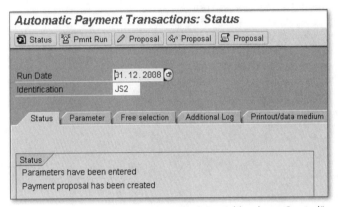

Figure 3.30 Status Message "Payment Proposal has been Created"

You can edit the payment proposal via the Proposal button.

Task sharing per accounting clerk The system now displays the Accounting clerk dialog box (see Figure 3.31). If you select All accounting clerks, the system selects all payments of a payment proposal run for processing. To only process the payments of the payment proposal that are assigned to a specific accounting clerk, select the Selected accounting clerk option and enter the corresponding ID. If you want to process all payments that aren't assigned to an accounting clerk, select the Selected Accounting Clerk option and don't enter any ID.

[+] **Task Sharing**

Particularly if a large number of vendors and customers are included in a payment proposal list, it makes sense to use the selection of accounting clerks to enable task sharing. A prerequisite is that the respective accounting clerks are also stored in the master data of the subledger account.

If you press the Enter key, the system takes you to the overview of the payment run. The first level displays a list of the individual payment media and exceptions for each business partner.

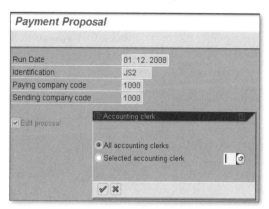

Figure 3.31 Dialog Box for Selecting the Accounting Clerks

The example shown in Figure 3.32 is not that complex. It refers to the enterprise, Testcompany, which is not supposed to be paid. The payment volume of the proposal run is €0.

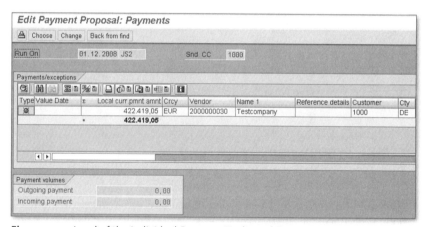

Figure 3.32 Level of the Individual Payment Media and Exceptions

You can view the corresponding open item if you double-click on a row within the exceptions. At the business partner level, you can see in Figure 3.33 that the Testcompany example involves the clearing process of vendor 2000000030 and customer 1000, that is, from a vendor that is also a customer.

Clearing of customers/ vendors

When you double-click on a line item, the system provides information on why this item has been included in the exception list. You can remove

Removing the payment block

the payment block here. Then, the item would be included in the actual payment run. Note that there are also payment blocks that you cannot remove in the payment proposal.

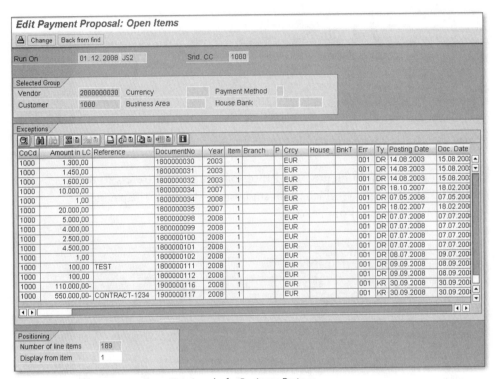

Figure 3.33 Exception Level of a Business Partner

[+] **Temporary Payment Blocks**

By double-clicking the line item, you can navigate to the payment information of this document item. You can set a payment block or change the payment method. If you set the payment block, the corresponding open item is not paid during this payment run. This modification applies to the specified payment run only. You change neither the original document nor the master record of the business partner. That means the next payment run considers this item again.

In the example, the payment proposal determines the balance from receivables and payables and identifies the exception documented in Figure 3.34. The payment cannot be made, because in total a debit balance, that is, a receivable, exists.

However, the `Reallocate...` button enables you to pay the selected item nevertheless. For this purpose, manually define a payment method including bank data, analogous to Figure 3.35. In the example, the system is supposed to generate a check from bank account 1000 GIRO of house bank 1000 DEUTSCHE BANK.

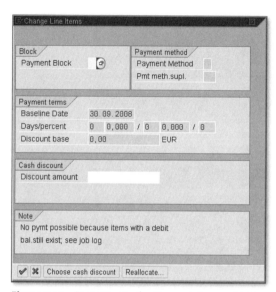

Figure 3.34 Exception in the Payment Proposal List

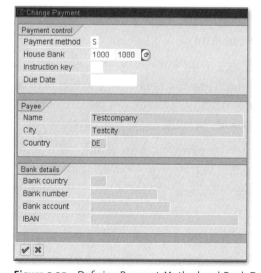

Figure 3.35 Defining Payment Method and Bank Data

After the changes have been saved, the updated payment proposal list provides the corresponding information. In the example shown in Figure 3.36, this is the second row, with an amount of €550,000 that has to be paid. The debit balance in the first row, which is not supposed to be paid, is then increased by this value.

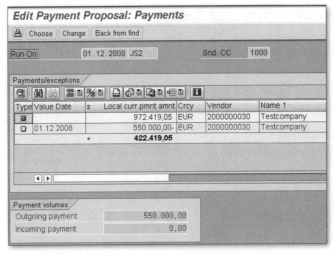

Figure 3.36 Updated Payment Proposal List

When the processing of the payment proposal list has been completed, clearing entries and payment media can be generated.

3.7.5 Executing the Payment Run

After you have processed the proposal list, you can schedule the payment run using the 🖳 Payment Run button. The amount of €550,000 is cleared in the vendor account with an automatically generated payment document. Accordingly, the status message illustrated in Figure 3.37 changes.

You start the printing of a check by performing an additional manual step, that is, clicking the 🖳 Printout button. The clearing transaction is documented through clearing document 2000000052 in the vendor line item list shown in Figure 3.38.

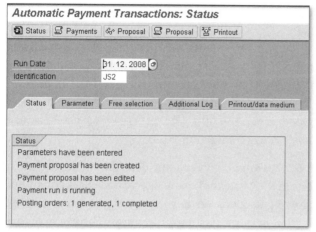

Figure 3.37 Status Message

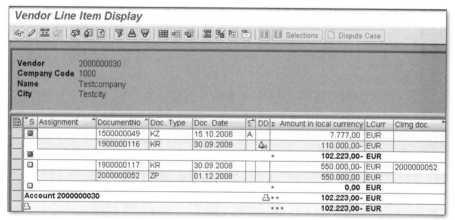

Figure 3.38 Vendor Line Item List

Parallel Process   **[+]**

The SAP system creates the clearing document and payment medium in parallel and independently of each other. You should consider this aspect particularly when you reconfigure the payment run. If the Customizing is set incorrectly, the system may clear items on the credit side without generating a payment medium subsequently.

In addition to the automated payment run, you can also trigger the process manually.

3.8 Manual Outgoing Payments

The basis of manual outgoing payments are usually payables that exist in the SAP system. In individual cases, advance payments can also be made without posted payables. This is referred to as a *payments on account*. You access the initial screen of outgoing payments via the menu path ACCOUNTING • FINANCIAL ACCOUNTING • ACCOUNTS PAYABLE • POSTING • OUTGOING PAYMENTS • POST (Transaction F-53).

Chapter 6, Section 6.5.2, Outgoing Payments, describes in detail similar business transactions in the context of manually created checks or ad-hoc payments. The following sections further discuss the *complete clearing*, *residual item*, and *partial payment* posting procedures. The examples are based on payables of €11,000 including an input tax of €1,000.

3.8.1 Complete Clearing

For complete clearings, the SAP system generates the screen shown in Figure 3.39. In the initial screen of the Enter Outgoing Payments transaction, you enter the document header as usual. The input in the Clearing text field appears for the clearing item in the vendor account. Compared to the previous document entry, the bank data is new.

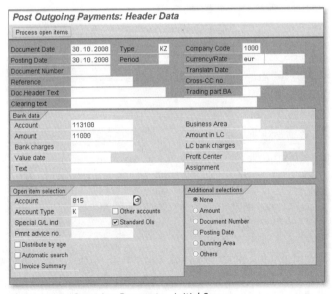

Figure 3.39 Outgoing Payments—Initial Screen

The outgoing payments are implemented through one of the defined house banks. The SAP system maps transactions in this bank account in a G/L account. You can enter the corresponding G/L account number in the Account field in the Bank data area. You then have to specify the payment amount and additional data. Additional selections enables you to include additional selection criteria (amount, document number, and so on). Outgoing payments through the house bank

The system supports you in specifying the offsetting entry in the vendor account. Consequently, you only need to enter the vendor account and the K account type (vendor). The SAP system supports you with a list of the open items that are supposed to be assigned. When you press the ⏎ key, the system opens the next screen, which displays the existing open items selected by the system in the account (see Figure 3.40). Depending on the setting in the editing options, you have to assign the corresponding open items by double-clicking on the payment amount fields. The example in Figure 3.41 shows the assignment of an open item with an amount of the outgoing payments of €11,000. The 2% cash discount is not used here.

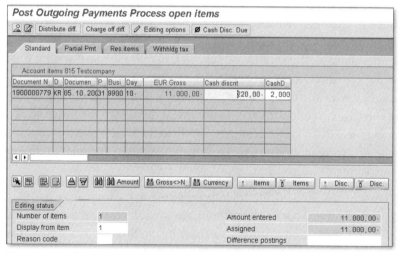

Figure 3.40 Outgoing Payments—Selecting the Open Items

The entered amount and the assigned amount are identical in the example. Therefore, the document can be posted. You can call the document Simulating documents overview of the outgoing payments using the Document Overview button. Only the entered item of the outgoing payments is displayed. You can view the vendor item, which has been automatically generated by the system, via the menu path DOCUMENT • SIMULATE.

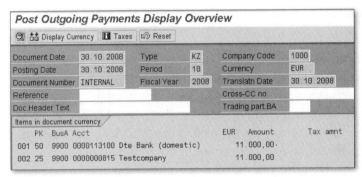

Figure 3.41 Outgoing Payments—Document Overview

Postings in the SAP system

The objects involved are a vendor from the FI-AP component and the general ledger from the FI-GL component. First, the "enter incoming invoice" activity leads to a credit entry for the "vendor" SAP object. The SAP system created an automatic entry to the reconciliation account defined in the vendor master record. The system posted the document and simultaneously closed the open item with the outgoing payment. The "payables" G/L account is not cleared, because the SAP system only stored the balance of the reconciliation account. The actual clearing process takes place for the "vendor" SAP object. The corresponding offsetting entry is posted in the G/L account that is defined in the initial screen (see Figure 3.39). Both documents are linked to each other through a 10-digit clearing number (in this example, this is the document number of the payment), as you can see in Figure 3.42.

Tolerance limits for difference postings

Differences that exceed the tolerance limits for postings may occur in the payment transaction. These limits are the tolerances defined by the accounting clerks and business partners in the SAP system during the system configuration. This could have been done for several reasons, for example, because a partial amount was paid (as in the example in the following section).

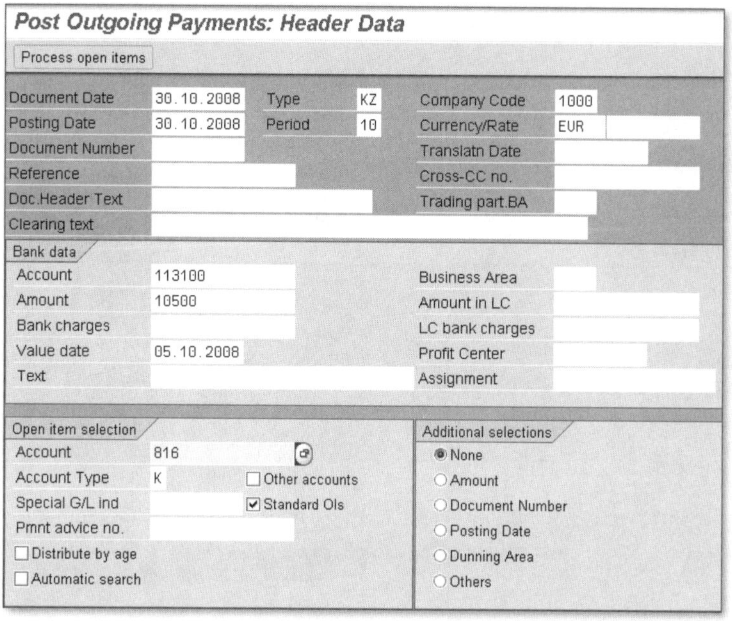

Post Outgoing Payments: Header Data

Process open items

Document Date	30.10.2008	Type	KZ	Company Code	1000
Posting Date	30.10.2008	Period	10	Currency/Rate	EUR
Document Number				Translatn Date	
Reference				Cross-CC no.	
Doc.Header Text				Trading part.BA	
Clearing text					

Bank data

Account	113100		Business Area	
Amount	10500		Amount in LC	
Bank charges			LC bank charges	
Value date	05.10.2008		Profit Center	
Text			Assignment	

Open item selection

Account	816		**Additional selections**	
Account Type	K	☐ Other accounts	◉ None	
Special G/L ind		☑ Standard OIs	○ Amount	
Pmnt advice no.			○ Document Number	
☐ Distribute by age			○ Posting Date	
☐ Automatic search			○ Dunning Area	
			○ Others	

Figure 3.42 Line Item Display after Outgoing Payments

When processing the open items, the following options are available in such cases:

- **Posting as a residual item**
  For residual item formations, the system closes the original open item and simultaneously generates a new open item with the remaining amount.

- **Posting as a partial payment**
  In this case, the original open item is not cleared. The SAP system posts the payment with an invoice reference. For this purpose, it enters the invoice number in the Invoice Reference field of the payment items.

3.8.2 Residual Items

In contrast to complete clearings, here a payment amount exists below the open item. The transaction is nearly the same as for the payment of the total amount described in Section 3.8.1, Complete Clearing. The initial screen is populated as shown in Figure 3.43.

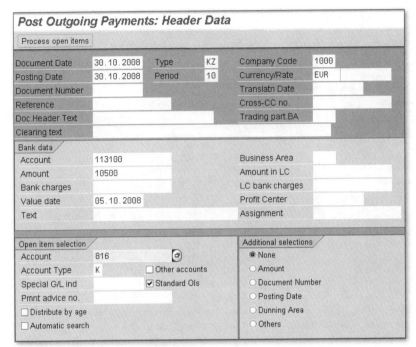

Figure 3.43 Outgoing Payments—Initial Screen for the Residual Item Formation

When you press ⌨Enter⌨, the system navigates you to the list of the selected items. From the processing of the open items, you must go to the Residual Items tab. In the Residual Items column, you enter the amount of the residual item. Alternatively, you can copy the remaining amount calculated by the system by double-clicking on the Residual Items field.

In the example, an outgoing payment of €10,500 leads to a residual item of €280. This is due to the proportionally accepted cash discount amount.

You can either first simulate or directly post the document. However, in both cases the system outputs the message that the item of the residual item still has to be corrected. For residual items, the SAP system requires you to make an entry in the text field of the document item (required entry field).

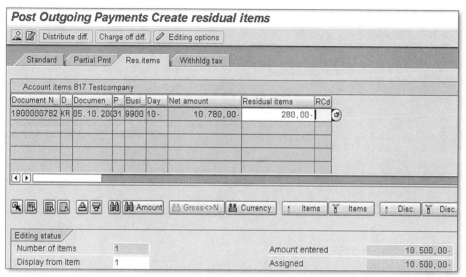

Figure 3.44 Residual Item for Outgoing Payments—List of the Selected Items

Post Outgoing Payments Display Overview

Document Date	30.10.2008	Type	KZ	Company Code	1000
Posting Date	30.10.2008	Period	10	Currency	EUR
Document Number	INTERNAL	Fiscal Year	2008	Translatn Date	30.10.2008
Reference				Cross-CC no.
Doc.Header Text				Trading part.BA

Items in document currency

	PK	BusA	Acct		EUR	Amount	Tax amnt
001	50	9900	0000113100	Dte Bank (domestic)		10.500,00-	
002	36	9900	0000000817	Testcompany		285,71-	1I
003	50	9900	0000276000	Discount received		194,81-	19,48- 1I
004	25	9900	0000000817	Testcompany		11.000,00	
005	50		0000154000	Input tax		19,48-	1I

Figure 3.45 Outgoing Payments—Residual Item Screen

Then, you can post the document. Figure 3.46 shows the process in the line item display. The original open item has been cleared, and the system has generated a new residual item.

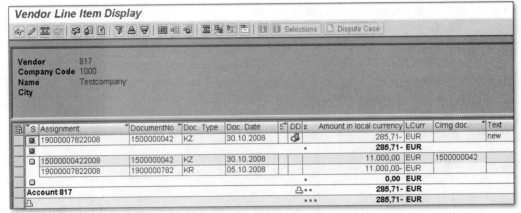

Figure 3.46 Residual Item for Outgoing Payments—Document Overview

In addition to the complete clearing and the described residual item formation, there are further options for posting outgoing payments.

3.8.3 Partial Payment

Differences may occur in a payment transaction for several reasons, for example, owing to the payment of a partial amount. When processing the open items, the user can post the outgoing payments as partial payments in such cases. For partial payments, the original open item is kept, and the system posts the payment to the vendor account and links it internally with the open item. To enter a partial payment, you follow the same menu path as for the residual item formation or for the payment of the total amount of an invoice. You populate the initial screen in the same way as for a residual item formation.

Pressing the [Enter] key takes you to the next screen. Now, you first have to assign the respective invoices to outgoing payment. This can be done by double-clicking on the corresponding field in the amount column of the displayed item list (see Figure 3.47). Then, select the Partial Payment tab (see Figure 3.48).

In the Payment amount column, you enter the amount of the partial payment. Alternatively, you can double-click on an amount to copy it. Figure 3.49 shows this process in the line item display.

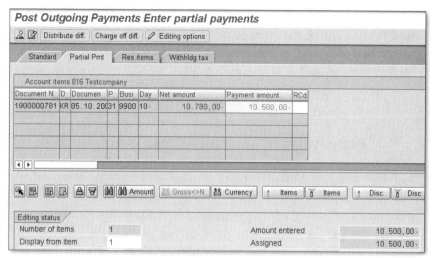

Figure 3.47 Partial Payment for Outgoing Payments

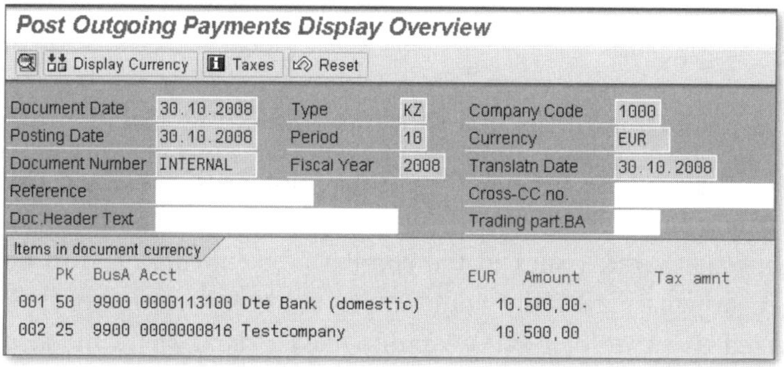

Figure 3.48 Outgoing Payments—Partial Payment Screen

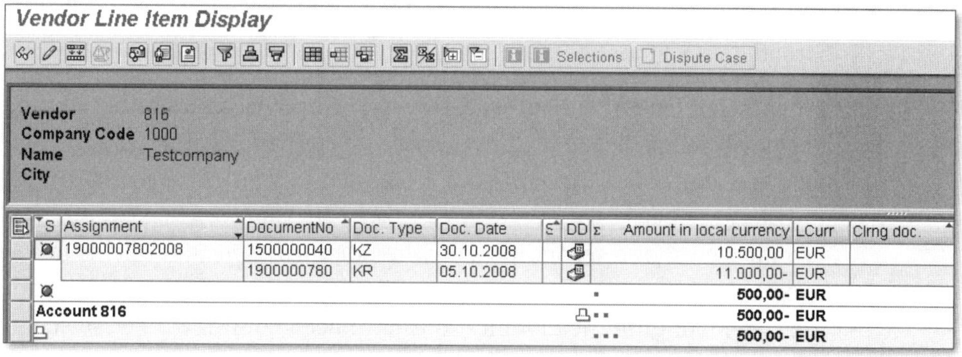

Figure 3.49 Line Items after a Partial Payment

The two items are indicated as open and linked to each other with identical content in the Assignment field. You can evaluate manual or automated outgoing payment postings—independently of whether they are implemented as complete clearings, residual items, or partial payments—with reports in SAP ERP.

3.9 Evaluations in Accounts Payable Accounting

SAP ERP and SAP NetWeaver BW provide a wide range of predefined evaluations. The information on the following pages merely represents examples and is only a fraction of the many possibilities available. The transparency of the due payables enables you to avoid expensive vendor credits by making the payments including deductions of cash discounts in time. Of course, a basic prerequisite for this is a sufficient liquidity of the enterprise. However, before it comes to the payment you must ensure that the payee is correct.

3.9.1 Confirmation of Critical Modifications

Risk management

Of course, an enterprise generally trusts its employees. However, risk management is supposed to identify and classify risks and initiate possible countermeasures. Issues in the context of payments need to be monitored particularly carefully. For example, not every accounting clerk is authorized to create or modify vendor master data. The same also applies to the execution of the actual payment program and the subsequent transfer of the payment medium to the bank. Task sharing in the entire business process is useful here and reduces the possibility of fraudulent actions.

In this context, SAP ERP provides several alternatives of security checking principles requiring at least two persons. For example, Transaction FK09 via the menu path ACCOUNTING • FINANCIAL ACCOUNTING • ACCOUNTS PAYABLE • MASTER DATA • CONFIRMATION OF CHANGE • LIST requires a confirmation of a second person when defined "sensitive" fields in the vendor master record are modified. The SAP system blocks the vendor for payment until the modifications have been confirmed. The selection screen shown in Figure 3.50 enables you to select the vendors that still need to be confirmed.

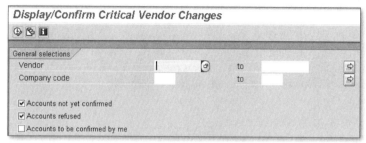

Figure 3.50 Displaying/Confirming Critical Modifications

When you click on the ⊕ button, the system executes the selection run and displays the results list from Figure 3.51.

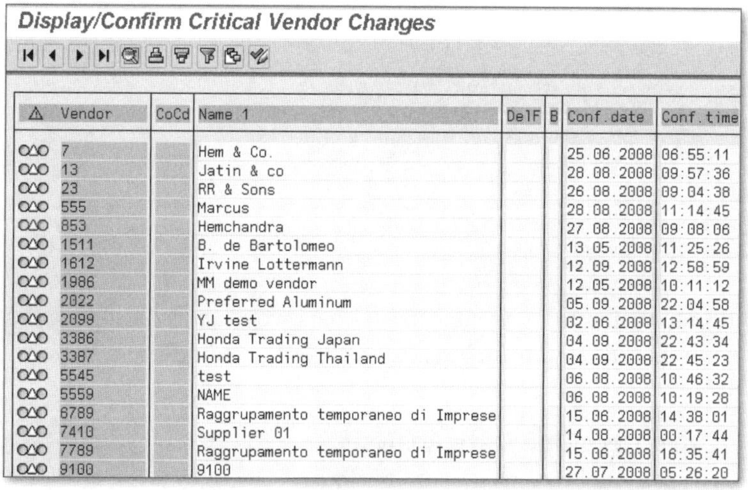

Display/Confirm Critical Vendor Changes

⚠	Vendor	CoCd	Name 1	DelF	B	Conf.date	Conf.time
∞	7		Hem & Co.			25.06.2008	06:55:11
∞	13		Jatin & co			28.08.2008	09:57:36
∞	23		RR & Sons			26.08.2008	09:04:38
∞	555		Marcus			28.08.2008	11:14:45
∞	853		Hemchandra			27.08.2008	09:08:06
∞	1511		B. de Bartolomeo			13.05.2008	11:25:26
∞	1612		Irvine Lottermann			12.09.2008	12:58:59
∞	1986		MM demo vendor			12.05.2008	10:11:12
∞	2022		Preferred Aluminum			05.09.2008	22:04:58
∞	2099		YJ test			02.06.2008	13:14:45
∞	3386		Honda Trading Japan			04.09.2008	22:43:34
∞	3387		Honda Trading Thailand			04.09.2008	22:45:23
∞	5545		test			06.08.2008	10:46:32
∞	5559		NAME			06.08.2008	10:19:28
∞	6789		Raggrupamento temporaneo di Imprese			15.06.2008	14:38:01
∞	7410		Supplier 01			14.08.2008	00:17:44
∞	7789		Raggrupamento temporaneo di Imprese			15.06.2008	16:35:41
∞	9100		9100			27.07.2008	05:26:20

Figure 3.51 Overview of Critical Modifications

This list indicates that numerous master record changes still have to be confirmed. The confirmation date indicates the date from which this process step is pending.

Bank and Account Number

Information on the bank or account number is particularly well suited to impose a security checking principle requiring at least two persons. However, because this data is maintained at the client level and because multiple company codes in the SAP system may share the master data, you have to pay attention to potential interactions. For example, if an accounting clerk who is responsible for enterprise A changes the bank details of a vendor, this modification causes a temporary payment block for all other company codes at the client level.

The example in Figure 3.52 shows the detailed status of a master record that has not been confirmed yet. The Changes to Sensitive Fields button displays the details before and after the modification of the master record. Based on this information, the modification can be confirmed or rejected.

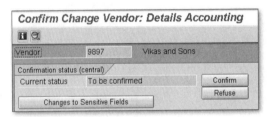

Figure 3.52 Confirming Details

In addition to maintaining vendor master data, you can also list payables in the open item due date analysis listed according to different blocks.

3.9.2 Open Item Due Date Analysis

This analysis is supposed to map the payables structure of an enterprise in sorted lists within periods. This enables you to view the expected outgoing liquidity in advance. The menu path Accounting • Financial Accounting • Accounts Payable • Information System • Reports for Accounts Payable Accounting • Vendor Items • Open Items Due Date Analysis first takes you to a selection of the company codes that are supposed to be considered on a freely selectable key date. In the example in Figure 3.53, the payables of company code 1000 that exist on 04/10/2008 are supposed to be selected.

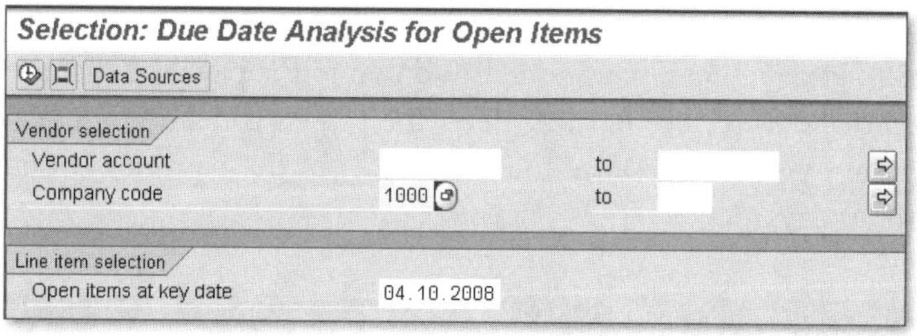

Figure 3.53 Selection for the Open Item Due Date Analysis

Analysis of the liquidity requirement

The result of this selection is illustrated in Figure 3.54. The drill-down report shows a sorted list with intervals of 30 days on the selected key date. The result includes payables that are already due (past) or items that will be due in the future (not due). This indicates that a considerable liquidity requirement of about €2 million already exists for a short-term period of 0 to 30 days.

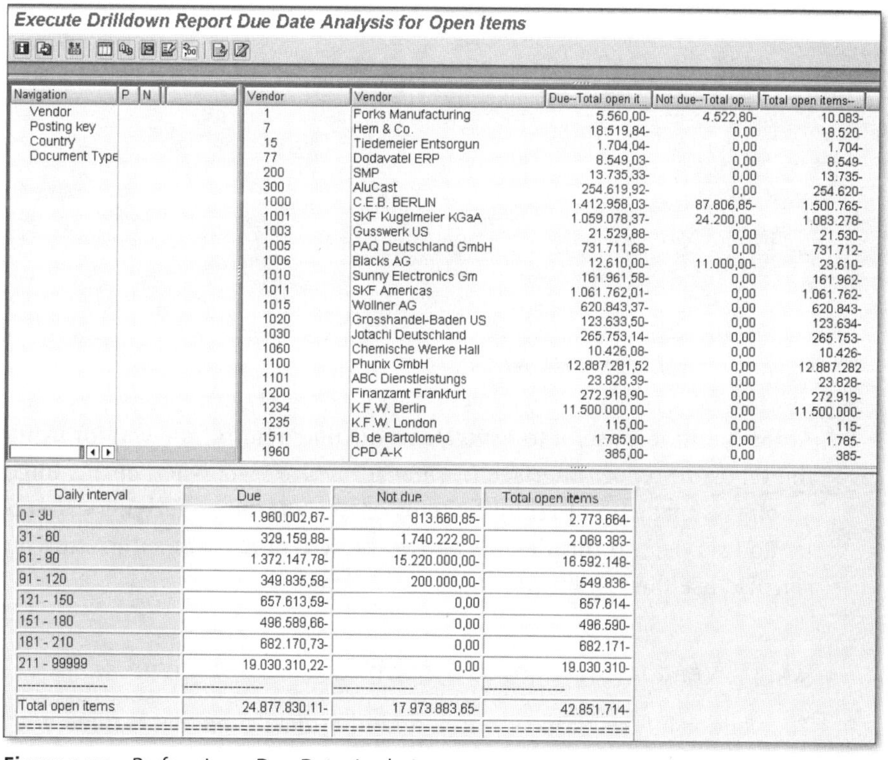

Vendor	Vendor	Due--Total open it...	Not due--Total op...	Total open items--...
1	Forks Manufacturing	5.560,00-	4.522,80-	10.083-
7	Hem & Co.	18.519,84-	0,00	18.520-
15	Tiedemeier Entsorgun	1.704,04-	0,00	1.704-
77	Dodavatel ERP	8.549,03-	0,00	8.549-
200	SMP	13.735,33-	0,00	13.735-
300	AluCast	254.619,92-	0,00	254.620-
1000	C.E.B. BERLIN	1.412.958,03-	87.806,85-	1.500.765-
1001	SKF Kugelmeier KGaA	1.059.078,37-	24.200,00-	1.083.278-
1003	Gusswerk US	21.529,88-	0,00	21.530-
1005	PAQ Deutschland GmbH	731.711,68-	0,00	731.712-
1006	Blacks AG	12.610,00-	11.000,00-	23.610-
1010	Sunny Electronics Gm	161.961,58-	0,00	161.962-
1011	SKF Americas	1.061.762,01-	0,00	1.061.762-
1015	Wollner AG	620.843,37-	0,00	620.843-
1020	Grosshandel-Baden US	123.633,50-	0,00	123.634-
1030	Jotachi Deutschland	265.753,14-	0,00	265.753-
1060	Chemische Werke Hall	10.426,08-	0,00	10.426-
1100	Phunix GmbH	12.887.281,52	0,00	12.887.282
1101	ABC Dienstleistungs	23.828,39-	0,00	23.828-
1200	Finanzamt Frankfurt	272.918,90-	0,00	272.919-
1234	K.F.W. Berlin	11.500.000,00-	0,00	11.500.000-
1235	K.F.W. London	115,00-	0,00	115-
1511	B. de Bartolomeo	1.785,00-	0,00	1.785-
1960	CPD A-K	385,00-	0,00	385-

Daily interval	Due	Not due	Total open items
0 - 30	1.960.002,67-	813.660,85-	2.773.664-
31 - 60	329.159,88-	1.740.222,80-	2.069.383-
61 - 90	1.372.147,78-	15.220.000,00-	16.592.148-
91 - 120	349.835,58-	200.000,00-	549.836-
121 - 150	657.613,59-	0,00	657.614-
151 - 180	496.589,66-	0,00	496.590-
181 - 210	682.170,73-	0,00	682.171-
211 - 99999	19.030.310,22-	0,00	19.030.310-
------------------	----------------	----------------	----------------
Total open items	24.877.830,11-	17.973.883,65-	42.851.714-
==================	================	================	================

Figure 3.54 Performing a Due Date Analysis

You can better analyze these values using the navigation within the drill-down report. Figure 3.55 illustrates a drill-down to the payables that are due to vendor 1000 (C.E.B. Berlin). Here, the screen is nearly identical to the general overview, because the major part of the payables is due within 0 to 30 days.

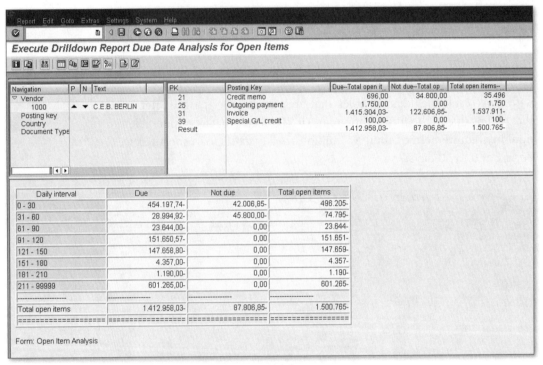

Navigation	P	N	Text		PK	Posting Key	Due--Total open it..	Not due--Total op..	Total open items-..
▽ Vendor					21	Credit memo	696,00	34.800,00	35.496
1000	▲ ▼		C.E.B. BERLIN		25	Outgoing payment	1.750,00	0,00	1.750
Posting key					31	Invoice	1.415.304,03-	122.606,85-	1.537.911-
Country					39	Special G/L credit	100,00-	0,00	100-
Document Type					Result		1.412.958,03-	87.806,85-	1.500.765-

Daily interval	Due	Not due	Total open items
0 - 30	454.197,74-	42.006,85-	496.205-
31 - 60	28.994,92-	45.800,00-	74.795-
61 - 90	23.644,00-	0,00	23.644-
91 - 120	151.650,57-	0,00	151.651-
121 - 150	147.658,80-	0,00	147.659-
151 - 180	4.357,00-	0,00	4.357-
181 - 210	1.190,00-	0,00	1.190-
211 - 99999	601.265,00-	0,00	601.265-
Total open items	1.412.958,03-	87.806,85-	1.500.765-

Form: Open Item Analysis

Figure 3.55 Drill-Down to a Vendor

At this point it is useful to navigate to the line items of the vendor using the report-to-report interface to view at invoice level whether this huge amount is made up of multiple items or to view the underlying deliveries and services. If this flexible and versatile report is not sufficient, you can also use the vendor information system.

3.9.3 Vendor Information System

The vendor information system is a kind of data cube that is filled with up-to-date information at regular intervals. You can view, rotate, and turn this cube from different perspectives. Consequently, the evaluations that are stored and structured according to topics in this cube are considerably well suited for analyses. In the SAP system, you can access the vendor information system via the menu path ACCOUNTING • FINANCIAL ACCOUNTING • ACCOUNTS PAYABLE • INFORMATION SYSTEM • TOOLS • SHOW EVALUATION.

The data cube of the vendor information system is static and always refers to a specific point in time. Via the menu bar entry, EXTRAS • DAY/TIME ON, you can display the creation time. The evaluations don't consider the posting procedures after this point in time. You therefore need to perform updates at regular intervals. The following sections describe the due date analysis as an example from the three evaluations shown in Figure 3.56.

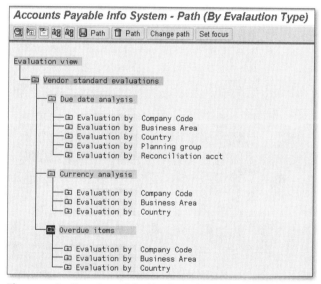

Figure 3.56 Overview of the Vendor Information System

You can access the due date analysis via the following views:

▶ Company code

▶ Business area

▶ Country

▶ Planning group

▶ Reconciliation account

The fixed, defined data cube provides these dimensions as standard evaluations. The example that is illustrated in Figure 3.57 uses the company code as the display format.

A list of the company codes that exist in the system including the respective payments that are currently due or will be due in the future maps the structures and may indicate faulty processes within a group with worldwide operations.

```
Due date analysis
 ▼  ▲  🔍 📖 🏱 🔲  ⊞ Total OIs  ⊞ OIs due  ⊞ OIs not due
```

Client IDES-ALE: Central FI Syst		Key date: 29.09.2008 Values in: EUR	
Company Code	Due	Not due	Total OI's
IDES US INC	64.634.650,65-	60.958,74-	64.695.609,39-
Company 1000	21.930.526,96-	201.363,77-	22.131.890,73-
IDES Canada for 4500	3.195.329,18-	0,00	3.195.329,18-
IDES AG NEW GL	2.602.519,00-	2.000,00-	2.604.519,00-
IDES New Zealand	2.385.313,41-	91.572,19-	2.476.885,60-
IDES Australia SR	1.633.696,72-	0,00	1.633.696,72-
IDES Retail GmbH	762.896,15-	0,00	762.896,15-
재고평가 테스트	724.000,00-	0,00	724.000,00-
IDES AG	490.000,00-	0,00	490.000,00-
IDES Retail INC US	233.685,40-	0,00	233.685,40-
IDES Training AC Gr. 19	200.000,00-	0,00	200.000,00-
IDES Brasil 7001	178.423,71-	0,00	178.423,71-
Group 26	119.950,00-	0,00	119.950,00-
IDES Training AC206	100.000,00-	0,00	100.000,00-
IDES France	89.951,00-	0,00	89.951,00-
IDES España	73.572,00-	0,00	73.572,00-
IDES Argentina	63.085,18-	0,00	63.085,18-
IDES Japan 5000	62.219,77-	0,00	62.219,77-
Australian Real Estate	33.408,86-	0,00	33.408,86-
IDES UK	17.374,96-	0,00	17.374,96-
IDES France affiliate	3.000,00-	0,00	3.000,00-
SMS	2.985,23-	0,00	2.985,23-
SAP A.G.	2.589,25-	0,00	2.589,25-
IDES US INC New GL	2.339,79-	0,00	2.339,79-
Services Logistics SP	1.282,99-	0,00	1.282,99-
Good Food	1.220,59-	0,00	1.220,59-
IDES Training AC Gr. 24	1.160,00-	0,00	1.160,00-
SP POST	999,00-	0,00	999,00-
CP Beverage	888,03-	0,00	888,03-
IDES México, S.A. de C.V.	831,63-	0,00	831,63-
IDES Training AC Gr. 18	700,00-	0,00	700,00-
Country Template AT	482,67-	0,00	482,67-
Empresa México "A"	17,48-	0,00	17,48-
Total	99.549.099,61-	355.894,70-	99.904.994,31-

Figure 3.57 Due Date Analysis per Company Code

If the due (to be paid) proportion of the total open item balance is disproportionally high, this may be due to a poorly structured invoice receipt process. Figure 3.58 illustrates an example of a demo system in which the total open item balance is due as of company code IDES Australia. This is based on the fact that no new incoming invoices with a date of required payment are entered in this test company code, and outgoing payments are not made for older invoices. In contrast, some items are not yet due for the second company code on top, Company 1000. With a double-click you can navigate to the display shown in Figure 3.58. This view allows for analyses per vendor and provides subsequent drill-down options to the vendor's line items.

Overall, the evaluations for critical master record modifications, the open item due date analysis, or the vendor information system provide useful support for the daily work of the accounts payable accountant.

Due date analysis

▼ ▲ ◎ 📖 ▽ 🗎 | 📊 Total OIs | 📊 OIs due | 📊 OIs not due

Client   IDES-ALE: Central FI Syst   Key date: 29.09.2008
Company Code Company 1000   Values in: EUR

Vendor	Due	Not due	Total OI's
K.F.W. Berlin	11.500.000,00-	0,00	11.500.000,00-
Vendor 01 GB	7.000.200,00-	0,00	7.000.200,00-
IT Service SpA	4.365.891,48-	0,00	4.365.891,48-
Global Business Properties	3.126.760,00-	0,00	3.126.760,00-
C.E.B. BERLIN	1.523.400,98-	43.004,07-	1.566.405,05-
SKF Kugelmeier KGaA	1.059.078,37-	24.200,00-	1.083.278,37-
SKF Americas	1.061.762,01-	0,00	1.061.762,01-
PAQ Deutschland GmbH	737.744,92-	0,00	737.744,92-
Wollner AG	620.843,37-	0,00	620.843,37-
JTC Corporation	584.640,00-	0,00	584.640,00-
Finanzamt Frankfurt	273.014,00-	0,00	273.014,00-
Jotachi Deutschland AG	265.753,14-	0,00	265.753,14-
AluCast	211.619,92-	0,00	211.619,92-
Sunny Electronics GmbH	161.961,58-	0,00	161.961,58-
Stromlieferant	134.231,96-	0,00	134.231,96-
Grosshandel-Baden USA	123.633,50-	0,00	123.633,50-
American Express	110.200,00-	0,00	110.200,00-
Shinozaki Tsutomo	101.000,00-	0,00	101.000,00-
Sapsota Company Limited	86.834,00-	0,00	86.834,00-

Figure 3.58   Due Date Analysis of the Vendors in a Company Code

3.10   Conclusion

The core process of accounts payable accounting includes efficient data entry and posting of incoming invoices. Depending on in which department this process step is performed and depending on the structure of the invoices, different SAP transactions are used. The next process step involves manual or automated outgoing payments. In particular, the two-level procedure with the proposal run enables you to obtain a good overview of the outstanding invoices. The necessary evaluations that provide transparency for future liquidity requirements for outgoing payments round off accounts payable accounting.

Accounts receivable accounting manages the customer receivables. This chapter provides a comprehensive description of the programs of SAP ERP Financials that help you keep the period between billing and incoming payments as short as possible.

4   Accounts Receivable Accounting

This chapter first describes the basic business principles of accounts receivable accounting, and then it outlines the SAP subledger FI-AR (Accounts Receivable) and details the business process that starts with the order creation and ends with the incoming payments. The focus is on the functional innovations of the current Release SAP ERP 6.0. In this context, this chapter describes some components of SAP Financial Supply Chain Management (FSCM) — SAP Credit Management, SAP Collections Management, SAP Dispute Management, and SAP Biller Direct — based on an example that is used throughout the chapter.

4.1   Business Principles

For subledger accounts you differentiate between customer accounts or customers and vendor accounts or vendors. In contrast to general ledger accounting, in which you only manage the total of receivables for the financial statement, you use accounts receivable accounting to record all details regarding the business transactions, such as invoices, credit memos, and incoming payments. The interaction between the sales department and accounts receivable accounting assumes a significant role here. The sales employees are interested in sales orders and sales volume, and they receive incentives in the form of bonus payments for their work.

The task of accounts receivable accounting is to convert the invoice amount that was agreed on by contract with the customer into cash

Total loss on receivables

receipt. The general rule still applies: "Sold and delivered goods remain a gift until they are paid." Enterprises solve this goal conflict between the sales department and accounts receivable accounting by means of a clearly defined receivables management. This management includes rules on how to proceed in certain cases. Besides the worst-case event—insolvency of one or more customers or total loss on receivables—this management aims to optimize the working capital.

Period outstanding of receivables If, for example, customers pay too late and don't pay the full invoice amount, this results in a delayed cash receipt, and the enterprise must keep its business activities running with borrowed money. This process in turn causes costs in the form of interest. A key figure that is mentioned more and more often is the DSO (days sales outstanding) value, that is, the period outstanding of receivables. A value that is as low as possible indicates an effective receivables management.

Process costs A third aspect in addition to the losses on receivables and interest charges concerns the process costs in receivables management: How much time and hence money is invested internally to go from the sales order to the cash receipt. You shouldn't underestimate the time required for internal communication in this context. A highly transparent and clear process is helpful here. You should definitely avoid a ping-pong game of questions and counter-questions between the sales department and financial accounting. This calls for clear responsibilities and goals. Sales departments and their bonus and payment goals are increasingly measured based on an effective receivables and working capital management. This alleviates the goal conflict of tasks between the sales department and financial accounting and ensures that all people involved pull together into one direction.

SAP's FI-AR software component provides a multitude of options to map receivables management efficiently and transparently. Furthermore, SAP FSCM of Release SAP ERP 6.0 is supplemented with further options for credit limit checks, the dunning procedure by telephone, and dispute case processing.

4.2   FI-AR Component

The SAP system includes two components or subledgers to save customer data and to implement an efficient receivables management on this basis:

- ▶ FI-AR (accounts receivable)
- ▶ FI-CA (contract accounting)

This dualism is due to the fact that enterprises use different business models—business to business (B2B) and business to consumer (B2C)—in practice.

Historically, accounts receivable accounting was originally developed for the B2B area. Industrial enterprises have industrial enterprises as customers whose number is considerably smaller than in the B2C business model. The data processing of processes, such as invoice posting, incoming payments, or dunning procedures, requires more CPU time with an increasing customer base; however, it runs in an acceptable time window. FI-AR and the general ledger are connected in real time.

Mass accounting with FI-CA

The B2C business model primarily concerns SAP industry solutions for telecommunication enterprises, electricity providers, and the media segment. One challenge is to map millions of end customers quickly and efficiently. Here, the data model and the existing programs for FI-AR quickly reach their (time) limits. This is where FI-CA (contract accounting) emerged, which is based on the industry solutions for mass accounting. The processes and hence the programs, such as invoice posting, dunning procedures, or incoming payments, are developed for these industries specifically for the FI-CA subledger. Furthermore, FI-AR and the general ledger are asynchronous; that is, they are connected to the background processing with a time delay.

To simplify the examples provided in the next sections, a B2B business model with the FI-AR component is used as the basis. The substeps shown can be transferred to a B2C business model with FI-CA to a certain extent only.

The FI-AR component keeps and manages account-based customer data. Furthermore, the component is an integral part of sales and distribu-

FI-AR

tion controlling. Sales and financial accounting have similar information requirements, for example, credit standing or payment history. Accounts receivable accounting provides not only the basis for proper accounting, but also data for an effective credit management through a close integration with the SD (sales and distribution) module and information for the optimization of the liquidity planning through a connection with the cash management and forecast.

Account analyses, alarm reports, due date lists, and flexible dunning are available for the open item management. The associated correspondence can be customized to the specific requirements of the enterprise. An incoming payment can be assigned to the corresponding receivables manually on the screen or by electronic means. By means of the payment program, you can automate both the debit memo procedure and the payment of credit memos. To document the processes in accounts receivable accounting, you can use account balances, journals, balance audit trails, and numerous standard reports. For key date valuations you revaluate foreign currency items, determine customers on the credit side, and scan the balances established this way for remaining terms.

Before you can execute these functions, you must define the customers' general information. The next section deals with the master data topic in more detail.

4.3   Master Data

The master data of customers is made up of three parts. The general data is maintained at the client level. This data is available for all company codes. At this level, you specify the name of the subledger account in subledger accounting, the tax number, and the bank details.

Data that is important for individual company codes is specified in the company code area. This includes the account number of the reconciliation account in the general ledger, the terms of payment, and the settings for the dunning procedure. For integrated use with the SD module (sales and distribution), you are provided with additional fields for the customer's master record. These fields contain information that is required for handling business transactions in the sales and distribution area and that is used exclusively in the SD module. This data includes the terms of delivery, price list type, and remarks regarding the customer. These specifications control the order processing, the shipping data, and the billing information, provided that these business transactions are recorded by means of a transaction to SD.

The SAP system provides a special master record type for one-time customers. In contrast to the "regular" master records, this master record does not contain specific data of the business partner, such as the address or bank details. This information is entered for each business transaction during document entry. When posting to a one-time account, the system automatically navigates to an entry screen to enter the business partner's specific data of.

One-time customer

One-Time Account **[+]**

Avoid one-time customers or one-time accounts wherever possible and reasonable. It decreases the transparency, and when a customer places a second or third order with your enterprise, you will find out that a general master record would have paid off.

4.3.1 Creating a Customer Account

For G/L accounts you have the option to record master record data from the SAP menu tree centrally in one process or incrementally in three steps. The central processing is available via the menu path ACCOUNTING • FINANCIAL ACCOUNTING • ACCOUNTS RECEIVABLE • MASTER DATA • CENTRAL MAINTENANCE • CREATE/CHANGE/DISPLAY (Transactions XD01/XD02/XD03).

For the incremental processing, you first maintain the general data at the client level and then the data in the company code. You perform the processing of data from the sales and distribution segment within the SD module. Another option is to go from the customer master record in FI to the corresponding sales area using the GOTO functionality. To maintain the individual areas you must select the menu path ACCOUNTING • FINANCIAL ACCOUNTING • ACCOUNTS RECEIVABLE • MASTER DATA • CREATE/CHANGE/DISPLAY (Transactions FD01/FD02/FD03).

Central maintenance

10-digit customer
number
In the dialog shown in Figure 4.1 you must enter the customer's account number and corresponding company code. The account number is assigned by the SAP system (internal number assignment) depending on the value of the account group. In general, the account number can be a 10-digit numeric or alphanumeric value with letters. This example uses the customer number CMS0000099. The key CMS in front of the number indicates the group of customers within a specific business segment.

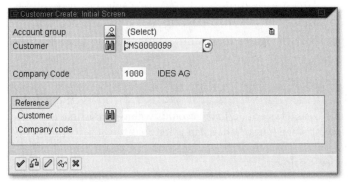

Figure 4.1 Create Customer

[+]

Meaningful Keys

Number descriptions with a meaning, also referred to as meaningful keys, are generally controversial. If the number already considers evaluation purposes, these specifications help you select and evaluate all customers of a business segment with the CMS key. However, you should be aware that the actual free customer number range consists of 10 minus three specified digits in such a structure. The question then is what happens if more than 9,999,999 customers exist in this business segment. Then, exceptions to the rule apply that must also be considered in simple reporting.

If you don't specify the company code when you create a customer, that is, if you leave this field empty, you can only maintain the client-specific area. The creation of a master record makes it imperative to specify the account group, which then controls the further recording of the master record, for example. You use the template technique by entering an account number that exists in the SAP system and the corresponding company code in the respective fields. If you press the ‹Enter› key, the system takes you to the maintenance of the customer account. The screen shown in Figure 4.2 appears, which is already filled with values in this example.

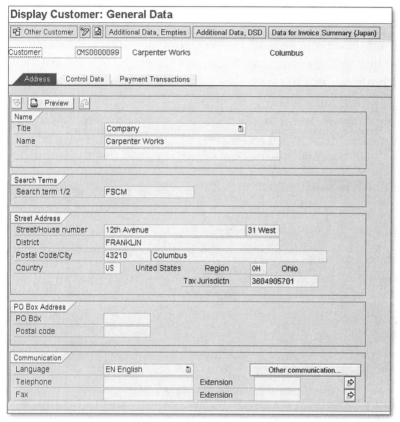

Figure 4.2 Maintenance of a Customer Account: General Data—Address

▶ **Name/Street Address**

The reports and correspondence in the SAP system access this address data. Depending on the report, it then appears in the address and salutation of correspondence or in the report lists.

▶ **Search Terms**

In this field, you can enter a freely selectable term that is used for the search for master records with the matchcode. To ensure that the field is filled uniformly, it is recommended that you specify rules. For the standard matchcode, this is the primary key with which you can search for master records most rapidly.

▶ **Language (Communication)**
Here, you define the language in which the correspondence is written.

The tabs shown contain further master record fields that are summarized according to content aspects. Figure 4.3 shows the Control Data tab, which you can also access via the F8 function key.

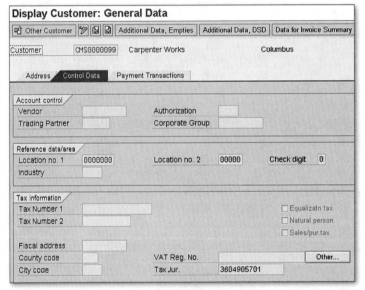

Figure 4.3 Maintenance of a Customer Account, Control Data—General Data

▶ **Account control (Vendor)**
If a business partner is both a vendor and a customer, you're provided with the option to have the system clear receivables and payables automatically (automatic payment program or dunning). In this case, you must enter the account number of the customer in the vendor master record and vice versa. If these fields are filled, the system displays a field called Clearing with ... in the Account Management tab for the company code data. Clearing is not possible until this field is activated.

In the Payment Transactions tab, you can make the settings shown in Figure 4.4:

▶ **Bank Details**

It is mandatory to enter the bank details if you use bank transfers or other payment methods of the payment program. If the automatic payment program is supposed to consider the automatic debit, you must additionally select the corresponding field. In this case, the automatic dunning procedure does not apply.

▶ **Alternative payer**

If you enter the customer's account number here, all payments are made using the bank details of this business partner (bank transfers, automatic debit, credit memos). This field exists in the general part, in the company code area, and at the document level. The specification that is more detailed applies (in this list in ascending form).

▶ **Bank type**

If you define multiple bank details in a customer master record, you can differentiate them by means of any four-digit abbreviation (partner bank type). If you want to pay an open item using the customer's specific bank details, you must define the corresponding abbreviation in the line item (see Figure 3.16). The payment program of the SAP system controls the customer's specified bank details.

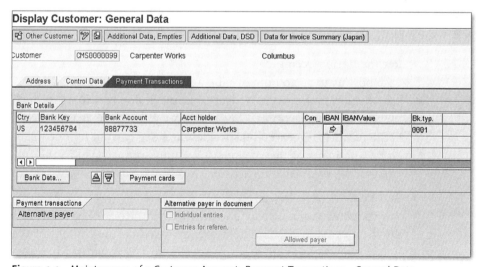

Figure 4.4 Maintenance of a Customer Account, Payment Transactions—General Data

The second part of the customer master record, the company code area, is accessible via the Company Code Data button.

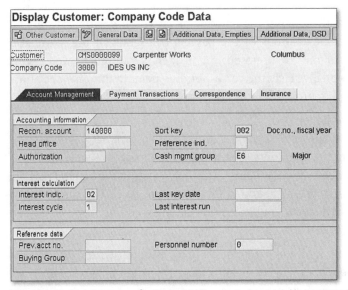

Figure 4.5 Maintenance of a Customer Account, Account Management—Company Code Data

First, the SAP system generates the screen shown in Figure 4.5 with the Account Management tab in the foreground. Here, you can make various settings for the account management in the general ledger and subledger.

▶ **Reconciliation account**

Each posting to an account of subledger accounting automatically creates an entry to the general ledger. This integration is ensured through the reconciliation account. The field status group in the master record of the reconciliation account specifies the screen layout for document entry. The items of the customer's account are managed in the currency of the reconciliation account.

▶ **Sort key**

You use sort keys to display line items. Usually, the SAP system sorts the documents in the line item display based on the content of the ASSIGNMENT field in the document. This sort key controls how the

ASSIGNMENT field is automatically filled during document entry if it is not populated with a value from another source.

▶ **Authorization**
In this field, you can specify who receives change or read authorization for this account.

▶ **Head office**
In some industries, sales take place in branch offices, but the accounting of all branches is managed centrally. To implement this, you must create a master record in the SAP system both for the head office and for the branch. In the branch's master record, you must enter the corresponding account number in the Head office field. The order management is performed by the branch. The transaction figures are then automatically posted to the head office's account. The account number of the branch concerned is recorded in the document items. For head office accounts, you should enter the sort key 004 (branch account number) that ensures a sorting of the line items according to branches. This variant of the sort key ensures that the entry of the Branch Account Number field is copied to the Assignment line item field.

To enter further data of a customer master record, go to the next tab. Figure 4.6 shows the Payment Transactions tab, which you can also call via the [F8] function key.

▶ **Terms of payment**
This key is used for orders, purchase orders, and invoices and provides information about dunning and payment transactions. The value entered here is used as a default value for the document entry.

▶ **Tolerance group**
You make specifications for granting of cash discounts and for the handling of payment differences for each tolerance group. This entry affects dunning and entry of payment transactions. For manual closing, the payment differences are accepted by the system up to the defined tolerance, and the items are closed.

▶ **Payment history record**
If you activate this field, the system records the customer's payment history. This is important for credit management.

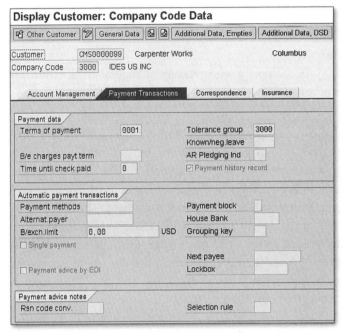

Figure 4.6 Maintenance of a Customer Account, Payment Transactions—Company Code Data

▶ **Payment methods**
Here, you can find the payment methods that are allowed for this business partner if the automatic payment program is used. If a payment method for the incoming payment is entered here, for instance, B (bank direct debit) or A (automatic debit), this business partner is not considered by the automatic dunning program.

▶ **Payment block**
An entry in this field causes a block of the account for payment transactions. In the automatic payment program, the block is effective if it is set either in the master record or in the document. If the block is set in the master record, all open items of this customer are transferred to the exception list.

[+] **Various Blocking Keys**

The * blocking key (asterisk) causes the system to ignore all open items of the account; the + key (plus) causes the system to ignore all open items for which no payment method has been explicitly specified in the document.

▶ **Single payment**

This checkbox determines that all open items of this business partner are paid or collected separately. This prevents multiple open items being cleared jointly with one payment medium.

▶ **Clearing with vendor**

This checkbox is only displayed if a value is entered in the Vendor field in the general part of the Control Data tab. However, an actual clearing within the automatic SAP procedure only takes place if this field is selected.

▶ The next tab contains more fields that refer to the customer master data. You can also use the F8 function key to go to the Correspondence tab. The SAP system creates a screen as shown in Figure 4.7.

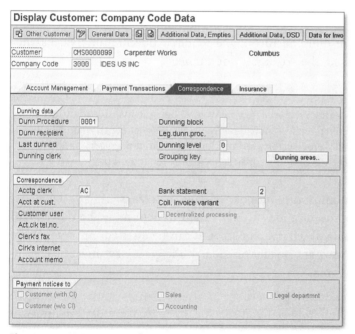

Figure 4.7 Maintenance of a Customer Account, Correspondence — Company Code Data

▶ **Dunning Procedure**

A central control factor of SAP's dunning program is the dunning procedure that you must define in the business partner master record. Dunning procedures are independent of the company code and can be used by all company codes within a client. Only the assignment of the dunning notices to the individual dunning procedures is controlled separately for each company code. If this business partner is supposed to be considered by the automatic dunning program, you must define a dunning procedure here.

This dunning procedure contains the following settings:

▶ **Dunning frequency/dunning interval**
A dunning interval is defined for each dunning procedure. It determines the dunning frequency, that is, the minimum number of days that must elapse after a dunning run before an account can be dunned again. To determine whether an account is included in a dunning run, the dunning program saves the date of the last dunning run in the master record. Based on the date and the dunning interval, the dunning program specifies whether the account is supposed to be considered in the dunning run. If the required dunning interval has not been reached, the account is not dunned.

[+] **Adhering to Dunning Intervals**

A dunning is either created if new items have become overdue in the account or if the dunning level of individual items has been changed manually. Customers shouldn't receive any further dunnings within a specific period (dunning interval). This period frequently is between 7 and 14 days.

▶ **Grace day/minimum number of days in arrears**
These day specifications are only used to determine the due date of open items and whether an account can be dunned. An item whose days in arrears are smaller or equal to the grace days must be considered as not due.

▶ **Number of dunning levels**
For each dunning level you can specify how many days in arrears a line item must be to reach the corresponding dunning level. The dunning level determines the associated dunning notice, for example.

▶ **Processes to be dunned**
Here, you specify whether the standard and/or special G/L transactions are dunned with a procedure. Special G/L transactions include,

for example, bill of exchange payment requests, payment requests, down payments, and down payment requests.

► **Dunning block**

If you select this field, this business partner is not considered within a dunning run of the automatic dunning program. For this purpose, you must enter a blocking key in the Dunning block field of the master record or of the document item. For the blocking key, you define descriptive texts that indicate the reason for the block. Blocked accounts or items are not considered in the dunning run and are output in an exception list including the blocking reason. You can remove or add dunning blocks within the scope of the dunning proposal processing.

► **Dunning level**

This field is usually set by the dunning program. In exceptional cases, you can change the dunning level manually. The dunning level influences the next dunning run. If the dunning level is 0, the system uses the minimum number of days in arrears that are specified in the dunning procedure to calculate the necessary days in arrears; for all other dunning levels, the system uses the grace days.

► **Dunning clerk**

The name of the clerk whose ID is indicated in this field is printed on the dunning notices. The dunning clerk and the accounting clerk can be two different people.

► **Accounting clerk**

The name of the clerk whose ID is indicated in this field appears on all correspondence documents sent to the business partner. Additionally, it is printed on the dunning notices, if the Dunning clerk field is not filled.

The next tab contains additional fields on the insurance topic. Press the F8 function key to go to the tab. The SAP system creates a screen as shown in Figure 4.8.

► **Policy number**

In this field, you can define the link to an export credit insurance policy.

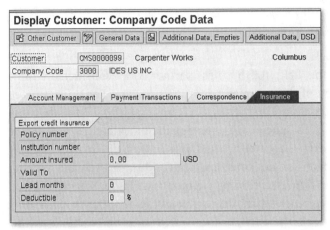

Figure 4.8 Maintenance of a Customer Account, Insurance—Company Code Data

► **Institution number**
Depending on where you contracted your export credit insurance, you can define a number for the institution here, for example, 01 for Creditreform.

► **Amount insured**
Here, you can define the value of your insurance.

► **Valid To**
The policies have a time limit and must be renewed at regular intervals. Here, you can enter the necessary date.

► **Lead months**
For this signal factor, you must maintain the maximum date of required payment to be granted for your customers.

► **Deductible**
Most export credit policies include a deductible share of the policyholder. This rate is between 20 and 40% depending on the insurance risk.

[+] **Risk Insurances**

An export credit insurance makes sense if you have customers with higher risk regarding loss on receivables, for example, in politically unstable countries. Furthermore, an export credit insurance is helpful to outsource parts of the receivables management.

> For example, the process step of a credit limit check is not that important any longer if large parts of the receivables are insured anyway. As far as the SAP functionality of SAP ERP is concerned, you should consider the Insurance tab of the customer master record as a storage location for contract information. If you want to use an export credit insurance, you need to use an SAP partner solution to automate the necessary process steps

With this information in the general data and the company code data, you can use a customer for postings. In the initial phase of a business relationship, you must define the master data in the SAP system. At the end of a business relationship, however, you may require the opposite.

4.3.2 Blocking a Customer Account

The master record of a customer contains multiple fields for blocking the account. For accounting, you have the option to block the account in one or more company codes. A dunning or payment block can be set at the company code level (see Figure 4.9). You can set and undo the block flag any time via the menu path ACCOUNTING • FINANCIAL ACCOUNTING • ACCOUNTS RECEIVABLE • MASTER DATA • BLOCK/UNBLOCK (Transaction FD05).

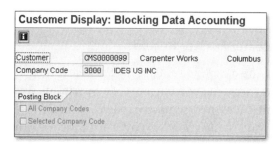

Figure 4.9 Block at the Company Code Level

Alternatively, you use the central maintenance to block or unblock customers for accounting and sales in one step: ACCOUNTING • FINANCIAL ACCOUNTING • ACCOUNTS RECEIVABLE • MASTER DATA • CENTRAL MAINTENANCE • BLOCK/UNBLOCK (Transaction XD05). For customers, the following block types exist: posting block, order block, delivery block, and billing block (see Figure 4.10).

Central block

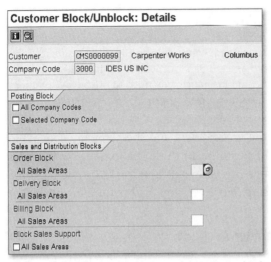

Figure 4.10 Central Block for Company Codes and Sales

A posting block means that no FI document can be created in the selected company codes. An order block means that no sales order can be created in the selected sales areas. A delivery block prevents the delivery in the selected sales areas. The billing block ensures that no invoice is created and sent to the customer. In addition to setting different blocks, you can also archive the customer master records.

4.3.3 Archiving of Customer Master Records

The subledgers provide you the option to set flags for the deletion of all master record data (All areas checkbox) or company code–specific master data of certain company codes (Selected company code checkbox). This is illustrated in Figure 4.11. You set deletion flags by selecting the menu path ACCOUNTING • FINANCIAL ACCOUNTING • ACCOUNTS RECEIVABLE • MASTER DATA • SET DELETION FLAG (Transaction FD06).

In the Deletion blocks area, you can make two selections. They have the following effect:

▸ **General data**
This flag prevents the deletion of general data from the master record by the archiving program.

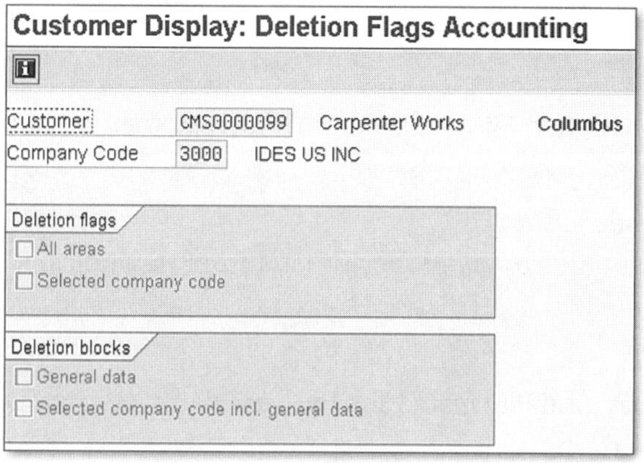

Figure 4.11 Setting Deletion Flags

▸ **Selected company code including general data**
   With this flag you determine that the company-specific data of the master record must not be deleted. If this flag is set, none of the associated general data is deleted.

Alternatively, you can also implement the deletion flag centrally (see Figure 4.12). This is done by selecting the menu path ACCOUNTING • FINANCIAL ACCOUNTING • ACCOUNTS RECEIVABLE • MASTER DATA • CENTRAL MAINTENANCE • SET DELETION FLAG (Transaction XD06).

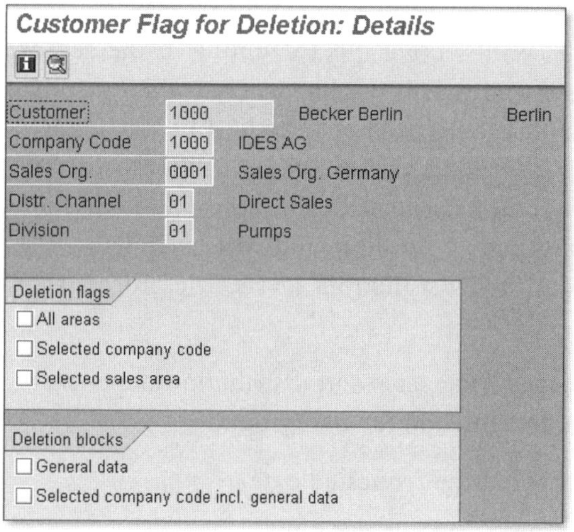

Figure 4.12 Setting the Deletion Flag Centrally

Selecting an option in the Deletion flags area has the following effects:

▶ **All areas**
This flag causes the deletion of all data from the customer master record.

▶ **Selected company code**
This flag specifies that only company-specific data from the indicated company code is deleted.

▶ **Selected sales area**
This flag indicates that all data created for the specified sales area is deleted in the master record.

Dependent data   The master data is deleted by means of the program for archiving customers or vendors. This program archives the master records flagged for deletion provided that no dependent data exists. Once you've defined the basis with the master data and clarified, for example, whether one-time customers are allowed, how numbers are assigned to customers (continuous or meaningful key), and which fields of the customer master record are to be maintained and how, it is time to have a look at an integrated business transaction.

4.4   Overview of the Integrated Business Transaction

When you examine the accounts receivable accounting in the context of integrated business transactions, this usually concerns the individual steps from order entry to incoming payments (order to cash). Integration also means that the information flow involves different departments. This example includes the departments of sales and distribution, accounts receivable accounting, controlling, and treasury. Figure 4.13 illustrates the various departments at the four levels. The process steps are performed from left to right.

Incoming orders   During the incoming orders in the sales and distribution department, two critical checks are implemented in the background:

▶ Can the goods be delivered at the requested date?

▶ Does the customer have a sufficient credit limit?

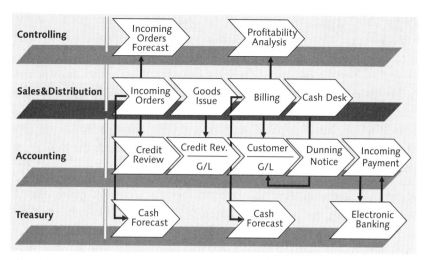

Figure 4.13 Integrated Business Transaction Order to Cash

If these check routines are successful, you can receive the order directly; otherwise you need to interact with the customer prior to the order receipt or order confirmation. For example, if goods can be delivered only a few days later, you should change the terms of delivery. The same applies if the customer has already fully used his credit limit; then you must change the terms of payment, you may require a cash payment. A successful incoming order impacts the future cash inflow of an enterprise. With the date of required payment, you are provided with a date for the planned cash receipt. This piece of information is significant for the treasury department. The controlling department can identify planned revenues for the products, x, y, and z, already in the forecast, by means of the incoming orders.

Goods issue

In real life, the next step of the process chain, the goods issue, is carried out days, weeks, or even months after the incoming order.

Billing

 At this time, the goods are removed from storage and delivered to the customer. Depending on the period between the incoming order and the planned goods issue, it makes sense to recheck the customer's credit standing. If you approved an order again under the current aspects, then the goods issue would result in stock issues.

Receivables management As the third step in the process chain, the billing documents the deliveries and services provided as a receivable in the accounts receivable accounting. The customer is requested to pay within the period that was agreed on for the incoming orders. At the same time, this information is forwarded internally to the controlling and treasury departments. The billing status is much more meaningful than the incoming orders status for a profitability analysis of the products, x, y, and z, or for a liquidity planning. At this point, the order is processed, the goods are delivered, and the billing brings the cash receipt closer.

A common saying in receivables management is "Delivered goods remain a gift until they are paid." This statement clearly indicates that the last steps of the order to cash process are decisive for the success or failure of an enterprise. Typically, a customer receives written dunning notices in multiple dunning levels after the date of required payment has been reached. In practice, you use three to four dunning levels with dunning intervals of 7 to 14 days. Frequently, customers incorporate this knowledge in the planning of payments to extend the actually agreed date of required payment. Only when they receive the third or last dunning notice, do they pay. This procedure certainly doesn't apply to all industries globally, but it applies sometimes—depending on the customer-vendor relationship in the industry.

Dunning procedure by telephone In addition to the dunning procedure by mail, the dunning procedure by telephone has established itself in the past few years. Before the date of required payment is reached, employees call the customers with high receivables to ask whether they were satisfied with the quality of the delivery and service and whether they could assume a punctual incoming payment. This procedure not only has the benefit of determining dispute cases at an early stage, but also better enforces the justified receivable with the phone call than with a dunning notice. As a side effect, you can take justified complaints seriously at an early stage and consequently increase customer satisfaction and service quality.

Cash receipt The final step of the process chain takes place when the customer pays, the payment is credited to the enterprise account, and the information is available via an electronic bank statement. Payment notes indicate which bills are supposed to be paid with the cash receipt. These notes are used for an automatic clearing of the original bill. If the payment notes don't provide any or sufficient information, you must implement a postprocessing step. This postprocessing step may be that you start the search internally.

If you consider the entire process from incoming orders to incoming payment, this period is usually assessed with the days sales outstanding (DSO) indicator. The lower the indicator, the better the internal process. This is a good starting point for every enterprise. The next sections describe the new options of SAP ERP Financials.

4.5 Monitoring Credit Lines with SAP Credit Management

The process step of the credit limit check is established between the FI and SD modules. If the credit limit is utilized, the credit control blocks the delivery or provision of services in logistics until the incident is clarified. Usually, the accounting and sales departments communicate with each other and try to find a solution. Accounting aims to keep the sum of loss on receivables low, and sales strives to conclude the deal that is relevant for its bonus. An effective credit management system helps identify changed behavior of existing customers and avoid a total loss on receivables at best. For new customers, you should classify and minimize the risks based on external assessments. To be able to use these optimization options, it is important to have all relevant information about the business partner available centrally and in real time. This includes internal information on existing customers with regard to payment history, dunning levels, and order volume and external information regarding their score. Based on sales threshold values in the business relationships, it is usually decided whether a customer is monitored by means of SAP Credit Management. Here as well, costs are generated that must be compared with an economic benefit. Based on this initial situation, the next sections describe the options of SAP ERP Financials.

Accounting and Sales

Create order Select the menu path LOGISTICS • SALES AND DISTRIBUTION • SALES • ORDER • CREATE to navigate to Transaction VA01, which is illustrated in Figure 4.14. A standard order is supposed to be recorded with order type OR. Organizational data is populated as optional fields in this example. An order is entered for the sales organization in USA, the Final customer sales distribution channel, and the Cross-division division.

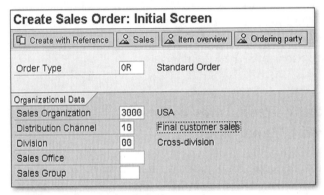

Figure 4.14 Create Sales Order

Availability check When you press ⌷Enter⌷, the system takes you to the order entry screen (see Figure 4.15). Again, Carpenter Works, customer number CMS0000099, is used as the customer. The order includes 10 monitors with material number M-12. Once these details are entered, the system starts an availability check for the requested delivery date, 4/3/2009, in the background. If this check fails, the system displays another transaction with a selection of when the monitors can be delivered and how many. This is not the case in this example, and all monitors can be delivered on the requested delivery date.

Credit limit check A second check in the background refers to the goods value of the order and includes a reconciliation with the credit limit defined for this customer. In the case shown in Figure 4.16, this credit limit check is negative. The credit lines were exceeded twice: for credit segment 3000 (USA Philadelphia) and for the globally valid credit segment 0000.

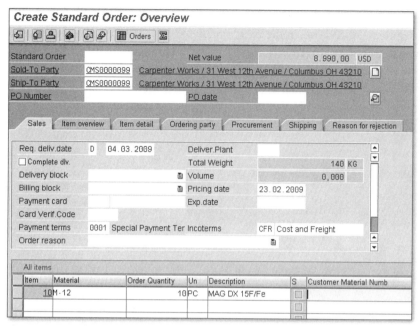

Figure 4.15 Define Sales Order with Details

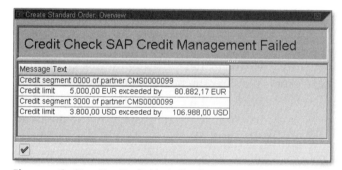

Figure 4.16 Negative Credit Limit Check

As a response, you can generally increase the credit limit. This makes sense when you want to make higher sales with an existing score. It is also possible to increase the credit limit temporarily for a seasonal business. To support your decision, you can check the master data of the business partner via the menu path ACCOUNTING • FINANCIAL SUP-PLY CHAIN MANAGEMENT • CREDIT MANAGEMENT • MASTER DATA • BUSI-

NESS PARTNER MASTER DATA. Figure 4.17 shows the details for the credit segment 3000. The credit limit calculated with $3,800 is considerably exceeded with an amount of $101,798. The assessment of the credit limit amount is based on a rule set for business customers (B2B). There, you must scrutinize the result of the calculation or scoring.

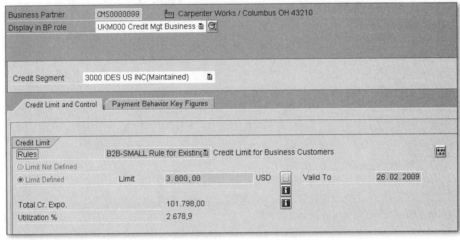

Figure 4.17   Master Data for Credit Management—Credit Line

After you've selected the general data and navigated to the Credit Profile tab, you can view further details for the calculation of the credit limit (see Figure 4.18). Overall, the assessment of customer CMS0000099 (Carpenter Works) is very negative. With a score of 38 and consequently a classification in the risk class of high default risks, you should assess the business activities critically. D&B, the external rating agency, shares this view and gives a rating of FF, which indicates a very low score. You could click on the Import Data button to request a current assessment of the credit agency.

External credit agencies are indispensable for ratings, particularly for new customers. Because internal information is usually not available yet, it is common practice to buy this information.

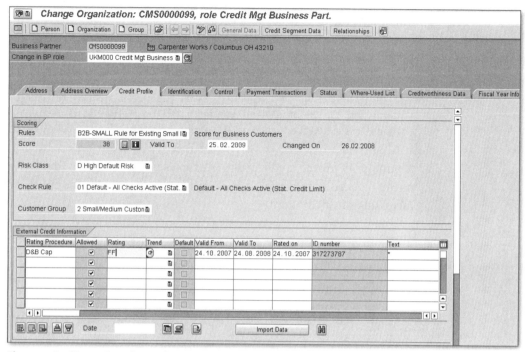

Figure 4.18 Master Data for Credit Management—Scoring

External Information on Score

[+]

Credit agencies, such as D&B, Creditreform, and Bürgel, provide compressed information by means of ratings and/or details, such as business formation or financial statements of the previous years. The alignment of the customer-specific credit strategy can vary greatly. A mixture of internal and external information can include the following:

▶ The external rating, for instance, AA+, includes a weighting of business information and is copied on a one-to-one basis. This is one of the factors in the new customer's score.

▶ Detailed business information is queried and weighted separately. This is one of the factors in the new customer's score.

▶ A mixture of external rating and business information takes place as the assessment factors.

▶ Information from multiple credit agencies is compared.

> Ultimately, the cost-benefit question arises. A complete avoidance of loss on receivables is not possible even with the best credit strategy—at least not without negatively influencing the business operations in the long term. An enterprise's primary goal is still to sell goods and services. The benefit is in the reduction of losses on receivables; that is, you use the value corrections of the past years and assume a percentage *x* as the potential benefit for the credit information. On the other hand, you must also consider the costs. A simple rating is less expensive than complete enterprise information.

A portal role for the credit manager enables you to obtain an overview of the blocked orders and a quick decision on accepting the orders or increasing the credit limit.

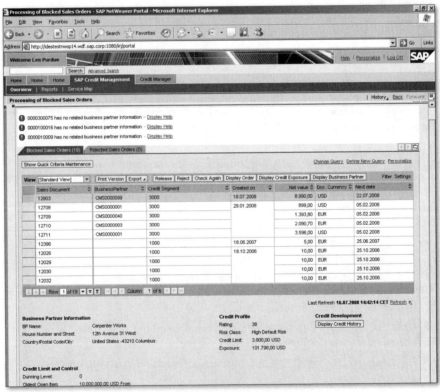

Figure 4.19 Overview of the Blocked Sales Orders in the Portal

All blocked sales orders are listed at a glance in Figure 4.19. Sales document 12903 in this example reflects the operation for customer

CMS0000099 (Carpenter Works). If you require further information in addition to the net value of $8,990, you can either have the system display the sales order in detail or select Personalize to add information to the standard view. In the lower part of the screen, you can view all information about the business partner and the credit profile at a glance. You can click on the Display Credit History button to obtain further details. Figure 4.20 shows three basic categories to illustrate why the credit limit was exceeded.

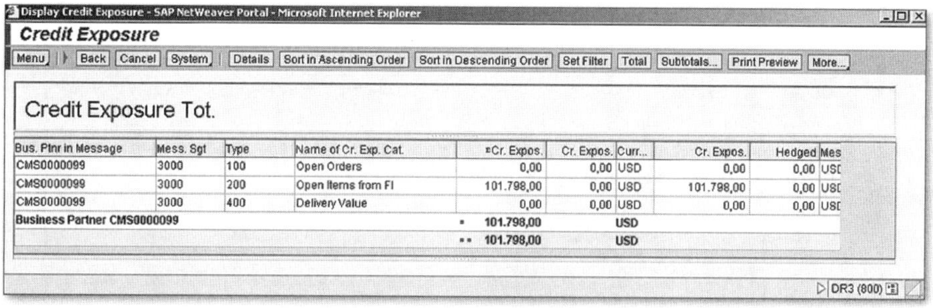

Figure 4.20 Details on the Credit Exposure in the Portal

The categories Open Orders and Delivery Value have a credit exposure of zero, which means it is not a temporary order boom. It doesn't seem to be a seasonal effect where the customer has many orders on hand that completely utilize the existing credit limit. The reverse seems to be the case. The orders are processed and delivered, but the invoices are still open and unpaid in accounting. A historical development of the credit score provides further information on whether the order should be performed.

Seasonal business

A role for decision support is provided in the portal precisely for cases like these. The upper part of Figure 4.21 displays the blocked orders. If you select an entry, in this case the entry for Crocodile Enterprise, the system displays the credit master data and a score history in the middle area.The lower part of the figure provides details on the credit exposure utilization. In case of Crocodile Enterprise, which has a continuously decreasing credit exposure, the decision can also be negative, and a sales order may be rejected. For Carpenter Works (CMS0000099), the situation looks much better. Order 12711, with a value of $8,990, can be accepted thanks to a continuously improving internal credit exposure.

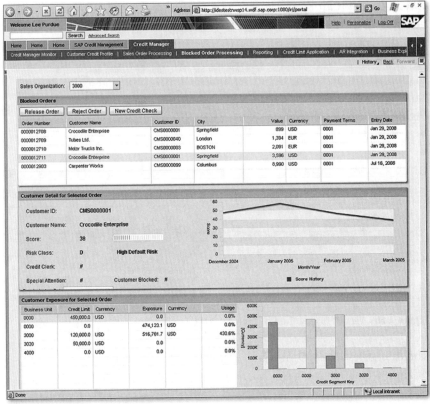

Figure 4.21 Decision Support for Blocked Orders in the Portal

Actions only in
exceptional cases
Credit managers should only take action in exceptional cases. To achieve this and to not impair the live sales and logistics process, you must fulfill basic prerequisites. A presegmentation is implemented based on black and white lists. Connected, associated enterprises and very good customers always automatically obtain a sufficient credit limit due to their membership in the white list. This prevents orders not being accepted and deliveries not being made. For enterprises that are on the black list it is the other way around. Here, you usually enter enterprises that have already filed for insolvency or are about to do so. According to this rough segmentation, a rule set applies that can consider different valuation procedures. In addition to the valuation procedures, further dimensions for defining a credit check strategy include different risk classes, check rules, and credit groups. A combination of these criteria enables you to perform a highly detailed segmentation. This forms the basis for

the various scoring models. Collected internal and external information is weighted and valuated according to the customer segmentation. The aim is to find criteria for automatic determination of a reasonable credit limit. By means of new roles in the portal, the credit manager can view all information at a glance, which enables him to make quick decisions that are based on comprehensive information.

Imagine that a cargo ship carrying a goods delivery is going to leave the port of Hamburg in 30 minutes. You as the credit manager must decide whether your enterprise's goods, which are worth €10 million, are shipped or not. This is a far-reaching and difficult decision. If you misjudge the situation, the goods are gone and you can't expect any cash receipt. A misjudgment could also be to not deliver the goods and lose a large order and possibly the customer.

Fortunately, receivables management includes not only the process step of credit limit monitoring, but many more substeps on the way to cash receipt.

4.6 Customer Interaction with SAP Biller Direct

After a successful check of the credit limit, you accept the order and then bill it. The process step of billing involves the printout of the bill or—for a high billing volume—the transfer of the billing data using electronic data interchange (EDI) for subsequent printout of the collective bill. Here, you perform one of the many interactions with the customer. In the dialog with the customers, you exchange various information, such as:

▶ Bills

▶ Current status of the customer's open items for reconciliation of accountings

▶ Specifications about which payments belong to which items

▶ Changes of the master data, that is, address or payment method

SAP Biller Direct enables an accounts receivable accounting via the Internet and an electronic interaction between the business partners. In the SAP ERP backend, you must first define the access rights. The business

Accounting via the Internet

partner receives a user name and a password, and has authorizations for the assigned company code or customer. For access via the Internet, you only require a browser that displays information from the SAP backend in real time. Therefore, SAP Biller Direct has no data storage, but communicates with the SAP ERP system directly.

The following pages continue the example of the customer Carpenter Works. The initial step provides an overview of the items that exist for an account. The accounts receivable accountant selects the selection screen of the line item list via ACCOUNTING • FINANCIAL ACCOUNTING • ACCOUNTS RECEIVABLE • ACCOUNT • DISPLAY/CHANGE ITEMS. Figure 4.22 shows a limitation to customer CMS0000099 (Carpenter Works) in company code 3000 (IDES USA) and the key date 7/13/2008. At this point, the order of 10 monitors is already delivered and invoiced. Pressing the F8 key executes the selection.

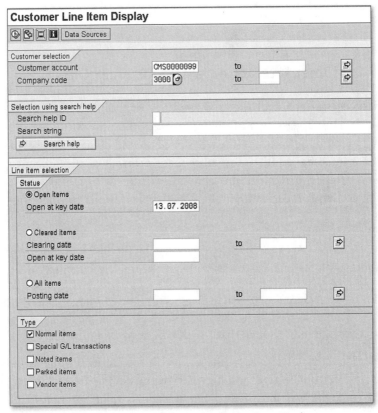

Figure 4.22   Selection Screen of the Customer Line Item Display

The result of two open items is shown in Figure 4.23. A total of $10,778 is distributed across two open invoices. Because the columns Case ID and Processor have no value, there is no dispute case; that is, they are regular open invoices that must still be paid by the customer.

Customer Line Item Display

Customer	CMS0000099
Company Code	3000
Name	Carpenter Works
City	Columbus

S	Ty.	DocumentNo	Doc. Date	Net due date	Reference	Invoice ref.	Clearing date	Clmg doc.	∑	Amount in local cur.	LCurr	Case ID	Processor	Text for
⚙	RV	1400000001	27.02.2008	27.02.2008	0090036725	1400000001				1.798,00	USD			
	DR	1800000061	13.07.2008	13.07.2008		1800000061				8.990,00	USD			
⚙									•	10.788,00	USD			
Account CMS0000099										10.788,00	USD			
									•••	10.788,00	USD			

Figure 4.23 Open Items of Customer CMS0000099

Carpenter Works has direct access to the accounts receivable accounting of its business partner. In cases in which the participants would coordinate via telephone or email, Carpenter Works' accounting department can access its customer account by means of the self-service. Figure 4.24 illustrates the logon screen of SAP Biller Direct. A clerk at Carpenter Works can access individual data from its customer account by means of a user ID and a password.

Self-Service

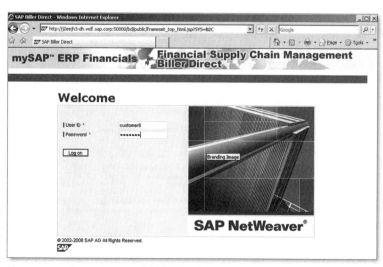

Figure 4.24 Logon Screen of SAP Biller Direct

195

In principle, an external business partner is provided with the following display and change functions by default:

- Bills to be approved
- Open bills
- Credits
- Paid bills
- Payments
- Payment advice note
- Dispute cases
- Address data
- Bank data
- Credit cards
- Automatic debit authorization
- Confirm balances
- Display profile
- Change password
- Display history of SAP Biller Direct activities
- Switch account

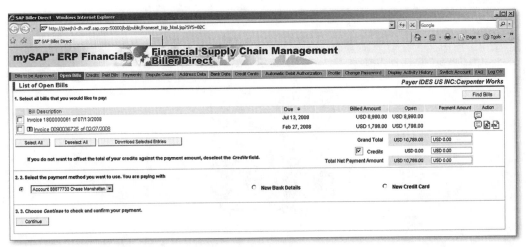

Figure 4.25 Overview of Open Invoices

The upper part of Figure 4.25 displays the individual released functions of this example. It is not always reasonable, desired, or accepted by the counterpart to have such a wide range of functions available as a self-service.

Carpenter Works can now access the original invoice in PDF format and use it as an invoice copy, for example. Figure 4.26 shows the access to a PDF that is already stored in the SAP ERP archive. You can download structured invoice data as an XML document. If it is provided with a qualified electronic signature, you can create an original posting on this basis and omit the paper printout. Finally, a function exists for the payment of the open invoice using a credit card or automatic debit. The specialized financial press frequently refers to these functions as EBPP (electronic bill presentment and payment). Whether and in which form EBPP is used depends on the customer structure and the acceptance of the technology.

Download PDF

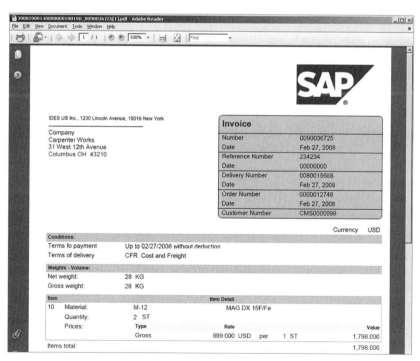

Figure 4.26 Display Invoice Details as PDF

The communication that is provided by SAP Biller Direct is versatile. As already described, you can check an invoice and then decide to not pay it owing to delivery defects, for example. In this constellation, a dispute case as shown in Figure 4.27 can be created directly by the customer, Carpenter Works. In addition to the classification as Damaged Goods and a note with a more detailed description, you can upload a file that includes a document or image, for example.

According to Figure 4.28, the dispute case was created. At this point, a workflow with an electronic file for the dispute case starts in the SAP ERP backend of the IDES US business partner.

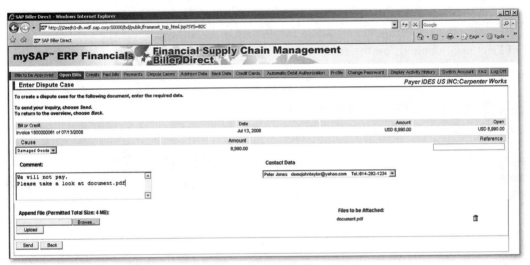

Figure 4.27 Enter Dispute Case in SAP Biller Direct

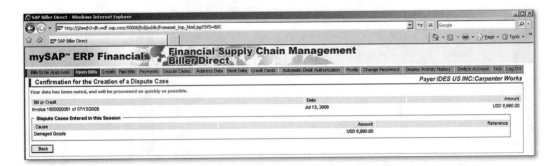

Figure 4.28 Confirmation of the Attachment

For the customer, Carpenter Works, the status of the dispute cases remains transparent. Figure 4.29 illustrates the overview screen for this interaction.

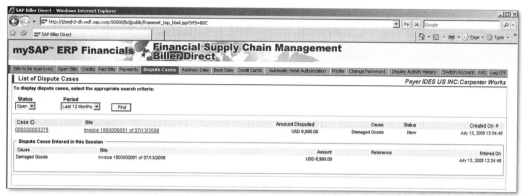

Figure 4.29 Overview of the Open Dispute Cases

SAP Biller Direct provides the customer, Carpenter Works (CMS0000099), with interaction options to display invoices, to download, and, in this example, to start and monitor a dispute case. To access this information, you require fewer calls or emails to accounts receivable accounting than previously. The "Create dispute case" action is already displayed to the accounts receivable accountant of IDES US in the line item display (Figure 4.30) and can be viewed by selecting the menu path ACCOUNTING • FINANCIAL ACCOUNTING • ACCOUNTS RECEIVABLE • ACCOUNT • DISPLAY/ CHANGE ITEMS.

Customer Line Item Display

Customer	CMS0000099
Company Code	3000
Name	Carpenter Works
City	Columbus

	S	Ty	DocumentNo	Doc. Date	Net due date	Reference	Invoice ref.	Clearing date	Clrng doc.	Σ	Amount in local cur.	LCurr	Case ID	Processor
		RV	1400000001	27.02.2008	27.02.2008	0090036725	1400000001				1.798,00	USD		
		DR	1800000061	13.07.2008	13.07.2008		1800000061				8.990,00	USD	3375	ACCOUNTANT2
										*	10.788,00	USD		
	Account CMS0000099										10.788,00	USD		
										**	10.788,00	USD		

Figure 4.30 Open Items Including Information on the Dispute Case

The dispute case is transparent and obvious for all parties involved. The core of SAP Dispute Management is to recognize dispute cases across department and company boundaries and to process and solve them.

4.7 Clarifying Payment Deductions with SAP Dispute Management

Dates for prolonging required payments

Enterprises are confronted with dispute cases if underpayments exist on the customer side or if notified payment deductions are submitted by the customer through debit memos or complaints. The processing times for clarifying a case are an important factor for when you can record a cash receipt. In some industries, it is common practice to initially question the agreed price to win another three weeks for the date of required payment after the subsequent clarification. Dispute cases that involve individual small items of an invoice that lead to a complete nonpayment are particularly annoying. If a customer claims a payment deduction, you should be able to clarify it as fast as possible. Dispute cases can be divided into three categories:

▸ **The customer informs the enterprise proactively.**
The complaints department, the account manager, and accounting must each be able to initiate a dispute case.

▸ **The customer claims payment deductions.**
The SAP system unsuccessfully tries to settle a number of invoices by means of an electronic bank statement. SAP Dispute Management can automatically generate a dispute case with the associated items, indicate the difference, and forward it to the clerk defined in the customer master record.

▸ **The customer holds the payments back.**
In this scenario, the open items become overdue after the terms of payment have expired. Here, a dispute case can be created automatically before the dunning notice.

Electronic record

All three categories create a dispute case that directly remains connected to the open item or the business transaction. It is not a hard copy of a snapshot that triggers a workflow. Rather, it is an intelligent electronic record that can be sent by the enterprise and automatically closes again if a cash receipt for the open item or business transaction is available, for example.

For the example of Carpenter Works (CMS0000099), the first category applies—the customer informs proactively. Independent of the way the dispute case was initiated, you can get an overview of the existing dispute cases via the menu path ACCOUNTING • FINANCIAL SUPPLY CHAIN MANAGEMENT • DISPUTE MANAGEMENT • DISPUTE CASE PROCESSING (see Figure 4.31).

SAP Dispute Management

Case ID	Customer	Reason	Ext. ref.	Case Title	Status Descr.	Disputed	Priority
3375	CMS0000099	0001			New	8,990.00	
3347	8886	0007			New	150.00	High
3326	COL012	0007		Problem with pricing	New	2,000.00	Medium
3316	COL099	0000			New	600.00	Medium
3302	COL001	0001		not stayed	New		Medium
3288	COL007	0000			New		Medium
3287	COL007	0000			New	1,200.00	Medium
3286	COL007	0000			New		Medium
3285	COL007	0000			New	1,450.00	Medium
3225	8888	0001	SX-555		New	950.00	
3221	COL020	0000	REF6767	facture toujours impayée.Client injoignable	New	13,800.00	Medium
3204	COL001	0007		Pricing issues	New	1,000.00	Medium
3201	8886	0007	0090037073	demo elextrolux2	New	965.41	High
3181	8889	0002	12345		New	3,484.50	
2803				Contenzioso	New		
2802				Contenzioso	New		Low
2681	COL001	0000		Anders	To be collected	500.00	High
1861	8889	0001			New	2,787.60	
1803	8801	0007		Accidently paid invoice	New		Medium
1802	8801	0000		Dispute case for credit memo	New		Medium
1801	8887	0000		Mother of all dispute	New		Medium

Figure 4.31 "My Dispute Cases" Overview

In the example of Carpenter Works (CMS0000099) and dispute case 3375, with a value of $8,990 that was initiated by the customer, the processing starts with the ACCOUNTANT2 user in the My Dispute Cases overview. Each case is identified with a unique continuous case ID. The classification of the reason for the dispute case helps you analyze the payment deduction cause. Ideally, this leads to a process improvement and prevents future dispute cases.

Internal and External Reasons for Dispute Cases [+]

The reason for dispute cases is usually not down to the customer, but is frequently due to internal process weaknesses.

For example, there can be customers that don't pay their invoices because they don't understand them or because they think that they contractually agreed to something else. If this occurs often, it may be because the invoice doesn't contain sufficient detailed information.

First, the customers don't pay the invoices at all, and then they pay with a delay. This may be because customer master data, such as the address, is defined incorrectly in the system. The invoice contains wrong information, so the customer cannot log on to the SAP ERP system and pay. An improved master data maintenance process can remedy this weakness.

If you replace the written dispute notes with electronic dispute management, you not only decrease the time until the internal case clarification, but you also obtain additional information that helps you detect process weaknesses and quantify their costs. A pragmatic approach is to use the case overview illustrated in Figure 4.31 and to form group totals for each cause category. This way, you get an indication of how often the individual categories occur and with which intrinsic value. A final assessment of the costs is only possible when the dispute cases are closed and when it becomes clear whether a cash receipt or credit memo was created.

The ACCOUNTANT2 processor selects case 3375 by double-clicking on it, and the system displays the details screen shown in Figure 4.32. The electronic record is displayed including all necessary information. These are, for instance:

▶ Customer
▶ Company code
▶ Status
▶ Reason
▶ Original disputed amount
▶ Disputed amount
▶ Credited
▶ Paid
▶ Cleared manually
▶ Automatically written off

By means of the configuration, you can hide information not required and show further details, such as the profit center. The principle is that you have everything at hand at a glance.

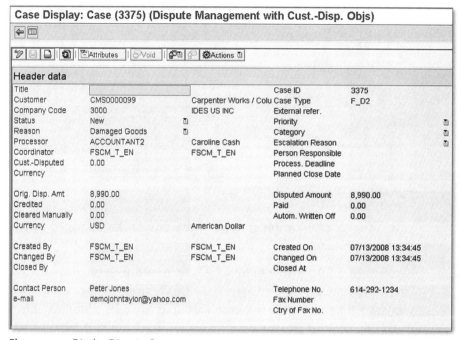

Figure 4.32 Display Dispute Case

A planned date of closure and escalation reasons emphasize the meaning of the dispute case processing process step. For example, if cases up to an amount of $10,000 are not solved within seven days, the system can automatically send a correspondence (escalation) to the responsible manager. The internal processing time usually decreases if this procedure is known within the enterprise.

Consequently, the dispute case is more than "just a workflow" between the departments. Rather, it is an electronic record that contains all information regarding a transaction. If you click on the Linked Objects button, the system provides markers to data that is already defined in the system, for example, the customer master data of customer CMS0000099 (Carpenter Works) or the document of the open disputed item. A double-click brings you to the document display (Transaction FB03) or the display of the customer account (Transaction FD03).

Linking of information

The dispute case that was created using SAP Biller Direct contains a document, *document.pdf*, that was uploaded and stored by the customer. Double-clicking on the file name opens Adobe Acrobat Reader, and you can access this information.

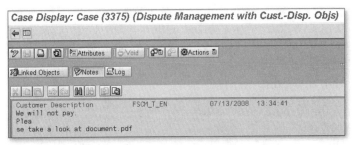

Case Display: Case (3375) (Dispute Management with Cust.-Disp. Objs)			

Hierarchy	Element Type	Visibility	Last Processed	Node I
▽ 🗂 Linked Objects			FSCM_T_EN / 07/13/200...	
▽ 🗂 Business Partner		All Roles		3
CMS0000099 (Customer)	Customer	All Roles	FSCM_T_EN / 07/13/200...	4
▽ 🗂 Disputed Objects		All Roles		5
3000 1800000061 2008 001 (Invoice)	Accounting Document Line Item	All Roles	FSCM_T_EN / 07/13/200...	7
▽ 🗂 Various		All Roles		23
🗋 document.pdf	Document Templates	All Roles	FSCM_T_EN / 07/13/200...	24

Figure 4.33 Objects for the Dispute Case

This is very useful for understanding the case of the Damaged Goods dispute case reason.

If you click on the arrow button [F12], you return to the dispute case overview. The example in Figure 4.34 shows the customer's note that was entered using SAP Biller Direct. Each note provides additional information on the user and the time of creation and cannot be changed retroactively. You can therefore clearly trace who did something and when in the SAP system.

Case Display: Case (3375) (Dispute Management with Cust.-Disp. Objs)

Customer Description   FSCM_T_EN   07/13/2008 13:34:41
We will not pay.
Plea
se take a look at document.pdf

Figure 4.34 Notes in the Dispute Case

Extensive log function · The Log button provides another overview of the processing steps that were implemented for the dispute case. In the lower section of Figure 4.35, you can clearly view the first attribute changes. The dispute case with an amount of $8,990 was initiated with the FSCM_T_EN technical user via SAP Biller Direct. The SAP system automatically determined Caroline Cash as the first processor based on the customer master data. Only a few minutes later, at 14:04, Caroline Cash accessed the dispute case for the first time.

Case Display: Case (3375) (Dispute Management with Cust.-Disp. Objs)

Date	Time	User	Activity	Old Value	New Value	Attribute Name
07/13/2008	14:20:51	Caroline Cash	Access to Case Notes			
07/13/2008	14:20:43	Caroline Cash	Access to Case Notes			
07/13/2008	14:20:28	Caroline Cash	Access to Linked Objects			
07/13/2008	14:20:28	Caroline Cash	Display Case			
07/13/2008	14:20:25	Caroline Cash	Access to Linked Objects			
07/13/2008	14:20:25	Caroline Cash	Display Case			
07/13/2008	14:13:52	Caroline Cash	Access to Case Notes			
07/13/2008	14:13:45	Caroline Cash	Access to Case Notes			
07/13/2008	14:13:39	Caroline Cash	Access to Linked Objects			
07/13/2008	14:13:39	Caroline Cash	Display Case			
07/13/2008	14:13:33	Caroline Cash	Access to Linked Objects			
07/13/2008	14:13:33	Caroline Cash	Display Case			
07/13/2008	14:04:18	Caroline Cash	Access to Linked Objects			
07/13/2008	14:04:18	Caroline Cash	Display Case			
07/13/2008	14:04:17	Caroline Cash	Access to Linked Objects			
07/13/2008	14:04:16	Caroline Cash	Display Case			
07/13/2008	13:34:46	FSCM_T_EN	Attribute Change		American Dollar	Currency
07/13/2008	13:34:46	FSCM_T_EN	Attribute Change	0.00	8990.00	Disputed Amount
07/13/2008	13:34:46	FSCM_T_EN	Attribute Change	0.00	8990.00	Orig. Disp. Amt
07/13/2008	13:34:46	FSCM_T_EN	Attribute Change		FSCM_T_EN	Coordinator
07/13/2008	13:34:46	FSCM_T_EN	Attribute Change		Damaged Goods	Reason
07/13/2008	13:34:46	FSCM_T_EN	Attribute Change	00	New	Status
07/13/2008	13:34:46	FSCM_T_EN	Attribute Change		Caroline Cash	Processor

Figure 4.35 Log of the Dispute Case

Seamless Documentation   **[+]**

You can even log the display of a dispute case. This way, you can specify the time from the first notice to the final processing.

If you are in the change mode, you have the option to define internal and external notes for the case via the Notes button. Initially, external information is marked with an "*" and you can view it via SAP Biller Direct or correspondence. The example shown in Figure 4.36 indicates that the customer doesn't want to pay for the damaged goods. After a telephone conversation regarding the situation, the processor enters the solution suggestion in the dispute case. The customer either returns the goods or pays a remaining amount of $1,000 for the goods.

Internal and external notes

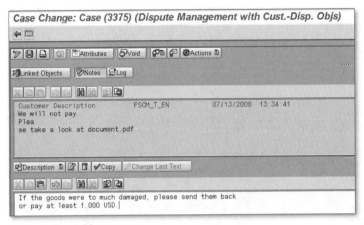

Figure 4.36 Adding Notes

By posting a credit memo via the menu path ACCOUNTING • FINANCIAL ACCOUNTING • ACCOUNTS RECEIVABLE • DOCUMENT • POST CREDIT MEMO, the discount is documented in the receivable (see Figure 4.37).

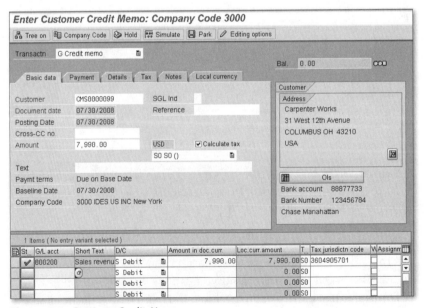

Figure 4.37 Posting a Credit Memo

The invoice of $8,990 now has a credit memo of USD 7,990. If you select the menu path ACCOUNTING • FINANCIAL ACCOUNTING • ACCOUNTS

RECEIVABLE • ACCOUNT • CLEAR, the system carries out a residual item formation for the customer account CMS0000099 (see Figure 4.38). In the figure, you can also view the dispute case 3375, which is automatically reduced by the amount of the credit memo. So, $1,000 is now open and to be disputed.

Clear Customer Create residual items

| Distribute diff. | Charge off diff. | Editing options | Create Dispute Case |

| Standard | Partial Pmt | Res.items | Withhldg tax |

Account items CMS0000099 Carpenter Works

Assignment	Document N	D.	P.	Document D	Day	Case	Processor	Status	Net amount	Residual items	RCd
0080015688	1400000001	RV	01	02/27/2008	132				1,798.00		
1600000012008	1600000001	DG	11	07/30/2008	17-				7,990.00-		
1800000612008	1800000061	DR	01	07/13/2008	5-	3375	ACCOUNTANT2	New	8,990.00	1,000.00	

Figure 4.38 Clearing the Original Invoice and Forming a Residual Item

In the dispute case overview, which is available via ACCOUNTING • FINANCIAL SUPPLY CHAIN MANAGEMENT • DISPUTE MANAGEMENT • DISPUTE CASE PROCESSING, the dispute case automatically changes with the clearing process—this is a major benefit of the electronic record that is directly connected with the open items. Figure 4.39 illustrates the current status, Being Processed, with the original and the remaining disputed amount.

Disputed amount reduction

SAP Dispute Management

Case ID	Customer	Reason	Ext. ref.	Case Title	Status Descr.	Σ Disputed	ΣOrig. Disp. Amt	Priority	Processor	Coordinator
3375	CMS0000099	0001			Being Processed	1,000.00	8,990.00		Caroline Cash	FSCM_T_EN
3347	8886	0007			New	150.00	150.00	High	Caroline Cash	ACCOUNTANT1
3326	COL012	0007		Problem with pricing	New	2,000.00	2,000.00	Medium	Caroline Cash	ACCOUNTANT1
3316	COL099	0000			New	600.00	600.00	Medium	Caroline Cash	AHRENSA
3302	COL001	0001		not stayed	New			Medium	Caroline Cash	ACCOUNTANT1
3288	COL007	0000			New			Medium	Caroline Cash	AHRENSA
3287	COL007	0000			New	1,200.00	1,200.00	Medium	Caroline Cash	AHRENSA

Figure 4.39 Updated Overview of the Dispute Cases

If the entire open item is written off or cleared, the dispute record closes automatically. This is another benefit compared to conventional workflows. Activities are only required if there is still need for dispute. In the case processing, you can double-click on the dispute case to open the current detail view (see Figure 4.40). The essential information is clear:

- ▸ Original disputed amount – $8,990

- ▸ Credited – $7,990

- ▸ Disputed amount – $1,000

- ▸ Processor – Caroline Cash

- ▸ Linked objects – Invoice and credit memo

Via the defined notes and documents, any third person can quickly trace each process of the case. Additionally, the log provides further detail information.

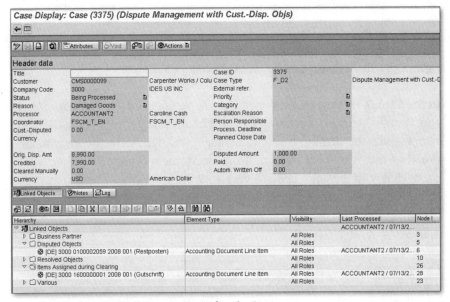

Figure 4.40 Detailed Dispute Case After the Posting

[+]

Documentation of the Decision Basis for Credit Memos

Public accountants and auditors are increasingly interested in the causes that have lead to the credit memo creation. The reason for this is the question of whether posted sales actually contained their expected value in the past. For example, you can sometimes observe the phenomenon of rapidly increasing sales figures at the end of a quarter or a year, which is then followed by an unusually high number of credit memos at the beginning of the subsequent period. This situation is known as *window dressing*. SAP Dispute Management provides all information that is required to answer this question efficiently.

In the Carpenter Works example, the original invoice still has an open remaining amount of $1,000. Additionally, there are other invoices, that is, receivables toward the customer. The internal process in accounts receivable accounting continues in parallel. There are dispute cases that must be solved, and overdue open items are forwarded to the dunning process. The next step is SAP Collections Management, which includes dunning by telephone.

4.8 Dunning Procedure by Telephone with SAP Collections Management

Today, you can send dunning notices by mail with every SAP ERP solution. This standard results in a decreasing acceptance by the customer. Initial dunning notices are ignored almost by default; usually the last dunning notice provides the desired result. The dunning process by mail possibly delays the incoming payment by weeks. SAP Collections Management in SAP ERP 6.0 provides new functions that enable you to become active prior to the written dunning notice.

Of course, it is not profitable to immediately call customers in case of a delay in payment. Effort and benefit are balanced only as of a certain receivable volume. An effective early receivables management is based on a transparent process. As a prerequisite, the software identifies, categorizes, and prioritizes the customers based on previously defined collection strategies. For example, if a customer has receivables of a minimum $100,000 that are due within 10 days, a collection process is started for this customer.

Collection strategies

If the customer is already at the second dunning level, the priority of this case among those to be processed is moved ahead. If SAP Credit Management identifies the customer as a risk case, the case moves to the top quarter of processing. For this purpose, you must first collect the relevant information regarding the customer in arrears, for example, open postings, incoming payments, dunnings, or risk assessment. Then, you call the customer. The aim of this call is to remind the customer of the payment and make arrangements for the promise to pay or dispute cases. The process is documented—and put forward again in cases of broken arrangements.

You can find SAP Collections Management under ACCOUNTING • FINANCIAL SUPPLY CHAIN MANAGEMENT • COLLECTIONS MANAGEMENT. In the Worklist subitem, you can find the daily tasks for the dunning procedure by telephone. As illustrated in Figure 4.41, the SAP system determined the customers that processor A is supposed to call today. Processor B can use the same menu path to obtain his personal worklist.

Worklists with priorities

SAP Collections Management not only distributes the work across processors, but it also prioritizes the individual lists at the same time. In the Priority column in Figure 4.41 you can clearly see the different values and groupings:

▶ Management

▶ Compulsion

▶ Solve Problem

▶ Reminder

Focus on customer contacts

The receivables clerks' worklists provide comprehensive information on the customers to be contacted. The employee gets an overview based on this information about the receivables, made and broken promises to pay, risk classes, credit limits, dispute cases, and the current dunning level. Additionally, SAP Collections Management suggests an amount to be collected. This amount doesn't need to cover the due open receivables. The amount decreases by current promise to pay, credit memos, or disputed open items, if necessary. The dynamically generated worklist considers current broken promises to pay and current incoming payments of accounting or dispute cases that the complaints department solved. SAP Collections Management assumes the receivables clerks have several organizational or administrative tasks and enables them to focus on customer contact.

The Carpenter Works example has the priority Solve Problem. A telephone call is considered less important because the company appears almost at the end of the telephone list. Owing to the receivable of $2,798 minus the open disputed amount of $1,000, the processor can expect a promise to pay of $1,798. In comparison to the other customers in the list, this amount is rather low.

Worklist

Valuation acc. to Strategy

Due Date Grid

Partner	Short Name of Business Partner	Priority	Currency	Σ Outstanding	Σ Overd.	Σ Overd.	Σ Overdue	Σ To Be Collected	Σ Promised	Σ Broken	Σ Disputed Amount
COL113	Copperfield Ltd. / Denver	Management	USD	11.400,00	2.700,00	8.700,00	0,00	11.400,00	11.400,00	11.400,00	3.800,00
COL106	Jetherjam Corp. / Las Vegas	Management	USD	8.700,00	2.900,00	5.600,00	200,00	8.700,00	5.600,00	5.600,00	200,00
COL007	Harikana AG / 10000 Berlin	Management	EUR	3.550,00	0,00	0,00	0,00	3.550,00	900,00	900,00	0,00
COL011	VBP Elektro AG / 10000 Berlin	Management	EUR	3.050,00	0,00	0,00	0,00	3.050,00	2.300,00	2.300,00	0,00
COL014	Futura AG / 04103 Leipzig	Management	EUR	2.190,00	0,00	0,00	0,00	2.190,00	1.390,00	1.390,00	0,00
COL013	Electronica AG / 80000 München	Management	EUR	9.900,00	0,00	0,00	0,00	6.100,00	6.400,00	6.400,00	5.700,00
COL101	Electronics Ltd. / Miami FL	Management	USD	6.900,00	4.200,00	1.600,00	1.100,00	6.500,00	1.100,00	700,00	400,00
COL006	Maximum Energy / 50000 Köln	Management	EUR	8.600,00	0,00	0,00	0,00	8.600,00	5.800,00	5.800,00	200,00
COL008	Elektronik & Media GmbH / 20000 Hannover	Management	EUR	3.170,00	0,00	0,00	0,00	3.170,00	400,00	400,00	400,00
COL012	Beste Konsumgüter AG / 60000 Frankfurt	Compulsion	EUR	6.900,00	0,00	0,00	0,00	6.300,00	3.700,00	3.700,00	600,00
COL003	Mediastars AG / 69190 Walldorf	Compulsion	EUR	2.980,00	0,00	0,00	0,00	2.980,00	0,00		700,00
COL109	AllYouNeed Ltd. / Boston	Compulsion	USD	7.400,00	1.400,00	6.000,00	0,00	5.900,00	6.000,00	6.000,00	1.500,00
COL104	Pharmania Ltd. / Dallas	Compulsion	USD	4.700,00	2.300,00	2.400,00	0,00	4.700,00	2.400,00	2.400,00	0,00
COL110	Jefferson's Electronics Ltd. / New York	Compulsion	USD	3.880,00	1.300,00	1.600,00	980,00	3.880,00	2.580,00	2.580,00	0,00
COL009	Glambert & Partner GmbH / 69100 Heidelberg	Compulsion	EUR	6.100,00	0,00	0,00	0,00	6.100,00	4.500,00	4.500,00	0,00
COL010	Schmidt & Söhne GmbH / 35000 Wetzlar	Compulsion	EUR	3.470,00	0,00	0,00	0,00	3.470,00	2.580,00	2.580,00	0,00
COL111	Smith & Smithies Ltd. / San Francisco	Compulsion	USD	3.000,00	0,00	1.600,00	1.400,00	3.000,00	2.300,00	2.300,00	600,00
COL107	BuyHere Ltd. / Los Angeles	Compulsion	USD	1.550,00	0,00	1.550,00	0,00	1.550,00	1.550,00	1.550,00	250,00
COL102	More & More Ltd. / New York	Compulsion	USD	2.950,00	900,00	1.850,00	200,00	2.950,00	2.050,00	2.050,00	200,00
COL112	Devonshire Best Produtcts Corp / La Grange	Compulsion	USD	2.500,00	0,00	1.100,00	1.400,00	2.500,00	1.400,00	1.400,00	1.400,00
COL020	Meilleurs Ordinateurs SA / F- Paris	Compulsion	EUR	106.601,00	1.500,00	26.500,00	18.600,00	32.800,00	16.300,00	0,00	2.201,00
COL004	Gastronomica GmbH / 80000 München	Compulsion	EUR	4.200,00	0,00	0,00	0,00	4.200,00	200,00	200,00	200,00
COL005	Samt & Seide AG / 70000 Stuttgart	Compulsion	EUR	3.850,00	0,00	0,00	0,00	3.850,00	2.450,00	2.450,00	1.150,00
COL002	Elektromarkt GmbH / 69190 Walldorf	Compulsion	EUR	2.900,00	0,00	0,00	0,00	2.150,00	950,00	950,00	950,00
COL015	Heller & Partner GmbH / 01067 Dresden	Compulsion	EUR	1.650,00	0,00	0,00	0,00	1.650,00	350,00	350,00	350,00
COL105	ConsuMe Ltd. / Phenix	Compulsion	USD	4.000,00	1.100,00	2.900,00	0,00	4.000,00	2.900,00	2.900,00	0,00
COL103	Feelgood Products Ltd. / Philadelphia	Solve Problem	USD	2.330,00	1.200,00	1.130,00	0,00	2.330,00	1.130,00	1.130,00	150,00
CMS0000099	Carpenter Works / Columbus OH 43210	Solve Problem	USD	2.798,00	0,00	0,00	0,00	1.798,00	0,00	0,00	1.000,00
COL114	Black & White Corp / Colorado	Solve Problem	USD	600,00	0,00	600,00	0,00	600,00	600,00	600,00	0,00
COL098	Meyer Logistik / 60000 Frankfurt	Reminder	EUR	1.200,00	1.200,00	0,00	0,00	1.200,00	0,00	0,00	0,00
COL115	Harper & Harper Corp. / San Diego	Reminder	USD	2.000,00	1.600,00	400,00	0,00	2.000,00	0,00	0,00	0,00

Figure 4.41 A Processor's Worklist

If you select a row, you can use the Valuation according to Strategy option to find out why a customer appears on the worklist at a particular position. As you can see in Figure 4.42, the amount of Carpenter Works is negligible. According to the defined collections strategy, the customer only appears on the list because it is valuated with a high risk class.

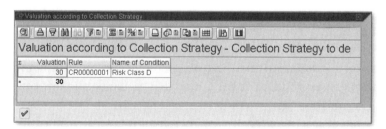

Valuation according to Collection Strategy

Valuation according to Collection Strategy - Collection Strategy to de

Σ	Valuation	Rule	Name of Condition
	30	CR00000001	Risk Class D
⊪	**30**		

Figure 4.42 Valuation of Carpenter Works According to the Strategy

Scoring with multiple criteria

The risk class D (high risk) results in a score of 30, which is sufficient for the priority Solve Problem. If you compare this customer with another customer who is in the upper area of the list owing to a higher priority, various criteria apply. Figure 4.43 shows a customer with a score of 90. For example, this customer has a broken promise to pay, overdue amounts larger than $1,000, and a credit limit utilization over 80%.

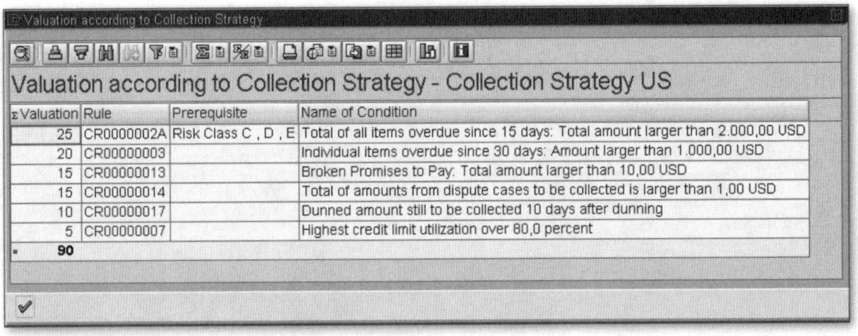

ΣValuation	Rule	Prerequisite	Name of Condition
25	CR0000002A	Risk Class C , D , E	Total of all items overdue since 15 days: Total amount larger than 2.000,00 USD
20	CR00000003		Individual items overdue since 30 days: Amount larger than 1.000,00 USD
15	CR00000013		Broken Promises to Pay: Total amount larger than 10,00 USD
15	CR00000014		Total of amounts from dispute cases to be collected is larger than 1,00 USD
10	CR00000017		Dunned amount still to be collected 10 days after dunning
5	CR00000007		Highest credit limit utilization over 80,0 percent
90			

Figure 4.43 Valuation of Another Customer

[+]

SAP Collections Management Is Not New

The process of dunning by telephone has been established in many enterprises and industries. Based on experience and a certain gut instinct, accounts receivable accountants or sales employees know who they should call. If you don't exceed a certain number of customers, you usually know the customer and his behavior very well. This instinct is systematized via the defined collections strategies; the tasks are distributed fairly via the worklists, and the results are made transparent later on.

To contact the customer, the receivables manager double-clicks on an entry to navigate from the worklist that contains several customers to be contacted to the detail view of an individual customer. In contrast to the list of open items that displays a customer's status in terms of accounting, the detail view shows an aggregated view of the original amount of the business transaction and the open amount remaining including partial payments or residual items. Consequently, the detail view contains less information than a traditional open items list, and it saves time otherwise spent searching for details. Therefore, it is ideally suited for contact by telephone. The receivables clerk can view all basic customer information on one screen during the telephone conversation:

▶ Invoices

▶ Payments

▶ Promise to pay

▶ Dispute cases

▶ Contact data

▶ Resubmission

In the Carpenter Works example, Figure 4.44 displays two rows with the original invoices. The difference from a classic open items list becomes clear in document number 1800000061. Based on the amount of $8,990, only $1,000 is open owing to the credit memo. In contrast to an invoice that can consist of a multitude of payments and credit memos, this overview provides the most important information in compact format—an essential difference from the open items list. This saves time in preparing for the call.

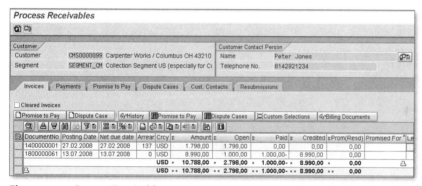

Figure 4.44 Process Receivables

This information is not lost despite the aggregation. You can click on the History button to drill down to the original documents in the SAP system. SAP Collections Management uses all information that exists in Accounts Receivable (FI-AR). This becomes clear if you click on the Refresh button, which is located in the top-left corner of Figure 4.44. If new invoices, credit memos, or payments are posted for Carpenter Works, this information is available in real time after you've clicked on the Refresh button.

Drill down

[+] **Real-Time Processing and Integration**

In the meantime, add-on solutions are available from SAP partners that cover the collections management business process. The classic benefits of integration, that is, that you can drill down document details or refresh information in real time, is usually not available there.

Integration of SAP Collections and Dispute Management

The integration of SAP Collections Management with SAP Dispute Management is almost accepted as a matter of course. On the one hand, you can consider the number and amount of dispute cases for the creation of worklists, and on the other hand, you are provided with further information for dispute cases in the detail processing of a customer. The dispute case that has been created so far is displayed if you select the Dispute Cases tab in Figure 4.45 (Carpenter Works example). The Dispute Case button enables you to jump from SAP Collections Management to SAP Dispute Management.

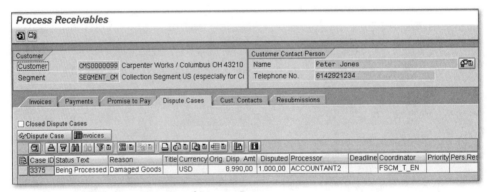

Figure 4.45 Overview of Dispute Cases

Telephone integration

Once all relevant information is available, you can call the customer. The Invoices tab, which is illustrated in Figure 4.46, is the starting point. The upper-right corner of the screen provides information on the contact person. Peter Jones, telephone number 614-292-1234, is the contact at the accounts payable accounting department of Carpenter Works. If you don't want to dial this number manually, it is possible to integrate your telephone system with the SAP system—abbreviated as CTI (computer and telecom integration) among experts. The goal of the call is to receive a promise to pay from the customer. In the negative case—if you cannot obtain a promise to pay from the customer—this is usually based on a specific reason. If the customer in this example hadn't notified the seller about the delivered damaged goods via the Internet, the call from collections management would have been the starting point of the dispute case. If the customer is satisfied with the delivery and service, you can expect the cash receipt soon. This is the case in the Carpenter Works example. The enterprise is supposed to transfer $2,798 by 9/1/2008. This transfer clears two invoices completely, and you can close the dispute case created via the Internet.

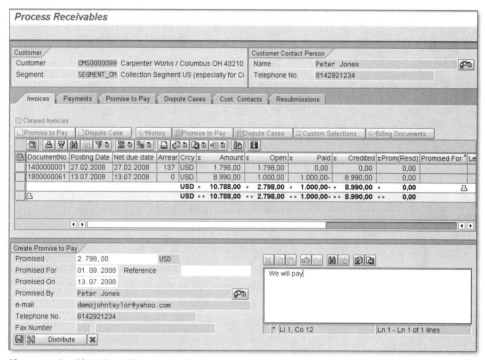

Figure 4.46 Obtaining a Promise to Pay

You can create promises to pay simultaneously for multiple invoices. Once the information is stored, it is available for creating the worklist in SAP Collections Management and the scoring in SAP Credit Management. Figure 4.47 shows the promise to pay given for 9/1/2008. If this documented date elapses, the promise to pay is considered broken. As a result, you can reduce the credit limit in SAP Credit Management via

Broken promises to pay

the automatic scoring. Additionally, you are required to call the customer again. The collections strategy considers this fact for the creation and prioritization of worklists.

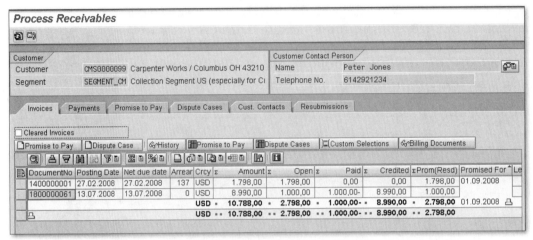

Figure 4.47 Overview including Promise to Pay

After the telephone call and when you leave the transaction by pressing F3, you must document the collected customer contact. Figure 4.48 shows the default values for the Carpenter Works example. In addition to the current date, the SAP system automatically generates the information in the note field. The given promise to pay forms the basis. You can add additional details in the free text field. This documentation makes it easier for you to trace the progress and result of this transaction later on. The categories of results, Customer Reached or Customer not Reached, that are defined in the solution with regard to the call, determine the display in the worklist and provide the collections manager with statistics for his group or individual employees.

Integration with other components

If you reached a customer and obtained a promise to pay, this customer is automatically sorted out of the open receivables and into the list of satisfied payments. SAP FSCM Collections Management is an essential element for the interplay of Accounts Receivable, SAP Credit Management, and the dispute cases in SAP Dispute Management.

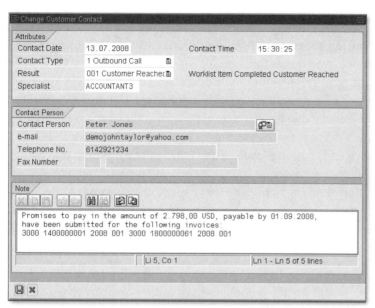

Figure 4.48 Change Customer Contact

A proactive approach for receivables management reduces the receivables and the loss on receivables, and contributes to better planning of liquidity. Furthermore, you can use the dunning procedure by mail as an alternative or supplement to SAP Collections Management.

4.9 Dunning Procedure by Mail

The purpose of business dunning is to have the debtor make the due payment without legal support on the creditor's side. A creditor usually proceeds as follows:

1. Reminder by sending a copy of the invoice or an account statement

2. Dunning notice including the due date of the debt and request for payment

3. Notification of collection implemented by a collection agency

4. Assignment to a collection agency

5. Last dunning notice with threat of legal actions

4.9.1 Introduction to the Dunning Program

SAP's dunning program selects the due open items of business part-ner accounts, determines the dunning level of the respective account or documents, and creates dunning notices. The dunning procedures are independent of the company code and define the dunning interval, the grace days for the due date determination, and the number of dunning levels. The system includes dunning procedures with different dunning frequencies and dunning levels. The names of the dunning procedures in the SAP system have four digits. If no incoming payment is recorded after multiple dunning notices have been sent to a business partner, legal measures must be taken where necessary and depending on the amount. In this case, you must define the corresponding date manually in the appropriate business partner master record.

The dunning program in the SAP system passes through multiple suc-cessive steps and includes both manual and automatic processes (see Figure 4.49):

1. **Maintain parameter**
   To trigger an automatic dunning, you must specify the key date for the due date check and which accounts the dunning program is sup-posed to check. The dunning program creates a dunning proposal that you can edit on the screen.

2. **Create dunning proposal**
   This is implemented automatically by the SAP dunning program.

3. **Edit dunning proposal**
   The user can specify the dunnings he wants to edit. Here, he can select according to processor or dunning level, for example. In the dunning proposal, the user can decrease the dunning level of the individual items. Additionally, he can release items or accounts for dunning for which a dunning block is defined. To keep the result of a dunning run transparent, you can log all implemented changes.

4. **Print dunning letter**
   The dunning level and the dunning date of the line items as well as the account concerned are not updated until the print of the dun-nings. Therefore, the dunning proposal can be repeated as often as you like. Not only customers, but also vendors can participate in a

dunning procedure. A joint assessment of customer and vendor items takes place if this is set accordingly in the master records of the business partner.

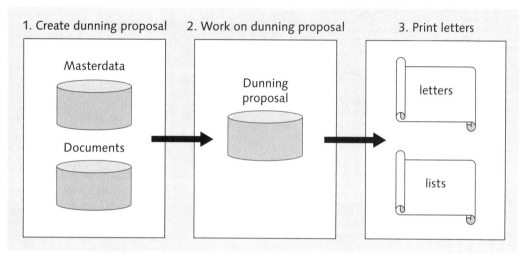

Figure 4.49 Dunning Flow

After you've gotten to know the basic structure of the dunning program, you are introduced to the application.

4.9.2 Maintaining Parameters

You access the initial screen of the dunning program via the menu path ACCOUNTING • FINANCIAL ACCOUNTING • ACCOUNTS RECEIVABLE • (ACCOUNTS PAYABLE) • PERIODIC PROCESSING • DUNNING (Transaction F150). First, enter the date of the dunning run and an identification. You can add a sequential number to the identification feature to distinguish between different dunning runs on the same date. The example shown in Figure 4.50 has 8/31/2008 as the date and IDES as the unique identification for the processor responsible.

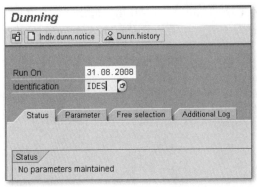

Figure 4.50 Dunning Program—Initial Screen

[+] **Dunning Date**

The date of the dunning run is also the date that appears in the dunning letters (dunning print). This date is part of the basic data of a dunning run that is specified manually in the Parameter tab. The Status tab only reflects a temporary status at the beginning of a running action. Therefore, you must press the Enter key to "refresh" the status.

Maintain basic data

To enter basic data, navigate to the Parameter tab. The following entries are mandatory:

▶ **Dunning date**
This date appears in the dunning letters. The SAP system uses it to calculate the days in arrears.

▶ **Documents posted up to**
All documents posted up to this date are checked for the due date during this dunning run (the Posting date in the document header is decisive here).

▶ **Company Code**
The system only considers the documents of the company codes that are entered here. It is possible to enter single values or intervals.

▶ **Customer account (vendor account)**
The dunning run considers the accounts of the customers or vendors that are entered here.

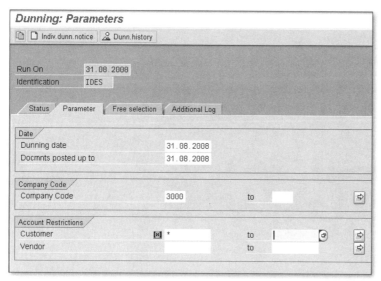

Figure 4.51 Entry of the Parameters of a Dunning Run

With the parameters of Figure 4.51, the system processes all customer accounts of the company codes 3000 on 8/31/2008 in this dunning run. In the next tab, Free selection, you can define fields at the document level or from the business partner master records as additional selection criteria. You enter the name of the database field in the Field Name column. The SAP system supports the search via the F4 help. Figure 4.52 illustrates the selection options.

Free selection

The example refers to the information from the customer master record. Figure 4.53 shows the selection fields available. If you select the Exclude Values field in the Free selection tab, this dunning run doesn't include the documents with the corresponding criteria from the Values columns.

In this example, the customer accounts with the reconciliation account 141000 are not selected for the dunning run. In real life, this could be an affiliated enterprise that is not supposed to receive dunning letters. In the next tab, you can define settings for the additional log. You specify the business partner for which a log is to be created.

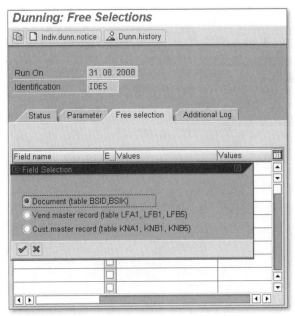

Figure 4.52 "Free Selection" Tab

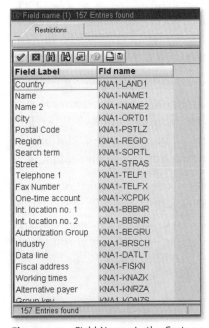

Figure 4.53 Field Names in the Customer Master Record

The log displays the processing logic of the dunning program with a high level of detail. The creation of an additional log requires CPU time and memory space; therefore, you should use it in exceptional cases only. If you make no entry here, the system doesn't create any additional log. According to the example in Figure 4.54, the system is supposed to create an additional log for all customers.

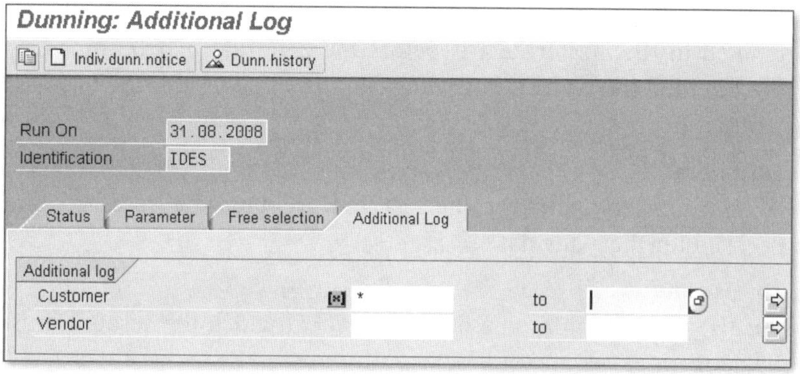

Figure 4.54 "Additional Log" Tab

Click on the Save button and navigate to the Status tab. There, the system informs you that the parameters were maintained (Figure 4.55).

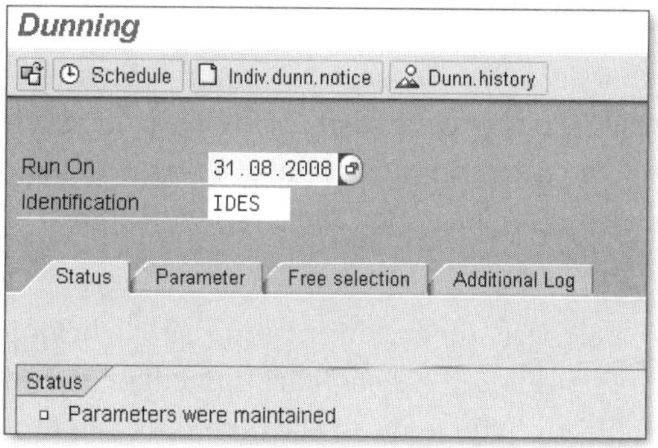

Figure 4.55 "Parameters Were Maintained" Status

Once all basic data has been entered, you can schedule the dunning proposal.

4.9.3 Creating the Dunning Proposal

After you've entered the parameters of the dunning run, you trigger the proposal run. This proposal run is an automatic procedure and basically consists of three steps:

1. **Select accounts**
   First, you check whether a dunning procedure is entered in the business partner master record. If the last dunning run's date that is defined in the master data is before the date that is determined by the dunning interval, this dunning run doesn't consider the business partner.

2. **Dun items**
   All documents found for the selected accounts are searched and checked for their due date.

3. **Dun accounts**
   Finally, you determine the dunning level at which the account must be dunned.

The result of this process is a dunning proposal list that can be edited.

Required computing power

A high number of customers to be dunned requires corresponding computing power for the SAP system. In order to not impair the daytime operation of the SAP system users, you usually schedule the dunning proposal for background processing. In some cases, the required computing power is only available at night. The scenario could look as follows: You maintain the selection parameters, that is, the basic data, on Thursday afternoon, schedule the proposal run for the evening, and have it processed by the system at night. On Friday morning, you can then edit the dunning proposal list.

You can schedule or immediately start the dunning proposal by clicking on the Schedule button (see Figure 4.56). Select Start immediately, and then click on the Schedule button if you want to start the dunning program in the foreground. In this case, the Start immediately field superimposes the entries of the Start date and Start time fields that are responsible for the background processing.

Skip dunning proposal list

If you select the Dunning print with scheduling? field, the dunning proposal list is no longer available for editing. If this is not intended, you can use this field to combine multiple steps in the SAP system. In this case, the OutputDevice field becomes mandatory.

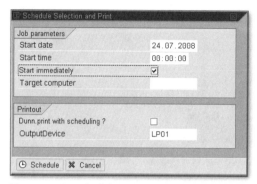

Figure 4.56 Schedule Dunning Proposal

Dunning Proposal and Dunning Print   **[+]**

Proceed with caution if you combine the work steps dunning proposal and dunning print. If you implement an automatic dunning that is based on existing, possibly incorrectly maintained data, good customers could unintentionally receive dunning letters with threats of legal actions. To prevent these errors affecting your business relationships, it usually makes sense to apply the dual-control principle by means of the dunning proposal.

Figure 4.57 illustrates the "Dunning selection Running" status message of the started dunning proposal run.

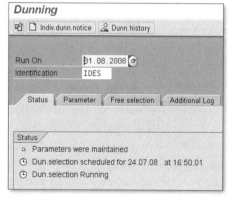

Figure 4.57 Dunning Selection Running" Status Message

Press Enter several times until the system displays the "Dunning selection is complete" message. Once the selection program is complete, both the status message and the interaction options change. Figure 4.58 shows these functions with additional buttons.

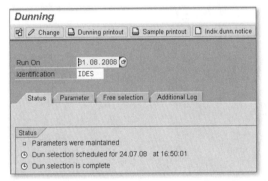

Figure 4.58 "Dunning Selection Is Complete" Status Message

The dunning proposal is created and can be processed.

4.9.4 Processing the Dunning Proposal

At this point, you can still delete the complete dunning proposal without any consequences. If the dunning selection led to an undesired dunning proposal, you don't need to rework it in a time-consuming, manual process. You can delete the dunning run, adapt the selection criteria, and take another look at the dunning proposal. If dunning letters have already been created for the next run, it is not possible to simply delete the dunning run. For the dunning proposal, you have the option to block accounts or items for dunning or change dunning levels. For editing, click on the Change button or follow the menu path EDIT • PROPOSAL • EDIT.

This opens the input mask shown in Figure 4.59. In this selection screen, you can select various options within a dunning proposal. Individual accounting clerks each work with a defined part of the dunning proposal. For example, you can select individual customers or vendors, dunning levels, or company codes. It is also possible to enter a two-digit accounting clerk ID to restrict the processing to business partners whose master records in the SAP system contain this ID. If you don't make any further entries in this screen, the system displays all dunning documents.

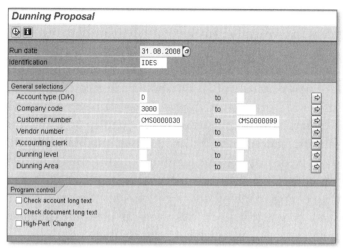

Figure 4.59 Selection Options for the Dunning Proposal

The customers within the number range CMS0000000 to CMS0000099 of company code 3000 are selected in this example. If you click on the Execute button, the system displays the selected part of the dunning proposal (see Figure 4.60).

Dunning Proposal

| ⏮ ◀ ▶ ⏭ | 🖉 Change dunning notice | 🖉 Change master data | 🖉 Change texts | 🗔 🖨 🗑 🔽 🔃 🗂 📈 💹 🔂 |

```
IDES US INC                Change dunning notices          Time 17:02:20    Date  24.07.2008
New York               Dunning run 31.08.2008/IDES      RFMAHN21/ACCOUNTANT1 Page        1
```

Che	AccTy	Account	CoCd	Clerk	Area		Dun Dunning block		T		
	DocumentNo Year Itm	Net due date			Arrear	Old dunLe	Dun Lock	C T		Amount in FC	Crcy
☐ D	CMS0000030	3000	AC		1						
1800000023 2005	1 02.05.2005	1.217				1	X		5.000,00	USD
1800000022 2005	1 11.05.2005	1.208				1	X		400.000,00	USD
* T										
									405.000,00	USD
☐ D	CMS0000040	3000	AC		1						
1800000025 2005	1 11.05.2005	1.208				1	X		21.000,00	USD
1800000024 2005	1 11.05.2005	1.208				1	X		350.000,00	USD
* T										
									371.000,00	USD
☑ D	CMS0000099	3000	AC		1						
1400000001 2008	1 27.02.2008	186				1	X		1.798,00	USD
100004648 2008	1 13.07.2008	49				1	X		1.000,00	USD
* T										
									2.798,00	USD
**										
									778.798,00	USD

Figure 4.60 Selected Part of the Dunning Proposal

Change dunning
proposal The selected part displays three customers' items. For each line item, you can view the days in arrears, the amount, and the new dunning level. Carpenter Works, customer number CMS0000099, has two open items that are both supposed to be included in dunning. The amount of $1,000 results from the original amount of $8,990 and a credit memo of $7,990. Additionally, there is a dispute case that is currently being processed and a promise to pay. In the configuration of the dunning program, this information can automatically result in an item that cannot be dunned. Then it would not be displayed in the dunning proposal. This is not the case in this example. In the list, select the customer CMS0000099 and then click on the Change dunning notice button. This takes you to the change mode shown in Figure 4.61. There, you can block the complete customer, Carpenter Works, or individual items for dunning.

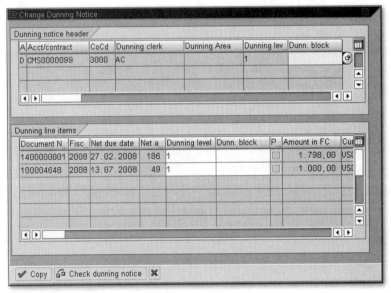

Figure 4.61 Change Dunning Notice

A dunning block set here only affects this dunning run and is not recorded to the master record or the document item.

Temporary Dunning Block   [+]

Dunning blocks set at this time are only valid for this dunning run. The changes only apply to the dunning proposal and do not affect the originally posted document or the maintained master record. If you decide to delete the dunning run after you've made changes to the dunning proposal, that is, after you've blocked some customers and items, you also delete the block information defined in the dunning proposal.

You can use the matchcode function ([F4] key) to call a list of possible block reasons. Figure 4.62 illustrates some variants.

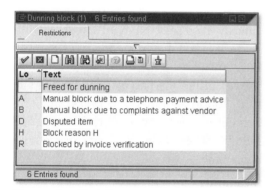

Figure 4.62 Block Reasons

To complete the processing, click on the SAVE button and then click on the BACK button twice to return to the initial screen of the dunning program. After you've edited the dunning list, you can have the system display all changes that have been implemented in this dunning run. For this purpose, the system provides the following four reports that you can access via the menu paths listed below. The system only displays those change lists that have been created within one dunning run.

Changes are logged

▶ GOTO • BLOCKED ACCOUNTS

▶ GOTO • BLOCKED ITEMS

▶ GOTO • ACCOUNT CHANGES

▶ GOTO • ITEM CHANGES

Besides the change lists, the optional additional log provides further options. You can have the system display the created additional log prior

Additional log

to printing; for this purpose select the menu path EXTRAS • DUNNING RUN
LOG. This log indicates the progress of the dunning run. The following
problems frequently occur:

► **No dunning procedure exists,** not **dunnable**
No dunning procedure is defined in the master data of the business
partner. In this context, the program cannot determine at which interval and levels the customer is supposed to be dunned. If these basic
parameters are missing, this results in the exclusion from the selection run. Maintain the master data of the business partner with a
valid dunning procedure to remove the cause.

► **Account XYZ is blocked by dunning run 31012008 TEST**
The business partner has already been selected in an active dunning
proposal. This is possibly a selection run that is no longer current, but
is still active. The date 1/31/2008 and the ID, TEST, suggest this. To
delete the dunning run, select it using the parameters, Execute ON
and Identification, and then choose Dunnings and Delete dunning
run from the menu bar. Each business partner can exist in one active
dunning proposal only. These blocks can emerge if you execute multiple dunning runs at the same time.

► **Amount not sufficient for dunning**
The amount has fallen below the minimum amount defined in the
dunning procedure that is necessary for dunning. Sometimes a high
credit memo can result in the balance of a customer account becoming a payable. The same can occur if the customer is also a vendor and
you've defined a clearing. If you owe your business partner money, a
dunning is not justified; this is indicated with this message.

► **Account has payment method for incoming payment**
In the customer account, you've defined an automatic debit or a debit
memo procedure for the payment methods. Because the payment run
enables you to collect money yourself, it is not due to the customer
that the documents have become overdue. In this case, dunning
would not be justified.

Figure 4.63 shows an example of the incremental procedure of the dunning program and its comprehensive documentation in the additional
log.

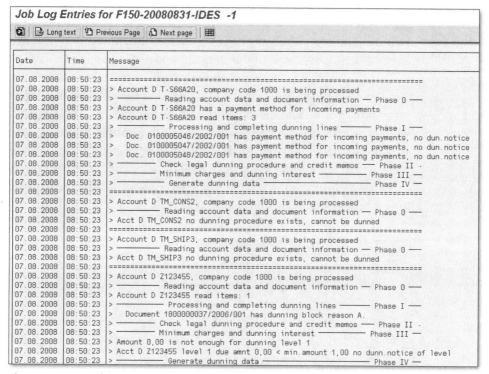

Job Log Entries for F150-20080831-IDES -1

| | Long text | Previous Page | Next page | |

Date	Time	Message
07.08.2008	08:50:23	===
07.08.2008	08:50:23	> Account D T-S66A20, company code 1000 is being processed
07.08.2008	08:50:23	> ———————— Reading account data and document information — Phase 0 —
07.08.2008	08:50:23	> Account D T-S66A20 has a payment method for incoming payments
07.08.2008	08:50:23	> Account D T-S66A20 read items: 3
07.08.2008	08:50:23	> ———————— Processing and completing dunning lines ———— Phase I —
07.08.2008	08:50:23	> Doc. 0100005046/2002/001 has payment method for incoming payments, no dun.notice
07.08.2008	08:50:23	> Doc. 0100005047/2002/001 has payment method for incoming payments, no dun.notice
07.08.2008	08:50:23	> Doc. 0100005048/2002/001 has payment method for incoming payments, no dun.notice
07.08.2008	08:50:23	> ———— Check legal dunning procedure and credit memos —— Phase II ·
07.08.2008	08:50:23	> ———————— Minimum charges and dunning interest ———— Phase III —
07.08.2008	08:50:23	> ———————— Generate dunning data ———————————— Phase IV —
07.08.2008	08:50:23	===
07.08.2008	08:50:23	> Account D TM_CONS2, company code 1000 is being processed
07.08.2008	08:50:23	> ———————— Reading account data and document information — Phase 0 —
07.08.2008	08:50:23	> Acct D TM_CONS2 no dunning procedure exists, cannot be dunned
07.08.2008	08:50:23	===
07.08.2008	08:50:23	> Account D TM_SHIP3, company code 1000 is being processed
07.08.2008	08:50:23	> ———————— Reading account data and document information — Phase 0 —
07.08.2008	08:50:23	> Acct D TM_SHIP3 no dunning procedure exists, cannot be dunned
07.08.2008	08:50:23	===
07.08.2008	08:50:23	> Account D Z123455, company code 1000 is being processed
07.08.2008	08:50:23	> ———————— Reading account data and document information — Phase 0 —
07.08.2008	08:50:23	> Account D Z123455 read items: 1
07.08.2008	08:50:23	> ———————— Processing and completing dunning lines ———— Phase I —
07.08.2008	08:50:23	> Document 1800000037/2006/001 has dunning block reason A.
07.08.2008	08:50:23	> ———— Check legal dunning procedure and credit memos —— Phase II ·
07.08.2008	08:50:23	> ———————— Minimum charges and dunning interest ———— Phase III —
07.08.2008	08:50:23	> Amount 0,00 is not enough for dunning level 1
07.08.2008	08:50:23	> Acct D Z123455 level 1 due amnt 0,00 < min.amount 1,00 no dunn.notice of level
07.08.2008	08:50:23	> ———————— Generate dunning data ———————————— Phase IV —

Figure 4.63 Log of the Dunning Run

If errors occur during a dunning run, you should reimplement the dunning run and create a job log. In this case you should proceed as follows:

1. Eliminate errors.

2. Delete the dunning proposal (DUNNINGS • DELETE DUNNING RUN).

3. Have the system recreate the dunning proposal.

Keep Log [+]

It is recommended that you don't delete the dunning proposal and thus the log until you are sure all errors are eliminated. Only then do you have the option to find clues about the error causes in the log.

Once you've completed editing and you are sure the customers contained in the dunning proposal are to receive a dunning letter, you can implement the next step.

4.9.5 Printing Dunning Letters

Sample printout of
the dunning print With the dunning print, you change the selected dunning proposal. The date and the highest level of dunning are updated in the master data of the customer account. The same applies to all open items that are supposed to be dunned. If you assume that this is the case for thousands of accounts, you should thoroughly consider this step of dunning print. Before you start this process by clicking on the Dunning Print button, you can still work in the test mode via Sample print and have the system generate a sample printout of the dunning letter for some customers. Figure 4.64 illustrates the sample print selection screen. The example is limited to the known customer, CMS0000099.

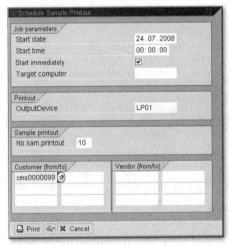

Figure 4.64 Selection Screen for the Sample Printout

If you click on the glasses icon, the system directly displays the print preview shown in Figure 4.65. All relevant information that exists in the customer master record is added to this standard letter. Because this example shows the first dunning, the dunning text is still rather friendly. Depending on the dunning level, you can use different text modules. You may remember the basic parameter of the dunning run and the selection field, consider Documents up to. You can find this information again in the dunning letter. Postings up to and including 8/31/2008 are considered. If the amounts due have been paid in the meantime, the customer can disregard the letter.

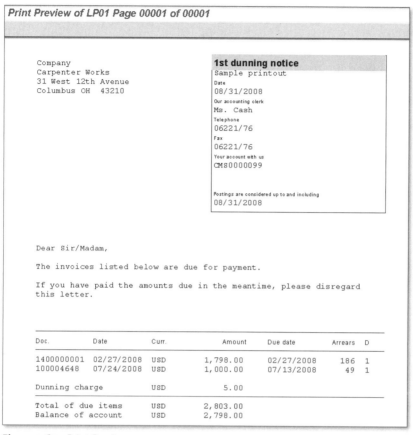

Figure 4.65 Print Preview

The dunning charge of $5 is not posted, but only stated in the dunning letter. This is supposed to emphasize the request for quick payment. Additionally, you can also charge dunning interests. For higher amounts and days in arrears, in this example, 186 or 49 days, this dunning interest can reach a considerable size.

Dunning charges and interests

Dunning Interests and Dunning Charges in Practice

In contrast to dunning charges, the customers usually pay the dunning interests—certainly because the corresponding laws support the creditor in this respect. From the technical point of view, you can calculate and post dunning interests in the SAP system. For dunning charges, you can implement a calculation but no posting in the standard version.

[+]

If the sample printout is completed successfully, you can print all dunnings by means of the corresponding button. The Schedule Print dialog box opens (see Figure 4.66). If you select Start immediately, the system starts the dunning printout in dialog mode. Otherwise, you must specify the start date and the start time for the background processing, and you must specify the output device. As usual, LOCL represents the specified standard Windows printer.

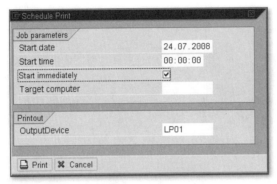

Figure 4.66 "Schedule Print" Dialog Box

If you click on Print, the Status tab appears (see Figure 4.67).

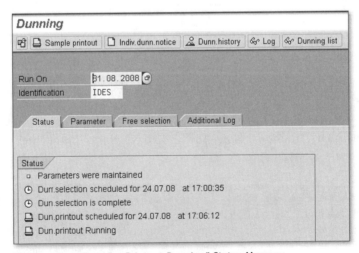

Figure 4.67 "Dunning Printout Running" Status Message

Electronic Dunnings

You don't always require written, paper-based dunning letters. In real life, the trend is to use existing email addresses and fax numbers to reduce costs. SAP Note 328124 provides support for the configuration.

After the dunning printout has been performed without any errors, the system automatically updates the master records and the dunned documents. You specify the dunning level and dunning date (see Figure 4.68).

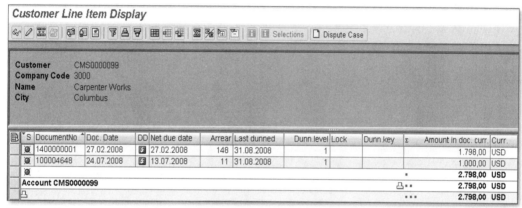

Figure 4.68 Document Item after the Dunning Printout

After the dunning printout, the business partner master record includes the current dunning run and the highest dunning level of the dunnings created for this business partner (see Figure 4.69).

The dunning procedure by mail is an instrument that is provided to you in receivables management in combination with SAP Collections Management and SAP Dispute Management. To give you a transparent overview of the customers and receivables, the system provides extensive evaluation programs.

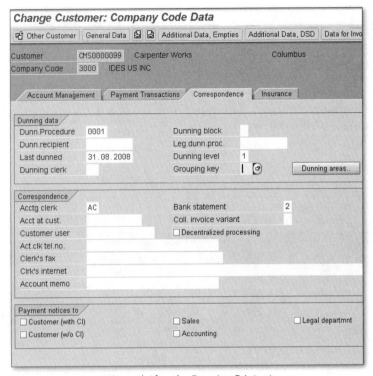

Figure 4.69 Master Record After the Dunning Printout

4.10 Evaluations in Accounts Receivable

Detailed reporting generates transparency

SAP ERP and SAP NetWeaver BW have a wide range of predefined evaluations. The information on the following pages merely represents examples and is only a fraction of the many possibilities available. Particularly in the area of receivables, transparency is worth a lot of money.

4.10.1 Customer List

You can answer the question about which customers are defined as master data in the system by evaluating the customer list. You can find the customer list under the menu path INFO SYSTEMS • ACCOUNTING • FINANCIAL ACCOUNTING • ACCOUNTS RECEIVABLE • REPORTS ABOUT ACCOUNTS RECEIVABLE ACCOUNTING • MASTER DATA • CUSTOMER LIST. Figure 4.70

shows the selection screen in which the system is supposed to output all customers of company code 3000 including their addresses, banks, and dunning data.

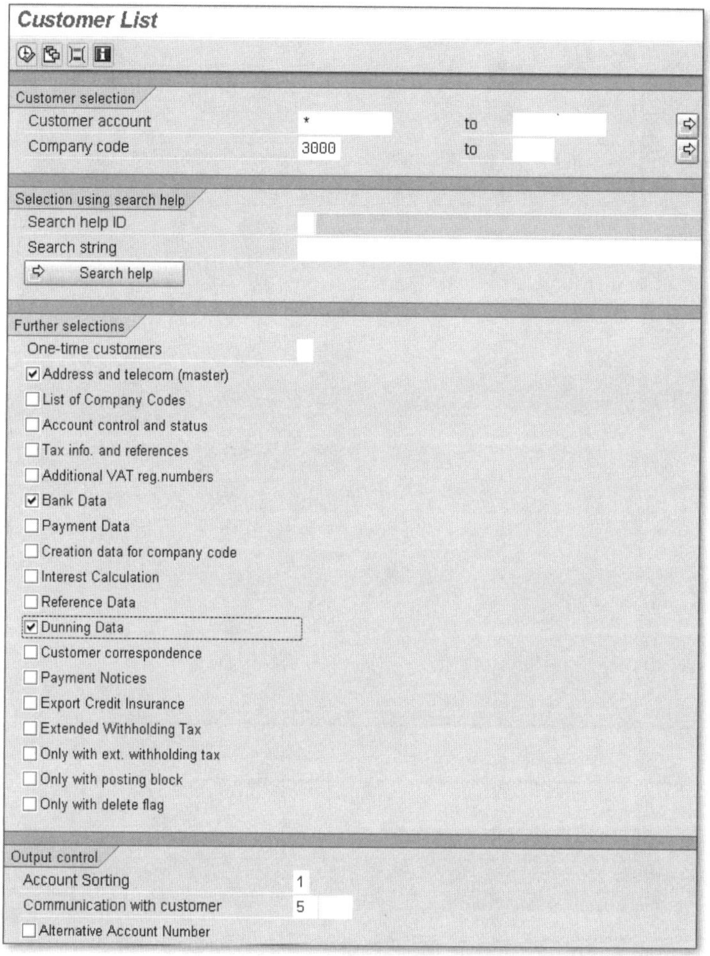

Figure 4.70 Selection Screen for the Customer List

Figure 4.71 shows the results list. It displays the defined master data of the general and the company code segment for customer CMS0000099 (Carpenter Works).

If you don't require detailed information, such as address, bank, and dunning data, and don't choose them in the selection, the results list looks as shown in Figure 4.72. This view only contains the customer number, the search term, the account group, the opening date, and the person who created it — the result is a very compact view.

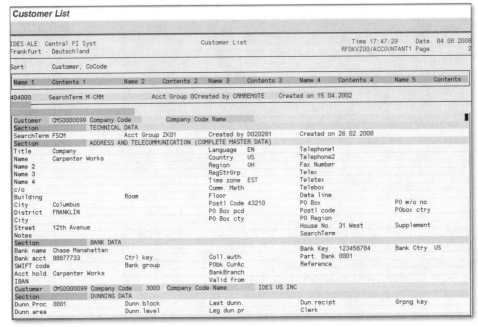

Figure 4.71 Customer List — Results List

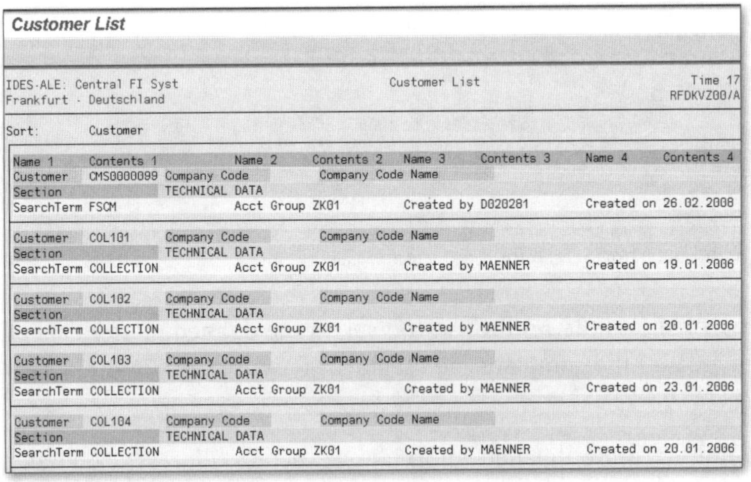

Figure 4.72 Customer List — Minimum Value of the Results List

You can use the Binoculars button to start a detailed search. In the example in Figure 4.73, the system searched for and found customer number CMS0000099.

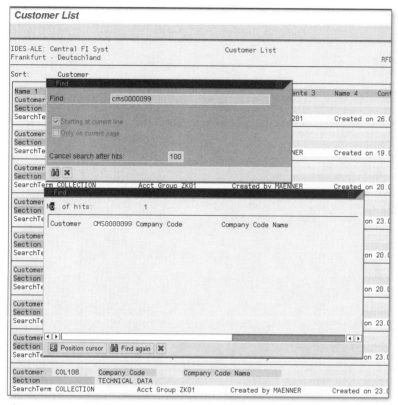

Figure 4.73 Search Function

In addition to the master data as the basis of accounts receivable accounting, it is necessary to keep an eye on the transaction data.

4.10.2 Customer Balances

The customer's balances enable you to draw conclusions about how much business has been done with individual customers. The term *sales*, which is defined by quantity times price is avoided here intentionally. Each attempt to calculate this value with another measurement method in accounting has some weak points and vagueness. You can find the

Definition of "sales"

evaluation of the customer balances under the menu path INFO SYSTEMS • ACCOUNTING • FINANCIAL ACCOUNTING • ACCOUNTS RECEIVABLE • REPORTS ABOUT ACCOUNTS RECEIVABLE ACCOUNTING • CUSTOMER BALANCES • CUSTOMER BALANCES IN LOCAL CURRENCY.

The example shown in Figure 4.74 illustrates a selection of all customers with company code 3000. A time limitation exists for periods 1 to 16 of fiscal year 2008.

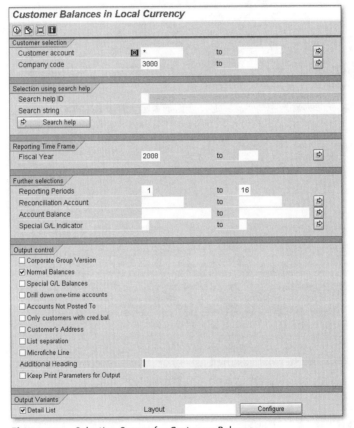

Figure 4.74 Selection Screen for Customer Balances

Figure 4.75 displays the results list with a compact list of the customers, their balance carryforward, and the debit and credit items. If the accumulated balance is positive, no receivable exists toward the customer. If the balance is negative, a payable exists owing to down payments, credit memos, or overpayments.

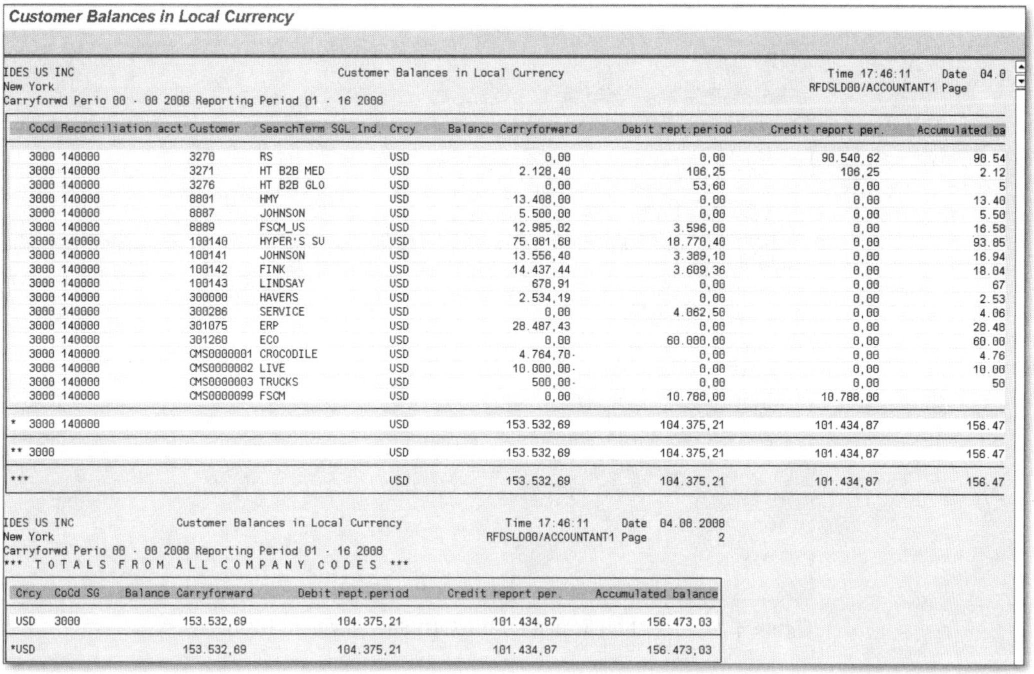

Customer Balances in Local Currency

IDES US INC Customer Balances in Local Currency Time 17:46:11 Date 04.0
New York RFDSLD00/ACCOUNTANT1 Page
Carryforwd Perio 00 - 00 2008 Reporting Period 01 - 16 2008

CoCd	Reconciliation acct	Customer	SearchTerm	SGL Ind.	Crcy	Balance Carryforward	Debit rept.period	Credit report per.	Accumulated ba
3000	140000	3270	RS		USD	0,00	0,00	90.540,62	90.54
3000	140000	3271	HT B2B MED		USD	2.128,40	106,25	106,25	2.12
3000	140000	3276	HT B2B GLO		USD	0,00	53,60	0,00	5
3000	140000	8801	HMY		USD	13.408,00	0,00	0,00	13.40
3000	140000	8887	JOHNSON		USD	5.500,00	0,00	0,00	5.50
3000	140000	8889	FSCM_US		USD	12.985,02	3.596,00	0,00	16.58
3000	140000	100140	HYPER'S SU		USD	75.081,60	18.770,40	0,00	93.85
3000	140000	100141	JOHNSON		USD	13.556,40	3.389,10	0,00	16.94
3000	140000	100142	FINK		USD	14.437,44	3.609,36	0,00	18.04
3000	140000	100143	LINDSAY		USD	678,91	0,00	0,00	67
3000	140000	300000	HAVERS		USD	2.534,19	0,00	0,00	2.53
3000	140000	300286	SERVICE		USD	0,00	4.062,50	0,00	4.06
3000	140000	301075	ERP		USD	28.487,43	0,00	0,00	28.48
3000	140000	301260	ECO		USD	0,00	60.000,00	0,00	60.00
3000	140000	CMS0000001	CROCODILE		USD	4.764,70-	0,00	0,00	4.76
3000	140000	CMS0000002	LIVE		USD	10.000,00-	0,00	0,00	10.00
3000	140000	CMS0000003	TRUCKS		USD	500,00-	0,00	0,00	50
3000	140000	CMS0000099	FSCM		USD	0,00	10.788,00	10.788,00	
* 3000	140000				USD	153.532,69	104.375,21	101.434,87	156.47
** 3000					USD	153.532,69	104.375,21	101.434,87	156.47
***					USD	153.532,69	104.375,21	101.434,87	156.47

IDES US INC Customer Balances in Local Currency Time 17:46:11 Date 04.08.2008
New York RFDSLD00/ACCOUNTANT1 Page 2
Carryforwd Perio 00 - 00 2008 Reporting Period 01 - 16 2008
*** T O T A L S F R O M A L L C O M P A N Y C O D E S ***

Crcy	CoCd	SG	Balance Carryforward	Debit rept.period	Credit report per.	Accumulated balance
USD	3000		153.532,69	104.375,21	101.434,87	156.473,03
*USD			153.532,69	104.375,21	101.434,87	156.473,03

Figure 4.75 Results List of the Customer Balances

The total of the balance usually indicates the sales. You can find comprehensive information and details on products and services in the evaluations of the SD module.

4.10.3 Customer Payment History

To be able to generate an incoming payment from the sales, it is very important to monitor the customer's payment history in receivables management. Follow the menu path Info Systems • Accounting • Financial Accounting • Accounts Receivable • Reports for Accounts Receivable Accounting • Customer Payment History to access the selection options shown in Figure 4.76.

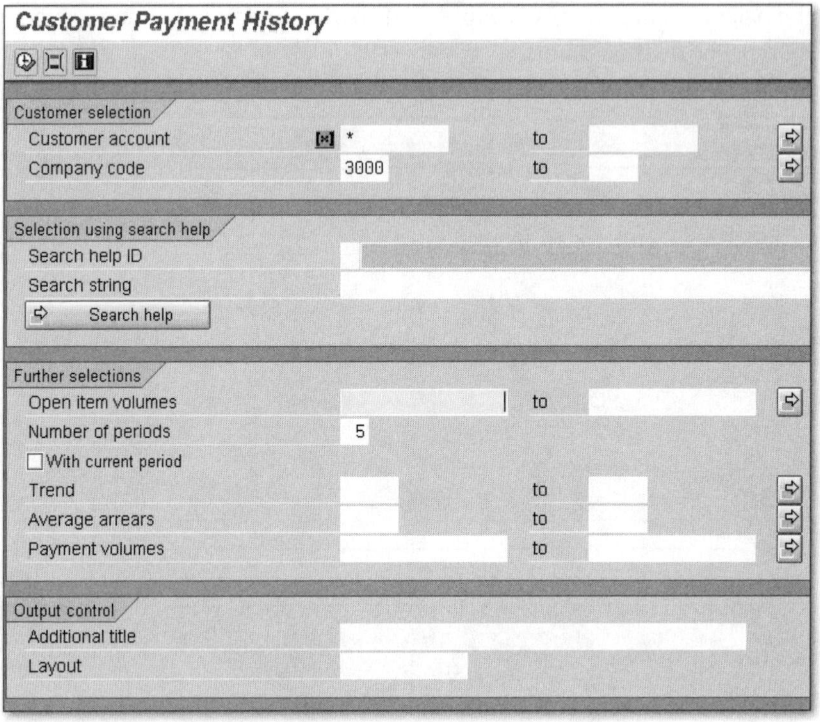

Figure 4.76 Selection Screen for the Customer Payment History

Days in arrears

In addition to the usual selection fields, such as customer or company code, you can also limit your search to suspected problem cases in the Further selections area. The open item volume and the average days in arrears can be an indication and hence a selection criterion. The result (see Figure 4.77) shows some customers and their payment history, distributed across multiple historical periods. For customers 3001, 3018, and 3050 the days in arrears are within a certain period. Days in arrears marked with a minus sign indicate payments before the due date. For customer 3000, the situation is similar, although this customer also has two peak values with 329 and 737 days in arrears, that is, beyond the date of required payment. The high amount of more than $500,000 was paid rather punctually with only eight days in arrears.

```
┌──────────────────────────────────────────────────────────────────────┐
│  Customer Payment History                                              │
│ ┌────────┬────────┬─────────────────┐                                 │
│ │Graphics│Forecast│ ▦ ▦ ▦ ▦ ▦       │                                 │
│                                                                        │
│ IDES US INC         Customer Payment History    Time 17:41:49  Date 04.08.2008│
│ New York                                        RFDOPR20/ACCOUNTANT1 Page    1│
│                                                                        │
│ Customer  CoCd Name 1                      Customer Type              │
│           Street                           Backlog    Arrears         │
│           PostalCode City                        Balance Carryforward Crcy│
│ Month Year Number Pmnts with csh disc. Arrear Without cash discnt Arrear│
│                                                                        │
│ 3000       3000 Thomas Bush Inc.           Net payer although cash dsct│
│            1 1 2800 South 25th Ave         8 Days        8 Days        │
│            60153    MAYWOOD                              0,00  USD     │
│    9 2002    4         7.900,00    30.          0,00       0           │
│   12 1997    1         9.017,97   329           0,00       0           │
│   10 1996    1             0,00     0        6.640,63      1.          │
│    9 1996    4             0,00     0      516.187,17      8           │
│    7 1996    2           927,84    14.         318,75      9.          │
│    5 1996    2             0,00     0        4.060,00      3.          │
│    3 1996    1         1.150,00   737       21.000,00    362           │
│                                                                        │
│ 3001       3000 Industrial Supplies Inc.   Net payer although cash dsct│
│            1 1345 Main St.                 0 Days                      │
│            23456    VIRGINIA BEACH                       0,00  USD     │
│    5 1996    1             0,00     0      193.375,00      0           │
│                                                                        │
│ 3018       3000 Fremont Supplies           Cash discount taken where possible│
│            1310 West Avenue                31 Days                     │
│            94061    REDWOOD CITY                         0,00  USD     │
│    8 2002    2           168,00    31           0,00       0           │
│                                                                        │
│ 3050       3000 Bush Holdings, Inc.        Cash discount taken where possible│
│            1 1 408 Michigan Avenue         9. Days       0 Days        │
│            60611    CHICAGO                              0,00  USD     │
│    6 2000    1         8.077,13    30.          0,00       0           │
│   12 1996    1             0,00     0       40.321,88      3.          │
│   10 1996    1        14.288,50    32.          0,00       0           │
│    9 1996    1         7.144,25    15        8.446,88      7           │
│    8 1996    1             0,00     0       31.476,59      3           │
│    5 1996    1        90.312,50     6.          0,00       0           │
│    4 1996    1         4.000,00     5           0,00       0           │
└──────────────────────────────────────────────────────────────────────┘
```

Figure 4.77 Results List of the Customer Payment History

A changing payment history can be an indication of the customer's liquidity issues. If you recognize this in time, you can change the terms of payment, for example, prepayment or down payments, as countermeasures.

4.10.4 Accounts Receivable Info System

Long before SAP NetWeaver BW was provided as a special reporting tool, a similar approach was implemented in SAP ERP. The accounts receivable info system is a kind of data cube that is filled with up-to-date information at regular intervals. You can view, rotate, and turn this cube to view it from different perspectives. Consequently, the evaluations that

Periodic information acquisition

are stored and structured according to topics in this cube are considerably well suited for analyses. You can access the accounts receivable info system via the menu path ACCOUNTING • FINANCIAL ACCOUNTING • ACCOUNTS RECEIVABLE • INFO SYSTEM • TOOLS • SHOW EVALUATION.

The following sections describe the three most important subject areas as examples from the six evaluations shown in Figure 4.78.

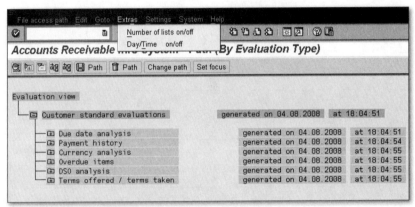

Figure 4.78 Accounts Receivable Info System—Overview

The data cube of the accounts receivable info system is static and always refers to a specific point in time. Via the menu path EXTRAS • DAY/TIME ON, you can display the creation time. The evaluations don't consider the posting procedures after this point in time. You therefore need to perform updates at regular intervals.

DSO Analysis

The period between the billing and the incoming payments is referred to as DSO (days sales outstanding). In receivables management, this key figure is an indicator to measure and hence monitor the customer's payment behavior. The DSO analysis in the accounts receivable info system allows an analysis based on the complete client (group) or the individual credit control areas (see Figure 4.79).

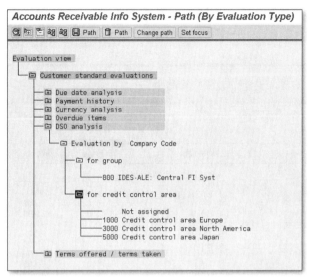

Figure 4.79 DSO Analysis for Group/Credit Control Area

In this example, the client (group) is to be evaluated. A double-click on the corresponding field takes you to Figure 4.80, a DSO analysis at the level of the respective company codes. The average DSO values are extremely high in the test system. The reason is that the sample calculations usually don't have any incoming payment. In real life, the DSO values are usually in the two-digit days range. In this example, we want to analyze the IDES AG company code in more detail.

DSO analysis

Client   IDES-ALE: Central FI Syst   Key date: 29.06.2008
                                                        Values in: EUR

Company Code	Balance	Sales	DSO days
IDES Japan 5000	880,51	0,00	9.999,0
IDES US INC	136.516,23	3.329,31	1.230,1
IDES AG	6.231.575,79	373.861,98	500,0
IDES Netherlands	2.170.100,01	556.166,66	117,1
Total	8.539.072,54	933.357,95	274,5

Figure 4.80 DSO Analysis At Company Code Level

If the average DSO values of a company code increase, it makes sense to use a more detailed display. If you double-click on the row of the company code, the system takes you to the next evaluation level, a customer list (see Figure 4.81).

```
DSO analysis
▼ ▲ ⊕ ☷

Client      IDES-ALE: Central FI Syst          Key date: 29.06.2008
Company Code IDES AG                            Values in: EUR
```

Customer	Balance	Sales	DSO days
Andrea Lindsay	8.280,00	0,00	9.999,0
Best Products	7.800,00	0,00	9.999,0
Elektromarkt GmbH	2.900,01	0,00	9.999,0
Mediastars AG	2.979,99	0,00	9.999,0
Gastronomica GmbH	4.200,00	0,00	9.999,0
Samt & Seide AG	3.849,99	0,00	9.999,0
Maximum Energy	8.600,01	0,00	9.999,0
Harikana AG	3.549,99	0,00	9.999,0
Elektronik & Media GmbH	3.170,01	0,00	9.999,0
Glambert & Partner GmbH	6.099,99	0,00	9.999,0
Schmidt & Söhne GmbH	3.470,01	0,00	9.999,0
VBP Elektro AG	3.050,01	0,00	9.999,0
Beste Konsumgüter AG	6.900,00	0,00	9.999,0
Electronica AG	9.900,00	0,00	9.999,0
Futura AG	2.190,00	0,00	9.999,0
Heller & Partner GmbH	1.650,00	0,00	9.999,0
Mc Crown	1.813,95	0,00	9.999,0
Winterfield's	199.308,59	4.599,99	1.299,8
Michael Lehmann	21.335,90	519,99	1.230,9
Frank Johannsen	21.183,03	553,80	1.147,5
Lampen-Markt GmbH	557,85	16,38	1.021,7
Motomarkt Stuttgart GmbH	1.265.158,51	38.180,22	994,1
Christal Clear	437,20	13,41	978,1
Karsson High Tech Markt	652,00	20,37	960,2
First Hyper's Supermark	90.242,76	3.312,00	817,4
Elektromarkt Bamby	331.635,24	13.493,52	737,3
Institut fuer Umweltforsch	1.743.233,23	101.085,97	517,4
Becker AG	1.002.996,41	211.184,91	142,5
Food Wholesale Inc.	1.552,34	776,17	60,0
Nudelfabrik GmbH	541,34	270,67	60,0
Becker Berlin	3.700,00-	99,99-	0,0
Omega Soft-Hardware Markt	58,73-	0,96	0,0
CBD Computer Based Design	164.876,04-	0,00	0,0
Amadeus	284.056,11-	0,00	0,0
C.A.S. Computer Applicatio	381.735,32-	66,39-	0,0
SudaTech GmbH	18.601,77-	0,00	0,0
Software Systeme GmbH	3.288,03-	0,00	0,0

Figure 4.81 DSO Analysis for Customer Account

This point constitutes the end of the static information of the accounts receivable info system. With another double-click you go to the current line items of the customer. In addition to the DSO analysis, which strongly focuses on the client, company code, and customer, the analysis of overdue items particularly relates to the individual business transaction or document.

Overdue Items

The analysis of the overdue items is the second evaluation of the accounts receivable info system that is supposed to be described here. At the first selection level, you can also select the business area in addition to the group and the credit control area (see Figure 4.82).

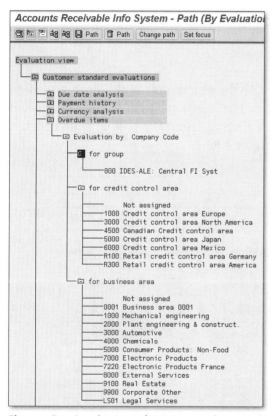

Figure 4.82 Overdue Items for Group, Credit Control Area, or Business Area

This example analyzes the overdue items of business area 1000 (mechanical engineering). With a double-click, the system takes you to the next evaluation level, the display for the company code (see Figure 4.83). In the context of the selected business area 1000 (mechanical engineering) and the three company codes, you can view the interest calculation numerator, days in arrears, and amount.

Overdue items

▼ ▲ ⊕ ⊞ ▽

Business area Mechanical engineering			Key date: 29.06.2008 Values in: EUR
Company Code	Int.calc.num.	Days in arr.	Amount
IDES Netherlands	511.071.284	1.303	39.217.850,00
IDES Filiale 1 IT Ko.1000	341.556.030	1.859	18.370.505,00
IDES AG	18.575.832	430	4.322.705,59
Total	871.203.146	1.407	61.911.060,59

Figure 4.83 Overdue Items for Company Code

These key figures are based on the data records in the demo system. In a real-life situation, they would be considerably smaller. Again, we want to analyze the values of the IDES AG company code in more detail. A double-click takes you to Figure 4.84.

Overdue items

▼ ▲ ⊕ ▽

Business area Mechanical engineering Company Code IDES AG				Key date: 29.06.2008 Values in: EUR
Doc.number	Due	Int.calc.num.	Days in arr.	Amount
100010174	12.01.2004	7.339.548	1.630	450.279,00
100000609	14.03.2005	1.484.076	1.203	123.364,61
100004393	17.10.2002	▌845.292	2.082	40.600,00
100004392	17.10.2002	338.117	2.082	16.240,00
1400000052	11.01.2007	255.813	535	47.815,60
1400000071	01.02.2007	228.217	514	44.400,20
1400000012	01.03.2007	199.186	486	40.984,80
1400000038	26.04.2007	195.893	430	45.556,50
1400000016	17.03.2007	186.852	470	39.755,64
1400000119	14.09.2007	182.872	289	63.277,54
1400000063	14.06.2007	179.009	381	46.983,94
1400000051	11.01.2007	177.802	535	33.234,00
1400000075	14.02.2007	176.504	501	35.230,36
1400000096	04.08.2007	175.476	330	53.174,40
1400000018	17.03.2007	171.921	470	36.578,93
1400000069	01.02.2007	171.718	514	33.408,10
1400000031	08.04.2007	168.311	448	37.569,40
100003807	07.10.2002	167.502	2.092	8.006,78
1400000061	14.06.2007	165.748	381	43.503,31
1400000044	15.05.2007	163.396	411	39.755,64
1400000029	08.04.2007	163.274	448	36.445,20
1400000077	28.06.2007	158.559	367	43.204,20
1400000070	01.02.2007	153.740	514	29.910,60
1400000010	01.03.2007	147.603	486	30.371,00
1400000116	09.09.2007	146.562	294	49.851,00
1400000050	11.01.2007	146.236	535	27.333,90
1400000058	03.06.2007	143.305	392	36.557,40
1400000057	03.06.2007	142.865	392	36.445,20
1400000030	08.04.2007	133.999	448	29.910,60
1400000076	28.06.2007	133.754	367	36.445,20
1400000137	07.10.2007	132.604	266	49.851,00
1400000040	26.04.2007	132.176	430	30.738,60

Figure 4.84 List of Overdue Items in the Mechanical Engineering Business Area and the IDES AG Company Code

Thanks to the list of the individual documents including their interest calculation numerator and days in arrears, in this example it is easy to determine the business transaction that is supposed to be examined more closely. With another double-click you go to the original document that represents the highest interest calculation numerator. Figure 4.85 shows that this demo system document is from the year 2003.

Analyze the interest calculation numerator

Display Document: Data Entry View

Document Number	100010174	Company Code	1000	Fiscal Year	2003
Document Date	28.11.2003	Posting Date	28.11.2003	Period	11
Reference	0090034329	Cross-CC no.			
Currency	EUR	Texts exist	☐	Ledger Group	

Co	Item	PK	S	Account	Description	Amount	Curr.	Tx	Cost Center	Order	Profit Center
1000	1	01		1032	Institut fuer Umweltforschung	450.279,00	EUR	A0			
	2	50		800000	Sales revenues - dom	116.319,00-	EUR	A0			1010
	3	50		800000	Sales revenues - dom	85.038,80-	EUR	A0			1010
	4	50		800000	Sales revenues - dom	6.830,80-	EUR	A0			1010
	5	50		800000	Sales revenues - dom	242.090,40-	EUR	A0			1010

Figure 4.85 Document Overview

The combination of a posting amount of €450,279 and an overdue amount since 2003 results in this high interest calculation numerator, which negatively affects the average value of the company code and the business area. In real life, such old receivables are presumably already written off or adjusted in their value.

In addition to the analysis of overdue items, exchange rate fluctuations and their effects are another important aspect in receivables management.

Currency Analysis

If a receivable exists in a foreign currency, the gain or loss from exchange rate fluctuation is implemented at the time of incoming payments. You can use the currency analysis of the accounts receivable info system to illustrate the effects of the current exchange rates in advance. The example in Figure 4.86 illustrates the exchange rate receivables per country: exchange rate changes in Germany for Euros and in the USA for dollars.

Review exchange rate effects

Currency analysis

Client IDES-ALE: Central FI Syst

Key date: 29.06.2008
Values in: EUR

Country	Total historical	Total current	Ex.rate diff. for current
United States	54.516,67	46.596,61	7.920,06·
Germany	245.000,40·	215.747,57·	29.252,83
Total	190.483,73·	169.150,96·	21.332,77

Figure 4.86 Currency Analysis for Country

If you double-click on "Germany," you can further analyze the exchange rate changes of almost €30,000. Figure 4.87 illustrates the next evaluation level, the customer overview. The customer, Frank Hiller, is conspicuous. Historically, the receivable amounted to €181,197; currently it is €151,653.

Currency analysis

Client IDES-ALE: Central FI Syst
Country Germany

Key date: 29.06.2008
Values in: EUR

Customer	Total historical	Total current	Ex.rate diff. for current
Becker Berlin	4.166,50	3.875,97	290,53·
Norbert Neumann	3.086,93·	3.086,93·	0,00
Susanne Schenk	2.745,89·	2.745,89·	0,00
Ina Imhof	1.440,53·	1.440,53·	0,00
Udo Uhland	33.621,08·	33.621,08·	0,00
Stefan Schäfer	1.630,32·	1.630,32·	0,00
Wanja Wagner	1.958,25·	1.958,25·	0,00
Ulla Ungerer	1.050,67·	1.050,67·	0,00
Zoltan Ziegler	953,51·	953,51·	0,00
Bernd Berger	2.884,08·	2.884,08·	0,00
Markus Miller	930,58·	930,58·	0,00
Michaela Meier	769,51·	769,51·	0,00
Susanne Schmid	649,32·	649,32·	0,00
Wolfgang Weber	1.288,49·	1.288,49·	0,00
Sabine Schulze	966,35·	966,35·	0,00
Herbert Huber	608,44·	608,44·	0,00
Matthias Mayer	1.163,19·	1.163,19·	0,00
Barbara Beckmann	948,50·	948,50·	0,00
Rolf Rothmann	1.234,80·	1.234,80·	0,00
TCC AG	4.997,93·	4.997,93·	0,00
Ferdinand Fichtel	1.666,98·	1.666,98·	0,00
Dirk Breitner	409,04·	409,04·	0,00
Ellen Effner	511,28·	511,28·	0,00
Richard Dürer	388,56·	388,56·	0,00
Susanne Lehmann	490,88·	490,88·	0,00
Oliver Lipp	388,56·	388,56·	0,00
Steffen Ott	613,56·	613,56·	0,00
Peter Zimmer	572,64·	572,64·	0,00
Frank Hiller	181.197,03·	151.653,67·	29.543,36
Total	245.000,40·	215.747,57·	29.252,83

Figure 4.87 Currency Analysis for Customer

You can further analyze the individual documents by double-clicking on the customer name (see Figure 4.88).

Customer Line Item Display

	St	Ty	DocumentNo	Doc. Date	Net due dt	Reference	Clearing	Clrng doc	Amt in loc.cur.	LCurr	Case ID	Processor
☐		DA	1600000167	02.10.2000	02.10.2000				89.889,73-	EUR		
☐		DA	1600000163	02.10.2000	02.10.2000				90.816,42-	EUR		
									180.706,15-	EUR		
** Account 1000000010									180.706,15-	EUR		

Customer: 1000000010
Company Code: 1000
Name: Frank Hiller
City: Berlin

Figure 4.88 Foreign Currency Posting of the Customer

Two business transactions in foreign currency result in the previously presented total receivable. The documents originate from the year 2000 and were probably posted in Euros with a relative low exchange rate after the currency changeover in Europe. Double-click to open the document overview and display the foreign currency amount in dollars or the local currency amount in Euros. Additionally, the document header indicates the exchange rate used (EUR/USD). Figure 4.89 illustrates this. The reduction of the receivable in Euros is based on the previous indirect quotation of 1.07 and a current exchange rate of approximately 1.50.

Receivables in foreign currency

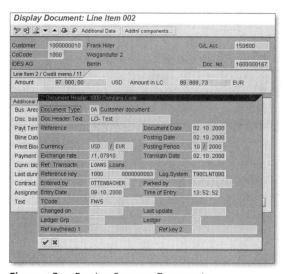

Figure 4.89 Foreign Currency Document

Focus on risks The loss from exchange rate fluctuation is implemented later with the incoming payment. The currency analysis helps you keep an overview of the possible risks and the losses and gains from exchange rate fluctuations during the period between the billing and the incoming payment.

To ensure that you can make analyses and decisions on the basis of current data, you need to continuously update the accounts receivable info system.

Updating the Info System

You can update the data source of the accounts receivable info system via the menu path ACCOUNTING • FINANCIAL ACCOUNTING • ACCOUNTS RECEIVABLE • INFO SYSTEM • TOOLS • SET • CREATE EVALUATION. Initially, the system takes you to the overview shown in Figure 4.90. There, you can define the background job for the update.

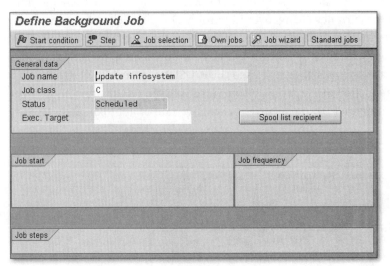

Figure 4.90 Define Job

You go to the details screen shown in Figure 4.91 by clicking on the Step button. The system automatically suggests the program name and variant for an update run. If you click on the Save button, you return to the job overview.

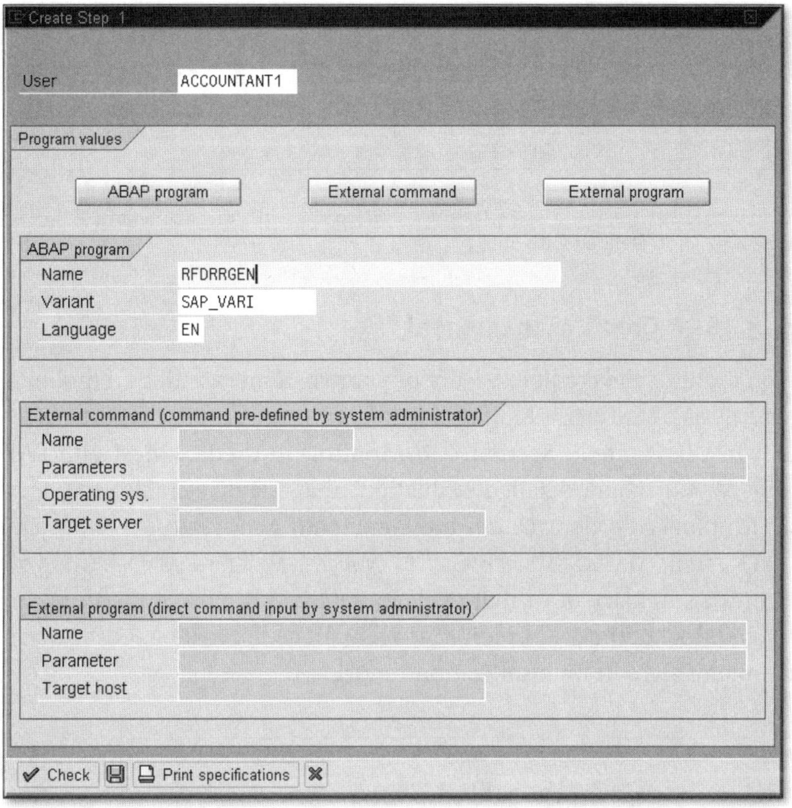

Figure 4.91 Create Step

In the lower part of Figure 4.92, you can see that a step was successfully defined for the defined job, UPDATE_INFOSYSTEM. Finally, you must specify when and how often the system is supposed to implement the update. That can be done using the Start condition button. If you define a periodic job, you don't need to repeat this manual technical work in the future.

Define the step

The accounts receivable info system provides you with a total of six reports to support you in the analysis of receivables. In addition, there are further evaluations that you require for the business operation in Accounts Receivable.

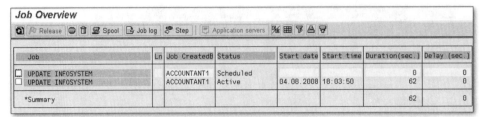

Figure 4.92 Job Defined with Step

4.10.5 SAP Credit Management

Monitoring the credit limit utilization

If you monitor the credit exposure of your customers with a credit limit, the analysis of the credit limit utilization constitutes an important instrument in this context. Section 4.5, Monitoring Credit Lines with SAP Credit Management, detailed evaluations that enable a credit limit decision for blocked orders. Under the menu path ACCOUNTING • FINANCIAL SUPPLY CHAIN MANAGEMENT • CREDIT MANAGEMENT • LIST DISPLAY, you can find a summary of further evaluations that provide you with a general overview of the SAP Credit Management area. Figure 4.93 shows an example of a credit limit utilization report.

SAP Credit Management: Display List of Credit Limit Utilization

List of Credit Limit Utilization

Without Extract

Icon	Utilization %	Risk Class	Partner	Block	Crcy	Exposure Amount	Cr. Expos.	Credit Limit	Hedged	Calculated
	142,5	D	COL113		USD	3.400,00	11.400,00	8.000,00	0,00	0,00
	140,7	D	CMS0000001		USD	16.270,52	56.270,52	40.000,00	0,00	38.000,00
	100,0	C	CMS0000007		USD	0,00	30.000,00	30.000,00	0,00	0,00
	100,0	C	CMS0000009		USD	0,00	30.000,00	30.000,00	0,00	0,00
	99,3	C	CMS0000022		USD	1.000,00-	141.000,00	142.000,00	0,00	42.000,00
	96,7	D	CMS0000012	X	USD	10.000,00-	290.000,00	300.000,00	0,00	25.000,00
	96,7	C	COL106		USD	300,00-	8.700,00	9.000,00	0,00	0,00
	82,8	B	CMS0000008		USD	1.202,00-	5.798,00	7.000,00	0,00	0,00
	81,0	D	CMS0000030		USD	95.000,00-	405.000,00	500.000,00	0,00	20.000,00
	77,1	E	CMS0000040		USD	114.448,99-	385.551,01	500.000,00	0,00	39.000,00
	69,0	D	COL101		USD	3.100,00-	6.900,00	10.000,00	0,00	0,00
	61,7	B	COL109		USD	4.600,00-	7.400,00	12.000,00	0,00	0,00
	51,7	D	COL110		USD	3.620,00-	3.880,00	7.500,00	0,00	0,00
	50,0	A	CCAU000001		USD	250,00-	250,00	500,00	0,00	500,00
	47,3	D	CMS0000099		USD	2.002,00-	1.798,00	3.800,00	0,00	3.800,00
	47,0	C	COL104		USD	5.300,00-	4.700,00	10.000,00	0,00	0,00
	41,5	B	8889		USD	23.418,98-	16.581,02	40.000,00	0,00	40.000,00
	39,4	B	CMS0000010		USD	322.000,00-	209.000,00	531.000,00	0,00	531.000,00

Figure 4.93 Credit Limit Utilization

This list is sorted in descending order based on the degree of utilization. Business partners with a percentage of approximately 100% or more are the most interesting ones. The credit block indicates which customer does not receive deliveries (CMS0000012 in this example). Additional information, such as the risk class or the absolute exposure amount, complements the overview.

Additional guarantees

Based on this list, you can decide for which customers it would be useful to have additional guarantees with guarantees of payment, letters of credit, or export credit insurances.

Supplementary to the receivables management and in addition to the evaluations in SAP Credit Management, the following section presents some reports from SAP Dispute Management.

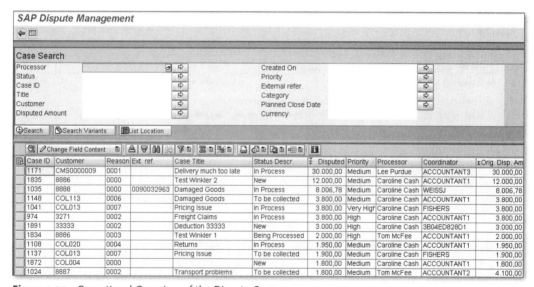

Figure 4.94 Operational Overview of the Dispute Cases

4.10.6 SAP Dispute Management

Evaluations in SAP Dispute Management are carried out in the SAP ERP system, on the one hand, and in SAP NetWeaver BW, on the other. In SAP ERP, you can find an operational overview of the dispute cases under ACCOUNTING • FINANCIAL SUPPLY CHAIN MANAGEMENT • DISPUTE MANAGEMENT • EDIT DISPUTE. Figure 4.94 lists the dispute cases in ALV

Operational overview in SAP ERP

format. The disputed amount in descending order was selected as the sorting criterion. Additionally, you can view the processing status, the processor, the coordinator, and the Escalation Reason column. You can also display further information without any problems. You can view the details of the dispute case by double-clicking on an entry in the list.

Further analyses take place in SAP NetWeaver BW. The standard version contains content that includes the following reports:

▶ Analysis for priorities and time grid (see Figure 4.95)

▶ Analysis for values and life (see Figure 4.96)

▶ Customer analysis (see Figure 4.97)

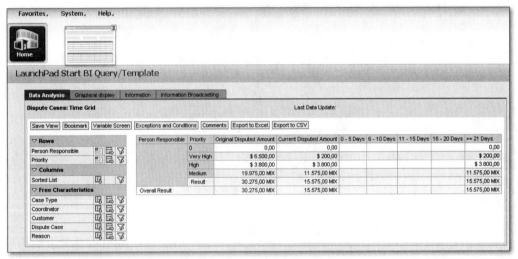

Figure 4.95 Analysis for Priorities and Time Grid

Analysis of the processing duration

Find out how long it takes to close dispute cases or which customers have dispute cases and how these were solved. If there are dispute cases that do not result in credit memos in principle, this may be due to your internal process steps.

In contrast to SAP Dispute Management, only evaluations in SAP NetWeaver BW exist for SAP Collections Management.

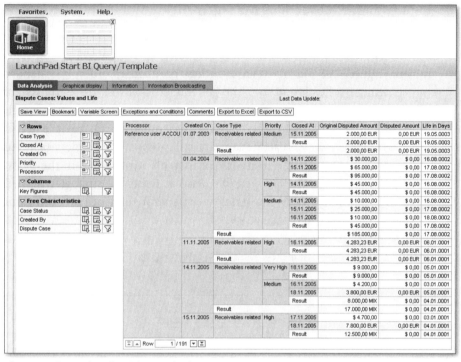

Figure 4.96 Analysis for Values and Life

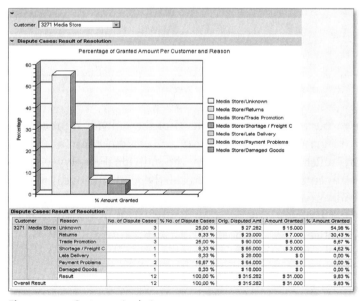

Figure 4.97 Customer Analysis

4.10.7 SAP Collections Management

Capacity utilization
of the employees The primary aim of evaluations in the collections management area is to make the work output that was generated through worklists transparent. Figure 4.98 illustrates an overview, grouped according to calendar weeks and collection group. The generated entries in the worklists are compared with the calls made. A percentage value indicates how much work has been done. In real life, this value should always be little below 100%. This ensures a realistic capacity utilization of the employees in the business process. If the value is considerably lower—like in the demo system—this can have two possible reasons. Either the strategies defined in the system generate too much work and/or there are not sufficient people available to do the work.

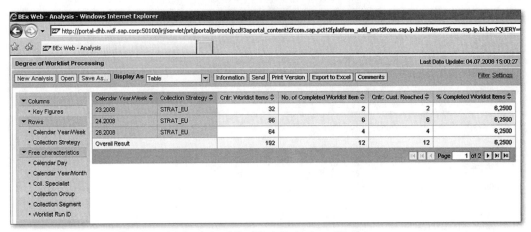

Figure 4.98 Analysis of the Work Output per Week

Shared server
center context It is also possible to evaluate at the level of the individual processors analogous to Figure 4.99. In this context, you could check in a targeted manner how much work was done by the individual employees. In a shared service center organization, particularly good employees receive additional bonuses based on this information. In some countries, this person-related evaluation is assessed as critical from the labor law–related perspective.

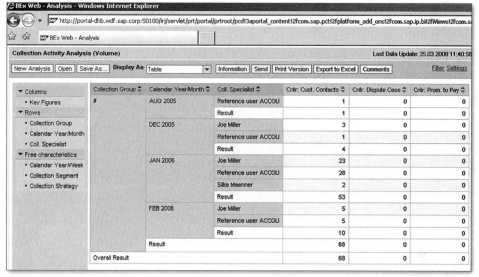

Figure 4.99 Analysis of the Collection Groups

These evaluations provide you with a multitude of options. The standard reports should cover most of the requirements necessary in real life.

4.11 Conclusion

Accounts receivable accounting ensures the cash flow of an enterprise by turning receivables into incoming payments. Two proverbs characterize this task area and the associated area of conflict: On the one hand, they say, "The customer is always right;" on the other hand, "Sales remain a gift until the goods are paid." This is the context in which the accounts receivable accountant works, and he is supported with SAP's innovations, such as SAP Credit Management, SAP Collections Management, and SAP Dispute Management. Reporting created in SAP NetWeaver BW is also useful to keep the current situation under control, particularly if the economic environment deteriorates regionally or globally and losses on receivables are possible.

Asset accounting concerns the management of complex fixed assets that are at the long-term disposal of an enterprise for the purpose of value creation. This chapter describes programs that can be used in SAP ERP Financials for the efficient and transparent organization of asset management.

5   Asset Accounting

This chapter describes the basic principles of asset accounting and the SAP subledger FI-AA (Asset Accounting). Asset Accounting, alongside accounts payable accounting and accounts receivable accounting, is one of the most important subledgers in accounting. The more asset-intensive an enterprise, the more significant the FI-AA component is. Tangible fixed assets are managed not only on the basis of their physical location, but on their value. In addition to local accounting principles, complex fixed assets are frequently valuated in accordance with IFRS or U.S. GAAP. In this context, the depreciation posting run and its parallel valuation is a main feature within Asset Accounting. The program for the depreciation posting run, which is a special new feature in Release ERP 6.0, is described in greater detail in Chapter 7, Closing Operations.

5.1   Business Principles

Fixed assets can be divided into tangible fixed assets, intangible fixed assets, and financial assets. Tangible fixed assets are complex fixed assets (buildings, machines, and so on) that are at the long-term disposal of an enterprise. Intangible assets are, for example, patents and licenses, whereas financial assets are shares in other enterprises, long-term securities, and long-term loan and mortgage claims. Traditional asset accounting encompasses the complete asset history, from the purchase order or initial acquisition (possibly managed as an "asset under construction" (AuC) through to retirement. The system calculates the values for depre-

Mapping tangible fixed assets

ciation, interest, insurance and other purposes between these two points in time and then makes these values available in many different forms in the asset accounting information system (AAIS). The calculation process for these values is automated to a large extent. In addition, an evaluation facilitates depreciation forecasting and the simulated development of asset values.

Country versions The FI-AA component is designed for international use in many countries and across a wide range of industries. In other words, no country-specific valuation rules have been hard-coded, which is especially beneficial for asset depreciation. At present, parallel valuation approaches in accordance with local and international depreciation regulations are the norm. The capitalization criteria for an asset in accordance with local regulations and the capitalization criteria for an asset in accordance with International Accounting Standards (IAS) largely correspond to each other. This means that, apart from some minor exceptions for intangible assets, there are no relevant (practical) differences between the capitalization prerequisites of both. When implementing an SAP system, the main task is to map the organization and structures of the enterprise in the system. In an SAP system, the organizational structures are divided according to the areas within an enterprise, each of which can be defined independently. However, to integrate the SAP systems, it is necessary to assign individual areas and their organizational structures to each other. The next section describes the organizational units of the FI-AA component and their assignments.

5.2 The SAP Software Component FI-AA

Integration considerations FI-AA (Asset Accounting) is used to manage and monitor tangible fixed assets within the SAP system. As part of the many integration relationships within the SAP system, data is transferred not only from other systems directly to asset accounting, but also from Asset Accounting to other systems. Therefore, when acquiring assets, it is possible to assign the invoice receipt and goods receipt in the materials management (MM) module   directly to the assets in the FI-AA component. Also, depreciation and interest can be transferred directly to Financial Accounting (FI) and cost accounting (CO). Like accounts receivable accounting and accounts payable accounting, Asset Accounting is also treated as a sub-ledger of Financial Accounting. However, for the FI-AA component to cover all legal and accounting requirements, it is necessary to define some organizational elements.

5.2.1 Chart of Accounts and Chart of Depreciation

The chart of depreciation summarizes the valuations permitted for each depreciation area (local law, tax depreciation, IAS, and so on). In other words, it describes the purpose of the calculation. The chart of depreciation, therefore, is a directory of depreciation areas organized according to business management requirements. The assignment of a company code to a chart of depreciation is independent of its assignment to a chart of accounts. Each company code uses exactly one chart of accounts and one chart of depreciation whereby a fixed relationship has not been defined between the chart of accounts and the chart of depreciation. This means that several company codes can use the same chart of accounts even though they are assigned to different charts of depreciation (and vice versa). Because asset accounting corresponds to the company code definition in general ledger accounting, it is essential to first set up a company code in FI. A chart of depreciation is then assigned to the company code (see Figure 5.1).

In the system, you can define several charts of depreciation for asset accounting. In general, a chart of depreciation is set up for each country and used by all company codes associated with this country. You must first copy this chart of depreciation from the reference chart of depreciation available in the system. The following objects are linked to a chart of depreciation:

Assignment per country

▶ Depreciation areas

▶ Investment support measures

▶ Depreciation keys

▶ Characteristics of transaction types

For reference purposes, SAP supplies country-specific charts of depreciation (sample charts of depreciation) in which different depreciation areas have been fully maintained.

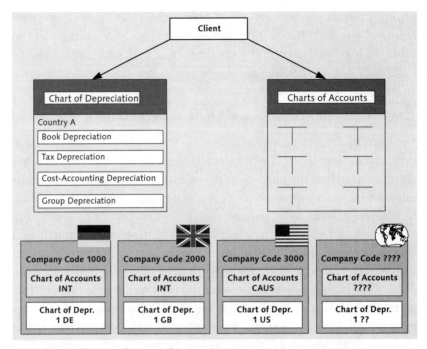

Figure 5.1 Definition of Charts of Depreciation

5.2.2 Depreciation Area

A depreciation area shows the valuation of a fixed asset for a particular purpose. It stores any information concerning the valuation of a complex fixed asset. The SAP component FI-AA provides the following options:

- Up to 99 depreciation areas can be used, in parallel, for each asset.
- If required, the values of a depreciation area can be posted automatically in FI.
- Depreciation areas can be used without restriction. There are no technical specifications.

Parallel valuations Each depreciation area permits the use of all forms of depreciation, interest, and revaluation calculation. Different depreciation areas can manage the same values and depreciation parameters, but show them in different currencies. You can use depreciation areas for various different valuations of all asset balances and transactions. Consequently, different valuation approaches exist for the following issues and business requirements:

- Local balancing of accounts in accordance with regional requirements

- The balance sheet for tax purposes (if another valuation is permitted)

- The balance sheet in accordance with IAS (if the valuation is necessary)

- Managerial accounting

- Parallel financial reporting (for example, as part of a group's balancing of accounts)

As shown in Figure 5.2, separate transaction figures are managed for each asset and depreciation area (asset balance sheet values, depreciation, net book values, and so on). Depreciation area 01 implements online postings to the general ledger, and documents are transferred on a one-to-one basis. This means that, during online posting, each original document assigned to an asset is posted to exactly one asset, without summarization.

Real-time integration

Asset xy in Year 2000		
	Balance Sheet Value	Depreciation	Net Book Value
Book Depreciation	100,000	40,000	60,000
Tax Depreciation	100,000	40,000	60,000
Cost Accounting Depreciation	100,000	10,000	90,000
Parallel Depreciation	100,000	10,000	90,000

Figure 5.2 Depreciation Areas of an Asset

[+] **Online Integration of Depreciation Area 01**

Only depreciation area 01, which is the master depreciation area in Asset Accounting, facilitates online integration into general ledger, accounts payable, or accounts receivable accounting.

Values can be posted periodically to other areas, and collective documents are written. If you have your own chart of depreciation when configuring the system, you deactivate any depreciation areas that you do not require, and you add depreciation areas that do not yet exist. You can also reactivate deactivated depreciation areas at any time.

5.2.3 Valuation Parameters

The FI-AA component provides a highly flexible design for individual depreciation areas. This is achieved through the use of a large number of valuation parameters, which you can use to define various factors that influence the calculation of depreciation. These factors are listed in Figure 5.3.

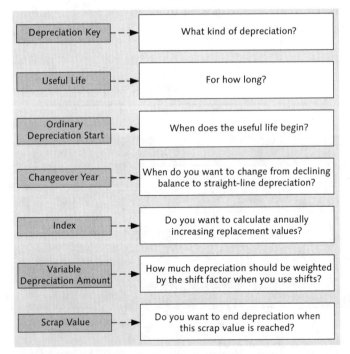

Figure 5.3 Valuation Parameters of a Depreciation Area

266

5.2.4 Value Transfer to General Ledger

When configuring the SAP system, you specify if and how values are posted from depreciation areas to the general ledger. When defining each individual depreciation area, you need to answer the following questions (see Figure 5.4):

▶ Will any values be posted?

▶ Will the asset balances be posted in real time and the depreciation values be posted periodically?

▶ Will the asset balances and depreciation values be posted periodically?

▶ Will only the depreciation values be posted periodically?

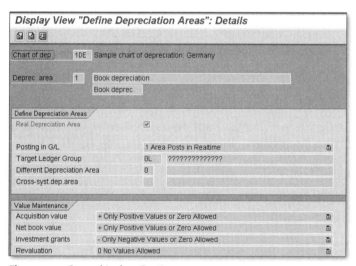

Figure 5.4 General Ledger Postings

For depreciation area 01, the system specifies that asset balances must be posted to the general ledger in real time. During periodic posting to the asset balance sheet account, you can also post values from other depreciation areas to the general ledger. The relevant depreciation areas can also post their asset balance sheet values from depreciation area 01 and still calculate other depreciation values and post them to the general ledger. In general, depreciation values are entered periodically and posted to the general ledger. You can also define depreciation areas that do not forward any values to the general ledger. Such areas are used for internal evaluation purposes only (for example, a depreciation area for tax depreciation).

5.2.5 Derived Depreciation Areas

The areas discussed above are known as real depreciation areas. In contrast, the system also uses derived depreciation areas. A derived depreciation area can consist of two or more real depreciation areas, which are linked by addition or subtraction. One possible use of derived depreciation areas is the calculation of reserves for special depreciation as a difference between legally permitted depreciation and specific depreciation in accordance with local law. Each time a posting is made and a depreciation value changes, the net book value rules for a derived depreciation area are checked in its real depreciation areas. If these basic definitions have been made in the FI module, you must consider the CO module to use FI-AA successfully.

5.2.6 Integration into Controlling

An asset is assigned to a cost accounting object (see Figure 5.5). It is therefore possible to use the following cost accounting objects:

- Cost center
- (Internal) order (real or statistical)
- Activity type

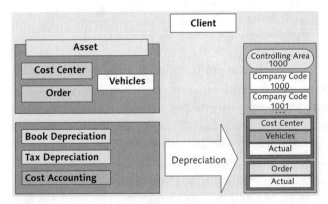

Figure 5.5 Assigning an Asset to Cost Accounting

You can post depreciation values from any depreciation area to cost accounting. For cost-accounting depreciation of an asset, you can use one of the following three options:

CO objects for depreciation postings

- Debiting a cost center
- Debiting a (real) order
- Debiting a cost center and a statistical order

> **Posting Depreciation Costs to Several CO Object Characteristics** **[+]**
>
> Example: If you want to post depreciation costs to several cost centers, you must allocate or distribute them in the CO module if, for example, a building is used by several departments and the various areas are to be debited with the depreciation costs. You can only ever define one CO object characteristic in an asset master record.

If you define a cost center and internal order in the master record of an asset, only the internal order is debited with the depreciation costs. Other SAP components may be used in addition to the FI and CO modules.

5.2.7 Integration Considerations

As part of the many integration relationships within the SAP system, data is transferred not only directly from modules to asset accounting, but also from Asset Accounting to other modules. For example, when acquiring assets or producing them in-house, the invoice and goods receipt or the withdrawal of material from the warehouse in the MM module is assigned directly to the assets in the FI-AA component. On the other hand, depreciation and interest can be transferred directly to Financial Accounting (FI) and Controlling (CO). Maintenance activities that must be capitalized can be settled from the PM module (plant maintenance) to the relevant assets. Figure 5.6 illustrates the interaction between various modules.

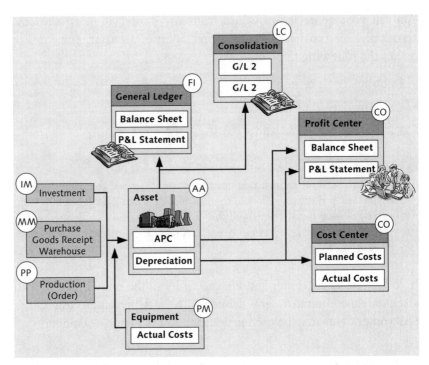

Figure 5.6 Integration Overview for FI-AA

Assets under construction

An asset is initially supplied by a vendor or produced in-house. The latter scenario concerns the asset under construction object. In this case, a third party (vendor object) supplies parts of the asset or provides services. If you deploy Investment Management (IM) or Controlling (CO), you can use a capital investment order or a special internal order to enter internal services. You can assign material withdrawals directly to the asset under construction object or initially to the corresponding internal order. At first, the corresponding order is settled in periodic intervals to the associated asset under construction before a special transaction is used to capitalize it to one or more assets. In the in-service phase, the asset is depreciated periodically in accordance with defined rules, and the calculated depreciation values are posted accordingly. At the same time, the CO object (cost center or order) defined in the asset master record is debited with the depreciation costs. This continues until the end of the asset's life when it is either scrapped or sold to a customer.

The definition of a chart of accounts and a chart of depreciation and the integration considerations of Controlling (CO), Materials Management (MM), Plant Maintenance (PM), and Investment Management (IM) provide a solid foundation for defining the master data in the next step.

5.3   Master Data

If you consider the various subledgers in the SAP system, the master data in every area represents an important starting point for subsequent business transactions. The master record information defined in Asset Accounting is particularly important. When structuring fixed assets in the SAP system, you can choose from the following three structural concepts:

- ▶ **Balance sheet level**
  The SAP system offers a three-level hierarchy at the balance sheet level. Here, a distinction is made between the balance sheet version, the balance sheet item, and the general ledger account.

- ▶ **Group level**
  At the group level, asset classes are used to structure fixed assets. The assets are structured according to legal or business requirements. Each asset belongs to exactly one asset class. Account determination is used to assign each asset to an individual balance sheet item.

- ▶ **Asset-related level**
  The SAP system offers a four-level hierarchy at the asset-related level. The group asset makes it possible to group a number of assets together for the purpose of a common valuation and depreciation. This is useful for complex machines and production lines, for example. The main asset number represents a complex fixed asset that is to be valuated independently. Below the main asset number, asset subnumbers can be used to further divide the asset into its asset components. These allow subsequent asset-related acquisitions to be considered separately. The lowest level consists of the transaction data that belongs to the relevant master record (line item).

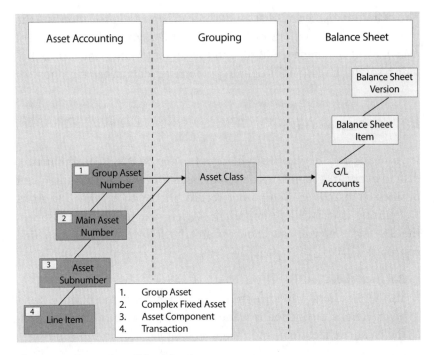

Figure 5.7 Structuring of Fixed Assets

5.3.1 Group Level: Asset Class

Complex fixed assets with comparable properties such as a common balance sheet account in the general ledger belong to the same asset class. Each asset created must reference exactly one asset class. Therefore, there is at least one asset class for "low-value assets" and one for "assets under construction." You can define control parameters and default values in each asset class.

Account determination
In Asset Accounting, asset classes are used to control account determination. Therefore, the account determination function must be defined in each asset class. The G/L accounts of the relevant chart of accounts, which are to be automatically posted for the various business transactions, are defined for this account determination (see Figure 5.9).

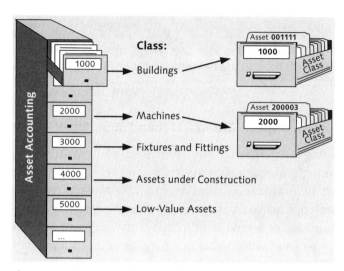

Figure 5.8 Using Asset Classes to Structure Assets

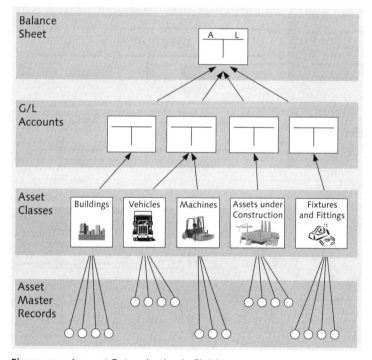

Figure 5.9 Account Determination in FI-AA

273

Asset Classes

Keep the number of asset classes in your SAP system as low as possible. In the asset master record, you can use many additional evaluation criteria for evaluation purposes.

5.3.2 Asset-Related Level: Group Asset and Subnumber

In addition to using asset classes to structure assets, you can also structure assets by using group assets or asset subnumbers. If you want a common depreciation calculation for several individual assets, you can group these assets together to form one group asset. However, if a complex fixed asset consists of several asset components that are to be valuated separately, you can divide a complex fixed asset into subnumber master records.

One reason for doing this may be to facilitate separate value developments for subsequent acquisitions or partial aggregates. Figure 5.10 shows how asset subnumbers are handled for subsequent acquisitions.

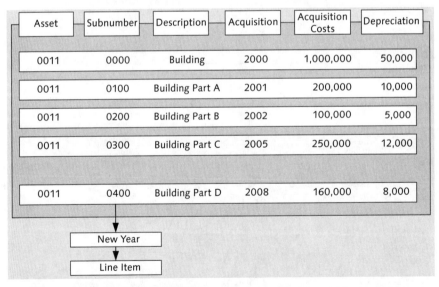

Asset	Subnumber	Description	Acquisition	Acquisition Costs	Depreciation
0011	0000	Building	2000	1,000,000	50,000
0011	0100	Building Part A	2001	200,000	10,000
0011	0200	Building Part B	2002	100,000	5,000
0011	0300	Building Part C	2005	250,000	12,000
0011	0400	Building Part D	2008	160,000	8,000

New Year

Line Item

Figure 5.10 Subsequent Acquisitions

In the system, a group asset is created as a separate master record. The relevant field in the asset master record is used to establish a connection between an asset and the group asset.

5.3.3 Creating Asset Master Records

Once structures have been defined for a group of tangible fixed assets, you can create master data under the menu path ACCOUNTING • FINANCIAL ACCOUNTING • FIXED ASSETS • ASSET • CREATE • ASSET (Transaction AS01). This menu path offers two alternatives:

▶ **Specification of company code and asset class**
The asset class delivers the most important parameters for the master record.

▶ **Specification of a reference**
The reference master record delivers the most important parameters for the master record.

The example provided in Figure 5.11 does not use a reference. In asset class 3200 for computers, we want to create five master records for company code 1000 in one step.

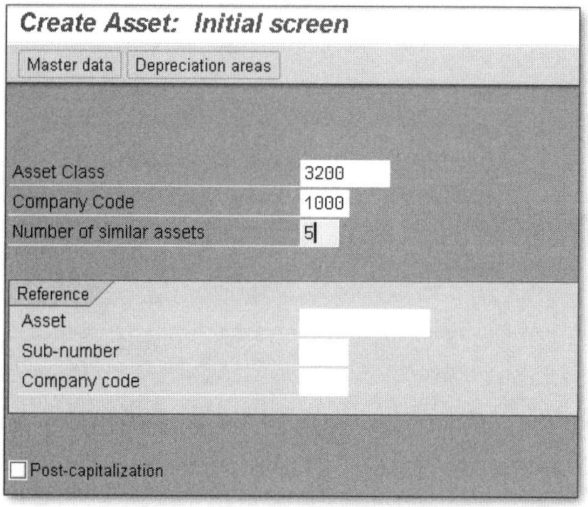

Create Asset: Initial screen

| Master data | Depreciation areas |

Asset Class	3200
Company Code	1000
Number of similar assets	5

Reference
Asset	
Sub-number	
Company code	

☐ Post-capitalization

Figure 5.11 Creating an Asset Master Record

You press ⌜Enter⌝ to access the screen on which you enter the master data (see Figure 5.12). Here, you define general asset data on the first tab page.

General Data

Inventory number

Account determination is transferred from the asset class that you have entered and cannot be changed. In this example, this is account determination 30000 for fixtures and fittings. All acquisition, retirement, depreciation, gain, and loss accounts are defined behind the configuration. The Inventory number field is optional. In some enterprises, the asset number corresponds to the inventory number. In such cases, no values are entered. If the FI-AA component has been implemented and if an enterprise has already affixed inventory number barcode stickers to its assets, it makes sense to enter this information in the Inventory number field.

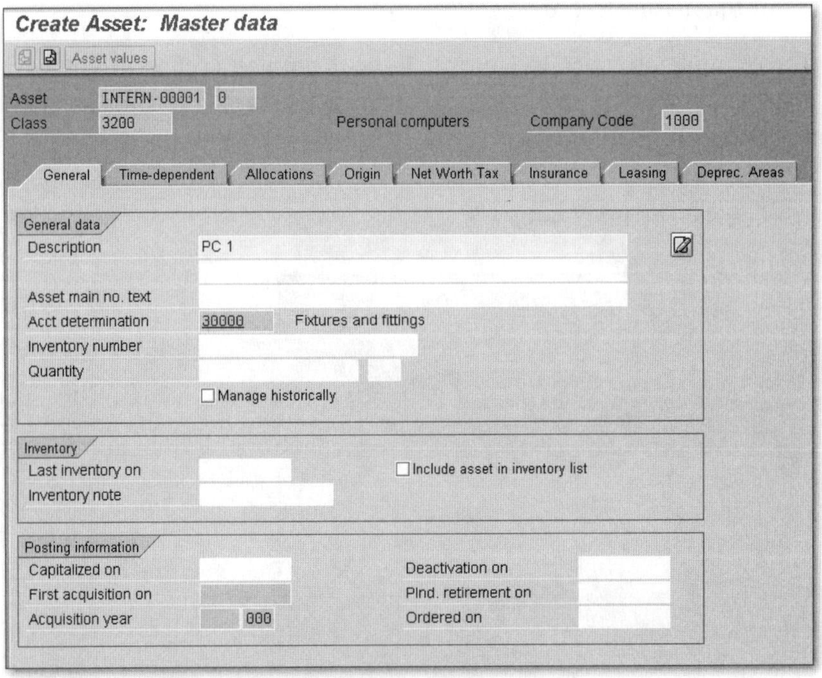

Figure 5.12 Creating an Asset—Initial Screen

Five PC master records are created in the example shown. If the Quantity field is used, a master record can also be used for quantity management. In this case, you would create only one master record for five PCs. However, one disadvantage associated with this method is the lack of traceability. For example, the selection criteria for the location or cost center are no longer available. This form of structuring may make sense for low-value assets where, for example, stools and tables are not managed with separate master records, but rather as one quantity. The system automatically maintains the data in the Posting information area the first time an acquisition is posted. Some of the information in an asset master record is managed as time-dependent data on the next tab page.

Quantity management

Time-Dependent Data

The time-dependent data is particularly important when allocating an asset in cost accounting. If depreciation is monthly, the system considers the current CO object. Figure 5.13 shows the tab page that contains the time-dependent data of an asset master record.

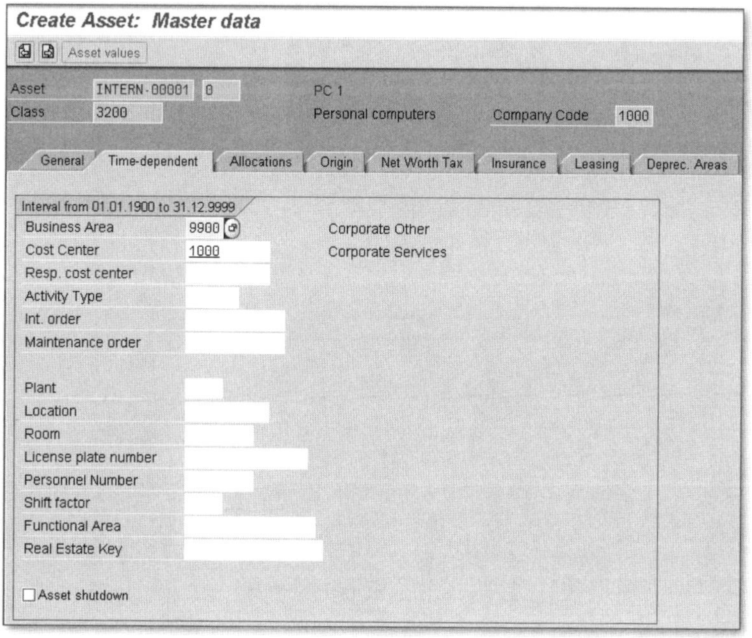

Figure 5.13 Time-Dependent Data

In this example, we want to post the depreciation values for PC1 to cost center 1000. Depreciation area 9900 is automatically determined from the master record for the cost center. In addition to depreciation, this area also contains the asset balance sheet values for creating business area balance sheets, if required. Optional fields for time-dependent data are also available. The Allocations tab page in the asset master data provides numerous options for later selections and evaluations.

Allocations

For evaluation purposes, there are up to five freely definable evaluation groups. Only four are shown in the example provided in Figure 5.14. Evaluation groups 1 and 2 have been defined. In addition, an asset super number can be used to summarize or "compound" several asset master records (for evaluation purposes).

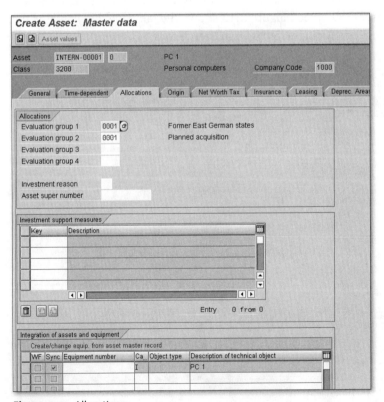

Figure 5.14 Allocations

The lower screen area shows the integration of assets and equipment into the Equipment Management module EAM (Enterprise Asset Management). If you save the asset master record, the contents are transferred to this module, and a master record is also generated.

Origin

Usually, the Origin tab is automatically filled when an asset is purchased. The vendor master record for the purchasing document is transferred to these fields.

Net Worth Tax

In some countries, there is a special form of taxation on fixed assets. If you require functions for a tax on nonincome values or net worth tax, you need the contents of this tab page. If your country does not have this special form of taxation, you can hide the entire master record tab.

Insurance

In certain cases, it is useful to insure valuable complex fixed assets. Figure 5.15 shows the information needed to manage insurance contracts.

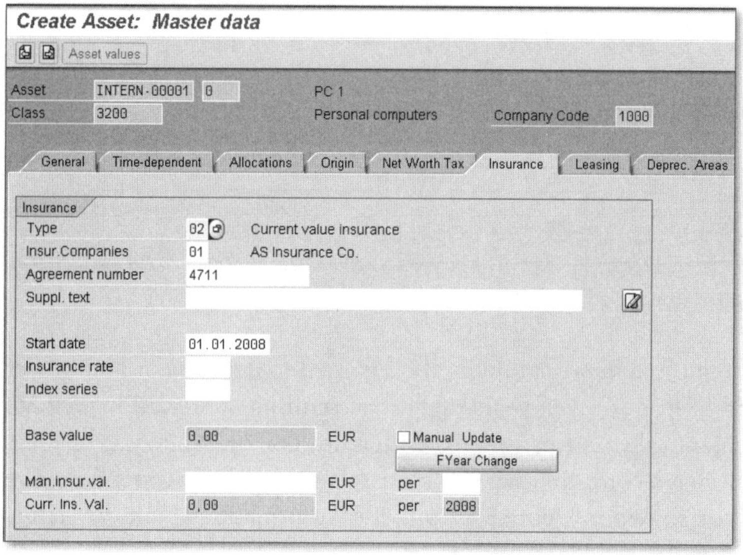

Figure 5.15 Insurance

Leasing

If you are the lessee of a complex fixed asset, you can enter information about the leasing contract on this tab page. Posting functions are available, but only to a limited extent.

[+]   **Leasing Management**

In FI-AA, the management of leasing contracts is rather rudimentary. If contracts change or if there are different valuation approaches for local law or IAS, the limitations of the software component FI-AA quickly become apparent. SAP therefore has its own solutions for lessors and lessees.

Valuation

When you create an asset master record, default values are transferred from the relevant asset class or reference master record. You can change or enhance these values. Figure 5.16 shows this valuation-relevant data for an asset master record.

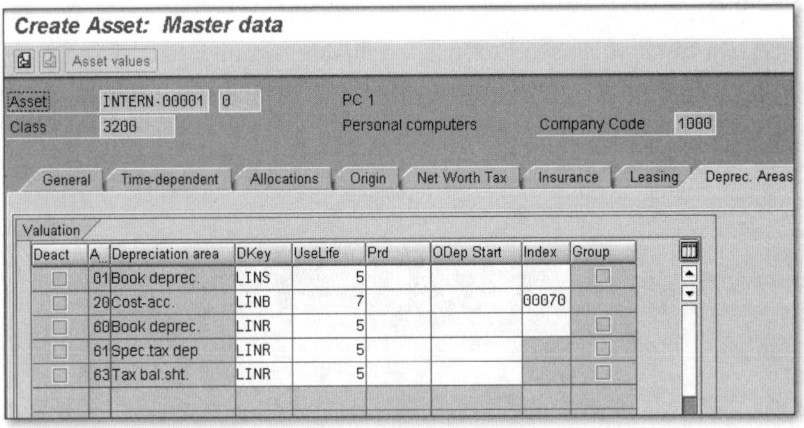

Figure 5.16   Valuation

The straight-line depreciation method is used to depreciate the PC over a period of five or seven years. In cost accounting depreciation area 20, replacement values are considered with index 00070. When you save the asset master record, the five similar assets are generated together. The dialog box shown in Figure 5.17 provides information about the status.

280

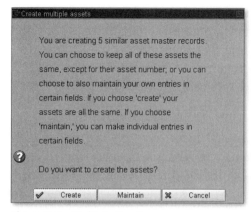

Figure 5.17 Multiple Creation

In practice, some input fields are maintained separately. The following five options are considered:

▶ Asset description

▶ Inventory number

▶ Business area

▶ Cost center

▶ Evaluation groups 1 to 5

If you choose Maintain, the system displays a dialog box in which you can maintain specific data for each asset. The system then transfers the entry that you made here to each cell in the column. You can now maintain the information individually for each asset (see Figure 5.18).

Multiple creation of master records

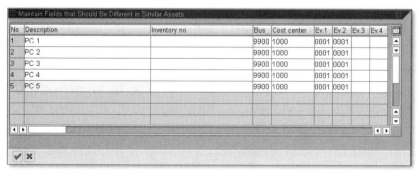

Figure 5.18 Multiple Selection — Maintaining Fields

Once these fields have been maintained and saved (using Save), the SAP system generates five new asset master records in one step. Acquisition postings can be maintained from this point onward. Also, the master records can be changed at any time.

5.3.4 Changing an Asset Master Record

The system generates a change document each time an asset master record is changed. This document contains a list of all modified fields and the number of changes in each field. The name of the person who made the changes is saved along with the old and new field content. To access the Change Asset transaction, follow the menu path ACCOUNT-ING • FINANCIAL ACCOUNTING • FIXED ASSETS • ASSET • CHANGE • ASSET (Transaction AS02).

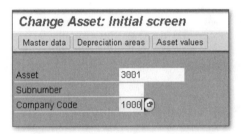

Figure 5.19 Changing an Asset—Initial Screen

Change document Press [Enter] to access the next screen (see Figure 5.20). You can now make changes on the relevant tab pages. To access the change documents, follow the menu path ASSET • DISPLAY • ASSET (from the Assets folder).

Once you have entered the asset number and, if necessary, the subnumber, you can access the change documents under the menu path ENVI-RONMENT • CHANGE DOCUMENTS • FOR CREATION.

You then double-click Asset Location, for example, to select one of the fields that have been changed (see Figure 5.21).

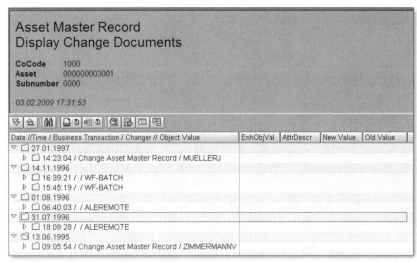

Figure 5.20 List of Fields Changed for an Asset

Display Change Document Item

Asset Master Record

Keyword	Technical Value	Prepared Value
Change doc. object	ANLA	ANLA
Object value	10000000000030010000	Asset: 3001-0 Schreibtisch Häussler normal
Document number	0000056778	
Date	27.01.1997	
Time	14:23:04	
Name	MUELLERJ	Joerg Mueller
Department		Olbert
Transaction code	AS02	Change Asset Master Record
Table Name	ANLZ	Time-Dependent Asset Allocations
Table Keys Long	8001000000000003001000099991231	To: 99991231
Field Name	WERKS	Plant
Attribute Descr.		Plant
New value	1300	1300
Old value	1100	1100
Change Indicator	U	Changed

Figure 5.21 List of Changes Made to a Field

This figure lists all of the changes made to this field since the master record was created. If you double-click on a specific change, the system displays details about this change (see Figure 5.22).

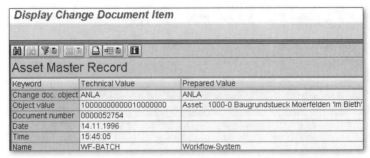

Figure 5.22 Detailed Information about a Change Made to a Field

5.3.5 The Asset Subnumber

If a complex fixed asset consists of several asset components, it may make sense, for technical reasons, to manage these asset components as subnumbers of an asset. Figure 5.23 shows this relationship.

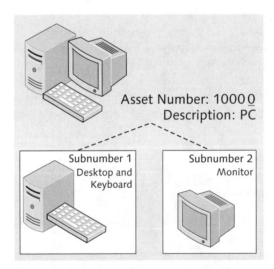

Figure 5.23 Overview of Asset Subnumber Management

To enter an asset subnumber (see Figure 5.24), follow the menu path ACCOUNTING • FINANCIAL ACCOUNTING • FIXED ASSETS • ASSET • CREATE • SUBNUMBER • ASSET (Transaction AS11). Press Enter to enter the master data (see Figure 5.25).

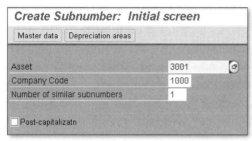

Figure 5.24 Creating a Subnumber—Initial Screen

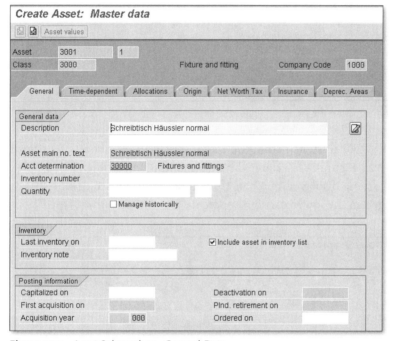

Figure 5.25 Asset Subnumber—General Data

Depending on how the relevant asset class has been configured, the data is copied from the master record of the main asset number and can still be changed, if necessary.

5.3.6 Blocking an Asset Master Record

Large enterprises, in particular, have very specific task sharing between accounts payable accounting and asset accounting. In these cases, new asset master records are requested long before an invoice receipt or acquisition posting. An effective method for preventing incorrect postings in the system is available under the menu path ACCOUNTING • FINANCIAL ACCOUNTING • FIXED ASSETS • ASSET • BLOCK. You can only post the acquisition after the master record has been checked (from a technical perspective) and released (unblocked). The preparatory work from Asset Accounting is performed, but incorrect postings are avoided. Figure 5.26 shows the initial screen of the transaction.

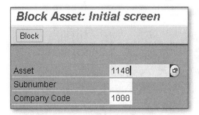

Figure 5.26 Blocking Assets—Request Screen

Preventing incorrect postings

Press [Enter] to switch from the initial screen to the processing screen shown in Figure 5.27. Here, the information concerning the complex fixed asset is displayed in a concise manner, and the acquisition lock is managed in the lower part of the screen.

Block Asset: Processing screen

Asset	1148	0	test1		
Class	1100		Buildings	Company Code	1000

General data

Description	test1

Acct determination	10000	Real estate and similar rights
Inventory number		
Quantity	0,000	

Posting information

Capitalized on		Deactivation on	
First acquisition on			
Acquisition year	0	Plnd. retirement on	

Acquisition lock

○ None
⦿ Locked to acquis.

Figure 5.27 Blocking Assets—Processing Screen

In practice, there are many more conceivable scenarios in addition to the aforementioned case of task sharing between accounts payable accounting and asset accounting. If you no longer require an asset master record, you can delete it under the menu path ACCOUNTING • FINANCIAL ACCOUNTING • FIXED ASSETS • ASSET • DELETE.

The following sections assume that the master records created earlier are also required and that the associated asset transactions already exist.

5.4 Asset Transactions

The business transactions for asset accounting are subdivided into transactions that cause a change in stock (acquisitions and retirements) and transactions that affect net income (depreciation and write-ups). To create an asset history sheet at the end of the year, an enterprise requires additional information (in other words, the "transaction type").

5.4.1 Transaction Types for Asset Transactions

The transaction type determines the type and content of a transaction. It controls the following points:

▶ Account assignment

▶ Which value fields are updated in which depreciation areas

▶ The assignment of the corresponding asset history sheet group

▶ Whether it concerns a debit or credit posting

▶ The document type

Each transaction type is assigned to exactly one transaction type group. Here, the main control properties of a transaction type (for example, which value fields or which associated G/L accounts) are derived from the assigned transaction type group. In addition, the transaction types categorize the possible business transactions (acquisitions, investment support measures, down payments, and so on). Note that the transaction type groups are fixed and cannot be changed. You can only define your own transaction types if you want to consider transactions in evaluations separately.

Fixed transaction type group

5.4.2 Document Types for Asset Acquisition

The document type is a two-digit alphanumeric key that is freely defined in Customizing. Exactly one number range is assigned to each document type (document storage). Account types are defined for each document type and must be used when creating a document. Document type AA means the document is posted as a gross amount, that is, without deducting a cash discount, whereas document type AN means the document is posted as a net amount, that is, with the cash discount amount deducted from the capitalization amount. The two examples provided below highlight the difference between these procedures.

Vendor Net Procedure

Example: The invoice amount is €10,000, and a cash discount of €500 (5%) is applied. Because there is a net posting, the value of asset 4711 immediately decreases by the invoice amount less the cash discount. In this example, the acquisition posting is €9,500.

Gross Procedure

Enhanced function in the new general ledger

With this method, an invoice amount of €10,000 is immediately forwarded to the complex fixed asset as an acquisition posting. The cash discount amount only reduces the acquisition costs of the complex fixed asset when the vendor payment (including the cash discount) has been made. Report SAPF181 is used to adjust the values at the end of the period. Section 5.6.2, Better Support for the Gross Procedure, describes the new general ledger's functional enhancement to the gross procedure.

5.4.3 Posting an Asset Acquisition

Acquisition costs and production costs are key terms in asset acquisition. They include the acquisition price and the incidental acquisition costs less the acquisition price reductions. Here, incidental acquisition costs are those costs needed to make an asset operational, whereby sales and administration costs and other overhead costs are only included in the acquisition costs if they can be attributed directly to the acquisition of the asset. Within an enterprise, the acquisition posting can be made in the department that is mainly responsible for the transaction. SAP ERP provides three options here (see Figure 5.28):

▶ In the FI-AA component with integrated accounts payable accounting without a purchase order reference

▶ In the FI-AA component without integrated accounts payable accounting and without a purchase order reference

▶ In the MM module (Materials Management) with integrated accounts payable accounting and a purchase order reference

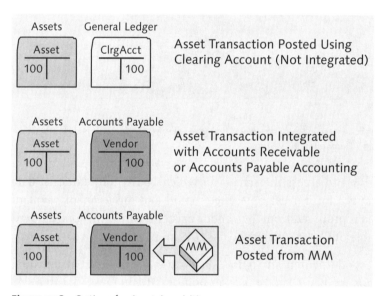

Figure 5.28 Options for Asset Acquisition

5.4.4 FI-AA with Integrated Accounts Payable Accounting Without a Purchase Order Reference

The "asset to vendor" posting is frequently made by accounts payable accounting, and it fulfills all of the requirements for Financial Accounting and Asset Accounting. When posting to the vendor account or asset account, the corresponding G/L accounts are automatically updated via the defined account determination (payables or asset balances). To enter an asset acquisition integrated with accounts payable accounting, follow the menu path ACCOUNTING • FINANCIAL ACCOUNTING • FIXED ASSETS • POSTINGS • ACQUISITION • PURCHASE • WITH VENDOR (Transaction F-90).

Here, you enter the relevant document header data, for example, the document date or document type (here: gross posting). You also enter the vendor (posting key 31 and vendor number) in the first line item. Figure 5.29 shows the initial entry screen for an integrated asset acquisition.

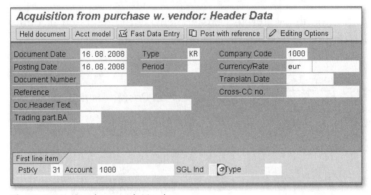

Figure 5.29   Purchase with Vendor

Personal value range

Press ⌈Enter⌉ to access the screen on which you enter additional data about the vendor, for example, the amount and the terms of payment (the value is proposed from the vendor master record). The total amount is a payable of €1,100, inclusive of a 10% input tax.

In the second line item in Figure 5.30, you enter the asset acquisition, that is, posting key 70 and the asset number. If you press ⌈F4⌉, the system displays your personal value range for Asset Accounting. Because, in this example, the five master records for the computer were initially created by the same user, they automatically appear in the personal value range.

Once you have selected an asset master record, you must enter a transaction type. To do this, you press ⌈F4⌉ to access a selection screen. In this example, transaction type 100 for acquisition postings was selected.

Even when there is a large number of transaction types, it is still easy to note the most important ones: 100—acquisition, 200—retirement, and 300—transfer.

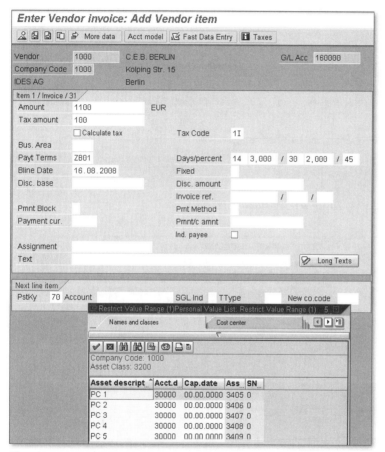

Figure 5.30 Purchase with Vendor—Initial Screen

If you press Enter, the system displays another screen on which you enter additional data. The complex fixed asset has a value of €1,000 and is operational for the enterprise as of 09/01/2008 (see Figure 5.32). Here, you use the reference date to define the start depreciation date.

Reference date as a capitalization date

291

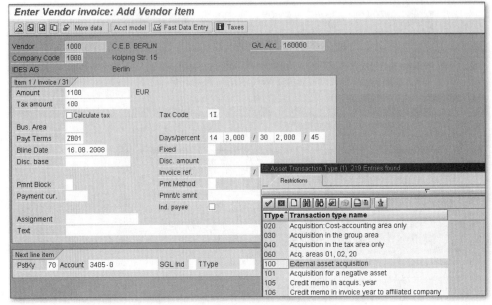

Figure 5.31 Purchase with Vendor—Transaction Types

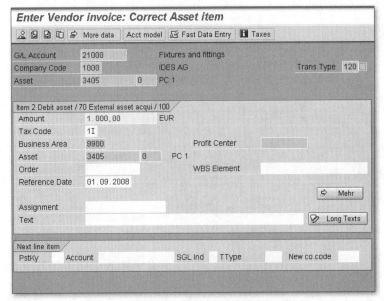

Figure 5.32 Purchase with Vendor—Entering an Asset Item

The first time an acquisition is posted, the system automatically writes the following information to the master record:

▸ Date on which the asset was capitalized (reference date)

▸ Initial acquisition date (reference date)

▸ Acquisition year and acquisition period (posting date)

The system derives the ordinary depreciation start date from the reference date of the acquisition posting in connection with the defined period control method (depreciation key) and then writes this date to the depreciation areas of the asset master record. The system uses the depreciation start date and the defined depreciation parameters to determine the planned annual depreciation and planned interest. If additional transactions are posted in the current year, these values are updated accordingly. In the case of an asset acquisition integrated with the accounts payable accounting component, the vendor is noted in the origin data of the master record.

The Asset Explorer transaction under the menu path ACCOUNTING • FINANCIAL ACCOUNTING • FIXED ASSETS • INFO SYSTEM • REPORTS ON ASSET ACCOUNTING • INDIVIDUAL ASSET menu path shows exactly how the acquisition is reflected in Asset Accounting. Proof of origin

Figure 5.33 shows asset 3405 with an acquisition value of €1,000. In addition, ordinary depreciation of €67 is already planned. If calculations are based on a useful life of five years, annual depreciation is 20%, that is, €200. Because 09/01/2008 was set as the asset value date, the depreciation period in 2008 is four months. Annual depreciation of €200 equates to €66.66 over a four-month period.

Using the Comparisons tab page, it is possible to look to the future. Figure 5.34 shows the value development of asset 3405. Other valuation approaches could be shown simultaneously in addition to depreciation area 01.

If, for organizational reasons, your enterprise cannot have integrated acquisition postings in accounts payable accounting and asset accounting, you can use a clearing account for acquisition postings.

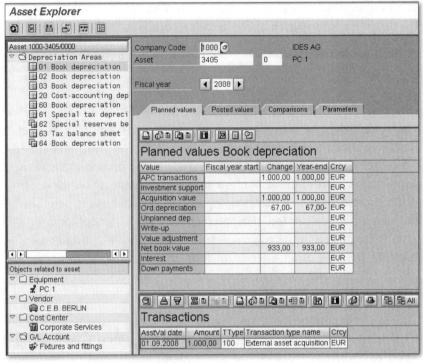

Figure 5.33   Asset Explorer—Planned Values

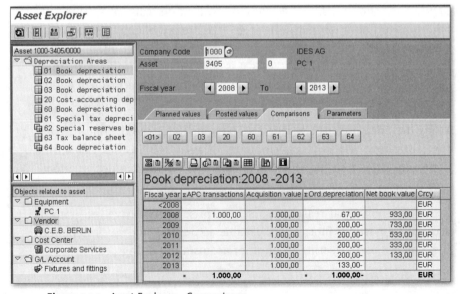

Figure 5.34   Asset Explorer—Comparisons

5.4.5 FI-AA Without Integrated Accounts Payable Accounting and Without a Purchase Order Reference

Posting of the asset acquisition is not integrated with accounts payable accounting. Instead, a clearing account is used. Figure 5.35 shows the initial screen of Transaction ABZON, which you can access via the menu path ACCOUNTING • FINANCIAL ACCOUNTING • FIXED ASSETS • POSTINGS • ACQUISITION • PURCHASE • ACQUISITION W.AUTOM. OFFSETTING ENTRY menu path.

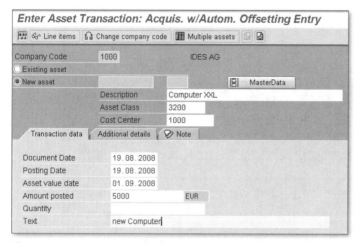

Figure 5.35 Acquisition with Clearing Account—Initial Screen

You use this SAP transaction to decide whether to use an existing master record or create a new master record.

However, you do not have the option of creating an asset master record directly from accounts payable accounting. In the example provided, we want to create a new master record with the description "Computer XXL," asset class "3200," and cost center "1000." If we want to maintain additional data, we can select MasterData. The relevant asset transaction data (for example, the capitalization amount and the asset value date) completes the entry screen for acquisition postings via a clearing account.

[+] **Clearing Account**

The clearing account must be managed on an open item basis, so that the account can be cleared. The clearing account is then cleared in a separate step, either manually under the menu path ACCOUNTING • FINANCIAL ACCOUNTING • FIXED ASSETS • POSTINGS • ACQUISITION • PURCHASE • CLEARING OFFSETTING ENTRY (Transaction F-91) or using the program SAPF124.

You can still check the document before posting (see Figure 5.36) under the menu path EXTRAS • SIMULATION.

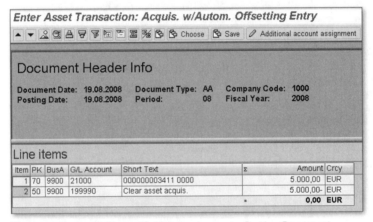

Figure 5.36 Acquisition with Clearing Account—Posting Document

Posting method with clearing account The SAP object "asset" from the FI-AA component is debited and, at the same time, the account determination defined in the asset master record is used for a posting to the associated balance sheet account 21000. The offsetting entry was made in clearing account 199990 (defined in the system), which is cleared when the invoice receipt is subsequently entered in Transaction F-91. Here, the SAP object "vendor" is also credited, and there is an automatic entry to the reconciliation account defined in the vendor master record.

If this method of acquisition posting does not satisfy the requirements of your enterprise, there is a third option, which involves Asset Accounting and Materials Management.

5.4.6 Acquisition in MM with Integrated Accounts Payable Accounting and a Purchase Order Reference

When the FI-AA component is integrated with the MM module, an asset acquisition can be posted using a purchase order handling. In this scenario, you can assign the purchase order or the purchase requisition directly to the asset. In the case of a goods receipt or invoice receipt, the system automatically capitalizes the asset. For account assignment category A (asset), you must enter an asset master record for the purchase order. Figure 5.37 shows a purchase order for a monitor. You define account assignment category A in the column next to item ID 10.

Purchase order with account assignment category A

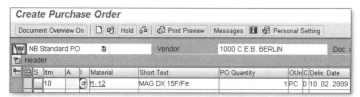

Figure 5.37 Purchase Order with Account Assignment Category A

If there is no master record, you can create an asset directly from the purchase order (see Figure 5.38).

Figure 5.38 Creating an Asset from a Purchase Order

For this account assignment, the system does not update any values or line items. Therefore, you can still change the account assignment up until the first goods receipt or invoice receipt. However, a "commitment" is generated for the "asset" object with account assignment. When you enter the purchase order, you can decide whether the system will capitalize the asset when you post the goods receipt or invoice receipt. Here, the Non-valuated GR selection means the goods receipt is not to be valuated for this item. Figure 5.39 shows the complete purchase order.

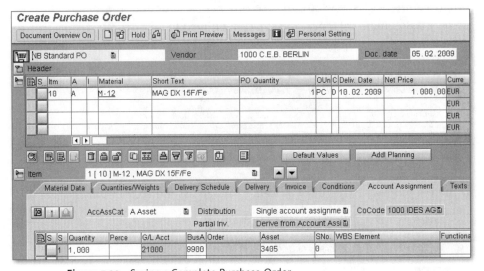

Figure 5.39 Saving a Complete Purchase Order

In this example, the asset is capitalized when you post the invoice receipt (nonvaluated goods receipt):

▸ **Valuated goods receipt**
When you post the goods receipt, the asset is capitalized with the value from the purchase order. The system automatically corrects any differences between the purchase order value and the invoice amount. For a goods receipt, the system posts the offsetting entry in the GR/IR clearing account (goods receipt/invoice receipt). For an invoice receipt, the clearing account is cleared.

▸ **Nonvaluated goods receipt**
The asset is not capitalized until the invoice is received. However, the system uses the goods receipt date as the capitalization date. In the

case of a goods receipt, the system does not generate an FI document, only an MM document (quantity). For an invoice receipt, the system generates the individual line items and updates the value fields.

The invoice receipt is entered in the invoice verification component in logistics (see Figure 5.40).

Logistical invoice verification enables the system to check a new incoming invoice against existing information (for example, the purchase order or goods receipt). This option is available under the menu path LOGISTICS • MATERIALS MANAGEMENT • INVOICE VERIFICATION • INVOICE VERIFICATION • DOCUMENT CREATION • ADD INVOICE (MRHR). You enter the document date, the document type (usually IR), and the relevant company code on this initial screen. The associated purchase order number, delivery note number, goods receipt document number, or account number of the vendor is then required to establish a reference to the purchase order, thus enabling the system to perform invoice verification. If a goods receipt has not been posted at that time, the invoice is automatically blocked for payment. This example does not contain any quantity or price differences.

Invoice receipt and capitalization

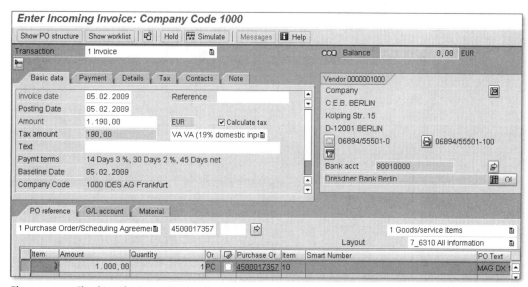

Figure 5.40 Checking the Incoming Invoice

The simulation in Figure 5.41 shows the account assignment lines to be expected. $1,000 is posted to G/L account 21000 (fixtures and fittings). The account determination of the "monitor" asset is named as the source.

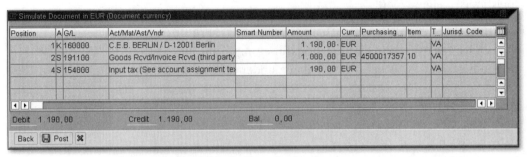

Figure 5.41 Simulating the Incoming Invoice

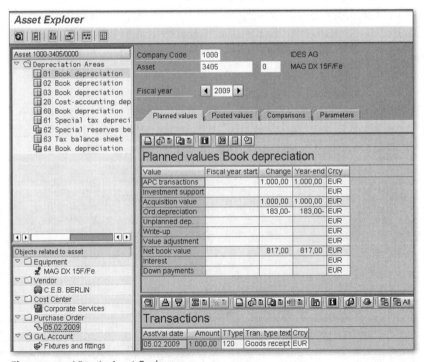

Figure 5.42 View in Asset Explorer

If the document has been posted, you can simulate the complete transaction in Asset Explorer. The Objects related to asset section in Figure 5.42 also shows a link to the purchase order—another pleasant side effect of the integration scenario involving the MM and FI-AA modules.

Acquisition postings can be made when the MM module or accounts payable accounting is integrated or when a clearing account is not integrated. A fourth option is available in addition to these three procedures. Complex fixed assets that are still in the process of being created can be managed as assets under construction (AuC). Examples include unfinished buildings or incomplete software implementations. On the date of completion, an asset under construction becomes a complex fixed asset that is available to the enterprise and can be depreciated. a stringent check is performed on this group of assets during the closing process, it will be discussed in greater detail in Chapter 7, Closing Operations.

Asset under construction

If the complex fixed asset is acquired in Asset Accounting, it runs through a depreciation life cycle until its retirement.

5.4.7 Depreciation

The wear and tear of a machine, computer or, in general, any complex fixed asset is recorded as depreciation in the balance sheet. Property is an exception because as it is not subject to wear and tear. Within the FI-AA component, it is necessary to differentiate between the following two depreciation types:

▸ Ordinary depreciation

▸ Unplanned depreciation

Ordinary depreciation is a periodic, scheduled, recurring loss in value. Chapter 7, Closing Operations, provides a detailed description of the depreciation posting run. In contrast to ordinary (planned) depreciation, unplanned depreciation is based on extraordinary circumstances. Because it does not concern a planned activity, we will use an example to take a closer look at unplanned depreciation.

The menu path ACCOUNTING • FINANCIAL ACCOUNTING • FIXED ASSETS • POSTINGS • MANUAL VALUE CORRECTION • UNPLANNED DEPRECIATION

Permanent decrease in value

301

leads you to the transaction shown in Figure 5.43. In this example, we want to adjust the value of the recently acquired computer in the year of acquisition, for exceptional reasons such as a user-inflicted hard disk defect. It is therefore necessary to permanently decrease the value of the complex fixed asset.

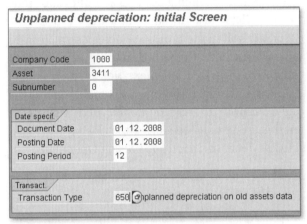

Figure 5.43 Unplanned Depreciation—Initial Screen

You press Enter to enter additional asset item data (see Figure 5.44). In this example, the value of the asset is to be decreased by €2,000, and the asset value date is 12/01/2008 for depreciation area 01.

Create Asset Transaction: Unplanned depreciation on new acquisition

Line Items

Asset	3411	0	Computer XXL
Company Code	1000		

Trans. Type 650 Unplanned depreciation on new acquisition

Posting data
Amount posted 2000 EUR
Asset val. date 01.12.2008

Additional details
Text broken Display

Reference

Figure 5.44 Entering an Asset Transaction

Transaction Type [+]

If unplanned depreciation concerns a complex fixed asset that was acquired in the same fiscal year, select transaction type 650 (unplanned depreciation on new acquisition) as shown in this example. If depreciation takes places the following year, use transaction type 660 (unplanned depreciation on old asset data), which the system proposes by default.

If you press [Enter], the entry is confirmed and the system runs through various screens with valuation approaches for each depreciation area. Figure 5.45 shows depreciation area 03 (U.S. GAAP). You can choose to make an identical decrease in value for each area.

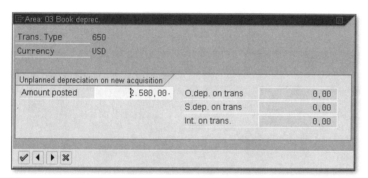

Figure 5.45 Entering an Asset Transaction for Each Depreciation Area

Once the system has processed all of the depreciation areas, it returns to the original overview in Figure 5.44. If you want to change valuation methods in one of the deprecation areas before the posting, select Line Items to make such changes. Figure 5.46 shows an overview of the areas posted.

If all of the values are entered correctly, the SAP system initially posts the document to the subledger only. It is then transferred to the general ledger the next time the system performs a planned, periodic depreciation posting run. The Asset Explorer transaction under the menu path ACCOUNTING • FINANCIAL ACCOUNTING • FIXED ASSETS • INFO SYSTEM • REPORTS ON ASSET ACCOUNTING • INDIVIDUAL ASSET shows an indirect effect of the transaction on the planned values (see Figure 5.47).

303

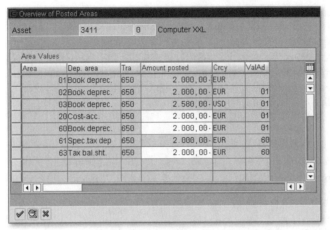

Figure 5.46 Overview of the Areas Posted

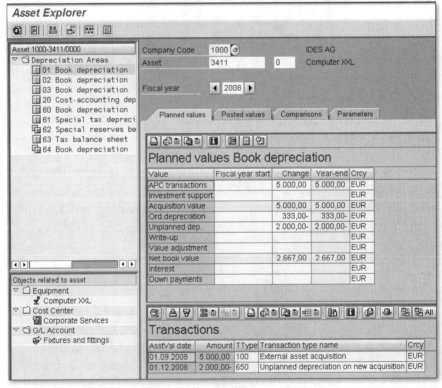

Figure 5.47 Planned Values in Asset Explorer

> **Planned Values and Posted Values** [+]
>
> Asset Explorer distinguishes between two categories, *planned values* and *posted values*, to distinguish between valuation approaches in FI-AA (planned values) and FI-GL (posted values).

Acquisition and subsequent depreciation are just two aspects of the life cycle of a complex fixed asset. One final consideration is asset retirement.

5.4.8   Asset Retirement

A nonrevenue asset retirement is identical to scrapping. Ideally, you would like revenue generated from the sale of an asset to exceed its book value. In this scenario, we use the term *gains*. Conversely, if revenue falls short of the book value, this is deemed to be a loss. There are three different ways to post the retirement of an asset in the SAP system:

Gain and loss

▶ With or without revenue

▶ With or without a customer

▶ As a complete or partial retirement

The following sections describe these options in more detail.

Asset Retirement with Revenue and Customer

The following example shows a complete retirement with revenue obtained from selling an asset to a customer. The system automatically calculates the loss and adjusts the corresponding asset balance and proportional accumulated depreciation. The asset value date and the period control method of the depreciation key are used to determine the asset value period of the asset retirement. The proportional accumulated depreciation calculated as a result of the retirement is withdrawn for the specific period. At the same time, the system also posts the asset retirement. Therefore, a gain or loss is the balance of the asset retirement amount, the accumulated depreciation amount, and the revenue obtained from the customer for the asset. This example uses the following values:

Asset balance	*242,000*
Depreciation	*72,600*
Revenue	*130,000*
Loss	*39,400*

The menu path ACCOUNTING • FINANCIAL ACCOUNTING • FIXED ASSETS • RETIREMENT • RETIREMENT WITH REVENUE • WITH CUSTOMER provides the option of posting the receivables posting to the customer, the revenue posting, and the asset retirement in one step.

Revenue account for asset retirements On the next screen (see Figure 5.48), you enter the relevant document header data such as the document date or document type. The first step is to enter the customer item. This is done by entering the corresponding posting key (usually 01) and the customer account number. You then press Enter to enter the remaining customer item data (see Figure 5.49). You have to enter the amount and customer item data here before you can enter the asset item. The corresponding posting key is 50 because it is a revenue item. In this example, the G/L account is 820000 (Proceeds from disposal/sale fixed assets).

If you press Enter, the system displays the screen shown in Figure 5.50.

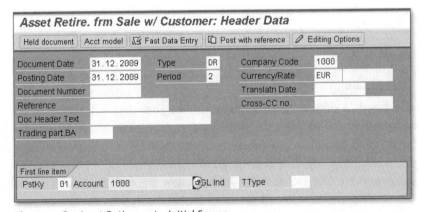

Figure 5.48 Asset Retirement—Initial Screen

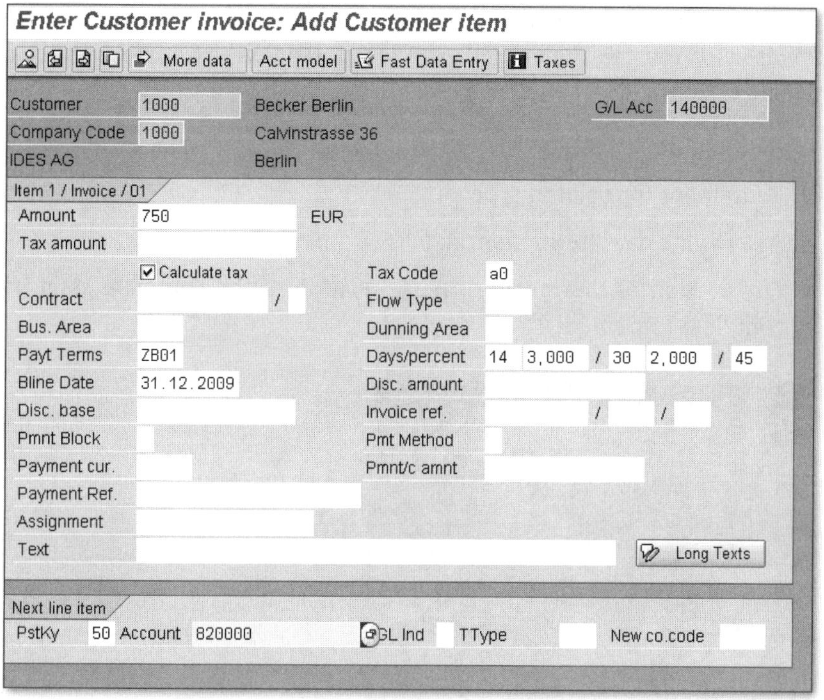

Enter Customer invoice: Add Customer item

  ☒ 🖫 ▣ ▯ ⇨ More data   Acct model   🖳 Fast Data Entry   🔢 Taxes

Customer	1000	Becker Berlin	G/L Acc	140000
Company Code	1000	Calvinstrasse 36		
IDES AG		Berlin		

Item 1 / Invoice / 01

Amount	750		EUR					
Tax amount								
	☑ Calculate tax		Tax Code	a0				
Contract		/	Flow Type					
Bus. Area			Dunning Area					
Payt Terms	ZB01		Days/percent	14	3,000	/ 30	2,000	/ 45
Bline Date	31.12.2009		Disc. amount					
Disc. base			Invoice ref.		/	/		
Prnt Block			Pmt Method					
Payment cur.			Pmnt/c amnt					
Payment Ref.								
Assignment								
Text					📝 Long Texts			

Next line item

PstKy   50   Account   820000   🔘GL Ind   TType   New co.code

Figure 5.49   Asset Retirement—Customer Item

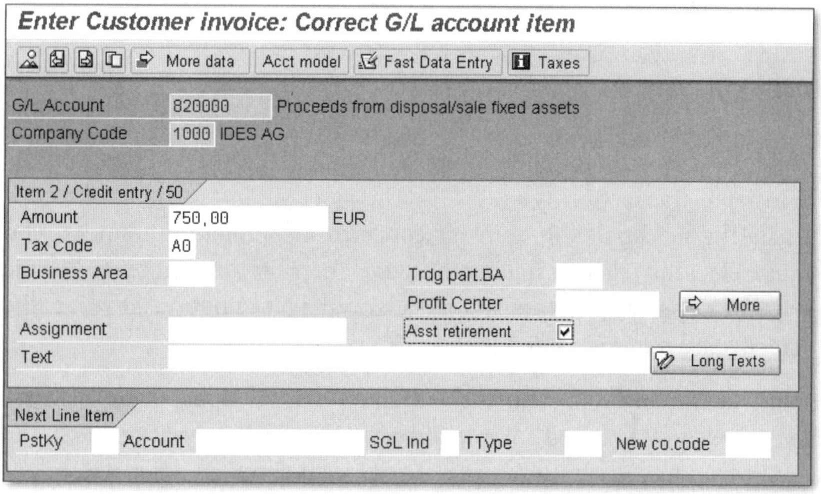

Enter Customer invoice: Correct G/L account item

  ☒ 🖫 ▣ ▯ ⇨ More data   Acct model   🖳 Fast Data Entry   🔢 Taxes

G/L Account	820000	Proceeds from disposal/sale fixed assets	
Company Code	1000	IDES AG	

Item 2 / Credit entry / 50

Amount	750,00	EUR		
Tax Code	A0			
Business Area		Trdg part.BA		
		Profit Center		⇨ More
Assignment		Asst retirement	☑	
Text			📝 Long Texts	

Next Line Item

PstKy   Account   SGL Ind   TType   New co.code

Figure 5.50   Asset Retirement—Revenue Item

When posting to the revenue account, you must select the Asset retirement field. You can then enter the relevant data on the next screen (see Figure 5.51):

- Asset number
- Retirement transaction type
- Asset value date (retirement date)
- The portion of the retiring part in relation to the complete asset or complete retirement

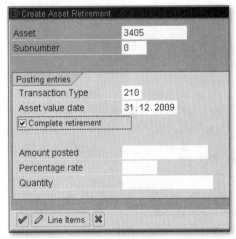

Figure 5.51 Asset Retirement—Asset Information

Complete or partial retirement

You now enter the number of the retiring asset in the SAP system; the associated transaction type is 210. The asset value date is used to calculate the net book value. If this concerns a complete retirement, you must select the relevant field. Otherwise, enter the amount posted or the retirement percentage rate. Then click on the NEXT button to access the screen shown in Figure 5.52.

If the document is posted, the retirement date is updated in the asset master record. A retired complex fixed asset is no longer available in the enterprise. In the next example, we want to show an asset retirement that does not directly reference a buyer (customer).

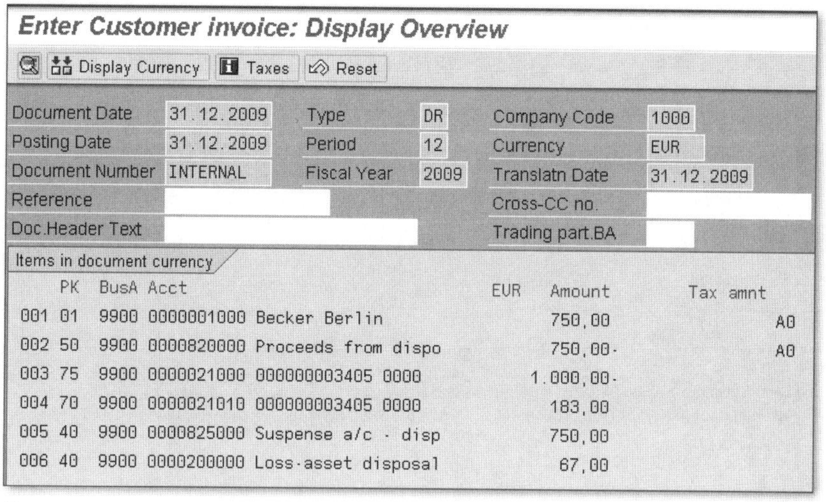

```
Enter Customer invoice: Display Overview

  🔍 📊 Display Currency   ℹ️ Taxes   🖉 Reset

  Document Date    31.12.2009   Type      DR    Company Code    1000
  Posting Date     31.12.2009   Period    12    Currency        EUR
  Document Number  INTERNAL     Fiscal Year 2009 Translatn Date  31.12.2009
  Reference                                      Cross-CC no.
  Doc.Header Text                                Trading part.BA
  Items in document currency
      PK  BusA Acct                         EUR   Amount     Tax amnt
  001 01  9900 0000001000 Becker Berlin           750,00           A0
  002 50  9900 0000820000 Proceeds from dispo     750,00-          A0
  003 75  9900 0000021000 000000003405 0000      1.000,00-
  004 70  9900 0000021010 000000003405 0000       183,00
  005 40  9900 0000825000 Suspense a/c · disp     750,00
  006 40  9900 0000200000 Loss·asset disposal      67,00
```

Figure 5.52 Asset Retirement—Simulated Document

Asset Retirement with Revenue Without a Customer

Under the menu path ACCOUNTING • FINANCIAL ACCOUNTING • FIXED ASSETS • RETIREMENT • RETIREMENT WITH REVENUE • WITHOUT CUSTOMER, you can post an asset retirement that does not reference a customer.

The initial transaction is shown in Figure 5.53. Here, you can define the asset number, document date, posting date, and asset value date in a clear and concise manner.

In the example, it is Christmas time and we want to sell the computer that was acquired for €5,000 and whose value has decreased by €2,000 (due to exceptional circumstances) for €100. If you consider the planned and incurred depreciation of €333, there is a total loss of €2,567. Figure 5.54 shows the entire posting document as part of a simulation.

Sales without a customer may make sense for small amounts or cash sales. If the complex fixed asset remains the property of one of the enterprises within the group, this is deemed to be a transfer, not a sale.

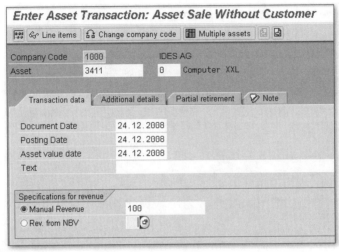

Figure 5.53 Asset Sale Without a Customer

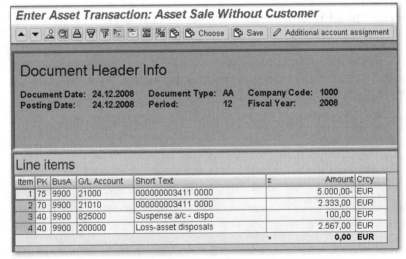

Figure 5.54 Sale Without a Customer—Simulating a Document

5.4.9 Asset Transfer

Transfer or asset transfer

Depending on the underlying business transaction, the FI-AA component distinguishes between intracompany-code transactions (transfers) and transactions between different company codes (asset transfers).

310

There are several possible reasons for a transfer:

▸ A master record was created in or posted to the wrong asset class.

▸ There has been a change of location and you need to change non-modifiable organizational allocations in the master record (for example, the business area).

▸ You want to split up an asset.

▸ You want to settle an asset under construction.

If a new master record is created within the transfer transaction, you can use field transfer rules to determine which of the input fields are to be transferred from the source asset to the master record of the target asset. The following example concerns a transaction under the menu path ACCOUNTING • FINANCIAL ACCOUNTING • FIXED ASSETS • RETIREMENT • TRANSFER.

On the initial screen of the transfer (see Figure 5.55), you enter the asset number that you want to transfer and the asset value date, which is used to calculate the net book value. If the asset to which you want to transfer exists already, you must specify another asset number. Otherwise, you can enter the new asset master record here.

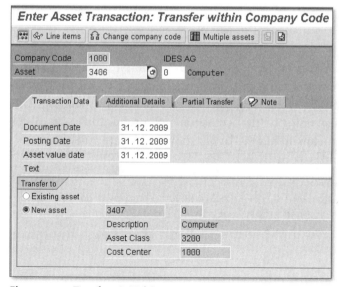

Figure 5.55 Transfer—Initial Screen

Transfer variant
defines the
transaction When you switch to the Additional Details tab page, the system displays the screen shown in Figure 5.56. Here, you can enter the document type and transfer variant. These enable you to control whether the transfer variant concerns an intracompany-code transfer or a cross-company-code asset transfer and how the asset values are transferred from the sending asset to the target asset.

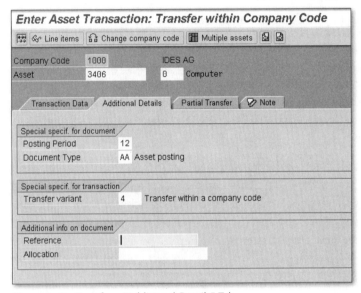

Figure 5.56 Transfer—"Additional Details" Tab

Because only 50% is to be reposted in this example, you must switch to the Partial Transfer tab page (see Figure 5.57). On this tab page, you enter the percentage rate of the partial transfer or corresponding posting amount, depending on the acquisition and production costs. In this example, the document has the layout shown in Figure 5.58.

[+] **Business area balance sheets**

If business area balance sheets are active in your company code, you cannot simply change the field in the asset master record. Furthermore, complete balance sheets require transfers from and to business areas.

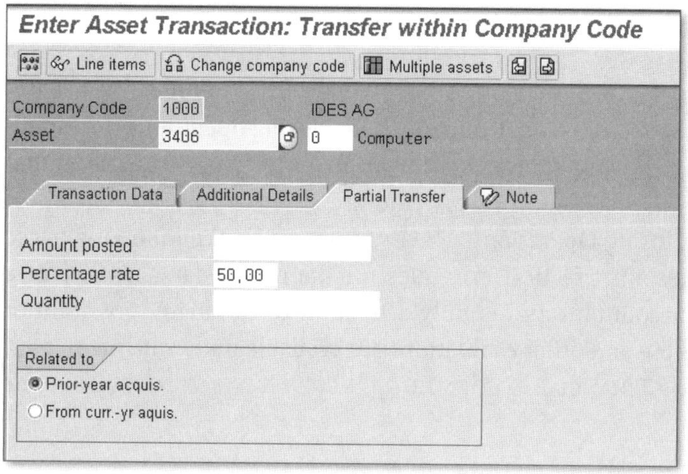

Figure 5.57 Transfer—"Partial Transfer" Tab Page

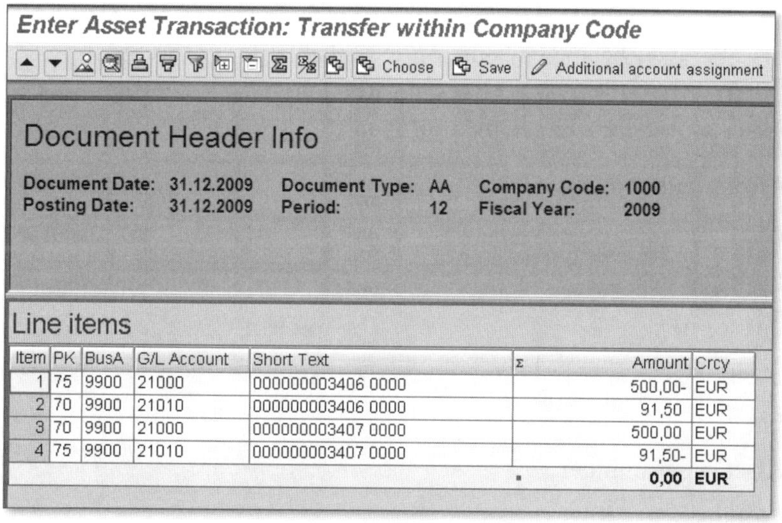

Figure 5.58 Transfer—Accounting Document

Irrespective of whether you use a transfer, acquisition, or retirement to clearly represent business transactions, numerous evaluations are available in the FI-AA component.

5.5 Evaluations in Asset Accounting

SAP ERP and SAP NetWeaver BW have a wide range of predefined evaluations for asset accounting. Evaluations for closing operations (for example, the asset history sheet, lists for an inventory, or evaluations that concern the depreciation posting run) are described in more detail in Chapter 7, Closing Operations. The information on the following pages merely represents practical examples for the day-to-day activities of a fixed asset accountant and is only a fraction of the many possibilities available. These and other evaluations are available under the menu path ACCOUNTING • FINANCIAL ACCOUNTING • INFO SYSTEM • REPORTS ON ASSET ACCOUNTING.

5.5.1 Asset Balance

With a view to obtaining a fast, compact overview of complex fixed assets, the asset balance evaluation is available under the menu ASSET BALANCE • ASSET LIST • ASSET BALANCE. The following sorting criteria can be used to preselect the recipient of the list:

- Asset number
- Asset class
- Business area
- Cost center
- Plant
- Location
- Asset super number
- Worklists

Creating groups Irrespective of whether you are the cost center manager, plant manager, or department manager of a business area or department at location XY, a corresponding asset balance evaluation is available for each target group. Figure 5.59 shows the selection screen, which is sorted according to asset number. For company code 1000, we want to list individual assets for the key date 12/31/2008. Alternatively, the asset groups could also be summarized together.

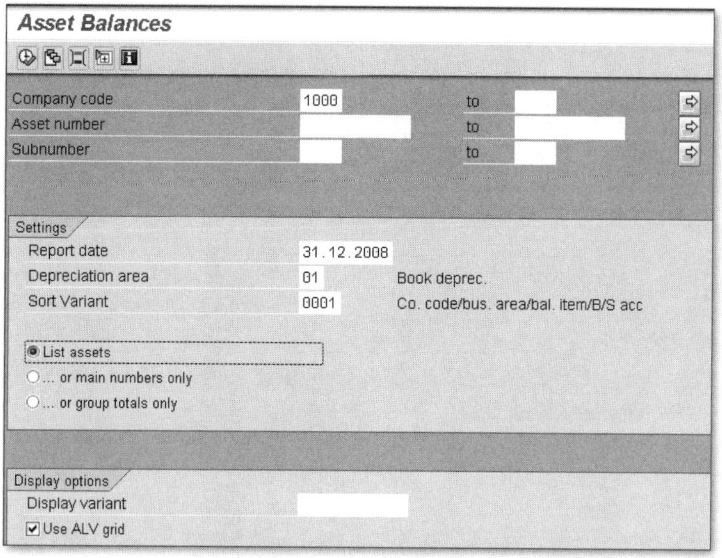

Figure 5.59 Selection Screen for Asset Balances

Figure 5.60 shows a list of asset balances. In accordance with the sorting key on the selection screen, the following different asset classes are listed consecutively:

- ▶ 3000 – Fixtures and fittings
- ▶ 3100 – Vehicles
- ▶ 3200 – Personal computers

These three groups belong to the same balance sheet item and are also accumulated on the basis of the sorting key. The values in the columns for the acquisition value, accumulated depreciation, and book value refer to the depreciation area selected, namely depreciation area 01 (U.S. GAAP). A corresponding book value of €0 shows that these assets have already been fully depreciated, but are still available to the enterprise. In other words, they have not been retired, which is frequently the case in a demo system, but very much an exception in practice.

The next report will show which assets were previously master records, but had no acquisition value.

Asset Balances

Asset Balances - 01 Book deprec.

Report date: 31.12.2008 - Created on: 19.08.2008

Asset	SNo.	Capitalized on	Asset description	Σ	Acquis.val.	Σ	Accum.dep.	Σ	Book val.	Crcy
Asset Class 3100 Vehicles				*	153.000,00	*	153.000,00-	*	0,00	EUR
3240	0	17.05.1995	Apple Macintosh Laptop		1.968,47		1.968,47-		0,00	EUR
3256	0	25.04.1997	Laptop		2.000,71		2.000,71-		0,00	EUR
3258	0	25.04.1997	Laptop		2.000,71		2.000,71-		0,00	EUR
3362	0	05.11.2001	PC 02		1.800,00		1.800,00-		0,00	EUR
3363	0	05.11.2001	PC 03		1.800,00		1.800,00-		0,00	EUR
3364	0	05.11.2001	PC 04		1.800,00		1.800,00-		0,00	EUR
3365	0	05.11.2001	PC 05		1.800,00		1.800,00-		0,00	EUR
3259	0	25.04.1997	Laptop		2.000,71		2.000,71-		0,00	EUR
3361	0	01.11.2001	PC 01		1.800,00		1.800,00-		0,00	EUR
3366	0	05.11.2001	PC 06		1.800,00		1.800,00-		0,00	EUR
3257	0	25.04.1997	Laptop		2.000,71		2.000,71-		0,00	EUR
Asset Class 3200 Personal computers				*	20.771,31	*	20.771,31-	*	0,00	EUR
Acquisition:Acquis. and production costs 21000 Office equipment				**	237.022,58	**	237.022,58-	**	0,00	EUR
Balance sheet item 1032031 Acquisition value				***	237.022,58	***	237.022,58-	***	0,00	EUR
Business Area 7000 Electronic Products				****	7.426.538,67	****	1.997.634,56-	****	5.428.904,11	EUR
2039	0	01.01.1995	PC-Prüfgerät		45.760,62		45.760,62-		0,00	EUR
2042	0	01.01.1995	Werkzeugsatz für PC-Prüfung		16.105,69		16.105,69-		0,00	EUR
2040	0	01.01.1995	PC-Prüfgerät		45.760,62		45.760,62-		0,00	EUR
2041	0	01.01.1995	Werkzeugsatz für PC-Prüfung		16.105,69		16.105,69-		0,00	EUR
Asset Class 2000 Machines decl. depr.				*	123.732,62	*	123.732,62-	*	0,00	EUR
Acquisition:Acquis. and production costs 11000 Machinery and equip.				**	123.732,62	**	123.732,62-	**	0,00	EUR
Balance sheet item 1032021 Acquisition value				***	123.732,62	***	123.732,62-	***	0,00	EUR
3272	0	04.08.1997	PC-Prüfgerät		4.348,21		4.348,21-		0,00	EUR
Asset Class 3000 Fixture and fitting				*	4.348,21	*	4.348,21-	*	0,00	EUR
3228	0	01.01.1995	Mercedes MB100D (Einsatzfahrzeug techn. Support)		50.905,89		50.905,89-		0,00	EUR
3229	0	01.01.1995	Mercedes Benz MB100D (Einsatzfahrzeug PC-Service)		50.905,89		50.905,89-		0,00	EUR
3231	0	01.01.1995	Mercedes Benz MB100D (Werkstattf.mit Spezialeinr.)		52.333,79		52.333,79-		0,00	EUR
3354	0	30.04.1999	VW Transporter		21.985,55		21.985,55-		0,00	EUR

Figure 5.60   List of Asset Balances

5.5.2   Directory of Unposted Assets

When tasks are shared between Asset Accounting and accounts payable accounting (acquisition with clearing account), it is particularly important to always have an overview of those master records that can be used for acquisition postings. You can access the relevant transaction (see Figure 5.61) by following the menu DAY-TO-DAY ACTIVITIES • INTERNATIONAL • DIRECTORY OF UNPOSTED ASSETS.

In the example provided, the selection is made in company code 1000 until the key date 12/31/2008.

If some assets have older dates, they can usually be blocked or deleted. A list of current master records is helpful for business transactions planned for the future. The evaluations entitled Directory of Unposted Assets and Asset Balances are merely two examples. Other evaluations are available under the same menu path.

The next section describes the practical effects of the SAP General Ledger on Asset Accounting in more detail.

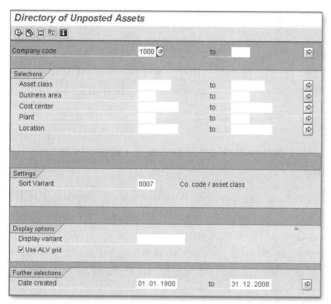

Figure 5.61 Selection Screen for the Directory of Unposted Assets

Directory of Unposted Assets

Directory of Unposted Assets

Assets | Break down grp. asset

Directory of Unposted Assets

- Created on: 19.08.2008

Asset	SNo.	Created on	Created by	Asset description
1160	0	02.06.2008	I033202	Vehicles
1161	0	28.07.2008	I809095	Banda transportadora
1148	0	22.10.2007	I033543	test1
1154	0	29.01.2008	D035500	Gebäude 2
2187	0	03.12.2002	ZUERKER	Asset for 4230
2188	0	03.12.2002	ZUERKER	Asset for 4230
2189	0	03.12.2002	ZUERKER	Asset for 4230
2304	0	16.10.2007	D000145	Beutelmaschine MB01
2309	0	01.07.2008	I041233	Asset Revaluation-001
2310	0	03.07.2008	I041233	Asset Revaluation-001
2314	0	28.07.2008	I054184	demo Affinity2
2307	0	29.01.2008	I003565	Pizza Machine
3005	1	10.03.2008	I041233	Group Asset1-1
3414	0	05.02.2008	I036794	Proton Waja 1.8
3921	0	02.06.2008	I053443	Camry
3922	0	08.06.2008	I043127	Road show truck group 17
3922	1	08.06.2008	I043127	Road show truck group 17
3922	2	08.06.2008	I043127	Road show truck group 17
3412	0	23.01.2008	D035500	Computer
3416	0	11.02.2008	D035500	Computer
3417	0	11.02.2008	D035500	Computer
3418	0	11.02.2008	D035500	Computer
3419	0	11.02.2008	D035500	Computer
3420	0	11.02.2008	D035500	Computer
3421	0	11.02.2008	D035500	Computer
3422	0	11.02.2008	D035500	Computer

Figure 5.62 Directory of Unposted Assets

317

5.6 Effects of New General Ledger on FI-AA

Even though the SAP General Ledger is a new optional component in SAP ERP Financials, its use is increasingly widespread. At this point, however, it is enough to mention just some of its features in conjunction with FI-AA.

5.6.1 Use of Delta Depreciation Area for Parallel Financial Reporting

Ledger approach in new G/L

Asset Accounting and its various depreciation areas support parallel financial reporting. SAP R/3 predominantly consisted of various asset balance sheet accounts and depreciation accounts that were mainly assigned to the depreciation area for each accounting principle. The new general ledger changes this defined storage location. Instead of different accounts, ledgers are now associated with the depreciation area for each accounting principle. However, the ledger approach in the SAP General Ledger also requires a new delta depreciation area in Asset Accounting. The following example highlights the need for this new delta depreciation area.

In this scenario, our test company IDES in company code 0005 capitalizes the "hardware" complex fixed asset in the "fixtures and fittings" asset class.

Account	Description	Debit	Credit	U.S. GAAP	Local GAAP
21000	Fixtures and fittings	20,000		0L	L6
160000	Payables		20,000	0L	L6

Table 5.1 Acquisition of the "Hardware" Complex Fixed Asset

As the posting record in Table 5.1 clearly shows, a single posting document updates both ledgers. The acquisition is posted using the Blank ledger group as the common valuation approach. If you consider the different depreciation postings in accordance with Local GAAP and U.S. GAAP, Table 5.2 clearly shows that the ledger approach in the SAP General

Ledger works with identical accounts for different valuation approaches. This makes the structure of the chart of accounts lean and clear.

Account	Description	Debit	Credit	U.S. GAAP	Local GAAP
211100	Depreciation of tangible fixed assets	5,000		OL	No posting
21010	Accumulated depreciation of fixtures and fittings		5,000	OL	No posting
211100	Depreciation of tangible fixed assets	4,000		No posting	L6
21010	Accumulated depreciation of fixtures and fittings		4,000	No posting	L6

Table 5.2 Depreciation Posting for the "Hardware" Complex Fixed Asset

The need for an additional delta depreciation area in Asset Accounting quickly becomes apparent when selling a complex fixed asset. In our example, the sales revenue value is €10,000, that is, a loss of €5,000 in accordance with depreciation area 01 (U.S. GAAP) and a loss of €6,000 for depreciation area 60 (Local GAAP). Accounts receivable postings are always permanently associated with depreciation area 01 for all accounting principles. This results in the posting record described in Table 5.3.

Sales require a delta depreciation area

Account	Description	Debit	Credit	U.S. GAAP	Local GAAP
21010	Accumulated depreciation of fixtures and fittings	5,000		OL	L6
825000	Clearing of asset retirement	10,000		OL	L6
200000	Loss from asset retirement	5,000		OL	L6
21000	Fixtures and fittings		20,000	OL	L6

Table 5.3 Retirement of "Hardware" Complex Fixed Asset

This posting method updates an "incomplete" valuation approach in every nonleading depreciation area even though there is another valuation for Ledger 6 (L6). An additional depreciation area is required in asset accounting to correct this issue in the general ledger as part of periodic posting of balance sheet values (see Table 5.4).

Account	Description	Debit	Credit	U.S. GAAP	Local GAAP
21010	Accumulated depreciation of fixtures and fittings		1,000	No posting	L6
200000	Loss from asset retirement	1,000		No posting	L6

Table 5.4 Adjustment in Non-Leading Depreciation Area

In addition to this change, the SAP General Ledger in Asset Accounting provides an additional new feature for the gross procedure.

5.6.2 Better Support for the Gross Procedure

Readjustment at period end

If an enterprise purchases a complex fixed asset, the system generates a purchasing document that facilitates a cash discount deduction for the incoming invoice when an outgoing payment is made. In many countries, the cash discount amount reduces the acquisition and production costs for the complex fixed asset— a fact that must be considered in Asset Accounting. Previously, the entire invoice amount was activated during the gross procedure in SAP R/3. Example: If a complex fixed asset costs €100,000 and the input tax is €10,000, the total payable is €110,000. For outgoing payments, cash discounts can only be posted in certain cases and in certain amounts. Three percent reduces the payable by €3,300 to €106,700, the net price of the complex fixed asset by €3,000, and the input tax by €300. In SAP R/3, however, the asset is still listed as amounting to €100,000 in Asset Accounting, even though it should only be €97,000 after the outgoing payment. In SAP R/3, the acquisition and production costs were not reduced until adjustment postings were made (that is, adjustments made at the end of the period). The SAPF181 program was previously used for this purpose.

As shown in Figure 5.63, new options are available in the SAP General Ledger, thanks to document splitting. The original document itself already contains information about how amounts are to be proportionately deducted from complex fixed assets in the case of cash discount deductions. When the outgoing payment is posted, the complex fixed asset in Asset Accounting is immediately reduced to €97,000. This result is shown in Figure 5.63.

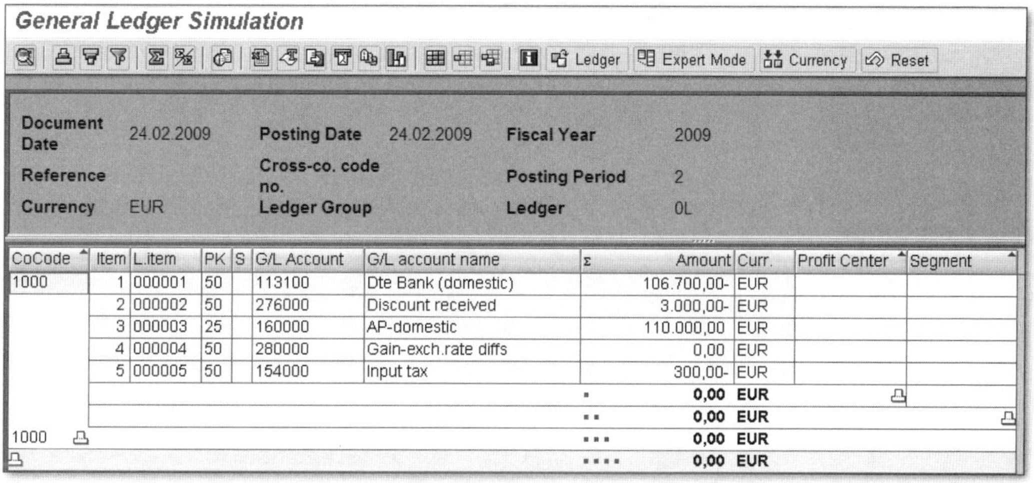

General Ledger Simulation

Document Date	24.02.2009	Posting Date	24.02.2009	Fiscal Year	2009
Reference		Cross-co. code no.		Posting Period	2
Currency	EUR	Ledger Group		Ledger	0L

CoCode	Item	L.item	PK	S	G/L Account	G/L account name	Σ	Amount	Curr.	Profit Center	Segment
1000	1	000001	50		113100	Dte Bank (domestic)		106.700,00-	EUR		
	2	000002	50		276000	Discount received		3.000,00-	EUR		
	3	000003	25		160000	AP-domestic		110.000,00	EUR		
	4	000004	50		280000	Gain-exch.rate diffs		0,00	EUR		
	5	000005	50		154000	Input tax		300,00-	EUR		
							•	0,00	EUR		
							• •	0,00	EUR		
1000							• • •	0,00	EUR		
							• • • •	0,00	EUR		

Figure 5.63 Online Adjustment for Incoming Payment

There is no need for a periodic activity for Asset Accounting. Therefore, less effort at the end of a period is just one advantage associated with the SAP General Ledger.

It also gives Asset Accounting enhanced functions in parallel financial reporting and the gross procedure. The use of these functions is optional, but should be considered when designing a SAP General Ledger.

5.7 Conclusion

The SAP component FI-AA makes it possible to heavily automate Asset Accounting. The defined master data, which, in this context, already provides a great deal of information about any future asset development (depreciation), is the basis for such automation. The depreciation run determines and posts valuation approaches that can also be processed for each complex fixed asset and, at the same time, for local law, IFRS, and U.S. GAAP. The new general ledger introduces a modified delta posting logic here. Furthermore, the evaluations delivered in FI-AA provide a transparent overview of not only the master records, but also value development.

Bank accounting concerns the management of enterprise liquidity. This chapter describes the programs in SAP ERP Financials that simplify processes and provide the necessary transparency.

6 Bank Accounting

This chapter describes the business principles of bank accounting, which are the basis for representing central bank accounting tasks within an enterprise. The following sections will provide examples to illustrate SAP programs such as the electronic bank statement, check deposit transaction, cash journal, and bill of exchange management.

In addition to some detailed improvements, the new SAP ERP Financials release has an important new feature that enables enterprises to send payment media and receive bank statements. In the past, these process steps were outside the SAP system. SAP Bank Communication Management, which is available as of ERP 6.0 Enhancement Package 2, now enables the entire process to be mapped within the SAP system. This chapter also discusses the Single Euro Payments Area (SEPA) and the evaluation options for liquidity management and the monitoring of outgoing checks.

6.1 Business Principles

Bank accounting is a subarea of Financial Accounting. All business transactions concerning enterprise banking are entered and managed here. The main role of bank accounting is to process and document all payment transactions, that is, all cash inflows and outflows. Such a concise definition may lead you to believe that bank accounting is unimportant. However, it is actually extremely significant. If an enterprise is doing well but has zero liquidity, it is, in effect, insolvent. Even if an enterprise can avoid bankruptcy, insolvency comes with its own major business disadvantages. It is the responsibility of the bank accounting department to retain an overview of all incoming and outgoing payments at all times and to ensure that the enterprise has liquid funds on an ongoing basis.

Treasury In practice, bank accounting is frequently a subarea of the treasury department, which is also concerned with guaranteeing and using liquid funds. Unlike accounts payable accounting, accounts receivable accounting, or asset accounting, the bank accounting (FI-BL) module is not a subledger in the traditional sense. Instead, detailed information is stored in the general ledger and in the subledgers of accounts payable accounting and accounts receivable accounting.

6.2   The FI-BL Component

The FI-BL component (Bank Ledger) manages bank master data in a central SAP bank directory. In addition to the enterprise's own house banks, the commercial banks of the vendors and customers are defined in the system. The commercial banks of customers or vendors must be maintained in their master data and in the internal SAP bank directory. SEPA will alter some things here because it will replace the national special features of 31 countries with one uniform standard. In addition to the master data, payment transaction adjustments are also necessary. With SAP Bank Communication Management (BCM), SAP ERP 6.0 Enhancement Package 2 provides a new solution for bank communication. FI-BL is also concerned with cash balance management for checks and bills of exchange. Here, incoming and outgoing payments are documented in electronic bank statements. Lastly, bank accounting can use the many standard evaluations contained in SAP ERP. The following sections will provide examples to illustrate individual functions.

6.3   Master Data

An enterprise's house bank As is the case in all SAP ERP modules, master data also plays a key role in bank accounting (FI-BL). Payments received or authorized by company codes are processed in banks known as house banks. The transactions on this bank account are then mapped in the SAP system to a G/L account. You can define and process house banks in Transaction FIBHU under the menu path ACCOUNTING • FINANCIAL ACCOUNTING • BANKING • MASTER DATA • BANK CHAINS • HOUSE BANKS • PROCESS. Figure 6.1 shows the selection screen for processing house banks. You can clearly see the mandatory Company code field, which specifies the level at which house banks are defined.

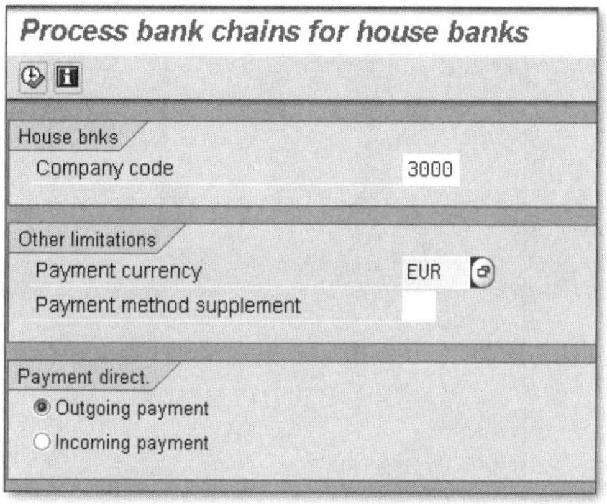

Figure 6.1   Processing House Banks

If you press F8, the system displays an overview of all house banks (see Figure 6.2). Company code 3000 has 10 house banks with subaccounts in different currencies.

Using subaccounts

Using Good Judgment when Selecting House Banks   [+]

In practice, enterprises try to keep the number of house banks as low as possible. Consequently, each house bank processes a large volume of transactions, which is generally associated with lower charges and internal administration costs (for example, when integrating bank statement data or payment medium files).

In light of the credit crunch in 2008, it may be dangerous to have too few business partners as house banks. Optimizing costs and reducing house banks may actually increase the risk of an enterprise not securing the necessary lines of credit, especially if two house banks merge, but the lines of credit agreed on with each bank are not automatically added together.

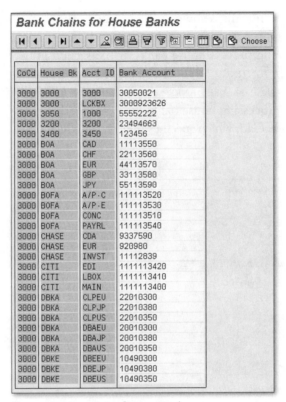

Bank Chains for House Banks

CoCd	House Bk	Acct ID	Bank Account
3000	3000	3000	30050021
3000	3000	LCKBX	3000923626
3000	3050	1000	55552222
3000	3200	3200	23494663
3000	3400	3450	123456
3000	BOA	CAD	11113550
3000	BOA	CHF	22113560
3000	BOA	EUR	44113570
3000	BOA	GBP	33113580
3000	BOA	JPY	55113590
3000	BOFA	A/P-C	111113520
3000	BOFA	A/P-E	111113530
3000	BOFA	CONC	111113510
3000	BOFA	PAYRL	111113540
3000	CHASE	CDA	9337590
3000	CHASE	EUR	920980
3000	CHASE	INVST	11112839
3000	CITI	EDI	1111113420
3000	CITI	LBOX	1111113410
3000	CITI	MAIN	1111113400
3000	DBKA	CLPEU	22010300
3000	DBKA	CLPJP	22010380
3000	DBKA	CLPUS	22010350
3000	DBKA	DBAEU	20010300
3000	DBKA	DBAJP	20010380
3000	DBKA	DBAUS	20010350
3000	DBKE	DBEEU	10490300
3000	DBKE	DBEJP	10490380
3000	DBKE	DBEUS	10490350

Figure 6.2 Overview of House Banks

Manual transfer of bank data

Now that all of the house banks have been defined for incoming and outgoing payments, we should discuss the internal SAP bank directory in greater detail here. As you saw in Chapters 3 and 4, which dealt with accounts payable and accounts receivable accounting, you define information concerning the business partner's bank in the master data. Any information entered here is subject to a check against the internal SAP bank directory. This ensures that incorrect entries are kept to an absolute minimum. Such a procedure requires a bank directory that is updated on a continuous basis. A program for transferring data directly to the SAP system is available under the menu path ACCOUNTING • FINANCIAL ACCOUNTING • BANKING • MASTER DATA • BANK MASTER RECORD • TRANS-

FER BANK DATA. The report here reads a file in ASCII format and can convert the formats of the following countries directly:

- Austria
- Canada
- Great Britain
- South Africa
- Denmark
- Spain
- Switzerland
- Germany
- Italy
- USA

If you require other country formats, you can use a user exit to adjust the import interface. Alternatively, you can use Transaction BIC to transfer the bank directory from a BIC file. The report is used to transfer a bank directory that contains the bank data of several countries into the SAP system (table BNKA). If the bank data is insufficient, you can manually supplement this data in the system. Figure 6.3 shows the relevant transaction, which is available under the menu path ACCOUNTING • FINANCIAL ACCOUNTING • BANKING • MASTER DATA • BANK MASTER RECORD • CREATE.

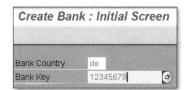

Figure 6.3   Creating a Bank

In this example, we want to create a country-specific eight-digit bank number for Germany. The rest of the bank data is then entered on the screen shown in Figure 6.4. In the case of foreign payment transactions, the SWIFT code uniquely identifies a bank worldwide.

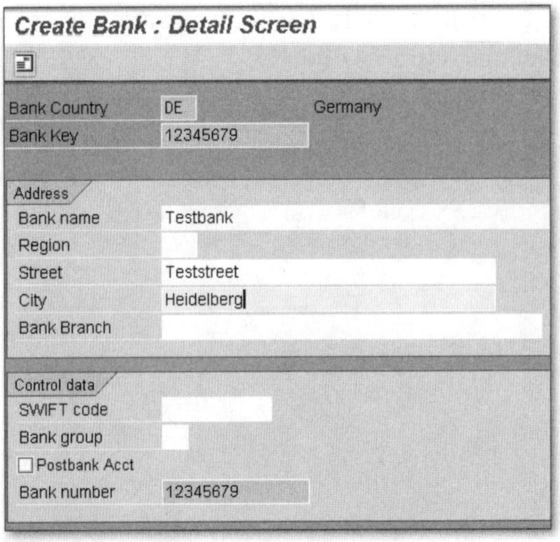

Figure 6.4 Creating a Bank—Detail Screen

Bank directory in SAP ERP

Once the data has been saved, this bank can be used as both a house bank and a bank for customers or vendors. Consequently, the bank directory grows continuously. The options of importing or manually maintaining bank master data as a house bank or as a bank for business partners in the bank directory are inextricably linked to SEPA. This means a significant change to the master data of payment transactions conducted in Euros.

6.4   Consequences of Introducing SEPA

New payment formats

SEPA affects Euro payment transactions in 31 countries. This new standard, which has been introduced for all bank transfers (European Credit Transfer, ECT) as of 01/28/2008, will replace national payment methods and payment media after a period of coexistence. The procedure for SEPA debit memos (European Direct Debit, EDD) will be adopted in 2009. The new XML payment formats are based on a common standard in accordance with ISO 20022. Here, the underlying concept is faster, more cost-effective foreign payment transactions in 31 countries.

The SAP system requires some adjustments to produce SEPA-compliant data media. Once again, the master data plays an important role here. In Figure 6.5, Transaction FK02 shows the bank key and account number of the vendor C.E.B. Berlin.

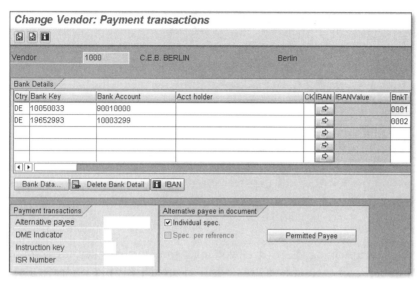

Figure 6.5 A Business Partner's Bank Information

National account numbers will be replaced with an International Bank **IBAN structure** Account Number (IBAN). You will be able to enter this field information in the master record. The IBAN consists of a country code, check digit, bank code, and account number. The SAP system can generate this new information as a proposal (see Figure 6.6).

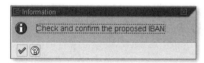

Figure 6.6 IBAN Proposal

The system issues this warning message for a reason. From time to time, the result of the mathematical algorithm does not correspond exactly to the IBAN assigned by the bank. We recommend that, at the very least, you compare the result with the data generated in Figure 6.7.

IBAN—Offering by External Providers **[+]**

When master data reaches a certain volume, manual maintenance is no longer efficient.

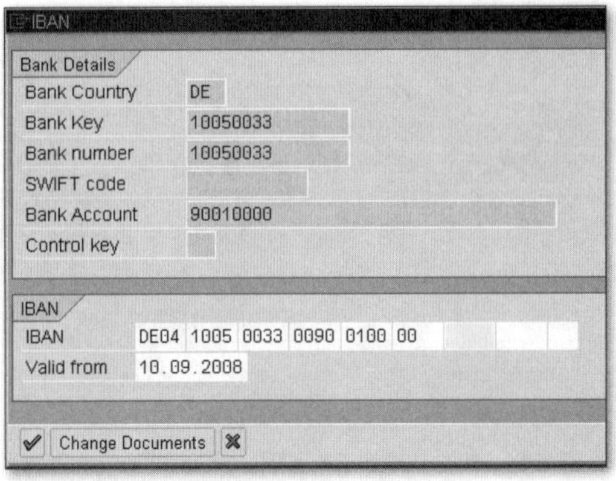

Figure 6.7 Generated IBAN

Future master data maintenance

When maintaining master data, you must enter the bank key, the account number, and the defined IBAN. This approach is valid if master data already exists for business partners. However, new vendors and customers may know only their IBAN, and not their bank key or bank number. This situation will arise more and more frequently in the future. Therefore, master data such as the bank key and bank number will not necessarily be defined first in the SAP bank directory. To obtain an IBAN abbreviation when entering data, you must maintain table TIBAN_WO_ACCONO in Transaction SM30 (see Figure 6.8).

IBAN without a bank account number

If you click on the Maintain button, you can activate IBAN maintenance without a bank account number. Figure 6.9 shows this easy and transparent configuration.

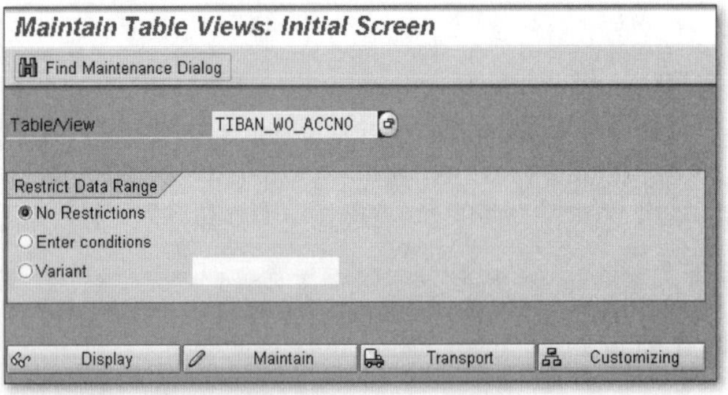

Figure 6.8 Table Maintenance

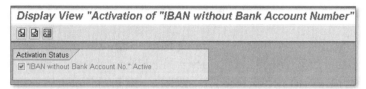

Figure 6.9 IBAN Without a Bank Account Number

This setting enables you to maintain the IBAN of a business partner in the bank directory without having to enter the bank number.

Change Vendor: Payment transactions

Vendor 1000 C.E.B. BERLIN Berlin

Bank Details

Ctry	Bank Key	Bank Account	Acct holder	CK	IBAN	IBANValue	BnkT
DE	10050033	90010000			⇨		0001
DE	19652993	10003299			⇨		0002
					⇨		

Bank Data... | Delete Bank Detail |

IBAN Converter

IBAN Entry
IBAN

Bank Details
Bank Country — ☑ Acct Number Unknown
Bank Key
Bank number
SWIFT code

Payment transactions
Alternative payee
DME Indicator
Instruction key
ISR Number

Figure 6.10 Direct IBAN Entry

For payments in the new SEPA format, the IBAN will form the basis for future Euro payment transactions. When master data is defined with this information, this covers just one small part of the topics of SEPA and payment transactions. The new European Credit Transfer and European Direct Debit formats will have to be configured. In addition, some enterprises will also ask basic questions about how bank communication will look with the new XML files.

6.5   Payment Transactions and Bank Communication

Planning liquidity

One of the main tasks of bank accounting is to ensure smooth and efficient processing of payment transactions. In addition to incoming payments, which are usually processed in an electronic bank statement (see Section 6.6, Processing Bank Statements), it is also necessary to plan outgoing payment amounts. The liquidity forecast evaluation (see Section 6.10.1) plays an important role here. Once the cash management specialist has obtained an overview of the liquidity available, the payment program can be planned under the menu path ACCOUNTING • FINANCIAL ACCOUNTING • BANKING • ENVIRONMENT • SETTINGS • ENTER AVAILABLE AMOUNTS FOR PAYMENT PROGRAM. Figure 6.11 shows different house banks and the available amounts for the payment program. The payment run planned and performed by accounts payable accounting (see Chapter 3, Accounts Payable Accounting) accesses this information and only pays due invoices if doing so does not exceed the available amount for each house bank.

In the following sections, we will provide examples to illustrate manual incoming and outgoing payments.

Display View "Available Amounts for Payment Program": Overview

Paying company code   3000   IDES US INC

Available Amounts for Payment Program

House bank	Account ID	Days	Currency	Available for outgoing pay..	Scheduled incoming paym..
3000	3000	5	USD	99,999,999.00	999,999,999.00
3200	3200	5	USD	99,999,999.00	0.00
BANK1	CHECK	5	USD	1,000,000.00	0.00
BANK1	OTHER	5	USD	1,000,000.00	0.00
BANK2	CHECK	5	USD	1,000,000.00	0.00
DBKA	DBAEU	999	EUR	999,999,999.00	999,999,999.00
DBKA	DBAJP	999	JPY	999,999,999,999	999,999,999,999
DBKA	DBAUS	999	USD	999,999,999.00	999,999,999.00

Figure 6.11   Entering Available Amounts for Payment Program

6.5.1   Incoming Payments

Assigning incoming payments

Incoming payment posting can be an automated or manual process. Bank accounting is faced with the same dilemma; it must find out which offsetting items are suitable for the debit posting on the cash receipt account. This may concern several invoices whose absolute amount may also differ from the incoming payment amount. To provide a better overview, the example shown over the next few pages will use a manual incoming payment to clear a manually posted customer invoice.

First, Transaction FB70 is used to enter a customer invoice manually. Figure 6.12 shows a receivable amounting to $5,959. The Reference field is particularly important here. If, for example, a business transaction has a contract number, you can enter this number here and then use it later to find the relevant invoice when an incoming payment is made. You can also use the document number generated by the system to identify the invoice, depending on the information that the customer supplies with the incoming payment.

Transaction F-28 can be used to post incoming payments manually. The electronic bank statement (see Section 6.6) automates this transaction. First, the header information is entered for the debit posting on the cash receipt account. The value date is 08/21/2008 for G/L account 113107, and the amount is $5,959.

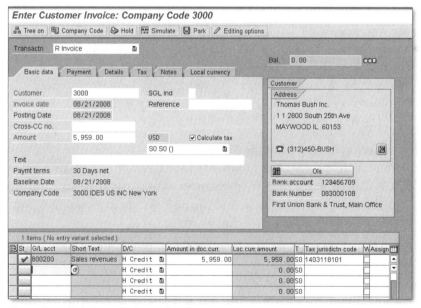

Figure 6.12 Entering a Customer Invoice

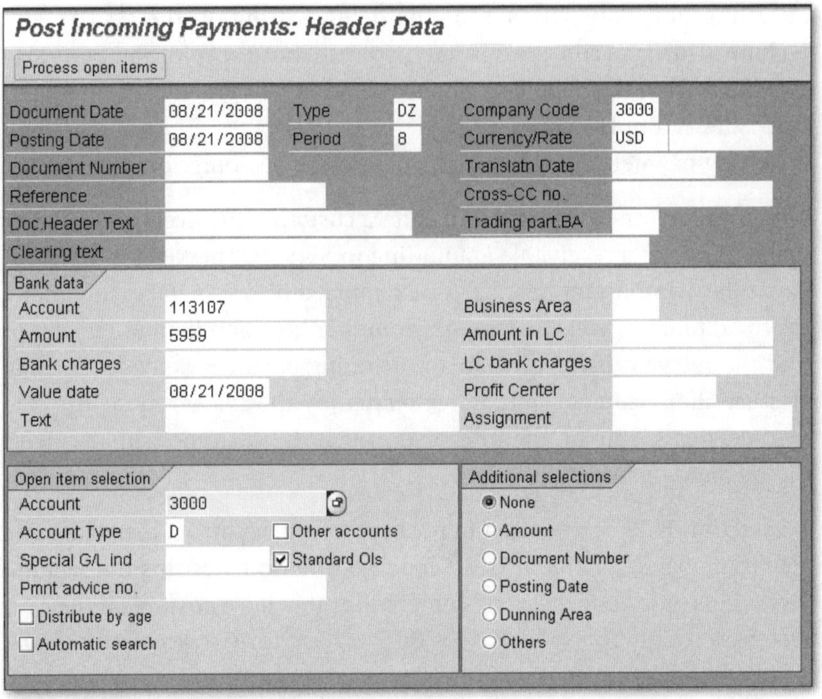

Post Incoming Payments: Header Data

Process open items

Document Date	08/21/2008	Type	DZ	Company Code	3000
Posting Date	08/21/2008	Period	8	Currency/Rate	USD
Document Number				Translatn Date	
Reference				Cross-CC no.	
Doc.Header Text				Trading part.BA	
Clearing text					

Bank data

Account	113107	Business Area	
Amount	5959	Amount in LC	
Bank charges		LC bank charges	
Value date	08/21/2008	Profit Center	
Text		Assignment	

Open item selection

Account	3000	
Account Type	D	☐ Other accounts
Special G/L ind		☑ Standard OIs
Pmnt advice no.		
☐ Distribute by age		
☐ Automatic search		

Additional selections

- ◉ None
- ○ Amount
- ○ Document Number
- ○ Posting Date
- ○ Dunning Area
- ○ Others

Figure 6.13 Entering Header Data

Handling differences

The system's search for customer account 3000 begins in the lower section of Figure 6.13. In this case, it is a relatively easy and unique search. The customer account is known, exactly one invoice is to be cleared, and there are no amount differences. Unfortunately, these ideal scenarios do not always occur in reality. Instead, it is necessary to distinguish between the following scenarios:

▸ **Underpayment within the tolerance**
You can define tolerance groups in the SAP system. A tolerance group is assigned to each individual customer in the customer master record at the company code level, and the SAP system automatically posts minor differences to a predefined account.

▸ **Underpayment above the tolerance and creation of a partial payment**
In the clearing transaction, an accounting clerk can decide how to deal with payment differences. Partial payments are one option. They

involve linking incoming payments with invoices. Only one assignment takes place and all items remain open.

▸ **Underpayment above the tolerance and creation of a residual item**
Unlike the partial payment, the original items are cleared for residual items. Another difference is that a proportional cash discount is granted for this procedure.

▸ **Payment on account**
The customer has been found, and you are completely free to choose the invoices that are to be cleared with the incoming payment. A payment on account makes sense in such cases. There is no clearing. Instead, a posting is made from the customer's incoming payment account. This item is then entered on the credit side of the customer account and can be used for open item account maintenance if the right information is available.

Sample Calculation for Partial Payment and Residual Items			[Ex]
Invoice	1,000	(3% cash discount)	
Incoming payment	800		
Partial payment	200		
Invoice	1,000	(3% cash discount)	
Incoming payment	800	(3% of 800 is 24)	
Residual items	176	(200 minus 24)	

In this sample incoming payment, the customer is already known, one invoice is to be cleared, and there are no amount differences. Figure 6.14 shows the ideal scenario and hints at other options such as partial payment, residual items, and payment on account.

Unlike manual incoming payments, which are relatively rare, postings that concern manual outgoing payments are more and more common.

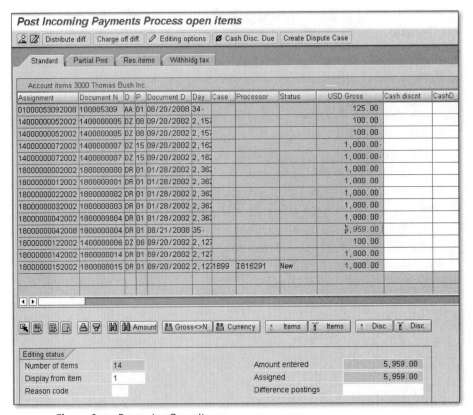

Figure 6.14 shows the following table in the interface:

Post Incoming Payments Process open items

Distribute diff. | Charge off diff. | Editing options | Ø Cash Disc. Due | Create Dispute Case

Standard | Partial Pmt | Res.items | Withhldg tax

Account items 3000 Thomas Bush Inc.

Assignment	Document N	D	P	Document D	Day	Case	Processor	Status	USD Gross	Cash discnt	CashD
01000053092008	100005309	AA	01	08/20/2008	34 -				125.00		
14000000052002	1400000005	DZ	08	09/20/2002	2,157				100.00		
14000000052002	1400000005	DZ	08	09/20/2002	2,157				100.00		
14000000072002	1400000007	DZ	15	09/20/2002	2,162				1,000.00 -		
14000000072002	1400000007	DZ	15	09/20/2002	2,162				1,000.00 -		
18000000002002	1800000000	DR	01	01/28/2002	2,362				1,000.00		
18000000012002	1800000001	DR	01	01/28/2002	2,362				1,000.00		
18000000022002	1800000002	DR	01	01/28/2002	2,362				1,000.00		
18000000032002	1800000003	DR	01	01/28/2002	2,362				1,000.00		
18000000042002	1800000004	DR	01	01/28/2002	2,362				1,000.00		
18000000042008	1800000004	DR	01	08/21/2008	35 -				5,959.00		
18000000122002	1400000006	DZ	06	09/20/2002	2,127				100.00		
18000000142002	1800000014	DR	01	09/20/2002	2,127				1,000.00		
18000000152002	1800000015	DR	01	09/20/2002	2,127	1899	I816291	New	1,000.00		

◀ ▶

Amount | Gross<>N | Currency | Items | Items | Disc. | Disc.

Editing status

Number of items	14	Amount entered	5,959.00
Display from item	1	Assigned	5,959.00
Reason code		Difference postings	

Figure 6.14 Processing Open Items

6.5.2 Outgoing Payments

Outgoing payment posting can be an automated or manual process. Chapter 3, Accounts Payable Accounting, describes automated payment transactions in the context of accounts payable accounting. In this section, it concerns unscheduled actions at short notice such as manual payments by check or ad hoc payments.

Payment by Check

Figure 6.15 shows a vendor invoice in Transaction FB60. The vendor C.E.B. requires a payment of $9,999.

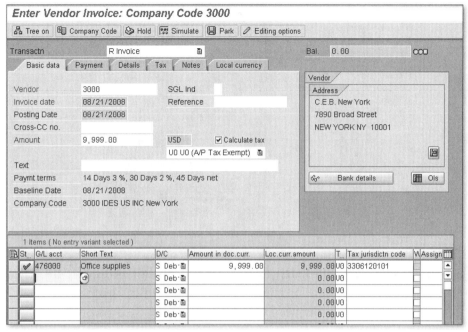

Figure 6.15 Entering a Vendor Invoice

Printing Ad Hoc Checks [Ex]

Imagine that one of C.E.B.'s freight forwarders arrives at your accounting department and requests immediate payment for the goods being delivered. The receivable has been authorized, but the payment cannot be made using petty cash (see Section 6.7, Cash Journal) because it concerns such a large amount of money. One possibility is to write a check that can be cashed immediately by a nearby bank.

The SAP system supports this procedure in Transaction F-58 or under the menu path ACCOUNTING • FINANCIAL ACCOUNTING • ACCOUNTS PAYABLE • POSTING • OUTGOING PAYMENT • POST + PRINT FORMS. Figure 6.16 shows the basic settings for payment method C (check) and house bank 3000. The option to calculate the payment amount is selected in the Processing type section of the screen.

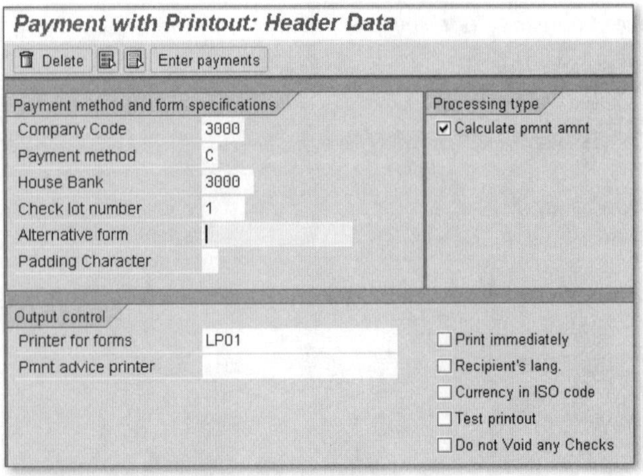

Figure 6.16 Payment with Printout

Entering a
payment If you click on the Enter payments button, the system displays the header data entry screen for bank accounting shown in Figure 6.17. Vendor 3000 (C.E.B.) is defined as the payee.

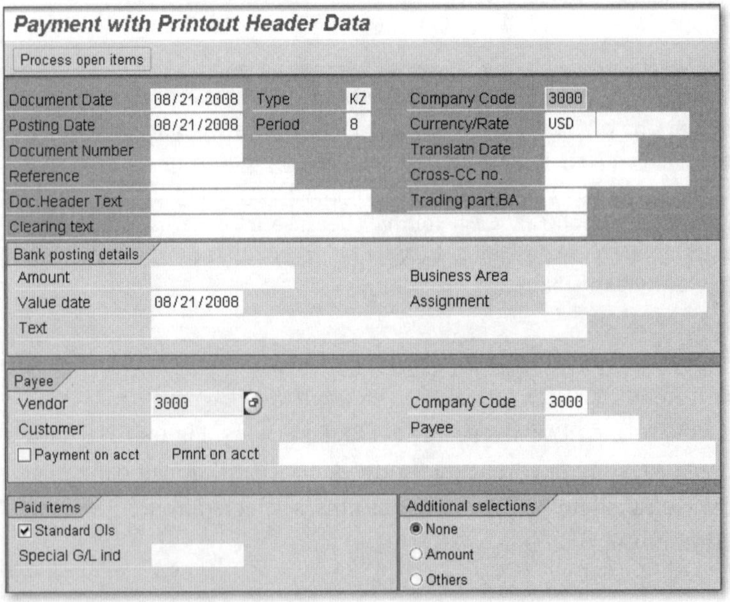

Figure 6.17 Entering Header Data

When you click on the Process open items button, the program navigates to the open item processing screen shown in Figure 6.18.

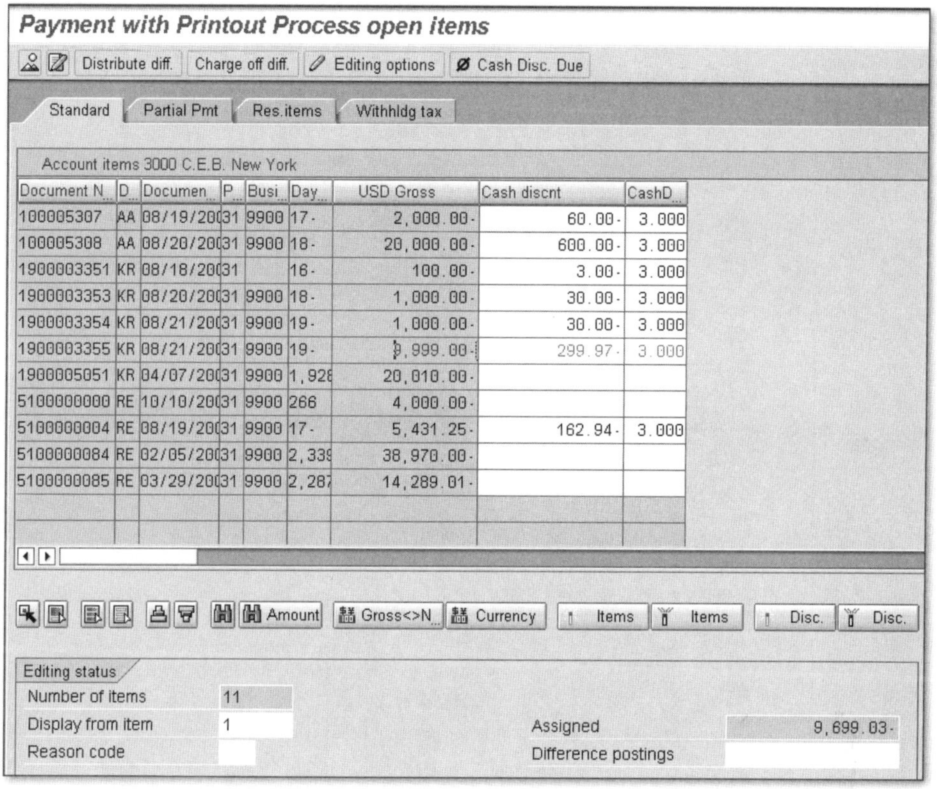

Payment with Printout Process open items

Distribute diff. | Charge off diff. | Editing options | Cash Disc. Due

Standard | Partial Pmt | Res.items | Withhldg tax

Account items 3000 C.E.B. New York

Document N	D	Documen	P	Busi	Day	USD Gross	Cash discnt	CashD
100005307	AA	08/19/20	31	9900	17-	2,000.00-	60.00-	3.000
100005308	AA	08/20/20	31	9900	18-	20,000.00-	600.00-	3.000
1900003351	KR	08/18/20	31		16-	100.00-	3.00-	3.000
1900003353	KR	08/20/20	31	9900	18-	1,000.00-	30.00-	3.000
1900003354	KR	08/21/20	31	9900	19-	1,000.00-	30.00-	3.000
1900003355	KR	08/21/20	31	9900	19-	9,999.00-	299.97-	3.000
1900005051	KR	04/07/20	31	9900	1,928	20,010.00-		
5100000000	RE	10/10/20	31	9900	266	4,000.00-		
5100000004	RE	08/19/20	31	9900	17-	5,431.25-	162.94-	3.000
5100000084	RE	02/05/20	31	9900	2,339	38,970.00-		
5100000085	RE	03/29/20	31	9900	2,287	14,289.01-		

Amount | Gross<>N | Currency | Items | Items | Disc. | Disc.

Editing status			
Number of items	11		
Display from item	1	Assigned	9,699.03-
Reason code		Difference postings	

Figure 6.18 Processing Open Items

You can now select all of the items due for payment by double-clicking on them. These items are then cleared with the outgoing payment posting. If the transaction is saved, the SAP system generates a check (see Figure 6.19).

Assigning items

However, it is not always advisable to use a check as a payment medium for payments at short notice.

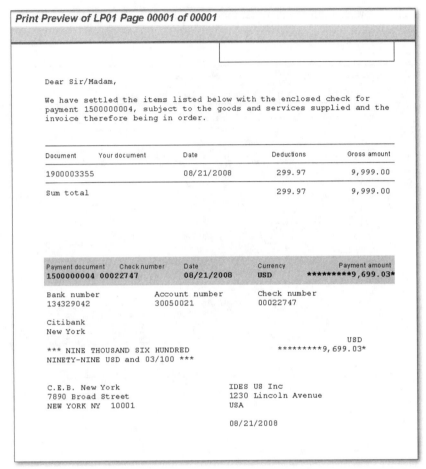

Figure 6.19 Check View

Ad Hoc Payment

As an alternative to payments by check, you can generate a bank transfer for an ad hoc payment in Transaction FIBLFFP. This scenario does not require an invoice on the vendor account for clearing purposes. Figure 6.20 shows a bank transfer of €1,000 to vendor 1000.

To ensure that this flexible option is not abused, it may be important to monitor which payment files are to be used within bank communication.

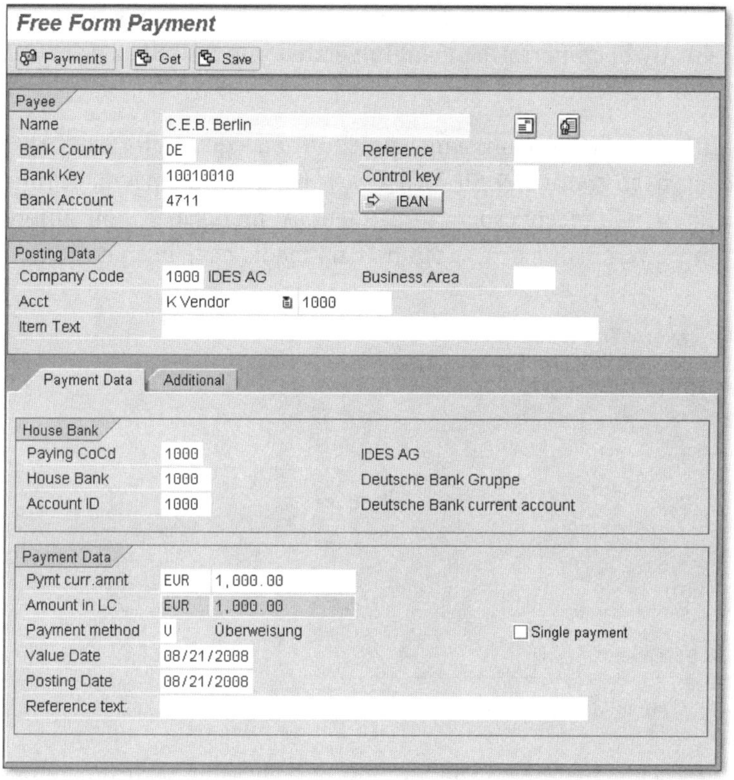

Figure 6.20 Ad Hoc Payment

6.5.3   Bank Communication

If payment transactions concern bank transfers or automatic debits, it is necessary to transfer payment medium information to the relevant house banks. In the 1990s, the standard process involved sending the data medium disk by post to the relevant bank. Since then, electronic data interchange (EDI) has been established as a new standard whereby special banking software data is used to transfer data from a PC. SAP systems based on SAP ERP 6.0 can use Enhancement Package 2 (released in 2007) to communicate directly with a bank. SAP Bank Communication Management (BCM)—sometimes also known by the project name Bank Relationship Management—provides new functions for the approval and release process of payment files and direct bank communication. Once the process has been established, the new SAP BCM functions schedule

SAP Bank Communication Management

a payment run in Transaction F110. Figure 6.21 shows a payment run that has already been performed and integrated into SAP Bank Communication Management.

The Identification field

The Identification field obtains a new function and significance here. This example has been configured in such a way that all of the payment runs with the ID AL will receive special treatment. At first glance, you simply see that only two posting orders but no data media have been created.

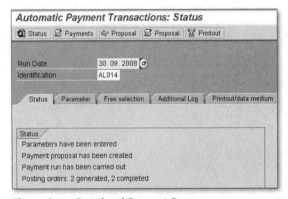

Figure 6.21 Completed Payment Run

Data medium created at a later time

Because the payment run in this example has already been integrated into SAP Bank Communication Management, the data media are no longer created in the payment run (F110), which is usually the case. This has numerous advantages, which we will discuss in greater detail with this example. Here, there is an outgoing payment of €105,500 for two vendors. To access the overview shown in Figure 6.22, follow the menu path EDIT • PAYMENT • DISPLAY.

Grouping payment media

If the payment medium is created later than it was previously, the enterprise's payment runs can be grouped together at random. SAP Bank Communication Management enables you to separate a payment run into several payment media or to group several payment runs together. This function is available under the menu path ACCOUNTING • FINANCIAL ACCOUNTING • FINANCIAL SUPPLY CHAIN MANAGEMENT • BANK COMMUNICATION MANAGEMENT • EDIT • MERGE PAYMENTS (Transaction FBPM1). Here, you can perform worthwhile preparatory work for the subsequent release process. If, for example, you define groupings for important or very important payments, you can determine whether it is necessary to adopt a principle of dual or triple control. Alternatively, if you want all of the outgoing payments resulting from payment runs to be approved from a central location, they can be merged into one payment. These are just two examples of the new options that did not exist previously with the payment program Transaction F110.

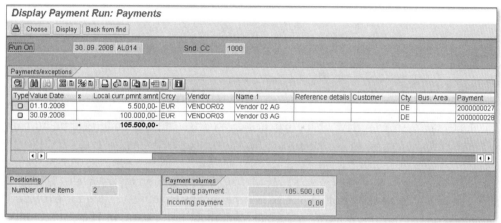

Figure 6.22 Displaying Payments to Be Made in the Payment Run

Figure 6.23 Merging Payments – Selection Screen

Both the defined configuration and the sample selection made in Figure 6.23 result in a payment run being grouped into one batch. This action is confirmed by the message shown in Figure 6.24.

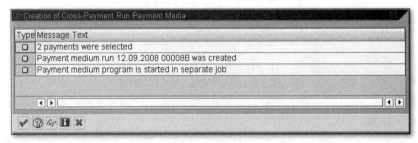

Figure 6.24 Confirmation of Merged Payments

Rules for the release process An overview of the batches created is available under the menu path ACCOUNTING • FINANCIAL ACCOUNTING • FINANCIAL SUPPLY CHAIN MANAGEMENT • BANK COMMUNICATION MANAGEMENT • STATUS MANAGEMENT • BATCH AND PAYMENT MONITORING (Transaction BNL_MONI). The overview shown in Figure 6.25 contains the example created for €105,500, which now has 51 as its batch number. In the Status or File Date column, you can see that a payment file has not been created yet. The grouping and release rules defined in the configuration are indicated in conjunction with the earlier payment groupings, namely 47 to 51. This example uses several rules. On the one hand, a distinction is made between payments ranging between €2 million and €10 million. Another rule is used for payments that do not fall into this category, but are above €5,000. Finally, grouped payments below this limit are made directly without any additional approval.

Batches

BatNo	#Pay	Rule description	Status	Batch Amount	Curr	House Bk
47	1	High Value Payments Merge ID BCM* (> 5.000 EUR) - Two Approvers	Payment medium created	6.000,00	EUR	1000
49	1	High Value Payments Merge ID AL* (2.000.000 to 10.000.000 EUR)	Payment medium created	15.000.000,00	EUR	1000
50	2	Low and Medium Value Payments Merge ID AL* (< 2.000.000 EUR)	Payment medium created	2.300,00	EUR	1000
51	2	High Value Payments Merge ID BCM* (> 5.000 EUR) - Two Approvers	Payment batch created	105.500,00	EUR	1000

Figure 6.25 Batch and Payment Monitoring

As an alternative to the display shown in Figure 6.25, a new SAP Portal role offers similar options in a different, more transparent display. If you do not use the SAP Portal, you are only concerned with the traditional display, which we will continue to use as the preferred display throughout this book.

SAP Portal role

If one or more batches require approval, it makes sense to use a notification function to notify the people responsible. Because time is ultimately money, you can also configure this function. If you double-click batch 51 in Figure 6.25, the system will display the two vendors due for payment. You can use the function shown in Figure 6.26 to double-check an outgoing payment for any unusually high individual amounts before it is approved. By this stage, the vendor invoices have already been cleared in accounting. Here, SAP Bank Communication Management merely provides "a second pair of eyes." The first check to determine whether invoices are to be paid is still subject to the payment run (Transaction F110) and the Payment Proposal List function.

A second pair of eyes

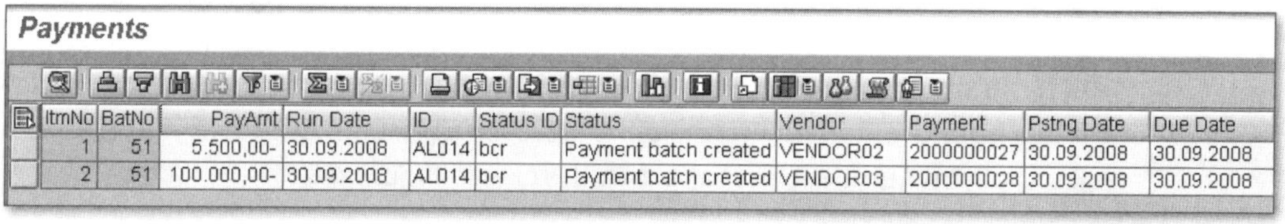

	ItmNo	BatNo	PayAmt	Run Date	ID	Status ID	Status	Vendor	Payment	Pstng Date	Due Date
	1	51	5.500,00-	30.09.2008	AL014	bcr	Payment batch created	VENDOR02	2000000027	30.09.2008	30.09.2008
	2	51	100.000,00-	30.09.2008	AL014	bcr	Payment batch created	VENDOR03	2000000028	30.09.2008	30.09.2008

Figure 6.26 Detailed Payment List

If some individual due payments are a little unclear to you or if you want to check incoming invoices at random, you can click on the 🔲 icon, which will take you directly to the source documents in accounts payable accounting. The example provided in Figure 6.27 shows the clearing document for the payment. The document type KR represents a vendor invoice that the payment program has cleared with the payment document (document type ZP).

Double-checking invoices

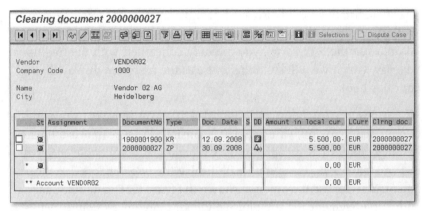

Figure 6.27 Clearing Document for the Payment

Principle of dual control

If you press [F12] twice, the system returns to the general overview. The principle of dual control has been defined for the payment runs that were merged to form batch 51. You can now click on the 👬 icon to display the group of people authorized to approve payments. This function clearly identifies who is responsible for approving payments within the enterprise. In practice, several employees are usually responsible, in order to provide vacation and illness coverage. In the example taken from the demo system, only the user Christian Approver can approve payments at the first approval level (see Figure 6.28).

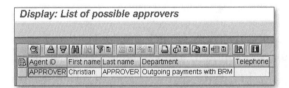

Figure 6.28 List of Possible Approvers

Once Christian Approver has been informed, he logs on to the SAP system as the next work step. Payments are approved in Transaction BNK_APP (ACCOUNTING • FINANCIAL ACCOUNTING • FINANCIAL SUPPLY CHAIN MANAGEMENT • BANK COMMUNICATION MANAGEMENT • PROCESSING • APPROVE PAYMENTS).

The previous example is listed as batch number 51 in the overview shown in Figure 6.29. If an approver requires additional information, he can also display the vendors and clearing documents.

> **Additional Options: Withholding Payments**
>
> At this point, the first approver can also withhold payment of individual items. If, for example, €100,000 will not be available in the house bank until a few days time, the payment amount for Vendor 3 can be withheld. In the example, the immediate payment of a lower amount (€5,500) to Vendor 2 would still be possible. This advantage is the result of the very late creation of the payment medium. However, this function should not replace proper planning of the amounts available before the payment run as well as targeted processing of the proposal list. Enterprises can and will only withhold amounts in exceptional circumstances, without reversing the payment run and associated clearing documents.

Therefore, nothing indicates that this step is the final approval step for a payment. Consequently, other people follow the user Christian Approver in a second step.

Figure 6.29 Overview of Payment Batch Approval

To approve a payment, you can click on the 🖋 icon. The approval is then confirmed in a message (see Figure 6.30).

Approval of the transaction

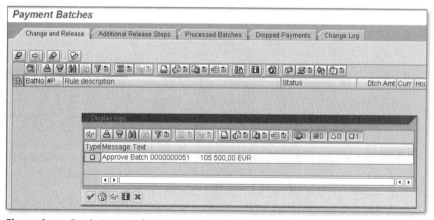

Figure 6.30 Batch Approved

Once the processing step has been saved, a digital signature is provided, thus documenting the transaction. In this example, the user authorizes the signature by entering his user ID and password (see Figure 6.31).

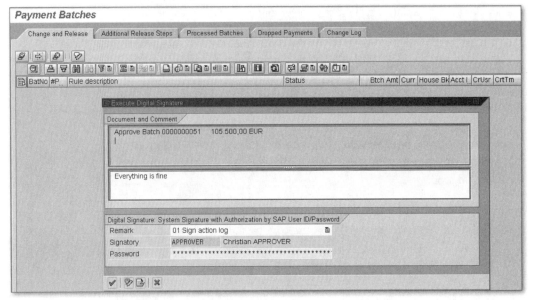

Figure 6.31 Documenting the Transaction

Because of the amount and its defined configuration, the payment grouping (batch) created under the sequential number 51 is subject to the principle of dual control. The first signature assigns the status In Approval to the transaction in payment monitoring (Transaction BNK_MONI) as shown in Figure 6.32.

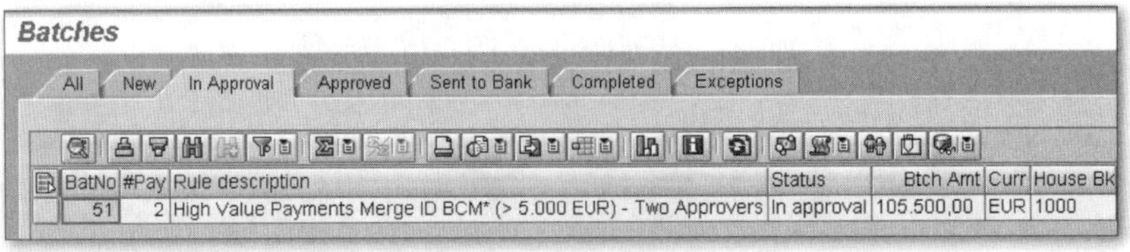

Figure 6.32 Batch in Approval

When you click on the 🏢 icon, the system displays a list of approvers required for the second step. Figure 6.33 shows that, once again, this example concerns only one person.

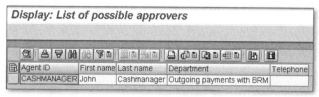

Figure 6.33   List of Possible Approvers, Part 2

Task Sharing

Frequently, the principle of dual control is such that the list of approvers for the first level (signature) contains more people than in the list of approvers for the final release. Consequently, several employees can perform a preliminary check, and the head of department can be responsible for the final approval.

In our example, John Cashmanager is responsible for approving the final release of the payment. In Transaction BNK_APP (see Figure 6.34), this status is shown for Final approval step, which is entered on the Additional Release Steps tab page.

Final Release

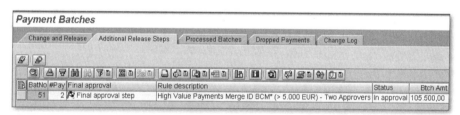

Figure 6.34   Final Approval of Payment

A signature also documents the transaction. When you click on the 🖾 icon, the system shows the various steps within the approval procedure (see Figure 6.35).

Digital signature

Status Change History

Date	Time	Status	Name	Action
12.09.2008	23:18:56	Released in company	CASHMANAGER	Active
12.09.2008	23:18:56	Payment medium created	CASHMANAGER	Active
12.09.2008	23:18:56	In approval	CASHMANAGER	InActive
12.09.2008	23:18:56	Released in company	CASHMANAGER	InActive
12.09.2008	23:14:41	In approval	APPROVER	Active
12.09.2008	23:14:41	Payment batch created	APPROVER	InActive
12.09.2008	23:05:53	Payment batch created	CASH	Active

Figure 6.35   Status Change History

Once all of the security measures for outgoing payments have been fulfilled, the system generates the payment file. You can then click on the icon to display the content of the data medium (see Figure 6.36).

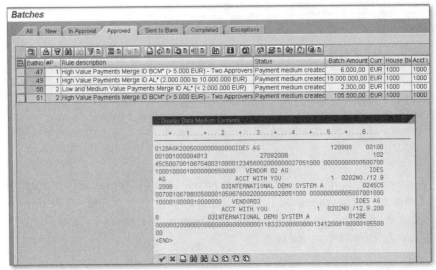

Figure 6.36 File Display

Sending the data medium

If there is a direct connection between the SAP system and the relevant bank, the payment medium is immediately sent directly to the house bank. Figure 6.37 shows that the status also changes in the SAP system.

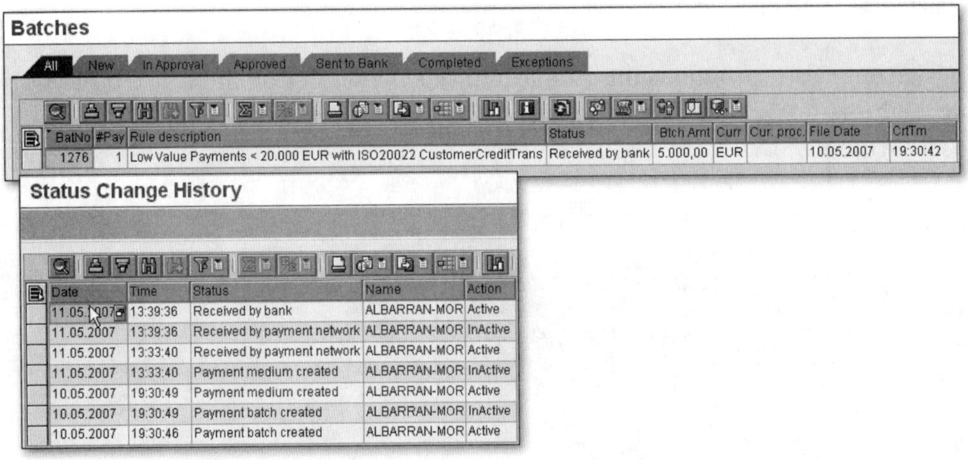

Figure 6.37 File Sent

If you use SAP Bank Communication Management to send payment files to your house banks, you can also use it to receive electronic bank statements.

Bank statements received

Bank Statement Monitor

| Company Code | 0001 |
| House Bank | DB |

	Proc.Stat.	Diff.Sts	Ser.No.Sts	Recon.Sts	CoCd	Hous.	Acct ID	CM acct	Crcy	Ctry	Bank number	Bank Account	G/L Account	Stmt date	Opening balance
	⬛OO	OOⅠ	OOⅠ	OOⅠ	0001	DB	GIRO	DBGIRO	EUR	DE	10020030	548334	113100	11.05.2007	787.322,68
	⬛OO	⬛OⅠ	OOⅠ	OOⅠ	0001	DB	US$	DBDOLLAR	USD	DE	10020030	148334	113150	12.04.2007	0,00
	⬛OO	⬛OⅠ	OOⅠ	OOⅠ	0001	DB	WERTH	DBGIRO	EUR	DE	10020030	123456789	113100	24.05.2007	2.008,00
									EUR						
									USD						

Figure 6.38 Bank Statement Monitor

Transaction FTE_BSM (ACCOUNTING • FINANCIAL ACCOUNTING • FINANCIAL SUPPLY CHAIN MANAGEMENT • BANK COMMUNICATION MANAGEMENT • STATUS MANAGEMENT • BANK STATEMENT MONITOR), shown in Figure 6.38, enables the bank accounting department to obtain an exact overview of which bank statements are present as a file and which have been imported and/or processed.

6.6   Processing Bank Statements

The more transactions there are on bank accounts, the more important it is to retain an overview. The bank statements of house banks provide not only the bank accounting department with valuable information about the status quo of the liquid funds available, but especially the accounts receivable accounting department, which is also involved. Incoming payments for receivables gives enterprises more room to maneuver within the credit limit and may make telephone or written reminders redundant. This leads to close collaboration between both departments (bank accounting and accounts receivable accounting) when processing bank statements. In practice, the bank information is generally imported in electronic form. Transaction FF_5 under the menu path ACCOUNTING • FINANCIAL ACCOUNTING • BANKING • INCOMING • BANK STATEMENT • IMPORT is used for this purpose.

Status of liquid funds available

Figure 6.39 shows the various options provided by this transaction. First, you select the format of the electronic bank statement. Different file formats are available, depending on the country or bank.

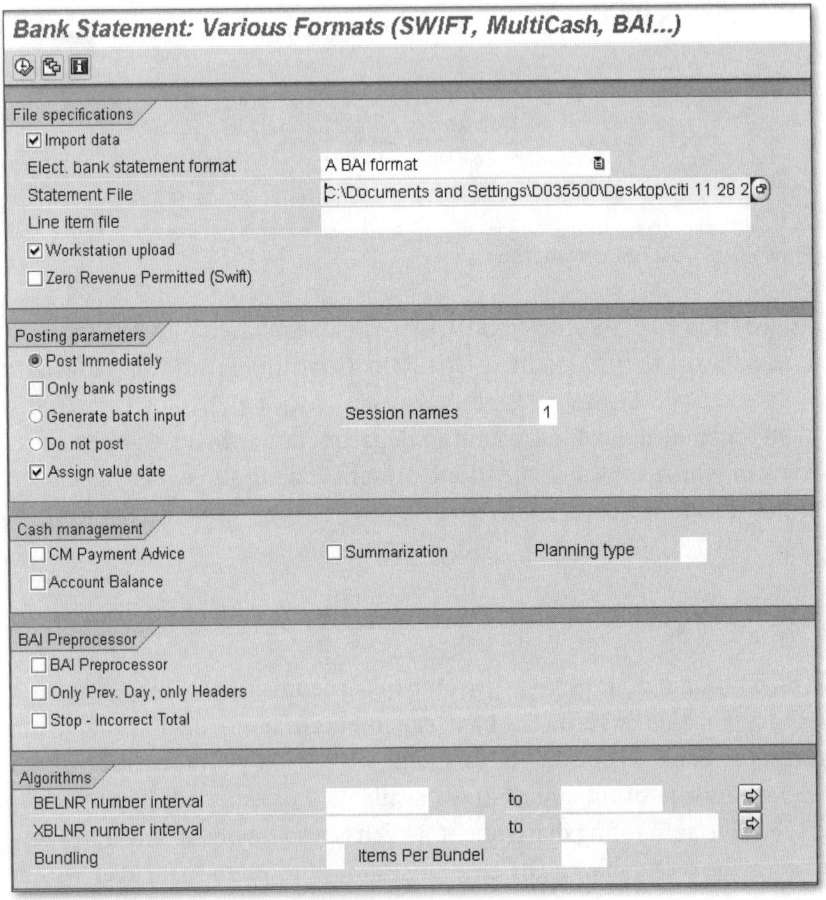

Figure 6.39 Importing a Bank Statement

Postprocessing procedure

The posting parameters enable you to determine if and how you want the data to be posted. If this is a test, it makes sense to select the Do not post option. Depending on the type of postprocessing, we recommend that you use the batch input procedure or select Post Immediately. If several people are active for a house bank in postprocessing, the older batch input procedure is unsuitable because only one accounting clerk can ever call the session here. In postprocessing, the Post Immediately procedure provides a dialog list from which several items can be processed simultaneously.

Irrespective of the procedure, you should take a closer look at the posting method used. Figure 6.40 outlines a brief scenario. If an enterprise receives money from a customer for a receivable, this results in two posting documents: debit the bank and credit the cash receipt and debit the cash receipt and credit the customer. You can always implement the first posting transaction directly; it provides the bank accounting department with important information about the house bank's account balance at present. Posting method

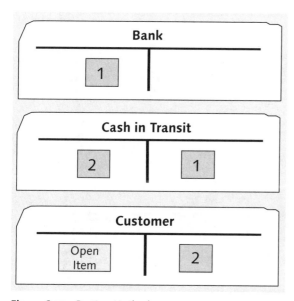

Figure 6.40   Posting Method

The second posting (to the customer) can be more difficult. The system automatically makes the posting, depending on whether an open item can be found and cleared. When postprocessing bank statements, accounts receivable accountants try to determine the customer and item(s) for which a cash receipt was intended.

The postprocessing screen is available in Transaction FEBA_BANK_STATEMENT under the menu path ACCOUNTING • FINANCIAL ACCOUNTING • BANKING • INCOMING • BANK STATEMENT • POSTPROCESS.

Figure 6.41 shows the starting point for this transaction. Because some enterprises have many house banks, each with a large number of bank statements, it makes sense and may even be necessary to make a selection before accessing the postprocessing screen. In our example, we want to call the bank statements of company code 3000, house bank 3000 (Citibank), and the checking account created there with the account ID 3000.

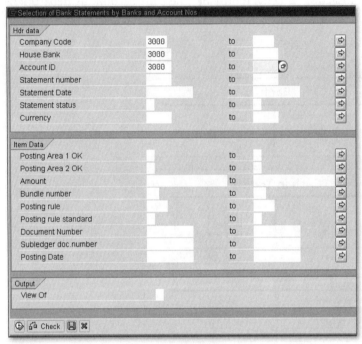

Figure 6.41 Postprocessing—Bank Selection

Automatically created document

The left-hand side of Figure 6.42 shows the bank statement numbers from the selection. In our example, we want to take a closer look at Bank Statement 2. The right-hand side of the screen shows transaction number 195. Therefore, the system automatically identified and posted $5,959. In addition, posting area 1 references the document number.

Postprocessing

When you double-click the number in posting area 1, the postprocessing transaction navigates to the document display. Figure 6.43 shows a bank transfer between two Citibank accounts.

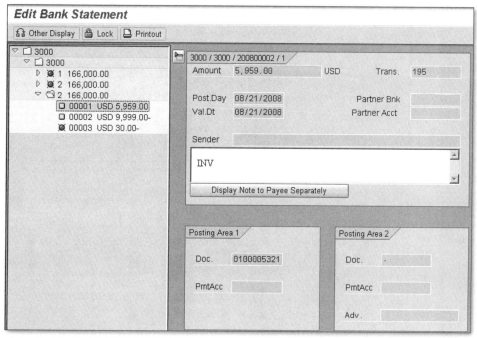

Figure 6.42 Postprocessing—Overview

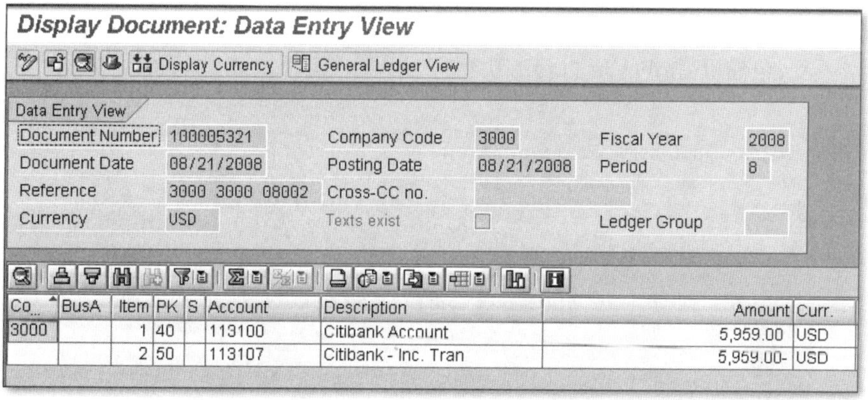

Figure 6.43 Displaying a Document

If you press F12, the second sale amount in Figure 6.44 also references direct processing. Based on the transaction and/or note to payee, $9,999 could be classified as a check posting.

Analysis of the note to payee

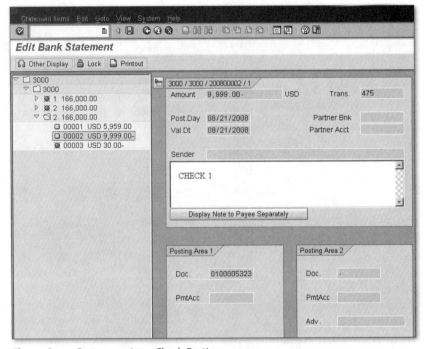

Figure 6.44 Postprocessing—Check Posting

If you double-click this entry, the system takes you back to the posting document shown in Figure 6.45.

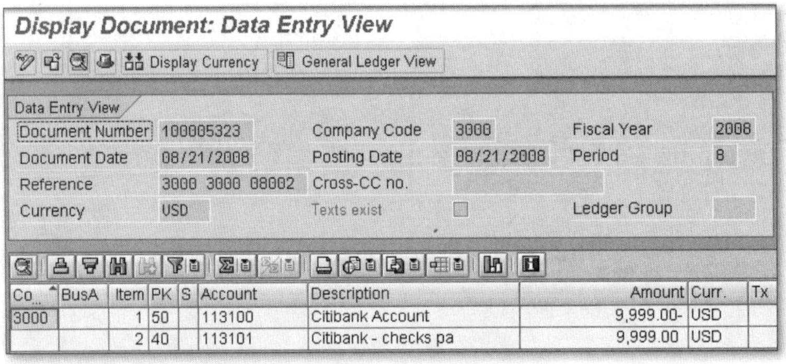

Figure 6.45 Displaying a Document—Check Posting

It is not always possible to fully automate a posting. If the business transactions are not known or only partially defined, manual postprocessing is necessary.

Degree of Automation   **[+]**

In general, 80–90% of all transactions in a bank statement can and are automatically posted by the system. If all process codes have been defined, optimization begins through the note to payee. Search strings can be used to improve the rate of processing (for example, if the license plate number of a company car belonging to an enterprise always contains a particular sequence or if abbreviations such as "FEE" or "Charge" in the note to payee imply bank charges).

The SAP system could not automatically post the third sale amount on the bank statement. Figure 6.46 shows that neither posting area 1 nor 2 has a document number for a debit amount of €30.

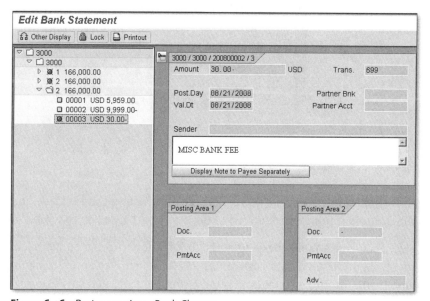

Figure 6.46   Postprocessing—Bank Charges

The note to payee indicates bank charges. Postprocessing takes place by placing the cursor on the sale amount and selecting Save. The program then navigates to the posting screen shown in Figure 6.47. Here, you see

Manual posting of bank charges

that an initial account assignment to G/L account 479000 (Bank Charges) was successful. However, the system could not perform an automatic posting in the background because cost accounting account assignments were missing.

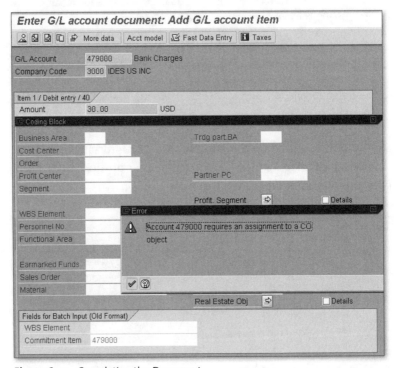

Figure 6.47 Completing the Document

If, for example, you specify a cost center, the posting can be made and the document number is entered in posting area 1 (see Figure 6.48).

Drill down to a single document

Here, you can double-click the entry to drill down to the single document. Figure 6.49 shows cost center 1000, which was entered manually. In the future, a default account assignment defined in Customizing and consisting of a P&L account and a cost accounting object will ensure that the electronic bank statement is automatically posted in the background.

The electronic bank statement is important for all transactions processed using house banks. You can also use cash journals to process incoming and outgoing payments.

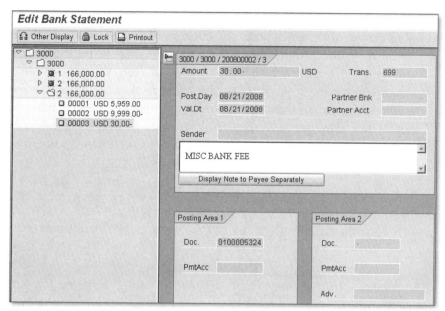

Figure 6.48 Completed Postprocessing

Co...	BusA	Item	PK	S	Account	Description	Amount	Curr.	Tx	Cost Center	Order	Profit Center
3000	9900	1	40		479000	Bank Charges	30.00	USD		1000		3402
		2	50		113100	Citibank Account	30.00-	USD				

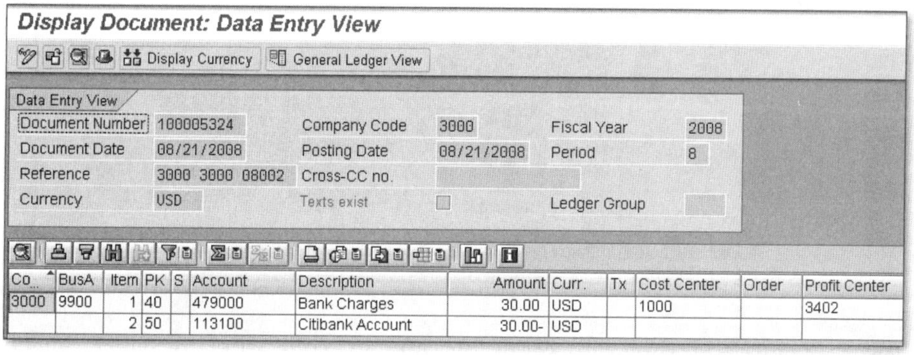

Figure 6.49 Document View—Bank Charges

6.7 Cash Journal

In practice, some business transactions are processed directly using cash, for example, if a vendor has delivered his goods to your enterprise but requires immediate payment before handing them over to you, or if a customer primarily uses cash to pay his receivables. These transactions also include smaller purchases such as office supplies, which are not invoiced but instead are paid using petty cash. The business transactions are versatile, which poses the question of how to document these transactions and include them in the balance sheet. Ultimately, your auditor will determine whether paper-based data recording or electronic data recording (by using a spreadsheet program) fulfills today's basic requirements for accurate bookkeeping and the necessary compliance requirements. In the SAP system, bank accounting can also manage cash journals under the menu path ACCOUNTING • FINANCIAL ACCOUNTING • BANKING • INCOMING • CASH JOURNAL (Transaction FBCJ).

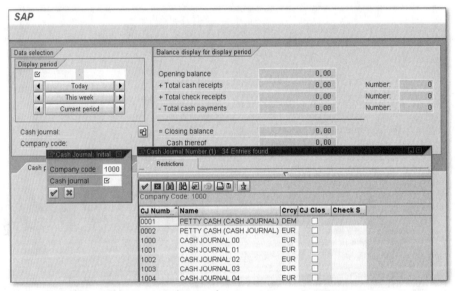

Figure 6.50 Selecting a Cash Journal

Small subledger accounting   Figure 6.50 shows the set up for company code 1000, for which several cash journals have been configured. A cash journal is an example of small subledger accounting. You can choose to record detailed information in the subledger only or also in the general ledger. In our example, a separate G/L account is assigned to each cash journal. Therefore, the many cash journals are also separated in general ledger accounting, in a consistent and transparent manner. However, one disadvantage here is a chart of accounts that contains more accounts than necessary. Alternatively, all cash journals can reference one G/L account. In this case, only subledger accounting provides information about the current financial status of each cash journal.

In our example, we have selected cash journal 1030 in company code 1000. This cash desk is managed in Euros and shows an opening balance of €20,000 on 08/21/2008. The Cash payments, Cash receipts, and Check receipts tabs represent the three possible categories of business transactions (see Figure 6.51). The transactions have been designed in such a way that the information will make sense to you even if you are not an accountant. Posting keys, debit amounts or credit amounts are not required here because this was the only way to ensure broad acceptance of the cash journal by users.

Documenting individual transactions

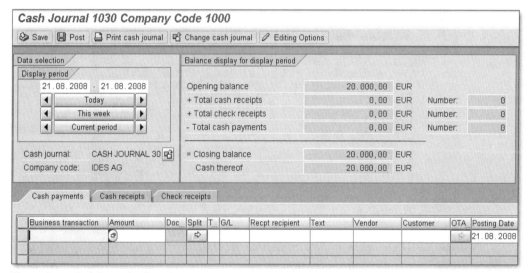

Figure 6.51 Cash Journal—Overview

For bank accounting purposes, there is a direct connection between the cash journal and the G/L account. In our example, cash journal 1030 is connected to account 100130. Figure 6.52 shows that the opening balance of €20,000 in the subledger corresponds to the total amount for the posting documents.

Connecting the cash journal to the G/L account

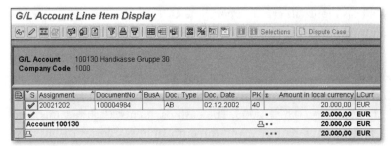

Figure 6.52 Connection to the General Ledger

To establish a connection between simple data entries and completed posting records, it is necessary to define business transactions for the cash payments, cash receipts, and check receipts categories. Figure 6.53 lists some of these transactions.

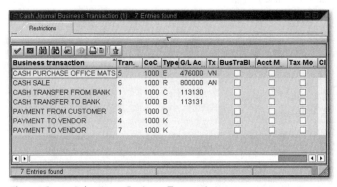

Figure 6.53 Selecting a Business Transaction

Overview of defined business transactions

The categories determine that receipts produce debit postings and payments produce credit postings. The offsetting account for the cash journal is defined in the business transaction itself. In our example, we want to purchase office materials to the value of €50. First, you select the CASH PAYMENTS tab. If you press F4, the system displays the business transactions that exist, including the CASH PURCHASE OFFICE MATS entry, the defined P&L account 476000, and the tax code. Only a limited knowledge of bookkeeping is required for the entry shown in Figure 6.54.

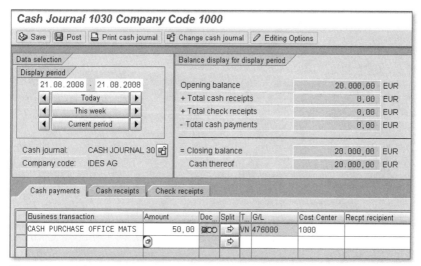

Figure 6.54 Selecting a Business Transaction that Will Determine the Account Assignment

At this point, the transaction is entered in the cash journal only. When you save the information, there is a cash outflow and the subledger balance is reduced accordingly. If this is successfully reconciled with the physical cash desk, a posting takes place, that is, the general ledger is updated at the end of the day. Figure 6.55 shows an example of two business transactions that have been entered and, in the meantime, saved in cash book 1030. The closing balance at the physical cash desk must be €19,200. These entries have not been transferred to the general ledger yet.

Transfer to general ledger

A cash payment from a customer is entered in a separate business transaction. Because the payment concerns a large amount, you want to confirm receipt of the money. You must decide whether you want to clear the incoming amount directly with the open invoices in accounts receivable accounting or instead perform a payment on account as shown in the example. Figure 6.56 shows the entry made, including additional information in the Receipt recipient field.

Cash payment from a customer

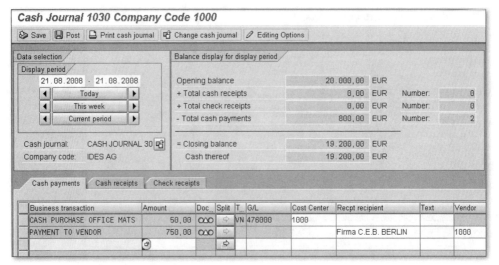

Figure 6.55 Saved Business Transactions

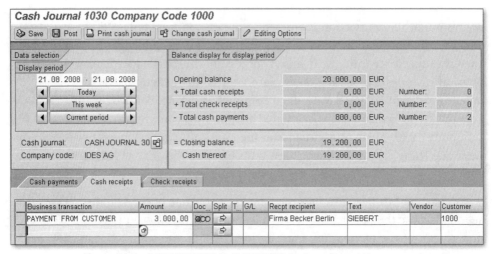

Figure 6.56 PAYMENT FROM CUSTOMER Business Transaction

Status of data entry If you select CONFIRMATION, the system displays an information message (see Figure 6.57). The status Entered is insufficient for the confirmation printout. The entry must have at least the status Saved or, even better, the status Posted.

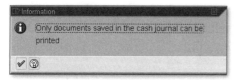

Figure 6.57   Information Message

Once these minor hurdles have been cleared, the confirmation printout becomes an easy-to-use function in the cash journal. Figure 6.58 shows a sample confirmation printout.

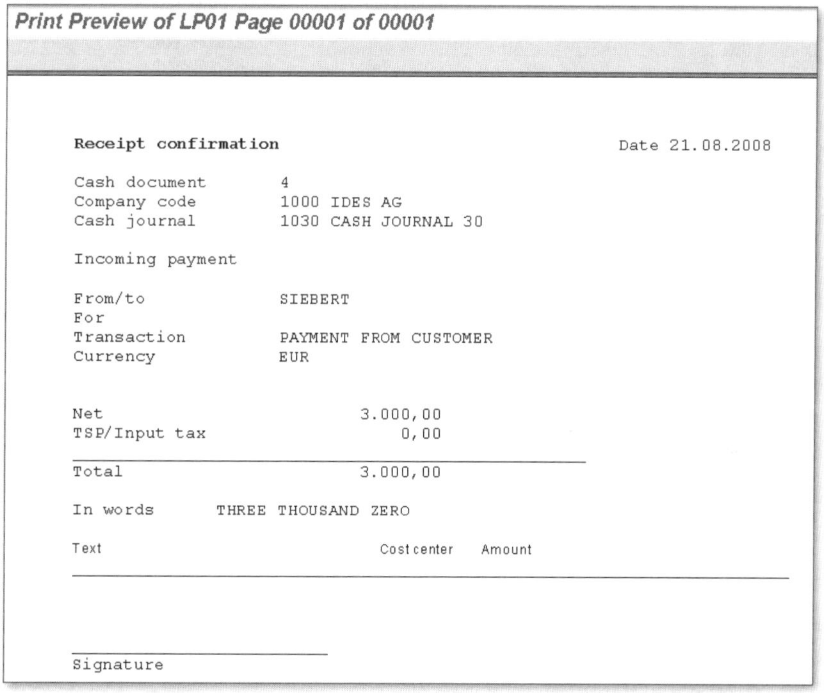

```
Print Preview of LP01 Page 00001 of 00001


        Receipt confirmation                      Date 21.08.2008

        Cash document       4
        Company code        1000 IDES AG
        Cash journal        1030 CASH JOURNAL 30

        Incoming payment

        From/to             SIEBERT
        For
        Transaction         PAYMENT FROM CUSTOMER
        Currency            EUR


        Net                         3.000,00
        TSP/Input tax                   0,00
        _____

        Total                       3.000,00

        In words      THREE THOUSAND ZERO

        Text                        Cost center    Amount
        _____



        _____
        Signature
```

Figure 6.58   Confirmation Printout

If the entries in the cash journal obtain the status Saved at the end of the day, they are transferred directly to general ledger accounting. In our example of petty cash book 1030, every business transaction and associated entry can then be found in G/L account 100130. Figure 6.59 shows both the outgoing payments of €50 and €750 and the incoming payment of €3,000.

Transfer to general ledger

If we return to the cash journal and double-click an entry, the system displays an additional window that reflects the link between the subledger and the general ledger (see Figure 6.60).

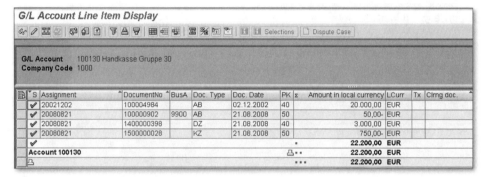

Figure 6.59 Transfer to General Ledger

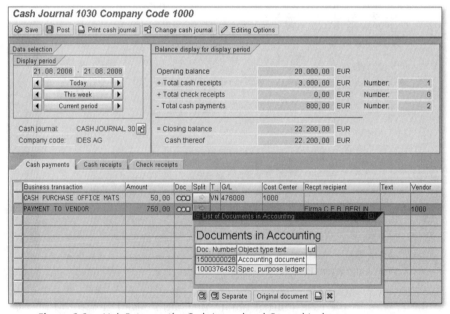

Figure 6.60 Link Between the Cash Journal and General Ledger

Reversal posting

Consequently, there is considerably greater transparency in cash journals. If, for example, no payment is made and the money is returned to petty cash, this is documented using a reversal (see Figure 6.61), which adopts the mechanisms of the general ledger. You must enter a reversal reason and reversal date here (see Figure 6.62).

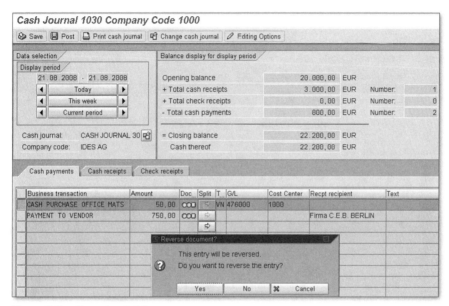

Figure 6.61 Reversing Entries

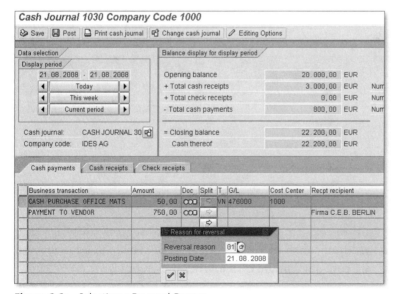

Figure 6.62 Selecting a Reversal Reason

If the posting period is open and the document can be posted, the reversal is documented in both the general ledger and subledger. Figure 6.63 shows the cash journal, and Figure 6.64 shows the G/L account after the reversal.

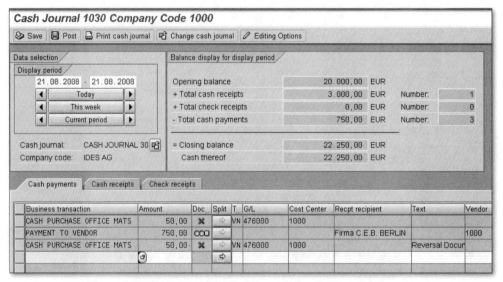

Figure 6.63 Overview of the Cash Journal after the Reversal

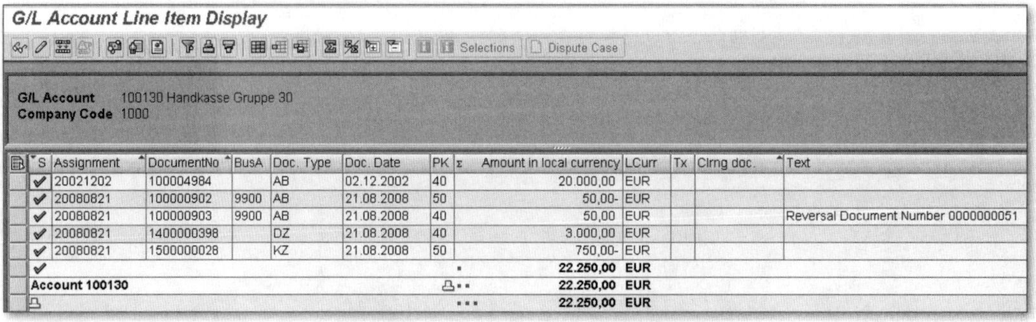

Figure 6.64 General Ledger View after the Reversal

If you want to evaluate these documents in a list, you can select Print cash journal in the cash journal. All transactions, including the reversal posting, are contained in the cash journal shown in Figure 6.65.

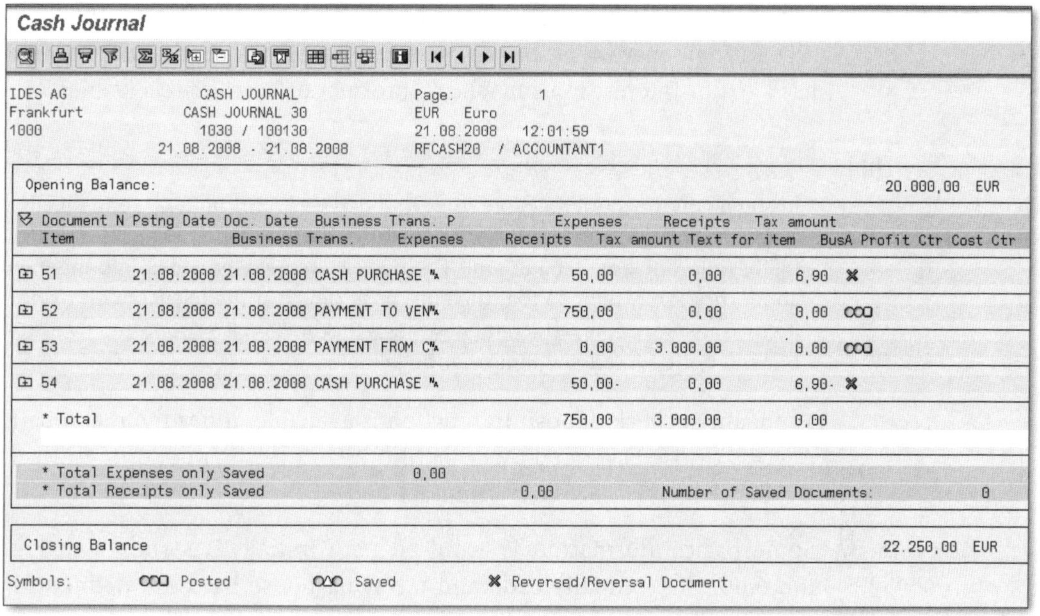

Figure 6.65 Cash Journal

Our example has introduced you to some of the many features of the cash journal. To summarize, the cash journal reduces any additional manual effort, it may avoid the need for an interface, and it achieves the new, required transparency through detailed documentation. Transaction FBCJ was re-created for Release 4.6 and has undergone many enhancements since then.

6.8   Check Deposit Transaction

Checks are used, to a greater or lesser extent, as a means of payment, depending on the country and industry. Manual check deposits are used to enter any checks received. Incoming checks need to be managed efficiently to transfer them to the house bank as quickly as possible. The goal here is an optimized value date on the bank account, so that no loss of interest is incurred. In an enterprise, information from incoming checks is gathered, as centrally as possible, in a check deposit list that is not posted immediately. Changes can be made at any time before the posting process begins. As of this time, both the checks and the central check

Optimized value date

deposit list are transferred to the house bank. In addition to the bank accounting department, the accounts receivable accounting department has a major interest in using check information to clear receivables.

[+]

> **Country Specifics**
>
> In some countries (for example, the United States), it is unusual to manually enter checks in the SAP ERP system. Instead, customers send checks directly to the relevant house bank, and the bank statement provides information about the cash receipt so that the enterprise can clear the relevant debit-side items. This procedure, which is known as a lockbox, is also supported by SAP, but will not be discussed in further detail here.

The manual check deposit transaction is available under the menu path ACCOUNTING • FINANCIAL ACCOUNTING • BANKING • INCOMING • CHECK DEPOSIT • ENTER MANUALLY (Transaction FF68).

Central check deposit list

Some basic information is required here initially. As shown in Figure 6.66, the company code and receiving house bank are defined for the central check deposit list. The transaction determines the posting method. In our example, there are two posting records:

▸ Debit the check deposit account and credit the clearing account.

▸ Debit the clearing account and credit the customer.

The value date refers to an estimated value date that will have a considerable effect on SAP reporting. Let's consider the current and future liquidity of the enterprise. In our example, a check receipt (check credit memo) is planned for 08/23/2008.

If you press ⌨Enter⌨, you can then enter check information in the list shown in Figure 6.67. In general, you can use the bank key and bank account number to identify the customer master record. If the check contains additional information such as reference document numbers, it is possible to identify the documents to be cleared in the SAP system, thus reducing the manual postprocessing effort considerably.

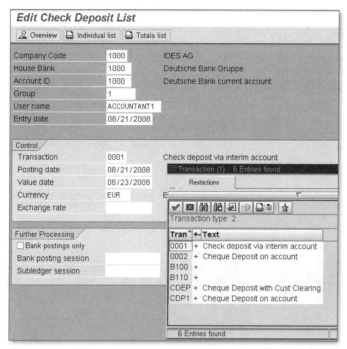

Figure 6.66 Editing a Check Deposit List

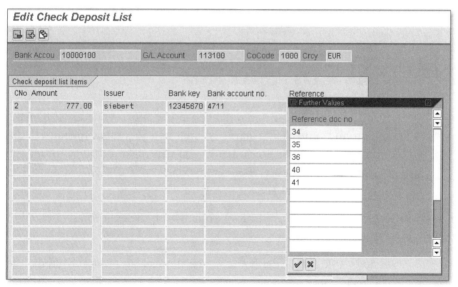

Figure 6.67 Entering Items

Clearing Several Invoices

At first, only one field for the reference document number is displayed on the entry screen. In practice, however, one check frequently clears several invoices. If you double-click the REFERENCE DOC NO. field, the system displays another window in which you can enter additional values.

If you press F12, you return to the general overview, which you can then save. You can then click on the 🔍 icon to view the current processing status (see Figure 6.68).

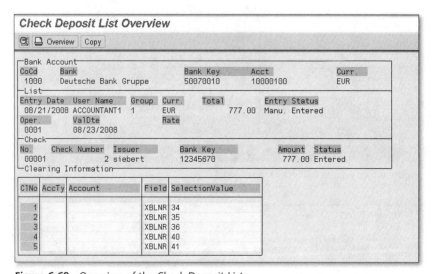

Figure 6.68 Overview of the Check Deposit List

Creating postings Because the transaction has not been posted yet, you can still make changes at any time. If the status is Final and you want to transfer the incoming checks to the house bank, you can make postings under the menu path CHECK DEPOSIT TRANSACTION • POST • INDIVIDUAL LIST. The result is the posting list shown in Figure 6.69.

Processing batch input sessions In accordance with the settings, two batch input sessions are created in our example:

▶ Session 1000-1000 (debit the check deposit account and credit the clearing account)

▸ Session \1000-1000 (debit the clearing account and credit the customer)

Update Account Statement/Check Deposit Transaction

IDES AG   Check deposit list posting   Time 14:06:27   Date 08/21/2008
Frankfurt   Processing Statistics   RFEBBU00/ACCOUNTANT1 Page   1

Posting Ar	Bank Key	Account Nu	Sessn	Group	FB01	FB05	PmtAcc	No Posting	Error	Total	Total Deb.	Total Cred
Bank Accounting	50070010	10000100	1000-1000		1	0	0	0	0	1	777.00	0.00
* Bank Accounting					1	0	0	0	0	1	777.00	0.00
** Bank Accounting					1	0	0	0	0	1	777.00	0.00
Subledger acctng	50070010	10000100	/1000-1000		0	1	0	0	0	1	777.00	0.00
* Subledger acctng					0	1	0	0	0	1	777.00	0.00
** Subledger acctng					0	1	0	0	0	1	777.00	0.00
***					1	1	0	0	0	2	1,554.00	0.00

Figure 6.69 List of Postings Created

The system should then be able to create one G/L account posting without errors. The second account assignment depends on the quality of the information on the check. It must contain the customer and the open items. Transaction SM35 provides an overview of the batch input sessions created (see Figure 6.70).

Batch Input: Session Overview

Selection criteria
Sess.: *   From: To: Created by: ACCOUNTANT1

Session name	Stat.	Created By	Date	Time	Creation Progra.	Lock Date	Authorizat.	Trans.			Screens
/1000-1000		ACCOUNTANT1	08/21/2008	14:06:27	RFEBBU00		ACCOUNTANT1	1	0	0	5
1000-1000		ACCOUNTANT1	08/21/2008	14:06:26	RFEBBU00		ACCOUNTANT1	1	0	0	5

Figure 6.70 Overview of the Batch Input Sessions

As expected, the "debit the check deposit account and credit the clearing account" posting can be made successfully. The session and its "debit the clearing account and credit the customer" posting record is selected and recorded by pressing [F8]. The content shown in Figure 6.71 appears on the next screen.

Displaying the posting method

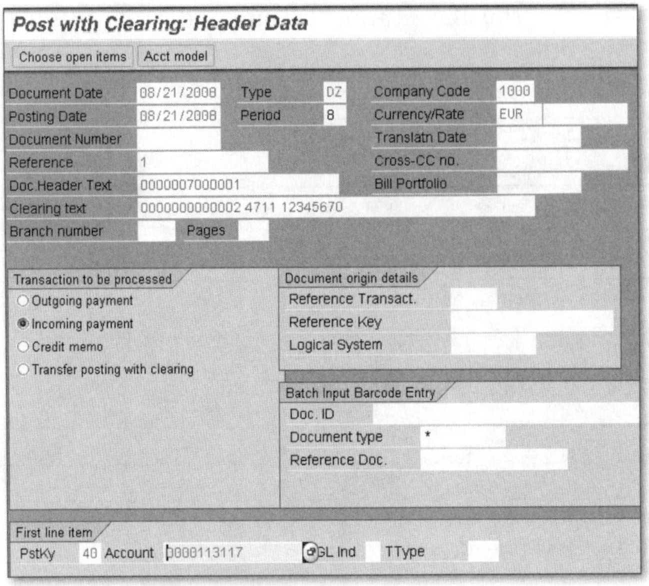

Figure 6.71 Post with Clearing

Value date   In addition to the header information, the figure below shows the start of the first document item. The header data of the incoming payment is correct. G/L account number 113117 is used as a clearing account. If you press Enter, the debit item is completed in the next view. Figure 6.72 shows the estimated value date in addition to the check amount.

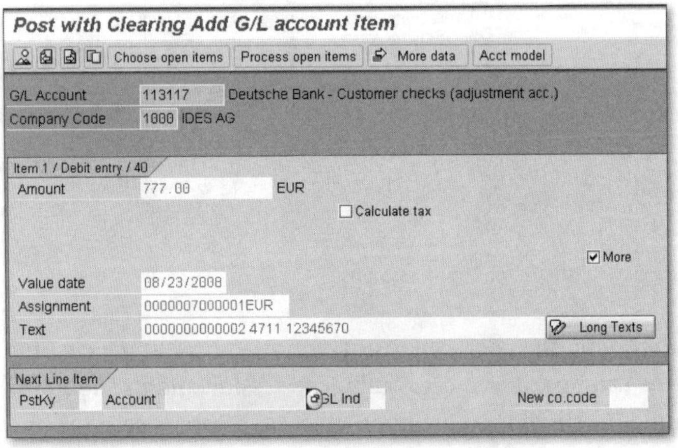

Figure 6.72 Entering the G/L Account Item

When you press ⌈Enter⌉ again, the batch input session navigates to the selection screen for open items. In the case of Figure 6.73, no customer could be found.

Once again, you can press ⌈Enter⌉ to change the selection conditions. In the example shown in Figure 6.74, the search for invoice items begins at this time.

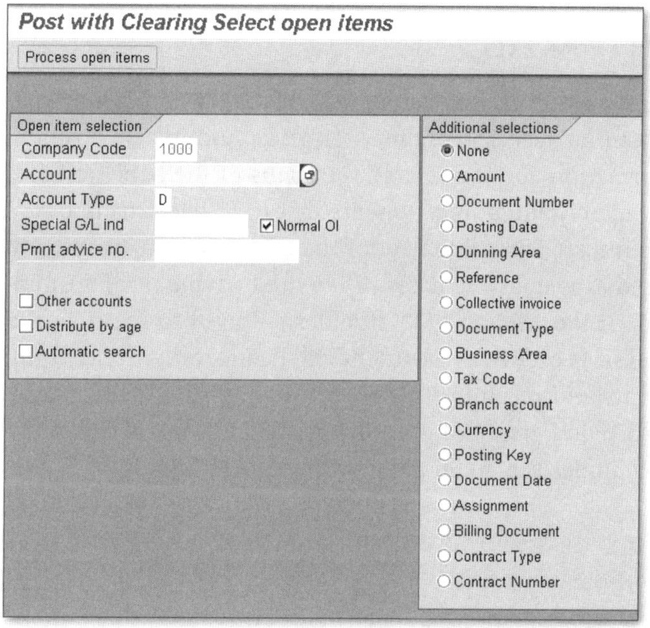

Post with Clearing Select open items

Process open items

Open item selection		Additional selections
Company Code	1000	● None
Account		○ Amount
Account Type	D	○ Document Number
Special G/L ind	☑ Normal OI	○ Posting Date
Pmnt advice no.		○ Dunning Area
		○ Reference
☐ Other accounts		○ Collective invoice
☐ Distribute by age		○ Document Type
☐ Automatic search		○ Business Area
		○ Tax Code
		○ Branch account
		○ Currency
		○ Posting Key
		○ Document Date
		○ Assignment
		○ Billing Document
		○ Contract Type
		○ Contract Number

Figure 6.73 Selecting Open Items

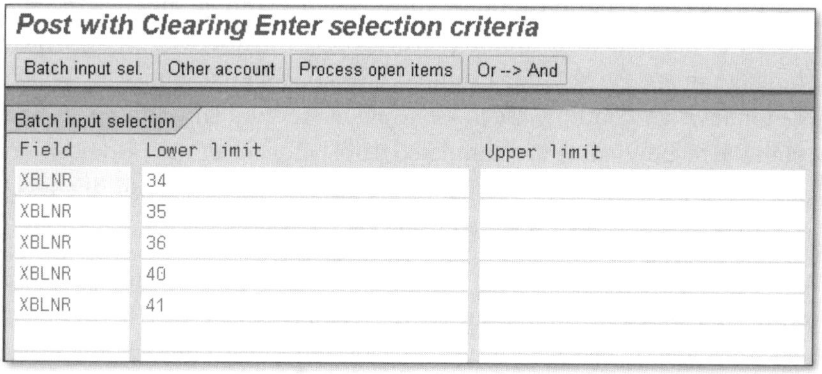

Post with Clearing Enter selection criteria

Batch input sel. | Other account | Process open items | Or --> And

Batch input selection

Field	Lower limit	Upper limit
XBLNR	34	
XBLNR	35	
XBLNR	36	
XBLNR	40	
XBLNR	41	

Figure 6.74 Selection Conditions

6.9   Evaluations in Bank Accounting

SAP ERP and SAP NetWeaver BW have a wide range of predefined evaluations for bank accounting. The information on the following pages merely represents practical examples for the day-to-day activities of a cash management specialist and is only a fraction of the many possibilities available.

6.9.1   Liquidity Forecast

Advantages associated with integration

The bank accounting department can use the Liquidity Forecast evaluation to obtain a central overview of the enterprise's current cash position. It provides information about not only the status of the bank account, but also incoming and outgoing payments that have been made or are planned for the future. The value date of the check deposit transaction is also considered as well as the dates of required payment for customers and vendors. If the MM and SD modules are used to manage purchase orders and sales orders, this content will be incorporated as future planned payments and receipts. This report highlights the advantages associated with SAP integration. In the SAP system, this important evaluation is available under the menu path ACCOUNTING • FINANCIAL SUPPLY CHAIN MANAGEMENT • CASH AND LIQUIDITY MANAGEMENT • CASH MANAGEMENT • INFO SYSTEM • REPORTS ON CASH MANAGEMENT • LIQUIDITY ANALYSES • LIQUIDITY FORECAST.

Changing the liquidity

In Figure 6.75, company code 1000 with a sorted list according to days is selected as the selection and display criterion. This makes sense for very short-term considerations. Alternatively, the data can be summarized at a weekly or monthly level for long-term forecasts. The delta display, which shows changes, is used, for example, for subledger accounts for which cash inflows and outflow are to be displayed individually and not as one total. We recommend an accumulated display for the entire cash position (for example, for bank accounts). In the output control, the scaling level is 3; that is, the display is scaled into "EUR 1,000" steps.

Cash inflows and outflows

When you press ⌞F8⌟, the criteria selected earlier produce the result list shown in Figure 6.76. In the summarized display (09/14/2008) for banks and subledger accounts, positive amounts denote cash inflows and negative amounts denote cash outflows. In our example, we want to take a closer look at the planned cash inflow of €92,000 on 09/22/2008. To do this, we double-click the entry.

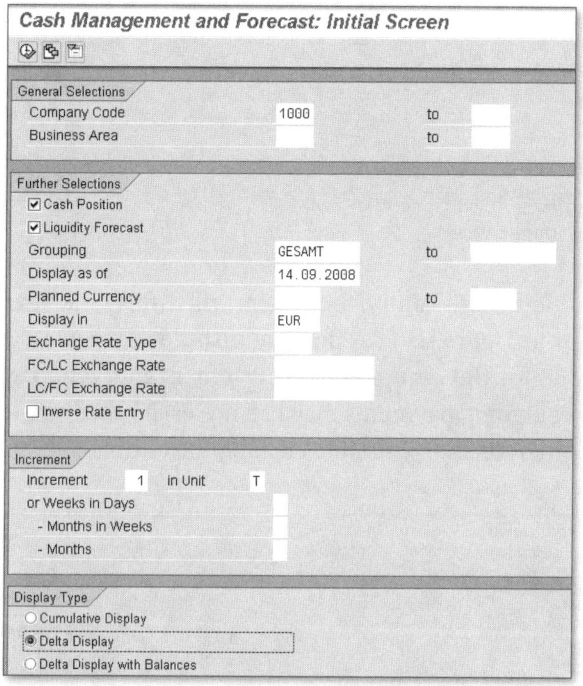

Figure 6.75 Initial Screen for Cash Management and Forecast

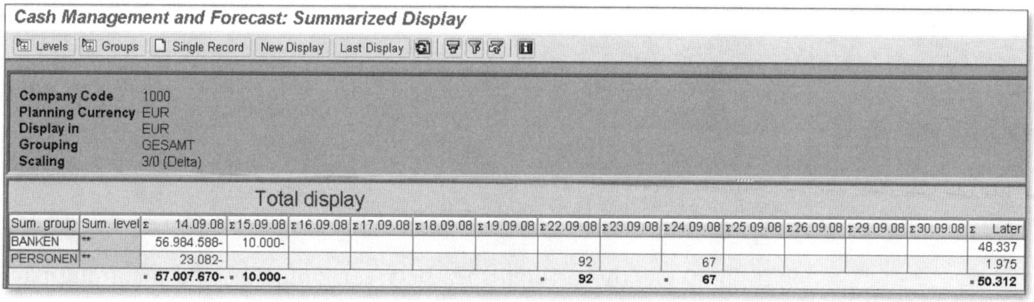

Figure 6.76 Summarized Display for Cash Management and Forecast

Figure 6.77 shows that, at the subledger account level, changes are assigned to the vendor/customer area only.

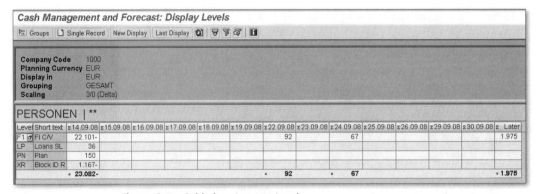

Figure 6.77 Subledger Account Level

Customer and vendor evaluation level

Once again, if you double-click the entry, the system will display the next evaluation level shown in Figure 6.78. A positive cash flow of €92,000 is expected on 09/22/08 for the grouping F1—Customers and Vendors. Because incoming and outgoing payments may balance each other out, it is advisable to check other details by double-clicking the entries.

Figure 6.78 Overview for Vendors and Customers

Figure 6.79 clearly distinguishes between outgoing and incoming payments. In row A1 (Domestic), a cash disbursement of less than €1,000 is planned for 09/22/2008. The defined scaling produces the result 0– on the screen. The revenue side in row E2 (Domestic) shows a planned cash receipt of €92,000 for 09/22/2008.

Display Individual Memo: Open Items in Liquidity Forcast

Group: E2 Domestic customers / Level: F1 Posting of purchasing & sales

CoCd	Plan. day	Curr.	Amount	BusA	Customer	Name 1	DocumentNo	Year	Itm
1000	20.09.2008	EUR	49.851,00	1000	1032	Institut fuer Umweltforschung	1400000127	2008	1
1000	20.09.2008	EUR	23.907,80	1000	1032	Institut fuer Umweltforschung	1400000128	2008	1
1000	20.09.2008	EUR	18.222,60	1000	1032	Institut fuer Umweltforschung	1400000126	2008	1

Figure 6.79 Individual Memo Display

You can double-click the entry to analyze whether it concerns one large due invoice or several smaller due invoices from one or more customers. The document displayed in Figure 6.80 shows that this entry concerns one customer with three invoices.

Display Document: Data Entry View

Taxes   Display Currency   General Ledger View

Data Entry View

Document Number	1400000127	Company Code 1000	Fiscal Year 2008
Document Date	17.07.2008	Posting Date 17.07.2008	Period 7
Reference	0090036876	Cross-CC no.	
Currency	EUR	Texts exist ☐	Ledger Group

Co...	Item	PK	S	Account	Description	Amount	Curr.	Tx
1000	1	01		1032	Institut fuer Umweltforschung	49.851,00	EUR	A0
	2	50		800000	Sales revenues - dom	49.851,00-	EUR	A0

Figure 6.80 Document Display

If SD integration is active, you can also drill down to the billing item (Figure 6.81).

Invoice (F2) 90036876 (F2) Display: Overview of Billing Items

Accounting   Billing documents

F2 Invoice (F2)	90036876	Net Value	49.851,00 EUR
Payer	1032	Institut fuer Umweltforschung / Bernauer Strasse 12 / DI	
Billing Date	17.07.2008		

Item	Description	Billed Quantity	SU	Net value	Material
10	Pumpe PRECISION 103	15	PC	49.851,00	P-103

Figure 6.81 Billing Item

Sixth evaluation
level

Starting with the original document, the user is already at the sixth evaluation level in bank accounting. If the billing document is required, the user can call it here (Figure 6.82).

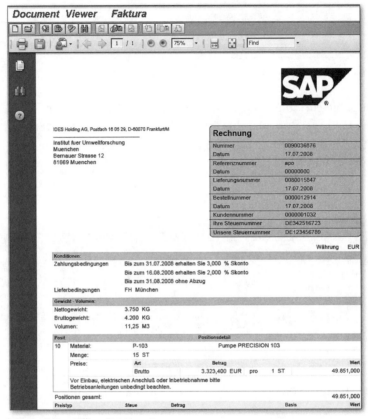

Figure 6.82 Billing Document

In an integrated SAP system, all of the information is just one double-click away. This is also the case for evaluations that concern the check register.

6.9.2 Check Register

Using checks

The question that comes to the fore when using a check register is which checks are used for which vendor transaction.

Internal Audits

Internal auditors regularly use this evaluation to prevent fraud within an enterprise. Even if the principle of dual control is applied to bank transfer media, checks can be created on any printer in the enterprise.

You can restrict selections by company code, house bank, and if necessary, by check number under the menu path ACCOUNTING • FINANCIAL SUPPLY CHAIN MANAGEMENT • CASH AND LIQUIDITY MANAGEMENT • CASH MANAGEMENT • INFO SYSTEM • REPORTS ON CASH MANAGEMENT • LIQUIDITY ANALYSES menu path. Figure 6.83 shows all of the selection options for the check register.

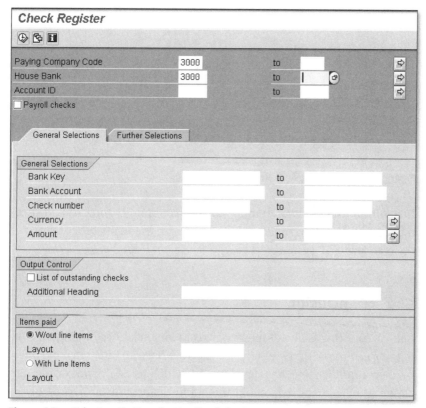

Figure 6.83 Selection Options for the Check Register

Result list provides details

The result list clearly shows which payments were made with individual checks (see Figure 6.84). You can double-click an entry to access the payment document and the original invoice. You can also determine which SAP user produced the check.

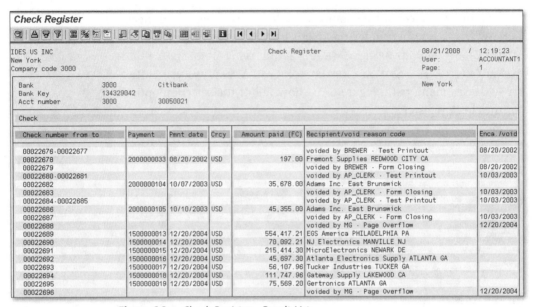

Figure 6.84 Check Register—Result List

In addition to these two sample evaluations (liquidity forecast and check register), the bank accounting department can use many other reports in the standard SAP system.

6.10 Conclusion

Bank accounting is one of the key areas in Financial Accounting. In challenging economic times, enterprises need to have an integrated overview of their liquidity. Further developments such as SAP Bank Communication Management help avoid integration gaps and can represent the entire process in the SAP system on a continuous basis. Furthermore, the principle of dual control during the approval procedure fulfills the current compliance standards for final payment release.

A closing provides information about an enterprise's current financial situation. This chapter describes the programs in SAP ERP Financials that can be used to automate the activities involved in the closing process and to enable a fast close.

7   Closing Operations

This chapter begins by examining the basic business principles underpinning closing operations. It then describes many SAP programs that you can use to reduce the manual effort involved in individual closings. It also provides tips for using organizational tools to accelerate the closing process in the SAP system.

7.1   Basic Business Principles

This section seeks to familiarize readers with the basic business principles on which closing operations are based.

All closing operations revolve around the financial statement, which consists of the balance sheet and profit and loss statement. The financial statement compares resources (assets) with claims (liabilities and owner's equity). Liabilities and owner's equity (the debit side of the balance sheet) provide information about the enterprise's source of funds, whereas assets (the credit side of the balance sheet) provide information about the disposition of funds. The financial statement contains value specifications only and does not include any quantity specifications. Liabilities and owner's equity can be broken down as follows:

Financial statement

▶ Fixed assets

▶ Current assets (inventory, receivables, cash)

Claims can be divided into:

- Stockholders' equity (capital stock, reserves)
- Outside capital (bonds, payables, provisions)

Prepaid/deferred items

In addition to liabilities and owner's equity, which are shown on the left-hand side of the balance sheet, and claims, which appear on the right, the balance sheet usually also includes prepaid and deferred items, that is, prepaid expenses and deferred income. These items delimit the profit and loss of one period from the profit and loss of the next. They include, for example, insurance premiums paid in advance (prepaid expenses) or rental income received in advance (deferred income). In both cases, the payment refers to a transaction that affects net income in the subsequent period.

In addition to the external year-end closing (i.e., the annual balance sheet and profit and loss statement), internal documentation, planning, and reconciliation calculations are often prepared. These are only used internally within the enterprise and are particularly flexible because they are not subject to legal restrictions. Closings can be prepared for various periods, for example, for a month, a quarter, or a year (year-end closing), and they serve the following purposes:

- Calculate tax liability
- Determine investment potential
- Calculate sale value

In this context, a fast close is an accelerated closing of the enterprise's books on a key date. Events that become known after the year-end closing cannot be incorporated.

[Ex]

Receivable Valuation

Enterprise A is in the process of preparing its financial statement for the fiscal year ending December 31. This process usually lasts until March or April of the following year. In mid-April, one of its major customers (B) declares insolvency. This information is known to A on April 30. It may seem obvious that the first thing to do is to write off the receivables that existed as of December 31. However, this is not a legally viable option. This situation has nothing to do with the balance sheet as of December 31. Both the cause of the event and the enterprise's knowledge of it date from the subsequent year. A timely year-end closing in March means that A does not have to even consider events that occur on April 30.

All enterprises have their own closing procedure document to help them complete this process of preparing the closing as quickly and efficiently as possible. In terms of IT support, the plan is usually stored in Microsoft Office applications (Word, Excel, Project) or, with the new SAP release, in the ERP system directly. A sample closing procedure document is provided in Appendix D to illustrate the essential business steps involved in an individual closing. The plan shows which activities need to be completed before and after the balance sheet date (usually December 31 each year). However, this example in no way claims to be complete or globally applicable.

The various closing plans enterprises use do not only contain the activities that take place in the SAP system. For example, the SAP system is not affected when the value of pension reserves is calculated by external experts. The following sections in this chapter focus on the activities in the closing process that are supported by SAP ERP Financials:

- Management of parked documents
- Maintenance of the goods receipt and invoice receipt account
- Posting of salaries and wages
- Posting of provisions
- Accrual and deferral postings
- Settlement of assets under construction
- Asset inventory
- Depreciation posting run
- Individual and flat-rate value adjustments
- Foreign currency valuation
- Interest calculation
- Manual and technical reconciliation
- Intercompany reconciliation
- Reclassification
- Balance confirmation
- Advance return for tax on sales and purchases
- Period control

▸ Control and monitoring of the closing process

▸ Balance carryforward

Parallel accounting

The transactions and programs provided for these activities in SAP ERP Financials can help you speed up your closing process. The results are particularly effective if you use parallel accounting principles for individual closings. If you do, programs such as the depreciation posting run for complex fixed assets, the foreign currency valuation of your receivables, flat-rate value adjustment, and reclassification are called numerous times and help you calculate or post valuations automatically, for example, for local law, IFRS and US-GAAP. The first section below discusses the business transactions in a posting period that are currently mapped incompletely in the SAP system. The document parking function, which is used by many enterprises, is useful in such cases.

7.2   Management of Parked Documents

There are various reasons for using parked documents. In terms of division of labor, it can be useful to simply park or save the documents of one employee or group of employees. A content check to determine account assignment (i.e., further processing in Controlling) can then be made by more qualified employees in the next step.

SAP authorization concept

In a second use case, the SAP authorization concept supports the posting function up to a defined amount and then switches to document parking as of this limit. In other words, a certain employee is not authorized to post documents over a certain amount and can only save, that is park, these documents instead. The content check is based on a principle of dual control involving a second employee.

Regardless of which situation applies to your enterprise (basic division of labor or an amount-dependent dual-control principle), it is always advisable to check the list of parked documents at the end of the posting period. This is because it is necessary to determine whether these documents (activities) belong to the current period for the purpose of calculating profits for the valid accounting period. If the period is technically closed, the posting date that has already been entered in the parked document usually has to be changed manually. To access the transaction

shown in Figure 7.1, select ACCOUNTING • FINANCIAL ACCOUNTING • GEN-
ERAL LEDGER • DOCUMENT • PARKED DOCUMENTS • POST/DELETE.

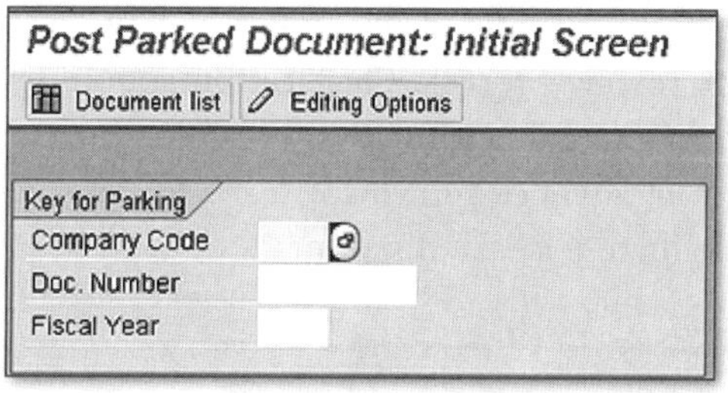

Figure 7.1 Posting a Parked Document

If you click on the Document list button, the selection screen shown in
Figure 7.2 is displayed. This provides you with an overview of all parked
documents and allows you to restrict the list by entering specific criteria.
In the example shown here, only the company codes from the fiscal year
2007 are selected. It is also useful to restrict the selection by processing
status. You can filter blocked documents or documents that are currently
in a release workflow. In our example, document status is not taken into
account in selecting the list.

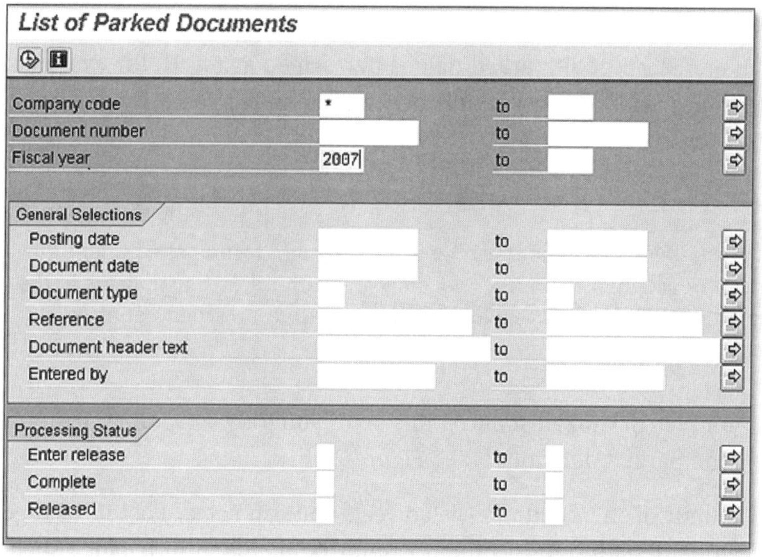

Figure 7.2 List of Parked Documents—Selection Screen

Document flow in the release approval procedure
Once you make your selection, the dialog list shown in Figure 7.3 appears. Thirteen parked documents are displayed in this example. Some vendor invoices with document type KR are blocked or are currently in a release procedure. The date of entry (Entered on) indicates how long the transaction has been in the review process. Clarification should be reached as soon as possible to enable a determination of profits for the valid accounting period, a correct advance return for tax on sales and purchases, and the option of deducting a cash discount.

Post Parked Documents: List

Status	SCCd	CoCd	Ty	DocumentNo	Year	Doc. Date	Posting Date	Entered on	User	Cp	Rel.ne	APth	Released by
	1000	1000	SA	100000129	2007	21.03.2007	21.03.2007	21.03.2007	OREGLIA1	☐	☐		
	1000	1000	SA	100000130	2007	21.03.2007	21.03.2007	21.03.2007	OREGLIA1	☑	☐		
	1000	1000	DR	1800000037	2007	23.05.2007	23.05.2007	23.05.2007	I034318	☑	☐		
	1000	1000	KR	1900000071	2007	18.06.2007	18.06.2007	18.06.2007	D036699	☐	☐		
	1000	1000	KR	1900000077	2007	09.07.2007	09.07.2007	09.07.2007	D035500	☑	☐		
🔒	3000	3000	KR	1900000044	2007	12.02.2007	12.02.2007	12.02.2007	I039731	☑	☑	3000	
🔒	3000	3000	KR	1900000057	2007	22.03.2007	22.03.2007	22.03.2007	WF-FI-C	☑	☑	3000	
🔒	3000	3000	KR	1900000058	2007	22.03.2007	22.03.2007	22.03.2007	WF-FI-C	☐	☑	3000	
🔒	3000	3000	KR	1900000059	2007	22.03.2007	22.03.2007	22.03.2007	I007782	☑	☑	3000	
🔒	3000	3000	KR	1900000060	2007	22.03.2007	22.03.2007	22.03.2007	WF-FI-C	☑	☑	3000	WF-FI-1
	3333	3333	KR	1900000058	2007	01.04.2007	25.04.2007	25.04.2007	I033202	☑	☐		
	6001	6001	DR	1800000008	2007	06.06.2007	06.06.2007	06.06.2007	MARIANO	☐	☐		
	AC10	AC10	KR	1900000001	2007	04.02.2007	04.02.2007	04.02.2007	C5038713	☐	☐		

Figure 7.3 List of Parked Documents—Document List

This dialog list offers several editing options. You can click on the ▣ icon to select all entries and send them for posting. When you do this, a complete check of all parked data is performed again. If, for example, the posting period or cost center originally entered is no longer valid, an error message appears.

[+] **Country-Specific Requirements for Document Entry**

When you delete a parked document, the assigned document number is not released or assigned to another document. As a result, a gap appears in the document journal. However, this is not permitted in certain countries (for example, Italy).

If you double-click on a list entry, this takes you directly to the screen for editing the parked document (see Figure 7.4).

Changing the document status
If all content of the document is correct, you can select Post to change the document status. A document cannot be included in balance sheet evaluations until it has been posted.

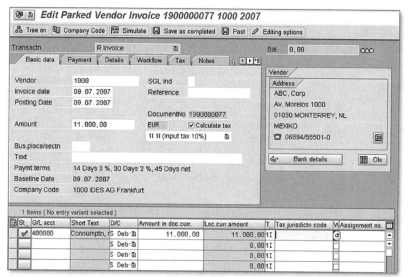

Figure 7.4 Editing a Parked Document

With a vendor invoice, this posted payable has the effect of adding to the debit side, whereas the expense items reduce income. Depending on the number and value of parked documents, they may constitute an important factor in providing an accurate representation of an enterprise's assets, financial situation, and performance. Once the parked documents have been processed, one of the first activities of the closing process is completed. This step is followed by automatic maintenance of the goods receipt/invoice receipt account.

7.3 Automatic Maintenance of the GR/IR Account

At the end of a posting period, the open transactions in the goods receipt/invoice receipt account must be processed correctly for the financial statement. We can distinguish between three scenarios in this context:

1. Ideally, both goods and receipts exist. Both items in the GR/IR clearing account balance out to zero and can be cleared (see Figure 7.5).

2. The vendor has delivered the goods but has not submitted the invoice. This incomplete transaction leads to an increase in the current assets on the credit side of the balance sheet, without showing a payable on the debit side.

3. Another possible scenario involves the reverse of this situation. In this case, the vendor has submitted the invoice, but the goods have not yet been received. This results in a payable on the debit side, without a corresponding disposition of funds on the credit side.

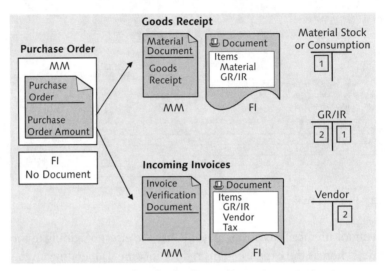

Figure 7.5 Posting Procedure for the GR/IR Clearing Account

It is absolutely essential that the GR/IR account is configured correctly under the menu path ACCOUNTING • FINANCIAL ACCOUNTING • GENERAL LEDGER • MASTER RECORDS • G/L ACCOUNTS • CENTRALLY. Line item display must be enabled in account management to ensure that each transaction can be evaluated.

Open item management If a transaction is complete, that is, if all documents for goods receipt and invoice receipt are in the system, management in the form of an open item account (OI account) is a very useful option. This allows all documents to be cleared, which makes it easier to detect incomplete transactions. The relevant items remain in the account as open items.

Selection of the correct sort key is essential for automatic clearing. The entry 014 (purchase order) copies the purchase order number and item identified in the MM module to the Assignment sort field (see Figure 7.7). This serves as a criterion for automatic balancing of goods receipt items and invoice receipt items. Figure 7.6 shows the correctly maintained GR/IR account 191100.

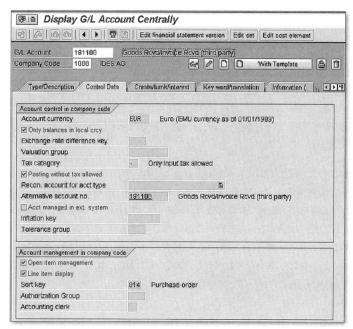

Figure 7.6 GR/IR Account Master Data

G/L Account Line Item Display

G/L Account 191100 Goods Rcvd/Invoice Rcvd (third party)
Company Code 1000

St	Assignment		DocumentNo	BusA	Type	Doc. Date	PK	Amount in local cur.	LCurr
☐ ✱	414-0100	00050	5000000122		WE	21.01.2000	96	785,34-	EUR
☐ ✱	414-0100	00050	5100000084		RE	02.02.2000	86	785,34	EUR
✱	414-0100	00050						0,00	EUR
☐ ✱	414-0100	00060	5000000122		WE	21.01.2000	96	926,46-	EUR
☐ ✱	414-0100	00060	5100000084		RE	02.02.2000	86	926,46	EUR
✱	414-0100	00060						0,00	EUR
☐ ✱	414-0100	00070	5000000122		WE	21.01.2000	96	819,09-	EUR
☐ ✱	414-0100	00070	5100000084		RE	02.02.2000	86	819,09	EUR
✱	414-0100	00070						0,00	EUR
☐ ✱	414-0100	00080	5000000122		WE	21.01.2000	96	683,09-	EUR
☐ ✱	414-0100	00080	5100000084		RE	02.02.2000	86	683,09	EUR
✱	414-0100	00080						0,00	EUR
☐ ✱	414-0100	00090	5000000122		WE	21.01.2000	96	413,12-	EUR
☐ ✱	414-0100	00090	5100000004		RE	02.02.2000	86	413,12	EUR
✱	414-0100	00090						0,00	EUR
☐ ✱	414-0100	00100	5000000122		WE	21.01.2000	96	427,95-	EUR
☐ ✱	414-0100	00100	5100000084		RE	02.02.2000	86	427,95	EUR
✱	414-0100	00100						0,00	EUR
☐ ✱	414-0100	00110	5000000122		WE	21.01.2000	96	388,58-	EUR
☐ ✱	414-0100	00110	5100000084		RE	02.02.2000	86	388,58	EUR
✱	414-0100	00110						0,00	EUR
☐ ✱	414-0101	00010	5000000051		WE	02.12.2000	96	1.971,03-	EUR
☐ ✱	414-0101	00010	5100000048		RE	05.01.2001	86	1.971,03	EUR

Figure 7.7 Open Items List for the GR/IR Clearing Account

In the next step, you retrieve the information about the open items in the account that is currently available at the end of the month.

Select ACCOUNTING • FINANCIAL ACCOUNTING • GENERAL LEDGER • ACCOUNT • DISPLAY ITEMS to display an overview of individual open transactions. If you select the Assignment column and click on the ☒ icon for control totals, an overview of existing goods receipts and invoice receipts is displayed. In the example shown in Figure 7.7, most transactions balance out to zero and can be cleared automatically. Document type WE indicates a goods receipt, whereas document type RE indicates an invoice receipt.

Automatic clearing   Manual clearing is generally avoided owing to the number of items involved. To access the automatic clearing function, select ACCOUNTING • FINANCIAL ACCOUNTING • GENERAL LEDGER • PERIODIC PROCESSING • AUTOMATIC CLEARING • WITHOUT SPECIFICATION OF CLEARING CURRENCY. Figure 7.8 shows the selection screen, where, in the example provided, company code 1000 for 2007 is to be maintained in special G/L account (191100) for goods an invoice receipts.

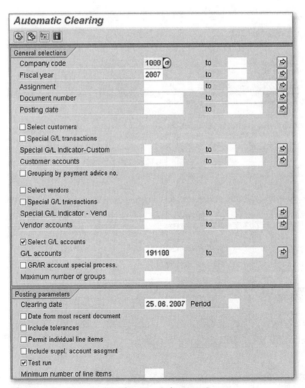

Figure 7.8 Automatic Clearing Selection Screen

The configuration is stored in the background for the G/L account to ensure that clearing is only executed if the Assignment characteristic is identical (as in our example of the purchase order number). Once you make your selection, the log shown in Figure 7.9 appears.

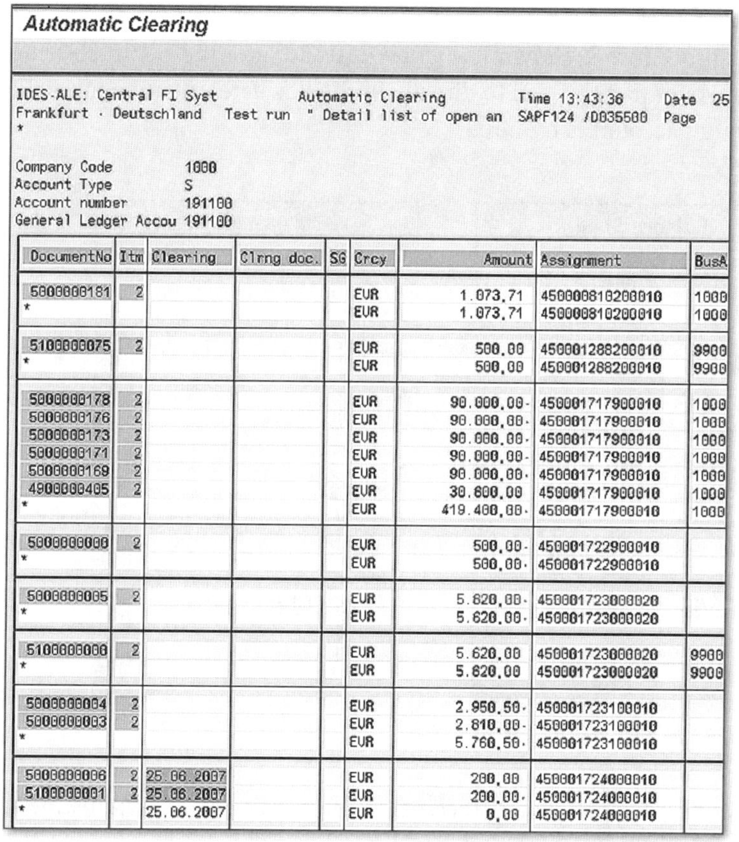

Automatic Clearing

```
IDES-ALE: Central FI Syst        Automatic Clearing        Time 13:43:38    Date  25
Frankfurt · Deutschland   Test run  " Detail list of open an  SAPF124 /D035580  Page
*

Company Code         1000
Account Type         S
Account number       191100
General Ledger Accou 191100
```

DocumentNo	Itm	Clearing	Clrng doc.	SG	Crcy	Amount	Assignment	BusA
5000000181	2				EUR	1.073,71	4500008182000010	1000
*					EUR	1.073,71	4500008182000010	1000
5100000075	2				EUR	500,00	4500012882000010	9900
*					EUR	500,00	4500012882000010	9900
5000000178	2				EUR	90.000,00-	4500017179000010	1000
5000000176	2				EUR	90.000,00-	4500017179000010	1000
5000000173	2				EUR	90.000,00-	4500017179000010	1000
5000000171	2				EUR	90.000,00-	4500017179000010	1000
5000000169	2				EUR	90.000,00-	4500017179000010	1000
4900000405	2				EUR	30.800,00	4500017179000010	1000
*					EUR	419.400,00-	4500017179000010	1000
5000000008	2				EUR	500,00-	4500017229000010	
*					EUR	500,00-	4500017229000010	
5000000005	2				EUR	5.820,00-	4500017230000020	
*					EUR	5.620,00-	4500017230000020	
5100000008	2				EUR	5.620,00	4500017230000020	9900
*					EUR	5.820,00	4500017230000020	9900
5000000004	2				EUR	2.950,50	4500017231000010	
5000000003	2				EUR	2.810,00-	4500017231000010	
*					EUR	5.760,50-	4500017231000010	
5000000006	2	25.06.2007			EUR	200,00	4500017240000010	
5100000001	2	25.06.2007			EUR	200,00-	4500017240000010	
*		25.06.2007			EUR	0,00	4500017240000010	

Figure 7.9 Automatic Clearing Log

The documents at the top of the screen that are grouped together below the Assignment field are incomplete, show a balance, and therefore could not be cleared. The lower part of the screen shows clearing documents dated 06/25/2007. For these documents, the values for the Assignment and Amount characteristics are identical. Or, to put it another way, an invoice receipt exists for the goods receipt, and the transaction is complete.

The Assignment selection characteristic

The relevant line items in the GR/IR account must be analyzed for all other business transactions, which are still incomplete. A goods receipt for which no invoice exists (scenario 2 above) must be shown as a debit item (delivered but not invoiced) on the balance sheet. An invoice receipt for which no goods receipt exists (scenario 3 above) must be shown as a credit item (invoiced but not delivered) on the balance sheet. The posting procedure is shown in Figure 7.10. Because the GR/IR clearing account is not to be posted to directly in the key date valuation, a GR/IR adjustment account is required.

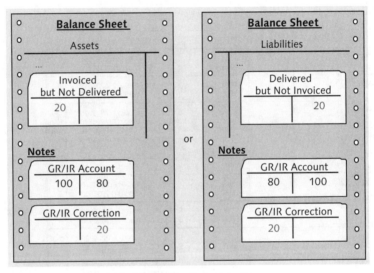

Figure 7.10 Posting Procedure for Key Date Valuation

The goods receipt/invoice receipt account (GR/IR) and adjustment account are shown in the same balance sheet item in the notes to the consolidated financial statements. This practical posting procedure results in a zero-balance line item. In our example, both the debit and credit amounts are equal to 100. In the following sections, an example in the SAP system is used to illustrate the subsequent steps of correct posting and balance sheet display.

Incomplete transactions can be reclassified automatically for the balance sheet. To do this, select ACCOUNTING • FINANCIAL ACCOUNTING • GENERAL LEDGER • PERIODIC PROCESSING • CLOSING • RECLASSIFY • GR/IR CLEARING. Figure 7.11 shows the essential selection and posting parameters.

GR/IR G/L account 191100 in posting code 1000 is selected for analysis. Postings for reclassification are to be saved in the RFWERE00 batch input session.

Analyze GR/IR Clearing Accounts and Display Acquisition Tax

Data Sources

G/L account selection

G/L account	191100	to	
Company code	1000	to	

Selection using search help

Search help ID

Search string

⇨ Search help

Parameters / Postings / Selections / Acq. tax

☑ Create Postings

Name of batch input session	RFWERE00
Ledger Group	
Document date	30.06.2007
Document type	SB
Posting date	30.06.2007
Month	
Reversal posting date	01.07.2007
Reversal period	
Posting header text	
☐ Post input tax	
Input tax code 0%	

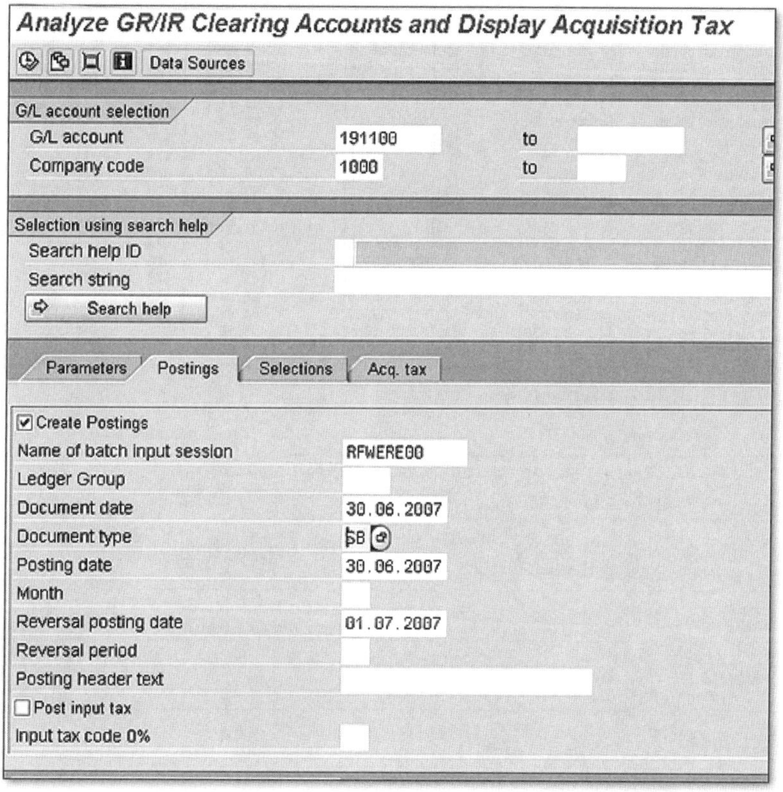

Figure 7.11 Selection and Posting Parameters for GR/IR Account Analysis

The key date for posting is 06/30/2007, after which reclassification postings arc reversed. A log is displayed when the analysis report has been run (see Figure 7.12). Based on the open items, the program attempts to group the documents so that complete transactions can be easily identified. In our example, this process has already been completed as part of automatic clearing. This is why only open business transactions are shown here.

If you click on the Postings button, the overview of reclassifications shown in Figure 7.13 is displayed.

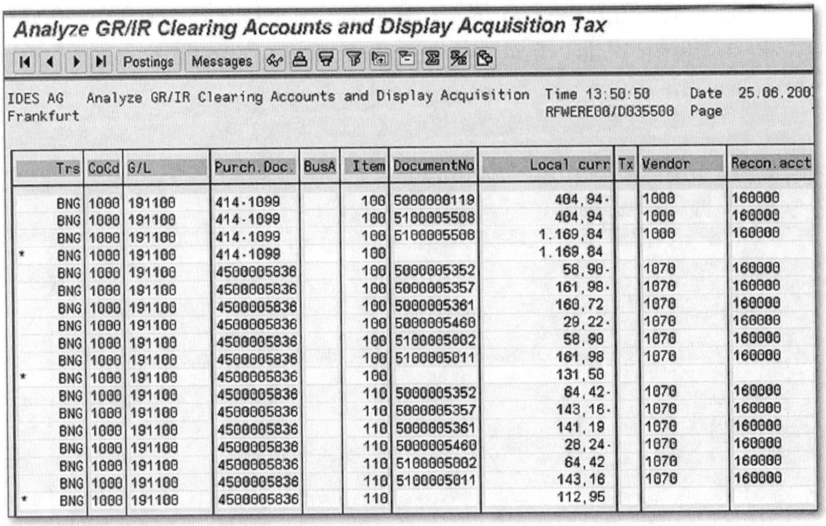

Analyze GR/IR Clearing Accounts and Display Acquisition Tax

```
IDES AG    Analyze GR/IR Clearing Accounts and Display Acquisition  Time 13:50:50      Date  25.06.200
Frankfurt                                                           RFWERE00/D035500   Page
```

	Trs	CoCd	G/L	Purch.Doc.	BusA	Item	DocumentNo	Local curr	Tx	Vendor	Recon.acct
	BNG	1000	191100	414-1099		100	5000000119	404,94-		1000	160000
	BNG	1000	191100	414-1099		100	5100005508	404,94		1000	160000
	BNG	1000	191100	414-1099		100	5100005508	1.169,84		1000	160000
*	BNG	1000	191100	414-1099		100		1.169,84			
	BNG	1000	191100	4500005836		100	5000005352	58,90-		1070	160000
	BNG	1000	191100	4500005836		100	5000005357	161,98-		1070	160000
	BNG	1000	191100	4500005836		100	5000005361	160,72		1070	160000
	BNG	1000	191100	4500005836		100	5000005460	29,22-		1070	160000
	BNG	1000	191100	4500005836		100	5100005002	58,90		1070	160000
	BNG	1000	191100	4500005836		100	5100005011	161,98		1070	160000
*	BNG	1000	191100	4500005836		100		131,50			
	BNG	1000	191100	4500005836		110	5000005352	64,42-		1070	160000
	BNG	1000	191100	4500005836		110	5000005357	143,16-		1070	160000
	BNG	1000	191100	4500005836		110	5000005361	141,19		1070	160000
	BNG	1000	191100	4500005836		110	5000005460	28,24-		1070	160000
	BNG	1000	191100	4500005836		110	5100005002	64,42		1070	160000
	BNG	1000	191100	4500005836		110	5100005011	143,16		1070	160000
*	BNG	1000	191100	4500005836		110		112,95			

Figure 7.12 GR/IR Account Analysis Log

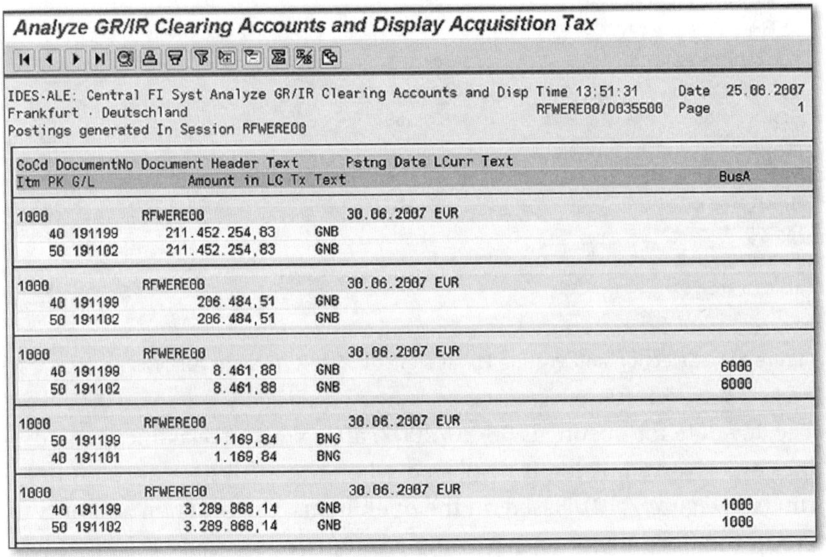

Analyze GR/IR Clearing Accounts and Display Acquisition Tax

```
IDES-ALE: Central FI Syst Analyze GR/IR Clearing Accounts and Disp Time 13:51:31     Date  25.06.2007
Frankfurt - Deutschland                                            RFWERE00/D035500  Page           1
Postings generated In Session RFWERE00

CoCd DocumentNo Document Header Text     Pstng Date LCurr Text
Itm PK G/L            Amount in LC Tx Text                                          BusA

1000            RFWERE00                 30.06.2007 EUR
    40 191199       211.452.254,83    GNB
    50 191102       211.452.254,83    GNB

1000            RFWERE00                 30.06.2007 EUR
    40 191199           206.484,51    GNB
    50 191102           206.484,51    GNB

1000            RFWERE00                 30.06.2007 EUR
    40 191199             8.461,88    GNB                                           6000
    50 191102             8.461,88    GNB                                           6000

1000            RFWERE00                 30.06.2007 EUR
    50 191199             1.169,84    BNG
    40 191101             1.169,84    BNG

1000            RFWERE00                 30.06.2007 EUR
    40 191199         3.289.868,14    GNB                                           1000
    50 191102         3.289.868,14    GNB                                           1000
```

Figure 7.13 Reclassifications Based on the GR/IR Account Analysis

If you select SYSTEM • SERVICES • BATCH INPUT • SESSIONS, you can view the reclassifications saved in the session that has just been generated (see Figure 7.14). In our example, session RFWERE00 contains 164 transactions, consisting of 82 reclassification postings for 06/30/2007 and the same number of reverse postings dated 07/01/2007.

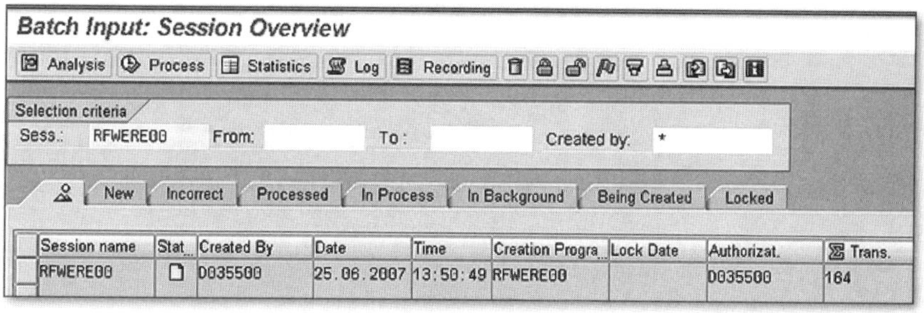

Figure 7.14 Batch Input Session for Reclassification

If the GR/IR account master data is configured correctly, in other words, if the line items, OI management, and sort keys are set up correctly, the SAP system is capable not only of clearing complete business transactions automatically, but also of correctly mapping incomplete transactions on the debit or credit side of the financial statement using GR/IR clearing posting. SAP ERP Financials provides efficient support in this regard, leaving you more time for other activities, such as the monthly posting of salaries and wages.

7.4   Transfer of Salaries and Wages

The HR department posts salaries and wages at the end of the month. This can be done via an interface using non-SAP software. Alternatively, payroll results can be transferred in a posting run to FI and CO using SAP ERP Human Capital Management (HCM) (previously SAP HR). As collective postings, these cannot be traced to individual employees from accounting. The sensitive information detailing how much each person earns remains protected within the HR system. This section illustrates how to recognize existing postings originating in SAP ERP HCM and explains possibilities opened up by using extensive authorizations in an integrated SAP system.

Payroll results in the posting run

In Transaction FB03, Display Document, you can select Document List to navigate to the screen shown in Figure 7.15. Here, the Reference Transaction field indicates the origin of the accounting document in the SAP ERP system. The keyword HRPAY indicates salaries and wages that are to be paid.

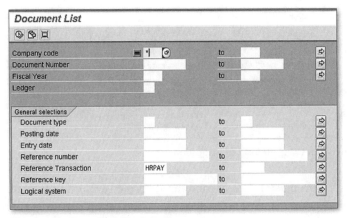

Figure 7.15 Document List Selection

From an accounting perspective, it may be very useful to be able to determine whether a monthly transfer of salaries and wages has already taken place. The list in Figure 7.16 shows some of these transactions.

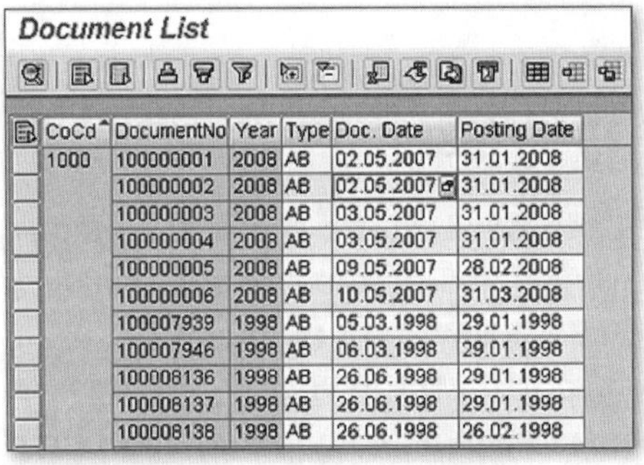

CoCd	DocumentNo	Year	Type	Doc. Date	Posting Date
1000	100000001	2008	AB	02.05.2007	31.01.2008
	100000002	2008	AB	02.05.2007	31.01.2008
	100000003	2008	AB	03.05.2007	31.01.2008
	100000004	2008	AB	03.05.2007	31.01.2008
	100000005	2008	AB	09.05.2007	28.02.2008
	100000006	2008	AB	10.05.2007	31.03.2008
	100007939	1998	AB	05.03.1998	29.01.1998
	100007946	1998	AB	06.03.1998	29.01.1998
	100008136	1998	AB	26.06.1998	29.01.1998
	100008137	1998	AB	26.06.1998	29.01.1998
	100008138	1998	AB	26.06.1998	26.02.1998

Figure 7.16 List of HRPAY Documents

If you double-click on one of these, the account assignment items of the transferred collective posting are then displayed (see Figure 7.17). In addition to the G/L accounts, you can identify additional account assignments, such as profit center, business area, and cost center. The processor in the accounting system is not usually authorized to access data beyond this point. Salaries and wages constitute sensitive data that is accessible to a very limited number of people. Therefore, many enterprises run a separate SAP ERP HCM system on a separate installation. However, if your role were that of tax auditor or HR employee, your work would only begin as of this point. You can select ENVIRONMENT • DOCUMENT ENVIRONMENT • ORIGINAL DOCUMENT to branch to SAP ERP HCM.

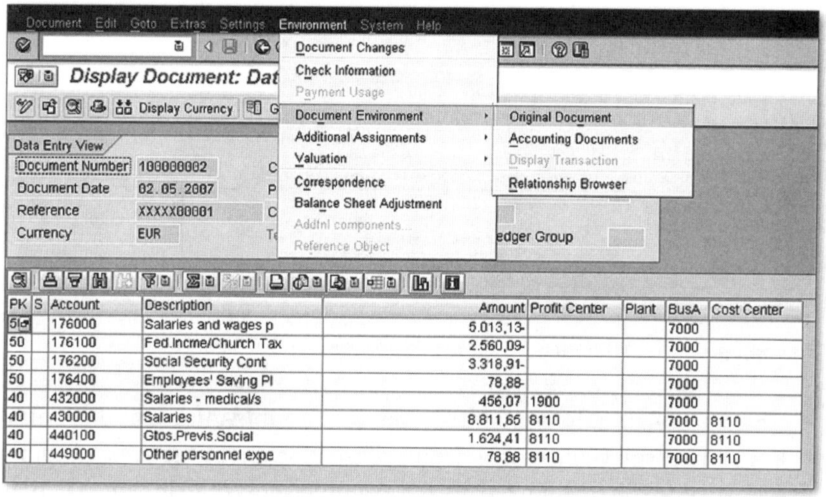

Figure 7.17 Document Overview

The payroll posting document that corresponds to the accounting document is displayed here as shown in Figure 7.18.

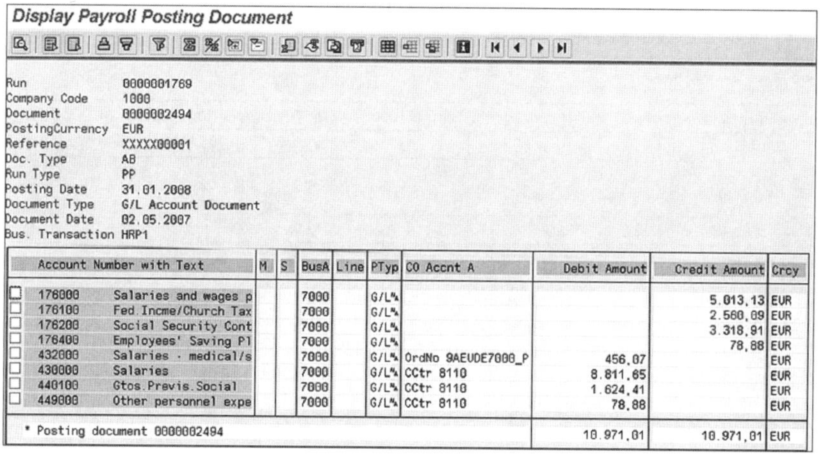

Figure 7.18 Payroll Posting Document

From here, you can access further details relating to this data, which would otherwise be available in summarized or encrypted form only. If you double-click on the item 176000 Salaries and Wages payable, the screen shown in Figure 7.19 appears, where details are listed for personnel numbers 1440 and 99986620.

Account Number with Text	CO Accnt	Wage Type Long Text	Pers.No.	Debit Amount	Credit Amount	Crcy
☐ 176000 Salaries and wages p		/559 Bank transfer	1440		3.712,80	EUR
☐ 176000 Salaries and wages p		/559 Bank transfer	99986620		1.300,33	EUR
* 176000 Salaries and wages p		/559 Bank transfer			5.013,13	EUR
**					5.013,13	EUR

Figure 7.19   Revision Information for the Payroll Posting Document

From the revision information, you can double-click on the entry 1,300.33 to display additional details of the portion of the gross amount that is payable (see Figure 7.20). This example shows the income tax that is to be paid.

27.06.2007 Employee's Payroll Results and Posted Amounts
       For a Period

Display of All Wage Types, Unsummarized

Pers.No.	Sequence Number	Status Ind	IN:Payroll Area	IN:Period	IN:PayTyp	IN:ID	IN:Date	FOR:Payroll Area	FOR:Period	FOR:From	FOR:To
1440	00150	A	02	10 2006				02	10 2006	01.10.2006	31.10.2006

Payroll Results (Table RT):

Wage Type	Wage Type Long Text	Amount	Crcy	Posted: Debit	Posted: Credit
/101	Total gross amount	6.039,88	EUR		
/102	Current remuneration SI	6.039,88	EUR		
/106	Regular gross tax amount	6.039,88	EUR		
/110	Payments/deductions	39,88-	EUR		
/147	Earned inc./garn.compar.	6.000,00	EUR		
/157	SI-exempt for 0 SI days	39,88	EUR		
/159	Gross trade tax	6.039,88	EUR		
/160	Mutual indem.soc. - gross	6.039,88	EUR		
/173	SI rel.cur.notional gross	6.039,88	EUR		
/201	Average bases	6.000,00	EUR		
/203	Average BAT previous yr.	6.000,00	EUR		
/204	Average contributions	6.000,00	EUR		
/207	Average days	0,00	EUR		
/208	Average hours	0,00	EUR		
/260	EE taxes	1.303,66	EUR		1.303,66
/261	Employee SI shares	983,54	EUR		983,54

Figure 7.20   Revision Information: Net to Gross

As you can see, it is always possible to retrace the various steps through which data has passed (i.e., follow an audit trail) if you have an integrated system and sufficient authorizations. In addition, it is always useful, from an accounting point of view, to have a basic knowledge of how the adjacent SAP ERP HCM system works and whether and when postings have been transferred from there to accounting. In contrast to the posting of salaries and wages, the values for accruals and deferrals are not calculated or posted automatically.

A transparent overall context

7.5 Provisions

In the context of closing operations, the question often arises as to whether and to what degree provisions are to be created. To answer this question, it is necessary to distinguish between various types of provision and probabilities of occurrence. Because of the type of provision involved, provisions for foreseeable losses owing to unsecured payables, threatened losses from wavering business, or warranties that are not legally enforceable must be created on the basis of local law and international accounting principles. Provisions for operating expenses, on the other hand, can only be created subject to certain conditions based on *International Financial Reporting Standards* (IFRS) or *United States Generally Accepted Accounting Principles* (US-GAAP). Local accounting principles may differ. Valuation variances arise in parallel accounting owing to different provision types and probabilities.

Differentiating probabilities of occurrence

Different Valuations Based on Different Accounting Principles   [Ex]

If a provision for foreseeable losses, such as a warranty case, is regarded as *probable*, it is included in the financial statement in accordance with US-GAAP. According to the IFRS accounting standard, an event is regarded as *probable* if its probability is categorized as greater than 50%. If its probability is between 30 and 70%, a provision ban applies under US-GAAP because the event is then categorized as *reasonably* probable. Local regulations may also vary.

Owing to the nature of provision postings, automatic valuation procedures cannot be used. The system has virtually no points of reference for performing a mathematical calculation in this context. In practice, calculations are usually made outside the SAP system (for example, in Excel) and then assigned manually as a G/L posting at the end of the period. One of the relevant transactions is shown in Figure 7.21. To access this screen, select ACCOUNTING • FINANCIAL ACCOUNTING • GENERAL LEDGER • DOCUMENT • ENTER G/L ACCOUNT DOCUMENT.

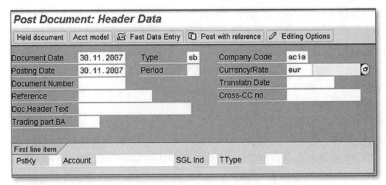

Figure 7.21 G/L Account Posting

<table>
<tr><td>**[+]**</td><td>**Input Help with Account Assignment Models**</td></tr>
<tr><td></td><td>You can put a lot of time and effort into entering each provision type and valuation for each accounting principle manually, or use a predefined account assignment model as a template to make this job much easier.</td></tr>
</table>

In the example shown, provisions are to be created on 11/30/2007 for company code ACIA. If you click on the Acct. Model button, the selection window shown in Figure 7.22 opens, where you can choose from among the various account assignment models available for this company code. In our example, account assignment model GL-SL03 can be used for company code ACIA, with EUR as the document currency and a provision posting as the business transaction.

Input help and memory aids

Predefined account assignment models do not only facilitate the process of entering data for recurring business transactions. They are also useful for implementing parallel accounting. With parallel accounting, the accounts approach must evaluate data based on each of the accounting principles. It can therefore easily happen that a posting is entered in accordance with local law, whereas the IFRS account assignment that is also required is forgotten. As you can see in Figure 7.23, the account assignment model proposes all of the relevant accounts for both local law (8xxxxxx) and IFRS (9xxxxxx). Account assignment models therefore help prevent such errors of omission in data entry.

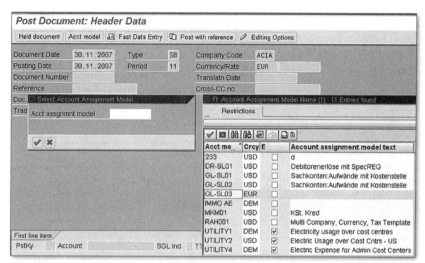

Figure 7.22 Selecting an Account Assignment Model

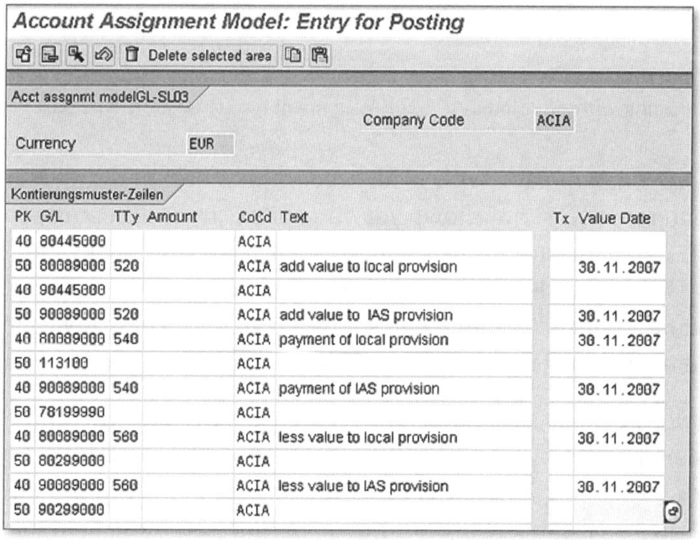

Figure 7.23 Account Assignment Model for Provision Postings

Transaction types as a prerequisite for the provision history sheet

Transaction Type is another additional account assignment field. This characteristic is essential for the creation of a provision history sheet from the SAP system directly after postings have been entered, but we'll get back to that later. In Figure 7.24, a provision of €30,000 is created for local law, and a provision of €20,000 is created in accordance with IFRS principles. Because this represents an allocation to provisions, an additional account assignment is made for the balance sheet account with transaction type 520. The unused lines in the account assignment model contain an amount of €0 and are deleted from the input screen after you confirm a warning message.

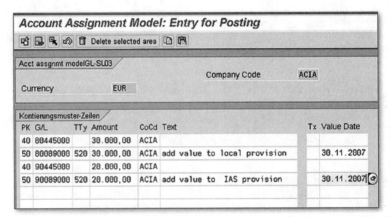

Figure 7.24 Posting with Additional Account Assignment for Transaction Type 520

Different financial statement versions

The SAP accounts approach with main account numbers and different financial statement versions allows you to express items differently in local and IFRS financial statements. If you select SYSTEM • SERVICES • REPORTING • RFBILA10, the selection screen shown in Figure 7.25 appears. In our example, a financial statement is to be created for company code ACIA based on a financial statement version ACI1 for local law.

The Others balance sheet item

The provision postings that have just been entered reduce the enterprise's retained earnings by €30,000 in accordance with local law. An item showing the same amount is listed under liabilities. Adjustments for an IFRS financial statement must not affect this and must therefore be expressed below the balance sheet items in the Others item. This is shown in Figure 7.26.

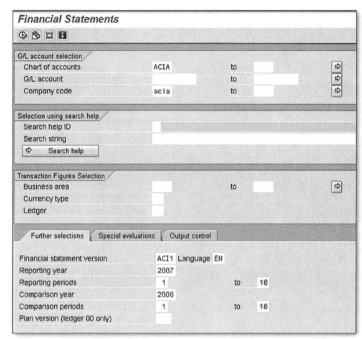

Figure 7.25 RFBILA10 Selection Screen

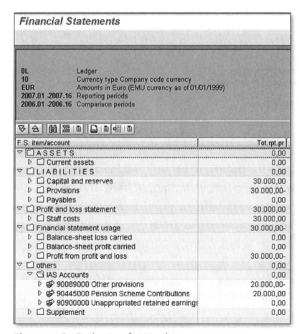

Figure 7.26 Evaluation for Local Law

The display is reversed in the IFRS financial statement version shown in Figure 7.27. Values of €20,000 are shown under liabilities. An item for retained earnings (profit) in the same amount is also shown. This time, it is the local valuations that appear below the balance sheet items in the *others* folder.

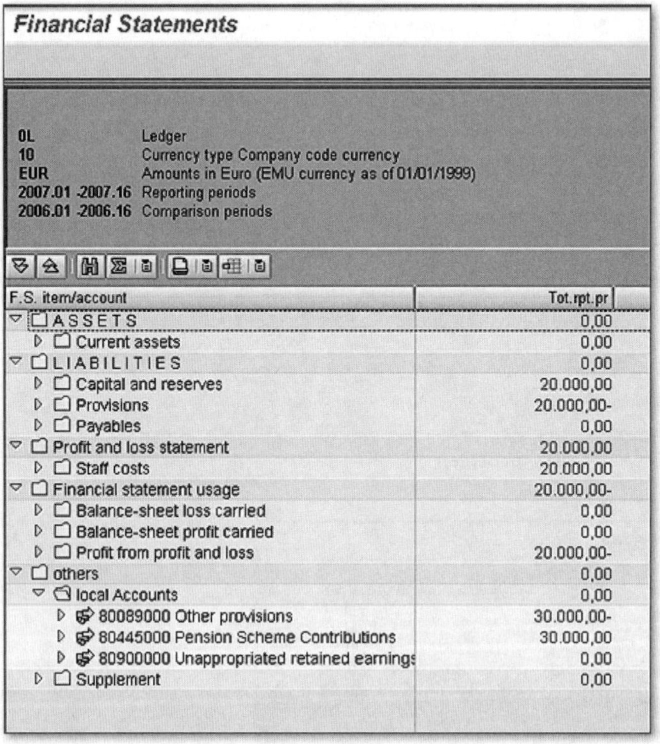

Financial Statements

OL	Ledger	
10	Currency type Company code currency	
EUR	Amounts in Euro (EMU currency as of 01/01/1999)	
2007.01 -2007.16	Reporting periods	
2006.01 -2006.16	Comparison periods	

F.S. item/account	Tot.rpt.pr
▽ ☐ A S S E T S	0,00
▷ ☐ Current assets	0,00
▽ ☐ L I A B I L I T I E S	0,00
▷ ☐ Capital and reserves	20.000,00
▷ ☐ Provisions	20.000,00-
▷ ☐ Payables	0,00
▽ ☐ Profit and loss statement	20.000,00
▷ ☐ Staff costs	20.000,00
▽ ☐ Financial statement usage	20.000,00-
▷ ☐ Balance-sheet loss carried	0,00
▷ ☐ Balance-sheet profit carried	0,00
▷ ☐ Profit from profit and loss	20.000,00-
▽ ☐ others	0,00
▽ ◁ local Accounts	0,00
▷ ☞ 80089000 Other provisions	30.000,00-
▷ ☞ 80445000 Pension Scheme Contributions	30.000,00
▷ ☞ 80900000 Unappropriated retained earnings	0,00
▷ ☐ Supplement	0,00

Figure 7.27 Evaluation for IFRS

This is a proven procedure for provision postings and evaluations in the context of parallel accounting and is a commonly used approach. Now let's return to the necessity of creating a provision history sheet and therefore also to the Transaction type characteristic. A provision history sheet is not currently provided in the SAP standard system.

[+] **Templates Provided in the Report Painter**

The Report Painter reporting tool provided in SAP ERP includes a template that can be easily adapted to meet individual requirements.

Transactions GRR2, Change Reports, and GRR3, Display Reports, provide an overview of the Report Painter reports that are delivered as standard (see Figure 7.28). Folder ZF1 is provided there as a basis for creating your own provision history sheet.

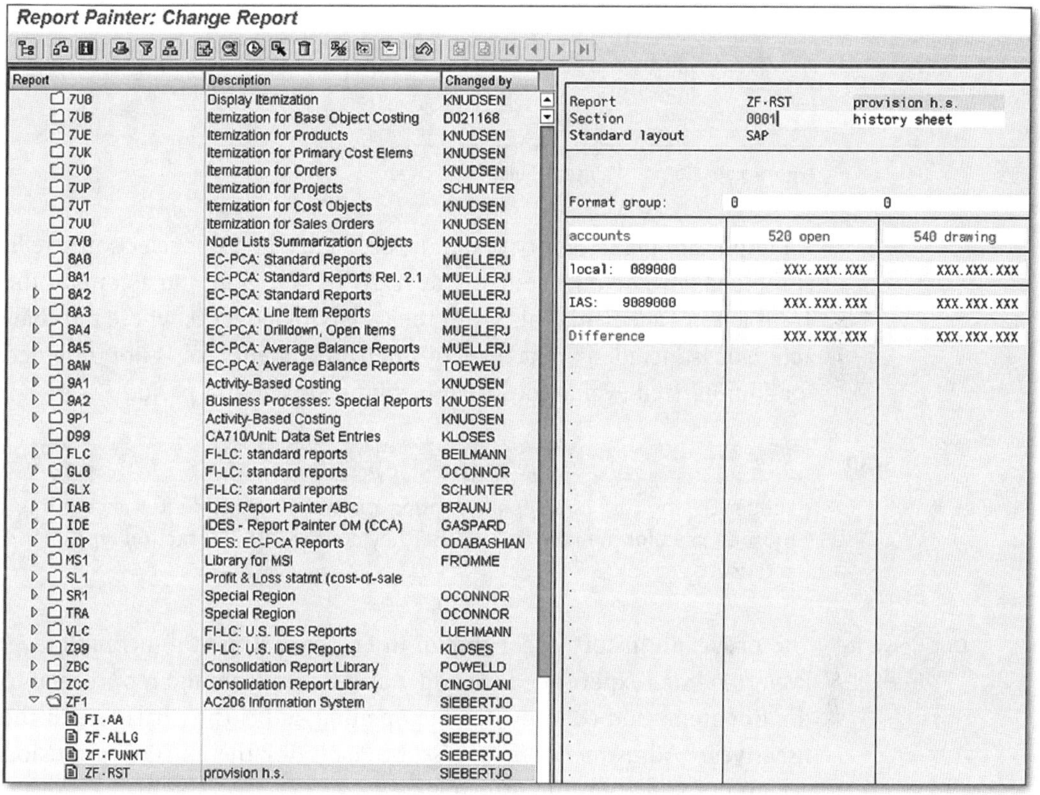

Figure 7.28 Report Painter—Overview

Local or IFRS provision accounts are defined for selection in the individual rows. The columns, meanwhile, filter the business transaction based on transaction type. If you press F8 to execute this report, the selection screen shown in Figure 7.29 is displayed.

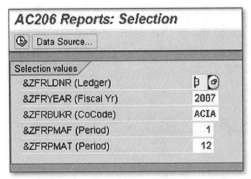

Figure 7.29 Report Painter—Selection Screen

An important default entry that must be changed on this selection screen is the Ledger. The data source that reads the program must contain the Transaction Type field. This is not the case with ledger 0, where the characteristic is included at the level of single documents but is not provided for summarized evaluations, that is, by fiscal year and period.

[+] **Selecting the Correct Data Basis**

Ledger 0F for cost of sales accounting or 8A for profit center accounting must be used for the reports because they contain the Transaction type characteristic.

Drill down to line items

The provision history sheet shown in Figure 7.30 is still incomplete. A Report Painter expert needs to add a drill-down from the report total to the line items and columns for the opening and closing balances in the fiscal year. Adjustments must also be made for the existing provision accounts and accounting principles used.

provision h.s.

Reports	accounts	520 open	540 drawing	580 elimination
GKV				
UKV	local: 089000	30.000-		
provision h.s.				
FI-AA	IAS: 9089000	20.000-		
	* Difference	10.000-		

Figure 7.30 Report Painter—Provision History Sheet Result

408

This example illustrates how provision postings can be made and how the basic framework for evaluating these is already in place in the system.

Like provisions, accruals and deferrals correctly represent the chronological boundaries between service and payment transactions in the profit calculation for the valid accounting period.

7.6 Periodic Accruals and Deferrals

From a business point of view, we can distinguish between accruals and deferrals as follows:

Accruals and deferrals

▶ With an accrual, the current service transaction is followed by a subsequent payment transaction. One example is rent that has to be paid at a later date, for example, at the end of the quarter ("other payables").

▶ The term *deferral*, on the other hand, is used if the current payment transaction is followed by a subsequent service transaction. For example, insurance coverage for a year is provided after an insurance premium is paid ("other receivables").

In SAP ERP Financials, there are two ways to map these transactions:

▶ With a recurring entry document

▶ With the Accrual Engine

In the conventional approach using a recurring entry document, the posting key, account, and amounts remain unchanged. This unchanging data is entered in a recurring entry document. The posting documents are then generated automatically on a regular basis. However, posting is not immediate. Instead, a batch input session is generated, which has to be processed subsequently.

The Accrual Engine is available as of SAP ERP and is intended to provide greater flexibility than recurring entry documents for accrual and deferral postings. With the Accrual Engine, accruals and deferrals, which are no longer defined on the basis of set values, are calculated automatically. If you adjust the values in the original document, adjustments are made automatically for all periods. Future accruals and deferrals can also be simulated. The new Accrual Engine, which is supported by an extensive information system, offers an alternative to conventional recurring entries. In the sections below, we examine both approaches in more detail using an example for the purpose of illustration.

7.6.1 Recurring Entry Documents

If you want to use the recurring entry method for accruals and deferrals, you must first create a recurring entry document for the system to use as a template. A recurring entry document is not an accounting document, and it therefore does not change the account balance. In the recurring entry document, you specify when a posting is to be generated with this document. Postings can be entered periodically or on specific, defined dates. To create the recurring entry document, select ACCOUNTING • FINANCIAL ACCOUNTING • GENERAL LEDGER (ACCOUNTS RECEIVABLE or ACCOUNTS PAYABLE) • DOCUMENT ENTRY • REFERENCE DOCUMENTS • RECURRING ENTRY DOCUMENT. The fields to be filled are explained below:

▶ **First run on**
This refers to the earliest date on which an actual document is to be generated.

▶ **Last run on**
This refers to the latest date on which an actual document is to be generated.

▶ **Interval in months/Run date**
If posting is to be executed periodically, the dates for the generation of actual documents are defined in these fields.

▶ **Run schedule**
If posting is to be executed at regular intervals rather than on specific dates, a run schedule must be defined in Customizing. This schedule specifies the individual dates for postings.

Figure 7.31 shows the header data in the recurring entry document. In the example provided here, a vendor rental invoice is to be posted automatically each month using a recurring entry document for the entire year 2007.

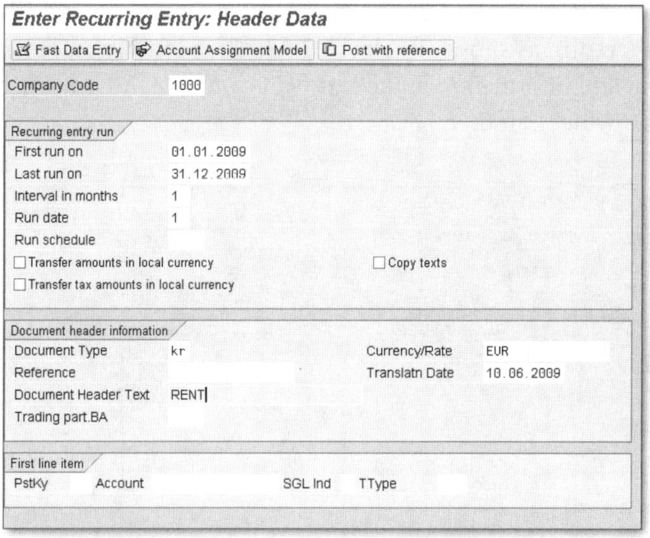

Enter Recurring Entry: Header Data

| 🖼 Fast Data Entry | 🖼 Account Assignment Model | 🖼 Post with reference |

| Company Code | 1000 |

Recurring entry run
First run on	01.01.2009
Last run on	31.12.2009
Interval in months	1
Run date	1
Run schedule	
☐ Transfer amounts in local currency	☐ Copy texts
☐ Transfer tax amounts in local currency	

Document header information
Document Type	kr	Currency/Rate	EUR
Reference		Translatn Date	10.06.2009
Document Header Text	RENT		
Trading part.BA		

First line item
| PstKy | Account | SGL Ind | TType |

Figure 7.31 Header Data in a Recurring Entry Document

If you specify posting key "40" (debit) and G/L account "470000" for occupancy costs, the input screen shown in Figure 7.32 is displayed, just as in the current posting program. Here, the monthly amount of €12,000, tax code V0, and cost center 1000 complete the first line item in the document.

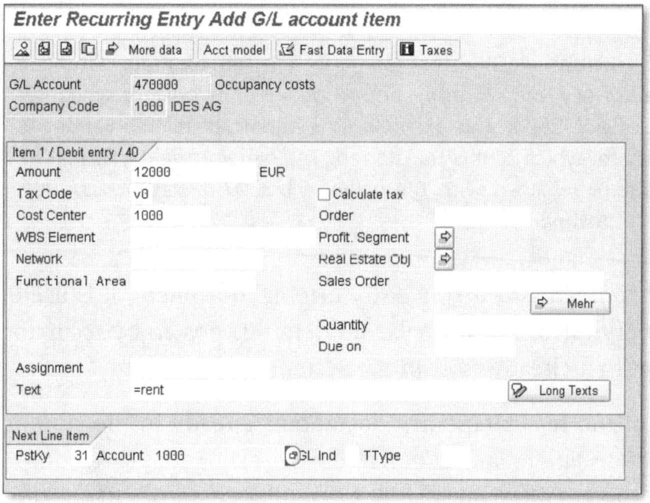

Enter Recurring Entry Add G/L account item

| 🖼 🖼 🖼 🖼 🖼 More data | Acct model | 🖼 Fast Data Entry | 🖼 Taxes |

| G/L Account | 470000 | Occupancy costs |
| Company Code | 1000 | IDES AG |

Item 1 / Debit entry / 40
Amount	12000	EUR
Tax Code	v0	☐ Calculate tax
Cost Center	1000	Order
WBS Element		Profit. Segment 🖼
Network		Real Estate Obj 🖼
Functional Area		Sales Order
		🖼 Mehr
		Quantity
		Due on
Assignment		
Text	=rent	🖼 Long Texts

Next Line Item
| PstKy | 31 | Account | 1000 | 🖼GL Ind | TType |

Figure 7.32 G/L Account Line Item in the Recurring Entry Document

The vendor line item is entered as the next document line item with posting key 31 (credit), as shown in Figure 7.33. The monthly amount, term of payment and information in the text field complete the recurring entry document, which can then be saved.

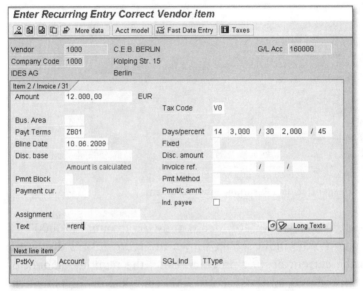

Figure 7.33 Vendor Line Item in the Recurring Entry Document

[Ex] **Dynamic Field Information.**

Dynamic fields, such as the information "=rent" in this example, are filled with actual data when the recurring entry document is posted, which allows for greater flexibility. In this example, it is important for the vendor to know the month for which rent is transferred. The dynamic field information "=rent" is therefore replaced with the values 01/2007, 02/2007, 03/2007, and so on during posting.

Once you have defined a recurring entry original document, it is useful to obtain an overview of the accruals and deferrals posted by recurring entry document that already exist in the system

To view a list of the recurring entry documents already in the system, select ACCOUNTING • FINANCIAL ACCOUNTING • GENERAL LEDGER (ACCOUNTS PAYABLE OR ACCOUNTS RECEIVABLE) • PERIODIC PROCESSING • RECURRING ENTRIES • LIST. At first glance, this report may not appear to be very comprehensive. However, it contains all of the information you need. Figure 7.34 shows the recurring entry original document that has just been created and a second vendor document for a monthly amount of $2,000.

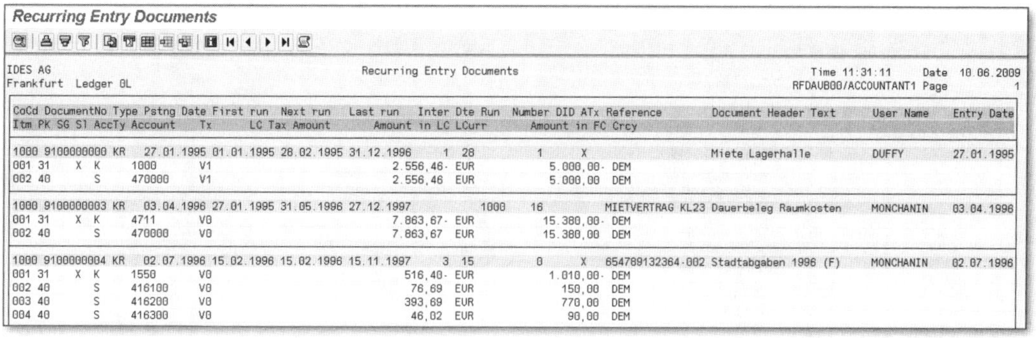

Figure 7.34 List of Recurring Entry Documents

To generate accounting documents from recurring entry original documents, it is not sufficient to simply schedule the recurring entry original documents. The recurring posting program also needs to be started at the correct intervals. To do this, select ACCOUNTING • FINANCIAL ACCOUNTING • GENERAL LEDGER (ACCOUNTS PAYABLE OR ACCOUNTS RECEIVABLE) • PERIODIC PROCESSING • RECURRING ENTRIES • EXECUTE. The entries on the selection screen shown in Figure 7.35 determine that the recurring entry postings that exist for company code 1000 as of 01/01/2007 are stored in the Rent batch input setting. By specifying a calculation period, you let the system know which recurring entry documents are to be included. If the date of the next posting run saved in the recurring entry document matches the calculation date entered or falls within the date range specified, the program places the data for the postings in the specified batch input session. A single accounting document is created for each recurring entry document in each program run. Therefore, a very long calculation period does not result in the generation of a large number of accounting documents (for example, Rent 1 – 12).

Posting runs at defined intervals

Improved Traceability of Postings with Batch Input Sessions   **[+]**

To ensure greater traceability, it is useful to retain access to the session for recurring entry documents for a certain period after it has been processed. To prevent the batch input session from being reorganized immediately, click on the Retain Processed Session button.

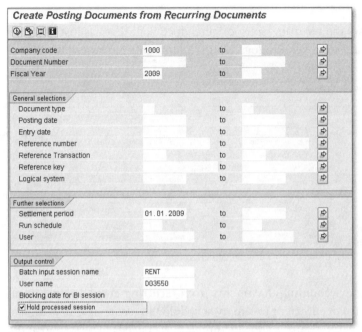

Figure 7.35 Executing the Posting of Recurring Entry Documents

After you run the recurring posting program, the Rent batch input session needs to be processed to execute the postings. To do this, select System • Services • Batch Input • Sessions. Figure 7.36 provides an overview of this transaction with the Rent batch input session, which contains a single accounting document.

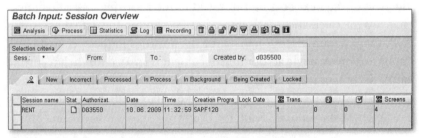

Figure 7.36 Executing the Posting of Recurring Entry Documents

When you process the session, the documents are sent for posting. The document contents (for example, account, posting period and cost center) are checked again at this point. The program replaces the dynamic text selected in our example ("=rent") with the information "Rental payment for 01/2007" (see Figure 7.37).

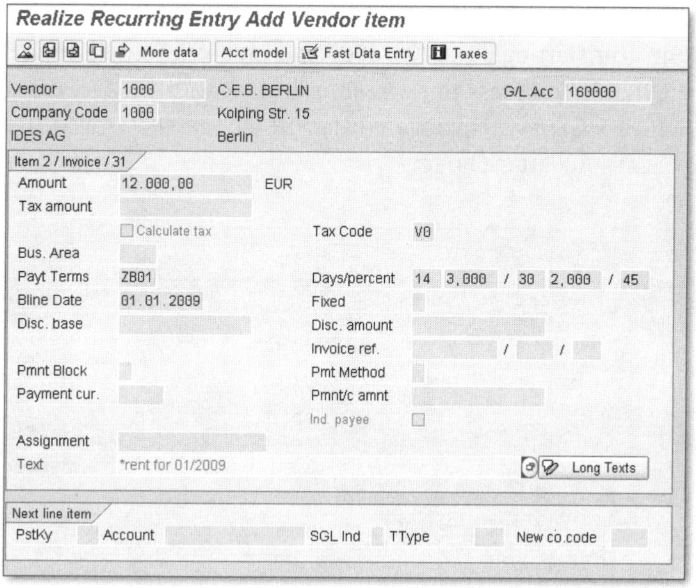

Figure 7.37 Posting Document

The Accrual Engine provides an alternative to the recurring entry document for accrual and deferral postings.

7.6.2 Accrual Engine

The Accrual Engine is a general tool for calculating and generating periodic accrual and deferral postings. Each of its application components is based on specific accrual and deferral scenarios, for which they offer an optimized user interface. Examples include:

Specific accrual/deferral scenarios

- Manual accruals in Financial Accounting
- Provisions relating to employee stock options
- Leasing accounting
- Intellectual property management

SAP develops and delivers application components of the Accrual Engine. Customer developments are not supported. Manual accruals and deferrals in Financial Accounting are discussed below as an example. In this scenario, the user enters the relevant business transaction (for example, an insurance policy, as an accrual object). The details of this object provide a basis for the posting. Figure 7.38 shows an insurance policy that is valid for one year starting on 07/01/2007 and involves a single annual premium of €1,200. To access this screen, select ACCOUNTING • FINANCIAL ACCOUNTING • GENERAL LEDGER • PERIODIC PROCESSING • MANUAL ACCRUALS • CREATE ACCRUAL OBJECT.

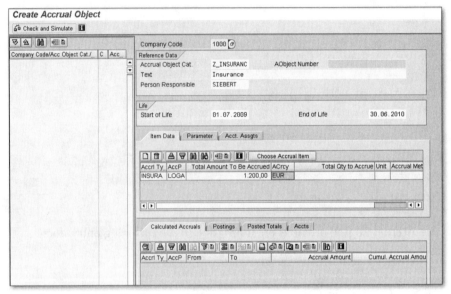

Figure 7.38 Creating an Accrual Object

Defining an accrual object

The Z_INSURANC accrual object represents a group of insurance policies in this case. The line item data indicates the type of accrual (INSURA) and the accounting principle applied (LOGA, for local requirements). Additional parameters for automatic postings at regular intervals are shown on the Account Assignment tab (see Figure 7.39). Here you can specify additional information, such as the business area, profit center, cost center order, and WBS element.

Running a simulation

Once the basic information has been entered, the Accrual Engine can run a simulation for the accrual object. If you select Check and Simulate, the selection window shown in Figure 7.40 appears, where you can specify a key date of your choice for the simulation.

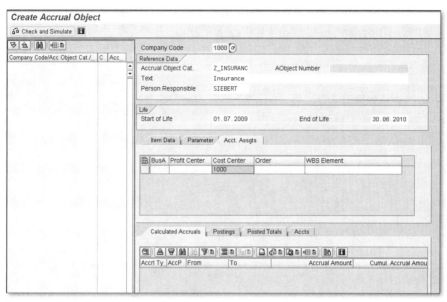

Figure 7.39 Maintaining Account Assignments

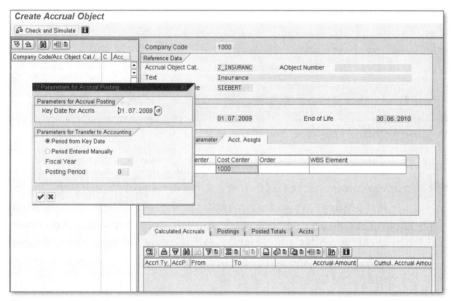

Figure 7.40 Key Date

Postings are not executed at this point. Figure 7.41 shows what the Accrual Engine would do as of July 1 to calculate the accrual for the amount of €1,200 over 12 months. As you can see, it would automatically post an amount of €100 each month.

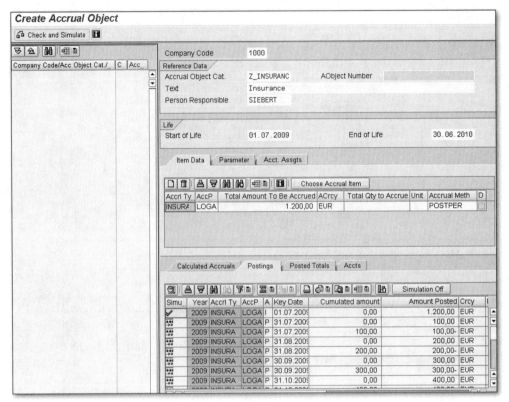

Figure 7.41 Displaying an Accrual Object

Grouping accrual objects

When you exit simulation mode, only the single annual amount of the insurance premium (€1,200) that has yet to be posted is shown. The list of actual postings grows each month. On the left of the screen shown in Figure 7.42, all accrual objects are maintained in groups based on object types. This provides a quick and clear overview of the accruals defined in the system and the actual postings that have already been processed by the Accrual Engine.

Access to the original document

You can double-click on any of the entries to access the original document that was posted (see Figure 7.43). Compared with the approach based on recurring entry documents, the Accrual Engine offers levels of clarity, transparency, and consistency that were not previously possible.

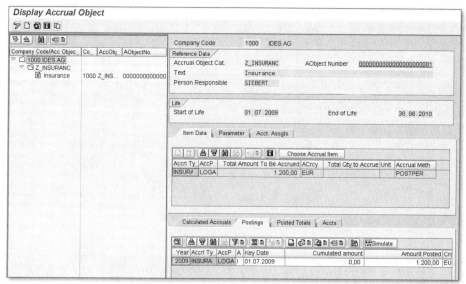

Figure 7.42 Grouping Accrual Objects

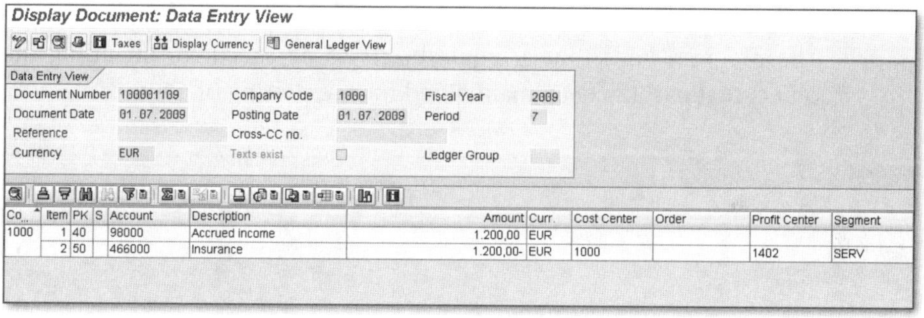

Figure 7.43 Drill-Down

Account 98000 (accrued income/deferred expenses) contains the total amount, which is reduced by €100 each month. For this to be posted automatically, you need to schedule a program for periodic posting as a background job. The example discussed on the following pages provides more detailed information about the results log, which is why posting is executed directly online at this point. The program is started for company code 1000 and the key date 07/31/2007 on the screen shown in Figure 7.44. To access this screen, select ACCOUNTING • FINANCIAL ACCOUNTING • GENERAL LEDGER • PERIODIC PROCESSING • MANUAL ACCRUALS • START PERIODIC ACCRUAL RUN.

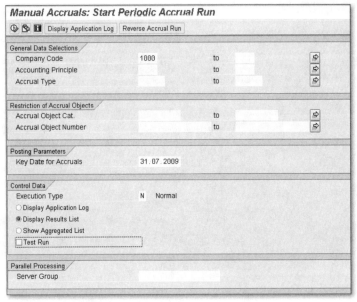

Figure 7.44 Starting Periodic Accrual Postings

The program finds four accrual objects to be executed, including the object that has just been maintained for the posting of €100.

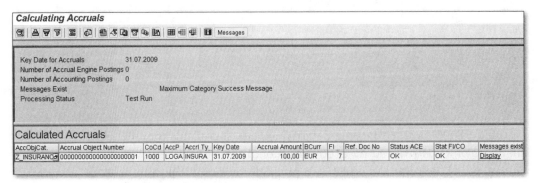

Figure 7.45 Posting List

If you double-click on this object, the posted line item is displayed (see Figure 7.46).

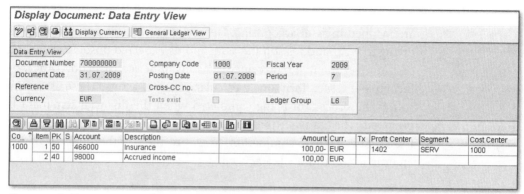

Figure 7.46 Posting List—Drill-Down

You can also display one or more accrual objects by selecting ACCOUNT-ING • FINANCIAL ACCOUNTING • GENERAL LEDGER • PERIODIC PROCESSING • MANUAL ACCRUALS • INFO SYSTEM • DISPLAY POSTED ACCRUALS • MANUAL ACCRUALS: DISPLAY LINE ITEMS IN THE ACCRUAL ENGINE.

You can now choose between two techniques for automatic accrual and deferral postings in the SAP system. The two options available are recurring entry documents and the Accrual Engine. If you are an existing SAP customer and are satisfied with the recurring entry postings defined in your system or if you use only a limited number of these, there is no reason to change at this stage. If, on the other hand, you are new to the subject and require a large number of deferral postings, the Accrual Engine offers benefits in terms of clarity, transparency, and the maintenance of accrual objects. However, you should be aware that you will initially need to invest more time in configuring this option.

Recommendations on the two SAP techniques

7.7 Asset Accounting

Many of the activities in the closing process relate to the FI-AA (Asset Accounting) subledger. The following topics are discussed in this section:

- Assets under construction (AuC)
- Asset inventory
- Depreciation posting run
- Asset history sheet

Complex fixed assets that are at the long-term disposal of an enterprise are mapped in asset accounting. Depreciation reduces acquisition costs owing to wear and tear on the asset and its expected obsolescence (and cost of investing in a replacement). Assets under construction (AuC), or incomplete assets, form one particular group of assets. These assets are still in the process of being completed when the financial statement is prepared. The status of these assets only changes to that of a complex fixed asset on their completion. They are then at the disposal of the enterprise and can be depreciated.

7.7.1 Assets Under Construction (AuCs)

Incomplete assets
During the closing process, assets under construction are normally checked and their status changed if necessary. The lifecycle of one of these assets is illustrated by the example below.

Select ACCOUNTING • FINANCIAL ACCOUNTING • FIXED ASSETS • ASSET • CREATE • ASSET to access the transaction for defining master data for assets. Figure 7.47 shows the selection of the special asset class 4000 for assets under construction.

Figure 7.48 shows the internal number assignment, textual description, and special account determination 40000 that are used to ensure that AuC balance sheet values are expressed correctly.

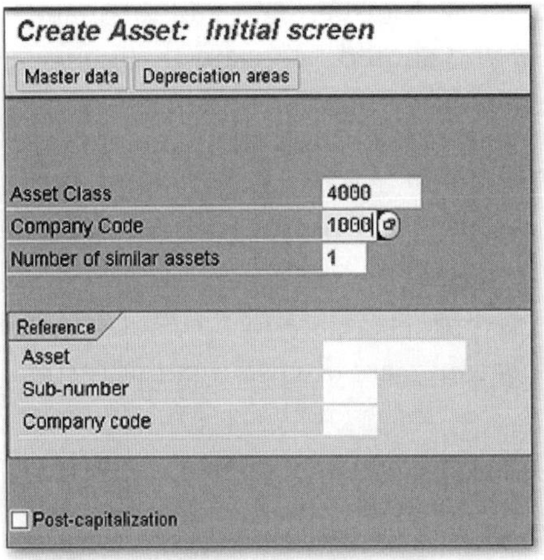

Figure 7.47 Asset Class 4000

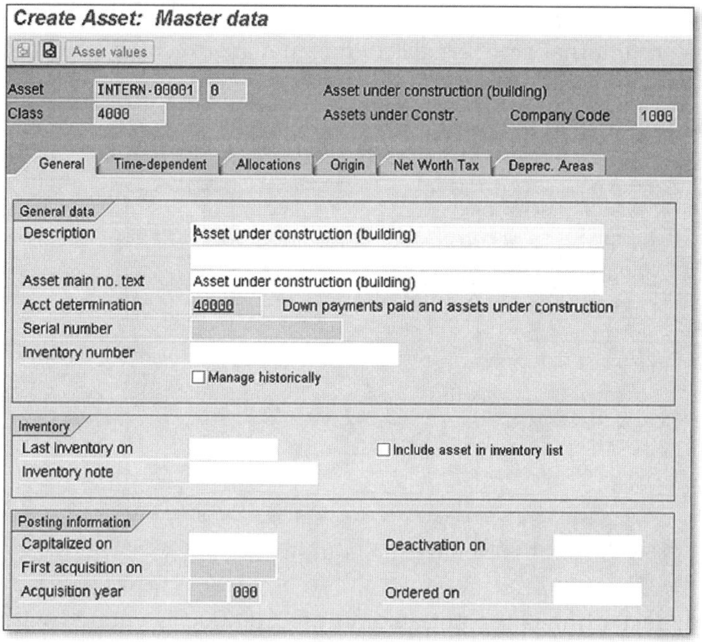

Figure 7.48 Account Determination 40000

If you select the Depreciation Areas tab, the unique nature of these assets becomes apparent. As Figure 7.49 shows, AuCs, as incomplete assets, cannot yet be depreciated.

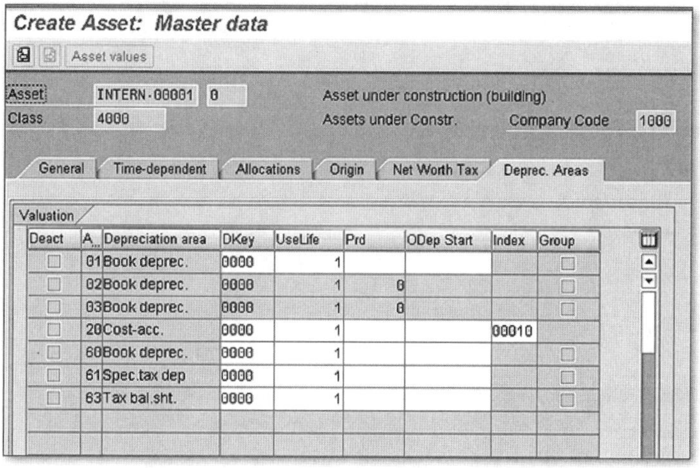

Figure 7.49 Depreciation is not Possible

Internal and external activities

You can execute postings by saving the AuC master record. Such postings usually concern internal or external activities and are executed as part of the asset creation process. The example in Figure 7.50 shows an external activity relating to vendor 1000 on 07/17/2007.

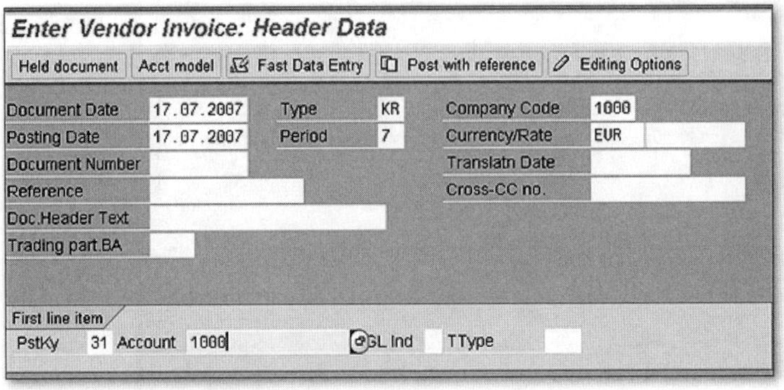

Enter Vendor Invoice: Header Data
Held document
Acct model
Fast Data Entry
Post with reference
Editing Options
Document Date
17.07.2007
Type
KR
Company Code
1000
Posting Date
17.07.2007
Period
7
Currency/Rate
EUR
Document Number
Translatn Date
Reference
Cross-CC no.
Doc.Header Text
Trading part.BA
First line item
PstKy
31
Account
1000
SGL Ind
TType

Figure 7.50 Vendor Invoice Header Data

If 10% is deducted for tax, a net amount of €100,000 is entered with posting key 70 and transaction type 100 (acquisition) in the master record of AuC 80000 that has just been created (see Figure 7.51).

Enter Vendor invoice: Add Vendor item
More data
Acct model
Fast Data Entry
Taxes
Vendor
1000
C.E.B. BERLIN
G/L Acc
160000
Company Code
1000
Kolping Str. 15
IDES AG
Berlin
Item 1 / Invoice / 31
Amount
110000
EUR
Tax amount
Calculate tax
Tax Code
1I
Bus. Area
Payt Terms
ZB01
Days/percent
14
3,000
30
2,000
45
Bline Date
17.07.2007
Fixed
Disc. base
Disc. amount
Invoice ref.
Pmnt Block
Pmt Method
Payment cur.
Pmnt/c amnt
Ind. payee
Assignment
Text
Long Texts
Next line item
PstKy
70
Account
80001
SGL Ind
TType
100
New co.code

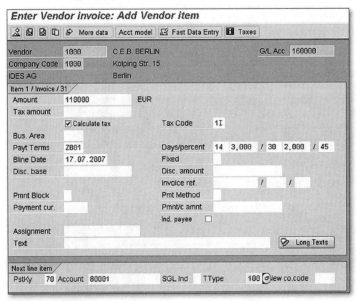

Figure 7.51 Vendor Invoice Item Data

Note also that an asset value date or capitalization date is not required. This is not the norm in asset accounting. As shown in Figure 7.52, the account determination for AuC 40000 for acquisition postings refers to G/L account 32000. The total amount of €100,000 would also appear in that account on the balance sheet date, provided that the status of our AuC did not change.

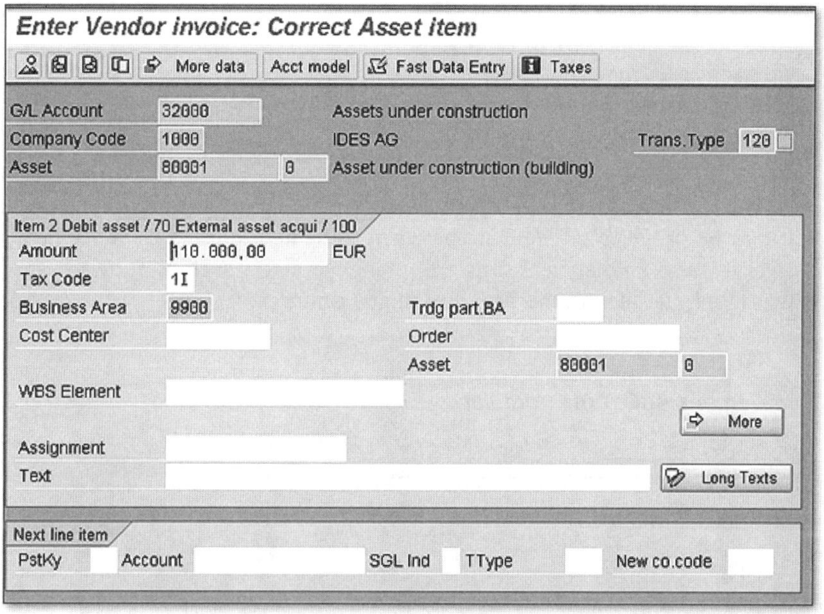

Figure 7.52 Vendor Invoice—Balance Sheet Account

In our example, a check run at the end of the period determined that the building can be used as of August 1. As a result, the status and value must be changed. Select ACCOUNTING • FINANCIAL ACCOUNTING • FIXED ASSETS • CAPITALIZE ASSET UNDER CONSTRUCTION • DISTRIBUTE to define distribution rules for the subsequent settlement of the asset in our example (see Figure 7.53).

Status change of an AuC

A line item list exists for AuC 80000 (building) in the configuration settings of asset class 4000. This setting is shown in Figure 7.54, where all transactions are listed as line items. At this point, it is possible, though not essential, to define a separate settlement rule for each transaction.

Line item list

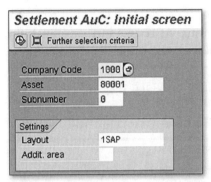

Figure 7.53 Settlement AuC—Initial Screen

Internal Activity

It may be useful to differentiate between settlement rules at the document level if, for example, the assets are intangible assets such as software, for which only certain internal activities can be capitalized.

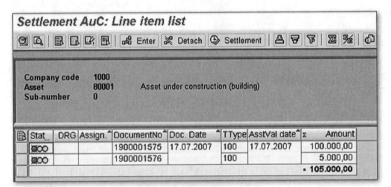

Figure 7.54 Line Item List for AuC Settlement

Defining settlement rules

In our example, both line items are selected and entered with an identical settlement rule (see Figure 7.55). According to this rule, the values of the AuCs are to be 100% capitalized. Asset 1147 (building 1) receives 70%, and asset 1148 (building 2) received 30%. The same effect would be achieved by using equivalence numbers in a ratio of 7:3.

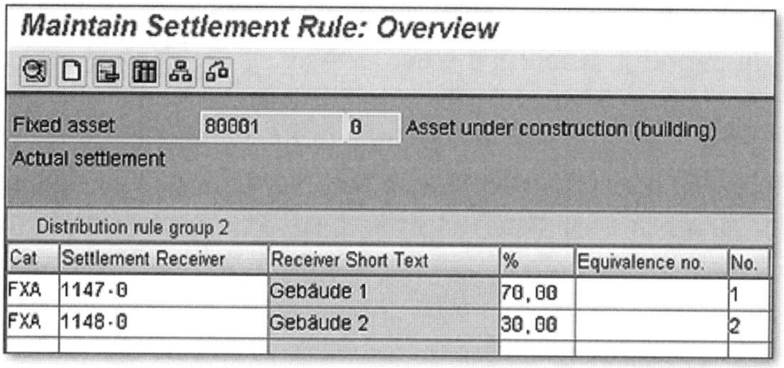

Maintain Settlement Rule: Overview

Fixed asset 80001 0 Asset under construction (building)
Actual settlement

Distribution rule group 2

Cat	Settlement Receiver	Receiver Short Text	%	Equivalence no.	No.
FXA	1147·0	Gebäude 1	70,00		1
FXA	1148·0	Gebäude 2	30,00		2

Figure 7.55 Settlement of AuCs—Maintaining Settlement Rules

The F12 key or Back button takes you to the previous line item list. You can click on the Save (Diskette) icon here to save your settings. When you exit the transaction, you can select ACCOUNTING • FINANCIAL ACCOUNTING • FIXED ASSETS • CAPITALIZE ASSET UNDER CONSTRUCTION • SETTLE to proceed with your closing operations. The initial screen for the settlement of assets under construction (see Figure 7.56) contains important information, specifically, the balance sheet display and the depreciation start date.

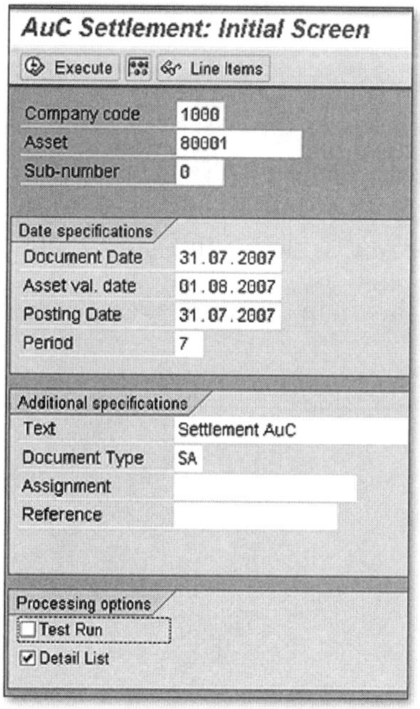

AuC Settlement: Initial Screen

Company code 1000
Asset 80001
Sub-number 0

Date specifications
Document Date 31.07.2007
Asset val. date 01.08.2007
Posting Date 31.07.2007
Period 7

Additional specifications
Text Settlement AuC
Document Type SA
Assignment
Reference

Processing options
☐ Test Run
☑ Detail List

Figure 7.56 Executing Settlement of AuCs—Selection Screen

A posting date of July 31 means that the AuC is credited at the end of
the month in period 7, whereas the two new assets are debited at the
same time. An amount of €0 is displayed as the balance on the key date
in the AuC balance sheet item. Depreciation of the two buildings starts
as of the following period (period 8) with the asset value date of August
1. Execution of a test or update run will explain the results shown in
Figure 7.57.

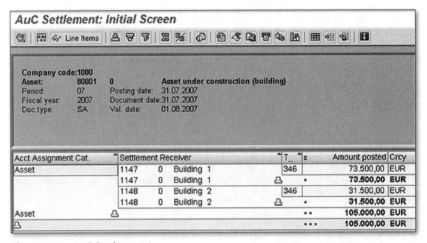

Figure 7.57 AuC Settlement Log

To exit the transaction, press [F3]. If you access the Asset Explorer, the
transaction is displayed in greater detail. To do this, select ACCOUNTING •
FINANCIAL ACCOUNTING • FIXED ASSETS • ASSET • ASSET EXPLORER. Here you
will see the intercompany transfer of the AuC as shown in Figure 7.58.

In Figure 7.59, acquisition postings are shown in the receiver asset, asset
1147.

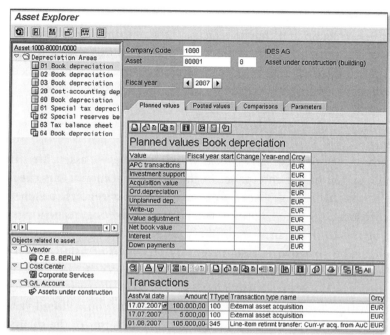

Figure 7.58 Asset Explorer with AuCs

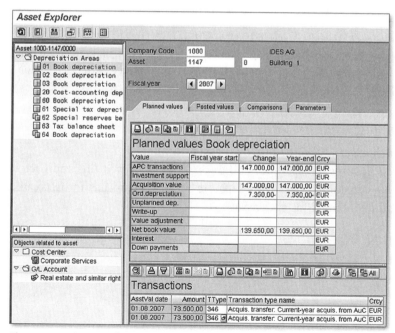

Figure 7.59 Asset Explorer with Building 1

At the month's end, you are in a position to change the status of assets under construction and thus to execute intercompany transfers in the financial statement and begin depreciation of the new fixed assets. In particular, if 100% of internal or external activities are not to be capitalized, this will have a significant impact on the profit and loss statement.

7.7.2 Asset Inventory

Checking responsibilities

The asset inventory regularly checks whether moveable assets are still at the disposal of the enterprise. In the simplest scenario, this check determines that changes need to be made to cost centers, business areas, or locations in the relevant data records. If fixed assets no longer exist owing to theft, an extraordinary asset retirement without revenue must be posted. The asset inventory process is occasionally very time-consuming and labor-intensive. If you select ACCOUNTING • FINANCIAL ACCOUNTING • FIXED ASSETS • INFO SYSTEM • REPORTS ON ASSET ACCOUNTING • INDIVIDUAL ASSETS in the SAP menu, you will find various reports for this purpose, which differ only in terms of the sorting used.

[+] | **The Role of Cost Center Managers**

The cost center manager is ideally suited to the task of coordinating or assuming partial responsibility for asset inventory. The cost center manager will be highly motivated to ensure that his area is only debited with depreciation postings relating to assets that still exist and are still in use.

There are various ways of managing assets:

▶ **Each asset is assigned its own asset number**
This ensures transparency and traceability. However, this approach is time-consuming because a separate master record has to be created and maintained for each asset.

▶ **Collective management**
With this approach, all identical assets are managed in a single master record. With collective management, the challenge is to ensure that each asset is uniquely identifiable.

Take, for example, a scenario where 20 computers are allocated to a cost center manager. If the only objective is to count the number of identical items, we can check these items off the list straight away. In practice, however, things are rarely that simple. For example, one computer may have been given to another business segment on loan or, for some inexplicable reason, only 19 of the 20 computers can be located. Such scenarios call for further action.

Individual management

Fixed assets are usually procured at various times and incur various acquisition and production costs. Therefore, each of the 20 computers has an individual depreciation and net book value. It is not possible to determine which equipment requires an intercompany transfer or where an asset retirement without revenue arises until it is established which equipment still exists. The process of clearly identifying each of these assets therefore comes first. This step can be speeded up by attaching a clearly visible sticker showing the equipment number to each asset. If a large number of movable assets are to be verified using this method, a mobile hand scanner can help read the information. A software program reads the data, compares it with the existing asset inventory, and creates action lists for any discrepancies or location changes. In addition to the conventional lists available in the SAP menu tree, SAP ERP Financials provides additional options for optimizing the asset inventory process. Take, for example, a solution implemented at SAP Germany, where employees receive an email notification instructing them to use the self-service asset inventory function (see Figure 7.60).

Collective management

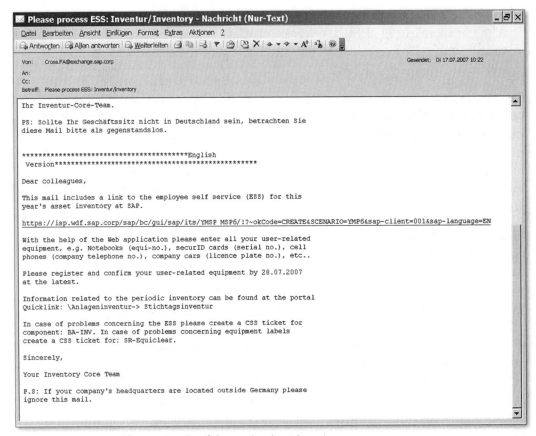

Figure 7.60 Email Concerning Asset Inventory

When you click on the link, the browser opens, showing a user-friendly interface that is also suitable for occasional users (see Figure 7.61).

The roadmap concept is intended to show users how many steps need to be completed. In our example, all of the data required can be entered and confirmed in six steps. After a brief introduction to the activities to follow, the user can click on the Continue button or select the second step to proceed. Figure 7.62 shows the Hardware category. Information about the laptop shown here (for example, description, equipment number, or location) needs to be confirmed or maintained in the asset master record. Additional office equipment can also be added electronically if required.

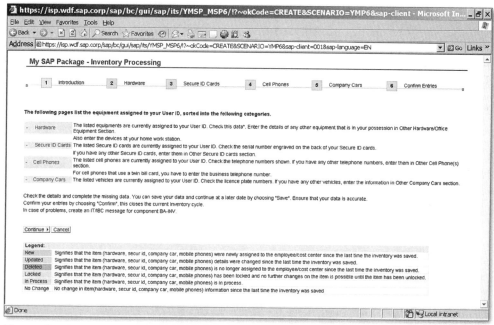

Figure 7.61 Asset Inventory—Introduction

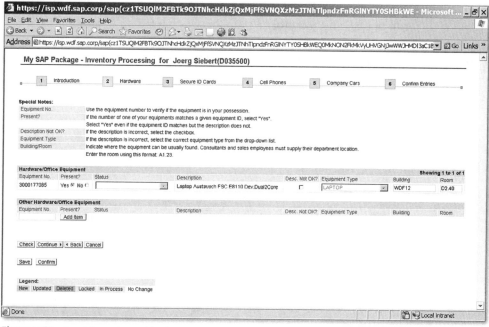

Figure 7.62 Asset Inventory—Hardware

In the next step, shown in Figure 7.63, the system checks for the existence of a secure ID card. This security tool enables Internet access at SAP Germany.

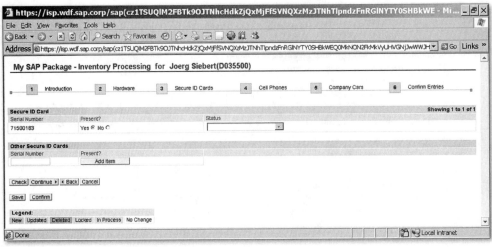

Figure 7.63 Asset Inventory—Secure ID Cards

Inventory control is then executed for the Cell Phones category. In this example, Figure 7.64 shows a change in cost center assignment because a cell phone, and therefore a number, was passed on to another person.

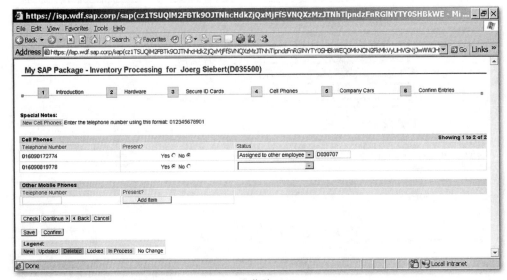

Figure 7.64 Asset Inventory—Cell Phones

In the penultimate activity, the status of the company car shown in Figure 7.65 is checked.

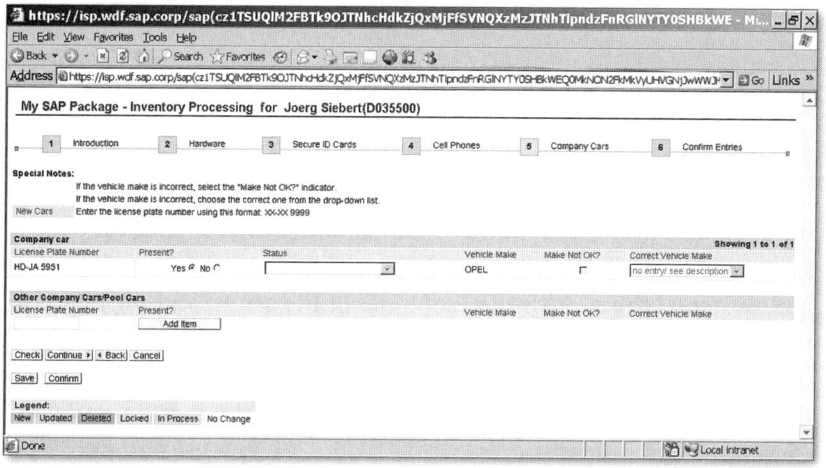

Figure 7.65 Asset Inventory — Company Cars

The final, sixth step brings together all of the entries made in the previous steps. Based on this electronically retrieved data, changes can be made to the locations, cost centers, and so on, and asset retirement postings can be entered (see Figure 7.66).

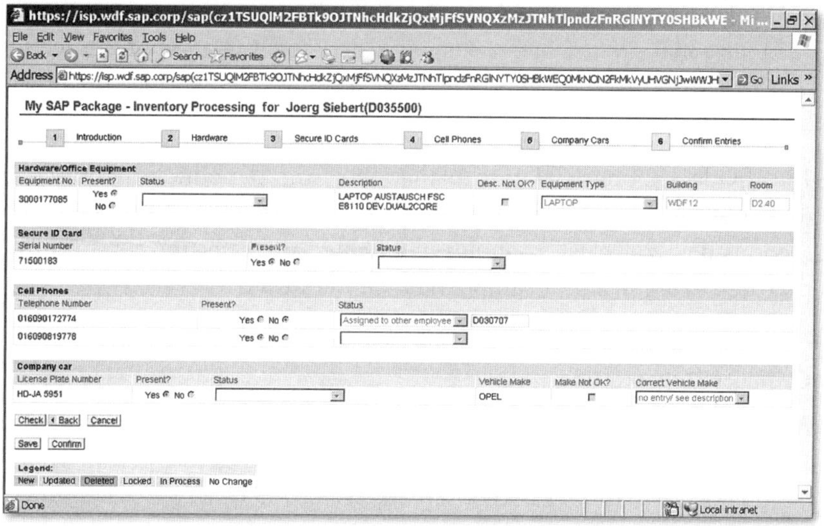

Figure 7.66 Asset Inventory — Confirm Entries

This is a structured workflow, which is ideally suited to occasional users. The web interface can also be enhanced for other fixed assets or queries if required. Overall, the new technical infrastructure of SAP ERP enables a new approach to asset inventory that can save time and money.

7.7.3 Depreciation Posting Run

The depreciation posting run is a periodic activity within Asset Accounting. It involves the transfer of valuations from FI-AA subledger accounting to general ledger accounting, where they can then be used for balance sheet evaluations. Depreciations for tangible assets need to be distributed systematically across the useful life of the assets, and the depreciation method used must correspond to the enterprise's consumption of the asset's economic usefulness. We can distinguish between various depreciation types within the FI-AA component. The most important of these are listed below:

► **Ordinary depreciation**
Ordinary depreciation refers to the reduction in the value of an asset over time owing to normal wear and tear. A range of methods can be used for this type of planned depreciation. These include straight-line depreciation, the declining-balance method, and the unit-of-production method of depreciation.

► **Unplanned depreciation**
Exceptional events, such as damage, that result in a long-term reduction in the value of an asset are mapped in the system using unplanned depreciation.

To provide a more detailed explanation of the periodic activity of the depreciation posting run within the context of the closing process, the sections below discuss examples of a depreciation posting run for ordinary depreciation and for unplanned depreciation.

Ordinary Depreciation

A complex fixed asset is acquired at a cost of €100,000 on 01/01/2007. Figure 7.67 shows how this business transaction is mapped in Transaction ABZON. To access this screen, select ACCOUNTING • FINANCIAL

ACCOUNTING • FIXED ASSETS • POSTING • ACQUISITION • EXTERNAL ACQUISITION • ACQUISITION W/AUTOM. OFFSETTING ENTRY.

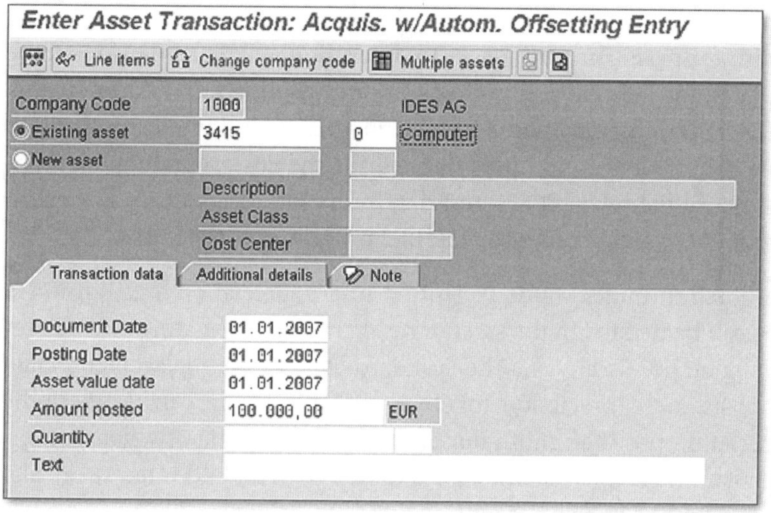

Figure 7.67 Entering the Asset Transaction

The icon allows you to simulate the document. The result of this simulation (see Figure 7.68) is an acquisition posting to balance sheet account 21000 (for fixtures and fittings) and a credit posting to clearing account 199999. Click on the icon to save the document. The asset is at the disposal of the enterprise as of 01/01/2007, is capitalized, and starts to depreciate owing to wear and tear.

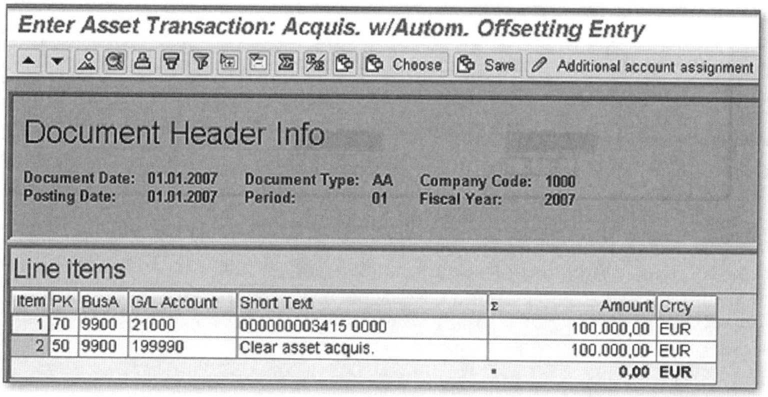

Figure 7.68 Entering the Asset Transaction—Simulation

437

Various valuation approaches
The various valuation approaches are evident in the asset master record. In depreciation area 01, the asset is subject to straight-line depreciation over a period of five years in accordance with US-GAAP specifications. Numerous parameters are defined when the depreciation areas are configured, for example, parameters to determine whether interest is to be calculated for the cost accounting area and whether depreciation below a value of zero is permitted. Depreciation values and interest are posted to the general ledger accounts defined for the corresponding depreciation area in the relevant account determination. An additional account assignment to a cost center or internal order is also permitted.

Index series for replacement values
If revaluation (indexing) is permitted in a depreciation area, an index series can be defined in the asset or asset class for calculating the replacement value per fiscal year. The system calculates the replacement value and posts the depreciation together with the interest in the periodic depreciation posting run. In our example, a useful life of seven years, a recalculation of replacement values (index 00070), and interest calculation are defined in cost accounting area 20 (see Figure 7.69).

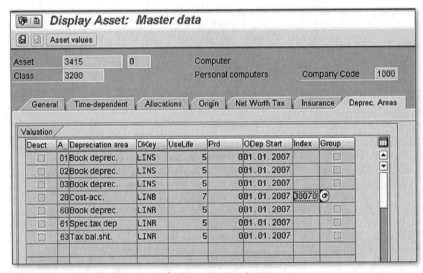

Figure 7.69 Asset Master Record—Depreciation Areas

Maintaining Index Series **[+]**

To maintain index series, select ACCOUNTING • FINANCIAL ACCOUNTING • FIXED ASSETS • ENVIRONMENT • CURRENT SETTINGS • MAINTAIN INDEX SERIES.

In this example, the result is a useful life of five years and therefore an annual depreciation of 20%, or €100,000. The acquisition cost is €20,000 for depreciation area 01. For cost accounting area 20, with a useful life of seven years, the depreciation amounts to €14,286, provided that the indexed replacement costs match the acquisition costs (index 100). Interest is also calculated based on depreciation key LINB. In our example, the interest amounts to 10% of half of the acquisition value of €100,000. This gives us the following simple calculation: €100,000 × 0.5 × 0.1 = €5,000.

This value should match the costs for fixed capital. Figure 7.70 shows the selection screen for the depreciation posting run, which you can access by selecting ACCOUNTING • FINANCIAL ACCOUNTING • FIXED ASSETS • PERIODIC PROCESSING • DEPRECIATION RUN • EXECUTE. The program is limited to processing 1000 assets in the test run. In this case, an annual depreciation run is executed in posting period 12/2007 in place of a regular monthly run. In practice, however, a monthly execution of this program is essential to ensuring an accurate determination of profits for the valid accounting period. In our example, we simply avoided a repeated division over 12 months.

The following configuration settings are required for the program to execute the calculation and the depreciation run to be subsequently posted:

Required configuration settings

► Chart of depreciation with the permitted depreciation areas

► Depreciation areas with the permitted depreciation methods and rules

► All asset classes with the permitted depreciation areas

► All asset classes with a defined automatic account determination

► Depreciation posting cycle (yearly, monthly, etc.)

► Details of the additional account assignments (cost center, order, etc.)

► Definition of a document type for depreciation postings

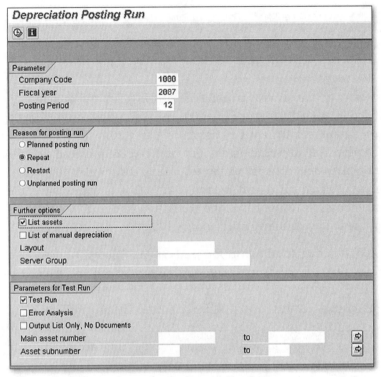

Figure 7.70 Selection Screen for the Depreciation Run

[+] | **Depreciation Posting Run**

If you have recently implemented Asset Accounting, you can execute a depreciation posting run to test that your configuration settings are complete.

New features in SAP ERP

In contrast to SAP R/3, the depreciation run program in SAP ERP is no longer based on processing in batch input sessions. The direct posting method is faster and can save you time if you have numerous assets. Another difference in the new release is the dialog list shown in Figure 7.71.

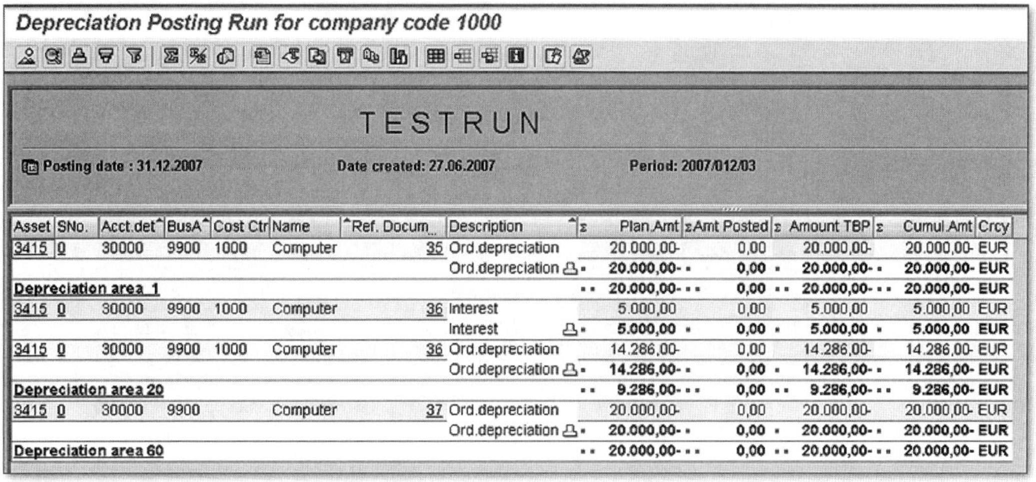

Depreciation Posting Run for company code 1000

TESTRUN

| Posting date : 31.12.2007 | Date created: 27.06.2007 | Period: 2007/012/03 |

Asset	SNo.	Acct.det	BusA	Cost Ctr	Name	Ref. Docum	Description	Σ	Plan.Amt	Σ	Amt Posted	Σ	Amount TBP	Σ	Cumul.Amt	Crcy
3415	0	30000	9900	1000	Computer	35	Ord.depreciation		20.000,00-		0,00		20.000,00-		20.000,00-	EUR
							Ord.depreciation	•	20.000,00-	•	0,00	•	20.000,00-	•	20.000,00-	EUR
Depreciation area 1								••	20.000,00-	•••	0,00	••	20.000,00-	•••	20.000,00-	EUR
3415	0	30000	9900	1000	Computer	36	Interest		5.000,00		0,00		5.000,00		5.000,00	EUR
							Interest	•	5.000,00	•	0,00	•	5.000,00	•	5.000,00	EUR
3415	0	30000	9900	1000	Computer	36	Ord.depreciation		14.286,00-		0,00		14.286,00-		14.286,00-	EUR
							Ord.depreciation	•	14.286,00-	•	0,00	•	14.286,00-	•	14.286,00-	EUR
Depreciation area 20								••	9.286,00-	•••	0,00	••	9.286,00-	•	9.286,00-	EUR
3415	0	30000	9900		Computer	37	Ord.depreciation		20.000,00-		0,00		20.000,00-		20.000,00-	EUR
							Ord.depreciation	•	20.000,00-	•	0,00	•	20.000,00-	•	20.000,00-	EUR
Depreciation area 60								••	20.000,00-	•••	0,00	••	20.000,00-	•••	20.000,00-	EUR

Figure 7.71 Dialog List for the Depreciation Posting Run

The test run is based on a single asset, a computer, with an acquisition cost of €100,000. Three reference documents, numbered 35, 36, and 37, are generated during the test run. If other assets with the same account determination existed in the same business area, three summarized reference documents would be generated in this example. One document can be assigned to depreciation areas 01, 20, and 60.

> **Summarization** [+]
>
> An individual posting document is not generated for each asset in the depreciation run. Instead, information is summarized where possible.

If you double-click on document number 32, the details for the G/L accounts to which the document is to be posted are displayed (see Figure 7.72). In this example, the current book value of the asset is not reduced in balance sheet account 21000 directly (for fixtures and fittings), but rather in a separate accumulated depreciation account (21010). Both accounts are expressed in an identical balance sheet item in the financial statement. This indirect method means that the original acquisition and production costs are clearly visible at all times in the balance sheet account. In addition, the accumulated depreciation account shows you the value of the cumulated depreciation. The net book value is calculated on the basis of an overall analysis.

Depreciation Posting Run for company code 1000
Choose
Save
Additional account assignment
Document Header Info
Document Date: 31.12.2007
Document Type: AF
Company Code: 1000
Posting Date: 31.12.2007
Period: 12
Fiscal Year: 2007
Ledger Group: 0L
Line items
Item PK BusA G/L Account Short Text Σ Amount Crcy
1 40 9900 211100 Ordinary depreciatio 20.000,00 EUR
2 75 9900 21010 ADP - fixts/fittgs 20.000,00- EUR
0,00 EUR

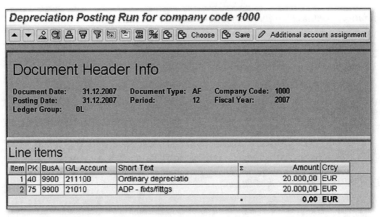

Figure 7.72 Reference Document 32 of the Depreciation Posting Run

Integration with Controlling

The depreciation is posted to tangible assets in P&L account 211100 in addition to balance sheet account 21010. If the P&L account is defined as a cost element, €20,000 is transferred to the cost center in Controlling (CO) that is defined in the asset master record. Alternatively, the depreciation amount including interest from depreciation area 20 can be transferred to CO. Figure 7.73 shows reference document 33. Your system configuration will determine which of the valuations is transferred to general ledger accounting. In many cases, only one valuation is used. In other words, the accounts are created as a cost element from either depreciation area 01 or depreciation area 20. Both postings are relevant for balance sheet evaluations.

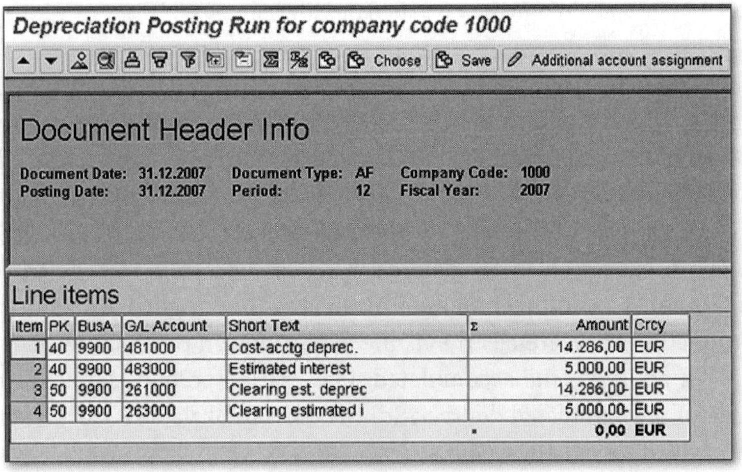

Depreciation Posting Run for company code 1000
Choose
Save
Additional account assignment
Document Header Info
Document Date: 31.12.2007
Document Type: AF
Company Code: 1000
Posting Date: 31.12.2007
Period: 12
Fiscal Year: 2007
Line items
Item PK BusA G/L Account Short Text Σ Amount Crcy
1 40 9900 481000 Cost-acctg deprec. 14.286,00 EUR
2 40 9900 483000 Estimated interest 5.000,00 EUR
3 50 9900 261000 Clearing est. deprec 14.286,00- EUR
4 50 9900 263000 Clearing estimated i 5.000,00- EUR
0,00 EUR

Figure 7.73 Reference Document 33 of the Depreciation Posting Run

The reference documents displayed are used for a simulation of the depreciation posting run, which is limited to 1000 assets. If you press F12 to return to the selection screen, you can press F9 there to start an update run in the background (see Figure 7.74).

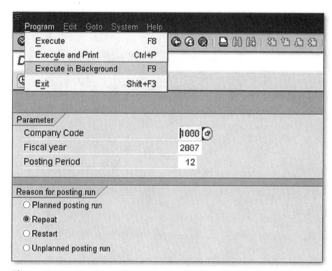

Figure 7.74 Starting a Depreciation Posting Run in the Background

In our example, the resulting log is sent to printer LOCL (Figure 7.75).

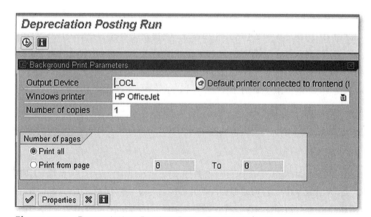

Figure 7.75 Depreciation Posting Run—Printer Selection

Scheduling the
run as a
background job Once you select a printer, you can schedule the depreciation run program. The program should be scheduled to run in the background, if possible at night, to avoid interfering with online postings. When scheduling this job, you need to take account of the number of assets involved and the corresponding effect on the program runtime and system load. Figure 7.76 shows the various options for starting the program.

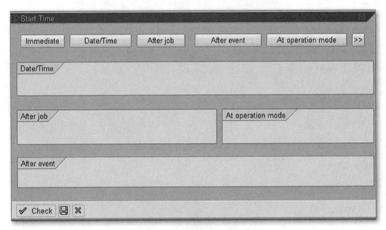

Figure 7.76   Scheduling the Depreciation Posting Run

Traceability of
posted values If you select ACCOUNTING • FINANCIAL ACCOUNTING • FIXED ASSETS • ASSET • ASSET EXPLORER, you can check, for each asset, whether a depreciation posting run resulted in postings. Our example concerns the Computer asset with asset number 3415 (see Figure 7.77). The depreciation posting run for this asset was scheduled and executed for the period 12/2007. Ordinary depreciation for depreciation area 01 is displayed on the Posted values tab. The document from the depreciation posting run is also displayed in the screen area below this. If you double-click on this entry, the summarized collective document (previously the reference document) is displayed.

The effects of the depreciation posting run are not shown on the Planned values tab. The values displayed there for ordinary depreciation originate in FI-AA subledger accounting. The 🔲 icon shown in Figure 7.78 displays additional details about the depreciation calculation.

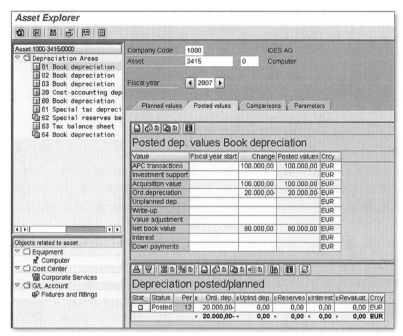

Figure 7.77 Posted Values in the Asset Explorer

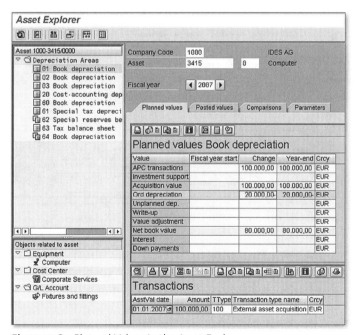

Figure 7.78 Planned Values in the Asset Explorer

It is useful to be able to display the postings and calculations that the system generated automatically, in particular for more obscure calculations.

Making sense of the calculated values

Let's look at the example of valuation area 20, where a useful life of seven years, indexed replacement values, and interest calculation are defined. Figure 7.79 shows acquisition and production costs (APCs) of €100,000, a depreciation amount of €14,286, and interest of €5,000. A summary of the calculation is shown in the lower screen area. In this example, the APCs are transferred as the base value because the index value is 100. If an index of 104 were defined instead, the base value would be €104,000 and the depreciation would be calculated on this basis. Because the computer has a useful life of seven years, the annual depreciation percentage is calculated as 100/7 = 14.2857%, which gives a depreciation of €14,286 for a base value of €100,000. The base value for the interest calculation amounts to half of the acquisition costs (€50,000). An interest rate of 10% would result in interest of €5,000 for the fixed capital. If the screen shown in Figure 7.79 does not provide sufficient information, you can click on the Calculation parameters, Depreciation Parameters, or Period information button to display additional details.

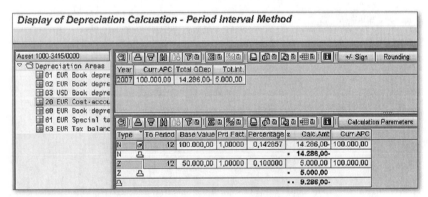

Figure 7.79 Depreciation Calculation in the Asset Explorer

The computer was acquired and depreciated using ordinary depreciation for various depreciation areas. Now that we've covered the basics of ordinary depreciation, we'll discuss an example of unplanned depreciation below.

ing was acquired in the year of depreciation (2007), transaction type 650 (depreciation on current-year acquisitions) is the correct transaction type. However, if the capitalization predates the year of depreciation, the only valid option is transaction type 640 (depreciation on prior-year acquisitions). If there is a mismatch between the year of acquisition and the transaction type selected, the error message shown in Figure 7.81 appears after you enter the manual depreciation.

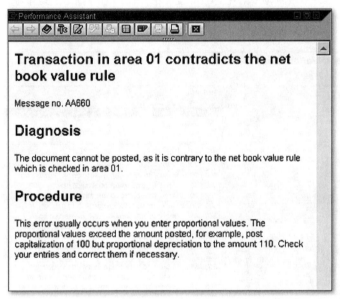

Figure 7.81   Error Message: Mismatched Acquisition Year and Transaction Type

Manual value correction

In this example, unplanned depreciation is executed for a new acquisition. The value adjustment of €80,000 is manually entered and posted for the relevant depreciation areas (see Figure 7.82).

General ledger integration

Initially, the document only exists in the FI-AA subledger. When the depreciation run is executed, both ordinary and unplanned depreciation is taken into account and transferred as a posting to the general ledger. The Asset Explorer shows that this depreciation run is still pending (see Figure 7.83). Both ordinary and unplanned depreciation values still have the status "planned."

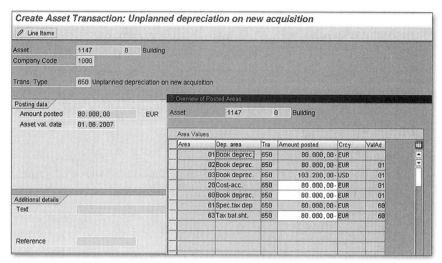

Figure 7.82 Entering an Asset Transaction

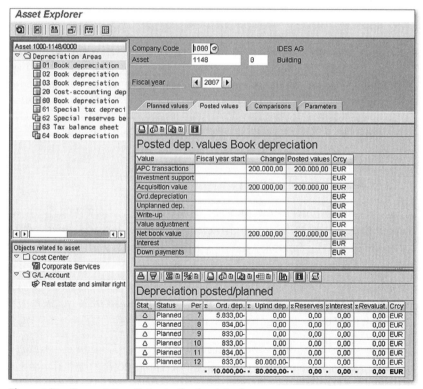

Figure 7.83 Depreciation Status in the Asset Explorer

Let's assume that the building was completed and ready for use by 01/01/2007. However, this information is not known to the asset accountant until period 7. By then, posting periods 1 to 6 are already closed. The question therefore arises as to what is to be done with the planned depreciation amounts for these periods. The system offers the following two methods for distributing the planned depreciation across the individual posting periods:

▶ **Smoothing method**
With the smoothing method, the depreciation is allocated equally among the remaining posting periods.

▶ **Catch-up method**
With the catch-up method, the depreciation due on transactions occurring within the fiscal year is posted as one total on the date of the transaction. In our example, a repeat posting of the depreciations due for periods 1 to 6 is executed in posting period 7.

[+]

> **Difference Between the Smoothing and Catch-Up Methods**
>
> If depreciation parameters are changed after the transaction and depreciations are posted, the depreciation posting run executed with the smoothing method divides the difference between the planned annual depreciation and the depreciation amount posted to date among the remaining posting periods in equal shares. If the catch-up method is used, the depreciation posting run posts this difference as one total in the current posting period.

7.7.4 Asset History Sheet

The relevant depreciations must be posted for the fiscal year in asset accounting. Asset Accounting also creates an asset history sheet, which is essential for the financial statement in accordance with legal requirements. To access the asset history sheet from the SAP menu, select ACCOUNTING • FINANCIAL ACCOUNTING • FIXED ASSETS • INFO SYSTEM • REPORTS ON ASSET ACCOUNTING • NOTES TO FINANCIAL STATEMENTS • INTERNATIONAL • ASSET HISTORY SHEET.

The selection screen that appears in shown in Figure 7.84. In the example shown, a report is executed for company code 1000 for the balance key date of 12/31/2008 based on the values in the FI-AA subledger. As you can see, the Depreciation posted switch is not set under Further settings.

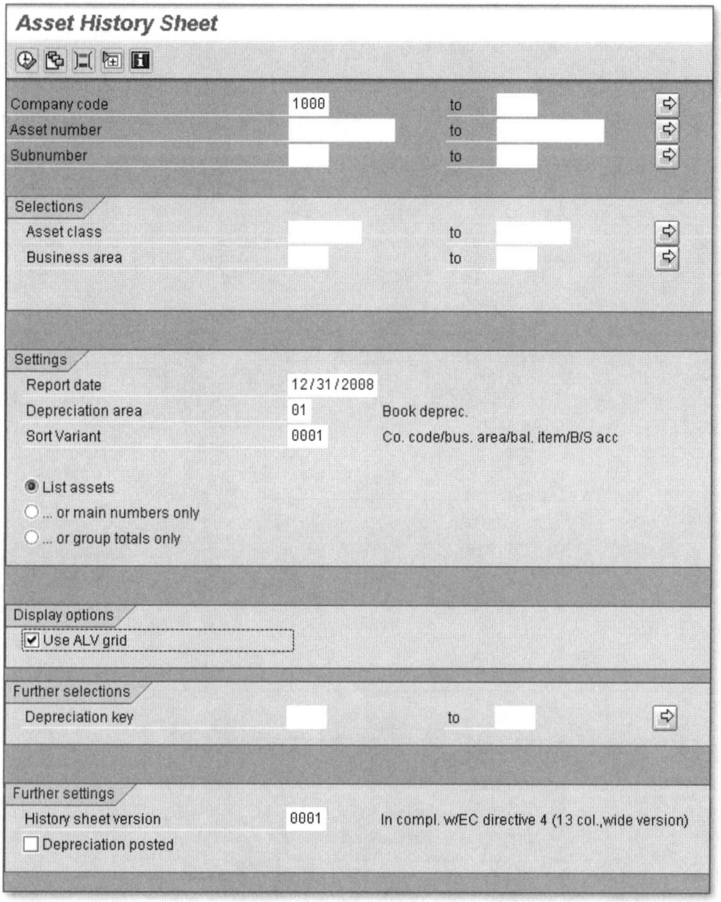

Asset History Sheet

Company code	1000	to		
Asset number		to		
Subnumber		to		

Selections

| Asset class | | to | | |
| Business area | | to | | |

Settings

Report date	12/31/2008	
Depreciation area	01	Book deprec.
Sort Variant	0001	Co. code/bus. area/bal. item/B/S acc

- ● List assets
- ○ ... or main numbers only
- ○ ... or group totals only

Display options

- ☑ Use ALV grid

Further selections

| Depreciation key | | to | | |

Further settings

| History sheet version | 0001 | In compl. w/EC directive 4 (13 col.,wide version) |
| ☐ Depreciation posted | | |

Figure 7.84 Selection Screen

We want to output a list containing values for depreciation area 01 (US-GAAP). Each row in the list represents an individual asset. In other words, the row structure is very granular. The asset history sheet version 0001 – HGB §268 is used to structure the columns. The result of the report is a list containing very detailed information, which is shown in Figure 7.85. Additional subtotals are calculated for the individual asset classes.

Legal requirements for the structure of the asset history sheet

You can also double-click on any of the assets to open the Asset Explorer and view more details of that asset. Take asset 2302 (robot welder), for example. If you double-click on this row, the details shown in Figure 7.86 are displayed. This feature is very useful if you want to track the details of the acquisition or depreciation.

Asset History Sheet

Asset History Sheet - 01 Book deprec.
in compl. w/EC directive 4 (13 col.wide version) (incomplete)

Report date: 12/31/2008 - Created on: 04/10/2008

Asset	Asset description	Cap.date	Σ	APC FY start	Σ	Dep. FY start	Σ	Bk.val.FY strt	SNo.	Σ	Acquisition	Σ	Dep. for year
1120	Betriebsgrundstück Werk Hamburg	01/01/1997		8,180,670.10		0.00		8,180,670.10	0		0.00		0.00
Asset Class 1000 Real estate			•	8,180,670.10	•	0.00	•	8,180,670.10		•	0.00	•	0.00
1113	NB-Fabrikgebäude 5	01/15/1996		6,646,794.45		1,595,231.45-		5,051,563.00	0		0.00		132,936.00-
1129	Montagehalle Werk Hamburg	01/01/1993		1,533,875.64		460,162.64-		1,073,713.00	0		0.00		30,678.00-
1138	Trafostation	05/31/1999		299,722.83		51,951.83-		247,771.00	0		0.00		5,994.00-
Asset Class 1100 Buildings			•	8,480,392.92	•	2,107,345.92-	•	6,373,047.00		•	0.00	•	169,608.00-
Acquisition:Acquis. and production costs 1000 Land and similar rig			••	16,661,063.02	••	2,107,345.92-	••	14,553,717.10		••	0.00	••	169,608.00-
Balance sheet item 1032011 Acquisition value			•••	16,661,063.02	•••	2,107,345.92-	•••	14,553,717.10		•••	0.00	•••	169,608.00-
2001	Fraesmaschine Maho 2323	11/01/1994		108,482.80		108,482.80-		0.00	0		0.00		0.00
2009	CNC Drehmaschine Gildemeister KFG	11/12/1994		159,011.78		159,011.78-		0.00	0		0.00		0.00
2012	Pressluft-Schraubanlage	05/23/1995		26,866.51		26,866.51-		0.00	0		0.00		0.00
2020	Schweißroboter MMKienzle 2000ROB17	01/01/1995		106,295.03		106,295.03-		0.00	0		0.00		0.00
2051	Getriebepumpe	01/01/1995		2,045.17		2,045.17-		0.00	0		0.00		0.00
2056	NB-Förderanlage 4	05/10/1996		61,355.03		61,355.03-		0.00	0		0.00		0.00
2130	Pressluft Schraubanlage	01/01/1990		7,869.38		7,869.38-		0.00	0		0.00		0.00
2131	Roboter für Montage	01/01/1990		15,338.76		15,338.76-		0.00	0		0.00		0.00
2132	Bohrmaschine	01/01/1990		23,008.13		23,008.13-		0.00	0		0.00		0.00
2166	Fertigungsroboter	06/03/1997		15,027.53		15,027.53-		0.00	0		0.00		0.00
2174	Fertigungsroboter	08/04/1997		10,581.52		10,581.52-		0.00	0		0.00		0.00
2182	Tauch und Trockenanlage	04/30/1999		300,639.63		263,060.63-		37,579.00	0		0.00		30,063.00-
2183	Steuerung T&T Anlage	04/30/1999		75,159.91		65,765.91-		9,394.00	0		0.00		7,515.00-
2190	Asset for AC040	01/01/2003		12,000.00		6,000.00-		6,000.00	0		0.00		1,200.00-
2302	Schweißroboter MMKienzle 2000ROB17	01/01/2003		106,295.00		53,147.00-		53,148.00	0		0.00		10,630.00-
Asset Class 2000 Machines decl. depr.			•	1,029,776.18	•	923,655.18-	•	106,121.00		•	0.00	•	49,408.00-
2107	Bohrmaschine WEBO 87-HT	08/22/1994		10,004.45		10,004.45-		0.00	0		0.00		0.00
2110	Elektro-Pumpe KN 2314	11/21/1994		15,850.05		15,850.05-		0.00	0		0.00		0.00
2113	Elektro-Pumpe KW 2314	11/29/1994		11,759.71		11,759.71-		0.00	0		0.00		0.00
2118	Elektro-Pumpe KW 2317	05/05/1994		23,008.13		23,008.13-		0.00	0		0.00		0.00
2119	Elektro Pumpe KW 2517	12/15/1994		19,429.09		19,429.09-		0.00	0		0.00		0.00
2121	Bohrmaschine ZU-890	05/01/1994		21,474.26		21,474.26-		0.00	0		0.00		0.00

Figure 7.85 Report

Figure 7.86 Drill-Down

The asset needs to be depreciated by €886 each month. This is shown in the asset history sheet as an annual depreciation of €10,630. The values are currently posted up to period 5 and planned for periods 6 to 12. However, the total amount is shown in the asset history sheet because of the selection criteria used. The values from the subledger (FI-AA) rather than the posted depreciated values (from general ledger accounting) were selected in our example. In practice, all depreciation posting runs should be executed at year end, and there should be no differences between subledger accounting and general ledger accounting.

7.8   Value Adjustments

At the end of a posting period, an enterprise must determine the value in real terms of the receivables that have been posted. The main business concern in this regard is whether a cash receipt can be counted on in each case. An enterprise may already be aware that some customers will be unable to pay owing to insolvency. For all other customers, empirical values based on past experience allow requirements for value adjustments to be detected and fulfilled. In the context of closing operations, a distinction is therefore made between individual value adjustments and flat-rate value adjustments.

Fulfilling requirements

7.8.1   Individual Value Adjustments

In cases (hopefully rare) where the debtor is insolvent, payment in full can no longer be expected for a delivery or a service rendered. This receivable must be classified as a doubtful receivable. According to the prudence concept, the year-end closing must take account of the risks and losses of which the enterprise is aware when preparing the annual financial statement. This is the case especially if the relevant facts predate the balance sheet date.

Prudence concept

Balance Sheet Preparation   [Ex]

An enterprise (FICO) is in the process of preparing its financial statement for the fiscal year ending December 31. This process usually lasts until March of the following year. In January, FICO learns that one of its customers (A) declared insolvency in December. In this case, an individual value adjustment is justified and necessary.

Allocation quota for cases of insolvency

In the SAP system, the process of individual value adjustment requires a manual posting. In cases of insolvency, an allocation quota usually applies; that is, a certain portion of the receivables may still be paid. In the best case scenario, this will be 100%; in the worst, 0%. Because the quota is still to be clarified when the value adjustment is performed, the tax amount must not be adjusted. The receivables are written off with a tax code of 0%. As soon as the allocation quota is clarified, the individual value adjustment is reversed. The open item is cleared by a cash receipt or depreciation of the remaining amount. The tax on sales and purchases is adjusted at this point.

Individual value adjustment

An example is discussed in detail in the following sections to explain, step by step, the various functions involved in individual value adjustment. Figure 7.87 shows the line item display for customer A with outstanding payments amounting to €100,246.58. If the enterprise (represented by company code 1000) is aware that customer A is insolvent, an individual value adjustment is required for the total amount of the receivables.

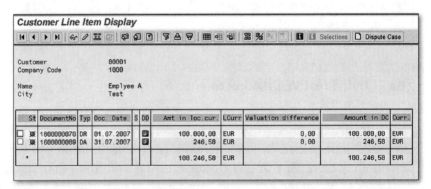

Figure 7.87 Customer Line Item Display

Customer account

To access the transaction for individual value adjustment, select ACCOUNTING • FINANCIAL ACCOUNTING • ACCOUNTS RECEIVABLE • DOCUMENT ENTRY • OTHER • TRANSFER WITHOUT CLEARING. The original customer receivable remains in the account, and its value is negated by an individual value adjustment. In this example, the document and posting date is 12/31/2007. Another important detail is posting code 19, which creates a credit item in the customer account and enables account assignment via a special G/L transaction. The item must not be posted to the usual customer clearing account. Instead, an alternative clearing account is selected with special G/L transaction E, "Reserve for bad debt" (see Figure 7.88).

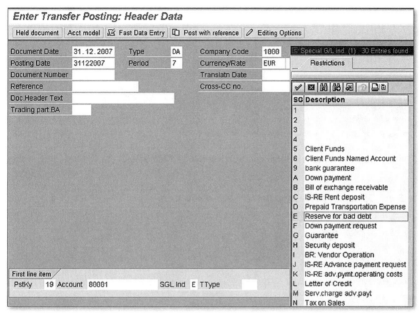

Figure 7.88 Special G/L Transaction "Reserve for Bad Debt"

In our example, the adjustment is not posted to customer reconciliation account 140000. Instead, special G/L transaction E is used for posting to account 142000 (for doubtful receivables). Individual value adjustments have a direct influence on the P&L statement. This is why an account assignment to account 210100 (for expenses from value adjustments to receivables) is effected with posting code 40 (debit posting) (see Figure 7.89).

Special G/L transaction E

In this example, the account is not created as a cost element in Controlling, and as you can see in Figure 7.90, it does not require additional account assignment.

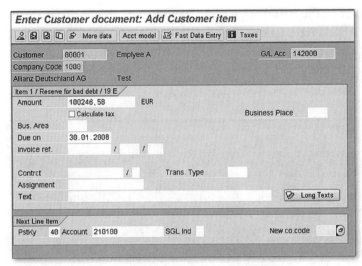

Figure 7.89 Alternative Reconciliation Account 142000

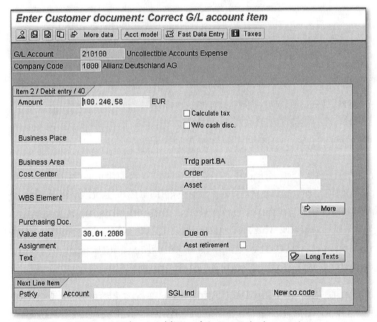

Figure 7.90 Posting Without Additional Account Assignment

Figure 7.91 shows all details of the scenario in the customer line item display. The original receivables still appear in reconciliation account 140000 as an open item. The individual value adjustment results in a total balance of 0 for the customer, whereas the amount of the receivables is expressed in account 142000 (doubtful receivables).

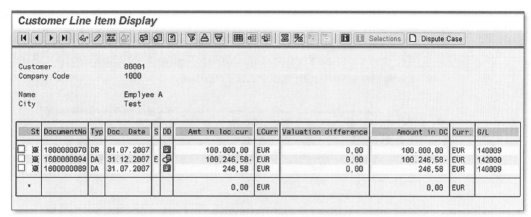

Figure 7.91 Line Item Display After the Individual Value Adjustment

Once all of the necessary adjustments have been made, the next step involves a flat-rate value adjustment.

7.8.2 Flat-Rate Value Adjustment

Unlike individual value adjustments, flat-rate individual value adjustments do not involve missed payments or insolvency. These cases must be posted manually as an initial step in the value adjustment process. Experience shows that a certain requirement also always exists for flat-rate value adjustment. The SAP system provides two methods:

Two types of flat-rate value adjustment

▶ **Manual flat-rate value adjustment**
This method is based on an estimate entered as a manual G/L account posting with the "Expense flat-rate value adjustment to value adjustment" posting record. Because the value adjustment is manual, this method is very flexible but error-prone.

▶ **Flat-rate individual value adjustment**
This term refers to a group of customers whose receivables are to be devalued as a batch using a predefined set of rules. This method is executed automatically. In the second step, the program for flat-rate individual value adjustments selects a group of receivables, calculates the required adjustment on the basis of empirical values or the reli-

ability of the accounting standard, and automatically assigns these receivables to an account.

Master data maintenance as a first step

Before receivables can be automatically valuated, the master data has to be maintained in accounts receivable accounting. In the company code data, the Account Management tab contains an indicator for subsequent flat-rate individual value adjustment. Figure 7.92 shows value adjustment key DN as a grouping characteristic.

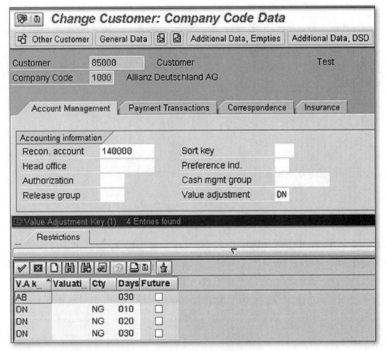

Figure 7.92 Value Adjustment Key in the Master Data

Value adjustment key

The value adjustment key can be user-defined. If, for example, it makes sense to group the customers by region, you could use the following keys:

- ▶ CN – Customers North
- ▶ CE – Customers East

▶ CW – Customers West

▶ CS – Customers South

The precise settings and functions associated with the value adjustment key are shown if you click on the blank page icon in the selection window listing the keys (see Figure 7.92). This brings you to the configuration settings for the application, where you can define new value adjustment keys, provided that you have sufficient authorization. As shown in Figure 7.93, the configuration settings also show additional information about existing entries.

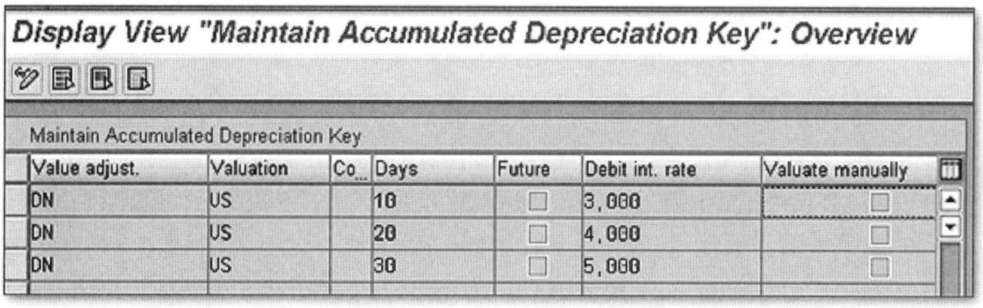

Display View "Maintain Accumulated Depreciation Key": Overview

Maintain Accumulated Depreciation Key

Value adjust.	Valuation	Co...	Days	Future	Debit int. rate	Valuate manually	
DN	US		10	☐	3,000	☐	
DN	US		20	☐	4,000	☐	
DN	US		30	☐	5,000	☐	

Figure 7.93 Value Adjustment Keys in the Configuration Settings

For example, value adjustment key DN is associated with a flat-rate devaluation for overdue receivables that increases over time. After 10 days, overdue receivables are devalued by 3%. After 20 days, this increases to 4%, and all receivables that are overdue by 30 days or more are devalued by 5%. These values are provided as an example only. In practice, past events are used as a basis for deciding how best to group characteristics and then make flat-rate individual value adjustments. Auditors often have specific ideas about how flat-rate individual value adjustments should be used. Remember that every Euro you include in this value adjustment reduces your enterprise's profits and therefore its tax liability. Other grouping characteristics for specific industries or customers of certain sizes are also possible.

Selecting the value adjustment key

The first requirement for making a valuation is a receivable in the accounts receivable accounting area. Figure 7.94 shows a posting of €110,000.

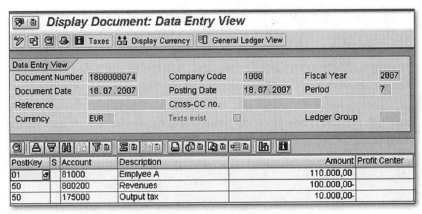

Figure 7.94 Outgoing Invoice with a Tax Rate of 10%

Flat-rate individual value adjustment is executed periodically and is processed by the system as part of the valuation run. The program is located in the SAP application menu under ACCOUNTING • FINANCIAL ACCOUNTING • ACCOUNTS RECEIVABLE • PERIODIC PROCESSING • CLOSING • VALUATE • FURTHER VALUATIONS. You can tell from this generic description that the program has several application areas. For example, it can also be used to carry out discounting and other customer-specific valuations. In short, the program performs the following functions for flat-rate individual value adjustment:

- Calculation of valuations based on a proposal list
- Creation of a checklist of values, including an option for making manual adjustments to individual values
- Key date valuation with subsequent reversal
- Update of document information

The example discussed in the following sections explains, step by step, the various functions involved in flat-rate individual value adjustment.

Before you can create a proposal list, you need to maintain the parameters for a valuation run. These parameters clearly identify who starts the program and when. In Figure 7.95, the program is started by user JE on 12/31/2007.

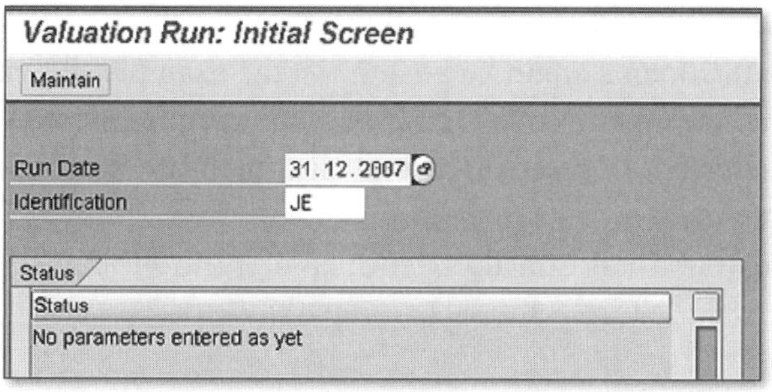

Valuation Run: Initial Screen

| Maintain |

| Run Date | 31.12.2007 |
| Identification | JE |

| Status |
| Status |
| No parameters entered as yet |

Figure 7.95 Valuation Run Identification

Click on the Maintain button to define the parameters for your valuation run. In our example (see Figure 7.96), we want to execute a valuation run with a key date of 12/31/2007. Valuation method 3 (flat-rate individual value adjustment) indicates the purpose of the program run. The amount to be valuated is to be posted to the accounts for the U.S. accounting standard on the key date of 12/31/2007 and automatically reversed by the program on 01/01/2008.

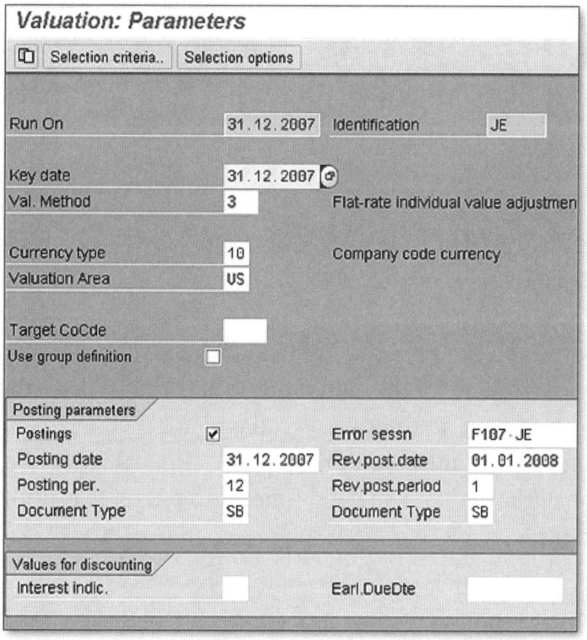

Valuation: Parameters

| Selection criteria.. | Selection options |

| Run On | 31.12.2007 | Identification | JE |

| Key date | 31.12.2007 |
| Val. Method | 3 | Flat-rate individual value adjustmen |

| Currency type | 10 | Company code currency |
| Valuation Area | US |

| Target CoCde | |
| Use group definition | ☐ |

| Posting parameters |
Postings	☑	Error sessn	F107-JE
Posting date	31.12.2007	Rev.post.date	01.01.2008
Posting per.	12	Rev.post.period	1
Document Type	SB	Document Type	SB

| Values for discounting |
| Interest indic. | | Earl.DueDte | |

Figure 7.96 Maintaining Parameters for the Valuation Run

Selection options In the selection options, you can specify the company codes and accounts to which the value adjustments are to be posted. In the example shown in Figure 7.97, a single company code (1000) and our sample customer number 81000 are selected. In practice, several customers are normally selected, either individually or as a range. Insolvent customers for which a manual value adjustment has already been included in the financial statement are to be excluded from the selection parameters.

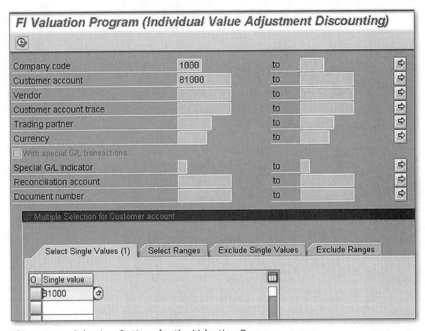

Figure 7.97 Selection Options for the Valuation Run

Releasing the valuation run In the selection options, you can press the [F8] key or choose the ⊕ icon to return to the basic parameters of the valuation. When you click on the save (diskette) icon, all of your settings are saved and are then available for use in a valuation run. As shown in Figure 7.98, this valuation run can be scheduled for or started at a specific time. Immediate execution is selected in our example.

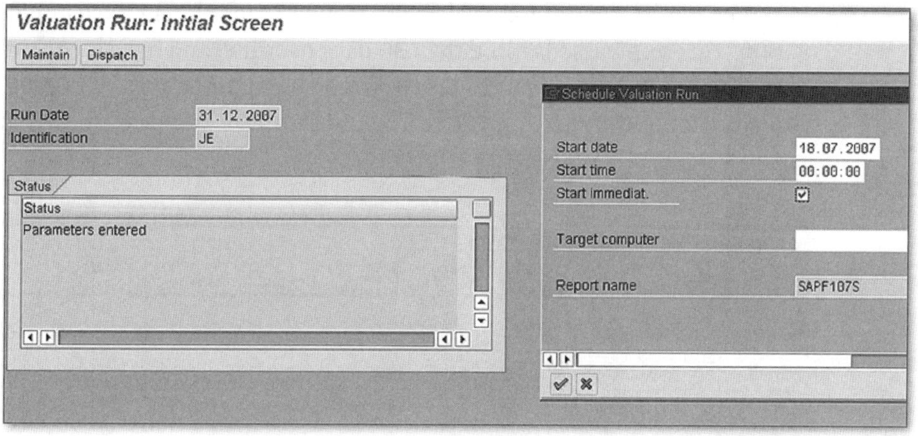

Figure 7.98 Executing the Valuation Run

Like the payment run and dunning run, the valuation run is a two-step process.

First, it produces a proposal that can be processed as part of a dialog   Proposal run
list. Figure 7.99 shows that, after the program was started, customers
and open items were selected in the background and a value adjustment
requirement was determined on the basis of the parameters defined. You
can click on the 🗑 icon to delete the existing data selection without any
consequences. You can click on the Display button to view the detailed
results of the proposal run or the Change valuations button to adjust the
values manually.

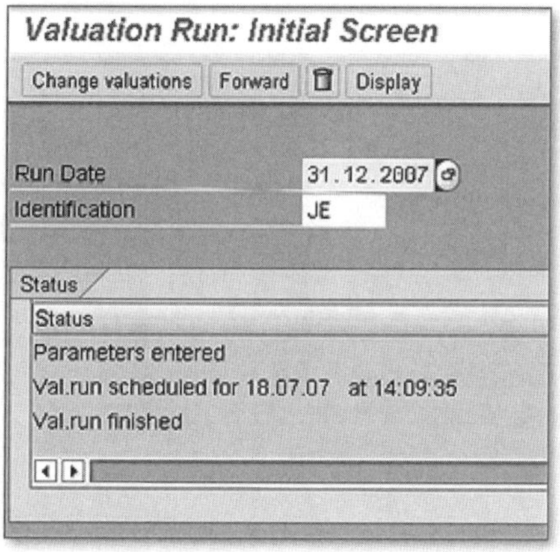

Figure 7.99 Status Information in the Valuation Run

In our example, the program selected an open item relating to customer 81000. This receivable is more than 30 days overdue, and its value therefore requires an adjustment of 5%. Based on a net amount of €100,000, the valuation difference is €5,000. The log for this example is shown in Figure 7.100.

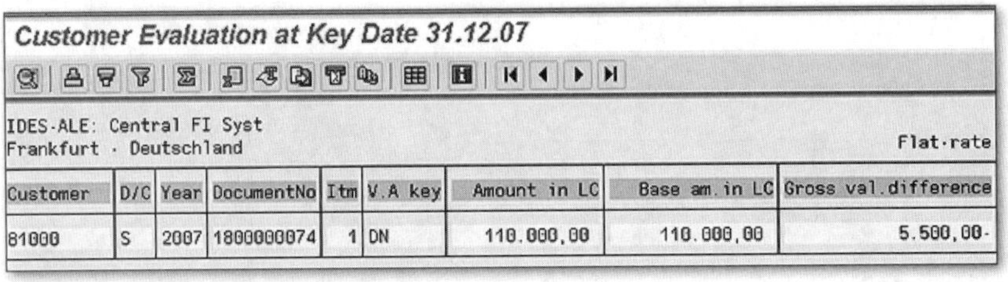

Customer Evaluation at Key Date 31.12.07

IDES-ALE: Central FI Syst
Frankfurt · Deutschland   Flat·rate

Customer	D/C	Year	DocumentNo	Itm	V.A key	Amount in LC	Base am. in LC	Gross val.difference
81000	S	2007	1800000074	1	DN	110.000,00	110.000,00	5.500,00·

Figure 7.100 Valuation Run Log

Sample postings If you and your auditor are satisfied with this valuation, you can make preparations for its transfer. Note that you can still delete the proposal run or adjust the values at this point. Before executing the update run, it is advisable to execute sample postings, as shown in Figure 7.101.

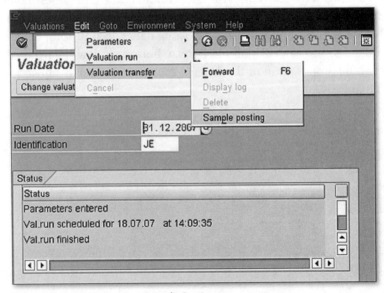

Figure 7.101 Valuation Run Sample Posting

As you can see in Figure 7.102, you can check the account determination and the total amount in the results of a sample posting.

```
Valuation Run: Initial Screen


Valuation of open items at key date

Posting for 1000 140009        EUR           5.000,00-
50 142100                      5.000,00
40 210100                      5.000,00
40 142100                      5.000,00
50 210100                      5.000,00
Company code total   1000      5.000,00-
```

Figure 7.102 Sample Posting Log

Because receivables account 140000 in the SAP system is usually defined as the reconciliation account, values cannot be posted to it directly. Therefore, an account assignment is made to balance sheet account 142100 (value adjustments to receivables), to which values can be posted directly. The correction is reflected in account 210100 in the profit and loss statement. As in the foreign currency valuation, the values are posted for evaluation on the key date of December 31 and then reversed on January 1.

Posting to the balance sheet account

Foreign currency valuation postings constitute another closing activity, which takes place after the individual and flat-rate value adjustment.

7.9 Foreign Currency Valuation

In the SAP system, the currency in which your independent accounting unit, that is, your company code, draws up its financial statements, is referred to as the local currency. Postings entered in a different currency need to be valuated on the relevant key date. The regulations for doing so may differ, depending on which accounting principles are applied. Under the IFRS and US-GAAP standards, the key date principle involves valuation using the exchange rate that is valid on the key date. This may conflict with local regulations that permit devaluation and prohibit upward revaluation.

Valuation on the key date

465

The universal program for foreign currency valuations of line items and balances is SAPF100, which you can access from the menu bar. Simply select SYSTEM • SERVICES • REPORTING. In short, this program performs the following functions:

▶ Calculation of valuation differences based on a proposal list

▶ Key date valuation with subsequent reversal

▶ Update of document information

The example discussed in the following sections explains, step by step, the various functions involved in foreign currency valuation.

[Ex]

Working with Foreign Currencies

If an enterprise that prepares its balance sheet in Euros makes a sale to a U.S. company in U.S. dollars, this receivable must be posted at the current exchange rate. In our example, the European enterprise makes a sale at an exchange rate of €1.60/$1. Figure 7.103 shows the relevant posting record for USD $1,000 or EUR €625.

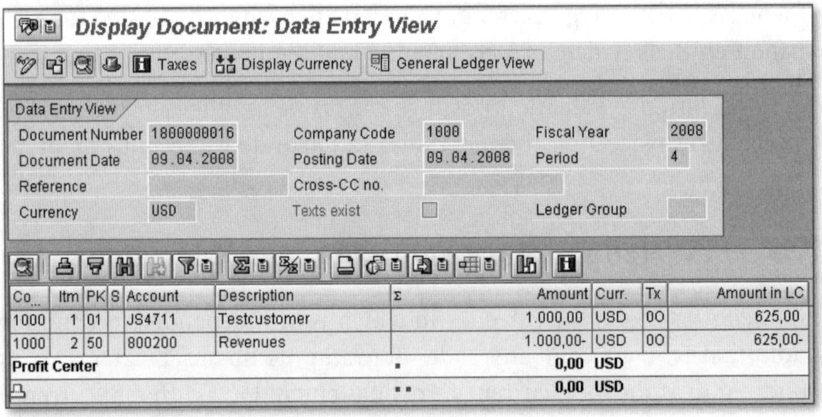

Figure 7.103 Invoice in Transaction Currency U.S. Dollars

Direct and indirect quotation

With indirect quotation, the cost of one unit of local currency (Euros) is given in units of the foreign currency (U.S. dollars). Thus, $1.60 is required to buy €1. Direct quotation, on the other hand, shows the cost of one unit of U.S. dollars in units of Euros, so, in this case, €0.625 is quoted as the price of buying $1. You can maintain the relevant exchange rates under ACCOUNTING • FINANCIAL ACCOUNTING • GENERAL LEDGER •

Environment • Current Settings • Enter Currency Exchange Rates using a Worklist. Figure 7.104 shows the indirect quotation for converting between Euros and dollars that applies as of 03/30/2008.

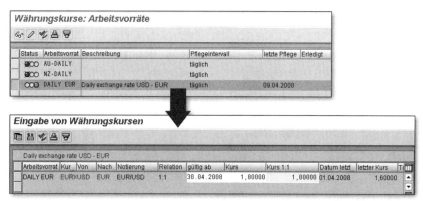

Figure 7.104 Maintaining Foreign Currency Rates

Foreign Currency Table   [+]

Technical table TCURR, which originated in R/3, is preserved in the latest release. However, in SAP ERP, it is now clearer and easier to use thanks to the new transaction, which is based on a worklist (see Figure 7.104).

For the sake of clarity, the indirect quotation also appears in abbreviated form with the special character "/" in the document header of a posted document in the SAP system (see Figure 7.105).

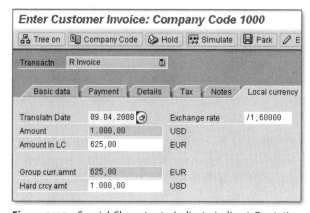

Figure 7.105 Special Character to Indicate Indirect Quotation

If we assume that documents exist in a foreign currency and that these were posted with direct or indirect quotation, a valuation must be executed for these documents on the key date with program SAPF100. You will find this program in the SAP menu under ACCOUNTING • FINANCIAL ACCOUNTING • ACCOUNTS RECEIVABLE • PERIODIC PROCESSING • CLOSING • VALUATE • FOREIGN CURRENCY VALUATIONS OF OPEN ITEMS (NEW). The same functions are also provided in accounts payable accounting and general ledger accounting. Figure 7.106 shows the general selection criteria or instructions for performing a valuation posting.

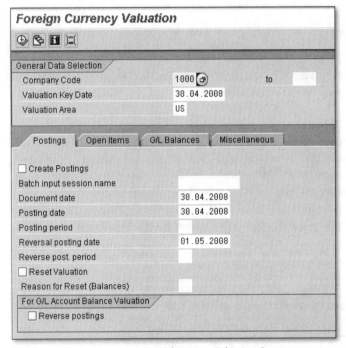

Figure 7.106 Foreign Currency Valuation—Selection Screenv

Valuation methods

Here, all documents with posting dates up to and including 04/30/2008 are selected for company code 1000. The valuation area (U.S. in this example) represents the defined valuation method and target accounts for the posting. The valuation method specifies how the valuation is to be executed. One of the following three methods is normally selected:

- ▶ Valuate in principle (key date principle)
- ▶ Lowest value principle
- ▶ Strict lowest value principle

The following example illustrates how each of these methods influences the valuation (see Table 7.1).

Valuation Methods				[Ex]

A receivable posted on April 30 at an exchange rate of €1.60/$1 is to be valuated on the relevant key dates for the valuation areas U.S. (US-GAAP), IA (IFRS), and LO (local GAAP) using the various methods available. The exchange rates on the key dates are as follows:

- ▶ 04/30 – €1.50/$1
- ▶ 10/30 – €1.60/$1
- ▶ 11/30 – €1.70/$1

Valuation area	Valuation method	09/30	10/30	11/30
US	Valuate in principle	1.50	1.60	1.70
IA	Lowest value principle	1.50	1.60	1.60
LO	Strict lowest value principle	1.50	1.50	1.50

Table 7.1 Overview of Valuation Area, Method, and Date

The postings are entered in a P&L account or adjustment account for receivables or payables because values cannot be posted directly to reconciliation accounts. The values are therefore posted to an adjustment account that is expressed in the same balance sheet item as the relevant reconciliation account.

Using adjustment accounts

The connection between the valuation area, method, and target account is only visible in the configuration settings. In the application itself, users cannot detect that a configuration is defined using key date valuation and target accounts 230010 (expense from valuation) and 140099 (adjustment account for receivables) for valuation area U.S.

[Ex]

Valuation of Receivables in Foreign Currencies

At the end of November, all receivables are to be valuated in accordance with the US-GAAP accounting standard, in other words, the key date principle. Because the date on which the document was originally posted with an indirect quotation of €1.60/$1, the strength of the Euro has risen against the dollar, and the exchange rate is now €1.80/$1.

For a receivable of $1,000, an adjustment of approximately €70 is required:

- April 9, 2008: $1,000 = €625 (€1.60/$1)
- November 30, 2007: $1,000 = €555 (€1.80/$1)

If valuation variances occur with parallel accounting, several valuation runs are required for each valuation area. The foreign currency program creates a batch input session with multiple postings for the US-GAAP accounting standard. The adjustment of €70 is posted with a posting date of 04/30/2008. Valuations in the local currency of the company code, adjusted for exchange rate fluctuations, are then possible for US-GAAP on this key date. To determine which documents result in adjustments in the foreign currency valuation run, refer to the program log (see Figure 7.107).

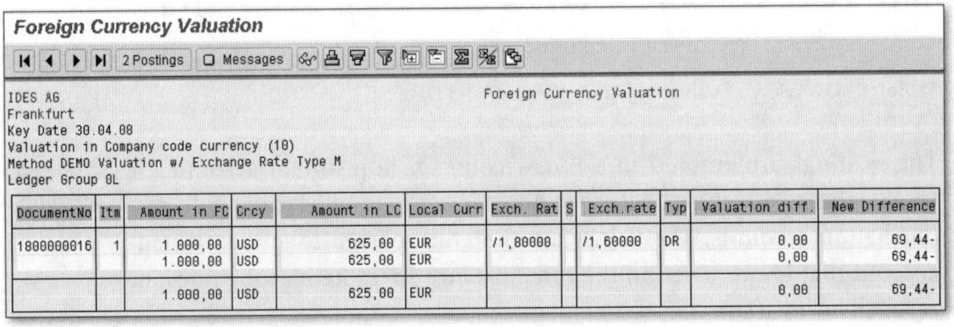
Foreign Currency Valuation

2 Postings | Messages

IDES AG
Frankfurt
Key Date 30.04.08
Valuation in Company code currency (10)
Method DEMO Valuation w/ Exchange Rate Type M
Ledger Group 0L

Foreign Currency Valuation

DocumentNo	Itm	Amount in FC	Crcy	Amount in LC	Local Curr	Exch. Rat	S	Exch.rate	Typ	Valuation diff.	New Difference
1800000016	1	1.000,00	USD	625,00	EUR	/1,80000		/1,60000	DR	0,00	69,44-
		1.000,00	USD	625,00	EUR					0,00	69,44-
		1.000,00	USD	625,00	EUR					0,00	69,44-

Figure 7.107 Foreign Currency Valuation—Log

Example

Two postings were generated. The first document posted is automatically reversed in the same run on the first day of the subsequent month.

Account	Description	Debit	Credit
230010	Expense from foreign currency valuation	$0 €70	
140099	Receivables adjustment		$0 €70

Table 7.2 Posting of Foreign Currency Valuation for November 30, 2008

Account	Description	Debit	Credit
140099	Receivables adjustment	$0 €70	
230010	Expense from foreign currency valuation		$0 €70

Table 7.3 Posting of Foreign Currency Valuation for April 30, 2008

The posting on April 30 serves as an accurate representation of the evaluations. Because an actual loss has not yet been confirmed, the posting is reversed (see Figure 7.108).

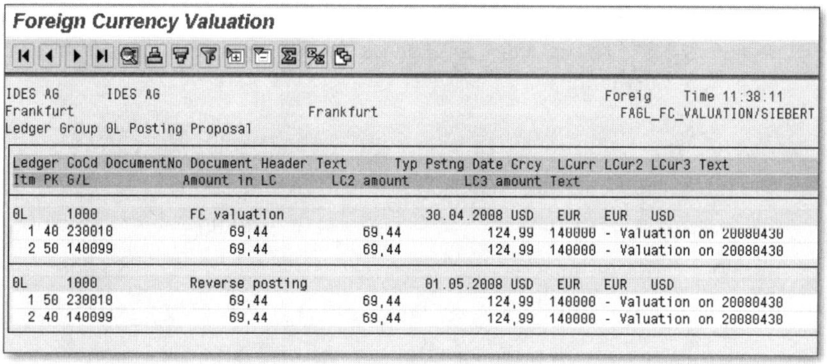

Figure 7.108 Foreign Currency Valuation — Postings

The display of the foreign currency amount as $0.00 takes a little getting used to. It may even be slightly annoying if the Local currency amount

Local currency and document currency

field is not displayed. The actual receivable in the document currency remains unchanged at $1,000. Only the local currency reflects the valuation variance, as shown in Figure 7.109.

The valuation only has an impact on the profit and loss statement in real terms when the payment is received.

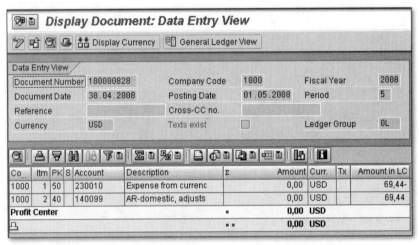

Figure 7.109 Automatically Generated Document

Example

A valuation is executed for April 30, which includes a reversal on May 1. The payment receipt for the receivable is to be posted on May 15. The exchange rate is €1.70/$1. The result is an expense of €37 owing to a loss from exchange rate fluctuations.

Account	Description	Debit	Credit
113100	Bank account	$1,000 €588	
140000	Receivables		$1,000 €625
	Loss from exchange rate fluctuations	$0 €37	

Table 7.4 Posting the Incoming Payment on May 15, 2008

This method is frequently used within a fiscal year. In some countries, however, it is not permitted to reverse a valuation at the end of the fiscal year. In this case, the valuation difference must be updated in the open item. To do this, select the Valuation for Balance Sheet Preparation checkbox in program SAPF100.

Example [Ex]

At the year end, the original receivable (€1.60/$1) is to be valuated for the financial statements at an exchange rate of €1.80/$1. A reverse posting is not permitted. Program SAPF100 is executed with the Valuation for Balance Sheet Preparation checkbox selected to update the valuation difference in the open item.

Account	Description	Debit	Credit
230010	Expense from foreign currency valuation	$0 €70	
140099	Receivables adjustment		$0 €70

Table 7.5 Posting on December 31, 2008

The payment is received in January 2009 when the exchange rate is €1.70/$1. This example shows how hidden reserves can be accumulated if the valuation on the balance sheet date is very low.

Account	Description	Debit	Credit
113100	Bank account	$1,000 €588	
140000	Receivables		$1,000 €555
	Gain from exchange rate fluctuation		$ €33

Table 7.6 Posting the Incoming Payment on January 27, 2009

To display the value with which the individual receivables are actually valuated, select ACCOUNTING • FINANCIAL ACCOUNTING • ACCOUNTS RECEIVABLE • ACCOUNT • DISPLAY ITEMS with the additional field VALUATION DIFFERENCE (see Figure 7.110).

The new general ledger requires a new valuation program As of the new SAP ERP release, report SAPF100 is no longer the program used for foreign currency valuation with the new general ledger. A new program was specially developed for the new release. In addition to a modified data structure, some key functional enhancements have been made for mapping a valuation for the purpose of preparing the financial statement. The next activity to be completed in an individual closing is automatic interest calculation for open items and balances.

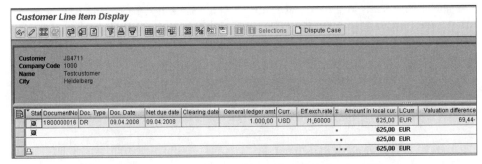

Figure 7.110 List of Open Items—Additional Field "Valuation Difference"

7.10 Interest Calculation

If we assume that the interest calculated by the financial institutions and credited to the bank accounts is correct, the subject of interest calculation is of relatively minor significance in the context of closing operations. Nevertheless, SAP ERP Financials provides functions for calculating and automatically posting interest based on account balances or line items. We examine these functions in detail here, based on the example of an employee loan.

A separate reconciliation account If you select ACCOUNTING • FINANCIAL ACCOUNTING • ACCOUNTS RECEIVABLE • MASTER DATA • DISPLAY, the company code data for employee A (or customer account 80000) is displayed as shown in Figure 7.111. On the Account Management tab, you can see that a special reconciliation account with the number 140009 is used for employee receivables. The interest calculation program essentially relies on the information specified under Interest Calculation on this tab. The interest indicator is subsequently used to determine the interest rate, and the interest cycle determines how often interest is calculated and posted.

The example continues in Figure 7.112, where employee A (customer account 80000) is granted a loan of €100,000 on 07/01/2007. In addition to asset account 140009 (employee receivables), this transaction is also documented in liability account 120000 (employee loans).

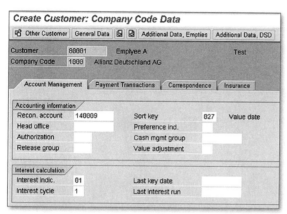

Figure 7.111 Master Data of Employee A, Customer Account 80000

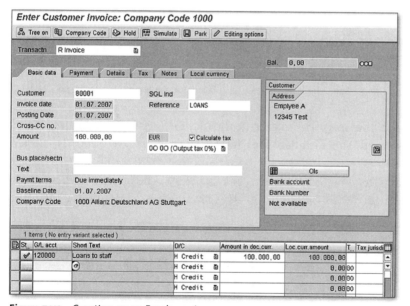

Figure 7.112 Granting on an Employee Loan

Select ACCOUNTING • FINANCIAL ACCOUNTING • ACCOUNTS RECEIVABLE • PERIODIC POSTING • INTEREST CALCULATION • ITEM INTEREST CALCULATION

Item interest calculation

• ITEM INTEREST CALCULATION to access the selection screen shown in Figure 7.113. First, a calculation test run is executed for 07/31/2007. In this case, interest indicator 01 corresponds to the master data of employee A (customer account 80000).

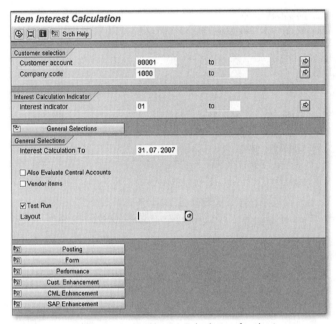

Figure 7.113 Selecting Item Interest Calculation for the Loan

When you press ⌷F8⌷ to execute the run, the log shown in Figure 7.114 is displayed. The document for €100,000 posted on 07/01/2007 is selected, and interest is calculated on the amount from 07/02/2007 to 07/31/2007, that is, for a period of 30 days, at a rate of 3%. The interest calculation formula 100,000 × 0.0/365 × 30 gives us an interest amount of €246.58.

Item Interest Calculation

Customer	0000080001
Company Code	1000
Interest Items	1
Date	17.07.2007
Person Responsible	D035500

	Except	Crcy	Interes	Clmg doc.	Year	DocumentNo	Itm	Int. From	Int.Calc.To	Days	Base.Amount of Int. Calc.	Interest Rate	Int. Amt without +/- Sign
		EUR	2		2007	1800000070	1	02.07.2007	31.07.2007	30	100.000,00	3,0000000	246,58

Figure 7.114 Interest Calculation Log for the Loan

Interest rates are highly susceptible to fluctuations. In our example, no values are posted when you execute a test run. This means changes can still be made by choosing ACCOUNTING • FINANCIAL ACCOUNTING • ACCOUNTS RECEIVABLE • ENVIRONMENT • CURRENT SETTINGS • ENTER TIME INTEREST TERMS. Figure 7.115 shows a selection of defined interest indicators, and thus also currency-dependent and time-dependent interest terms.

Defining interest terms

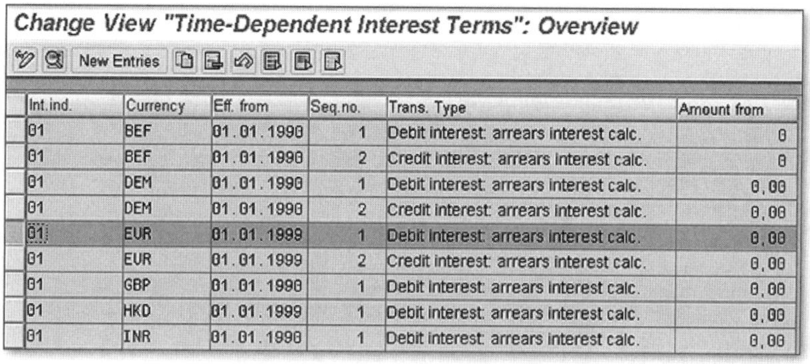

Change View "Time-Dependent Interest Terms": Overview

Int.ind.	Currency	Eff. from	Seq.no.	Trans. Type	Amount from
01	BEF	01.01.1990	1	Debit interest: arrears interest calc.	0
01	BEF	01.01.1990	2	Credit interest: arrears interest calc.	0
01	DEM	01.01.1990	1	Debit interest: arrears interest calc.	0,00
01	DEM	01.01.1990	2	Credit interest: arrears interest calc.	0,00
01	EUR	01.01.1999	1	Debit interest: arrears interest calc.	0,00
01	EUR	01.01.1999	2	Credit interest: arrears interest calc.	0,00
01	GBP	01.01.1990	1	Debit interest: arrears interest calc.	0,00
01	HKD	01.01.1999	1	Debit interest: arrears interest calc.	0,00
01	INR	01.01.1990	1	Debit interest: arrears interest calc.	0,00

Figure 7.115 Overview of Time-Dependent Interest Terms

The interest calculation program has used the entry Debit interest arrears interest calc. 01, Currency EUR, which is valid as of 01/01/1999, as a valid calculation parameter. If you double-click on this term, the detail screen shown in Figure 7.116 is displayed, showing an interest rate of 3% for the debit interest arrears interest calculation, which is independent of the amount.

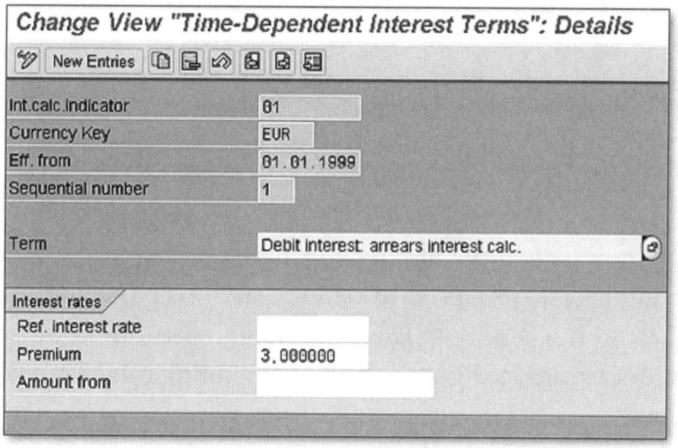

Change View "Time-Dependent Interest Terms": Details

Int.calc.indicator	01
Currency Key	EUR
Eff. from	01.01.1999
Sequential number	1
Term	Debit interest: arrears interest calc.

Interest rates

Ref. interest rate	
Premium	3,000000
Amount from	

Figure 7.116 Detail Screen for the Interest Term

Changes affect the next calculation run for line item interest. In our example, the existing terms are left unchanged, and an update run, including posting, is executed. To do this, select ACCOUNTING • FINANCIAL ACCOUNTING • ACCOUNTS RECEIVABLE • PERIODIC PROCESSING • INTEREST CALCULATION • ITEM INTEREST CALCULATION • ITEM INTEREST CALCULATION. Now let's look at the effects on the master data and the open items of the customer account. The key date of the last interest calculation is noted in the company code data (see Figure 7.117).

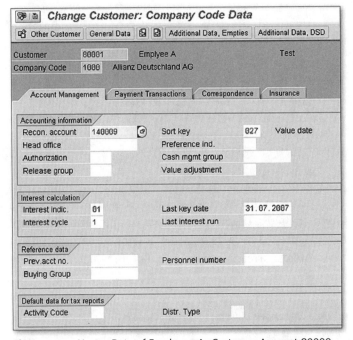

Figure 7.117 Master Data of Employee A, Customer Account 80000

The program has also processed interest of €246.58 in the item interest calculation (Figure 7.118).

The loan is a long-term loan and will not be included in dunning. However, a corresponding cash receipt is to be expected over the coming days to cover the interest amount. The SAP system also offers other automatic periodic activities in this area, such as a dunning run or repeat interest calculation.

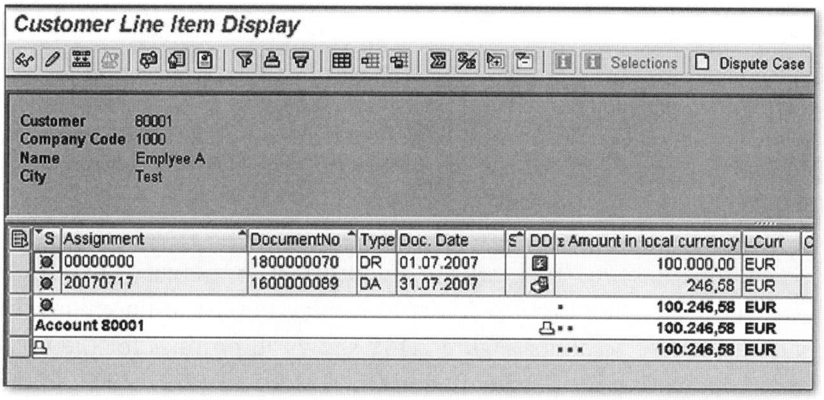

Figure 7.118 Line Item Display for Employee A, Customer Account 80000

7.11   Reconciliation Measures

The figures in Financial Accounting influence business decisions, share price, performance-based remuneration, and so on. An accurate mapping of business transactions and thus of the enterprise's assets, profitability, and overall financial situation is therefore essential. Reconciliation measures are intended to check the figures and ensure that they are correct. We can distinguish between the following two types of reconciliation measures:

▶ Manual checking of postings

▶ Technical reconciliation of transaction figures

Examples are provided in the following sections to explain these procedures.

7.11.1   Manual Checking of Postings

To err is human. Over the course of a fiscal year, we can reasonably expect incorrect postings to be made. These have a negative influence on the information value of Financial Accounting figures. However, checking all posting documents during the closing process is another matter. A balance must be achieved between the costs and benefits of reconciliation measures. One possible approach would be to restrict the check to certain accounts or amounts posted.

[Ex] **Example**

A complex fixed asset may have been accidentally posted directly to expenses without being capitalized. If the posting amount is €10,000 and the useful life is assumed to be five years, the annual profit calculated is too low by a figure of €8,000 (€10,000 posted as a direct expense against €2,000 depreciation).

Detecting incorrect postings

Select ACCOUNTING • FINANCIAL ACCOUNTING • GENERAL LEDGER • ACCOUNT • DISPLAY/CHANGE ITEMS to display the list of line items for a group of G/L accounts. Figure 7.119 shows all postings for the fiscal year 2007 within the posting period 01/01/2007 to 12/31/2007. In the selected accounts, you can click on the multiple selection icon ⇨ to view the details of the accounts where an incorrect posting is likely, for example, the building maintenance account.

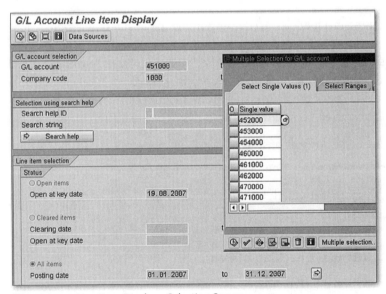

Figure 7.119 Line Item Display—Selection Screen

Line item display

If you execute the selection, hundreds or even thousands of items are displayed. If you select the Amount in local currency column and click on the ⬇ icon for sorting entries in descending order, the documents with the highest values are displayed at the top of the list (see Figure 7.120).

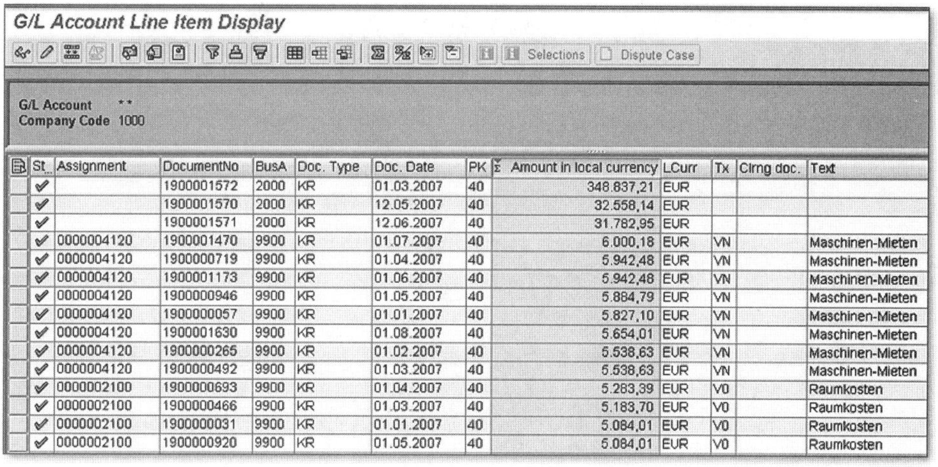

G/L Account Line Item Display

G/L Account **
Company Code 1000

St	Assignment	DocumentNo	BusA	Doc. Type	Doc. Date	PK	Amount in local currency	LCurr	Tx	Clrng doc.	Text
✓		1900001572	2000	KR	01.03.2007	40	348.837,21	EUR			
✓		1900001570	2000	KR	12.05.2007	40	32.558,14	EUR			
✓		1900001571	2000	KR	12.06.2007	40	31.782,95	EUR			
✓	0000004120	1900001470	9900	KR	01.07.2007	40	6.000,18	EUR	VN		Maschinen-Mieten
✓	0000004120	1900000719	9900	KR	01.04.2007	40	5.942,48	EUR	VN		Maschinen-Mieten
✓	0000004120	1900001173	9900	KR	01.06.2007	40	5.942,48	EUR	VN		Maschinen-Mieten
✓	0000004120	1900000946	9900	KR	01.05.2007	40	5.884,79	EUR	VN		Maschinen-Mieten
✓	0000004120	1900000057	9900	KR	01.01.2007	40	5.827,10	EUR	VN		Maschinen-Mieten
✓	0000004120	1900001630	9900	KR	01.08.2007	40	5.654,01	EUR	VN		Maschinen-Mieten
✓	0000004120	1900000265	9900	KR	01.02.2007	40	5.538,63	EUR	VN		Maschinen-Mieten
✓	0000004120	1900000492	9900	KR	01.03.2007	40	5.538,63	EUR	VN		Maschinen-Mieten
✓	0000002100	1900000693	9900	KR	01.04.2007	40	5.283,39	EUR	V0		Raumkosten
✓	0000002100	1900000466	9900	KR	01.03.2007	40	5.183,70	EUR	V0		Raumkosten
✓	0000002100	1900000031	9900	KR	01.01.2007	40	5.084,01	EUR	V0		Raumkosten
✓	0000002100	1900000920	9900	KR	01.05.2007	40	5.084,01	EUR	V0		Raumkosten

Figure 7.120 Line Item Display with Items Sorted in Descending Order

Sharing information

In some cases, the posting text is enough to indicate an incorrect posting. Otherwise, it makes sense to have the asset accountant recheck any unusually large amounts. In Figure 7.121, three documents are selected, which can be sent as an internal document by selecting List • Send.

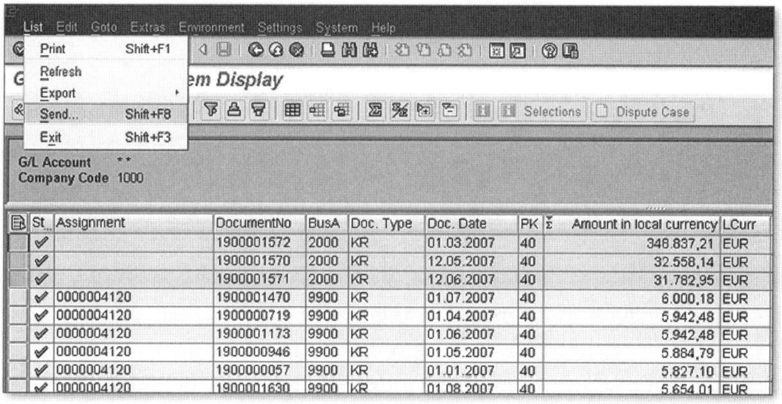

G/L Account **
Company Code 1000

St	Assignment	DocumentNo	BusA	Doc. Type	Doc. Date	PK	Amount in local currency	LCurr
✓		1900001572	2000	KR	01.03.2007	40	348.837,21	EUR
✓		1900001570	2000	KR	12.05.2007	40	32.558,14	EUR
✓		1900001571	2000	KR	12.06.2007	40	31.782,95	EUR
✓	0000004120	1900001470	9900	KR	01.07.2007	40	6.000,18	EUR
✓	0000004120	1900000719	9900	KR	01.04.2007	40	5.942,48	EUR
✓	0000004120	1900001173	9900	KR	01.06.2007	40	5.942,48	EUR
✓	0000004120	1900000946	9900	KR	01.05.2007	40	5.884,79	EUR
✓	0000004120	1900000057	9900	KR	01.01.2007	40	5.827,10	EUR
✓	0000004120	1900001630	9900	KR	01.08.2007	40	5.654,01	EUR

Figure 7.121 Selecting Items in the Line Item Display

You can send the contents to Asset Accounting directly without having to print the line item display or export it to a spreadsheet. In our example, the information is to be forwarded to the internal SAP user with the ID d035500. Alternatively, you can generate an email address or fax number directly. Figure 7.122 shows the screen for creating and sending the document.

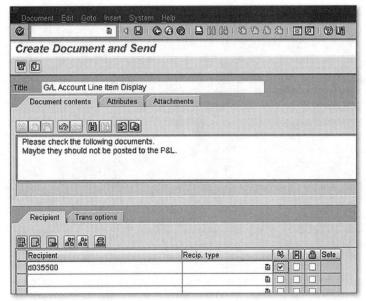

Figure 7.122 Creating and Sending a Document

Because the send type is defined as an express document, the internal SAP user in Asset Accounting is immediately informed in an action pane (Figure 7.123).

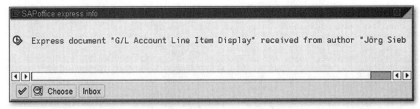

Figure 7.123 Action Pane Displaying Express Info

If the user chooses to display the internal message, it is displayed as shown in Figure 7.124.

A double-click on the attachments displays the attached list of line items. The previously selected sorting of documents is preserved in the list displayed. In addition, the three documents that were previously selected are still highlighted (see Figure 7.125).

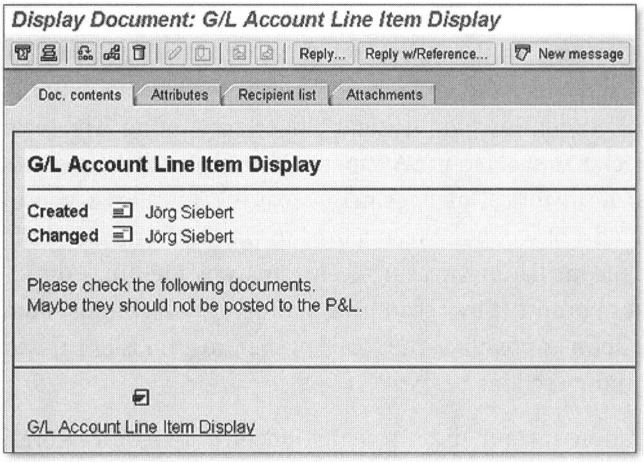

Display Document: G/L Account Line Item Display

Doc. contents | Attributes | Recipient list | Attachments

G/L Account Line Item Display

Created 🖃 Jörg Siebert
Changed 🖃 Jörg Siebert

Please check the following documents.
Maybe they should not be posted to the P&L.

G/L Account Line Item Display

Figure 7.124 Document Display

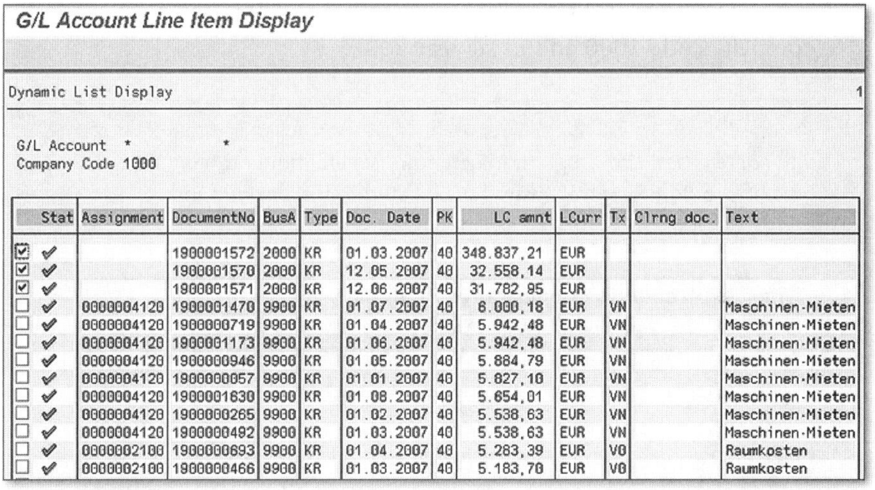

G/L Account Line Item Display

Dynamic List Display   1

G/L Account *   *
Company Code 1000

Stat	Assignment	DocumentNo	BusA	Type	Doc. Date	PK	LC amnt	LCurr	Tx	Clrng doc.	Text
☑ ✔		1900001572	2000	KR	01.03.2007	40	348.837,21	EUR			
☑ ✔		1900001570	2000	KR	12.05.2007	40	32.558,14	EUR			
☑ ✔		1900001571	2000	KR	12.06.2007	40	31.782,95	EUR			
☐ ✔	0000004120	1900001470	9900	KR	01.07.2007	40	6.000,18	EUR	VN		Maschinen-Mieten
☐ ✔	0000004120	1900000719	9900	KR	01.04.2007	40	5.942,48	EUR	VN		Maschinen-Mieten
☐ ✔	0000004120	1900001173	9900	KR	01.06.2007	40	5.942,48	EUR	VN		Maschinen-Mieten
☐ ✔	0000004120	1900000946	9900	KR	01.05.2007	40	5.884,79	EUR	VN		Maschinen-Mieten
☐ ✔	0000004120	1900000057	9900	KR	01.01.2007	40	5.827,10	EUR	VN		Maschinen-Mieten
☐ ✔	0000004120	1900001630	9900	KR	01.08.2007	40	5.654,01	EUR	VN		Maschinen-Mieten
☐ ✔	0000004120	1900000265	9900	KR	01.02.2007	40	5.538,63	EUR	VN		Maschinen-Mieten
☐ ✔	0000004120	1900000492	9900	KR	01.03.2007	40	5.538,63	EUR	VN		Maschinen-Mieten
☐ ✔	0000002100	1900000693	9900	KR	01.04.2007	40	5.283,39	EUR	VO		Raumkosten
☐ ✔	0000002100	1900000466	9900	KR	01.03.2007	40	5.183,70	EUR	VO		Raumkosten

Figure 7.125 List Display

The documents can now be checked by an expert, based on document numbers. In addition to this manual reconciliation measure for checking the accuracy of the content, a technical reconciliation is also performed.

7.11.2 Technical Reconciliation of Transaction Figures

Programs are written by humans and, despite rigorous testing, may contain errors. It is therefore very useful to reconcile transaction figures as part of your closing operations. This procedure involves comparing the debit and credit postings of the individual documents with the transaction figures from the relevant periods in accounts receivable accounting, accounts payable accounting, and general ledger accounting. The term sales volume check has evolved in SAP-speak. The results of the analysis report are saved in historical management records. This allows you to document the details of when the reconciliation was performed and the accuracy of the reconciliation measures. This analysis identifies differences that are not permitted by accounting standards, which must then be eliminated as soon as possible. The scope of the program is illustrated by an example in the sections below.

General check of postings

To access the transaction for the reconciliation of transaction figures, select ACCOUNTING • FINANCIAL ACCOUNTING • GENERAL LEDGER • PERIODIC PROCESSING • CLOSING • CHECK/COUNT • RECONCILIATION. This transaction is shown in Figure 7.126, where a selection has been made for company code 1000 and fiscal year 2007.

[+] | **Performance**

In some cases, the program may require several hours to complete its analysis. It should therefore always be executed in the background.

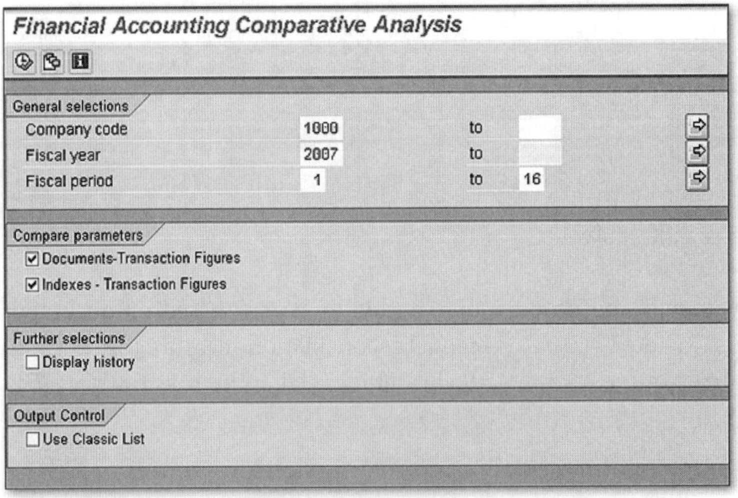

Figure 7.126 Reconciliation of Transaction Figures—Selection Screen

Documents and indexes (in other words, technical access options) are selected as reconciliation parameters. If other checkboxes are not selected, the compressed log shown in Figure 7.127 is displayed after a successful execution of the program.

> ### Blocking Posting Periods [+]
>
> Before calling the program, you should close the relevant posting periods. This excludes the possibility of errors occurring during the reconciliation of transaction figures owing to the posting of a new document.

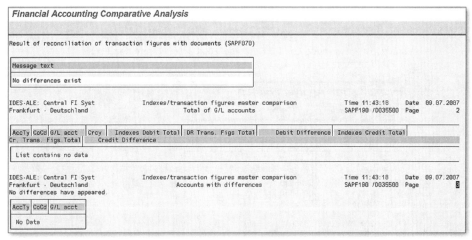

Figure 7.127 Reconciliation of Transaction Figures—Compressed Log

To view a detailed log with details for each account type, period, and company code (as shown in Figure 7.128), select the Use Classic List checkbox on the selection screen.

No differences are shown in our example. Press F12 to go back and change the screen output. Select the Display History checkbox on the selection screen to view the history maintained for the reconciliation, as shown in Figure 7.129.

This function tells you who started the program and when and shows you the result of the program run. You can also click on the Totals | Accounts buttons to display additional details of each run. In most cases, no differences are shown. However, if differences are detected, immediate action should be taken to correct them.

485

Financial Accounting Comparative Analysis

IDES AG — Reconcile Documents and Account Transaction Figures — Time 11:43:33 Date 09.07.2007
Frankfurt — Customers: Totals Across Company Code 1000 — SAPF070 /D035500 Page 1

Recon. in company code currency EUR

A T	CoCd	Local curcy	FY	FP FP	Item debit total	Account debit total	Debit difference	Item credit total	Account credit total	Credit difference
D	1000	EUR	07	01	438.115,88	438.115,88	0,00	256.402,86	256.402,86	0,00
D	1000	EUR	07	02	319.762,92	319.762,92	0,00	132.699,06	132.699,06	0,00
D	1000	EUR	07	03	525.380,14	525.380,14	0,00	131.413,80	131.413,80	0,00
D	1000	EUR	07	04	184.645,41	184.645,41	0,00	50.122.932,02	50.122.932,02	0,00
D	1000	EUR	07	05	13.766.765,77	13.766.765,77	0,00	14.315.534,50	14.315.534,50	0,00
D	1000	EUR	07	06	968.342,58	968.342,58	0,00	1.086.200,85	1.086.200,85	0,00
D	1000	EUR	07	07	2.343,52	2.343,52	0,00	75.750,02	75.750,02	0,00
D	1000	EUR	07	08	0,00	0,00	0,00	1.000.000,00	1.000.000,00	0,00
D	1000	EUR	07	09	10.000,00	10.000,00	0,00	0,00	0,00	0,00
D	1000	EUR	07	10	0,00	0,00	0,00	0,00	0,00	0,00
D	1000	EUR	07	11	0,00	0,00	0,00	0,00	0,00	0,00
D	1000	EUR	07	12	110.400,00	110.400,00	0,00	0,00	0,00	0,00
D	1000	EUR	07	13	0,00	0,00	0,00	0,00	0,00	0,00
D	1000	EUR	07	14	0,00	0,00	0,00	0,00	0,00	0,00
D	1000	EUR	07	15	0,00	0,00	0,00	0,00	0,00	0,00
D	1000	EUR	07	16	0,00	0,00	0,00	0,00	0,00	0,00
D	1000	EUR	07	**	16.325.756,22	16.325.756,22	0,00	67.120.933,11	67.120.933,11	0,00

Figure 7.128 Extended Log for the Reconciliation of Transaction Figures

Reconciliation Analysis History

Totals | Accounts

Entry Date	Time	User Name	Status
09.07.2007	11:43:33	D035500	OK
09.07.2007	11:43:14	D035500	OK
09.07.2007	11:37:20	D035500	OK
09.07.2007	11:37:03	D035500	OK
09.07.2007	11:36:31	D035500	OK
09.07.2007	11:34:01	D035500	OK
01.04.2007	03:46:48	SMITHALL	OK
29.03.2007	16:11:28	HEISSENBERG	OK
26.02.2007	04:04:07	VANESSA	OK

Figure 7.129 Historical Management for the Reconciliation of Transaction Figures

7.12 Intercompany Reconciliation

Internal business volumes generate a need for reconciliation measures

As soon as you have more than one company code, business transactions usually arise that extend across company code boundaries. These internal business volumes need to be eliminated in the consolidated financial statement, which gives rise to a latent need for the reconciliation of the individual balance sheets to determine, for example, whether the receivables of A also appear in the balance sheet of B as payables of the same amount. Previously, differences in intercompany accounts were largely determined in the consolidation procedure. An example is provided below to explain the process of intercompany reconciliation based on the individual closing.

In this example, company code 3000, IDES USA, receives a loan of $5,500 from its subsidiary, company code 1000 in the Netherlands. Figure 7.130 shows one side of this intercompany transaction. In a homogeneous SAP environment, cross–company code documents enable automatic posting to both company codes, so differences are prevented in the first place.

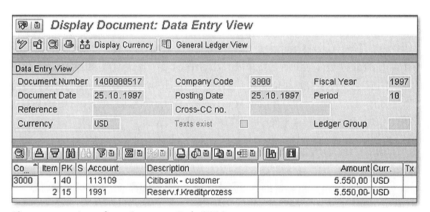

Figure 7.130   Loan from Company Code 3000

The posting record in company code 3000, IDES USA, consists of a debit account assignment for the OI-managed G/L account 113109 and a credit item of subledger account 1991. The liquid funds are available in the Citibank account, and the liability is represented by a credit posting in the subledger account. As soon as this transaction is posted, it is flagged for subsequent intercompany reconciliation. The Trading Partner field in the credit item is automatically filled with the value "1000," as you can see in Figure 7.131.

Required settings

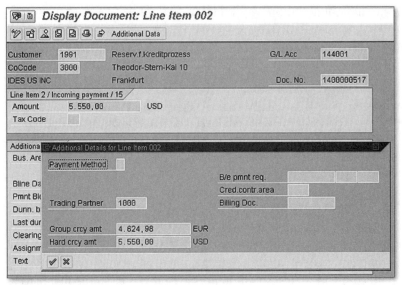

Figure 7.131 Trading Partner in the Posting Record

The trading partner data is copied from the master data of the subledger account. This data specifies that the business partner is an intercompany partner. The value uniquely identifies the relevant subsidiary. Figure 7.132 shows the general master data defined for customer 1991. To access this screen, select ACCOUNTING • FINANCIAL ACCOUNTING • ACCOUNTS RECEIVABLE • MASTER DATA • DISPLAY.

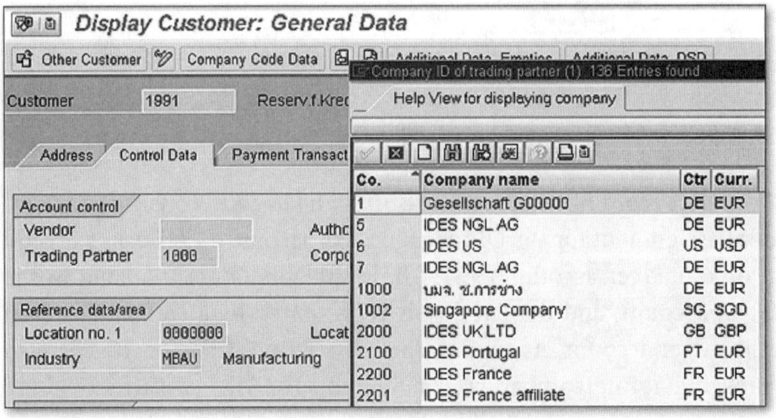

Figure 7.132 Trading Partner in the Master Record of the Subledger Account

Customer 1991 is the trading partner in the Netherlands. The account assignment in company code 3000, IDES USA, uses the relevant trading partner (1000) to identify the business transaction concerning the loan received. This identifying information is inherited by all posting items and is subsequently updated from the master data of the customer account.

The "Trading Partner" Field	[+]

Separate account groups should be created for intercompany subledger accounts. The TRADING PARTNER field is a required entry field in such cases. This configuration ensures a high level of data quality for intercompany postings. This makes it much easier to perform reconciliation at the level of G/L and subledger accounts.

It can be assumed that a corresponding receivable is posted in debit and that a cash outflow is posted in credit for subsidiary 1000, IDES Netherlands. If subsidiary 1000 in the Netherlands does not use an SAP system, reconciliation is essential at the period end. As a rule, the following three areas require reconciliation in the SAP and non-SAP systems:

▶ Accounts payable accounting

▶ Accounts receivable accounting

▶ General ledger accounting

Intercompany Reconciliation	[+]

Programs for reconciling receivables and payables have been available since R/3 Release 4.6. These programs are capable of comparing and reconciling internal business volumes within an SAP system. As of SAP ERP 2004, they can do the same thing regardless of the number and type of systems involved. Line items are loaded into a separate, flexible work area and, if possible, cleared automatically. Differences are identified and adjustment postings are triggered. Unexplained differences can be eliminated by automatic posting in the distributed SAP and non-SAP systems. This option rounds off the closing process perfectly. From a business perspective, you need to determine whether your distributed business units will agree to such a concept. In any case, the ultimate goal is still to enhance the quality of intercompany figures, thereby avoiding costly and time-consuming work and queries for consolidation.

Gathering
information

The programs for the various types of account reconciliation are organized into folders in the SAP application menu. In our example, our focus
is on the intercompany business transactions in the G/L accounts. To
access this screen, select ACCOUNTING • FINANCIAL ACCOUNTING • GENERAL
LEDGER • PERIODIC PROCESSING • CLOSING • CHECK/COUNT • INTERCOMPANY
RECONCILIATION: OPEN ITEMS. In the first step, the documents must be
downloaded from intercompany partners into a central data store. Figure
7.133 shows the selection screen for the Select Documents transaction.

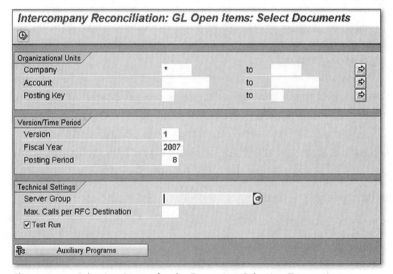

Figure 7.133 Selection Screen for the Document Selection Transaction

Central
information
storage

The Company organizational unit is associated with one or more company codes in your system configuration. In this example, company 6
represents company code 3000, in which the loan payable has been
posted in the 8/2007 posting period. This data is read in the Select Documents transaction and is saved in version 1 of the work area for intercompany reconciliations. To ensure a successful reconciliation, the corresponding data records of subsidiary 1000 (company 5) must also be read
by the intercompany reconciliation program. The log in Figure 7.134
shows the data records that have been imported from other companies.
You can see that no data has been loaded for companies AEN1 und AEN2
owing to a connection error.

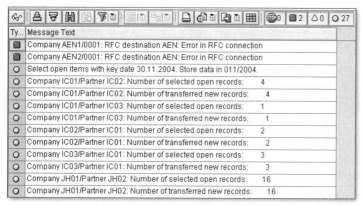

Ty...	Message Text	
▣	Company AEN1/0001: RFC destination AEN: Error in RFC connection	
▣	Company AEN2/0001: RFC destination AEN: Error in RFC connection	
○	Select open items with key date 30.11.2004. Store data in 011/2004.	
○	Company IC01/Partner IC02: Number of selected open records:	4
○	Company IC01/Partner IC02: Number of transferred new records:	4
○	Company IC01/Partner IC03: Number of selected open records:	1
○	Company IC01/Partner IC03: Number of transferred new records:	1
○	Company IC02/Partner IC01: Number of selected open records:	2
○	Company IC02/Partner IC01: Number of transferred new records:	2
○	Company IC03/Partner IC01: Number of selected open records:	3
○	Company IC03/Partner IC01: Number of transferred new records:	3
○	Company JH01/Partner JH02: Number of selected open records:	16
○	Company JH01/Partner JH02: Number of transferred new records:	16

Figure 7.134 Document Selection Log

An automatic clearing program is started in the Assign Documents transaction. The prerequisites for this are criteria such as identical amounts or the field contents of fields such as Reference or Assignment. The selection screen for the Assign Documents transaction is shown in Figure 7.135. Here you can specify the conditions necessary for successful clearing in the background. Your configuration settings are not visible to the user in this transaction.

Identifying differences

Intercompany Reconciliation: GL Open Items: Assign Documents

Organizational Units
Company   *   to
Trading Partner   to
Company's Accounts   to
Partner's Accounts   to

Version/Time Period
Version   1
Fiscal Year   2007
Posting Period   8

Technical Settings
Server Group
Max. Calls per RFC Destination
☑ Test Run

Auxiliary Programs

Figure 7.135 Assign Documents—Selection

Automatic and
manual clearing In our example, the G/L debit posting for company 6 (company code 3000) can be cleared automatically with a G/L credit posting for company 5 (subsidiary 1000) if, in addition to the amount, an identical transaction number is defined in the Document Text field. Note that this procedure is used in a self-contained work area for reconciliation purposes only. It has no effect on operational accounting. The log in Figure 7.136 shows how a large number of data records can be cleared automatically. The rules defined have located six data records relating to business transactions between companies IC01 and IC02 and, of these six, three could be cleared immediately. The next activity requires the Reconcile Documents Manually transaction.

Once you have loaded documents into the work area and the automatic reconciliation process is completed, start the Reconcile Documents Manually transaction. The selection screen for this transaction is shown in Figure 7.137. You can configure settings here for each company or account to be reconciled. In our example, a filter is not set because we want to display all companies and accounts. The value "EUR" is entered in the Display Currency field so that intercompany differences will be displayed in Euros.

Making differences transparent The real work begins now. On the left side of the screen shown in Figure 7.138, you can see a navigation tree, which represents the business relationships between the individual companies and trading partners. In this example, the folders representing companies 5 and 6 are open. Company 6, which represents company code 3000, has an intercompany business relationship with trading partner 1000, IDES Netherlands. The total intercompany difference is shown in the selected display currency as €4,302. The relevant line items are shown on the right side of the screen. In this case, a single document is shown, with an amount of $5,550, which corresponds to €4,302. You can select this document and click on the magnifying glass icon to drill down to the original document.

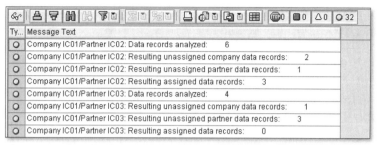

Ty...	Message Text
○	Company IC01/Partner IC02: Data records analyzed: 6
○	Company IC01/Partner IC02: Resulting unassigned company data records: 2
○	Company IC01/Partner IC02: Resulting unassigned partner data records: 1
○	Company IC01/Partner IC02: Resulting assigned data records: 3
○	Company IC01/Partner IC03: Data records analyzed: 4
○	Company IC01/Partner IC03: Resulting unassigned company data records: 1
○	Company IC01/Partner IC03: Resulting unassigned partner data records: 3
○	Company IC01/Partner IC03: Resulting assigned data records: 0

Figure 7.136 Log for the "Assign Documents" Transaction

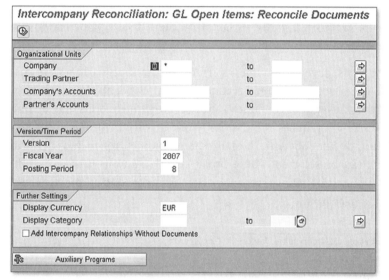

Figure 7.137 Selection Screen of the "Reconcile Documents Manually" Transaction

Figure 7.138 Overview of Differences in the "Reconcile Documents Manually" Transaction

No data record is displayed to show the situation from the perspective of partner 1000. This may be due to a variety of reasons:

- ▶ No posting was entered in the accounting system used by subsidiary 1000, IDES Netherlands.

- ▶ The posting was not entered in the correct accounting period, 08/2007.

- ▶ A posting was entered but was based on poorly maintained master data or did not include a reference to a trading partner.

- ▶ The current line items of the intercompany documents were not supplied or were only partly supplied by the subsidiary for use in the central reconciliation tool.

In most cases, several documents from both trading partners are displayed. The process of manual reconciliation now begins. Based on various criteria, the system generates a proposal for which items may belong together, which reduces the manual work involved. As shown in Figure 7.139, documents with the same transaction currency and identical amounts can be selected. These broad criteria allow you to work efficiently when using manual reconciliation as opposed to automatic clearing in the background.

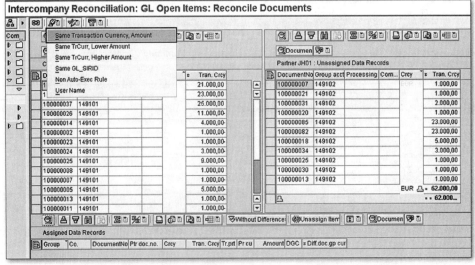

Figure 7.139 Clearing Items in the "Reconcile Documents Manually" Transaction

Figure 7.140 shows nine business transactions that need to be cleared. The user can approve and reject each of these individually.

Intercompany Reconciliation: GL Open Items: Reconcile Documents

Group	Co.	Crcy	Tran. Crcy	Tr.prt	Pr cu	Amount	DGC	Σ Difference
	JH02	EUR	23.000,00-	JH01		23.000,00	EUR	0,00
9							EUR •	0,00
	JH02	EUR	23.000,00-	JH01		23.000,00	EUR	0,00
8							EUR •	0,00
	JH02	EUR	5.000,00-	JH01		5.000,00	EUR	0,00
7							EUR •	0,00
	JH02	EUR	3.000,00-	JH01		3.000,00	EUR	0,00
6							EUR •	0,00
	JH02	EUR	1.000,00-	JH01		1.000,00	EUR	0,00
5							EUR •	0,00
	JH02	EUR	1.000,00-	JH01		1.000,00	EUR	0,00
4							EUR •	0,00
	JH02	EUR	1.000,00-	JH01		1.000,00	EUR	0,00
3							EUR •	0,00
	JH02	EUR	1.000,00-	JH01		1.000,00	EUR	0,00
2							EUR •	0,00
	JH02	EUR	1.000,00-	JH01		1.000,00	EUR	0,00
1							EUR •	0,00
							EUR ••	0,00

Figure 7.140 Proposal List in the "Reconcile Documents Manually" Transaction

If you look again at our example of the loan with a posting of $5,500 for one of the partners only, you can see that an intercompany difference that requires clarification exists at the end of the posting period. You can select the item and click on the letter icon to generate correspondence about the item. Figure 7.141 shows the selection of defined correspondence templates in the available languages.

Generating correspondence

After you select a template, an overview of the contact persons defined in the system for the subsidiary is displayed (see Figure 7.142). You can select one or more contact persons as the recipients of the correspondence.

495

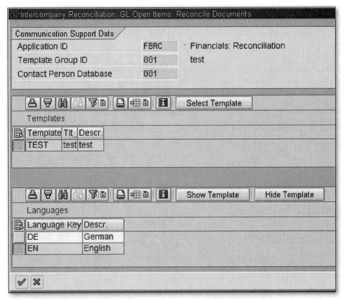

Figure 7.141 Correspondence Template in the "Reconcile Documents Manually" Transaction

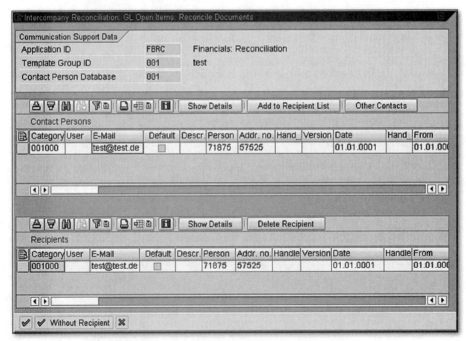

Figure 7.142 Reconcile Documents Manually—Contact Persons

Text templates and the relevant contact persons, including contact details, must already be defined in the configuration. It is then a very simple matter to create a letter, fax or, as in this example, an email containing the relevant information (see Figure 7.143).

Communicating differences

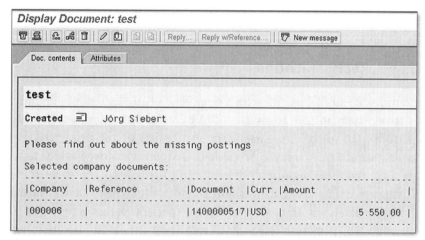

Figure 7.143 Correspondence Relating to the "Reconcile Documents Manually" Transaction

To improve traceability, each item that has already been included in a correspondence document is flagged with a status indicator, as shown in Figure 7.144.

Figure 7.144 Status Indicator in the "Reconcile Documents Manually" Transaction

A central overview of differences and related correspondence enables a more structured and transparent reconciliation process. Unexplained differences can be eliminated by an automatic posting in the distributed SAP and non-SAP systems. This option rounds off the closing process

Greater transparency in the overall process

perfectly. From a business perspective, you need to determine whether your distributed business units will agree to such a concept. An option for adjustment postings can help make intercompany processes more disciplined. In most cases, however, it will simply postpone clarification requirements until after the closing key date. In practice, human intervention is essential to clarify differences and reach agreement.

7.13 Reclassification

Customers with credit balances

To provide external parties with a clear view of an enterprise's liquidity, it is necessary to sort receivables and payables based on their validity periods. On the balance sheet date, it may also be the case that there are outstanding payables to be made to customers and receivables to be paid by vendors. Regrouping is required to accurately represent these customers with credit balances and vendors with debit balances in the financial statement. In the SAP system, a special program is provided to automatically perform these tasks of sorting by due date and regrouping, which is referred to as reclassification. An example is provided below to explain these functions in detail.

[+]

How the Reclassification Program Works

The program is also used if a customer or vendor's reconciliation account has changed during the fiscal year, for example, if a change of ownership has resulted in this subledger account being reassigned to the affiliated companies. In this scenario, receivables and payables are correctly reclassified and expressed in the balance sheet on the balance sheet date.

The line item display (ACCOUNTING • FINANCIAL ACCOUNTING • ACCOUNTS RECEIVABLE • ACCOUNT • DISPLAY ITEMS) clearly indicates whether the line items require sorting or reclassification. Figure 7.45 shows a customer account where a credit memo for €5,000 changes a positive balance into a negative balance. In short, it produces a payable rather than a receivable, which the system shows as an amount of €–1,000 in the account. In terms of chronological sorting, all three documents fall into the category of payables due within one year.

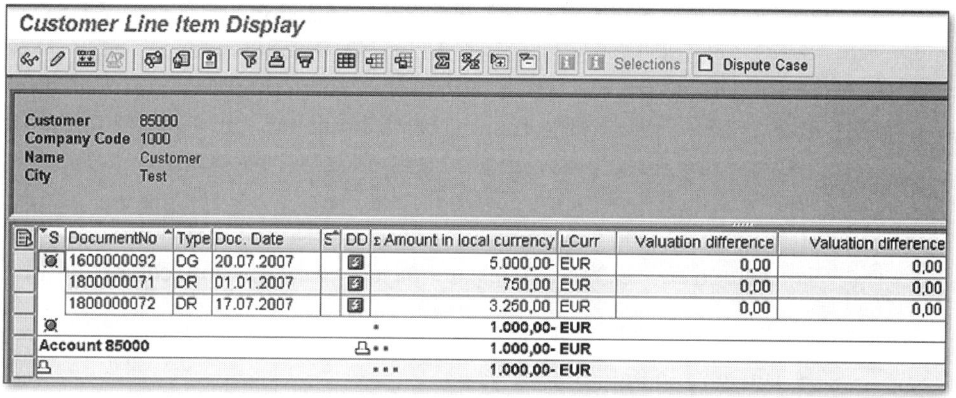

Customer Line Item Display

Customer   85000
Company Code 1000
Name   Customer
City   Test

S	DocumentNo	Type	Doc. Date	S	DD	Σ Amount in local currency	LCurr	Valuation difference	Valuation difference
	1600000092	DG	20.07.2007			5.000,00-	EUR	0,00	0,00
	1800000071	DR	01.01.2007			750,00	EUR	0,00	0,00
	1800000072	DR	17.07.2007			3.250,00	EUR	0,00	0,00
						1.000,00-	EUR		
Account 85000						1.000,00-	EUR		
						1.000,00-	EUR		

Figure 7.145   Line Item Display for a Customer with a Credit Balance

In this example, the program SAPF101 is started via the menu path SYS-
TEM • SERVICES • REPORTING. Figure 7.146 shows a range of parameters
for selection and posting control.

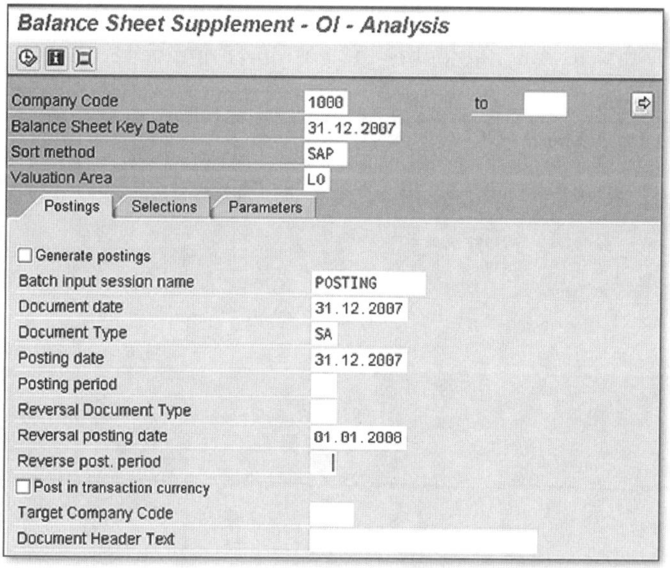

Balance Sheet Supplement - OI - Analysis

Company Code	1000	to	
Balance Sheet Key Date	31.12.2007		
Sort method	SAP		
Valuation Area	L0		

   Postings   Selections   Parameters

☐ Generate postings
Batch input session name	POSTING
Document date	31.12.2007
Document Type	SA
Posting date	31.12.2007
Posting period	
Reversal Document Type	
Reversal posting date	01.01.2008
Reverse post. period	

☐ Post in transaction currency
Target Company Code	
Document Header Text	

Figure 7.146   Postings in the Balance Sheet Supplement

In our example, any necessary adjustment postings must be entered by
12/31/2007. These postings are simultaneously reversed for the first day
falling within the next posting period because these reclassifications are

Posting reclassifi-
cations

not necessary for day-to-day business transactions. The Generate postings checkbox is not selected on the screen shown here because these are settings for a test run. In an update run, posting records are created for the specified data in the Posting batch input session. This session must then be processed (SYSTEM • SERVICES • BATCH INPUT). Figure 7.146 also shows that all documents posted for company code 1000 up to a posting date of 12/31/2007 are to be included. The selected sort method (SAP) is configured so that receivables and payables are categorized as follows:

▶ Due within one year

▶ Due within one to three years

▶ Due within more than three years

Sort methods can also be configured differently to give a more general or precise classification. The valuation area is linked to the account determination for parallel accounting. In our example, the value LO indicates local accounting standards.

Selection options The selection parameters shown in Figure 7.147 restrict the selection to account type D for customer accounts and customer number 85000.

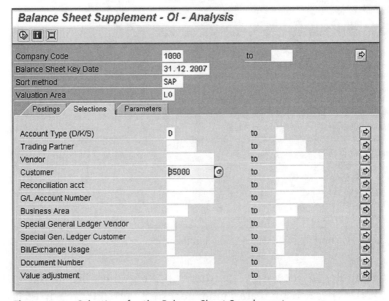

Figure 7.147 Selections for the Balance Sheet Supplement

On the next tab, parameters are set to indicate how the valuation is to be executed by the program. As shown in Figure 7.148, the selected customers are to be grouped together in a group posting in this case. Note that valuation type 5, Translation of Balances, is selected. This means receivables and payables are to be sorted on the basis of their due dates and are to be reclassified.

Grouping customers in a group posting

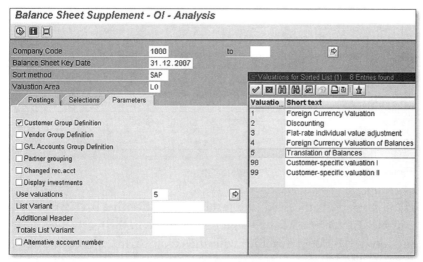

Figure 7.148 Parameters for the Balance Sheet Supplement

After you press F8 to run the program in the background, a log of the analysis is displayed (see Figure 7.149).

Balance Sheet Supplement - OI - Analysis

Allianz Deutschland AG   Balance Sheet Supplement · OI Analysis per 31.12.07   Time 13:52:09   Date 17.07.2007
Stuttgart   FAGL_CL_REGROUP/D035508 Page   1

Tr.Prt	AccTy	Prev.rec.1	Account	Description	Ac.	Crcy	Net due date	DocumentNo	Amount Valuated	Ty	Pstng Date
	D	140000	0000085000	Payables withi%	V02	EUR	20.07.2007	1600000092	5.000,00-	DG	20.07.2007
	D	140000	0000085000	Payables withi%	V02	EUR	01.01.2007	1800000071	750,00	OR	01.01.2007
	D	140000	0000085000	Payables withi%	V02	EUR	17.07.2007	1800000072	3.250,00	OR	17.07.2007
*		140000	0000085000		V02				1.000,00-		
**		140000	0000085000						1.000,00-		
***		140000							1.000,00-		
**** Target Comp. Code 1000									1.000,00-		

Figure 7.149 Analysis Log

The documents from the line item display are selected. Once again, a customer with a credit balance is shown in the account with €–1,000. If you now select Postings, the batch input session for the defined account assignments is displayed (see Figure 7.150).

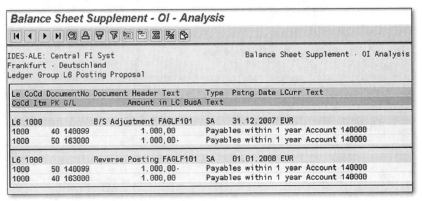

Balance Sheet Supplement - OI - Analysis

```
IDES-ALE: Central FI Syst                        Balance Sheet Supplement · OI Analysis
Frankfurt · Deutschland
Ledger Group L6 Posting Proposal

Le CoCd DocumentNo Document Header Text       Type  Pstng Date LCurr Text
CoCd Itm PK G/L              Amount in LC BusA Text

L6 1000            B/S Adjustment FAGLF101     SA    31.12.2007 EUR
1000    40 140099              1.000,00        Payables within 1 year Account 140000
1000    50 163000              1.000,00-       Payables within 1 year Account 140000

L6 1000            Reverse Posting FAGLF101    SA    01.01.2008 EUR
1000    50 140099              1.000,00-       Payables within 1 year Account 140000
1000    40 163000              1.000,00        Payables within 1 year Account 140000
```

Figure 7.150 Generated Batch Input Postings

Clearing account for transfer postings If the session is processed, the result is a balance that is classified as a payable. The debit account assignment is made in the receivables clearing account 140099. Together with the credit balance in reconciliation account 140000, this produces an overall balance of 0 on the credit (assets) side of the balance sheet. Account 163000 contains a second credit account assignment item on the debit (liabilities) side of the balance sheet (see Figure 7.151).

Display Document: Data Entry View

☑ ☑ ☑ ☑ ☑ Display Currency ☑ General Ledger View

Data Entry View						
Document Number	225	Company Code	1000	Fiscal Year		2007
Document Date	31.12.2007	Posting Date	31.12.2007	Period		12
Reference		Cross-CC no.				
Currency	EUR	Texts exist	☐	Ledger Group		L6

PK	S	Account	Description	Amount	Profit Center	Plant	BusA
40		140099	AR-domestic, adjusts	1.000,00			
50		163000	Cust.with a crd.bal.	1.000,00-			

Figure 7.151 Transfer Posting on December 31, 2007

As shown in Figure 7.152, a reverse posting is entered in the next posting period on 01/01/2008 (see posting date).

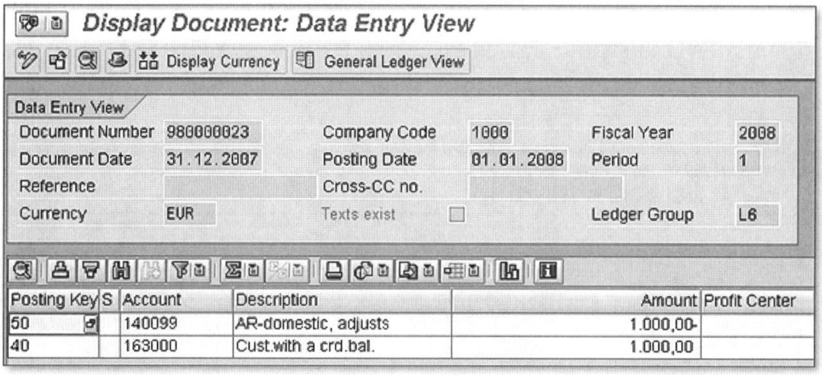

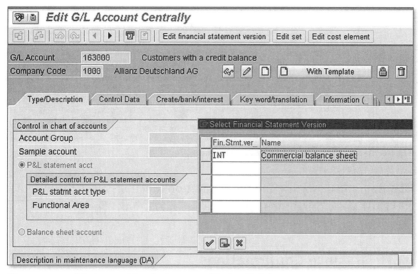

Figure 7.152 Reverse Posting on December 31, 2008

To view a precise representation in the balance sheet, select ACCOUNTING • FINANCIAL ACCOUNTING • GENERAL LEDGER • MASTER RECORDS • G/L ACCOUNTS • CENTRALLY (see Figure 7.153).

Figure 7.153 G/L Account for Customers with Credit Balances

If you select G/L account 163000 (for customers with credit balances) and click on the Edit financial statement version button, the exact item to be expressed in the balance sheet is shown in the relevant version (Figure 7.154). In our example, account 163000 is shown on the debit side under LIABILITIES • PAYABLES/OTHER LIABILITIES • OTHER LIABILITIES/ OTHER • DUE WITHIN ONE YEAR/OTHER.

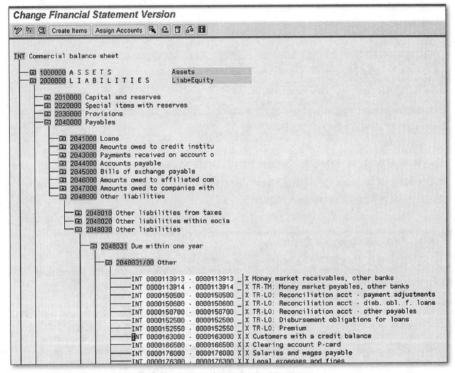

Figure 7.154 Display of the Financial Statement Version

These automatic sorting and reclassification functions make the program SAPF101 a key component of all closing operations.

7.14 Balance Confirmations

Checking the information value of the accounting figures
After the balance carryforward has been technically completed and the old fiscal year has been blocked, balance confirmations must be sent. The purpose of these letters is to check whether your individual business

partners can confirm the figures for the relevant receivables and payables. This should exclude the possibility of fictitious postings appearing on the balance sheet. This process verifies the information value of the figures in accounting. Its structure is outlined in Figure 7.155. Letters are sent to a selection of vendors and customers. Based on the figures in accounting, these are sent a letter and a listing of the line items from the relevant account. A standardized reply to be completed by the business partner is also attached to speed up the confirmation (or rejection) process. This information is returned directly to a supervisory unit, such as the internal audit department or the external auditor. The checklists that are generated at the same time as the letters enable a comparison of internal and external information. A summary detailing the response rate, the total number of items confirmed, and items requiring further clarification is documented in the results table. The example discussed in the following sections guides you through each step of the program.

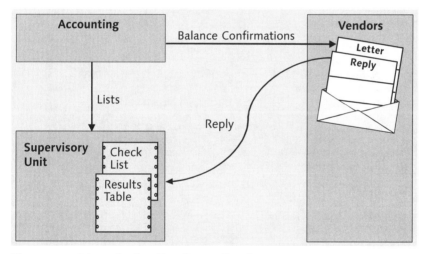

Figure 7.155 Balance Confirmation: Process Overview

You will find the programs SAPF130D and SAPF130K under ACCOUNTING • FINANCIAL ACCOUNTING • ACCOUNTS RECEIVABLE/ACCOUNTS PAYABLE • PERIODIC PROCESSING • CLOSING • CHECK/COUNT • BALANCE SHEET CONFIRMATION: PRINT in the SAP menu. Figure 7.156 shows the selection screen for a customer balance confirmation. In this example, a general selection is made for all customers belonging to company code 1000 on

Generating letters and checklists

12/31/2007. The query is restricted by several prerequisites that must be fulfilled. Under Further selections, the selection is further restricted to customers that generated sales of between €10,000 and 10,000,000 in the 2007 fiscal year. The sample size is also limited to the first 50 customers found. The letter will indicate that a reply is due by 01/31/2008.

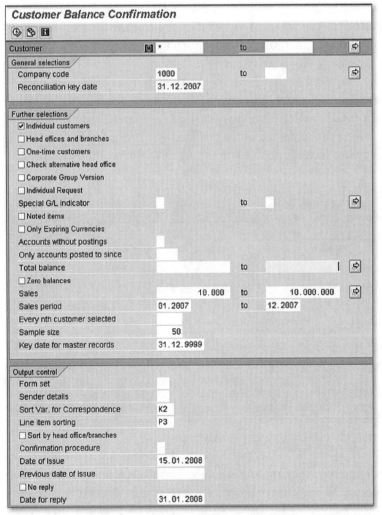

Figure 7.156 Selection Screen for the Customer Balance Confirmation

Figure 7.157 shows the printed balance confirmation letter, with the individual line items listed at the bottom.

IDES Holding AG, Postfach 16 05 29, D-[illegible]

Company
Customer 1000
Calvinstrasse 36
13467 Berlin-Hermsdorf

Balance confirmation

Date
09.07.2007
Your account with us
1000
Our accounting clerk

Telephone

Telefax

Your clerk
Frau Menges
Our account with you
500789

Balance confirmation on 31.12.2007

Dear Sir/Madam,

In connection with the checking of our year-end closing, we would ask you to compare the open items listed in the line item list from 31.12.2007 with your ledgers and to confirm the agreement with the balance on the last page of this letter up until the 31.01.2008. If, on checking, you discover any differences, please let us know so that the reasons for these differences can be ascertained.

Please find enclosed an envelope for your reply and statement of any differences found.

We look forward to hearing from you soon.

Yours sincerely

IDES Inc.

Itemization of open items

Figure 7.157 Letter with Itemization of Open Line Items

In addition to this letter, the program also generates a reply for the business partner (see Figure 7.158). Here, the overall balance can be confirmed or rejected by selecting a checkbox. The transaction is documented with the date and signed. The internal audit department is specified as the recipient in the address field at the top of the letter.

```
Firma                                    ┌─────────────────────────────┐
IDES AG                                  │ Reply                       │
Interne Revision (Internal Audit)        │ Date                        │
Lyoner Stern 23                          │                             │
60441 Frankfurt                          │ Clerk                       │
                                         │                             │
                                         │ Telephone                   │
                                         │                             │
                                         │ Telefax                     │
                                         │                             │
                                         │ Your account with us        │
                                         │ 500789                      │
                                         │ Your clerk                  │
                                         │                             │
                                         │ Our account with you        │
                                         │ 1000                        │
                                         └─────────────────────────────┘

This balance confirmation applies to:

Firma
Ides AG
Martin Steiner, Kathrin Walther,
Bernd Zecha, Dondogmaa Lchamdondog
IDES intern
Postfach 160529
60070 Frankfurt

The outstanding total balance on key date 31.12.2007 amounts to:

EUR               132.787,01        In your favor
CNY                11.000,00        In your favor

Please find herewith our reply, marked and explained below:

__  The balance, according to our books, agrees with the figure stated
    above.

__  The balance, according to our books, does not agree with the figure
    stated above.  An explanation of the differences can be found on the
    back page of this letter or is enclosed separately.
    Contact: Name              _____

          Telephone number     _____
```

Figure 7.158 Reply

The checklist shown in Figure 7.159 is provided for this supervisory unit. In this example, 17 customers are to be documented, representing a total volume of just under €1.2 million in receivables.

Print Preview of P313 Page 00002 of 00003

		18.300,00	EUR		total		
		18.300,00	EUR		18.300,00	EUR	
ROHRER01	Rohrer AG Gr.01					DE	
	13365	Berlin					
		18.070,75	EUR		total		
		18.070,75	EUR		18.070,75	EUR	
ROHRER30	Rohrer AG Gr.30					DE	
	13365	Berlin					
		570,48-	EUR		total		
		570,48-	EUR		570,48-	EUR	
SUPER-BIKE	Super-Bike					DE	
		München					
		50.456,00	EUR		total		
		50.456,00	EUR		50.456,00	EUR	
T-L64B17	SudaTech GmbH					DE	
	70563	Stuttgart					
		54.835,20	EUR		total		
		54.835,20	EUR		54.835,20	EUR	
T-L69A10	Hallmann Anlagenbau					DE	
	59067	Hamm					
		3.000,00-	EUR		total		
		3.000,00-	EUR		3.000,00-	EUR	
Sum total		1.172.550,81	EUR				
		1.100,00	EUR		11.000,00	CNY	
		1.170.573,04	EUR		1.170.573,04	EUR	
		877,77	EUR		600,00	GBP	

Figure 7.159 Checklist

The entire procedure is summarized in the results list, which is shown in
Figure 7.160. This indicates how many of the 17 customers replied and
what percentage of the receivables were confirmed as valid.

					Local	
Reconciliation date:	31.12.2007		Date of issue:		15.01.2008	
Additional text:			Reply date:		31.01.2008	

	Number of zero bals.	% number items		amount amount	Local curr ency doc. curr- ency	% %
Requested						
balance confirmations	0000000017 0000000000	100,00				
				1.100,00	EUR	0,09
				11.000,00	CNY	100,00
				1.170.573,04	EUR	99,83
				1.170.573,04	EUR	100,00
				877,77	EUR	0,07
				600,00	GBP	100,00
Sum total in local currency						
				1.172.550,81	EUR	100,00
Unreturned	_____					
			_____		EUR	
			_____		CNY	
			_____		EUR	
			_____		EUR	
			_____		EUR	
			_____		GBP	
Returned without confirmation						
- undeliverable	_____					
			_____		EUR	
			_____		CNY	
			_____		EUR	
			_____		EUR	

Figure 7.160 Results List

To ensure complete and comprehensive documentation, you can print the list of parameters used for the selection shown in Figure 7.161.

As a fraud avoidance measure, balance confirmation forms part of the overall corporate governance concept.

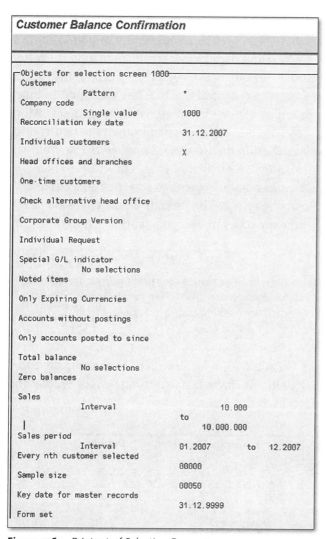

Figure 7.161 Printout of Selection Parameters

7.15 Period Control

To ensure that profits are calculated correctly for the valid accounting period, it is essential not only that the documents be posted to the correct period. The posting period must also be technically open. In other instances, you may want to prevent postings in a certain period once specific activities have been completed, for example, the advance return for

Technical opening in period control

511

tax on sales and purchases or auditor certification of the balance sheet. In the SAP system, these tasks are the responsibility of period control, which represents both technical and business functionality. It is often incorrectly assumed that period control comprises a central instance in the FI module. In fact, period control mechanisms are found in other modules also, for example, CO or MM (Materials Management). More about those later. First, we need to understand how FI period control works. This is explained using the example described below. You will find FI period control in the SAP menu under ACCOUNTING • FINANCIAL ACCOUNTING • GENERAL LEDGER • ENVIRONMENT • CURRENT SETTINGS • OPEN AND CLOSE POSTING PERIODS. The variants defined here are linked with one or more company codes in the configuration settings.

[Ex] | **Central Control of Company Codes**

With a single entry, you can open or close a month for posting for 100 company codes. If you do not want to use this type of central control, you need to create up to 100 variants for opening and closing the company codes and then maintain these in the FI period table.

Figure 7.162 shows variant ZZJS, which is linked with company codes 0005, 1000, and 2000. In this example, the posting periods 6/2007 and 7/2007 are open for all account types.

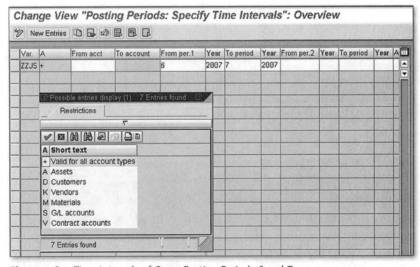

Figure 7.162 Time Intervals of Open Posting Periods 6 and 7

The character "+" stands for all account types as is always required as a basic selection option. Because the posting date is essential to ensure a correct determination of profits in the valid accounting period, this control table is used to perform an immediate verification when dates are entered in the document header (see Figure 7.163). In the example shown here, the fiscal year variant is the calendar year. When a posting date of 05/15/2007 is entered, the period 5/2007 is derived and sent for verification and an error message is immediately returned.

Selecting account types

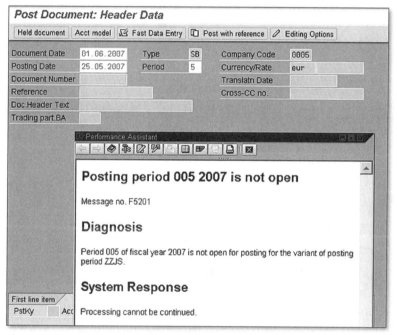

Figure 7.163 Document Entry in Period 5

Further refinements are also possible in the control table. As a second example, the periods 06/2007 and 7/2007 are open for general posting, but the additional entry K determines that only period 7/2007 is open for certain postings to vendor accounts. In this case, the accounts in question are those numbered 0000000001 to ZZZZZZZZZZ in the vendor master data (Figure 7.164).

Opening individual periods

If you select a posting date that does not fall within the open period, the error message shown in Figure 7.165 is issued. The system response is

Checking posting procedures in real time

the same in the case of restrictions defined for assets, customers, material accounts, G/L accounts or contract accounts.

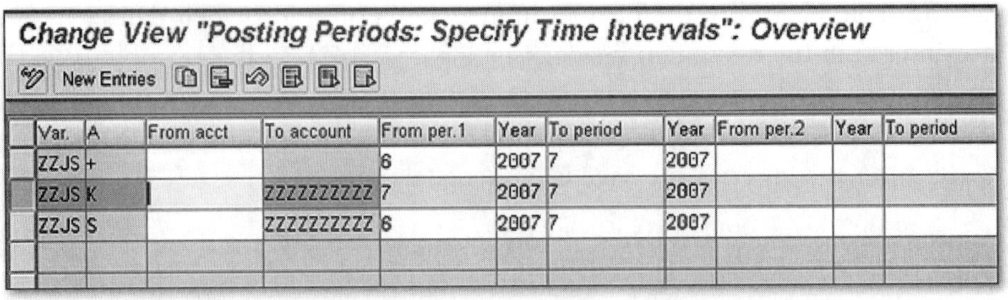

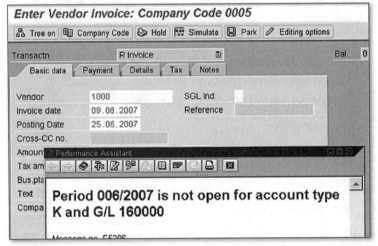

Figure 7.164 Open Posting Period for Accounts Payable Accounting

Figure 7.165 Error Message for Accounts Receivable Accounting

In addition to the standard posting periods discussed so far, special periods may also be defined, as illustrated in the following example. Once again, the fiscal year variant corresponds to the calendar year running from period 1, January, to period 12, December. In addition, periods 13, 14, 15, and 16 can be used for posting special closing entries. Figure 7.166 shows a scenario where all special periods are open, that is, 12/2007 to 01/2008.

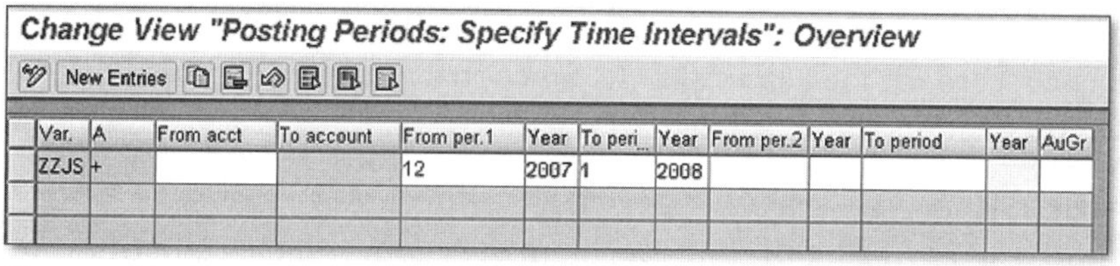

Change View "Posting Periods: Specify Time Intervals": Overview

New Entries

Var.	A	From acct	To account	From per.1	Year	To peri...	Year	From per.2	Year	To period	Year	AuGr
ZZJS	+			12	2007	1	2008					

Figure 7.166 Open Special Periods

If you want to open only these particular periods, it is recommended that you use the entire width of the table (as in Figure 7.167). Here, only the periods 12/2007 and 01/2008 are open.

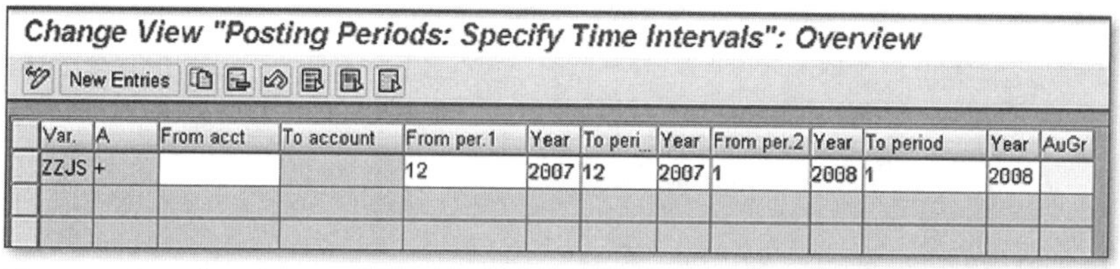

Change View "Posting Periods: Specify Time Intervals": Overview

New Entries

Var.	A	From acct	To account	From per.1	Year	To peri...	Year	From per.2	Year	To period	Year	AuGr
ZZJS	+			12	2007	12	2007	1	2008	1	2008	

Figure 7.167 Closed Special Periods

Restricting Selections with an Entry in the AuGr Column [+]

The column with the rather cryptic title AuGr (authorization group) can be used to place a restriction on the full potential offered by the control table. If you define an entry in this column, it is only possible for a user defined in the authorization concept (object F_BKPF_BUP) to enter postings in the interval range "From period 1" – "To period 1." An entry under AuGr therefore places a significant limit on the number of people involved in closing operations. This feature can also be used for special periods.

7.16 Tax on Sales and Purchases

Input tax and output tax

Deliveries and services that are entered in the system as posting documents over the course of a period usually contain document line items for input or output tax. At the period end, these amounts must be checked and totaled and the balance reported to the tax authorities as a receivable or payable. SAP general ledger accounting includes reporting functions that you will find very helpful in this regard. The program for advance returns for tax on sales and purchases (which is provided in many country-specific versions) posts the balance of input and output tax to a tax payable account, generates a log, and if required, provides an electronic data record for the authorities. Its functional scope is described in detail in the example provided below.

Select ACCOUNTING • FINANCIAL ACCOUNTING • GENERAL LEDGER • REPORT-ING to access the transaction for communication with the authorities and to access country-specific versions of the program for the advance return for tax on sales and purchases (see Figure 7.168).

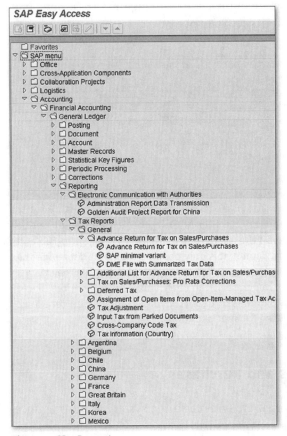

Figure 7.168 Reporting

To access the selection screen shown in Figure 7.169, select ACCOUNTING • FINANCIAL ACCOUNTING • GENERAL LEDGER • REPORTING • TAX REPORTS • GENERAL • ADVANCE RETURN FOR TAX ON SALES/PURCHASES • ADVANCE RETURN FOR TAX ON SALES/PURCHASES.

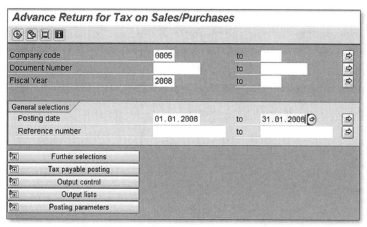

Figure 7.169 Selection Screen for the Advance Return for Tax on Sales/Purchases

In the example, the selection is limited to documents relating to input and output tax that were posted for company code 0005 in the period 01/01/2008 to 12/31/2008. Further restrictions can also be made, as shown in Figure 7.170.

Selecting the reporting period

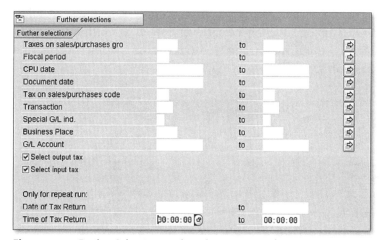

Figure 7.170 Further Selections in the Advance Return for Tax on Sales/Purchases

---

Creating Tax on Sales and Purchases Groups   **[+]**

A group of company codes can be grouped together as a tax on sales and purchases group. In this case, you no longer need to execute and report an advance return of tax on sales and purchases for each company code.

Posting to the tax payable account

In addition to the selection criteria, posting criteria must also be defined for the program. The accounts for input and output tax that are associated with the tax codes are cleared in a procedure that involves posting the balance to a defined tax payable account for receivables or payables due from or to the tax authorities. This procedure is saved to batch input session RFUMSV00, as shown in Figure 7.171.

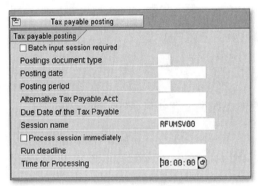

Figure 7.171 Tax Payable Posting for the Advance Return for Tax on Sales/Purchases

Before the session is processed and postings are executed, it is useful to be able to view a log showing a clear overview of as much information as possible. To output such as log, you can choose the selection criteria on the selection screen shown in Figure 7.172.

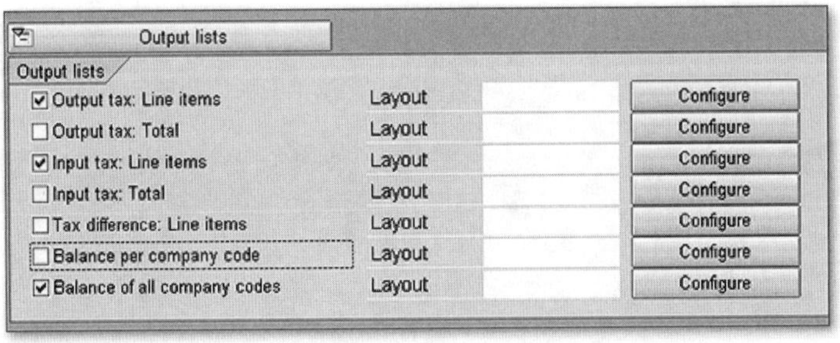

Figure 7.172 Advance Return for Tax on Sales/Purchases—Log

You then decide whether the program run is to be a test or update run in the screen shown in Figure 7.173. This screen also offers an option for communicating the results electronically to the tax authorities.

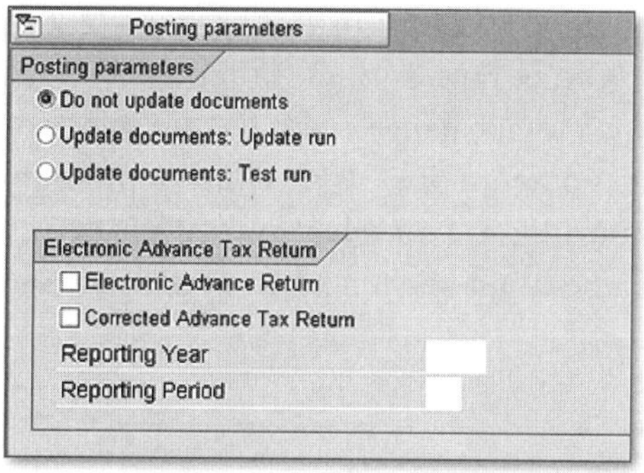

Figure 7.173 Posting Parameters for the Advance Return for Tax on Sales/Purchases

Once all of the settings are made, you can press [F8] to start the program in the background. It selects the documents and calculates the balance of input and output tax based on the tax code. The program then creates a batch input session for tax payable postings, generates a file for electronic communication with the authorities, and outputs the overall result in a log (see Figure 7.174).

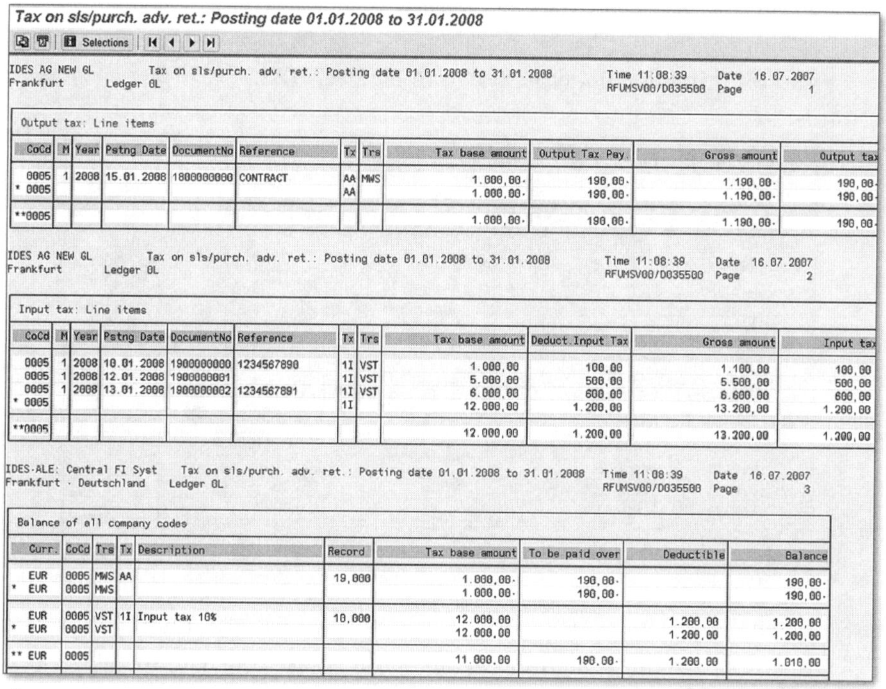

Calculation based on tax code

Figure 7.174 Log of the Advance Return for Tax on Sales/Purchases

For company code 0005, a document is found in the period 1/2008, which contains output tax of €190 (tax rate is 19%). In terms of input tax, three relevant documents with a total balance of €1,200 are selected. The calculation of tax payable gives a figure of €1,010, which represents a receivable due from the tax authorities. If you select SYSTEM • SERVICES • BATCH INPUT, you will find a batch input session to be processed (see Figure 7.175).

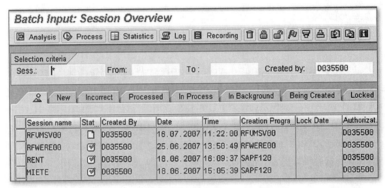

Figure 7.175 Batch Input—Session Overview

The resulting document is shown in Figure 7.182.

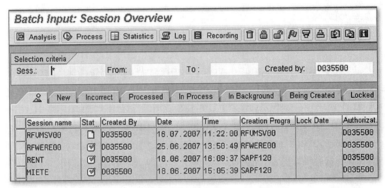

Figure 7.176 Tax Payable Posting

Electronic reporting After the receivable is posted as a balance of €1,010, the relevant data must be communicated to the tax authorities. You will find the transaction provided for this purpose in the SAP menu under ACCOUNT-

ING • FINANCIAL ACCOUNTING • GENERAL LEDGER • REPORTING • ELEC-
TRONIC COMMUNICATION WITH AUTHORITIES • ADMINISTRATION REPORT
DATA TRANSMISSION. The selection parameters shown in Figure 7.177
correspond to those used in our example for company code 0005 and
return type 1 (advance return for tax on sales/purchases) in the period
1/2008.

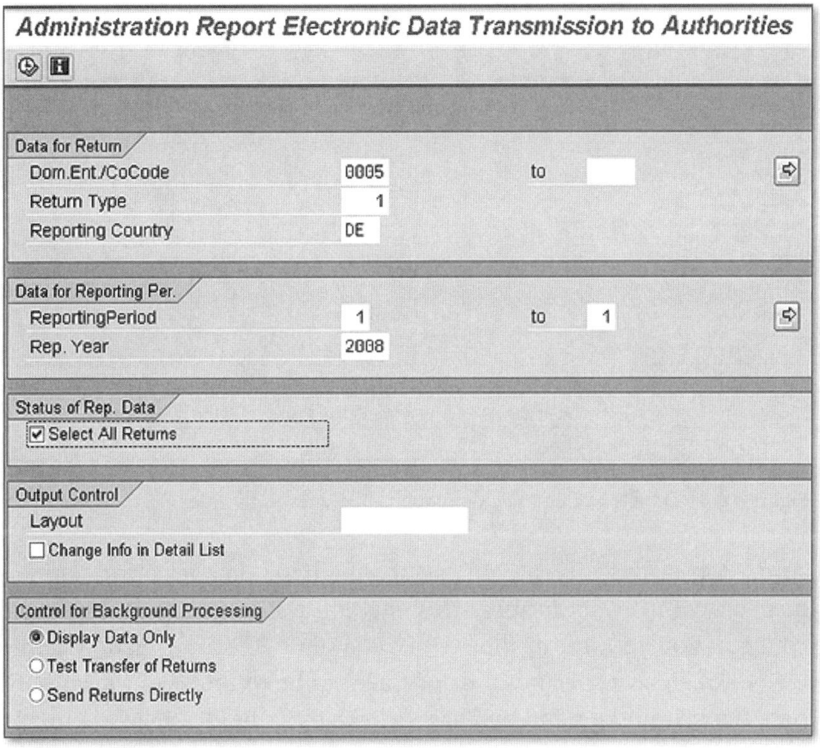

Figure 7.177   Selection Screen for Electronic Communication with Authorities

On the next overview screen, shown in Figure 7.178, you can see that
exactly one data record has been found. It has the status New and has
not yet been transferred.

If you place the cursor on this entry and click on the 🔲 icon, the detailed
overview shown in Figure 7.179 is displayed.

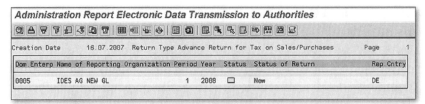

Figure 7.178 Electronic Communication with Authorities—Overview

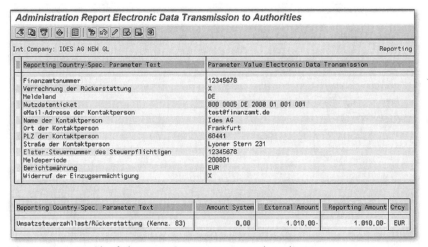

Figure 7.179 Details of Electronic Communication with Authorities

Logging the procedure

At the top of this screen, you can see the basic data used for communication with the authorities. This data must already be defined in the configuration settings of the SAP ERP system. The information in the lower screen area specifies the document to be returned to the authorities. The tax on sales and purchases payable can be classified as either a system amount (in other words, an amount calculated by the Advance Return for Tax on Sales/Purchases program described above) or an external amount. Values can be entered manually because an enterprise may not use the SAP system to manage all of its accounts but may still want to use the SAP reporting function. If the total amount of tax payable corresponds to the amount you want to declare, press F12 to return to the overview screen, where you can click on the 🖼 icon to communicate this information to the authorities. Both the status and the transfer log of your communication (either successful or failed) are then saved.

7.17   Balance Carryforward

As the fiscal year draws to a close, several technical activities must be completed in the SAP system. One of these is the balance carryforward. From an accounting perspective, the year-end closing means that the closing balance of the balance sheet accounts also serves as the initial balance in the next fiscal year.

However, things are more complicated for income statement accounts. In the new fiscal year, the opening balance in these accounts is always zero, that is, they start each year with "a clean sheet." This is certainly true of the profit and loss accounts at least. When the fiscal year changes, its balance is posted to one or more special retained earnings accounts. In most countries, however, the carryforward in the balance sheet and profit and loss statement accounts is not implemented as a posting in the SAP system. Instead, the balance of the last posting period is carried forward as the balance in period 0 of the new fiscal year without a posting record. An opening entry is only possible in certain countries where this is legally permitted. The example discussed in the following sections explains, step by step, how the balance carryforward procedure works.

Figure 7.180 shows bank account 113100 in the balance display transaction, which you can access under ACCOUNTING • FINANCIAL ACCOUNTING • GENERAL LEDGER • ACCOUNT • DISPLAY BALANCES in the SAP menu.

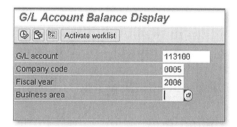

Figure 7.180   Selection Screen for G/L Account Balance Display

If you press F8 or click on the icon to execute the transaction, the balance overview shown in Figure 7.181 is displayed. At the start of the 2006 fiscal year, there is a balance carryforward of €60,000 in period 0. The changes made during the 16 posting periods during the 2006 fiscal year produce a cumulative balance of €–169,000. This value is required

Balance overview for each fiscal year

as the balance carryforward, and thus the opening balance, for the 2007 fiscal year.

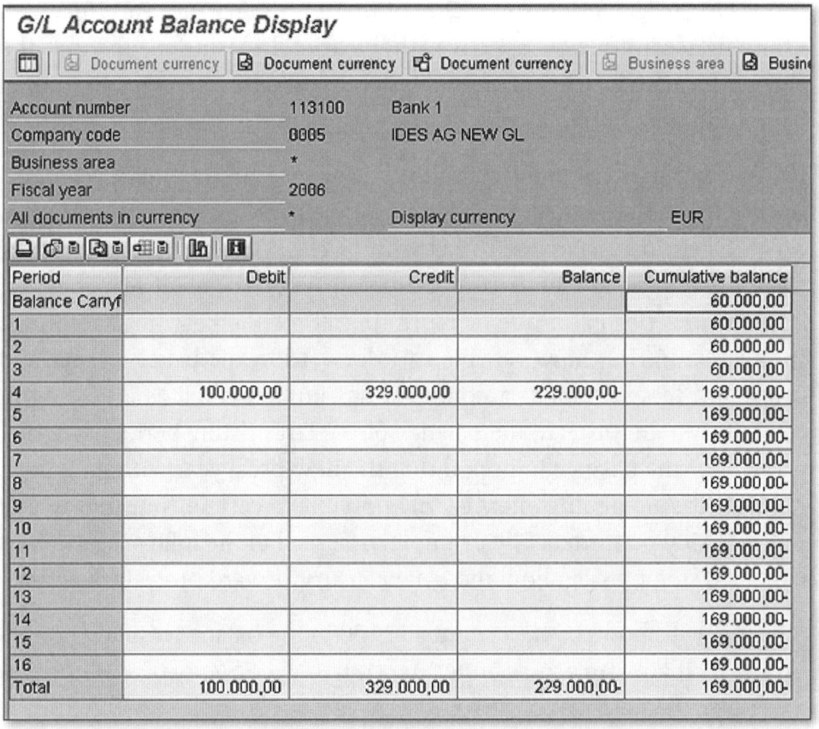

G/L Account Balance Display
Document currency
Document currency
Document currency
Business area
Busin
Account number
113100
Bank 1
Company code
0005
IDES AG NEW GL
Business area
*
Fiscal year
2006
All documents in currency
*
Display currency
EUR

Period	Debit	Credit	Balance	Cumulative balance
Balance Carryf				60.000,00
1				60.000,00
2				60.000,00
3				60.000,00
4	100.000,00	329.000,00	229.000,00-	169.000,00-
5				169.000,00-
6				169.000,00-
7				169.000,00-
8				169.000,00-
9				169.000,00-
10				169.000,00-
11				169.000,00-
12				169.000,00-
13				169.000,00-
14				169.000,00-
15				169.000,00-
16				169.000,00-
Total	100.000,00	329.000,00	229.000,00-	169.000,00-

Figure 7.181 Overview of G/L Account Balance Display

In this example, there is no balance carryforward, and there are as yet no postings for the new fiscal year 2007. Based on this initial situation, the information message shown in Figure 7.182 is displayed when you select the Display Balances menu option for fiscal year 2007.

Information
No data read for fiscal year 2007 (long text)

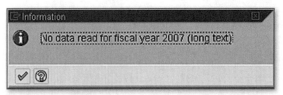

Figure 7.182 Information Message for G/L Account Balance Display

At this point, the question often arises as to whether it is even possible to post items in the new fiscal year if there is no balance carryforward. The answer is yes, and this scenario is illustrated in Figure 7.183.

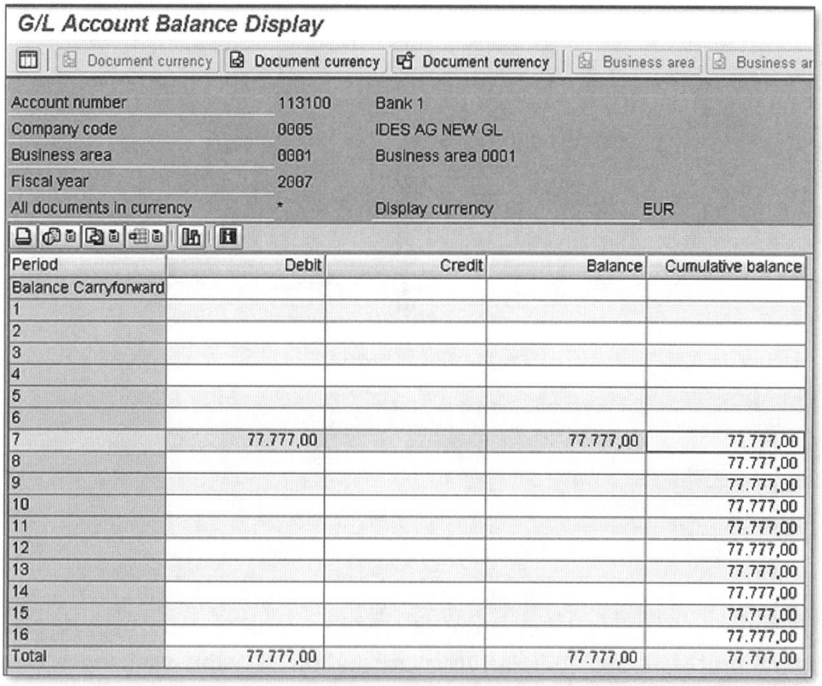
G/L Account Balance Display
Document currency
Document currency
Document currency
Business area
Business ar
Account number 113100 Bank 1
Company code 0005 IDES AG NEW GL
Business area 0001 Business area 0001
Fiscal year 2007
All documents in currency * Display currency EUR

Period	Debit	Credit	Balance	Cumulative balance
Balance Carryforward				
1				
2				
3				
4				
5				
6				
7	77.777,00		77.777,00	77.777,00
8				77.777,00
9				77.777,00
10				77.777,00
11				77.777,00
12				77.777,00
13				77.777,00
14				77.777,00
15				77.777,00
16				77.777,00
Total	77.777,00		77.777,00	77.777,00

Figure 7.183 G/L Account Balance Display—Posting Without a Balance Carryforward

Balance carryforward as a technical procedure

Postings can be entered in the new fiscal year independently of the balance carryforward, which is merely a technical procedure. The balance carryforward only influences the cumulative balance. In our example, the 2006 balance of €–169,000 is not carried forward, which means the overall picture of the bank account, including its representation on the end-of-quarter balance sheet, is not accurate. This situation can only be remedied by selecting Accounting • Financial Accounting • General Ledger • Periodic Processing • Closing • Carry Forward.

The selection screen in Figure 7.184 shows settings made for a balance carryforward for G/L accounts (ledger 0) in company code 0005 into the fiscal year 2007.

[+] **Balance Carryforward**

You use report SAPF010 to execute a balance carryforward for accounts payable and receivable. If you use additional ledgers, such as FI-SL and/or parallel currencies, you must use SAPFGVTR instead.

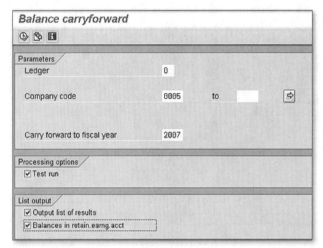

Figure 7.184 Balance Carryforward for G/L Accounts—Selection Screen

If you press [F8] to execute the transaction as an update run, the program processes a balance carryforward and displays the results in a compressed view (see Figure 7.185).

Figure 7.185 Balance Carryforward for G/L Accounts—Log

This log indicates whether the balance carryforward has been successfully completed. You can also click on the Balance sheet accounts and Retained earnings accounts buttons to display more details. The relevant details for our example are shown in the detailed list for balance sheet account 113100 in Figure 7.186. As you can see, the bank account contains a balance carryforward of €–169,000.

Display of balance sheet accounts

Year	CoCd	BusA	Account	Crcy	Trans.cur.	Co.cd.curr	Crcy2	Grp curr.	Curr3
2007	0005		31000	EUR	275.000,00	275.000,00	EUR	275.000,00	EUR
2007	0005		31100	EUR	275.000,00	275.000,00	EUR	275.000,00	EUR
2007	0005		31200	EUR	275.000,00-	275.000,00-	EUR	275.000,00-	EUR
2007	0005		32000	EUR	450.000,00	450.000,00	EUR	450.000,00	EUR
2007	0005		35000	EUR	45.000,00	45.000,00	EUR	45.000,00	EUR
2007	0005		35010	EUR	30.000,00-	30.000,00-	EUR	30.000,00-	EUR
2007	0005		70000	EUR	1.450.000,00-	1.450.000,00-	EUR	1.450.000,00-	EUR
2007	0005		85000	EUR	100.000,00-	100.000,00-	EUR	100.000,00-	EUR
2007	0005		113100	EUR	169.000,00-	169.000,00-	EUR	169.000,00-	EUR
2007	0005		113101	EUR	60.000,00-	60.000,00-	EUR	60.000,00-	EUR

Figure 7.186 Balance Carryforward for G/L Accounts—Balance Sheet Accounts

If you press F12 to return to the compressed log, you can then access the detailed list for the retained earnings accounts. As shown in Figure 7.187, the items in the profit and loss accounts from 2006 are posted to a retained earnings account (900000) and carried forward into 2007.

Assigning P&L accounts to a retained earnings account

Retained Earnings Account

[+]

With parallel accounting, there is no one, unique retained earnings account. If you use several accounts to map valuation differences (for provision postings, for example), you also require several retained earnings accounts. These can be maintained in the configuration settings in Transaction OB53 or in the master data of each P&L account. However, if you use a single retained earnings account, the field for master data maintenance is hidden (see Figure 7.188).

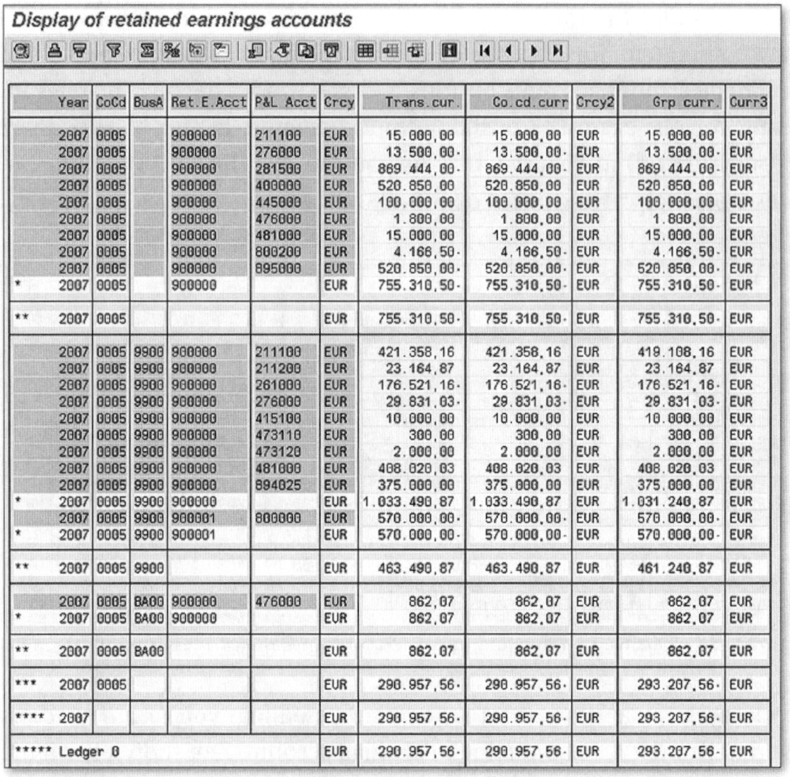

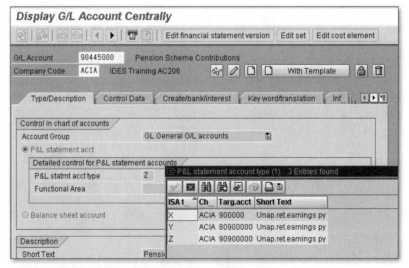

Display of retained earnings accounts

Year	CoCd	BusA	Ret.E.Acct	P&L Acct	Crcy	Trans.cur.	Co.cd.curr	Crcy2	Grp curr.	Curr3
2007	0005		900000	211100	EUR	15.000,00	15.000,00	EUR	15.000,00	EUR
2007	0005		900000	276000	EUR	13.500,00-	13.500,00-	EUR	13.500,00-	EUR
2007	0005		900000	281500	EUR	869.444,00-	869.444,00-	EUR	869.444,00-	EUR
2007	0005		900000	400000	EUR	520.850,00	520.850,00	EUR	520.850,00	EUR
2007	0005		900000	445000	EUR	100.000,00	100.000,00	EUR	100.000,00	EUR
2007	0005		900000	476000	EUR	1.800,00	1.800,00	EUR	1.800,00	EUR
2007	0005		900000	481000	EUR	15.000,00	15.000,00	EUR	15.000,00	EUR
2007	0005		900000	800200	EUR	4.166,50-	4.166,50-	EUR	4.166,50-	EUR
2007	0005		900000	895000	EUR	520.850,00-	520.850,00-	EUR	520.850,00-	EUR
* 2007	0005		900000		EUR	755.310,50-	755.310,50-	EUR	755.310,50-	EUR
** 2007	0005				EUR	755.310,50-	755.310,50-	EUR	755.310,50-	EUR
2007	0005	9900	900000	211100	EUR	421.358,16	421.358,16	EUR	419.108,16	EUR
2007	0005	9900	900000	211200	EUR	23.164,87	23.164,87	EUR	23.164,87	EUR
2007	0005	9900	900000	261000	EUR	176.521,16-	176.521,16-	EUR	176.521,16-	EUR
2007	0005	9900	900000	276000	EUR	29.831,03-	29.831,03-	EUR	29.831,03-	EUR
2007	0005	9900	900000	415100	EUR	10.000,00	10.000,00	EUR	10.000,00	EUR
2007	0005	9900	900000	473110	EUR	300,00	300,00	EUR	300,00	EUR
2007	0005	9900	900000	473120	EUR	2.000,00	2.000,00	EUR	2.000,00	EUR
2007	0005	9900	900000	481000	EUR	408.020,03	408.020,03	EUR	408.020,03	EUR
2007	0005	9900	900000	894025	EUR	375.000,00	375.000,00	EUR	375.000,00	EUR
* 2007	0005	9900	900000		EUR	1.033.490,87	1.033.490,87	EUR	1.031.240,87	EUR
2007	0005	9900	900001	800000	EUR	570.000,00-	570.000,00-	EUR	570.000,00-	EUR
* 2007	0005	9900	900001		EUR	570.000,00-	570.000,00-	EUR	570.000,00-	EUR
** 2007	0005	9900			EUR	463.490,87	463.490,87	EUR	461.240,87	EUR
2007	0005	BA00	900000	476000	EUR	862,07	862,07	EUR	862,07	EUR
* 2007	0005	BA00	900000		EUR	862,07	862,07	EUR	862,07	EUR
** 2007	0005	BA00			EUR	862,07	862,07	EUR	862,07	EUR
*** 2007	0005				EUR	290.957,56-	290.957,56-	EUR	293.207,56-	EUR
**** 2007					EUR	290.957,56-	290.957,56-	EUR	293.207,56-	EUR
***** Ledger 0					EUR	290.957,56-	290.957,56-	EUR	293.207,56-	EUR

Figure 7.187 Balance Carryforward for G/L Accounts—Retained Earnings Accounts

Figure 7.188 Maintaining a Retained Earnings Account

When you exit the logs of the balance carryforward program and look again at the account in our example (Figure 7.189), you will notice the difference in period 0 and in the cumulative balance.

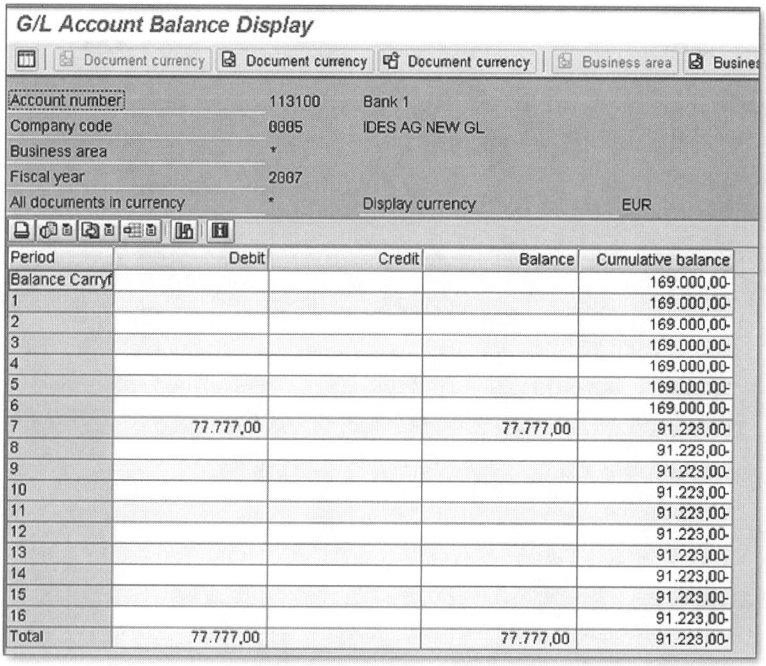

G/L Account Balance Display

| | Document currency | | Document currency | | Document currency | | Business area | | Busines |

Account number	113100	Bank 1
Company code	0005	IDES AG NEW GL
Business area	*	
Fiscal year	2007	
All documents in currency	*	Display currency	EUR

Period	Debit	Credit	Balance	Cumulative balance
Balance Carryf				169.000,00-
1				169.000,00-
2				169.000,00-
3				169.000,00-
4				169.000,00-
5				169.000,00-
6				169.000,00-
7	77.777,00		77.777,00	91.223,00-
8				91.223,00-
9				91.223,00-
10				91.223,00-
11				91.223,00-
12				91.223,00-
13				91.223,00-
14				91.223,00-
15				91.223,00-
16				91.223,00-
Total	77.777,00		77.777,00	91.223,00-

Figure 7.189 G/L Account Balance Display for Fiscal Year 2007 with a Successfully Completed Balance Carryforward

If postings are still being entered in the previous fiscal year (2006 in our example), these are automatically carried forward into period 0 in 2007. This is determined by the general conditions for the balance carryforward that were configured for our example. The technical procedure of a balance carryforward can, in principle, be executed or repeated at any point.

7.18   Conclusion

The automated valuation and posting procedures in the new SAP ERP release offer the highest possible level of system support for month-end, end-of-quarter, or year-end closings. Noteworthy new features in this release include functions for posting accruals with the Accrual Engine, web-based asset inventory, new and improved functions for intercompany reconciliation, and electronic tax returns for tax on sales and purchases. All of these enhancements have the capacity to facilitate a fast close by improving the efficiency and quality of closing operations.

Appendices

A Basic Principles of the SAP System

This appendix describes the navigation options in the SAP ERP system. It also explains the most important SAP concepts.

A.1 Operating SAP ERP

SAP categorizes the functional areas of an enterprise into accounting, logistics, and human resources. The individual functional areas are divided into modules (see Figure A.1). Every module has components, which have subcomponents.

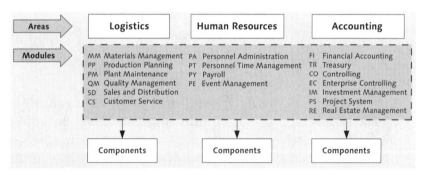

Figure A.1 Modules by SAP

The components are indicated by a multidigit ID that is based on the name of the component and added to the module. This book focuses on the components of the SAP FI module.

A.2 Introduction

In the SAP system, multiple users can use the same data basis at the same time. The SAP authorization concept enables you to customize the work area according to the requirements of the individual user. That means not every user is authorized to carry out the same transactions.

SAP modules

User authorizations

A.3 Logon

Once the SAP system has started, it displays the logon screen. The entries made here affect the complete user session.

Entries in the logon screen

You must specify the following details in the logon screen (see Figure A.2):

▶ **Client**
SAP refers to an enterprise as a client. Each client has a unique client number. This number ensures exclusive access to the data of the enterprise. During the session, you can only access this client's data.

▶ **User**
The system administrator specifies the user and user name. The administrator defines specific authorizations and settings for each user.

▶ **Password**
The password protects the data from unauthorized access.

▶ **Language**
SAP provides international software, that is, the system is available in various languages. If you don't make any entries here, the system automatically selects the language that is defined in the user master record. If you want to use a different language, enter the appropriate ID in this field.

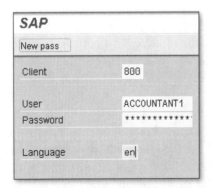

Figure A.2 Logon Screen of the SAP System

A.3.1 Password Rules

The assignment of passwords is subject to specific rules. Table A.1 illustrates which rules are specified by SAP and which rules can be modified by the customers.

Rules	Specification by
Minimum length: three characters.	Customers
Validity period (number of days after which the password has to be changed).	Customers
The first character isn't allowed to be "!" or "?".	SAP
The first three characters of the password aren't allowed to be identical to the first three characters of the user name.	SAP
The first three characters aren't allowed to be identical.	SAP
The first three characters aren't allowed to be blanks.	SAP
The password isn't allowed to be PASS or SAP.	SAP
Any characters that can be entered with the keyboard are allowed. The passwords are not case sensitive.	SAP
Users can change their password at most once a day. This restriction does not apply to administrators.	SAP
The new password isn't allowed to be identical to the user's last five passwords.	SAP

Table A.1 Password Rules

Navigation in Fields [+]

You can navigate from one field to another using either the mouse or the Tab key.

To change the password, you first have to enter the user ID and the current password.

The toolbar of the logon screen contains the New Password button. If you click on it, the dialog box shown in Figure A.3 appears. It prompts you to enter the new password in both fields. After you have confirmed this, the new password is valid from this point on.

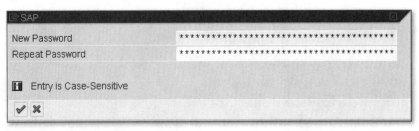

Figure A.3 Changing the Password

A.4 Logon Procedures

Specifications for the logon

You can specify the following for the logon procedure:

1. The client number. If this field already contains a number, you can accept or overwrite it.

2. The user name.

3. Your password. For security reasons, this procedure is hidden. You can trace the input via the cursor movement only.

4. The language. You can enter "EN" for English, for example, or leave the field blank. In this case, the system uses the specification in your user master record.

Press ⏎ after you have made all necessary entries.

A.5 User Interface

After you have logged on successfully, the user interface (Figure A.4) appears (SAP GUI). Now, the actual work in the SAP system begins.

Elements of SAP GUI

The user interface consists of the following components:

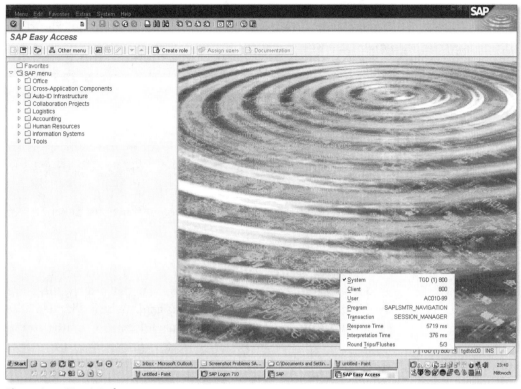

Figure A.4 User Interface

▶ **Menu bar**
The menu bar enables you to call commands or functions using the menu items.

▶ **Title bar**
The title bar contains the description of the current mode in which you are now.

▶ **Toolbar**
The toolbar contains the functions that are most frequently used. You can call these functions by clicking on the corresponding button. If the mouse pointer is positioned on a particular icon for a few seconds, a window opens that explains the function of the icon.

▶ **Command field**
You can directly enter the transaction code into the command field (see Figure A.5). This takes you to the desired application. The trans-

action code is a multidigit alphanumeric character string that maps the transaction. This enables you to navigate more quickly to the desired application than via the corresponding menu path.

Figure A.5 Command Field

► **Application toolbar**
The application toolbar consists of different functions, depending on the application.

► **Status bar**
The status bar displays messages, such as notes on incorrect entries. By double-clicking on these messages, you can display the corresponding long text. By clicking on the triangle (which is hidden here) in the status bar, you can view additional information on the current view.

► **Menu tree**
The menu tree takes you to the desired application.

A.6 Navigation

The SAP system provides various navigation options, which are introduced in the following sections.

A.6.1 Navigation via the Menu

Menu tree   The menu tree (Figure A.6) has a hierarchical structure. A menu path is defined by numerous menu items. You call a specific interface (application, transaction) or start a particular function with the last menu item of a menu path.

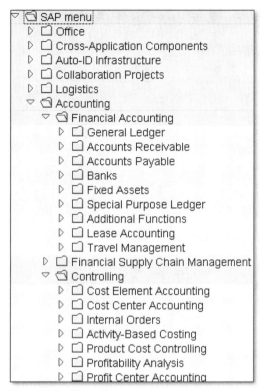

Figure A.6 Menu Tree

A.6.2 Navigation via Transaction Codes

The last menu item of a menu path always starts an application—or in SAP terminology—a transaction. Technically, the transaction is uniquely defined by the transaction code, which can also be displayed in the menu tree. This can be implemented via the menu path EXTRAS • SETTINGS • SHOW TECHNICAL NAMES.

Transaction

When you enter a transaction code in the command field and activate it with the [Enter] key, the system directly navigates to the required transaction. This enables you to work with the keyboard without requiring the mouse.

The transaction codes enable you to quickly navigate from one activity to the next. To display the transaction code in an application, follow the menu path SYSTEM • STATUS.

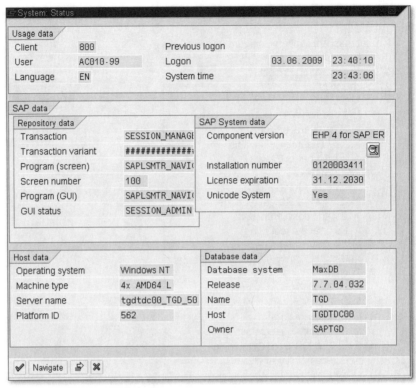

Figure A.7 Transaction Code

Transaction codes are alphanumeric combinations. They are not sorted systematically. If you want to navigate from one transaction to the next, you can do this either via the menu path or via the menu tree; you can also enter the following commands in the command field:

► **/n+ TCODE**
This way you navigate from the current transaction to another.

► **/o + TCODE**
Select this command if you want to open a new session with a different transaction.

► **S000**
This opens the Easy Access menu.

If you've only just started the SAP system and are still in the Easy Access menu, you can immediately enter the transaction code.

A.6.3 Favorites Maintenance

If you are in the SAP Easy Access menu, the menu tree lists so-called favorites to simplify the navigation. You can integrate transactions, reports, external files, and Internet addresses that you often use with the Favorites folder, which means you can create your own menu tree that meets your specific desires and requirements.

You integrate folders and external objects (files, programs, and Internet addresses) with the favorites via the menu path illustrated in Figure A.8.

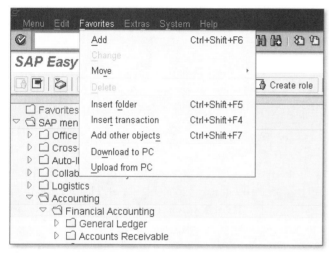

Figure A.8 Favorites Maintenance—Adding a Folder

Afterward, you must label the folders (see Figure A.9).

Figure A.9 Favorites Maintenance—Labeling a Folder

The easiest way to add transaction codes to the favorites is to click on the corresponding entry in the menu tree, keep the left mouse button pressed, and drag the entry to the desired position in the favorites list. Then, release the mouse button (drag-and-drop procedure).

Alternatively, you can also create the entry via the menu path FAVORITES • ADD TRANSACTION. A dialog box appears where you must specify the transaction code. The system then displays further instructions to complete the procedure.

Function keys You can also use the function keys in the toolbar to create favorites. Figure A.10 lists the meanings of the function keys.

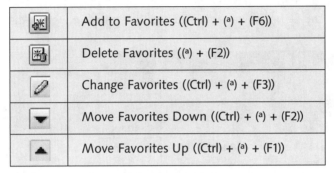

	Add to Favorites ((Ctrl) + (ª) + (F6))
	Delete Favorites ((ª) + (F2))
	Change Favorites ((Ctrl) + (ª) + (F3))
	Move Favorites Down ((Ctrl) + (ª) + (F2))
	Move Favorites Up ((Ctrl) + (ª) + (F1))

Figure A.10 Meanings of the Function Keys

In addition, you can maintain the favorites via the context menu, which you call with the right mouse button (see Figure A.11). Figure A.12 shows a possible result of the favorites maintenance.

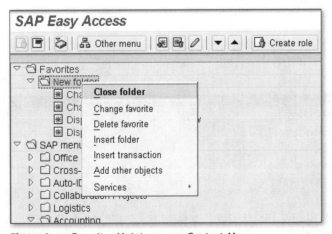

Figure A.11 Favorites Maintenance—Context Menu

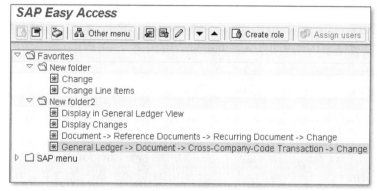

Figure A.12 Favorites Maintenance—Result

A.6.4 Navigation via the Toolbar

The SAP system uses a wide range of icons. In most cases, the toolbar is identical in the entire SAP system; however, you cannot use all icons everywhere. When icons have a gray background, they're inactive and you cannot use them.

If you want to know the meaning of a particular icon, position the mouse pointer on the button. The system then displays a small window that explains the meaning of the icon (tooltip).

Tooltip

A.7 Data Entry

SAP distinguishes between the overwrite mode and the insert mode. When you enter data, you usually use the overwrite mode. To insert characters, you use the insert mode. The status bar displays which mode is currently set. OVR indicates that the overwrite mode is set and INS that the insert mode is set (see Figure A.13).

Insert and overwrite mode

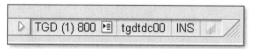

Figure A.13 Overwrite Mode in the Status Bar

In the SAP system, a distinction is made between the following types of fields:

▸ **Required entry field**
These fields require an entry. Otherwise the SAP system outputs an error message and requires an entry.

▸ **Optional entry field**
Here, the data entry is optional.

▸ **Display field**
These fields are used for information only.

Set data and
hold data

To facilitate repeated data entries, you can use two functions in the SAP system. They can be found under the menu paths SYSTEM • USER PROFILE • HOLD DATA or SYSTEM • USER PROFILE • SET DATA.

▸ **Hold data**
If you have filled numerous fields for an application, you can have the system remember these entries using the menu paths defined above. When you call the application the next time, the system enters this data as default values, but you can also overwrite these entries.

▸ **Set data**
Here, it is not possible to overwrite the held specifications. To disable this function, select the menu path SYSTEM • USER PROFILE • DELETE DATA.

A.8 User Settings

The individual user can maintain parts of his user master record at various places in the SAP system. The following sections describe the most important options.

A.8.1 User Interface Settings

Easy Access menu

The menu path EXTRAS • SETTINGS enables you to configure the display in the Easy Access menu.

If the favorites are maintained in such a way that they include all required transactions and reports, you can hide the SAP menu with a selection. You can display the transaction codes in the SAP menu or in the favorites by selecting the Show Technical Names option.

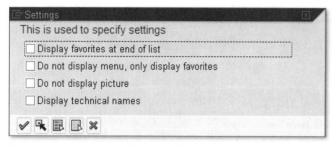

Figure A.14 Settings for the Main Menu

A.8.2 Options

The corresponding button takes you to the options. The corresponding settings are made in several tabs. In the first tab, you can define in which format system messages are output. If you select the corresponding checkbox, the system displays the message type in a dialog box, if the checkbox is not selected in the status bar. Here, you can also influence the functioning of the tooltips (inactive, slow, or immediate action; see Figure A.15). The Cursor tab provides additional setting options (see Figure A.16).

Figure A.15 User Master Record—Options

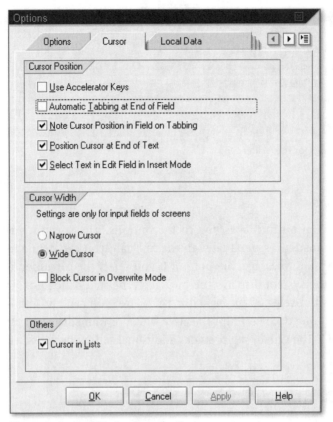

Figure A.16 User Master Record—Cursor

User master record The user master record usually provides the settings shown in Figure A.16. However, in the standard version of the SAP system, the first option is not selected. During data entry, this has the effect that the mouse pointer automatically jumps to the next input field when a field is completely filled. If this option is not selected, the mouse pointer "sticks" at the end of the field and needs to be moved to the next input field manually. As of Release 4.6, a field history is available. It can be configured in the Local Data tab (see Figure A.17).

When you have activated the field history, the SAP system stores the defined number of the previous entries for each input field and provides them in a list for selection the next time you enter data. For the setting from Figure A.17, this includes the previous five values respectively.

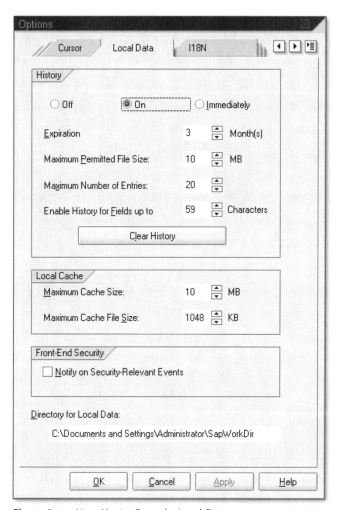

Figure A.17 User Master Record—Local Data

A.8.3 Personal Data

To maintain your address data and define default values follow the menu   **Address data**
path SYSTEM • USER PROFILE • PERSONAL DATA (Figure A.18). The first tab
merely contains your address data. This is required, for example, when
creating correspondence or working with SAP Office, for example.

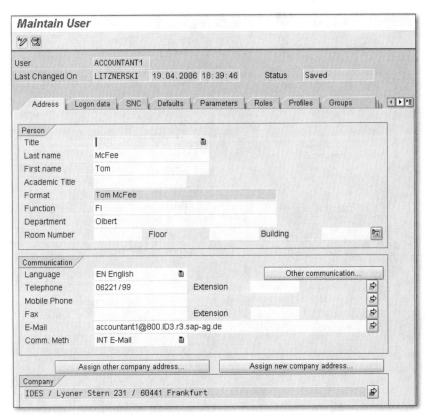

Figure A.18 User Profile—Address

Defaults   The Defaults tab (see Figure A.19) enables you to specify the printer name (it has to be explicitly defined by the SAP basis first). This way, you don't have to enter a printer name in the print output selection screen from the SAP menu. This also applies for the selection of Immediate Printing and Delete after Output. You can also define in which language the SAP system is supposed to start, if no specification has been made in the Language field.

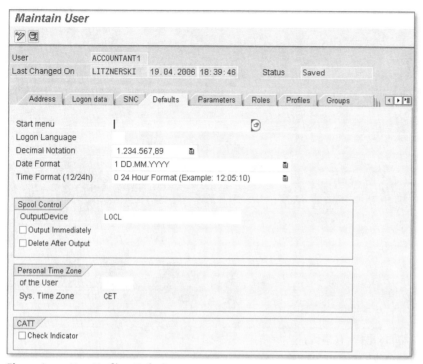

Figure A.19 User Profile — Defaults

The Parameters tab enables you to define default values for future activities in the SAP system. However, this is only useful if you frequently
enter the same value for a specific field. For example, the entries from
Figure A.20 have the system to always enter the value 00 in the Column
input field in any screen. It is a default value, which you can overwrite
anytime.

Default values

To define these default values, determine the parameter ID of the field.
For this purpose, position the mouse pointer on the field, and then call
the field help with the ⌐F1⌐ function key (Figure A.21).

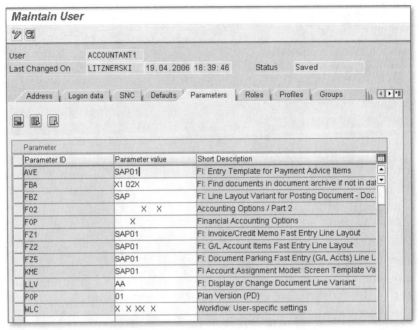

Figure A.20 User Profile—Parameters

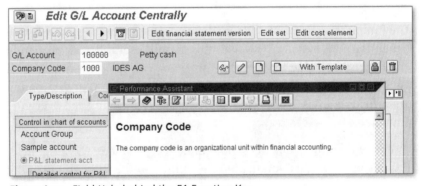

Figure A.21 Field Help behind the F1 Function Key

The parameter ID of the field is part of the technical data of this field. The system displays the data when you click on the Technical Information button (see Figure A.22).

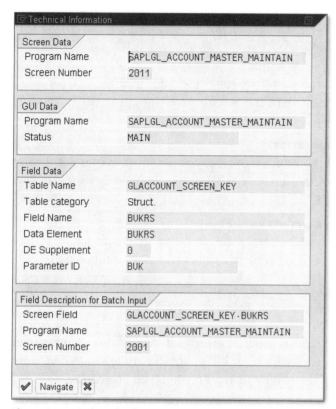

Figure A.22 Technical Information on a Field

A.9   Message Types

The SAP system uses messages to provide the user with information   Messages
(Figure A.23). For example, it indicates incorrect entries or successful
postings. It displays the messages either in the status bar or in a specific
dialog box. This setting is user-specific and can be implemented via the
customizing of the local layout.

Figure A.23   Message in the SAP System

There are different message types. The following types are especially important:

▶ **W message type (Warning)**
This message type warns you about a possibly incorrect entry. You can save the entry to which the message refers or ignore the warning by pressing Enter.

▶ **E message type (Error)**
In contrast to the W message type, you cannot save your entry when the system outputs this message, because the entry is wrong and has to be corrected.

▶ **I message type (Information)**
This message type indicates particularly important information, which you have to confirm before you can execute the next function.

A.10 Sessions

An SAP application that you use corresponds to a session. You can open multiple windows (sessions) for different tasks at the same time. However, you cannot open more than six sessions simultaneously.

You can open a new session with the corresponding button, by directly entering the transaction code in the command field, or via the menu path SYSTEM • GENERATE SESSION.

An additional window opens in the foreground. The new window is now the "active session." If your screen displays multiple sessions, you can go to a different application by simply clicking on the desired session.

You can navigate between the individual sessions using the Alt + Left or Alt + Right key combination. You can close the active session via the menu path SYSTEM • DELETE SESSION or by using the Alt + F4 key combination.

[!] **Warning**

Remember to save the entered data. The system won't prompt you to do this when you exit the session.

A.11 Storing Data

For an application that consists of several screens, the system only stores the data temporarily when you navigate between the screens. The system doesn't store the data in the corresponding database until you explicitly save it using the Save button or the [F11] function key.

If you are in the last input screen of the application and press [Enter] instead of using the Save button, the system displays a dialog box in which you're asked if you want to store the data.

A.12 The SAP Library

By following the menu path HELP • SAP LIBRARY, you can navigate to the SAP Library (Figure A.24). The SAP Library offers help on procedures and refers to additional subject areas. If you search for a term, enter the corresponding term in the field provided and click on the Show button or press [Enter]. The system then displays comprehensive documentation on the right or opens an additional window where you have to specify the term more precisely.

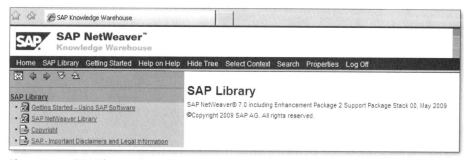

Figure A.24 SAP Library

A.13 The SAP Glossary

You can find the glossary under the menu path HELP • GLOSSARY. In contrast to the SAP Library, it only provides brief definitions of the concepts used in the system (similar to a lexicon).

A.14 Logoff

The logoff terminates a session in the SAP system. You can use the following logoff procedure anyplace within the SAP system:

▶ Saving not yet saved data

▶ Selecting the menu path SYSTEM • LOG OFF

The system displays a dialog box where you have to confirm the logoff (see Figure A.26).

After the confirmation, the system closes all SAP applications. To use a transaction code to log off, you must enter the following command into the command field: "/nend."

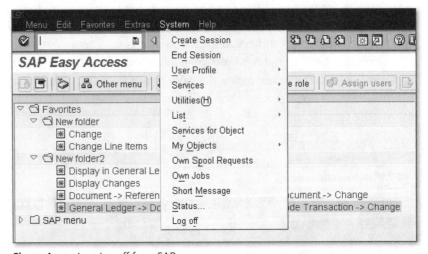

Figure A.25 Logging off from SAP

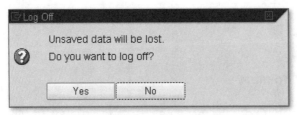

Figure A.26 "Log off" Dialog Box

B   Glossary

Account Assignment Model   The account assignment model is a template used to post documents. It contains items that are proposed as default values in the document to simplify data entry. An account assignment model can contain any number of line items, as well as the posted amount or an equivalence factor for proportional allocation of an amount.

Account Group   This object groups together attributes that control the creation and management of master data records. The account group determines which data is relevant for the master record and specifies a number range from which numbers are selected for the master records. An account group must be assigned to each master record.

Account Type   A key that indicates the accounting area to which an account belongs. Account types include customer accounts, vendor accounts, G/L accounts, asset accounts and material accounts. The posting key determines which account type is used.

Accrual/Deferral Posting   Accrual/deferral postings are adjustment postings that must be made at the end of a posting period. They are then reversed in the subsequent period. The accrual program posts the accrual/deferral to the G/L account and then indicates the date on which the reverse posting is to take effect. A reversal program is executed to select and reverse the relevant accrual/deferral documents.

Activity Type   Activity types classify the activities performed in the cost centers within a controlling area. These are measured in units of time or measurement. Example: machine time, working hours

Additional Account Assignment   An additional account assignment defines additional account assignment objects in the line item. These include the terms of payment, payment method, cost center, etc.

Analysis and Transfer Posting of GR/IR Clearing Accounts   This program (RFWERE00) analyzes GR/IR clearing accounts and creates adjustment postings to report business transactions correctly for balance sheet preparation.

Asset Class   The asset class is the main criterion used to classify fixed assets. It enables account determination and offers various number ranges and display options.

Assignment Field   The Assignment field is an additional reference field for line items. This field is provided for all line items posted. Line items can be sorted in the line item directory based on the value in this field. The assignment field is filled automatically (sort code in the master record) or manually (entry in a line item).

Automatic Account Assignment   An automatic function (in Financial Accounting) used in posting transactions, which allows the system to assign line items to the corresponding accounts without the user having to enter any data.

Balance Carryforward   At the end of the fiscal year, all balances of balance sheet items are carried forward (as the "balance carryforward") from the old year into the new year as the opening balance.

Balance Sheet Account Valuation   The RFSBEW00 program valuates G/L accounts that are managed in a foreign currency. The valuation takes place on a key date that is specified as a selection parameter.

Balance Sheet Adjustment (Program)   Program SAPF180 ensures that business areas record balances of zero. This is necessary when preparing balance sheets for each business area. If Profit Center Accounting is active, adjustments are made for profit centers also. The program retroactively assigns receivables, payables, taxes, and exchange rate differences to these units.

Bank Master Data   Information about a bank that is required to conduct business transactions with that bank. This information is stored in the bank directory, which contains information about all relevant banks. This information includes the bank name, its address, and country-specific details.

Baseline Date   The baseline date is the date on which the terms of payment take effect. The SAP ERP system permits individual changes to this date in accordance with customer requirements.

Bill of Exchange   A promise of payment in the form of an abstract payment paper that is separate from the original legal transaction.

Branch Account   An account that is used to represent the head office or branch relationship of a customer or vendor in the SAP system. Purchase orders, deliveries, or invoices entered for branch accounts are posted to the head office account. Each branch account must refer to a head office account.

Business Area   A business area is an organizational unit of external accounting that represents a separate area of operations or responsibilities within an enterprise and to which value changes recorded in Financial Accounting can be allocated.

Chart of Accounts   A schema used to classify all G/L account master records that are required within one or more company codes. The chart of accounts contains the account number, the account name, and control information for the G/L account master record. Various types of charts of accounts are available (see Operating chart of accounts, Group chart of accounts, Country-specific chart of accounts).

Clearing   A procedure whereby the open items of one or more accounts are indicated as cleared (paid). Open items can be cleared if the total credit amount used to clear the items equals the total debit amount of the items to be cleared in one or more accounts, in other words, if the balance of these debit and credit amounts is zero. For example, when a customer pays an invoice, you can clear the open items that correspond to that invoice.

Client   A client is a unit in an SAP ERP system that is self-contained in commercial, organizational, and technical terms and has separate master records and its own set of tables.

Company Code   The smallest organizational unit for which a complete, self-contained set of accounts can be drawn up for purposes of external reporting. This includes the recording of all relevant transactions and the generation of all supporting documents required for financial statements.

Controlling Area   A controlling area is an organizational unit within an enterprise, which represents a complete, self-contained system used for cost accounting purposes.

Correspondence   All analyses and reports that are sent to business partners are viewed as correspondence. Correspondence includes account statements, balance confirmations, individual and circular letters, document extracts, payments notices, and bill of exchange charges statements.

Cost Center   Cost centers are organizational units in which the costs incurred in specific areas of responsibility are collected. Cost centers are defined within a controlling area. A controlling area may consist of one or more cost centers.

Cost Element   Cost elements classify the consumption of production factors that is valuated in relation to business purposes within a controlling area.

Country-Specific Chart of Accounts   The country-specific chart of accounts offers an alternative account numbering structure for meeting local reporting requirements. It is also referred to as the "alternative chart of accounts."

Cross-Company Code Posting   A posting transaction involving several company codes. The system creates a document for each of the company codes involved. Cross-company code postings are used, for example, to process centralized purchasing or centralized payment transactions.

Drill-Down Reporting   A reporting tool that enables interactive data evaluation.

Document Change Rules   Documents can be changed on the basis of document change rules under the number of the original document. These rules determine which fields can be changed and the conditions under which this is permitted.

Document Principle   A principle that dictates that postings are always supposed to be stored in document form. The document is preserved as a coherent unit, which can be displayed at any time until it is archived.

Document Type   A key used to differentiate the various business transactions that are to be posted. The document type controls how the document is stored and defines the account types to which the documents will be posted. The document type is entered in the document header of all documents.

Dunning   A structured process for dunning customers. Customers are assigned to a dunning procedure, which specifies how and when they are to be dunned.

Exchange Rate Type   The exchange rate type allows you to define several exchange rates in the system and use these for various purposes. You can use the exchange rate type to define a buying rate, bank selling rate, and average rate to convert foreign-currency amounts, to define a rate for the conversion of financial reports, or to define a rate for a specific currency requirement within your enterprise.

Field Status   The aim of field statuses is to enable precise and efficient data entry. Using the field status function allows you to display the relevant combination of fields when you enter data. This eliminates errors that would occur if fields were to be included or excluded. Individual fields can be defined as required entry fields, optional fields, or hidden fields. These settings depend on the user-defined configuration.

Financial Statement Version   These versions are created to give structure to the balance sheet and the profit and loss (P&L) statement. Financial statement versions can be defined for a specific chart of accounts, a group chart of accounts or without an assignment. Charts of accounts are assigned to the positions at the lowest levels of the hierarchical structure.

Functional Area   An organizational unit in SAP ERP Financials that classifies areas of an enterprise by their business functions, for example, production, administration, sales and distribution, mar-

keting, or research and development, in accordance with the requirements of cost of sales accounting. Cost of sales accounting indicates exactly why and how costs are incurred in an enterprise by breaking costs down by functional area.

G/L Account Fast Entry   With standard posting by item, each G/L account item is displayed on a new screen with all available fields. With G/L account fast entry, item templates are displayed, in which only predefined fields are available. This restricted selection is generally only one or two lines long. As a result, many items can be displayed on a single screen, which enables faster entry of several items for standardized postings.

G/L Account Master Record   A data record containing information that controls how data is entered in a G/L account and how that account is managed. This information includes, for example, the currency in which the account is managed.

GR/IR Clearing Account   This G/L account contains postings for purchase orders for which goods have already been received but an invoice has not yet been received, as well as postings for purchase orders for which an invoice has been received but goods have not yet been received.

Group   A group is a consolidation unit to which company codes are assigned.

Group Chart of Accounts   The group chart of accounts groups together various charts of accounts for group accounting.

Input Tax   A tax charged by the vendor.

Internal Order   The use of internal orders allows the costs of specific procedures and tasks within an enterprise to be planned, recorded, monitored, and settled. The SAP system enables continuous monitoring of internal orders (from creation through planning and posting of actual costs to final settlement).

Invoice Verification   In invoice verification, vendor invoices are compared with the purchase order and the goods receipt.

Lockbox Processing   In the USA, payment transactions are largely handled using checks. To process these payments quickly, banks offer a lockbox service, which allows customers to send payments directly to the bank's lockbox. The bank deposits the checks and forwards the details of the check to the payees via file transfer.

Noted Item   A special item that does not change any account balances. A document is generated when a noted item is posted. The item can be displayed using the line item display. Certain noted items are processed by the payment program or dunning program. Example: down payment requests

Number Range   Within the SAP Financials modules, number ranges are configured to meet individual business requirements. Number ranges can be assigned internally or externally. Some number ranges are reserved for specific uses in SAP ERP. Number ranges are defined for master records and documents.

One-Time Account   An account that records the transaction figures for a group of business partners with whom you conduct business once only or rarely. A special master record is required for one-time accounts. Specific data relating to the business partner, such as address and bank details, is entered in the document itself rather than in the master record.

Open Item Management   Open item management stipulates that the items in an account must be cleared by other items in the same account. The relevant items must balance out to zero before they are cleared. The account balance is therefore always equal to the sum of the open items.

Open Item Valuation   Open item valuation (report SAPF100) performs a foreign currency valuation for accounts that are managed on an open item basis, for example, vendor accounts and customer accounts.

Operating Chart of Accounts   Each company code uses the G/L accounts of a single chart of accounts for account validation during document posting. This chart of accounts is referred to as the operating chart of accounts.

Operating Concern   The operating concern is the central element in profitability analysis. Controlling areas are mapped to a single operating concern for internal accounting.

Output Tax   A tax levied on customers.

Parked Document   An incomplete document can be stored temporarily and then posted at a later point in time by the same or a different user.

Payment Program   The payment program was developed for international payment transactions with customers and vendors, and it processes both incoming and outgoing payments. The program is very flexible, allowing you to define country-specific aspects of payments, such as payment method, payment form, or the specifics of data transfer.

Posting Code Currency/Local Currency   The currency of a company code, in which the document in posted. The SAP system always stores the company code currency.

Posting Key   Every line item posted is always associated with a single posting key. This posting key determines whether an item refers to a debit posting or a credit posting. The posting key controls the account type and influences the screen display.

Posting Period Variant   Company codes are assigned to a posting period variant. This variant defines which periods are open for posting.

Primary Cost Element   Primary cost elements are cost items or revenue items within a chart of accounts that have corresponding G/L accounts in Financial Accounting. A primary cost element must exist as a G/L account in the chart of accounts and as an account in Financial Accounting before it can be created.

Profitability Segment   Profitability segments represent the marketing and management views of an enterprise as distinct from the legal reporting views. Profitability segments are defined within an operating concern and are used in the profitability analysis module.

Profit Center   Profit centers collect the revenues and costs for the cost centers for which they are responsible.

Purchasing Organization   The purchasing organization is responsible for end-to-end processing of purchasing activities (for example, requests for quotation and purchase orders). The purchasing organization maintains information that is relevant for vendors and for pricing to support the most cost-effective acquisition of goods possible.

Reconciliation Account   The reconciliation account is a G/L account that is used to update the subledger accounts in parallel with the general ledger. A reconciliation account is defined in the company code segment of each subledger account master record. As a result, all postings to subledger accounts are also posted automatically to the general ledger reconciliation account.

Recurring Entry   Recurring entries are business transactions that are repeated on a regular basis. Recurring reference documents can therefore be created to accelerate periodic posting. These reference documents are then selected and processed periodically. Background processing is used for the actual process of updating the general ledger.

Reference Document or Reference Master Record   Reference documents or master records are documents or master records that have been posted and which can be used as a template for posting to facilitate data entry.

Report Tree Report trees are graphical representations of reports, structured by application area. SAP ERP contains standard reports for each area, which users can modify to suit their enterprises' individual business requirements.

Report Painter A programmed ABAP/4 generator, which you can use to define rows and columns in reports for customer-specific reporting. These can be defined in the Report Painter's GUI frontend.

Report Variant You can use a report variant to save pre-defined selection criteria for a report. You can define several report variants for each report. However, you can only use a single variant for each report. Report variants enable the use of default report settings to ensure consistent report output.

Sales Organization A sales organization represents a legal sales unit and is assigned to a company code. This assignment creates a connection between sales and distribution and financial accounting. Because a sales organization belongs to a single company code, all financial transactions relating to this sales organization are posted in this same company code. Several sales organizations can be assigned to the same company code.

Secondary Cost Element Secondary cost elements are maintained exclusively in Controlling (CO). They represent internal value flows, for example, internal

activity allocation, overhead rates, and settlement transactions.

Special G/L Indicator An indicator that identifies a special G/L transaction. Special G/L transactions include, for example, down payments and bills of exchange. Setting this indicator triggers the use of an alternative reconciliation account for special G/L transactions in the subledger. These transactions are not balanced with the receivables and payables from deliveries and services.

Special Period A special posting period that subdivides the last regular posting period for closing operations. You can define a maximum of four special periods per fiscal year in Financial Accounting.

SWIFT Code SWIFT stands for Society for Worldwide Interbank Financial Telecommunication. In the context of international payment transactions, the internationally recognized SWIFT code allows banks to be identified without details of their address or bank number. SWIFT codes are used mainly for automatic payment transactions.

Tax Code A two-digit code that represents information used to calculate and express tax on sales and purchases. The tax code controls the tax rate, tax type, and calculation type.

Term of Payment Terms of payment are defined as four-digit alphanumeric keys. Each term of payment consists of a maximum of three possible combinations of payment periods and cash discount percentage rates.

Transaction Currency This is the currency entered in the document header.

Valuation A balance sheet term that refers to the calculation of the value of all fixed and current assets and all payables at a specific time and in accordance with legal requirements.

Vendor Master Record A data record containing all of the information about a business partner. This information is required for processing business transactions, for example. It includes the business partner's address and bank details.

Vendor Net Procedure A posting procedure whereby the expected cash discount amount is applied as soon as the invoice is posted, accompanied by a reduction of the acquisition costs or material stock value. As a result, the exact acquisition values can be posted minus the cash discount amount.

Worklist When displaying account balances or line items, you can use worklists to quickly call up several accounts simultaneously. You can define worklists for the following objects: BU-KRS (company code), KUNNR (customer number), LIFNR (vendor number), and SAKNR (G/L account).

C   Menu Paths

C.1   Chapter 2—General Ledger Accounting

C.1.1   Master Data

Accounting • Financial Accounting • General Ledger • Master Data • Collective Processing

C.1.2   Documents in the SAP System

Accounting • Financial Accounting • General Ledger • Posting • General Posting

Accounting • Financial Accounting • General Ledger • Posting • Reference Document • Account Assignment Model

Accounting • Financial Accounting • General Ledger • Posting • Enter G/L Account Document for Ledger Group

C.1.3   Evaluations

Accounting • Financial Accounting • General Ledger • Info System • General Ledger (new)

Accounting • Financial Accounting • General Ledger • Info System • General Ledger Reports • Balance Sheet/Profit and Loss Statement/Cash Flow • General • Actual/Actual Comparisons

C.2   Chapter 3—Accounts Payable Accounting

C.2.1   Master Data

Accounting • Financial Accounting • Accounts Payable • Create Master Data

Accounting • Financial Accounting • Accounts Payable • Central Maintenance • Master Data • Block/Unblock

C.2.2 Entering Incoming Invoices

Accounting • Financial Accounting • Accounts Payable • Other Postings • General Invoice

Accounting • Financial Accounting • Accounts Payable • Posting • Invoice

Accounting • Financial Accounting • Accounts Payable • Posting • IR/GU Fast Entry • Invoice

Logistics • Materials Management • Invoice Verification • Document Entry • Add Incoming Invoice

C.2.3 Payment Transactions

Accounting • Financial Accounting • Accounts Payable • Periodic Processing • Pay

Accounting • Financial Accounting • Accounts Payable • Posting • Outgoing Payments • Post

C.2.4 Evaluations in Accounts Payable Accounting

Accounting • Financial Accounting • Accounts Payable • Master Data • Confirmation of Change • List

Accounting • Financial Accounting • Accounts Payable • Information System • Reports for Accounts Payable Accounting • Vendor Items • Open Items Due Date Analysis

Accounting • Financial Accounting • Accounts Payable • Information System • Tools • Show Evaluation

C.3 Chapter 4—Accounts Receivable Accounting

C.3.1 Master Data

Accounting • Financial Accounting • Accounts Receivable • Master Data
• Central Maintenance • Create/Change/Display

Accounting • Financial Accounting • Accounts Receivable • Master Data
• Central Maintenance • Set Deletion Flag

C.3.2 Overview of the Integrated Business Transaction

Logistics • Sales and Distribution • Sales • Order • Create

C.3.3 Monitoring Credit Lines

Accounting • Financial Supply Chain Management • Credit Management
• Master Data • Business Partner master Data

Accounting • Financial Accounting • Accounts Receivable • Account •
Display/Change Items

C.3.4 Clarifying Payment Deductions

Accounting • Financial Supply Chain Management • Dispute Management • Dispute Case Processing

Accounting • Financial Accounting • Accounts Receivable • Document •
Post Credit Memo

Accounting • Financial Accounting • Accounts Receivable • Account •
Clear

Accounting • Financial Supply Chain Management • Dispute Management • Dispute Case Processing

C.3.5 Dunning Procedure by Telephone

Accounting • Financial Supply Chain Management • Collections
Management

C.3.6 Evaluations

Info Systems • Accounting • Financial Accounting • Accounts Receivable • Reports about Accounts Receivable Accounting • Master Data • Customer List

Info Systems • Accounting • Financial Accounting • Accounts Receivable • Reports about Accounts Receivable Accounting • Customer Balances • Customer Balances in Local Currency

Info Systems • Accounting • Financial Accounting • Accounts Receivable • Reports for Accounts Receivable Accounting • Customer Payment History

Accounting • Financial Accounting • Accounts Receivable • Info System • Tools • Show Evaluation

Accounting • Financial Accounting • Accounts Receivable • Info System • Tools • Set • Create Evaluation

Accounting • Financial Supply Chain Management • Credit Management • List Display

Accounting • Financial Supply Chain Management • Dispute Management • Edit Dispute

C.4   Chapter 5—Asset Accounting

C.4.1 Master Data

Accounting • Financial Accounting • Fixed Assets • Asset • Create • Asset

Asset • Display (or Change) • Asset

Environment • Change Documents • For Creation

Accounting • Financial Accounting • Fixed Assets • Asset • Block

Accounting • Financial Accounting • Fixed Assets • Asset • Delete

C.4.2 Business Transactions

Accounting • Financial Accounting • Fixed Assets • Postings • Acquisition • Purchase • Clearing Offsetting Entry

Accounting • Financial Accounting • Fixed Assets • Postings • Manual Value Correction • Unplanned Depreciation

Accounting • Financial Accounting • Fixed Assets • Retirement • Retirement with Revenue • Without Customer

Accounting • Financial Accounting • Fixed Assets • Retirement • Transfer

C.4.3 Evaluations

Accounting • Financial Accounting • Fixed Assets • Info System • Reports on Asset Accounting • Individual Asset

C.5 Chapter 6—Bank Accounting

C.5.1 Master Data

Accounting • Financial Accounting • Banking • Master Data • Bank Chains • House Banks • Process

Accounting • Financial Accounting • Banking • Master Data • Bank Master Record • Transfer Bank Data

Accounting • Financial Accounting • Banking • Master Data • Bank Master Record • Create

C.5.2 Payment Transactions and Bank Communication

Accounting • Financial Accounting • Banking • Environment • Settings • Enter Available Amounts for Payment Program

Accounting • Financial Accounting • Accounts Payable • Posting • Outgoing Payment • Post + Print Forms

Accounting • Financial Accounting • Financial Supply Chain Management • Bank Communication Management • Edit • Merge Payments

Accounting • Financial Accounting • Financial Supply Chain Management • Bank Communication Management • Status Management • Batch and Payment Monitoring

C.5.3 Processing Bank Statements

Accounting • Financial Accounting • Banking • Incoming • Bank Statement • Import

Accounting • Financial Accounting • Banking • Incoming • Bank Statement • Postprocess

C.5.4 Cash Journal

Accounting • Financial Accounting • Banking • Incoming • Cash Journal

C.5.5 Check Deposit Transaction

Accounting • Financial Accounting • Banking • Incoming • Check Deposit • Enter Manually

C.5.6 Evaluations

Accounting • Financial Supply Chain Management • Cash and Liquidity Management • Cash Management • Info System • Reports on Cash Management • Liquidity Analyses • Liquidity Forecast

Accounting • Financial Supply Chain Management • Cash and Liquidity Management • Cash Management • Info System • Reports on Cash Management • Liquidity Analyses

C.6   Chapter 7—Closing Operations

C.6.1 Management of Parked Documents

Accounting • Financial Accounting • General Ledger • Document • Parked Documents • Post/Delete

C.6.2 Automatic Maintenance of the GR/IR Account

Accounting • Financial Accounting • General Ledger • Master Records • G/L Accounts • Centrally

Accounting • Financial Accounting • General Ledger • Account • Display Items

Accounting • Financial Accounting • General Ledger • Periodic Processing • Automatic Clearing • Without Specification of Clearing Currency

Accounting • Financial Accounting • General Ledger • Periodic Processing • Closing • Reclassify • GR/IR Clearing

C.6.3 Recurring Entry Documents

Accounting • Financial Accounting • General Ledger (Accounts Receivable or Accounts Payable) • Document Entry • Reference Documents • Recurring Entry Document

Accounting • Financial Accounting • General Ledger (Accounts Payable or Accounts Receivable) • Periodic Processing • Recurring Entries • List

Accounting • Financial Accounting • General Ledger (Accounts Payable or Accounts Receivable) • Periodic Processing • Recurring Entries • Execute

C.6.4 Accrual Engine

Accounting • Financial Accounting • General Ledger • Periodic Processing • Manual Accruals • Create Accrual Object

Accounting • Financial Accounting • General Ledger • Periodic Processing • Manual Accruals • Start Periodic Accrual Run

Accounting • Financial Accounting • General Ledger • Periodic Processing • Manual Accruals • Info System • Display Posted Accruals • Manual Accruals: Display Line Items in the Accrual Engine

C.6.5 Assets Under Construction

Accounting • Financial Accounting • Fixed Assets • Asset • Create • Asset

Accounting • Financial Accounting • Fixed Assets • Capitalize Asset under Construction • Distribute

Accounting • Financial Accounting • Fixed Assets • Capitalize Asset under Construction • Settle

Accounting • Financial Accounting • Fixed Assets • Asset • Asset Explorer

Accounting • Financial Accounting • Fixed Assets • Info System • Reports on Asset Accounting • Individual Assets

C.6.6 Depreciation Posting Run

Accounting • Financial Accounting • Fixed Assets • Posting • Acquisition • External Acquisition • Acquisition w/Autom. Offsetting Entry

Accounting • Financial Accounting • Fixed Assets • Environment • Current Settings • Maintain Index Series

Accounting • Financial Accounting • Fixed Assets • Periodic Processing • Depreciation Run • Execute

Accounting • Financial Accounting • Fixed Assets • Asset • Asset Explorer

Accounting • Financial Accounting • Fixed Assets • Posting • Manual Value Correction • Unplanned Depreciation

Accounting • Financial Accounting • Fixed Assets • Info System • Reports on Asset Accounting • Notes to Financial Statements • International • Asset History Sheet

C.6.7 Value Adjustments

Accounting • Financial Accounting • Accounts Receivable • Document Entry • Other • Transfer Without Clearing

Accounting • Financial Accounting • Accounts Receivable • Periodic Processing • Closing • Valuate • Further Valuations

System • Services • Reporting

C.6.8 Foreign Currency Valuation

Accounting • Financial Accounting • General Ledger • Environment • Current Settings • Enter Currency Exchange Rates using a Worklist

Accounting • Financial Accounting • Accounts Receivable • Periodic Processing • Closing • Valuate • Foreign Currency Valuations of Open Items (New)

C.6.9 Interest Calculation

Accounting • Financial Accounting • Accounts Receivable • Master Data • Display

Accounting • Financial Accounting • Accounts Receivable • Periodic Posting • Interest Calculation • Item Interest Calculation • Item Interest Calculation

Accounting • Financial Accounting • Accounts Receivable • Environment • Current Settings • Enter Time Interest Terms

Accounting • Financial Accounting • Accounts Receivable • Periodic Processing • Interest Calculation • Item Interest Calculation • Item Interest Calculation

C.6.10 Reconciliation Measures

Accounting • Financial Accounting • General Ledger • Account • Display/Change Items

Accounting • Financial Accounting • General Ledger • Periodic Processing • Closing • Check/Count • Reconciliation

C.6.11 Intercompany Reconciliation

Accounting • Financial Accounting • Accounts Receivable • Master Data • Display

Accounting • Financial Accounting • General Ledger • Periodic Processing • Closing • Check/Count• Intercompany Reconciliation: Open Items

Accounting • Financial Accounting • Accounts Receivable • Account • Display Items

System • Services • Reporting

Accounting • Financial Accounting • General Ledger • Master Records • G/L Accounts • Centrally

C.6.12 Reclassification

Accounting • Financial Accounting • Accounts Receivable/Accounts Payable • Periodic Processing • Closing • Check/Count • Balance Sheet Confirmation: Print

C.6.13 Period Control

Accounting • Financial Accounting • General Ledger • Environment • Current Settings • Open and Close Posting Periods

C.6.14 Tax on Sales/Purchases

Accounting • Financial Accounting • General Ledger • Reporting

Accounting • Financial Accounting • General Ledger • Reporting • Tax Reports • General • Advance Return for Tax on Sales/Purchases • Advance Return for Tax on Sales/Purchases

Accounting • Financial Accounting • General Ledger • Reporting • Electronic Communication with Authorities • Administration Report Data Transmission

C.6.15 Balance Carryforward

Accounting • Financial Accounting • General Ledger • Account • Display Balances

Accounting • Financial Accounting • General Ledger • Periodic Processing • Closing • Carry Forward

D Sample Closing Procedure Document

Description	Tasks	Done by
Distribution of the schedule	Distributing this year's closing procedure planning by email	October
Inventory preparation	Preliminary discussion of the inventory	November
Inventory instructions regarding all inventories	Creating a schedule Defining people responsible Checking the prices for raw materials, auxiliary materials, and expendable supplies Inventory update of remaining quantities	November
Physical inventory	As-is analysis of all warehouse stock Counting, weighing, measuring, estimating Recording in count lists	November
Prepostings	Forwarding information Entering prepostings	December
Checking the prepostings	Checking and controlling the stock values Signing and releasing	December
Final inventory posting	Evaluating raw materials, auxiliary materials, and expendable supplies Semifinished products Finished products Packing Evaluating acquisition and production costs Performing range-of-coverage devaluations	December
Checking the system-created inventory	Printing and forwarding lists Checking and manually correcting the lists, if required	December
Balance confirmation for all banks	Printing and sending the letters for the balance confirmations in time	December
Currency account	Setting currency accounts to €0 or evaluating them at the end of the year	December

Description	Tasks	Done by
Posting deadline for the sales system	Closing the invoicing for the old year	December
Rent and leasing obligations	Lists by: Real estate Technical systems and machines Fixtures and fittings Other	January
Reconciliation of bank balances	Reconciling and documenting bank balances	January
Listing checks in stock	Printing Checking Revision and forwarding	January
Losses on receivables and value adjustments	Notification by the management on expected losses via lists Issue Posting	January
Process cost provisions	Creating lists Letter to lawyers Obtaining confirmations	January
Reconciliation of financial accounts	Reconciliation in the accounting system by the posting deadline	January
Reconciliation of clearing accounts	Reconciliation Interest calculation as necessary	January
Cash management accounts	Reconciliation and intercompany validation Interest settlement with agreed interest rates	January
Cash on hand journal on the key date	Creation and confirmation by signature Creating copies and forwarding them	January
Credits	Listing the credit line by credit institution, life, remaining debts, and collaterals	January
Provisions	Requesting actuarial appraisals for guaranteed pension payments, anniversary bonuses, and semiretirements	January

Description	Tasks	Done by
Requesting accounts payable balance confirmation	Randomly requesting confirmations from the vendors on the key date minus one month	January
Prepaid/deferred items on the credit and debit side	Posting documents Copying Forwarding	January
Other receivables/payables	Posting documents Copying Forwarding	January
Posting deadline for the purchase system	Posting the remaining invoices for the old year	January
Settlement	Executing the last internal settlement	January
Investment subsidies	Official information Applications or calculation bases for investment allowances and subsidies	January
Posting deadline for financial accounting	Closing the postings for the old year	January

E   Additional Sources of Information

Books

Arif, Naeem; Muhammad, Sheikh Tauseef. *SAP ERP Financials: Configuration and Design.* SAP PRESS, 2008.

Bauer, Eric; Siebert, Jörg. *New General Ledger in SAP ERP Financials*. SAP PRESS, 2007.

Patel, Manish. *Discover SAP ERP Financials*. SAP PRESS, 2009.

Schöler, Sabine; Zink, Olaf. *SAP Governance, Risk and Compliance.* SAP PRESS, 2008.

F   The Authors

Heinz Forsthuber is an experienced SAP consultant and trainer, focusing on Controlling (CO) and Financial Accounting (FI). Currently, he works as an SAP in-house consultant in the public sector and is in charge of the FI, CO, and MM modules. Additionally, he is responsible for archiving and the user administration.

Jörg Siebert began working as a consultant and trainer in the Financial Accounting area in 1996, and moved to Financials Product Sales at SAP Germany in 2003. His activities consist of both SAP R/3 and the new components in SAP ERP Financials, such as Financial Supply Chain Management, Corporate Governance, and SAP NetWeaver BW. His extensive practical experience was gained as an SAP trainer and FI/CO consultant at Cap Gemini Ernst & Young and DCW Software. His certification as a consultant for SAP FI/CO and SAP SEM, his degree in information management, and his subsequent accounting qualification are the basis of Jörg's extensive technical competence.

Index

E

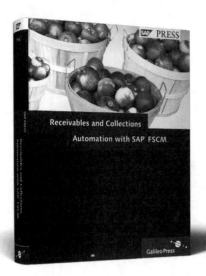

Teaches how to design, configure, and implement the FSCM Collections, Dispute, Credit, and Biller Direct components

Provides proven guidance and real case studies for extending an ERP Financials infrastructure with FSCM

Sreedhar Narahari

Receivables and Collections Automation with SAP FSCM

The primary purpose of the book is to provide finance team members, implementation project managers, and consultants with a comprehensive, practical guide to the FSCM applications available for automating the receivables and collections manage-ment functions. Focusing primarily on the core functions of the Biller Direct, Credit Management, Collections Management, and Dispute Management applications, the book offers readers a roadmap for implementation, integration, and customization.

approx. 450 pp., 79,95 Euro / US$ 79.95
ISBN 978-1-59229-245-5, Oct 2009

>> www.sap-press.com

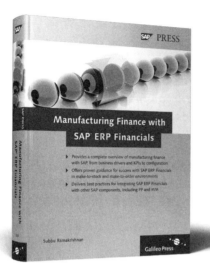

Provides a complete overview of manufacturing finance with SAP, from business drivers and KPIs to configuration and integration

Offers proven guidance for success with SAP ERP Financials in make-to-stock and make-to-order manufacturing environments

Subbu Ramakrishnan

Manufacturing Finance with SAP ERP Financials

The primary purpose of the book is to provide finance team members, implementation project managers, and consultants with a comprehensive, practical guide to the Finance functionality available for the manufacturing environment and the configuration and integration processes necessary for optimizing ERP Financials for manufacturing. Focusing primarily on the core functions of the Financial Accounting and Controlling components, the book provides readers with a holistic look at the business drivers, KPIs, configuration schemes, and technical issues relevant to the manufacturing finance function. It presents a solution-oriented view of manufacturing finance that includes the integration of ERP Financials components with other SAP applications critical to the manufacturing operation, such as Production Planning and Materials Management.

580 pp., 2009, 79,95 Euro / US$ 79.95, ISBN 978-1-59229-238-7

>> www.sap-press.com

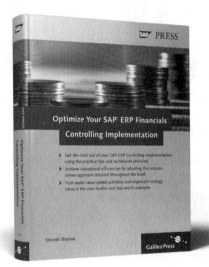

Get the most out of your SAP Controlling implementation using the practical tips and techniques provided

Learn how to make better management decisions by using the Controlling specific information in this book

Shivesh Sharma

Optimize Your SAP ERP Financials Controlling Implementation

This book will answer the question, What do I do with my SAP Controlling-related requirements once the implementation is complete? Therefore, it begins where implementation guides leave off. Using tested business processes it prepares readers to make the most of their Controlling implementation.

465 pp., 2008, 79,95 Euro / US$ 79.95
ISBN 978-1-59229-219-6

>> www.sap-press.com

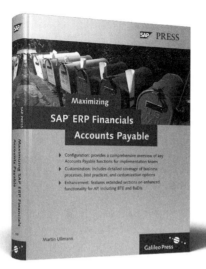

Configuration: provides a comprehensive overview of key Accounts Payable functions for implementation teams, consultants, project managers, and end-users

Customization: includes detailed coverage of business processes, best practices, and customization options

Martin Ullmann

Maximizing SAP ERP Financials Accounts Payable

Maximizing Accounts Payable in SAP ERP Financials is the definitive, comprehensive guide to implementing, configuring, and enhancing AP for project managers, executives, technical leads, and end-users (functional resources who actually interact on a daily basis with the configured system).Covering the configuration of every AP function, plus strategies for incorporating business processes, best practices, and additional SAP enhancements, this book provides the guidance and experience needed for maximizing the use and potential of the Accounts Payable module.

488 pp., 2009, 79,95 Euro / US$ 79.95
ISBN 978-1-59229-198-4

>> www.sap-press.com

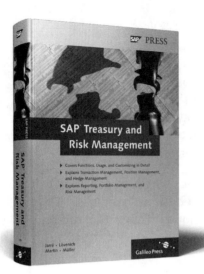

Uncover functionality, processes and complete customization details

Master transaction and position management with hedge management

Unlock the secrets of reporting, portfolio controlling and risk management

Fully up-to-date for SAP ERP 6.0

Sönke Jarré, Reinhold Lövenich, Andreas Martin, Klaus G. Müller

SAP Treasury and Risk Management

This comprehensive guide introduces you to the functionality and helps you quickly master the usage of SAP Treasury and Risk Management. Learn about the most important customization settings as well as typical use cases and get straightforward solutions to many of the most common problems. With volumes of detailed screenshots, in-depth overviews and practical examples, all components of the tool are covered in detail – from transaction and position management, to risk and performance analyses, to reporting and beyond. Plus, you'll also benefit from expert guidance on interfaces and integration as well as compliance requirements. The book is up-to-date for SAP ERP 6.0.

722 pp., 2008, 99,95 Euro / US$ 99.95
ISBN 978-1-59229-149-6

>> www.sap-press.com

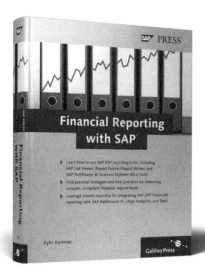

Understand and implement strategies for maximizing Financials reporting capabilities

Learn and apply best practices for simplifying, streamlining, and automating financial and management reporting

Leverage proven expertise concerning the integration of Financials reporting with BI, xApp Analytics, and Duet™

Aylin Korkmaz

Financial Reporting with SAP

This book provides finance and IT teams with best practices for delivering financial reports faster, more accurately, and in compliance with various international accounting standards. Featuring step-by-step coverage of all major FI reporting functions (including Sub-Ledger, Corporate Finance Management, and Governance, Risk & Compliance), this timely book will help you streamline and simplify financial business processes and automate financial and management reporting in SAP ERP Financials. It includes coverage of integrating FI reporting with Business Intelligence, xApp Analytics, and Duet™.

668 pp., 2008, 79,95 Euro / US$ 79.95
ISBN 978-1-59229-179-3

>> www.sap-press.com

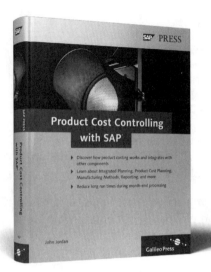

Discover how product costing works
and integrates with other modules

Learn about Integrated Planning,
Product Cost Planning,
Manufacturing Methods, Reporting,
and more

Reduce long run times during
month-end processing

John Jordan

Product Cost Controlling with SAP

If you are looking for a resource that shows you how to set up
Controlling for Product Costing and how it integrates with other
modules, this book is for you. This comprehensive resource is for anyone
in Financials, Production Planning, Purchasing, and Sales and Distribution
with an interest in the integrated areas of product costing. Learn how
overhead costs flow from financial postings to cost centers and then on
to manufacturing orders. Also learn about the material ledger, transfer
pricing, reporting, and discover how to address common problem areas,
including month-end processing, long run times, and message and
variance analysis.

572 pp., 2009, 79,95 Euro / US$ 79.95
ISBN 978-1-59229-167-0

Interested in reading more?

Please visit our Web site for all
new book releases from SAP PRESS.

www.sap-press.com